Gene Kilgore's

RANCH VACATIONS

The Complete Guide to Guest and Resort, Fly-Fishing, and Cross-Country Skiing Ranches in the United States and Canada

Fifth Edition

John Muir Publications
Santa Fe, New Mexico

John Muir Publications, P.O. Box 613, Santa Fe, New Mexico 87504

Printed in the United States of America
Fifth edition. First printing February 1999

Library of Congress Cataloging-in-Publication Data

Kilgore, Gene, 1953.
Gene Kilgore's ranch vacations : the complete guide to guest and resort, fly-fishing, and cross-country skiing ranches in the United States. -- 5th ed.
p. cm.
Includes index.
ISBN 1-56261-418-5
1. Resorts -- United States--Guidebooks. 2. Resorts--Canada, Western--Guidebooks. 3. Dude ranches--United States--Guidebooks. 4. Dude ranches--Canada, Western--Guidebooks. 5. Fly fishing--United States--Guidebooks. 6. Fly fishing--Canada, Western--Guidebooks. 7. Cross-country skiing--United States--Guidebooks. 8. Cross-country skiing--Canada, Western--Guidebooks. I. Title. II. Title: Ranch vacations.
TX907.2 .K55 1998
796.5'02573--dc21
98-55211
CIP

Editors: Marybeth Griffin, Nancy Gillan
Graphics Editor: Heather Pool
Production: Marie J. T. Vigil
Typesetter: Melissa Tandysh
Printer: Banta Company

Front cover photo of Echo Valley Guest Ranch, British Columbia—
© Ashworth Photo Group, Inc.
Back cover photo by Robert Holmgren

Distributed to the book trade by
Publishers Group West
Berkeley, California

The information in this book is subject to change without notice. We strongly recommend that you call ahead to verify the information presented here before making final plans or reservations. The author and publisher make no representation that this book is absolutely accurate or complete. Errors and omissions, whether typographical, clerical, or otherwise, may sometimes occur herein. All ranches are included without charge to them. The ranches that have photographs have paid an extra fee to help defray the cost of publication.

THE SPIRIT OF THE WEST

Out where the hand clasps a little stronger
Out where the smile dwells a little longer
That's where the West begins;

Where there's more of singing and less of sighing;
Where there's more of giving and less of buying,
And a man makes friends without half trying—
That's where the West begins.

—Arthur Chapman (1915)

"Somewhere out on the prairie is the greatest cowboy that's ever been. And when he lays his hands upon the ponies they shudder with an understanding skin. And he says, ponies, now ponies, don't worry. I have not come to steal your fire away. I want to fly with you across the sunrise and discover what begins each shining day."

—Jeffrey Bullock

WHAT RANCH GUESTS ARE SAYING:

"We are still filled with warmth, smiles, a few extra pounds, and all the wonderful and unforgettable memories of your ranch. We reminisce among ourselves and our friends about our cozy cabin, the yellow and orange marshmallow-eating rainbow trout, and the beautiful lake they lived in, rowboating, the lodge—never without a crackling fire on chilly days and nights—the sing-alongs, square-dancing, food, rodeos, prizes, guests, and all you great people who created such a relaxing and 'truly Western' experience for us."

—W.C.

"I count myself as one of the very fortunate to be among the pampered guests at Hidden Creek. You all contributed in a very real way to our experience. The ways you made every effort to help us feel like family were the most satisfying.... We love the way your kids' program not only entertains but educates about nature and the environment. The whole experience provides a great foundation for kids to help preserve what is most vulnerable in this age of high technology."

—N.G.

"In today's age, where 'service' businesses fall short of caring about their customers, yours puts the customers first—a simple concept that's rarely adopted. Today was my first day back at work and all I could think about was riding and the pure serenity at your ranch."

—J.R.

WHAT RANCHERS ARE SAYING:

"We stand in awe! You're like having all the railroads rolled into one and then accomplishing even more. You have worked marvels. Your book is done with such care, such insight, and with the knack, it would seem, of leading potential guests to the ranch that will be right. You've managed to lift awareness of dude ranching in the midst of all sorts of other vacation opportunities right to the top. And once that awareness takes hold, your book leads each person in the right direction. It's as if a friend were advising each person as to the place that would suit him best."

—J.M., Arizona

"I can only try and explain the degree to which your involvement and dedication to the Ways of the West and to those of us who share our hospitality has furthered our commitment to our purpose. Thank you."

—R.S., Wyoming

Contents

Foreword

The first guest ranch I ever visited was the Lazy K Bar Ranch nestled in the Crazy Mountains just north of Big Timber, Montana. I was a buck-toothed eight-year-old whose main interests were slingshots and TV Westerns. Kennedy had just been elected president, while Jello-rings, hula-hoops, and Elvis were still big. Hippies had not yet replaced beatniks in my native San Francisco, and many endangered species, including the nuclear family, were still intact.

On the way to the ranch I smelled the sagebrush and marveled at the huge clouds that sailed across the sky like small white countries unto themselves. Pronghorn antelope sprang away from us, melting into the heat mirage. Another 10 miles on the dusty road and we were at 5,000 feet, heading into a valley flanked by snowcapped peaks.

My father had first visited the Lazy K Bar Ranch in 1928 at the age of six. As we came through the front gates a barrel-chested, bowlegged cowboy named Spike Van Cleve greeted us. A Harvard dropout, Spike was the third generation in his family to own the ranch—which is now over a century old and still being operated by the Van Cleves.

The next two weeks were magical. My father taught me how to dangle a dry fly in Big Timber Creek for brown trout, while Spike showed me the way of the cowboy: "Always water your horse before you tend to yourself." As guests we herded cattle by day and listened to ghost stories at night. The Saturday-night square dance cured me of stage fright, and there was a memorable night encounter with a shadowy bear. Well, maybe it was just a noisy porcupine. During a day of branding I was allowed to ride a bawling calf until it bucked me off and stomped my ribs in—the perfect finale to a kid's vacation.

Over the next three decades I kept a print of Charlie Russell's painting *Bronc to Breakfast* on my dresser as I moved from New York, to Paris, and back to San Francisco. Whenever a big city got me down I would make week-long trips to that wild, cinch-busting country in order to fish the annual salmon-fly hatch on the Madison River, to watch the Fourth of July rodeos, or to ride at great guest ranches. The West so inspired me that in 1989 I spent six months journeying through Montana and published a travel memoir, *Ghost Hunting in Montana*.

Gene Kilgore and I went to school together, and re-connected on the 1989 Montana Centennial Cattle Drive which we both covered as journalists. In this extravaganza—really a week-long stampede—we mingled with 2,400 cowboys and 2,800 cows in a never-ending cloud of dust and high spirits. Someone observed that it was the largest gathering of horsemen since the Battle of Gettysburg. This is a long way of saying that Gene Kilgore really knows the West and its many spectacular ranches that invite city slickers as guests.

Since my first days in ranch country I have tried out a number of other places that range from simple, old-time, working ranches to fancy digs with hot tubs, skeet-shooting ranges, wine lists, and fishing wranglers. In the West you can experience the country as it was before the arrival of Lewis and Clark—and even before Clint Eastwood and Ralph Lauren. Bouncing along those ranch roads, pardner, you'll learn to love the mud bumps. And when you're bunking up, don't make a big fuss about the chipmunk living in your mattress—or else all the guests will be wanting one.

By the way, the breakfast ride to Grizzly Creek starts at seven, and I suggest you bring a fly-rod, or at least your camera, because the pancake-eating moose is back in our valley and one of the wranglers aims to rope it. Yee-hawwwww!

—Barnaby Conrad, III

Preface

This guide will open your eyes to a world of unforgettable pleasure, natural beauty, and wholesome fun. It will put you in touch with ranches and lodges throughout the United States and Canada, as well as top Western museums and annual Western events in North America.

Ranch vacations today offer much more than horseback riding. In fact, you don't even have to like horses or horseback riding to enjoy the properties described in this guide. Some ranches today offer fly-fishing, gourmet dining, tennis, swimming, white-water rafting, natural-history guides, massage, and more. Quite simply, what makes these vacations so special is their wholesome and unforgettable adventures in nature. Everyone—grandparents, children, singles, and families—can find a ranch vacation to suit them. Ranches offer facilities to professional groups, corporations, schools, and churches for seminars, retreats, and workshops. They also offer wonderful opportunities for family reunions, weddings, and honeymoons.

I began researching the first edition of this guidebook in 1979 while I was working as a cowboy for one of the largest cattle operations in the country, Miller Land and Livestock, about 75 miles south of Jackson Hole, Wyoming, and later as a dude wrangler for the one-and-only Frank Galey at his famous White Grass Ranch at the foot of the Tetons. I undertook this exciting project to share with people around the world a truly magnificent way of life.

Today, more than ever, people are seeking relief from the ever-increasing stresses of our fast-paced world. There is no better way for families and individuals to unwind, recharge batteries, gain perspective, reconfirm values, spend time with family members, meet interesting people from around the world, and, most of all, experience the natural beauty and tranquility of the outdoors than on a ranch vacation. As we approach the year 2000, I believe there will continue to be a reawakening and interest in our great North American wilderness heritage.

The more advanced we become technologically, the more we will crave the simpler pleasures of life. Nature, home-cooked meals, kindness, and sincere hospitality. This guide is not a history of ranch vacations. It is a friend that puts you in touch with a wonderful, unique group of properties and people who offer an incredible life-enhancing experience. A way of life. A vacation to be enjoyed by both the young and the young at heart.

Ranch vacations offer one of the greatest year-round vacation opportunities in the world today. Welcome to Gene Kilgore's Ranch Country.

Fifth Edition Thoughts

Welcome to our Fifth Edition of *Ranch Vacations*. We are proud to present you with our best edition ever, bringing you the latest and greatest of ranch country across North America.

I'm proud, very proud, to dedicate this edition to my mother, Mimi, who passed away December 11, 1997. Such an inspiration, such a spirit, and such a believer! Here's to you, Ma.

In 1979 I began researching *Ranch Vacations* in Wyoming. I was convinced that ranch country—the wide-open spaces, nature's beauty, wildlife, and old-fashioned hospitality were, next to the air we breathe and water we drink, the absolute greatest. Now, almost 20 years later, I am convinced more than ever.

Today we have more than 100,000 copies of our guide in print, and I am proud that we have been able to help so many people experience this magnificent way of life. We are also bringing travelers to ranch country through World-Wide Ranch Headquarters on the Internet at www.ranchweb.com—come and visit us.

It always amazes me how much change takes place over the course of two years—new ranches being created, ranches being sold, and new programs being developed. Probably the biggest change over the past two years has been the explosion of information available on the Internet. You will note that most every property in this book has e-mail and Internet addresses.

In this edition you will find many new ranches (even one in the Hawaiian Islands) and completely updated information on each ranch or lodge that we feature. We've uncovered some exciting properties for you and know that you'll enjoy discovering them as you mosey through the color section.

As the world turns, the explosive growth of technology has brought about tremendous changes in the way we do business, and where we can work and play. Over the past three years my travels have taken me across the country and to Europe and South America. Wherever I go, traveling men and women light up about the possibilities of visiting one of the properties in our book. Those who have already done it go on about the unforgettable experiences they had.

There were many highlights over the past several years, not the least of which was to see our young son turn three. That little boy—my favorite cowboy—has traveled to more ranches in North America than any little fellow I know. How special it is to see the wonder and joy in his eyes, and I am grateful to be able to share the best of ranch country with him. It is my hope with the Fifth Edition to bring ranch country to more children than ever before. Other highlights included meeting Henry Kravis, who has built one of the finest sporting lodges in the world; and Ted Turner, at CNN World Headquarters in Atlanta. His son Bo, who is a really first-class individual, now oversees one of the largest ranch operations in America. It was a busy couple of years on the "Gene Kilgore Ranch USA Tour" with a host of television shows, and radio in almost every major city across the country.

I am proud of what we have been able to accomplish and grateful to my wife, Regina, and son, William Francisco, for their inspiration, to my father and sister, and to the talented team that helps me. Particular thanks to all the ranch and lodge owners and you, our readers. Thank you!

Welcome to the best-ever Fifth Edition. Ride on, pardner!

Acknowledgments

There are many special people who have helped make this book such a success—over 100,000 copies in print now! Wow.

To all of you, family, friends, ranch and lodge owners, television and radio producers, newspaper and magazine writers, state and government agencies, all our readers along with all my associates, I say thank you!

I am especially grateful to my old friend Barnaby Conrad, III—a distinguished writer, author, and true Bohemian, who loves cowgirls, singing old cowboy tunes, and ranch life, too.

Extra-special thanks to my incredible colleagues up at Lake Tahoe—Sharon Peterson, who has typed all five manuscripts; Janice Tippin, who oversees and coordinates all my traveling, office, and publishing activities; and Kim Savoie in Sonoma—you three are fabulous. Thank you! Finally, to my editor and everyone at John Muir Publications—more happy trails!

The Kilgore Ranch Network—Real Estate Division

The Kilgore Ranch Network—Real Estate Division specializes in exclusive properties in North America and around the world. It consists of people who represent recreational and working ranch properties: guest ranches, wilderness lodges, and fly-fishing and cattle ranches.

Who Makes Up the Network

The Network consists of leading ranch and real-estate professionals. The Kilgore Network assists buyers and sellers in the acquisition and sale of premier properties.

Why Buyers and Sellers Use the Network

1. Knowledge and experience.
2. Powerful central source of ranch information.
3. Worldwide visibility in the marketplace.

If you're interested in buying or selling a . . .

- Dude/Guest Ranch
- Resort Ranch
- Wilderness Retreat
- Cross-Country Ski Ranch
- Fly-Fishing Lodge
- Working Cattle Ranch

Call or Write:

Kilgore Ranch Network—Real Estate
Worldwide Ranch Headquarters
PO Box 1919
Tahoe City, California 96145, USA
Phone: (916) 583-6926
Fax: (916) 583-6900
E-Mail: ranchman@ranchweb.com
Internet: http://www.ranchweb.com

"World-class ranches for world-class buyers."

The Kilgore Ranch Network—Travel Division

The Kilgore Ranch Network—Travel Division was developed in response to our worldwide readers who have requested extra assistance in selecting ranch vacations.

This service is designed for individuals, families, couples, and professional groups, as well as corporations, who wish to benefit from our expertise and firsthand knowledge over and above the information available in *Gene Kilgore's Ranch Vacations*.

Vacation Adventures Offered:

- Ranch vacations—all types
- Fly-fishing
- Pack trips
- Naturalist/wildlife-viewing
- National parks
- River rafting
- Cross-country and downhill skiing
- Snowmobiling

International Riding Adventures:

- Horseback Trips Worldwide

Kilgore Ranch Travel

Phone: (916) 583-6926
Fax: (916) 583-6900
E-Mail: ranchman@ranchweb.com
Internet: http://www.ranchweb.com

Introduction

Cowboys, Indians, horses, cattle, and ranches have been in my blood since I was five years old. The cowboy's rugged independence, his romantic lifestyle, together with the wide-open spaces, still capture our imaginations and conjure up images that hold a special place in all our hearts. More than ever ranches are in. Every year, Americans, Canadians, Europeans, and visitors from around the world trade in their city shoes for cowboy boots to dream about and experience this unique way of life.

One of the most remarkable things about a ranch vacation is the lasting impression it makes, especially on children. Take your children to the beach for a week. Ten years later ask them the name of it; they will have forgotten. Take them to a ranch, and for the rest of their lives they will remember its name and maybe even the names of their horses. And that's really true!

The history of ranch vacations can be traced to the days of Theodore Roosevelt's Rough Riders in the late nineteenth century. As the story goes, the Eaton Brothers—Howard, Willis, and Alden—established a hay- and horse-ranch near Medora, North Dakota, in 1879. Soon, friends from the East headed west by train to be a part of the Eatons' new and exciting life. Before they knew it, the Eatons were baby-sitting these big-city dudes, taking them out to help with the chores and cattle. The more the dudes did and the dirtier they became, the happier they were.

Word spread, and soon more of these early-day city slickers came out and fell in love with the rugged simplicity of the West and all it gave them. In those days visitors came by train, not for a week but for months at a time. One guest was so at home on the range that he asked Howard Eaton if he could pay room and board in order to stay on. This exchange of money gave birth to an industry.

The Eaton brothers realized the potential in dude ranching and hosting visitors with varying backgrounds and interests. In 1904, they moved their operation from the flatlands of North Dakota to the mountains of Wolf, Wyoming. Today, the Eaton Ranch is run by the third and fourth generations of the family.

Other ranchers soon got into the act. In 1926, the Dude Ranchers' Association held its first meeting. This association is more active today than ever. In 1934 a group of Colorado ranchers formed their own Colorado Dude & Guest Ranch Association. In 1989 ranchers in British Columbia, Canada, started the British Columbia Guest Ranchers' Association. Since then, many other associations have formed. All of these groups (not to mention all the first-rate fly-fishing, cross-country skiing, hunting, and outfitting organizations) are dedicated to preserving and maintaining high standards in their respective industries.

In general, the underlying theme of today's ranch vacation is the horse. Most of the properties included in this guide provide a variety of riding opportunities—for beginner, intermediate, and advanced riders. Every ranch is different, expressing the personality of the terrain as well as that of the host or owner.

Today, while most of the properties are preserving the Old West, many are keeping up with the present by offering modern amenities and services. Besides horseback-riding programs, many offer swimming, mountain biking, fishing, hiking, rodeos, tennis, skeet-shooting, hayrides, and even ballooning. Many realize the importance and enjoyment of learning and have incorporated naturalist talks, art, and photography workshops.

A ranch vacation also enables parents to vacation with their children, where both learn an appreciation for animals and nature. In addition, on a ranch vacation people of all ages and from all walks of life can interact socially, intellectually, and artistically in a marvelously wholesome, intimate, and unique atmosphere.

Accommodations range from very rustic cabins (even sleeping under the stars) to plush, modern suites. Some have natural hot-spring pools, golf, and tennis; others feature whirlpool spas, saunas, exercise equipment, and even massage.

Ranches that take guests include guest ranches, resort ranches, working cattle ranches, fly-fishing ranches, hunting ranches, and cross-country skiing ranches. They can be found throughout the United States and Canada. Most are in the western United States (Colorado, Wyoming, Montana, Idaho, California, and Oregon), the Southwest (Arizona and New Mexico), the Southeast (North Carolina), Texas, and New York state. In Canada, the majority are in the provinces of British Columbia and Alberta.

Ranches in the Southwest and Southeast will have different weather and landscapes from those in the Northwest. Native ranch customs, architecture, equipment, and clothing will vary, too. If you want to see adobe buildings and mesquite and enjoy arid, warm temperatures, there is a property in this guide for you. If the sawtoothed Rocky Mountains are more to your liking, you can experience that, too. Each region offers different attractions and activities. While the location and climate vary, one thing usually remains the same—down-home hospitality.

On Being a Good Dude

The term "dude" goes way back. Lawrence B. Smith, in his book *Dude Ranches and Ponies*, wrote, "'Dude' was applied to an outsider, city person, or tenderfoot; one who came from another element of society and locality; in short, a stranger as far as the West and its ways were concerned. As dude was applied to a male, so the word 'dudeen' later was made to fit the female, and the business of catering to them was called 'dude ranching.'"

If you feel uncomfortable being referred to as a "dude," you might like to know that President Theodore Roosevelt was one of the first men to receive this name. It could be said that everyone is a dude when traveling in unfamiliar territory. Most ranchers and guests would agree that the key ingredients to being a great dude are a love and respect for nature, a willingness to listen and learn, patience, and understanding. One rancher summed it up by saying, "The perfect dude is one who sees beauty, savors nature's peace and quiet, has compassion for his or her fellow man, and has an understanding for what the ranch host must contend with each day to make the ranch holiday seem effortless."

The perfect dude takes it easy the first two days at the ranch and works into the program slowly. "Relax, unwind, don't push too hard too fast," said one rancher to a young Wall Street broker. He added, "Remember, you'll be able to come back year after year for the rest of your life." Most of all, the ability to relax and have fun is essential to being the perfect dude.

Selecting a Ranch

The ranches included in this guide offer a wide range of choices. The most challenging part of your vacation will be selecting where you want to go. As rates are in constant fluctuation, we have chosen to use the following daily rate code:

$ = $0–$100 per person per day
$$ = $100–$150
$$$ = $150–$250
$$$$ = $250–$300
$$$$$ = $300–$400
$$$$$$ = $400 up

For the most part, rates listed are American Plan with meals, lodging, and activities included. Ranches that offer Modified American Plan and European Plan rates have been noted. When you're confirming your reservation, we recommend you verify the rates and exactly what they include. The symbol • preceding the rate code indicates that the ranch offers travel-agent commissions.

I recommend that first you turn to the color photographs at the center of the guide. Here you'll quickly get a feel for some of the beautiful properties listed. After you've looked these over carefully, mosey through the rest of the guide. To find ranches that offer your special interests, turn to the Special Ranch Features section. Then write or telephone the ranches that interest you. I suggest you telephone and speak personally with the owners or managers; you can get a pretty good feel for things by phone. Ask for a brochure and for the names of several past guests you might contact. Call them and ask what sort of time they had, if they have children, too, and if they have any special considerations like yours. Perhaps the most important thing of all in ranch travel is chemistry between owner/manager/staff and you, their guest.

Here are some questions you might like to look over before you call a ranch or lodge.

Gene Kilgore's Questions to Ask

Rates

- What are your rates?
- What is the tipping/gratuity policy?
- Are there special rates for families, children, seniors, and corporations?
- Do you have a non-riding rate?
- Are there off-season rates?
- Is there a minimum length of stay?
- Besides state and local taxes, what do your rates *not* include? What is the tipping policy? (Rates don't always include gratuities or all activities.)

Vacationing with Children (See Special Ranch Features "Children's Programs")

- What does the ranch's children's program include?
- What age must children be to ride? (Today's insurance regulations may not allow very young children to ride.)
- Is child care provided, and to what extent?
- Is this a child-oriented ranch?
- Can children ride with parents?
- Are parents welcome in children's activities?
- Can parents ride with children?
- Do children eat separately?
- Can children eat together?
- What are the qualifications of the child-care providers?
- Is baby-sitting available?

Horses and Riding

- Are riding lessons available?
- What kind of riding program does the ranch have?
- Is it open-meadow riding, or head-to-tail mountain-trail riding?
- Is the program best suited for beginners, or are there opportunities for intermediate and advanced riders, too?
- Are riding helmets required?

- Are riding helmets provided?
- Can I bring my own helmet?
- Are there non-riding days?
- Do I need my own cowboy boots, or is there a boot rental program?
- Do I get the same horse all week?
- Can I brush and saddle my own horse?
- Do the owners/managers take part in the riding program?
- How long are typical rides?
- If I'm a medium or advanced rider, can I jog or lope?
- How many wranglers and guests go out on rides at a time?
- Can I bring my own saddle?
- Can I bring my own horse?
- Do I ride all days of the week?
- Will I need to sign an assumption of risk or waiver form before riding?

Cattle Work

- How many cattle do you run?
- Do guests participate in all cattle activities?
- Can guests brand with the cowboys?
- Do you teach roping?

Miscellaneous

- Is there a staff naturalist?
- Are the activities of the ranch or lodge sufficient for non-riding or non-fishing members of a family?
- Will the ranch cater to special diets? (Some have vegetarian, low-salt, and low-cholesterol menus.)
- Will the ranch provide guest references?
- Are there special clothing requirements?
- Will the ranch provide a clothing/equipment list? (Usually standard procedure.)
- What equipment does the ranch provide? (Fishing rods, tennis rackets, etc.)
- Do I need a license to fish? Should I buy one before I arrive?
- What will the weather be like?
- Can we buy sundry items at the ranch? (Not all ranches have stores on the premises.)
- Do you provide airport, train, or bus pickup? (Many ranches are happy to pick you up. There is often a nominal charge.)
- Do you recommend rental cars? (In most instances, once you arrive you'll not want to leave the ranch. However, you may opt for flexibility and independence.)
- Are laundry facilities available? (Many ranches have laundry facilities; some will even do your laundry.)
- What is your liquor policy? (Many ranches ask that you bring your own wine or liquor. If desired, you can pick these up on your way, or the ranch will get them for you with advance notice. Some ranches offer wine and beer, and a number have fully licensed bars and extensive wine lists.)
- Are any foreign languages spoken?
- Are pets allowed?
- What is the elevation of the ranch?
- Are there wheelchair facilities?

- What is your smoking policy?
- Are there nonsmoking rooms?

Getting There

Whatever method of transportation you choose, it's a good idea to check with the ranch or lodge before you make travel plans. Your hosts will advise you about roads, major commercial airports, and private airstrips. Should you fly or take the train? They'll also tell you whether they will pick you up.

What to Wear

Clothing is an essential part of the ranch-vacation experience. It's important to pack correctly and bring clothes that will enable you to enjoy your Western experience—a pair of boots, several pairs of jeans, a good cowboy belt with buckle, a cowboy hat, several shirts, and a warm jacket are about all you'll really need. Over the years, after hundreds of miles on horseback and thousands of miles in automobiles and airplanes, I know quality clothing is better than quantity. (Well, I guess that goes for most everything in life.)

Here are a few Gene Kilgore clothing tips. Along with quality, think comfort. Invest in a good pair of boots and a cowboy hat. Make sure your boots are well-worn before you arrive—you don't want blisters. Buy at least three pairs of jeans and wash them at least four times, using softener. They'll be much more comfortable and will have faded a bit so you don't look quite so "green." Take along a warm jacket, a sweater, and even a vest. Early mornings and evenings can be cool.

Finally, when making your reservation, ask the ranch or lodge to send you a clothing list to help with your packing. And pardner, one last thing, don't forget a flashlight, some lip protection, mosquito repellent, and sunblock. The ranch or lodge you've selected will be more than happy to give you all the advice you require.

Definitions

ADRA (Arizona Dude Ranch Association): An association of Arizona dude ranches.

BCGRA (British Columbia Guest Ranchers' Association): An association of Canadian ranches in the province of British Columbia, formed in 1989 to market ranch vacations throughout Canada and the United States.

CDGRA (Colorado Dude and Guest Ranch Association): An association founded in 1934, made up solely of Colorado ranch and ranch resort properties dedicated to marketing and maintaining excellence in the Colorado guest-ranch industry. Members meet annually.

Cross-Country Skiing Ranch: A ranch that offers cross-country skiing opportunities. Trails are normally groomed with specialized, professional equipment. Instruction, guide service, and equipment are usually available.

Day Ranch: A ranch or ranch setting (maybe even a Western town) that offers travelers the opportunity to visit and enjoy the spirit of the Old West without providing overnight accommodations. Often horseback rides and full-meal service are available.

Dude: Any individual who is not in his or her natural environment. A business or pleasure traveler who is in another state or even a foreign country. Basically, a dude is you and me—we're all dudes in one way or another!

Dude/Guest Ranch: Usually a family-owned and -operated ranch with the primary objective of offering its guests a Western experience. Horseback riding is usually the main activity; hiking, fishing, and swimming are often included.

DRA (The Dude Ranchers' Association): An association of Western dude ranches, founded in

1926, dedicated to maintaining the quality and high standards of Western hospitality established by early ranches.

Fly-Fishing Ranch: A facility offering an extensive fly-fishing program with instruction and guides. Some ranches/lodges have on-premises tackle shops.

Hideaway Report: A privately published newsletter dedicated to the discovery of peaceful vacations and executive retreats for the sophisticated traveler. Author's Note: This monthly newsletter is highly esteemed by experts in the travel industry. All properties that have been featured in the *Hideaway Report* are so noted under "Awards."

Gymkhana: A series of games or events on horseback.

Hunting Lodge: A facility that specializes in seasonal big-game or bird hunting. Many of these lodges offer activities for non-hunting family members. Some provide full-service hunting and support facilities. Many have father–son programs.

IGDRA (Idaho Guest and Dude Ranch Association): An association of Idaho dude ranches.

MDRA (Montana Dude Ranch Association): An association of Montana dude ranches.

Naturalist: One who is trained in the appreciation and understanding of nature and the outdoor world.

Orvis-Endorsed: Orvis, the respected fly-fishing company, realized there was a need to check out and endorse top-notch fishing lodges with first-rate guides. Today, Orvis-endorsed lodges are monitored by Orvis personnel. These lodges provide complete fly-fishing guide services. Each has its own fly-fishing tackle shop. Orvis-endorsed lodges in this book are designated as such.

Pack Trip: An overnight, multiple-day, week-long, or month-long trip on horseback. All supplies, including food, tents, and equipment, are carried by horses, mules, or sometimes even llamas. Usually a magnificent wilderness experience.

PRCA (Professional Rodeo Cowboys Association): An association dedicated to promoting and setting the standards of the professional rodeo industry.

Resort Ranch: A facility that may or may not have a Western theme but does offer horseback riding. Usually the amenities are upscale, with a range of resort activities offered. Note: Some properties use "resort" in their names but may not offer resort amenities.

Rodeo: A cowboys' tournament or competition in which men and women compete in an arena; involves livestock (horses, steers, bulls) and barrel racing.

TGRA (Texas Guest Ranch Association): An association of Texas dude ranches.

Wagon Trains: Original or restored covered wagons that transport participants on day or overnight trips so they can experience the life of pioneers, explorers, and mountain men. (See Appendix for list of companies.)

Wilderness Lodge: In the heart of wilderness areas, these facilities offer a retreat from civilization. Generally, all supplies arrive by plane, boat, horse, or sometimes four-wheel-drive vehicle.

Wrangler: Originally, a cowboy who was hired on at a guest ranch to "wrangle" (herd and care for) horses and take dudes out on day and overnight rides. Today, a wrangler may be male or female, a college student or a cowboy. There is no telling what a wrangler's background might be. The important ingredient is that the wrangler is experienced with horses, and patient, understanding, and friendly with dudes.

WDRA (Wyoming Dude Rancher's Association): An association of Wyoming dude ranches.

WANTED

A Few Good Guests

You're about to begin one of your most exciting adventures: selecting the right ranch or lodge for you, your family, your friends, your company, or your clients. To begin, I ask you to sit back and relax, maybe prop your feet up on your desk or settle into your favorite chair in front of a blazing fire. Our goal is to help you by connecting you with a wide variety of properties across the United States and Canada. After you've looked at the beautiful color photos in the center of the guide and read about the ranches and lodges, contact those that interest you. Unlike any other holiday experience that I know of, the secret to this one is chemistry, just like a marriage. If the chemistry is good, the marriage is golden. If not, as an old cowboy told me, "Better saddle up and ride on."

So mosey through this guide, enjoy the color-photo section, make some calls, ask questions, and—*this is very important*—ask for references (former guests who have enjoyed the ranch or lodge and whom you may call). We also invite you to visit the Worldwide Ranch Headquarters on the Internet at http://www.ranchweb.com. You may have to do a little work, but just like a horseback ride, once you get in the saddle all kinds of exciting things can happen.

ONE OF GENE KILGORE'S FAVORITE RANCH SAYINGS

We have gentle horses for gentle people,
Spirited horses for spirited people,
And for people who don't like to ride,
We have horses that don't like to be ridden.
—Lake Mancos Ranch, Colorado

Guest and Resort Ranches
in the United States

Kachemak Bay Wilderness Lodge
China Poot Bay, Homer, Alaska

As the author, I've taken the liberty of including a few extra-special places that don't fit the exact mold of a ranch but do capture the spirit of adventure and wilderness. This is one of them. Michael and Diane McBride call on their special talents to enrich your vacation in North America's last great frontier—Alaska. Michael is a member of the prestigious Explorers Club and has 30 years of experience in Alaska's wilderness. He is a master guide, naturalist, licensed skipper, and bush pilot. His wife and partner, Diane, has a background in biology and will help you understand the natural history of the region. Kachemak Bay Wilderness Lodge on Cook Inlet is a hideaway in Alaska's wilderness. It is a place for nature lovers, fishermen, photographers, and those seeking the quiet solitude of lush forests and untracked beaches. Nestled among the towering spruce of China Poot Bay, the lodge commands a spectacular view of the surrounding mountain peaks, ocean, seabird rookeries, and seal herds on sand bars. Kachemak Bay lies at the end of the famous Kenai Peninsula, 100 air miles southwest of Anchorage, and is accessible only by seaplane or boat. You will see why it attracts so many world-famous photographers. The sea is at your feet, the forest at your back, and five glaciers rest in this magnificent region.

Address: P.O. Box 956 K, China Poot Bay, Homer, Alaska 99603
Telephone: (907) 235-8910; fax: (907) 235-8911
E-Mail: wildrnes@xyz.net
Internet: http://www.xyz.net/~wildrnes.htm
Airport: Homer
Location: seven air miles east of Homer
Memberships: Explorers Club, Interpretive Naturalists, Audubon Society
Awards: Listed in *America's Best 100* as "America's best wilderness lodge"; *Hideaway Report* 1996 calls it one of the 100 best destinations in the world
Medical: Homer South Peninsula Hospital, 15 miles; emergency helicopter service
Conference: 15
Guest Capacity: 15
Accommodations: Each of the four uniquely different cabins, with the names Cliff House, Stone House, Boat House, and Goose Point House, has its own wood-burning stove, electricity, homemade quilts, and full modern bathroom; baskets with California wine, Swiss chocolates, and fresh fruit await the arrival of all guests. The main lodge has a wonderful stone fireplace and also its own private guest room with full bath and private entrance. Private outdoor hot tub and sod-roofed Finnish sauna are about 50 feet from the lodge.
Rates: $$$$$$. American Plan. Ask about Chenik Camp (bear-viewing camp) and Mountain Lake Loon Song Camp for canoeing and hiking. Floatplane transportation extra.
Credit Cards: None. Personal checks accepted.
Season: May to October
Activities: The lodge is a naturalist's and fisher's haven. Ask about the superb guides in the areas of marine life, anthropology, botany, fishing, and kayaking. Observe and photograph marine mammals, seabirds, bald eagles, moose, bears, sea otters, and whales. Enjoy tide-pooling (29-foot tidal range); clams and mussels; fishing for trout, salmon, char, flounder, and halibut; kayaking, canoeing, and rowboating.
Children's Programs: Individualized. Best for children age eight and up.
Dining: Master chef; fresh seafood daily from the bay. Homemade bread and pastries. Delicious bouillabaisse gets rave reviews. Fine wine and beer served. Bring your own liquor or order in advance. Room service available.
Entertainment: Weekly natural-history slide program, piano, Michael plays a mean guitar and accordion.
Summary: Michael and Diane McBride run one of the premier wilderness lodges in the world. Besides an emphasis on personal service, they and their staff (all of whom have a special interest in and knowledge of the environment) offer a superb naturalist program, as well as interpretive naturalist and photography workshops. Outreach Chenik Camp is their remote sister lodge for observing brown bears near McNeil River Brown Bear Sanctuary.

Crystal Creek Lodge
Dillingham, Alaska

You've probably dreamed about Alaska—and with good reason. It's big, fresh, wild, free, and filled with adventure. This is a land of mountains, tundra, glaciers, and lakes, where the scenery is overwhelming and the wildlife untamed. Located amid all this is Crystal Creek Lodge. Owner Dan Michels and his fine staff offer men and women an Alaskan adventure/fishing experience second to none. At Crystal Creek you'll be treated like a king and get to see and fish as much of Alaska as you could possibly want in a week. If you're one of those who likes to really rough it or doesn't like to fly, this is probably not the place for you. The lodge offers all upscale amenities. Fly-out service each day via floatplane or helicopter with your guide is a major part of this exhilarating Alaskan experience.

Address: Box 92170K, Anchorage, Alaska 99509
Telephone: (800) 525-3153, (907) 245-1945; fax: (907) 245-1946
E-Mail: crystalc@alaska.net
Internet: http://www.crystalcreeklodge.com
Location: Bristol Bay area, southwest Alaska; 320 miles southwest of Anchorage, 15 miles northwest of Dillingham
Awards: Orvis-endorsed Lodge
Medical: Kanaknek Hospital in Dillingham, 20-minute helicopter flight
Conference: 20
Guest Capacity: 20
Accommodations: The 9,800-square-foot main lodge is the center of operation. There are 13 double-occupancy rooms on two levels (1–7 lower, 8–13 upper); room three is the most spacious. Each is modern with full amenities, including queen-size beds, full bathrooms (tub and shower combination) with plenty of hot water even though the lodge is powered by its own generator, and individual temperature controls. Because during the summer months it's light almost 20 hours a day, there are "blackout" shades in each room. Daily maid and laundry services are provided. The lodge also has changing and boot-drying rooms.
Rates: $$$$$$. Full American Plan. Sunday to Sunday with six days fishing and seven nights lodging. Includes everything except liquor, gratuity, and round-trip airfare to Dillingham.
Credit Cards: VISA, MasterCard
Season: Mid-June to mid-September
Activities: The lodge is right on Lake Nunavaugaluk in the center of southwest Alaska's Bristol Bay area, known for its large salmon runs and trophy-class trout, char, and grayling fishing. Four planes and one helicopter will take you and your guide to remote fishing areas. Here you'll fish for king, chum, sockeye, pink, and silver salmon, rainbow and lake trout, arctic char, arctic grayling, Dolly Varden, and northern pike. Fully equipped tackle shop in lodge and use of all appropriate rods, reels, tackle, and waders are included.
Children's Programs: Children welcome. Not recommended for children under age 10.
Dining: Excellent cuisine, cooked to order. After breakfast the chef will ask for your dinner preference from three different entrées that change daily. Streamside sack lunches (place your lunch order the night before), and occasionally your guide will prepare fresh-caught salmon. Complimentary house wine served with dinner. Fine wine list available.
Entertainment: After a full day of fishing and flying, most guests are delightfully worn out.
Summary: Crystal Creek Lodge offers excellent personal service, comfort, and superb daily fly-in/fly-out fishing. You'll see an abundance of wildlife. Highest aircraft and guide-to-guest ratio in Alaska. If you desire, your legal limit of freshly caught salmon will be cleaned, vacuum-packed, and frozen for your trip home. (Author's note: You should definitely like to fly and enjoy fishing. Avid photographers should bring plenty of film.)

Orvis

Circle Z Ranch
Patagonia, Arizona

THE DUDE RANCHERS' ASSOCIATION

ARIZONA DUDE RANCH ASSOCIATION

The Circle Z Ranch, founded in 1926, nestles in a picturesque mountain valley at 4,000 feet surrounded by steep canyons, colorful hills, and dramatic mountain backdrops. Unique to the ranch, and most unusual in southern Arizona, is a wonderful creek they call "Sonoita," which is bordered for miles by century-old cottonwood trees. This was Apache country, and relics of the Spanish conquistadors are still found. Hollywood has been here, filming *Broken Lance*, John Wayne's *Red River*, and television's *Gunsmoke*, to name a few. The Circle Z is romantic, with its adobe buildings reflecting the Spanish influence and early-West simplicity. Circle Z is run by delightful resident managers and has been owned since 1974 by Lucia Nash, who fell in love with it when brought here by her family as a child. Ranch-bred horses and a variety of trails coupled with delicious food and warm hospitality bring guests back year after year. Bird-watchers flock to the Circle Z to see some of the rarest species in the United States. You'll find all the easygoing pleasures of dude-ranch life at the Circle Z.

Address: P.O. Box 194, Dept. K, Patagonia, Arizona 85624
Telephone: (888) 854-2525, (520) 394-2525; fax: (520) 394-2058
E-Mail: info@circlez.com
Internet: http://www.circlez.com
Airport: Tucson; private planes at Nogales, eight miles away
Location: 60 miles south of Tucson, directly off Highway 82; 15 miles north of Mexican border
Memberships: The Dude Ranchers' Association, Arizona Dude Ranch Association
Medical: Carondelet Holy Cross Hospital, 15 miles
Guest Capacity: 40
Accommodations: Comfortable and attractive. There are seven adobe cottages with 27 rooms with private baths and showers (many with Mexican tile), a variety of bed sizes, and colorful rugs on wooden floors. Electric blankets are available. All rooms, suites, and cottages have individually controlled heat and outside entrances onto porches or patios. Laundry facilities available.
Rates: $–$$. American Plan. Weekend and off-peak rates available. Three-day minimum stay.
Credit Cards: None. Personal checks accepted.
Season: November to mid-May
Activities: Experienced wranglers lead twice-daily scenic and loping rides plus many all-day and picnic rides on a remarkable variety of trails across 6,000 acres of deeded ranch land and the contiguous Coronado National Forest. Ask about Ardent Riders Month in January and the weekly overnight pack trip with heated wall tents. The emphasis is on maintaining the atmosphere of an old-time family ranch: riding instruction, hiking, swimming in an outdoor heated pool, and an all-weather tennis court. Fishing in Lake Patagonia and an 18-hole championship golf course nearby.
Children's Programs: Although there is no planned children's program and child care is not provided, children are welcome. Ping-Pong, shuffleboard, horseshoes, basketball. Kids' cantina with pool table and jukebox. Most children under age five do not ride.
Dining: Meals are served in the dining room or on the patio of the main lodge. Variety of fine-quality cuisine. Ranch specialties include mesquite-grilled steaks, mild Southwestern dishes, home-baked breads, and desserts. Adobe cantina for adults has piano, game table, and large wooden deck for relaxing. BYOB. Children dine earlier in their own dining room.
Entertainment: Mostly rest and relaxation, but occasional country-music entertainers. Ranch has player piano with 100 tunes.
Summary: Riding is the main thing here, and if you choose, you may keep the same horse throughout your stay. Great for people who enjoy nature and won't miss TV and in-room telephones. Unstructured other than riding and meals. Bird-watcher's paradise at ranch and adjacent Nature Conservancy preserve. Nearby: Mining and ghost towns, an artisan village, Spanish mission, Mexican border-town shopping, and visits to Old West tourist towns of Tombstone and Bisbee. Spanish spoken.

See color photos, page 169.

Elkhorn Ranch
Tucson, Arizona

THE DUDE RANCHERS' ASSOCIATION

ARIZONA DUDE RANCH ASSOCIATION

The Millers' Elkhorn Ranch is old-time dude ranching at its best! At 3,700 feet, the ranch sits in a secluded valley, surrounded by the picturesque Baboquivari mountain range, with canyons, rolling hills, mesquite, and open desert to the east. The ranch is small and informal, well out of the city, with activities centering on the outdoors. It's a lovely part of the Southwest. The Miller family has been operating this riding ranch since 1945; today it's run by the third generation—Charley and Mary Miller. The Elkhorn offers unexcelled riding and a relaxed way of life for 32 guests. The ranch spirit encourages family group fun but offers lots of time to be alone if you wish. The cabins and ranch buildings are designed in the Southwestern architectural style. With 10,000 acres and over 100 horses, unlimited riding and hiking are assured. The less-adventurous can relax by the pool or outside each cabin. Bring your camera and binoculars—Arizona's birds are numerous.

Address: HC1 Box 97, Tucson, Arizona 85736
Telephone: (520) 822-1040
Internet:http://www.guestranches.com/elkhorn
Airport: Tucson
Location: 50 miles southwest of Tucson, off Route 286 between Mileposts 25 and 26
Memberships: The Dude Ranchers' Association, Arizona Dude Ranch Association
Medical: St. Mary's Hospital in Tucson, 50 miles
Guest Capacity: 32
Accommodations: Guests enjoy Southwestern-style cabins that vary from one to two bedrooms, some with sitting rooms and open fireplaces with mesquite firewood, all with private baths and electric heat. Cabins have tiled and cement floors with Mexican throw-rugs, some original art. Daily maid service and nightly bed turn-down service.
Rates: $$–$$$. American Plan. Special rates for stays of two or three weeks or longer. One-week minimum stay in high season tends to be Sunday to Sunday, four-night minimum stay in low season.
Credit Cards: None. Personal checks or traveler's checks accepted.
Season: Mid-November through April
Activities: Some of the best riding in the country. Each morning at breakfast, Charley Miller meets with guests to discuss riding interests and options. As Charley says, "If someone really wants to ride, we sure try to accommodate them." And he does! With more than 100 horses, all levels of guided riding are provided on desert or mountain trails. Lions' Hotel, Sycamore Canyon, and Mine Canyon are just a few of the favorites. Moonlight rides offered. Surfaced tennis court and kidney-shaped 50-foot heated swimming pool. Shuffleboard, table tennis, horseshoe-pitching, and a pistol/rifle range (bring your own guns) are offered, as well as bird-watching and hiking.
Children's Programs: Kiddie wrangler. No special program. No baby-sitting, but nannies are welcome. Prefer children old enough to ride (ages six and older).
Dining: Delicious home-cooked meals served buffet-style in the longhouse or on the patio. Cookouts on the trail, picnics in the desert, and dinners cooked on the barbecue. BYOB in cabins only.
Entertainment: Rest and relaxation. Stargazing, bridge, or enjoy the ranch's extensive library—you're pretty much on your own.
Summary: One of the nicest families in the business. Many repeat-guest families, couples, and singles. Newcomers always feel a part of the family. Superb desert and mountain riding. Excellent ranch-raised horses and one of the best ranch riding programs in the country. Beginners can learn here, and advanced riders can be challenged. Nearby: Arizona-Sonora Living Desert Museum, Kitt Peak Observatory, the Tohono O'odham Reservation, and old Spanish missions of San Xavier and Tumacacori.

Flying E Ranch
Wickenburg, Arizona

THE DUDE RANCHERS' ASSOCIATION

ARIZONA DUDE RANCH ASSOCIATION

Flying E Ranch, the "riding ranch," is a few miles west of Wickenburg. Since 1960, owner-manager Vi Wellik has been hosting families, couples, and singles who come to savor the ranch's wonderful spirit and friendly hospitality. As Vi says, "We've been hosting guests for 40 years and serving up our own brand of dude-ranch hospitality." Located in the Hassayampa Valley on the north edge of the Sonoran Desert, the Flying E rests on a 2,400-foot mesa at the foot of historic Vulture Peak. Warm days, starlit nights, beautiful desert scenery, relaxed ambiance, and privacy keep guests returning year after year. Come to ride, swim, play tennis, relax, or stroll the scenic walking paths. Flying E is one of the most immaculately kept ranches I've ever seen. Vi, her husband, Bill Bryant, her staff, and her "down-home" dude ranch are very special and will receive you with open arms!

Address: 2801 W. Wickenburg Way, Dept. K, Wickenburg, Arizona 85390-1087
Telephone: (520) 684-2690; fax: (520) 684-5304
E-Mail: vacation@flyingeranch.com
Internet: www.flyingeranch.com
Airport: Phoenix Sky Harbor. Private planes and executive jets land at Wickenburg Municipal Airport (Wellik Field), across from the ranch.
Location: On Highway 60, approximately 60 miles northwest of Phoenix and four miles west of Wickenburg's town center
Memberships: The Dude Ranchers' Association, Arizona Dude Ranch Association
Medical: Wickenburg Regional Hospital, five miles
Guest Capacity: 34-plus
Accommodations: Rooms are "squeaky clean," comfortable, electrically heated and air-conditioned, with delightful Western decor. All rooms have TVs, private baths, air-conditioning, electric blankets, refrigerators, and wet bars. Ask about the "family house" and the Southwest Suite.
Rates: • $$–$$$. American Plan. Children's rates available when occupying same room as parents. Horseback riding extra. Two-night minimum (November and December), three-night minimum (January to May), four-night minimum (all holiday periods).
Credit Cards: None. Personal checks, travelers checks and cash accepted.
Season: November 1 to May 1
Activities: Do as much or as little as you wish. You won't be programmed every minute. Two-hour morning and afternoon horseback rides to places like Mt. Everett, Robbers Roost, and Yucca Flats. Beginner, intermediate, and advanced rides. Instruction available. Breakfast cookouts, lunch rides, chuck-wagon feeds, and occasional hayrides. Beautiful heated pool, hot spa, exercise room, sauna, shuffleboard, basketball, volleyball, horseshoe-pitching, rock-hounding, and lighted tennis court. While many come to horseback ride, some prefer to experience the desert by foot on the many walking trails. Eighteen-hole championship golf course at nearby Los Caballeros Golf Club; guests play on ranch membership. Town offers outstanding Desert Caballeros Museum, art galleries, and fine Western stores.
Children's Programs: Children are parents' responsibility! No children's programs.
Dining: Hearty and genuinely good food served family-style in private dining room. Social hour with hors d'oeuvres each evening. BYOB. No bar.
Entertainment: Occasional "inter-ranch" square and line dancing in barn loft, and "dudeos" (games on horseback) in ranch area. A cozy living room with fireplace, entertainment center, and grand piano.
Summary: Vi says, "Flying E is a spirit," and so it is. The ranch staff is dedicated to sincere, friendly service. Because of this, most of the families, couples, and singles who come are repeat guests or friends of guests. For many, the ranch is their "Camelot of the Old West." The words of a recent new guest say it all: "There are places in life that make life a better place. In a very short time, I somehow felt at home there, on horseback, in beautiful country with the warmth of new friends who seem like old friends. Well done! Thank you! See ya soon."

See color photos, page 170.

Grapevine Canyon Ranch

Pearce, Arizona

THE DUDE RANCHERS' ASSOCIATION

ARIZONA DUDE RANCH ASSOCIATION

Grapevine Canyon Ranch, a working cattle ranch as well as a guest ranch, lies in the heart of Apache country at a 5,000-foot elevation. The ranch buildings, nestled in groves of Arizona oak, manzanita, and mesquite trees, are almost invisible in this wooded canyon, with mountains forming a three-sided backdrop. The ranch is owned and operated by Eve and Gerry Searle, whose philosophy can be summed up in two words: personal attention. Gerry, a longtime rancher, also spent many years in the movie industry, doubling for stars in stunt riding, including every episode of *High Chaparral*. Eve came to the United States from Melbourne, Australia, where she worked as a flight instructor. She has a cosmopolitan background, having lived in Europe, India, Australia, and Mexico before settling in Arizona. Grapevine is famous for its program of trail rides, seasonal cattle work, horsemanship seminars, horseback games, and all-day rides, for which riders and horses are transported to the trailhead in the forest wilderness; also history rides to abandoned ghost towns, Fort Bowie, and Chiricahua National Monument. One European couple summed up the ranch best: "As children we dreamed it, as adults we have lived it at Grapevine Canyon Ranch."

Address: P.O. Box 302 K, Pearce, Arizona 85625
Telephone: (800) 245-9202, (520) 826-3185; fax: (520) 826-3636
E-Mail: egrapevine@earthlink.net
Internet: http://www.beadude.com
Airport: Tucson
Location: 85 miles southeast of Tucson, off Interstate 10
Memberships: The Dude Ranchers' Association, Arizona Dude Ranch Association
Medical: Willcox Hospital, 40 miles
Conference: 25
Guest Capacity: 30
Accommodations: Two-room *casitas* or pleasant single-room cabins. Each is air-cooled; all are quiet and individually decorated in delightful country style with a Southwestern touch. Most are secluded in groves of Arizona oak. All are fully carpeted and equipped with full or three-quarter baths, coffeepots, stocked refrigerator, sun deck, and porch.
Rates: • $$$. Stocked refrigerator, sun deck, and porch. Three-night minimum stay.
Credit Cards: VISA, MasterCard, Discover, American Express. Personal checks accepted.
Season: Year-round including Christmas, Thanksgiving, and Easter. (Closed December 1–15)
Activities: Horseback riding is the most popular. Ride groups are small so riders with similar ability can ride together up to seven hours a day. Long and short rides, catering both to novice and experienced riders. Guests may unsaddle and brush their horses at the end of the day. For safety, a check-out ride to prove that you can handle a horse at speed is required before you can join the fast rides. Occasional cattle work. Beautifully curved swimming pool (heated April to October), and Jacuzzi. Sightseeing, including Mexico and legendary Tombstone. Hiking trails, over 90 species of birds, and a lake stocked with bass and catfish. Golf nearby (seven miles).
Children's Programs: No children under age 12.
Dining: Hearty ranch breakfasts cooked to individual order. Lunch and dinner are served buffet-style. Roasted Cornish game hens, chimichangas, barbecued pork and beef ribs, steak and roast beef, rich homemade desserts, and ice cream. Beer and wine available.
Entertainment: Video/TV room with film library, books, and magazines, occasional live country music. Dummy steer-roping, darts, recreation room with pool table and Ping-Pong.
Summary: Intimate guest ranch with extensive riding for the novice to the professional rider. International clientele. Emphasis is on personalized, friendly service. Relaxation, seasonal cattle work in the beautiful Arizona high country. Group and corporate programs available.

See color photos, page 171.

Grand Canyon Bar Ten Ranch
in Arizona near St. George, Utah

The lodge at the Bar Ten Ranch is located about nine miles from the north rim of the Grand Canyon. From this modern sandstone-brick lodge, you can see in the distance the grandeur of these red cliffs. For years, the Bar Ten Ranch has been a starting and ending point for guests on Colorado River rafting trips. The history and excitement of the Grand Canyon and the Colorado River are yours at the Bar Ten, a working cattle ranch that boasts 60,000 acres and 400 head of cattle. No telephones or oiled roads. Urgent messages are delivered by two-way radio from town. Tony and Ruby, along with their six children and family members, host guests who come to experience Colorado River rafting trips and the ranch tour packages. The Bar Ten offers a unique blend of remoteness and modern comforts. One guest wrote, "You have created an experience that enriches the lives of your guests! The Bar Ten Ranch is an unforgettable experience!" Hearty country meals, varied ranch activities, and hospitality provide guests with a lasting Grand Canyon and Western ranch experience!

Address: P.O. Box 910088 K, St. George, Utah 84791
Telephone: (800) 582-4139, (435) 628-4010; fax: (435) 628-5124
E-Mail: bar10@infowest.com
Internet: http://www.infowest.com/bar10
Airport: McCarren, Las Vegas; direct charter flights available; dirt airstrip on ranch (call in advance for flight information)
Location: 80 miles south of St. George, Utah (two-hour drive on dirt road, 30-minute flight); 200 miles east of Las Vegas (four-hour drive, one-hour flight; most guests fly)
Medical: Dixie Medical Center, St. George, Utah; helicopter available for emergencies
Conference: 60
Guest Capacity: 60
Accommodations: For the adventurous, there are covered wagons for private sleeping on the hillside behind the main lodge—great for couples. Surrounded by lawns and desert landscape, the two-story Bar Ten lodge has comfortable dormitory-style rooms with bunk beds and common bathrooms. The main floor of the lodge is home to the Bar Ten Trading Post, which sells river supplies, books, gifts, snacks, T-shirts, and other unique souvenirs.
Rates: • $$. American Plan. Includes everything except airfare and helicopter rides. Call for package rates.
Credit Cards: VISA, MasterCard
Season: April through October. Off-season rates available for groups.
Activities: The Bar Ten Ranch offers a variety of entertaining activities and tour packages, including Colorado River rafting trips, overnight packages consisting of one or more days at the ranch, cattle drives, horseback pack trips, and scenic flights combined with part- or full-day ranch adventures and/or a trip to the rim of the Grand Canyon. Ranch activities may include a Western demonstration, horseback riding, horseshoes, skeet-shooting, hiking, basketball, volleyball, and other group activities. Scenic helicopter rides available most days during the season (extra).
Children's Programs: No specific programs. Children under age eight not advised for river trips.
Dining: Cowboy breakfast, sandwich-bar lunch, chuck-wagon Dutch-oven dinners (i.e., potatoes, beef, homemade bread, vegetable, and dessert). BYOB.
Entertainment: The Bar Ten gang puts on a terrific patriotic show with singing, clogging, cowboy poetry, fiddle-playing, country songs with wranglers, and a slide show depicting the evolution of the Bar Ten. The show usually ends with watermelon and mingling.
Summary: Remote ranch located about nine miles from the north rim of the Grand Canyon, specializing in ranch and spectacular river-rafting packages and tours. Many guests come for the day, some overnight, and others stay longer for various adventure programs. Most guests arrive by helicopter or airplane. Other adventures include: cattle drives, horseback pack trips, overnight tours, and scenic flights. For family, business, seminars, and youth groups.

The Horseshoe Ranch on Bloody Basin Road
Mayer, Arizona

THE DUDE RANCHERS' ASSOCIATION

ARIZONA DUDE RANCH ASSOCIATION

One hundred square miles, a century-old brand, 1,700 head of cattle, cottonwoods, sycamores, and mesquite trees embracing the desert landscape—welcome to The Horseshoe Ranch, one of Arizona's oldest working cattle ranches that opens its gates to a limited number of guests from around the world who wish to experience real ranch life. At The Horseshoe, good old Western hospitality is alive and well with the Wilcox family. At 3,200 feet, the ranch is set on a stretch of the Agua Fria River, soon to be included in the Wild and Scenic National River System. It's a place where perennial live water flows, a rare and greatly prized thing in Arizona. Juniper-studded mountains rise to 6,000 feet and pueblos of Perry Mesa Tradition, a 1,000-year-old prehistoric Indian culture, are yours to discover. Dick Wilcox, wife Millie, daughter Charlotte, and their staff, are dedicated to enhancing lives and sharing the rich traditions of the West with men and women who come to ride this ruggedly beautiful landscape.

Address: HCR 34, Box 5005, Mayer, Arizona 86333
Telephone: (520) 632-8813; fax: (520) 632-8813
E-Mail: hranch@primenet.com
Internet: http://www.primenet.com\~hranch
Airport: Phoenix, with scheduled shuttle service by "Shuttle U" and ranch pickup at Cordes Junction
Location: 65 miles north of Phoenix on Interstate 17 to the Bloody Basin Road Exit (1½-hour drive). Nearest town is Cordes Junction.
Memberships: Cattle Growers' Association, The Dude Ranchers' Association, Arizona Dude Ranch Association
Medical: Phoenix Hospital, 65 miles; emergency helicopter service available
Guest Capacity: 10 adults; capacity is much higher if you "rent the ranch"
Accommodations: Eight large guest rooms in modern ranch homes, all with baths. Rooms are immaculate, and you sleep between sun-dried sheets. The main ranch has two large sitting rooms, each with stone fireplace, where guests gather for conversation and impromptu fun.
Rates: • $$$. American Plan. Three-day minimum stay, arrive any day.
Credit Cards: VISA, MasterCard
Season: The ranch has two regular guest seasons—Fall: October 1 to November 30; spring: early March to mid-May. Their *Rent the Ranch* program, where the ranch belongs just to your group, is available from December 1 until early March.
Activities: Activities are tailored to the cattle and the season. After dinner, one of the cowboys takes the topo map of the range and describes what needs to be done, where, and how to get there. Cowboy/guest team assignments are worked out to fit each individual's ability, strength, and inclination. Whether tenderfoot or top hand, there is always plenty to do. What you don't know, you'll learn! If you "rent the ranch," all activities are custom-planned to meet the needs of your group.
Children's Programs: No children under age 12 except when you "rent the ranch."
Dining: One table seats all. The extended ranch family gathers to enjoy abundant, hearty, ranch-style food and swap tales of the day's adventures. Mesquite-grilled steaks and Mexican specialties are favorites. The long Arizona growing season guarantees lots of fresh vegetables and fruit from the ranch garden and orchard. Ranch neighbors are invited for dinner from time to time—a great ranching tradition. BYOB.
Entertainment: No scheduled events. Photos, slides, and videos are sometimes used to support stories of earlier adventures. Guests and staff make their own fun. Laughs are never in short supply.
Summary: Old-time goodness with modern comforts. A wonderful rancher's ranch for experienced riders! One hundred square miles and 1,700 head of cattle. A place where the needs of the cattle shape each day, where you can learn about the business of ranching and savor sincere Western hospitality. Early to bed and early to rise. Ask about the *Rent the Ranch* program. Nearby: Sedona, Jerome, and the Grand Canyon.

See color photos, page 172.

Lazy K Bar Guest Ranch
Tucson, Arizona

THE DUDE RANCHERS' ASSOCIATION

ARIZONA DUDE RANCH ASSOCIATION

Just 16 miles northwest of Tucson, the Lazy K Bar Guest Ranch nestles against the Tucson Mountains overlooking the Santa Cruz Valley. Owned by Bill Scott and managed by Carol Moore, the ranch is run on the "Arizona Plan"—that is, all facilities and entertainment are included in one nightly rate with a three-night minimum stay. The Lazy K Bar is a well-rounded vacation destination offering riding, swimming, tennis, hiking, or relaxing—something for everyone in the family. Guests also enjoy the ranch's library, stocked with numerous books, and can meet before dinner at the ranch's Long Horn Bar for a cocktail. While rooms have no TVs or telephones, there is a large-screen TV in the main lodge. At the Lazy K Bar you will enjoy Arizona desert beauty and warm, family hospitality.

Address: 8401 N. Scenic Drive, Dept. K, Tucson, Arizona 85743
Telephone: (800) 321-7018, (520) 744-3050; fax: (520) 744-7628
E-Mail: lazyk@theriver.com
Internet: http://www.lazykbar.com
Airport: Tucson, private airstrip nearby
Location: 16 miles northwest of Tucson off Silverbell Road. Call ranch for directions.
Memberships: The Dude Ranchers' Association, Arizona Dude Ranch Association
Awards: AAA 2 Diamond
Medical: Northwest Hospital, 10 miles
Conference: 50
Guest Capacity: 65
Accommodations: The main lodge is the center for all social activities. Guests can stroll comfortably down the gravel paths from the lodge to single rooms and suites located in the nine adobe buildings. Each of the 23 rooms has individually controlled heat and air-conditioning, private bath, carpeting, and king, queen, or extra-long twin beds. Large family rooms are equipped with daybeds or sofa beds. Southwestern motif. Laundry facilities available.
Rates: • $$–$$$. American Plan. Rates depend on season and size of cottage. Children's rates. Minimum three-night stay. Trap-shooting, tennis lessons, riding lessons, and massage available at additional charge. Off-premises riding excursions can be arranged at additional charge.
Credit Cards: VISA, MasterCard, American Express, Discover. Personal checks accepted.
Season: Mid-September through mid-June. Mid-June through mid-July children's horsemanship camp.
Activities: Horseback riding through mountain and desert country. Two rides (slow and fast) twice a day all week. Weekly breakfast or lunch rides go into Saguaro National Park. Team penning, a horse-and-cattle activity with guest participation. Heated pool, two lighted tennis courts, Jacuzzi, volleyball, horseshoe-pitching, trap-shooting, shuffleboard, and basketball. Recreation room with billiards, Ping-Pong, and shuffleboard table. Excellent golf in Tucson, 10 minutes away.
Children's Programs: No special program. Kids under age six ride with supervision in arena. Baby sitting can be arranged at an hourly rate. Children are welcome.
Dining: Hearty ranch-style meals. Saturday night T-bone steaks are mesquite-broiled and served under the stars next to the ranch's 30-foot waterfall. Tuesday night favorite, "all-you-can-eat" barbecue rib cookout. Breakfast cooked to order, luncheon buffets, many great Mexican dishes. BYOB.
Entertainment: Nature talks, team-drawn hayrides, square dancing, Western music, country-Western dance lessons, TV room for viewing special programs, rodeos in town. Tucson evening entertainment within a 20-minute drive.
Summary: Casual, relaxed ranch. Riding program geared to individual ability with opportunities to increase your horse knowledge. Ranch is great for those who enjoy outdoor activities or just relaxing in the Arizona sunshine. A haven for bird-watchers. Sunday excursions to the Sonoran Desert Museum or Old Tucson Movie Studio. Other points of interest include San Xavier Mission, Colossal Cave, and Biosphere II.

See color photos, page 173.

Kay El Bar
Wickenburg, Arizona

THE DUDE RANCHERS' ASSOCIATION

ARIZONA DUDE RANCH ASSOCIATION

This lovely old guest ranch, established in 1926, is listed on the National Register of Historic Places. Today it is owned and operated by John and Nancy Loftis. What attracted them to the ranch was "the history, beautiful handmade adobe bricks, towering eucalyptus trees, the green grass, small size, and most of all the incredible charm!" The ranch offers a desert oasis with friendly hospitality where guests quickly feel like part of the family. Guests enjoy beautiful, varied riding terrain and a relaxed atmosphere with folks from around the world who share a love of the West, horses, and camaraderie! Welcome to the Kay El Bar Ranch.

Address: P.O. Box 2480 K, Wickenburg, Arizona 85358
Telephone: (800) 684-7583, (520) 684-7593; fax: (520) 684-4497
E-Mail: kelbar@juno.com
Internet: http://www.kayelbar.com
Airport: Phoenix Sky Harbor, 60 miles; private planes use Wickenburg Airport with a 5,000-foot airstrip, five miles
Location: 60 miles northwest of Phoenix off Route 89, five miles north of Wickenburg
Memberships: The Dude Ranchers' Association, Arizona Dude Ranch Association
Medical: Wickenburg Community Hospital, five minutes away
Guest Capacity: 24
Accommodations: The main lodge consists of eight rooms with private baths, a large living room, a bar, lots of books, and a big stone fireplace. There is also Homestead House, a two-bedroom, two-bath cottage with living room and fireplace, and a separate *casita* with two bedrooms, Casa Grande with sitting area and fireplace, and Casa Monterey with twin beds. Both have private baths and walk-in showers.
Rates: • $$–$$$. American Plan. Children's and special group rates available. Two-day minimum stay mid-October until mid-February. Four-day minimum stay mid-February to first of May and all holidays.
Credit Cards: VISA, MasterCard. Personal checks preferred.
Season: Mid-October to May 1
Activities: Very flexible riding program individualized to guests' abilities and interests. The Sonoran Desert terrain, with sandy washes, canyons, or rocky ridges, offers riding variety, beauty, and excitement. There are magnificent saguaro cactus and views to the distant mountain ranges. Two rides daily, except Sundays and holidays with morning rides only. All-day rides and riding instruction available. The hiking trail climbs to a lookout with panoramic views and beautiful sunsets. The new hot tub and heated swimming pool get lots of use. Hiking, bird-watching and plenty of wildlife-watching, including roadrunners, deer, javelina, coyotes, and big jackrabbits. Horseshoes, Ping-Pong, and other outdoor games. Golf at two fine golf courses and tennis nearby.
Children's Programs: Children join parents for ranch activities. Children must be age seven in order to ride.
Dining: Announced by the bell and served in the beautiful mission-like dining room. Wonderful home-cooked food including mesquite-grilled beef, pork chops, John's famous smoked ham, Mexican dishes, and a full roasted turkey dinner with all the trimmings. Fresh vegetables, fruit, and dessert specials. Weekly cookouts on the banks of the Hassayampa River. Licensed bar.
Entertainment: Informal program of cowboy singing, poetry, and storytelling in front of the crackling lodge fireplace. Ask John about the "Case of the Bulletproof Pancakes." Large library.
Summary: Wonderful historic dude ranch with a Spanish flair. On the National Register of Historic Places. Very cozy atmosphere in a lush desert environment. Singles, couples, and families will feel at home. Very casual. Only scheduled activities are meals and riding. Nearby: Desert Caballeros Museum, Joshua tree forest, mining museum, Gold Rush Days each February, Blue Grass Festival in November, cowboy poetry gathering in December. Local shopping, guided fishing on Lake Pleasant, top golfing nearby.

Merv Griffin's Wickenburg Inn and Dude Ranch
Wickenburg, Arizona

In 1995, entertainer Merv Griffin bought the Wickenburg Inn. Under his guidance the ranch offers cowboys, horses, horseback-riding lessons, family rides, cattle drives, hayrides, trail rides, cookouts, children's program, and family fun, along with other resort amenities such as swimming pool and spa, tennis, and nearby golf. As ranch manager Susanne Walsh says, "Merv fell in love with this ranch's beauty and location. In addition to his television shows and numerous business ventures, he raises Arabian and thoroughbred horses—which are very close to his heart. Merv has created a charming guest ranch atmosphere with a wonderful Western program, including some of the finest professional wranglers and horses in the business, first-class resort facilities, surrounded by a desert setting. The ranch combines the informality and the spirit of the Old West." In the world of dude ranching, Merv Griffin's new ranch is a bright-shining star.

Address: 34801 N. Highway 89, Wickenburg, Arizona 85390
Telephone: (800) 942-5362, (520) 684-7811; fax: (520) 684-2981
E-Mail: wickinn@primenet.com
Internet: http://www.merv.com
Airport: Phoenix Sky Harbor; Wickenburg for private aircraft, including jets
Location: 70 miles northwest of Phoenix, eight miles north of Wickenburg off Highway 89
Memberships: Arizona Dude Ranch Association, Arizona Hotel and Motel Association
Medical: Wickenburg Community Hospital, eight miles
Conference: 30–125. Two meeting rooms with audiovisual equipment. Ask for conference packet.
Guest Capacity: 150
Accommodations: In 1995, the ranch began extensive remodeling of the grounds and accommodations. The adobe *casitas* follow the natural contours of the desert and have their own Southwestern charm; each *casita* has a fireplace and some have private sun decks. In addition, there are nine lodge rooms, all with color TVs and telephones.
Rates: • $$–$$$$. American Plan. Includes several rides each day. Children under age five free. Special rates for groups. No minimum stay except during holidays.
Credit Cards: VISA, MasterCard, Discover, American Express
Season: Year-round, all holidays.
Activities: One of Merv's great loves is horses. As a result, the ranch built a professional rodeo arena and assembled fine horses and some of the best wranglers in the business, including a few professional competition cowboys. Daily walk, open-trail, and all-day rides with box lunch. Cookout and sunset rides. Weekly half-day cattle drives. Summer morning and evening riding. Expert riders can be challenged. Riding instruction. Beautiful two-level swimming pool with waterfall, and tennis courts. Resident naturalist and nature museum. Arts and crafts studio offering leather tooling, jewelry-making, and ceramics. Golf nearby.
Children's Programs: At Thanksgiving, Christmas, and spring break, special programs with counselor. Baby-sitting is available year-round. Call for details. Ask about the Little Wranglers program.
Dining: The ranch considers dining to be an important part of vacationing. Varied cuisines and full bar available year-round.
Entertainment: Ranch rodeos, Western dancing, nature hikes, desert jeep tours, and cookouts on Tuesdays and Saturdays.
Summary: In 1995, Merv Griffin's ranch began a new tradition of excellence. Beautiful desert setting with accommodations, riding, tennis, swimming, and nearby golf. Professional rodeo arena with regular events. Nearby town of Wickenburg and Desert Caballeros Western Museum.

See color photos, pages 174–175.

Price Canyon Ranch
Douglas, Arizona

On the northeastern slope of the Chiricahua Mountains (that's "big mountain" in Apache) at 5,600 feet, is the headquarters for Price Canyon Ranch. Backdropped by the Arizona mountains which rise to over 9,000 feet in the middle of the Coronado National Forest, the ranch attracts visitors with its wildlife and natural history. The ranch mixes ranching and hospitality on their 14,000-acre working cattle spread just 40 miles from the Mexican border. "Don't expect anything fancy." As owner Stanley explains, "We are not a dude ranch, but a working cattle ranch that takes a few paying guests at times." Guests participate in cattle roundups, work with livestock (depending on the time of year), and enjoy plenty of horseback riding. The Smiths raise 150 head of Texas longhorns, Brangus, and a mix of other cattle which adapt well to this high-desert climate. The terrain is desert mesa, with rolling grasslands, high mountain meadows, and bluffs. Summer temperatures can near the 90s; winter temperatures can drop into the 30s at night. Stanley's wife Pat, sums it up best: "Our guests are those who want to slow down from busy city life, who appreciate our sincere hospitality and, most of all, who want a chance to be a part of our family—sharing daily ranch life and our love of the great outdoors."

Address: P.O. Box 1065 K, Douglas, Arizona 85608
Telephone: (520) 558-2383; fax: (520) 558-2440
E-Mail: pcranch@gateway.net
Internet: http://www.agonline.com/pricecanyon
Airport: Tucson
Location: 150 miles southeast of Tucson, 42 miles northeast of Douglas
Memberships: National Cattleman's Beef Association, Arizona Dude Ranch Association
Medical: Hospital in Douglas, 42 miles
Guest Capacity: 24
Accommodations: Guests are put up in the family bunkhouse, an apartment with kitchen and an adjoining singles' bunkhouse, or the large, cozy, People's Barn with pool table. Ten RV and trailer hook-ups available in the live oak grove.
Rates: $–$$. American Plan.
Credit Cards: None. Personal checks and traveler's checks accepted.
Season: Year-round, including Christmas, Thanksgiving, and Easter
Activities: This is a working cattle ranch. Depending on the season, various types of work need to be done. Seasonal ranch activities include branding and roundups. If you don't want to participate you can enjoy open meadow and mountain trail rides. Fishing for catfish in pond, solar-heated swimming pool open in summer, and hiking. Small hot tub in private room to sooth aching muscles.
Children's Programs: Children under age 10 not encouraged unless special request is made.
Dining: Good, home-style ranch cooking. BYOB.
Entertainment: The People's Barn is always open for guests to watch TV, read, or play board games, pool, and piano. Rodeos in town at certain times of the year. Pretty much do your own thing after supper.
Summary: Low-key, easygoing 14,000-acre cattle and guest ranch for adults and older children who want to experience an informal program with lots of rugged mountains, oak trees, and scenic desert views. As Stanley says, "We take a few guests each week who wish to enjoy our rustic ranch and easygoing lifestyle." Bring your own horse if you wish. Horse stalls available. Ten RV hook-ups available. Nearby: historical sites, Indian lore, and Mexico just across the border. Pets allowed under supervision.

Rancho de la Osa
Sasabe, Arizona

ARIZONA DUDE RANCH ASSOCIATION

Rancho de la Osa is one of the rarest and most famous historic guest ranches, capturing the romance and history of Spain and Mexico as an old Spanish land grant. Here you are transported back in mind and spirit to a time when the Franciscans, *vaqueros*, and early Spanish settlers roamed this Sonoran desert along the Mexican border. In 1997 Richard and Veronica Schultz, art collectors, architectural aficionados, and international travelers, bought the ranch and have brought a sophisticated, elegant, friendly atmosphere to the world of guest ranching. Here folks enjoy and savor an ambiance rich in culture and diverse in artistic expression. Together with an incredible appreciation of the land with its natural beauty and high-desert serenity, guests can enjoy the al fresco spirit and the comforts found in finer hotels. Since the 1920s, as one of the great Spanish haciendas, Rancho de la Osa has entertained such personalities as Margaret Mitchell (author of *Gone With The Wind*) and U.S. Supreme Court Justice William O. Douglas. It is now home-away-from-home for a host of personalities, who come, as Richard says, "to chill out and rekindle their intellectual and artistic spirits" surrounded by the pristine 130,000-acre Buenos Aires National Wildlife Refuge.

Rancho de la Osa—relaxed, rich, and very special.

Address: P.O. Box 1 K, Sasabe, Arizona 85633
Telephone: (800) 872-6240, (520) 823-4257; fax: (520) 823-4238
E-Mail: osagal@aol.com
Internet: http://www.guestranches.com/ranchodelaosa
Airport: Tucson. Private planes call for details.
Train: Amtrak to Tucson
Location: 60 miles southwest of Tucson, directly on the Mexican border
Memberships: The Dude Ranchers' Association, Arizona Dude Ranch Association
Medical: St. Joseph's Hospital, Tucson
Conference: 42
Guest Capacity: 42
Accommodations: The old Southwest is captured in the 1860s hacienda, and in the guest rooms. Warm and inviting ambiance, Mexican antiques, and fine art. Three guest wings contain 18 individual guest accommodations. These unique structures are constructed of hand-formed adobe brick. Each room has a private entrance, its own kiva fireplace, and Mexican antiques and furnishings. Some rooms have courtyard gardens.
Rates: $$–$$$. American Plan. Group and off-season rates.
Credit Cards: VISA, MasterCard, Discover
Season: Mid-September to June
Activities: Rides on trails over many various kinds of terrain and include all-day rides to abandoned Presumido Trading Post (available only for week-long guests), a lunch ride to La Casa de las Rocas, and rides along the Mexican border or on the Antelope Trail. Individual instruction available. Birding is a popular activity on the ranch. The Buenos Aires Wildlife Refuge and Brown and Mustang Canyons provide fabulous opportunities for birders. Other activities include hiking, biking, swimming, stargazing, croquet, horseshoes, movies, art lessons (additional), dancing in the Cantina, relaxing in the Jacuzzi, and shoe branding.
Children's Programs: Adult-oriented ranch. Prefer well-behaved children ages 12 and older.
Dining: Southwestern gourmet cuisine—superb! Choice cuts of meats, along with home-baked breads and desserts. Fresh herbs, vegetables, and salad greens from the garden. Special meals with advanced notice. Full liquor license, extensive wine and premium tequila list. Espresso and cappuccino served (extra).
Entertainment: Resting and relaxing with good dinner conversation. Evening meal is a social gathering that usually lasts about two hours, with guests sitting around huge dining room with fireplace. Fine brandies and liqueurs.
Summary: A sophisticated al fresco Western experience. Elegance, Southwestern gourmet cuisine, wide-open spaces, 130,000 acres of wildlife preserve, artistic sensibility, and intellectual expression. Ask about riding, birding, art, history, photography, wine, and tequila-tasting.

See color photos, page 178.

Rancho de los Caballeros
Wickenburg, Arizona

Rancho de los Caballeros is one of the premier ranches in North America and is celebrating its 50th anniversary. Set amid 20,000 acres of beautiful desert scenery, the ranch has maintained a long tradition of excellence and continues to attract families and individuals who enjoy a host of recreational activities, first-rate personal service, and comfort. Los Caballeros is well known for its 18-hole championship golf course, consistently ranked in the top five in Arizona. Many guests come just to play golf, others to play tennis, ride horseback in the open desert country, sit by the pool, or just enjoy the relaxing atmosphere. The ranch offers superb conference facilities in the Palo Verde Conference Center, ideal for small and large groups up to 250 people. Rancho de los Caballeros means "Ranch of the Gentlemen on Horseback." Perhaps what it should really stand for is "excellence": great people, great resort amenities, great golf, and great riding.

Address: 1551 S. Vulture Mine Road, Wickenburg, Arizona 85390
Telephone: (800) 684-5030, (520) 684-5484; fax: (520) 684-2267
Internet: http://www.SunC.com
Airport: Phoenix Sky Harbor; private planes at Wickenburg Municipal Airport on a 5,000-foot paved runway, fuel available. Call ranch for details.
Location: four miles southwest of Wickenburg, 56 miles northwest of Phoenix on Highway 60
Memberships: Arizona Dude Ranch Association
Awards: Mobil 4 Star
Medical: Wickenburg Community Hospital, four miles
Conference: 150 (250 for day meetings); excellent 4,500-square-foot conference center. Ask for conference brochure.
Guest Capacity: 150
Accommodations: A variety of air-conditioned *casitas* with private baths, sun patios, and separate entrances. Each room is tastefully decorated in Southwestern style, including handcrafted furnishings from Mexico and Santa Fe. TVs and telephones in all rooms.
Rates: • $$$. American Plan. Children's (under age five free) and group rates. Golf and riding packages available. Rates vary depending on season and type of accommodations.
Credit Cards: None. Personal checks accepted.
Season: October through May
Activities: The ranch offers scenic beginner, intermediate, and advanced riding. Riding instruction on request. Breakfast, lunch, and dinner cookout rides. Four tennis courts with resident tennis pro, swimming, and guided nature walks with information on flora and fauna. Trap- and skeet-shooting extra (guns and instruction provided). Hot-air ballooning on-site, mountain biking, and jeep tours. Los Caballeros Golf Club with 18-hole course includes a head pro and several assistants, a driving range, pro shop, locker rooms, golf carts, and rental equipment. Food and beverages available at club grill.
Children's Programs: Excellent children's programs for kids ages five through 12—breakfast through lunch and during dinner if desired. Riding, swimming, and hiking during the day, and games in the evening. Baby-sitting is available for younger children (extra). Thanksgiving, Christmas, and holiday programs are popular.
Dining: Reserved individual tables. Menu features a four-course meal with five daily specials. Luncheon buffets served poolside. Full-service bar. Children may eat together or with their parents.
Entertainment: Cookouts twice a week, card and table games, billiards, line dancing, and movies. Nature walks, putting tournaments, and gymkhanas. Occasional cowboy poetry and singalongs. Stargazing with local astronomer. Musical entertainment Friday and Saturday evenings.
Summary: One of Kilgore's Best of the Best ranch resorts. This historic guest ranch and golf club offers championship 18-hole golf at one of the top five courses in Arizona. Golf and tennis pros on staff. Daily horseback riding. Excellent conference facilities for up to 250. Nearby: Wickenburg town for shopping, Desert Caballeros Western Museum, Vulture Mine, Hassayampa River Preserve (a nature preserve), and the scenic Sonoran desert.

See color photos, pages 176–177.

Tanque Verde Ranch
Tucson, Arizona

The Tanque Verde Ranch is a historic ranch dating to 1868 when the Carrillo family settled here and ran cattle up into the Rincon Mountains east of Tucson. Today, situated on 640 acres and bordered by the Coronado National Forest and the Saguaro National Park, the ranch continues to work 300 head of cattle on a 22,000-acre Forest Service lease. The ranch headquarters has evolved into one of the premier guest ranch/resorts in the Southwest, welcoming guests from around the world to a diverse program of riding, hiking, tennis, or just relaxing within a Sonoran-style architectural setting. Bob Cote and his dedicated staff provide guests with true Western hospitality every day of the year! They run a first-class operation and continue to receive the prestigious Mobil 4 Star award, as well as travel write-ups in countless magazines and newspapers from around the world. Guests explore the fascinating Sonoran Desert through a comprehensive daily naturalist study program. A beautiful new nature museum highlights the flora and fauna of the Sonoran Desert, complete with live-animal exhibits. The Cote family's philosophy is simple: provide the very best in friendly, professional service in an exciting and stimulating environment for the entire family. Tanque Verde Ranch is truly a luxurious oasis in the desert and without question one of the country's finest resort/guest ranches.

Address: 14301 E. Speedway, Dept. K, Tucson, Arizona 85748
Telephone: (800) 234-DUDE (3833), (520) 296-6275; fax: (520) 721-9426
E-Mail: dude@tvgr.com
Internet: http://www.tvgr.com
Airport: Tucson, 35 minutes
Location: 15 miles east of Tucson at the end of East Speedway. In the foothills of the Rincon Mountains.
Memberships: Arizona Dude Ranch Association
Awards: Mobil 4 Star, 300 Best Hotels in the World
Medical: Tucson Medical Center, 15 miles
Conference: 150; new conference facility, state-of-the-art multimedia computer interface, 6,800 square feet of meeting space. Conference director on-site. Sales packets available.
Guest Capacity: 150
Accommodations: Sixty-five *casita*-style rooms, from historic Ramada rooms to large, spacious deluxe suites with whirlpool tubs and Southwestern decor. Most with adobe-style fireplaces, private patios, and large picture windows. All with telephones. Laundry facilities available.
Rates: • $$$. American Plan. Rates vary with season. Activities/facilities are included in room rates.
Credit Cards: VISA, MasterCard, Discover, American Express
Season: Year-round, open all holidays
Activities: Over 130 horses with daily guided rides. Adults may ride with children in the children's program. Daily basic and intermediate horsemanship lessons. Slow scenic rides and loping for the advanced rider. Breakfast, all-day, and picnic rides. Fun-khanas in winter season. All riding and instruction included. Overnight pack trips during summer months (extra). Five professional tennis courts (one Omni court), outdoor heated pool, indoor health spa with pool, saunas, whirlpool, and exercise room. Fishing, hiking, and bird walks. Over 175 species of birds seen at ranch. Golf at nearby courses.
Children's Programs: One of the most comprehensive counselor-supervised children's programs for Buckaroos ages four to six and Wranglers ages seven to 11. Special summer camp sessions.
Dining: The Doghouse Saloon for happy hour. Family-style seating in beautiful Southwestern dining room. Continental and American cuisine worthy of Mobil 4 Star. Enormous lunch salad bar and 20-foot-long pastry and dessert table. Weekly barbecue cookouts in Cottonwood Grove. Wine and beer available at all meals (extra).
Entertainment: Nightly lectures by historians/naturalists, stargazing with astronomer, country-Western dancing, Bingo night.
Summary: Internationally renowned ranch resort famous for its extensive programs catering to guests of all ages. One of the largest riding stables. Lots of Southwestern historical charm. Superb children's program. Two full-time naturalists and nature museum. Educational and fun evening programs. Delightful gift shop.

White Stallion Ranch
Tucson, Arizona

THE DUDE RANCHERS' ASSOCIATION

ARIZONA DUDE RANCH ASSOCIATION

Just 17 miles from downtown Tucson, surrounded by rugged desert mountains, is White Stallion Ranch. In the 1960s, the True family bought this quiet, peaceful, 3,000-acre ranch, which looks out to Safford and Panther Peaks and the Tucson mountain range. "The only sounds you'll hear are those of the desert and the ranch," says Cynthia True, who along with her sons Russell and Michael and their families, oversee this lovely high-desert ranch. Guests are impressed with the warmth and beauty of the land and the Trues' famous hospitality. The ranch features a herd of purebred Texas longhorn cattle and a rodeo each week with team roping, a cutting-horse exhibition, steer-wrestling, and barrel racing. Many scenes from the television series *High Chaparral* were filmed here. Peacocks run free on the ranch, as do roadrunners.

Address: 9251 W. Twin Peaks Road, Dept. K, Tucson, Arizona 85743
Telephone: (888) WSRANCH (888-977-2624), (520) 297-0252; fax: (520) 744-2786
E-Mail: wsranch@flash.net
Internet: http://www.wsranch.com
Airport: Tucson
Location: 17 miles northwest of Tucson
Memberships: The Dude Ranchers' Association, Arizona Dude Ranch Association
Awards: Mobil 3 Star
Medical: Northwest Hospital, 11 miles
Conference: 30–75; 1,200 square feet
Guest Capacity: 50–75
Accommodations: White Spanish-style bungalows with adobe exteriors hold single rooms, suites, and a few deluxe suites and cabins. Each has a private bath, air-conditioning, and private patio with views through the cactus garden to the mountains and Saguaro National Park. There are no TVs or telephones. Six deluxe suites have high ceilings with exposed beams, antique Mexican furniture, whirlpool tubs, and fireplaces. Laundry facilities.
Rates: • $$–$$$. American Plan. Nightly, off-season, weekly, and children's rates available.
Credit Cards: None. Traveler's checks or personal checks accepted.
Season: September through May. Open Thanksgiving, Christmas, and Easter.
Activities: Russell takes great pride in matching horses with riders. Children and adults may, if they wish, brush and saddle their own horses. Except on Sundays, there are four rides a day, usually two fast and two slow, and all-day rides into Saguaro National Park. If you think you're a fast rider, the ranch has a riding test for you. Breakfast and mountain rides. Team-cattle penning in arena is extremely popular with guests. Guided nature walks with trained naturalists along foothills of the Tucson Mountain Range, guided hiking program. Swimming in key-shaped heated pool, shuffleboard, volleyball, basketball, two professional tennis courts, and indoor redwood hot tub. Golf nearby.
Children's Programs: Children of all ages are very much a part of the ranch programs and participate fully; they'll enjoy all the animals in the petting zoo. Children are parents' responsibility. Children under age five ride with parents.
Dining: Breakfast menu-style, lunch buffet, dinner family-style or buffet. Wednesday hayrides, desert cookouts, and the outdoor Indian oven. Lunch and dinner menus posted daily. Vegetarian and special diets provided with advance notice. Happy hour with hors d'oeuvres precedes dinner, when Cynthia introduces guests and bids farewell to those leaving in the morning. No smoking in dining room.
Entertainment: Bonfire with cowboy singer, stargazing, and wonderful naturalist talks. Ask about astronomy and speaker programs.
Summary: The Trues' brand of hospitality and warmth is very special! Excellent staff, immaculate grounds, delicious food, wonderful, private desert setting, and great value make White Stallion tops! Lovely Spanish-style ranch close to Tucson but isolated. Part of 100,000-acre game preserve adjacent to Saguaro National Park. Singles and families welcome.

OFFICE

Lost Spur Guest Ranch
Harrison, Arkansas

In 1989, T.J. and Lynn Hunter decided that the thing they both loved most was people. T.J. hails from Texas and his wonderful wife of 30 years from Vancouver, Canada. Both grew up on farms and ranches and have always shared a common love for people, the outdoors, and nature. In 1992 they were able to make their dream come true in Arkansas' Ozark Mountains. Like many, they had no idea that this part of the country was so beautiful; they now understand why it has been called one of the best-kept secrets in the United States. Here the pace is slow and the folks as friendly as they come. Lost Spur is a family place that serves up warm hospitality. Folks return for the pastoral beauty, the marvelous river that runs right through the ranch, and the small, intimate atmosphere.

Address: 8148 Lost Spur Road, Harrison, Arkansas 72601
Telephone: (800) 774-2414, (870) 743-7787; fax (870) 743-6686
Internet: http://www.lostspur.com
Airport: Springville, Missouri (commercial), 90 miles; Harrison, Arkansas (commuter flights); Fayetteville, Arkansas
Location: 17 miles northeast of Harrison; 42 miles south of Branson
Medical: Northwest Arkansas Medical Center, 17 miles
Guest Capacity: 30
Conference: 24
Accommodations: Four cedar cabins are set in the woods overlooking Crooked Creek and the Big Bluff. Cabins Two and Four each have one queen-size, two twin, and two bunk beds. Cabin One has two queen beds. Cabin Three has two queen and four bunk beds. Cabins are individually decorated. All have covered porches, swings, private baths, air conditioning, and heat. Ask about the Country Cottage.
Rates: $$. American Plan. Children's and off-season rates. Summer: Sunday to Saturday. Three- and six-day packages. Discounts for seniors and military. Group rates.
Credit Cards: VISA, MasterCard, American Express, Discover. Personal checks preferred.
Season: March through October
Activities: Lots to do for all ages. Spring-fed, crystal-clear Crooked Creek (a 30-foot-wide river) runs right through the property, so water activities are a unique highlight: swimming, fishing for smallmouth and largemouth freshwater bass, canoeing, tubing, and sunbathing; volleyball and basketball. Horseback rides go out twice a day—early morning and late afternoon—winding through the heavily wooded areas, crossing the creek and meadows. Watch for deer, wild turkeys, rabbits, and armadillos! You'll enjoy trying out your riding skills in the arena as well. Skeet-shooting available.
Children's Programs: A children's paradise. Great two-story children's tree house and playground. Kids love to catch crawdads in the creek. Swimming hole. Children are parents' responsibility. Grandson Ty will teach them how to rope.
Dining: Family-style meals served three times a day. Lynn's famous baked French toast, oatmeal pancakes with local fresh fruit: blackberries, blueberries, apples, and peaches. T.J.'s rib-eye chuck-wagon cookout and cowboy breakfast are highlights. Ask about the Crooked Creek fajita cookout.
Entertainment: Occasional nightly entertainment. Hayrides, cowboy country-Western impersonator, Country Blues playing authentic Ozark music. Line dancing. Homemade ice-cream social games.
Summary: Family guest ranch in the heart of the Ozark Mountains with oak, hickory, and sycamore trees. Private 116 acres at the end of a five-mile gravel road. Wonderful crystal-clear, spring-fed creek runs through ranch. Lots of great water activities. May see wild turkeys, deer, beavers, armadillos. Nearby: Silver Dollar City and famous Branson, Missouri.

Scott Valley Resort and Guest Ranch
Mountain Home, Arkansas

THE DUDE RANCHERS' ASSOCIATION

In the serenity of the Ozarks, amid 625 acres of beautiful meadows, woodlands, rocky cliffs, and spring-fed streams, is the Coopers' white, clean-cut, red-trimmed Scott Valley Guest Ranch, which began operation in 1953. Kathleen Cooper has shared the joys of her ranch and her down-home hospitality with people from around the country since 1985. Rated as one of the most popular vacation spots in the Ozarks, Scott Valley offers a variety of activities for its guests, including riding for beginning, intermediate, and experienced riders. Fishermen will enjoy some of the best fishing on the White (ranked fourth in the world for trout fishing) and North Fork Rivers, both famous for rainbow and brown trout. You'll feel the warm and friendly hospitality that is the secret of the Coopers' success. Children, too, will experience all the treasures of the great outdoors. Guests have been known to say, "It's just like home and being with family."

Address: Box 1447 K, Mountain Home, Arkansas 72654
Telephone: (870) 425-5136; fax: (870) 424-5800
E-Mail: svr@mail.ot.centuryinter.net
Internet: http://www.scottvalley.com
Airport: Springfield, Little Rock, Memphis, Mountain Home (via St. Louis, Missouri, or Dallas, Texas)
Location: six miles south of Mountain Home off Highway 5, 156 miles north of Little Rock, 196 miles west of Memphis
Memberships: The Dude Ranchers' Association
Awards: *Family Circle* Family Resort of the Year 1990, 1991, and 1992
Medical: Baxter County Regional Hospital, six miles
Conference: 65+; two rooms (1,200 square feet), off-season only
Guest Capacity: 65+
Accommodations: Each of the 28 one- or two-bedroom, motel-type guest rooms has a full bathroom with tub and shower, air-conditioning, electric heat, and daily maid service. Ask about the Hilltop Hideaway for the ultimate escape!
Rates: • $–$$$. American Plan. Children under age two free. Prefer one-week stay. Weekly family, group, senior, and military rates. Rates include horseback riding (canoes and boats on stays of three days or more).
Credit Cards: VISA, MasterCard. Travelers checks or personal checks accepted.
Season: March through November, including Thanksgiving, and Easter. Hilltop Hideaway year-round.
Activities: Scheduled horseback rides. Experienced riders should inquire about the spring and fall rides. The Coopers specialize in the smooth-gaited Missouri fox-trotters. Hiking, swimming in a heated pool or nearby lakes and streams. Ten minutes from world-class fishing on the White and Norfork Rivers, as well as boating and canoeing. Jet-skiing, sailing, and scuba diving available at nearby Lake Norfork (extra). Table tennis, badminton, tennis, volleyball, fitness room, and shuffleboard. Eighteen-hole golf course nearby.
Children's Program: Fully equipped playground and petting zoo with lots of animals. Ranch encourages families to interact with their children. Pony rides for children under age seven. Baby-sitting available.
Dining: Down-home, good cooking including biscuits and gravy, ham, great Mexican fare, cornbread, and chicken and dumplings, with meals for lighter appetites. Weekly dinner cruise on Lake Norfolk during summer season.
Entertainment: Some type of scheduled activity every evening. Be sure to ask Kathleen about the famous Western entertainment in Branson, Missouri. Summer entertainment is geared for families.
Summary: A haven for first-time ranch families to spend time together in a low-key, relaxing atmosphere with gaited horses and blue-ribbon trout fishing. Spring and fall months best for adults, singles, couples, and experienced riders. Ask about the Hilltop Hideaway. Arkansas is one of the best values you can find for your vacation dollar and is one of the United States' great hidden treasures. Nearby: Blanchard Springs Caverns, the Ozark Folk Center and Village 1890. Great antiquing.

Alisal Guest Ranch
Solvang, California

The Alisal is one of the great resort ranches in North America. This 10,000-acre paradise really has it all: 50 miles of riding trails, two par-72 championship golf courses, a private 96-acre lake, and seven tennis courts. In addition to first-class recreational amenities and lodging facilities, the ranch also has 2,000 head of cattle run separately from the guest operations. What also sets the Alisal apart is the level of personal service. General manager David Lautensack, who joined the ranch in 1993, has instilled a new spirit throughout the Alisal and personally gets out daily with his staff to meet and get to know his guests, in the true spirit of great ranching. The Alisal—a tradition of excellence.

Address: 1054 Alisal Road, Solvang, California 93463
Telephone: (805) 688-6411, reservations: (800) 425-4725; fax: (805) 688-2510
E-Mail: info@alisal.com
Internet: http://www.alisal.com
Airport: Los Angeles, 2½ hours; Santa Barbara with commercial jet service, 35 miles; Santa Ynez for private planes, five miles
Location: 40 miles northwest of Santa Barbara
Awards: *Family Circle* Family Resort of the Year, *Hideaway Report*
Medical: Santa Ynez Hospital, three miles
Conference: 150; 6,000 square feet of meeting space
Guest Capacity: 150–250
Accommodations: 73 cottages and garden rooms scattered around the grounds, which feature century-old sycamores, range from one-room studios to executive suites with nightly turn-down service. All are modern with high ceilings, fireplaces, and refrigerators. No TVs or telephones in the rooms, but TVs and pay phones are available in all public areas. Laundry service is available (extra).
Rates: • $$$–$$$$. Modified American Plan (including breakfast and dinner). A wide variety of seasonal activity packages is available. Ask about the Roundup Vacation Package. Two-night minimum-stay requirement.
Credit Cards: VISA, MasterCard, American Express
Season: Year-round
Activities: Two-hour trail rides go out twice each day, separated into walking, trotting, or loping over 50 miles of trails. Private rides and riding instruction available. Semiweekly breakfast rides, weekly guest rodeo (summer). Lake activities on 96-acre private Alisal Lake include fishing, boating, and windsurfing. The Ranch Golf Course (designed by Bill Bell), is a 72-par California classic which winds past stately oak, sycamore, and eucalyptus trees. The 72-par River Course follows the meanderings of the Santa Ynez River and provides a panoramic view of the foothills. Seven tennis courts. Pro shops for both tennis and golf. Heated pool and whirlpool. Volleyball, shuffleboard, and game room with table tennis and billiards.
Children's Programs: Daily arts and crafts program. Extensive summertime and holiday programs, a year-round petting zoo. Evenings are busy with Bingo, storytelling, and talent shows. Special events include the Giant Easter Bunny and egg hunt at Easter, the Fourth of July pageant, and Santa's visit with caroling and gifts at Christmas.
Dining: Dinner attire required. Served in the Ranch Room, the menu varies daily and features contemporary regional cuisine created by acclaimed chefs. Excellent wine selection. Summer lunches served poolside. Winter: lunches served in the main dining room or at the golf clubhouses. Limited room service available.
Entertainment: The Southwestern-decorated Oak Room, with a large stone fireplace and cathedral ceiling, provides nightly dancing, cocktails, and relaxation with live music. The large, adults-only library is for quiet reading. Large-screen TV available.
Summary: Superb resort ranch ideal for families, horseback riding, golf, fly-fishing; children's and wine-tour packages available. Also an excellent meeting environment for groups of up to 150 people from September to June. Nearby: Solvang Danish community, 30 local wineries, outlet shopping, and a large art community. Video available upon request.

See color photos, pages 180–181.

ALISAL RANCH
FIELD

Coffee Creek Ranch
Trinity Center, California

THE DUDE RANCHERS' ASSOCIATION

In the mid-1970s, Ruth and Mark Hartman sold their house in the San Francisco Bay Area and bought this riverside ranch in northern California. Coffee Creek Ranch, named after the creek that flows through the property, covers 127 acres at the base of the majestic Trinity Alps Wilderness Area. At 3,100 feet, Coffee Creek is in a river canyon, surrounded by a mountain wilderness area. The ranch is not far from Trinity Lake and 13 miles from the Trinity Center Airport.

Address: HC 2, Box 4940 K, Trinity Center, California 96091
Telephone: (800) 624-4480, (530) 266-3343; fax: (530) 266-3597
Internet: http://www.coffeecreekranch.com
Airport: Redding or Trinity Center (3,000-foot runway), for small planes only
Train: Amtrak to Redding. Contact ranch concerning Greyhound bus.
Location: 278 miles north of San Francisco, 72 miles northwest of Redding, 45 miles north of Weaverville off Highway 3
Memberships: The Dude Ranchers' Association, California Hotel & Motel Association
Medical: Weaverville Hospital, 45 miles
Conference: 50, conference folder available
Guest Capacity: 50
Awards: AAA 3-Diamonds; Honorable Mention, *Family Circle*
Accommodations: All 14 cabins have porches. Most two-bedroom cabins have one or two baths and wood-burning stoves. The one-bedroom, one-bath cabins have potbellied stoves to keep you warm and cozy. All cabins have showers, some with bathtub/shower combinations. Handicapped-accessible cabin or ranch-house room with front porch is also available. Daily maid service and laundry facilities are available.
Rates: • $$–$$$. American Plan. Summer horseback riding extra by the ride or weekly. Special rates for spring and fall include riding. Children's, teen, and senior rates available. One-week minimum stay during summer, Saturday to Friday. Two-day minimum stay spring, fall, and winter.
Credit Cards: VISA, MasterCard, American Express, Discover. Personal checks, cash, or traveler's checks accepted.
Season: Year-round, closed periodically between seasons
Activities: Coffee Creek offers scheduled riding in the summer, including breakfast and twilight rides. Ask about their more personalized riding program in the spring and fall. Picnic, all-day, and overnight rides including pack trips to mountain lakes. Guided hiking; fishing in stocked pond, Coffee Creek, Trinity Lake, and alpine lakes. Archery, badminton, shuffleboard, volleyball, trap-shooting, and rifle range (guns provided). Swimming in heated pool or in Coffee Creek and canoeing on the pond. Health club. Winter: wilderness cross-country skiing, snowmobiling, inner-tubing, ice fishing, sleigh rides, and dogsledding by request—all weather permitting.
Children's Program: Excellent youth program for ages three to 17. Specialized activities for various age groups. Wonderful international counselors. Baby-sitting during rides for children under age three.
Dining: All you can eat, family-style; fresh fruit, vegetables, and family recipes. Barbecues and steak fries. Ask about the "crazy cake." Beer and wine available. BYOB, but it must be kept in the cabins.
Entertainment: Horse-drawn hayrides, bonfires, Bingo, talent shows, gymkhanas, live music several times a week by the Coffee Creek band (The Rattlesnakes), square and line dancing. Rec room, pool table, table tennis, horseshoes, shuffleboard, and basketball. Satellite TV.
Summary: Family owned and operated with strong emphasis on families. Excellent youth program. Serious riders should consider early summer and fall. June and July have the best weather and lots of wildflowers. National Scenic Byway. Adults/singles-only weeks. You may bring your own horse. Fly-fishing instruction available. Conference room seats 40. Spanish, Dutch, German spoken. Handicapped facilities. Nearby: Trinity Center Western Museum, historical town of Weaverville, and Chinese "Joss House" temple.

Drakesbad Guest Ranch
Chester, California

Tucked away in the southeast corner of Lassen Volcanic National Park is a century-old guest ranch that is peaceful and quiet, the way it has always been. Forty-seven miles from the park's southwest entrance, Drakesbad is secluded in one of California's most scenic mountain valleys. Surrounded by thousands of acres of forest and oodles of lakes, this rustic ranch—knotty-pine lodge rooms with kerosene lanterns—is known for its hot springs that fill the ranch's swimming pool. This ranch is for those who like fresh mountain air, quiet surroundings, and limited electricity. Here the only schedule is when the meals are served. One guest commented, "We don't want too many people to know about Drakesbad because we enjoy it so much." There is only one major drawback to this old ranch—its popularity. It gets booked many months in advance. Great scenery, great staff, and lots of rest and relaxation. Drakesbad is very, very special!

Address: Drakesbad Guest Ranch, Lassen Volcanic National Park, Drawer K, end of Warner Valley Road, Chester, California 96020 (summer); 2150 Main Street, Dept. K, Suite 5, Red Bluff, California 96080 (year-round)
Telephone: Summer: dial operator and ask for Susanville operator, area code 530, then ask for Drakesbad 2. Be patient; this takes a while. Winter: (887) 439-0002; fax: (530) 529-4511.
Airport: Redding, Reno, or Sacramento; private planes into Chester, 17 miles
Location: 117 miles southeast of Redding off Highway 36 in Chester; 125 miles northwest of Reno
Medical: Seneca Hospital, Chester, 40 minutes
Guest Capacity: 75
Accommodations: 13 cabins and six lodge rooms. All are delightful with sinks, toilets, (some with showers), and wood floors. Kerosene lamps give an old-time ranch flavor, with some electricity; daily housekeeping is provided; bathhouse for cabins without showers.
Rates: $$. American Plan. Weekly rate for stays of seven nights or more. Horseback riding extra.
Credit Cards: VISA, MasterCard. Personal checks accepted.
Season: Early June to early October
Activities: This is not the place for someone who needs something to do every moment of the day. It is leisure-oriented and best suited for those who enjoy communing with nature and relaxing. Fishing, riding, hiking, and swimming in a modern pool heated by thermal volcanic heat, with temperatures averaging 95 to 100 degrees Fahrenheit. Daily horseback riding is available by reservation the night before. One-hour to all-day rides. Insurance and terrain require walking only. Helmets offered to those who wish to use them.
Children's Programs: Supervised children's program for ages six to 12 is available three afternoons each week. Parents are responsible for children.
Dining: Wonderful cuisine. Breakfast and dinner served in dining room; buffet or sack lunch. Menu is varied and features delightful, nutritious food. Special diets can be accommodated with advance notice. Weekly cookouts of ribs and steaks, with hamburgers and hot dogs for the kids. Beer and wine service at lunch and dinner.
Entertainment: Star-studded skies and marvelous fireside ranger chats.
Summary: A diamond in the rough. A remote, charmingly rustic ranch with hot-springs pool and hydrothermal area. Great for families, couples, and singles who want an unhurried environment in scenic and remote northern California. Hot-springs swimming, hiking, relaxing, and horseback riding are the main activities here. Excellent staff and very high percentage of repeat guests. Drakesbad Ranch is operated by California Guest Services, Inc., under a concession contract with the National Park Service, Department of the Interior. Nearby: Drakes Lake, Boiling Springs Lake, Devil's Kitchen, Pacific Crest Trail.

Greenhorn Creek Ranch
Quincy, California

Greenhorn Creek Ranch is in the Feather River country of the Sierra Nevada Mountains. To many, this part of northern California is a Shangri-la, with its rushing streams, magnificent pine forests, and crisp mountain air. This 640-acre ranch is surrounded by more than one million acres of Plumas National Forest and by vacation homes that have been built over the years. Founded in the mid-1960s, it was bought in 1995 by longtime guests Howard and Kathy Klein who, together with their general manager (also a longtime guest), have brought a new spirit to Greenhorn. The ranch provides Western vacations for families, couples, and singles. Greenhorn Creek Ranch offers wholesome family fun.

Address: 2116 Greenhorn Ranch Road, Quincy, California 95971-7010
Telephone: (800) 334-6939, (530) 283-0930; fax: (530) 283-4401
E-Mail: grnhorn@inreach.com
Internet: http://www.greenhornranch.com
Airport: Reno, 70 miles; private airplanes to Gansner, 12 miles
Location: 70 miles northwest of Reno on Highway 70, off Highway 395; 248 miles north of San Francisco
Memberships: Quincy Chamber of Commerce
Medical: Plumas District Hospital in Quincy, 12 miles
Conference: 60
Guest Capacity: 80
Accommodations: The main lodge is a two-story Western-looking structure with covered balcony and walkways. The second floor has 12 wood-sided motel-style rooms; the lower level houses the office and lobby, with a fireplace. There are 16 rustic cabins, usually reserved for families and groups with children. All cabins and lodge rooms have private bathrooms with showers and small decks with swings.
Rates: • \$–\$\$. American Plan. Various season and package rates. Discounts for groups of more than 10.
Credit Cards: VISA, MasterCard
Season: April through November
Activities: Horseback riding is the main activity at the ranch. A wide variety of scenic trails provides riders with a great view of some of Plumas County's prettiest areas. Two-hour rides go out twice each day through the big pines and along Greenhorn Creek. Children and adults usually ride separately, however they can ride together if they wish. Beginner and intermediate rides. A dinner ride on Sunday features a steak cookout in the big pines. Lunch ride on Tuesday serves up hamburgers along Greenhorn Creek. Wednesday is the guest rodeo. Thursday is an all-day ride to the beautiful Feather River area. If you don't wish to ride, you can hike along mountain trails. The ranch has a big fishing pond with large trout. Heated swimming pool and a hot tub surrounded by a large redwood deck. Horseshoes, volleyball, and softball. Nearby: golf courses and tennis courts are 20 minutes from the ranch.
Children's Programs: Children are the responsibility of parents. The ranch has a Kiddie Corral for small children with supervision by a Kiddie Wrangler; also features a petting zoo, a fishing pond, and playground.
Dining: Home-style cooking includes barbecues, steak-and-hamburger cookouts.
Entertainment: Recreation hall with bar area and dance floor, poker room, and game room full of some of the newest game machines for the kids. Also a large-screen TV. Relax by the pool or hot tub. Enjoy the bar area; beer and wine available. Live music and line dancing. Bingo.
Summary: Greenhorn Ranch is owned by Howard and Kathy Klein, who came to the ranch in the early 1970s as guests. They fell in love with the area and built a house next to the ranch to bring their family to this beautiful area. The Kleins offer a wholesome, low-key Western experience for families. The Greenhorn has become very popular for family reunions. Smoke-free policy preferred. Nearby: Lake Tahoe and Reno.

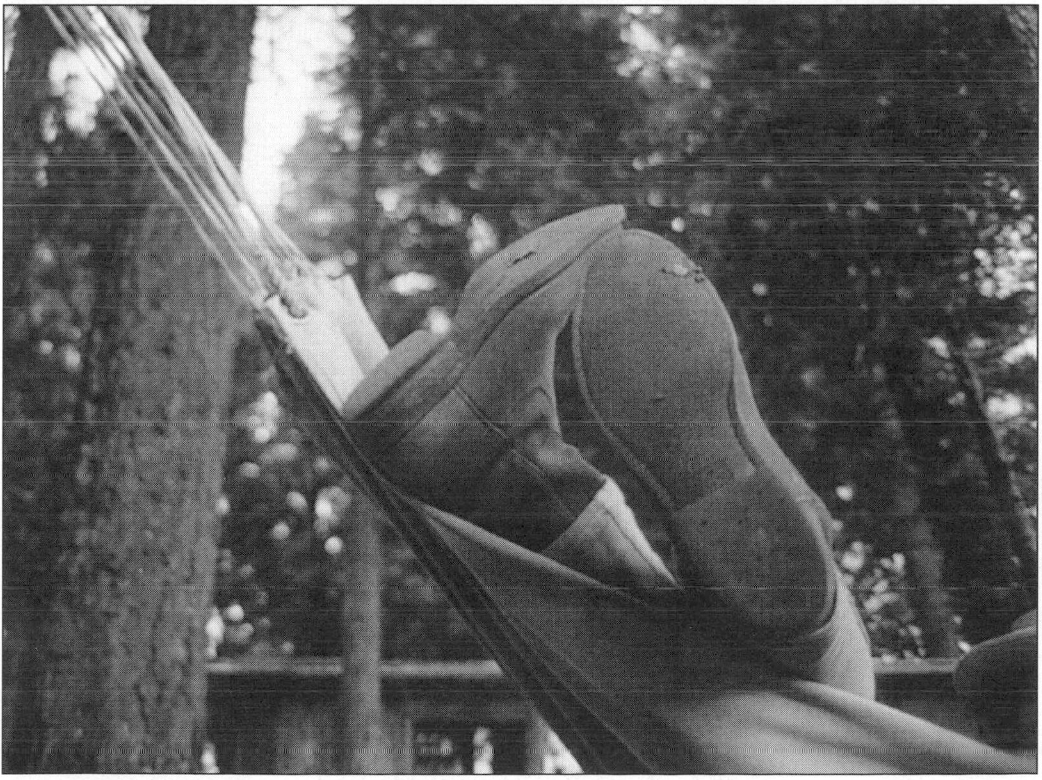

Highland Ranch
Philo, California

Highland Ranch is located in the beautiful wine and redwood country of northern California. Secluded and very private, the ranch sits above the Anderson Valley, known for fine wines and friendly vineyards. Highland Ranch is owned and hosted by George Gaines; following a successful international legal and business career, he bought it in the late 1980s and transformed it into a pastoral paradise. Here you'll find deer and other local wildlife, tall redwoods, fruit trees, wildflowers, and meadows divided by split-rail fences. The charming old yellow-and-white ranch house is the central gathering place, where guests relax by a crackling fire and savor subtle aromas from the kitchen. With its proximity to San Francisco, the Mendocino Coast, and some of California's finest wineries and towering redwoods, Highland Ranch is a slice of heaven and a piece of paradise.

Address: P.O. Box 150 K, Philo, California 95466
Telephone: (707) 895-3600; fax: (707) 895-3702
Internet: http://www.ranchweb.com/highland
Airport: San Francisco, Oakland, and Santa Rosa for commercial flights; Ukiah for private jets and small planes; Boonville for small planes only. Helicopter landing at ranch.
Location: 2½ hours north of San Francisco, six miles northwest of Philo off Highway 128
Medical: Ukiah Community Hospital, 24 miles
Conference: 12–20; 250-square-foot conference room
Guest Capacity: 22
Accommodations: Individual cabins and duplexes with various sleeping arrangements. Most have fireplaces and sitting areas; all have telephones, private baths, electric blankets, good towels, and very comfortable mattresses and pillows. Covered porches with rocking chairs.
Rates: $$$. American Plan. Two-day minimum stay.
Credit Cards: VISA, MasterCard, American Express. Personal and traveler's checks accepted.
Season: Year-round
Activities: Do as much or as little as you wish, from wine-tasting or bird-watching to reading your favorite book. Very individualized program. If you are looking for set schedules and planned activities, this is not the place for you. Wonderful riding on over 100 miles of trails through the towering redwoods or open meadows, along the ridges overlooking the Anderson Valley, or along the Navarro River. Rides are tailored to experience levels, and English saddles are available. Tennis on two surfaced courts, swimming in pool or three-acre pond, fishing, hiking, clay-pigeon shooting, or simply relaxing in four hammocks just outside the ranch house.
Children's Programs: Children are welcome with a family gathering. No formal programs.
Dining: Exceptional food, featuring local produce and fresh fish, is served family-style in the charming Old World dining room. Fabulous country breakfasts and lunches. Each evening George pours complimentary cocktails and Anderson Valley and international wines with dinner. Special menus upon request. The food is outstanding and so is the ambiance.
Entertainment: Many enjoy relaxing in hammock heaven while reading their favorite book. Others enjoy the extensive library and music collection. Some tune into the ranch's satellite TV. Great local Anderson Valley entertainment available.
Summary: Wonderful, small, very private ranch in northern California. Near Anderson Valley wineries and Mendocino Coast. Superb food, fine wine, great conversation, and hospitality. Excellent for individuals, couples, honeymoons, family gatherings, reunions, and small corporate groups. Local vineyards include Lazy Creek, Pepperwood Springs, Roederer, Husch, Navarro, Greenwood Ridge, and Scharffenberger. Be sure to stop by the Apple Farm for fresh apple cider. French and Italian spoken. Video available. Well-behaved pets are welcome.

See color photos, page 179.

Howard Creek Ranch
Westport, California

In 1867, after the Civil War, the early pioneer Howards received a land grant of thousands of acres along California's northern coast. They were the first settlers in the area and ran sheep and cattle and operated a sawmill, a blacksmith shop, and a dairy. This charming ranch inn is surrounded by bright green lawns and vibrant flowers and filled with antiques, offering a simple, wholesome getaway just off the highway. People come to unwind and enjoy the wilderness, the rustic setting, and the dramatic ocean and mountain views. Howard Creek is cheerful, friendly, country-like, and just 300 yards from the ocean. Current owners, Charlie and Sally, are in the process of restoring the old ranch barn. The ranch is a cozy nest, close to the sea and mountains with an abundance of wildlife and all the little homey touches that show someone cares. One guest summed it up: "It's beautiful, quiet, peaceful, and romantic."

Address: P.O. Box 121 K, 40501 N. Highway 1, Westport, California 95488
Telephone: (707) 964-6725; fax: (707) 964-1603
Internet: http://www.howardcreekranch.com
Airport: San Francisco, Santa Rosa
Location: Three miles north of Westport, 124 miles south of Eureka, 150 miles north of San Francisco
Memberships: Mendocino Coast Innkeepers Association, California Association of Bed and Breakfast Inns
Awards: Frommer's *The 100 Best Bed and Breakfast Homes in North America*; selected by *Vacation Magazine* as one of America's best romantic inns
Medical: Fort Bragg, 18 miles
Guest Capacity: 22
Accommodations: Two small cabins are next to Howard Creek and a meadow, and the Beach Cabin has an ocean view. There are four rooms in the New England–style white-sided ranch house: two open onto the second-story balcony through French doors (ask Sally about the Lucy Howard etching story), and two rooms face east. All accommodations reflect early California character with antiques and fresh flowers. Many have intricate handcrafted redwood detailing. You may listen to the pounding surf or gaze at the stars from skylights and picture windows. Inquire about the Boathouse Cabin. Some cabins and rooms have refrigerators and microwave ovens. All cabins have glass-doored woodstoves. Daily maid service.
Rates: $–$$. European Plan. Winter rates are also available.
Credit Cards: VISA, MasterCard, American Express
Season: Year-round
Activities: Guests enjoy the ambiance, the flowers, the hot tub overlooking the ranch (with German massage by reservation only), and most of all, the coastal enchantment, including whale-watching, birding, and tidal pools. There's also a solar-heated swimming pool and a long, sandy beach. Wonderful riding program in association with Ms. Lari Shea, winner of the prestigious Tevis Cup 100-mile endurance ride. Lari offers rides along the ocean beaches and coastal bluffs, and through a cattle ranch. Her Akhal-Teke/Russian Orlov-cross Arabians excel on the trails, as well as in dressage and jumping. Appies and quarter horses round out her stable of well-trained horses for both English and Western enthusiasts.
Children's Programs: Not children-oriented—an adult getaway.
Dining: Only breakfast is served: omelets and Sally's famous fresh blackberry-banana buttermilk hotcakes. Ranch-fresh eggs. Sally will help you with local restaurant selections.
Entertainment: Sit by the fireplace, read in the library, play the piano, or stroll across the 75-foot swinging bridge.
Summary: Ranch bed-and-breakfast on California's Mendocino coast. Excellent riding opportunities, both English and Western, on ocean beaches and scenic bluffs of the coastal mountains. Instruction with advance reservations. Massage available. Italian, Dutch, and German spoken. Pets allowed by prior arrangement. Nearby: Skunk Train through the redwoods, Mendocino shops, and Fort Bragg Harbor.

Hunewill Circle H Ranch
Bridgeport, California

THE DUDE RANCHERS' ASSOCIATION

With Lake Tahoe and Yosemite nearby, this old-time family cattle ranch has been taking guests since 1930. The ranch is situated in the lovely, green, wide-open cattle-ranching Bridgeport Valley in the heart of the Sierras, backdropped by the Sawtooth Ridge that marks the northeastern boundary of Yosemite National Park. It was founded by the great-great-grandparents of the present owners, the Hunewill family. The ranch runs about 2,000 head of cattle over 5,000 acres. While horseback riding is the main activity, hikers will find miles of trails, and fishermen enjoy nearby streams and lakes. The Hunewills say, "We love this ranch and our way of life." Families have been returning here for years. The ranch offers a beautiful setting, great hosts, and a low-key Western atmosphere.

Address: P.O. Box 368 K, Bridgeport, California 93517 (summer); 200 K Hunewill Lane, Wellington, Nevada 89444 (winter)
Telephone: (760) 932-7710 (summer), (775) 465-2201 (winter), or (775) 465-2325 (Stan and Jan)
E-Mail: hunewillranch@tele-net.net
Internet: http://www.hunewillranch.com
Airport: Reno; private airplanes, Bridgeport
Location: 115 miles south of Reno on Highway 395, 50 miles north of Mammoth, five miles southwest of Bridgeport on Twin Lakes Road
Memberships: The Dude Ranchers' Association
Medical: Mono Medical Clinic, five miles
Guest Capacity: 45
Accommodations: Bridgeport was one of the early gold-mining areas, so the ranch buildings have a Victorian flavor. There are 24 white cottages in the ranch quadrangle, each with private bath, electric and gas heat, carpeting, and porch. The ranch house is a lovely two-story Victorian, built in 1880 and surrounded by tall poplars. Laundry facilities available.
Rates: • $$. American Plan. Rates vary depending on accommodation and month. Children's rates. One-week minimum stay encouraged. Saturday to Saturday. Ask about three- and five-day packages.
Credit Cards: None. Personal checks accepted.
Season: May to late September
Activities: Riding is the main attraction. Three rides go out mornings and afternoons for beginning, intermediate, and advanced riders. Beginners (both children and adults) appreciate special rides designed to build confidence and skills with instruction-oriented wranglers and gentle horses. Beautiful wide-open-meadow rides. Ask about the rides to Eagle Peak, Buckeye Canyon, and Tamarack Lake. Riding helmets provided for those who wish. Breakfast and lunch rides. Any time the ranch does cattle work, guests are welcome to join in. Fishing in nearby streams and lakes (bring your own gear), nature walks, volleyball, and horseshoes. Tennis five miles away.
Children's Programs: Children are their parents' responsibility. Children are included in all ranch activities and have an enjoyable experience in a healthy outdoor environment. During adult riding times, youngsters ages six and under are watched by a Buckaroo Counselor and may be led on a gentle horse. Kids ages six to 11 go on beginning rides with adults.
Dining: Ranch-style, everyone eats together. Two barbecues each week. Don't miss the Hunewill's own mountain-spring well water. BYOB.
Entertainment: The Hunewill "Summer House" plays host to square dancing, skit night, impromptu singing, and music. Weekly gymkhana, roping lessons, and hayrides.
Summary: One of California's most renowned dude/cattle ranches. Great old California family. Riding is the main activity here. Very casual and low-key. Cattle roundup in mid-September. Spring and fall cattle-work weeks; cattle work and roping clinics. Bridgeport rodeo in July. Fall color rides and five-day November cattle drive. Massage available. Nearby: ghost towns of Bodie, Aurora, Lundy, and Buckeye Hot Springs, courthouse in Bridgeport.

See color photos, page 182.

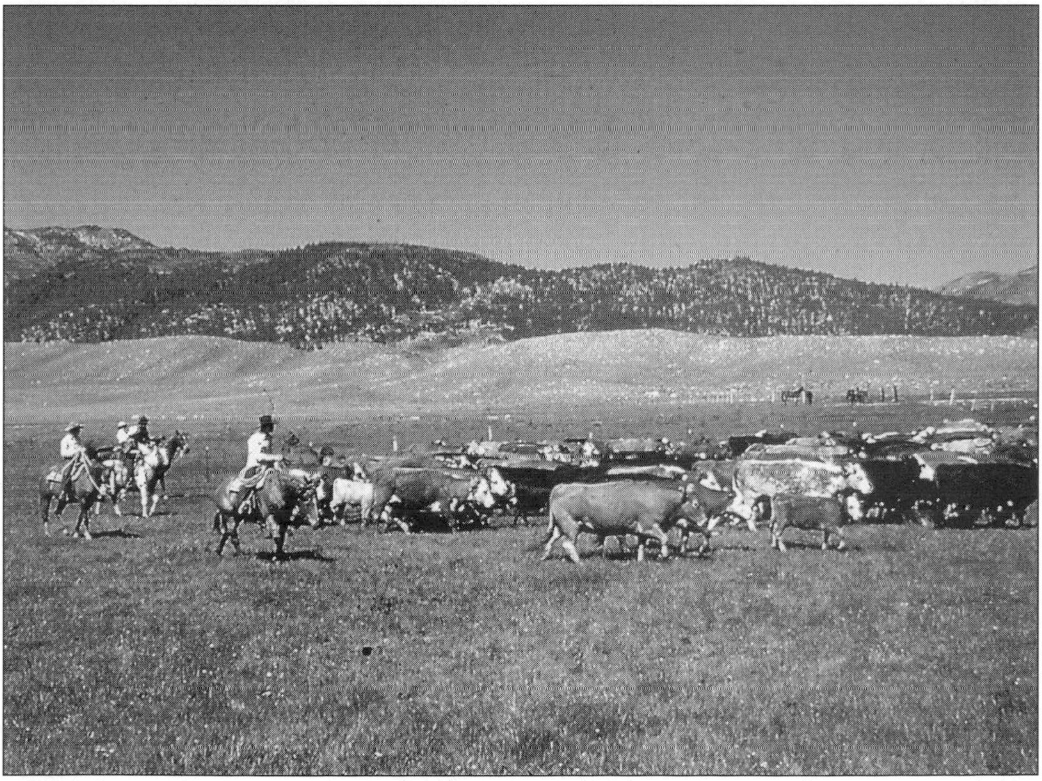

Rankin Ranch
Caliente, California

The Rankin Ranch is one of California's old ranching traditions. It is here in a secluded valley in southern California that Bill and Glenda, along with Bill's mother, ranch matriarch Helen Rankin, share their love for people and the West. The Rankin family has been in the cattle business since 1863. On 30,000 acres in northern Kern County, things are pretty much as they always have been—slow and easy is the pace, warm and friendly are the folks. Over the years lots of people have driven up over the winding, slow-going road and down into this beautiful grassy valley to spend time at the ranch. Those who return yearly have a real appreciation for country living and are able to leave their businesses and professions behind. Here it's quality family time.

Address: P.O. Box 36 K, Caliente, California 93518
Telephone: (805) 867-2511; fax: (805) 867-0105
Airport: Bakersfield, free transportation available with one-week stay
Location: 42 miles northeast of Bakersfield off Highway 58 via Caliente–Bodfish Road
Memberships: National Cattlemen's and Cattlewomen's Associations, California Historical Society
Awards: California 100 Year Club
Medical: Lake Isabella Hospital, 25 miles
Conference: 24; 1,500-square-foot meeting/rec room
Guest Capacity: 40
Accommodations: 14 comfortable, wood-paneled duplex cabins are named after sites on the ranch, like Lightner Flat, Ruby Mine, and Rankin Hill. Each cottage has a bath, carpeting, and picture windows. Daily maid service provided; cribs available on request.
Rates: • \$–\$\$\$. American Plan. Children's rates. Rates vary depending on time of year. One-night minimum stay policy.
Credit Cards: VISA, MasterCard, American Express, Discover. Personal checks accepted.
Season: Late March through early October
Activities: Daily one-hour morning and afternoon guided horseback trail rides are included. This is scenic mountain country, so most riding is at a walk. In meadow areas, some loping can be done. When there are cattle to be moved in the meadow, guests are invited to help the cowboys. FYI: this is not a weekly activity. Julia Lake and Walker Basin Creek are stocked with rainbow trout (bring your own fishing pole). There's tennis, archery, and hiking. The ranch has a lovely, shaded, heated-swimming-pool area where many guests enjoy swimming, reading, or just plain relaxing. Shuffleboard, table tennis, horseshoes, and volleyball are also available. Petting farm.
Children's Programs: Fully supervised seasonal children's programs 9 a.m. to 3:30 p.m. and 5:30 to 7 p.m. Excellent crafts program, talent shows, swim meets, picnics, and games. Ask about the kids' favorite afternoon-picnic Indian hike and bottle-feeding the baby calves. Baby-sitting available with advance notice.
Dining: Amid Rankin Ranch cowboy photos, guests enjoy three hearty ranch-style meals in the spacious, high-ceilinged dining room, the Garden Room. Don't come here to lose weight. Breakfast is served from 7:30 to 9 a.m. BYOB for adult patio party at 5:30 p.m. daily featuring the Rankin Ranch's famous guacamole dip and chips. Vegetarians will not be disappointed. One fun evening includes a hay-wagon ride, meadow barbecue, and horseshoe tournament. Ask about the Rankin Ranch Family Cookbook.
Entertainment: Something is planned each evening: square dancing, pool tournaments, hayrides, talent show, and indoor horse races. Rec room for all ages.
Summary: A great family running an old-time, working cattle ranch. Come here to relax, recharge, and enjoy wonderful easygoing Western hospitality and kindness. Lots of space, peace, and quiet. Excellent for celebrating special birthdays, anniversaries, and family reunions. Ask about Western Week in May. Europeans welcome. Featured in *Better Homes and Gardens, U.S. News and World Report* (video), and *Sunset* magazine. Spanish spoken. Nearby: the gold rush town of Havilah and white-water rafting on the Kern River.

See color photos, page 183.

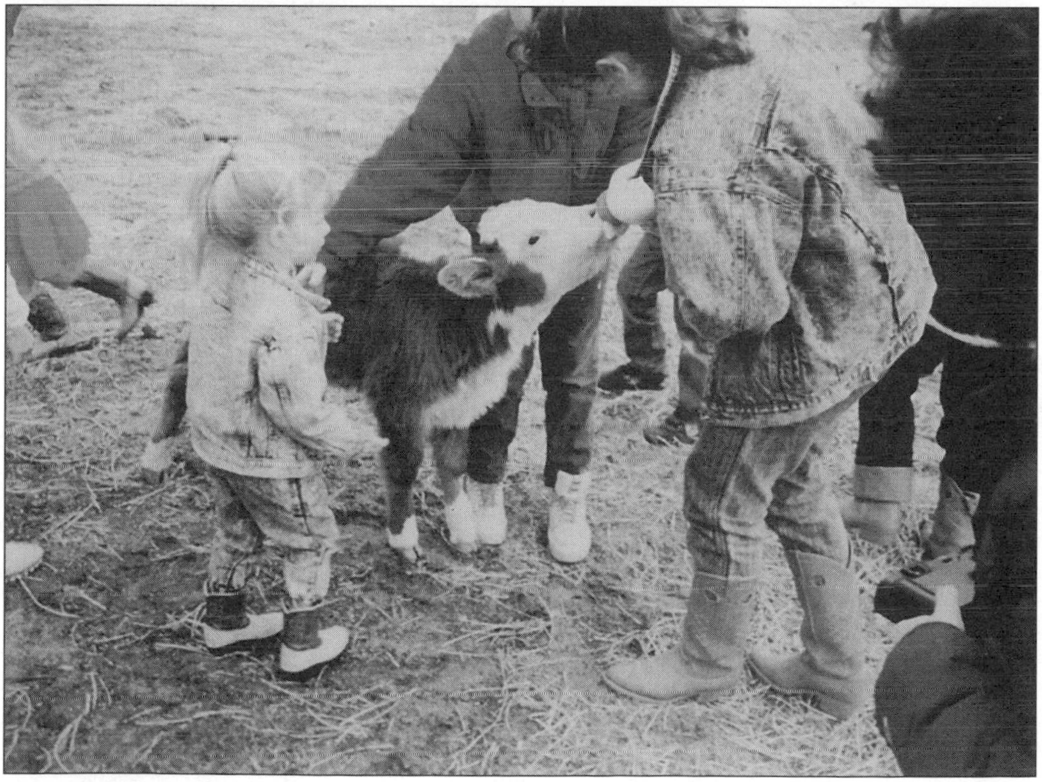

4UR Ranch
Creede, Colorado

The present owners bought the 4UR in the early 1970s. The same timeless qualities of nature, history, fly-fishing, and hospitality continue to make the 4UR Ranch a delightful experience. The ranch is high (8,500 feet) in the San Juan Mountains of southwestern Colorado, and the old CF and I Fluorspar Mine from the early 1900s keeps a watchful eye over it. For discriminating fly-fishing guests, there is private fishing on the Rio Grande and Goose Creek; the two Lost Lakes are at 11,000 feet. July and August are the ranch's busiest family months; September is a favorite for fishermen.

Address: P.O. Box 340K, Creede, Colorado 81130
Telephone: (719) 658-2202; fax: (719) 658-2308
E-Mail: 4urranch@amigo.net
Airport: Alamosa via Denver; 6,800-foot paved airstrip in nearby Creede with hangar facilities for guests
Location: 222 miles southwest of Denver, 60 miles west of Alamosa, eight miles southeast of Creede off Highway 149
Medical: St. Joseph's Hospital, Del Norte, 40 miles
Conference: 50, June and September
Guest Capacity: 50
Accommodations: Guest facilities consist of three delightfully remodeled 1950s cedar-shake mini-lodges. Rooms share a common breezeway porch, but each has its own entrance with numerous rockers. All rooms have private baths, thermostatic heating, daily maid service, and nightly bed turn-down. A family cottage is available at certain times. The main lodge, with its dining and living rooms, splendid valley views, bar, and game room, is the center stage for evening socializing. Laundry service is available (extra).
Rates: • $$$. American Plan. Includes all ranch activities except massage, sporting clays, raft trips, guided hikes, and fly-fishing instruction. Children's rates available. Children under age five free. Group and conference rates available. Seven-day minimum stay in July and August, Saturday to Saturday.
Credit Cards: VISA, MasterCard
Season: Early June through September
Activities: Fly-fishing, riding, and hiking are main activities. Fly-fishing on river and in alpine lakes with instruction available by request. Each evening fishermen roll the dice to select their own half-mile stretch of water for the following morning's fishing. BYO gear. Some flies and equipment available. Breakfast, morning, afternoon, and all-day horseback rides through very scenic country; most rides are walking. Some advanced rides. Heated swimming pool, log bathhouse with sauna, hot sulfur baths, whirlpool. Massage room with licensed massage therapist available. Tennis court, hiking, and rafting available. Thirteen-station sporting-clays course (ranch prefers you bring your own guns).
Children's Programs: Counselor for kids over age six. Full-day supervised program from 9 a.m. to 5 p.m. Junior Wrangler program teaches kids about horses. Baby-sitting provided with advance notice. Bring your own nanny if you wish full-time care. Children's gymkhanas.
Dining: Fisherman's early continental breakfast followed by regular full-course breakfast. Weekly breakfast ride along the Rio Grande with biscuits and gravy, scrambled eggs and ham, baked apples, and cowboy coffee. Once a week the ranch features a high-noon fish fry along Goose Creek. Gourmet backcountry picnics. Full-service bar and select premium wines.
Entertainment: Unscheduled. Lots of quality family time. Jeep-pulled hayrides, video movie classics (Westerns and Disney). Evening fly-tying.
Summary: Wonderful guest ranch on scenic Goose Creek, famous for its excellent fly-fishing; eight and one-half miles of private waters. Family-oriented during July and August; mostly adults during September. Hot sulfur pool. Special 4UR fly-fishing school. Old "Doc" buggy and four-seat surrey rides.

Aspen Canyon Ranch
Parshall, Colorado

CDGRA

Built in 1987, the ranch is bordered on three sides by Forest Service lands and overlooks the Williams Fork River, 50 feet below. It's a base camp for outdoor adventure. Today it is owned and operated by Steve and Debbie Roderick, along with their four children, ages 11, nine, seven, and four. A wonderful family spirit prevails here, offering those with and without children a place to ride, hike, fish, and relax. At Aspen Canyon Ranch the schedule is flexible, personal, and tailored to its guests. And that's just the way it is!

Address: 13206 County Road 3, Parshall, Colorado 80468
Telephone: (800) 321-1357; fax: (970) 725-0044, (970) 725-3600
E-Mail: acr@imageline.com
Internet: http://www.acr@imageline.com
Airport: Denver; private aircraft to Kremmling
Train: Amtrak to Granby
Location: 25 miles north of Silverthorne, 90 miles west of Denver. Ranch will send you a detailed map.
Memberships: Colorado Dude and Guest Ranch Association, Colorado Guides and Outfitters
Medical: Kremmling Hospital, 26 miles
Conference: 40
Guest Capacity: 40
Accommodations: Guests stay in three fourplex log cabins named Deer Lodge, Elk Lodge, and Trout Lodge, each on the banks of the Williams Fork River. All have comfortable accommodations, natural-gas fireplaces, flannel comforters, carpeting, refrigerators, coffeemakers, porches, and old-fashioned swings. You'll find a large jar of freshly baked cookies in your room each day. Ask about the three-bedroom Cliff House overlooking the Williams Fork River. The main lodge, with a wonderful porch, houses the dining and living rooms and two cozy fireplaces. Riverside hot tub and deck.
Rates: • $$$. American Plan. Children's, off-season, group, and winter rates available. Children under age three free. Full-time baby-sitting available. Cliff House bed-and-breakfast rates in winter.
Credit Cards: VISA, MasterCard, Discover
Season: Summer: late May through early October. Winter: snowmobiling mid-December to April.
Activities: Guests enjoy casting a line into the Williams Fork River for brook, brown, and rainbow trout. Three stocked ponds. Fishing gear available. Guides available on request. Scheduled easygoing mountain trail riding program. As Steve says, "We are flexible and try to meet our guests' expectations." Half-day and all-day riding, hiking (ask about the Lake Evelyn picnic hike). Mountain bikes available. Golf and ballooning 30 miles away. Ranch gymkhana, calf-roping, and barrel racing in rodeo arena. Rafting on the Colorado, Blue, Arkansas, and Clear Creek Rivers is available each week. Winter: ask about lunch/snowmobile program.
Children's Programs: Children's program for kids ages three to 12. Call for details.
Dining: Home-style ranch cooking. Everything is homemade! Special diets catered to. BYOB.
Entertainment: Sing-alongs, line and Western dancing, seasonal rodeos in town, and guest and staff gymkhanas.
Summary: Small, very friendly guest ranch for families who appreciate a wonderful family environment, river setting, and children's program. Terrific cabin amenities. Nearby: Breckenridge and Vail, and Rocky Mountain National Park for day trips.

Aspen Lodge Ranch Resort
Estes Park, Colorado

CDGRA

Aspen Lodge shines bright, both as a ranch resort for families during the summer and as a corporate retreat/meeting conference center in the off-season. Situated at 9,000 feet, at the base of the Twin Sisters Mountains, the lodge and guest cabins look out to Longs Peak. Fresh air, spectacular views, and the surrounding Rocky Mountain National Park make for a tremendous vacation opportunity for everyone. The focal point of Aspen Lodge is the main lodge. Built of lodgepole pine, this magnificent 33,000-square-foot structure is one of the largest log buildings in North America. With access to more than 1,600 acres of wooded mountainside and alpine lakes and meadows, Aspen Lodge Ranch Resort offers both summer and winter activities in proximity to one of Colorado's most famous national parks.

Address: 6120 Highway 7, Estes Park, Colorado 80517
Telephone: (800) 332-6867 nationwide, (970) 586-8133; fax: (970) 586-8133
E-Mail: aspen@aspenlodge.com
Internet: http://www.aspenlodge.com
Airport: Denver
Location: 10 minutes south of Estes Park, 65 miles northwest of Denver off I-25
Memberships: Colorado Dude and Guest Ranch Association
Awards: AAA 3 Diamond, *Official Hotel Guide*: Best Dude Ranch 1996, Delta Dream Vacation
Medical: Estes Park Hospital, seven miles
Conference: 150; excellent conference facilities
Guest Capacity: 150
Accommodations: The lodge features several hospitality suites and 36 guest rooms. Separate from the main lodge are 23 multiroom cabins with porches and great views.
Rates: • $$–$$$. American Plan. Horseback riding and some equipment rentals (mountain bikes) extra. Children's, conference, and group rates available. Check with ranch for special winter rates. Three-, four-, and seven-night packages in summer.
Credit Cards: VISA, MasterCard, American Express, Diners Club, Discover
Season: Year-round, open all holidays
Activities: Summer programs offer something for everyone. Trail-riding from the lodge into adjoining Rocky Mountain National Park. Also, advanced open-country riding available at the nearby ranch surrounded by 33,000 acres of Roosevelt National Forest. Ask about the overnight horseback campout. Week-long instructional program for kids and adults. Fishing in lake, hiking, climbing, and heated outdoor pool with whirlpool. Two lighted tennis courts. The Sports Center has weights and exercise room, two racquetball courts, game room, and Finnish sauna. River rafting and van tours can be arranged. Mountain bikes, volleyball, horseshoes. Eighteen-hole par-70 golf course nearby. Estes Park with shops and galleries is 10 minutes away. Winter: see Cross-Country Skiing chapter.
Children's Programs: Extensive (flexible) children's program 9 a.m. to 4 p.m. each day (except Sunday) that's fun as well as educational: Indian lore, pioneer lifestyles, moviemaking, and nature exploration. Baby-sitting available.
Dining: Beautiful Longs Peak is framed through the dining-room windows. The dining lodge offers "casual continental" to Colorado cuisine. Western bar and deck.
Entertainment: Hayrides, square dancing, barbecues, movies, two-stepping, weekend entertainers, and nature walks.
Summary: Ranch resort with access to 33,000 acres. Surrounded by the highest peaks of Rocky Mountain National Park. Abundant recreational activities with access to cultural opportunities of Estes Park 10 minutes away. Á la carte and week-long riding packages. Exciting children's program. A 33,000-square-foot multifaceted, multinational atmosphere. Off-season conference opportunities. Watch out for the elk! Indoor smoke-free policy.

Bar Lazy J Guest Ranch
Parshall, Colorado

THE DUDE RANCHERS' ASSOCIATION

CDGRA

The Bar Lazy J is the oldest continuously operating guest ranch in Colorado, and began entertaining guests in 1912, when it was known as the Buckhorn Lodge. It's situated right on the Colorado River at an elevation of 7,500 feet, about a half-mile from the little town of Parshall. In 1995, Jerry and Cheri Helmicki bought the ranch to share their love of the great outdoors with people from around the world. A unique feature of the ranch is the beautiful Gold Medal trout river, offering anglers the opportunity to fish right outside their cabin doors. Horseback riding is the main ranch activity. Each day riders have a choice of walking, trotting, or loping rides. Jerry and Cheri have put together a strong children's program with children's counselors and wranglers. At the Bar Lazy J you can ride, fish, read, or just get downright lazy and listen to the Colorado River sing its song right outside your cabin.

Address: P.O. Box N-K, Parshall, Colorado 80468
Telephone: (800) 396-6279, (970) 725-3437; fax (970) 725-0121
E-Mail: barlazyj@rkymtnhi.com
Internet: http://www.barlazyj.com
Airport: Denver
Location: 15 miles west of Granby, 100 miles northwest of Denver
Memberships: The Dude Ranchers' Association, Colorado Dude and Guest Ranch Association
Medical: Kremmling Hospital, 13 miles
Guest Capacity: 38
Accommodations: Guests stay in 12 cozy log cabins, accommodating two to eight people each. Each is named after wildflowers or fishing flies. Most have wooden floors, paneling, and enclosed covered porches overlooking the river, and all have rockers. Bathroom and thermostatically controlled heat in each. Nightly turn-down service and coffeemakers in each cabin.
Rates: • $$$. American Plan. Children's and off-season rates available. One-week minimum stay in June, July, and August, Sunday to Sunday. Three-day minimum stay in September.
Credit Cards: VISA, MasterCard. Personal checks and traveler's checks preferred.
Season: Late May through September
Activities: Most come here to fish, ride, and relax, and not necessarily in that order! Gold Medal fishing with weekly fishing clinic. Stocked fishing pond for kids and those who don't wish to fish the river. Horseback riding for many levels of experience. Breakfast, half-day, and all-day rides through the Arapahoe National Forest and open fields dotted with sage and grazing cattle, along the river, and through aspen groves. Small groups (eight or fewer) go out on each ride. Slow, medium, and fast rides. Other ranch activities include mountain biking, hiking, outdoor heated swimming pool, large Jacuzzi, shuffleboard, horseshoes, volleyball, and jeep trips. River rafting nearby.
Children's Programs: Extensive program from 8:30 a.m. to 5 p.m. each day. "Ranch Fun," for kids ages three and older, can be a full day of supervised ranch activity including horseback riding; the program is flexible and optional. Children's playroom where all craft activities take place. Children eat with their parents. Baby-sitting available for very young children (extra).
Dining: Meals are served family-style in the beautiful log dining room. Traditional family-style meals. A variety of vegetarian meals available too. Enjoy homemade soup, pies, cakes. BYOB.
Entertainment: Campfires, hayrides, volleyball, staff shows, and country dancing in the rec room barn.
Summary: The oldest continuously operating guest ranch in Colorado, located along the Colorado River. Lots of history. Buildings reflect wonderful old-time atmosphere. Great children's program, which allows parents a vacation, too. Great for families, couples, and singles who enjoy the outdoors without a highly structured program. All cabins overlook the river. Two-thirds of a mile of Gold Medal trout river, the Colorado, runs through the ranch.

See color photos, page 184.

C Lazy U Ranch
Granby, Colorado

THE DUDE RANCHERS' ASSOCIATION

CDGRA

The C Lazy U Ranch story began back in 1919. In 1988, the Murray family, who had been guests each year since 1959, bought their favorite home-away-from-home. They have ensured that the C Lazy U experience continues to be one of the best in the business today. C Lazy U mixes rustic luxury with old-fashioned informality. The facilities and food are Western, comfortable, and of superb quality. The ranch continues to receive the prestigious Mobil 5-Star and AAA 5-Diamond ratings. This 2,000-acre ranch has it all, from designer soap to therapeutic massage that will soothe your tired muscles and help you unwind. Very family-oriented, the ranch has different programs for children and adults. Families eat breakfast together, then the kids go off to work—to work at having the most fun they've ever had.

Address: Box 379, Granby, Colorado 80446
Telephone: (970) 887-3344; fax: (970) 887 3917
E-Mail: ranch@clazyu.com
Internet: http://www.clazyu.com
Airport: Denver International
Location: Six miles northwest of Granby off Highway 125, 95 miles west of Denver
Memberships: Colorado Dude and Guest Ranch Association, The Dude Ranchers' Association, Cross-Country Ski Association
Awards: Mobil 5 Star, AAA 5 Diamond
Medical: Granby Medical Center
Conference: 70; spring, winter, and fall
Guest Capacity: 110
Accommodations: The accommodations are comfortable and casual. Many cabins have fireplaces and vary from single rooms to family suites. Some have Jacuzzi bathtubs and stocked refrigerators. Full amenities include hair dryers, bathrobes, coffeemakers, humidifiers, nightly turn-down service, a fruit basket that's replenished daily, and a fire that's reset daily.
Rates: • $$$–$$$$$. Full American Plan. Off-season and group rates available.
Credit Cards: None. Personal checks or cash accepted.
Season: June through September. Mid-December through March. September is adults only.
Activities: Excellent progressive riding program: fast, medium, and slow rides, depending on rider's ability, and instructional rides for every level. Morning, afternoon, and weekly picnic rides. Some English riding. Horses are assigned for the week and matched to each rider's ability. Usually six to eight to a ride. Adults and children ride separately, except on the weekly family ride. Indoor riding arena; two LayKold tennis courts, with tennis pro who gives complimentary instruction; spring-fed, heated pool; indoor sauna and whirlpool; racquetball court; trap and skeet range (extra); fishing in stocked pond or Willow Creek (guided fishing can be arranged on the Colorado River); white-water raft trips (30 minutes away, extra); and golf nearby. Winter: see chapter on Cross-Country Skiing Ranches.
Children's Programs: Kids and adults do their own thing. Parents and kids love it! Extensive children's program for ages three to 12; teen program 13 to 17. Children eat together at lunch and dinner. Families with children under age three must bring their own nanny/baby-sitter. Ask about designated Baby Weeks.
Dining: Guests enjoy happy hour before dinner in the cozy lodge bar, often accompanied by live grand-piano background music. Two entrées each evening. Prime rib, steaks, fresh vegetables, and homemade breads. Poolside cookouts twice weekly. Special meals on request. Full wine service with dinner. Children eat before adults.
Entertainment: Something is planned each evening. Square dancing, cookouts, campfires, and sing-alongs. Cowboy singer, staff shows, Western band, and weekly "Shodeo"—part show, part rodeo.
Summary: One of the top and most celebrated year-round destination guest ranches. Premier children's programs for kids and teens. Superb for families and couples. September is adults-only month. October horsemanship clinic. Riding program both summer and winter. French, German, and Spanish spoken.

See color photos, page 185.

Colorado Trails Ranch
Durango, Colorado

THE DUDE RANCHERS' ASSOCIATION

CDGRA

Over the years Colorado Trails Ranch has had one of the finest reputations in the guest-ranching business. It has always been famous for its outstanding riding and children's programs. Today, Jeanie Ross and general managers Robin and Stan Williams, along with their marvelous staff, continue to offer families a truly exceptional program. Colorado Trails Ranch is geared to family fun and children. Located in the beautiful San Juan Mountains at 7,500 feet, just outside the famous mining town of Durango, the ranch offers a comprehensive Western riding program with certified riding instructors. An extensive guided fly-fishing program has been developed along four miles of private water on and near the ranch. At Colorado Trails you'll enjoy the Western Village, complete with trading post where they serve old-fashioned ice-cream treats next door to the opera house—you might just "ride into the romance of the Old West"!

Address: 12161 County Road 240, Durango, Colorado 81301
Telephone: (800) 323-3833, (970) 247-5055; fax: (970) 385-7372
E-Mail: CoTRanch@aol.com
Internet: http://www.colotrails.com
Airport: La Plata, 18 miles from ranch
Location: 12 miles northeast of Durango on County Road 240; 200 miles north of Albuquerque, New Mexico; 350 miles southwest of Denver
Memberships: The Dude Ranchers' Association, Colorado Dude and Guest Ranch Association, American Quarter Horse Association, American Humane Association, American Riding Instructors Association
Awards: *Family Circle* 1990 and 1991 Family Resort of the Year; 1988 American Humane Association's outstanding service in the field of humane education (Rosemary Ames Award)
Medical: Mercy Medical Center, Durango
Conference: 60; three different room setups, 4,800 square feet; mid-May, late September and October
Guest Capacity: 65 (33 rooms)
Accommodations: Guests can stay in four types of comfortably furnished cabins. All rooms have private bathrooms, carpeting, electric baseboard heat, and porches. Guest laundry is available.
Rates: • $$$. All-inclusive American Plan. Family, off-season, and nanny rates.
Credit Cards: VISA, MasterCard, American Express, Discover, Diners Club
Season: Late May to October
Activities: One of the best riding programs in the country. Western riding instruction for beginners through intermediate riders. Ask Robin about "Horsetalk." English riding available in the arena. Extensive fly-fishing program (see chapter on Fly-Fishing Ranches). Ask about Mesa Verde trip. Heated swimming pool, whirlpool spa, and fishing. Archery, rifle and trap-shooting (guns provided), hiking, and water-skiing on Lake Vallecito. Golf, rodeo, and float trips are available at extra cost.
Children's Programs: One of North America's best and most extensive programs for children ages five to 18. Kids eat together if they wish.
Dining: The dining room overlooks scenic Shearer Creek Valley and Eagle Ridge. Hearty ranch food and plenty of it. No bar. Drinking permitted in cabins only.
Entertainment: A program every evening, hayrides, cookouts, ice-cream socials, dances, professional rodeos, and melodrama in Durango.
Summary: One of the leading guest ranches in America. Outstanding ranch for families, teens, and children. Caring and personable staff. Full Western riding and fly-fishing programs. Ask about adult-only weeks, family reunions, and the exciting trip to Mesa Verde Indian Cliff Dwellings. Nearby: the famous Durango/Silverton narrow-gauge train.

See color photos, pages 186–187.

Coulter Lake Guest Ranch
Rifle, Colorado

THE DUDE RANCHERS' ASSOCIATION

CDGRA

Coulter Lake Guest Ranch is one of the few Western guest ranches that overlooks its own charming lake. The ranch is nestled in a small mountain valley on the western slope of the Rockies, deep in the White River National Forest at 8,100 feet. In operation since 1938, Coulter Lake retains that Old West flavor and is hosted today by Russ and Susan Papke and owned by Don Hock. Coulter Lake Guest Ranch is surrounded by some of Colorado's most spectacular mountain country, stretching for miles in all directions, virtually unchanged since Indian times. Forests of quaking aspen and spruce overlook meadows of wildflowers. Deer, elk, and other wildlife are abundant. Russ and Sue are year-round residents and have purposely kept the ranch small, intimate, and rustic. Family members of all ages, as well as singles, will love and savor this extra-special mountain hideaway.

Address: P.O. Box 906 K, Rifle, Colorado 81650
Telephone: (800) 858-3046, fax: (970) 625-1473
E-Mail: coulterlake@sopris.net
Internet: http://www.ranchweb.com/coulter
Airport: Grand Junction
Train: Amtrak to Glenwood Springs
Location: 21 miles northeast of Rifle beyond Highway 325
Memberships: The Dude Ranchers' Association, Colorado Dude and Guest Ranch Association, Colorado Snowmobile Association
Medical: Clagett Memorial Hospital, Rifle
Conference: 20 (spring and fall only)
Guest Capacity: 28
Accommodations: Eight cabins stand on the mountainside among the quaking aspen trees; Lakeside and Forest Haven are by the lake. They vary in size and can sleep from two to nine people. Each has a private bath, some with fireplaces, and most have porches. Ranch generates its own power (curling irons and hair dryers not recommended but can be used at the lodge).
Rates: • $$–$$$. American Plan. Children's and family rates available. Off-season and group rates.
Credit Cards: VISA, MasterCard, American Express, Discover, and Novus. Checks or cash preferred.
Season: Late May to October, mid-December to early April
Activities: Riding: short to all-day rides. Mondays and Tuesdays have morning and afternoon rides to Little Box Canyon, Long Park, and Pot Holes. Wednesdays and Fridays feature all-day rides to Irish Point and Little Hill. Hamburger twilight rides to Coulter Mesa on Thursdays. Weekly four-wheel-drive trips, fishing in stocked lake or in alpine streams and lakes (some fishing poles at ranch). The famous Coulter Lake rowboat races take place on Saturdays. Hiking and horseshoes, occasional cattle drives, lake swimming, and volleyball. Eighteen-hole golf, tennis, rafting, and hot springs in nearby Rifle and Glenwood Springs. Photographers should bring a lot of film! Plenty to do. Winter: meals and lodging for snowmobilers and cross-country skiers. Guided snowmobile rentals and tours are available but extra.
Children's Programs: Baby-sitters are available with advance notice. Three-mornings-per-week program for ages three to five including supervised Kiddie rides.
Dining: Hearty, family-style meals. Cookouts, including a supper ride to 10,000-foot Coulter Mesa. Saturday buffet, Wednesday grilled steak and fish. Special diets can easily be accommodated with advance notice. BYOB.
Entertainment: Sing-alongs, square dancing, melodrama, slide shows, and cowboy movies.
Summary: Delightful, small, family ranch. Remote setting, right on its own lake—no noise, no telephones. As Sue says, "We are low-key. If you enjoy good people, riding, and nature, give us a call." Adult-only weeks in early summer and fall. Ask about three-day packages and pack trips. Featured in *National Geographic Traveler* magazine 1995. Video available.

See color photos, page 188.

Deer Valley Ranch
Nathrop, Colorado

CDGRA

Deer Valley Ranch is bordered by 14,000-foot Mt. Princeton and Mt. Antero, with the Chalk Cliffs forming the backdrop. This Christian guest ranch has been in the same family since 1954. The DeWalt and Woolmington families, who now run the ranch, are committed to creating a very special atmosphere for all ages. The ranch places a strong emphasis on the family and does not allow any alcoholic beverages. Their ranch resort program is extensive and offers a variety of rates for many budgets, with special activities planned from dawn to late evening.

Address: Box K, Nathrop, Colorado 81236
Telephone: (800) 284-1708, (719) 395-2353; fax: (719) 395-2394
E-Mail: fun@deervalleyranch.com
Internet: http://www.deervalleyranch.com
Airport: Colorado Springs or Denver; private planes to Buena Vista, 10 miles
Location: 12 miles southwest of Buena Vista, 100 miles directly west of Colorado Springs on Highway 162
Memberships: Colorado Dude and Guest Ranch Association
Medical: Buena Vista Medical Clinic, 10 miles; Salida Hospital, 25 miles
Conference: 125 can meet in the two-story, 1,500-square-foot Centennial Hall or in two other meeting areas (off-season only).
Guest Capacity: 125
Accommodations: The 10-bedroom guest lodge is attached to a Western living room with a large fireplace and ranch dining rooms which look out on 14,269-foot Mt. Antero. The lodge also includes a spacious outdoor double deck for enjoying the mountain scenery. The 15 private family cabins, with historical mining names like St. Elmo and Tincup, sit among the ponderosa and piñon pines. They are two-, three-, and four-bedroom cottages with full kitchens, living areas, fireplaces, and decks.
Rates: • $–$$. Full American Plan in the lodge or modified European Plan in the cottages. All cabin guests are asked to eat one meal a day in the lodge, but they have the option of eating in their cabins as well. Horseback riding is charged on a per-ride basis or by the week. Children's rates for ages three to five and six to 12.
Credit Cards: None. Personal checks accepted.
Season: Year-round, open all holidays
Activities: Complete á la carte horseback riding options including instruction; one-, two-, and three-hour rides; and all-day rides above timberline near the Continental Divide. Fully guided hiking program includes pre-breakfast hikes daily, mountain climbs, and trail hikes through the San Isabel National Forest. Tennis court, free golf at two local courses, two hot-spring pools (90 to 95 degrees Fahrenheit), indoor and outdoor hot tubs. Fly-fishing instruction in Chalk Creek and fishing trips to regional rivers and high lakes, as well as family fishing in stocked ranch lake. Snowsliding, three-on-three basketball, nature hikes, family softball, rock hounding, gold-panning. Whitewater rafting on the nearby Arkansas River is extra.
Children's Programs: All ranch programs are scheduled for families to be together. Children ages four to 11 have the option of choosing four to six hours of their own programs each day. Two full-time children's directors plan hikes, crafts, swimming, and games. Special play area at the Western Town. Teen activities for ages 12 to 16 include overnight campout. Baby-sitting is extra.
Dining: Many cookouts and special meals. Special diets accommodated.
Entertainment: Programs every night. Square dancing, history talks, hayrides with campfires, Western music, and cowboy poetry. Western staff show with guest participation. Satellite TV in Centennial Hall and lots of Western videos. Sunday morning worship service. The Sunday evening hymn-sing is a highlight for many.
Summary: Christian family guest ranch for families, couples, single parents, and singles, with full program of ranch resort activities. You determine your own activities and even adjust your expenses by determining how many meals you want in the dining room and what riding you do. A complete family destination vacation. Be sure to ask about the Trading Post and the ranch cookbook.

Diamond J on the Fryingpan Lodge & Guest Ranch
Meredith, Colorado

The Diamond J dates back to the 1920s as a hunting and fishing lodge. Today it is a four-season getaway high in the Colorado Rockies. At 8,300 feet, the ranch is at the western base of the Continental Divide, surrounded by the White River National Forest. Under new ownership since 1997, it is now an Orvis-endorsed fly-fishing lodge. The Diamond J offers full summer and winter programs with plenty of activities for all, and is just one hour from Aspen. In addition to horseback riding and Gold Medal trout fishing, two of the attractions guests find exhilarating are visiting Ruedi Reservoir, four miles away, and the Jeep trip to the Continental Divide at 12,259 feet, where the air is wonderfully fresh and the view stretches as far as the eye can see.

Address: 26604 Fryingpan Road, Drawer K, Meredith, Colorado 81642
Telephone: (970) 927-3222; fax: (970) 927-5119
E-Mail: pmc@rof.net
Internet: http://www.djfryingpan.com
Airport: Aspen via Denver
Location: 45 miles from Aspen, 45 miles east of Glenwood Springs off Highway 82
Memberships: Orvis-endorsed fly-fishing lodge
Medical: Aspen and Glenwood Springs, about 45 minutes
Conference: 35
Guest Capacity: 35
Accommodations: The ranch has a cozy two-story, nine-room lodge and 14 log cabins. Each cabin is decorated in rustic Western style with fireplaces, stoves, and gas heat. Cabins were recently redecorated and bathrooms remodeled. Smoke-free policy.
Rates: $$$. American Plan. Off-season rates. Private riding lessons and guided fly-fishing extra.
Credit Cards: VISA, MasterCard
Season: Year-round, including holidays
Activities: Summer program includes guided horseback riding. Half-day and all-day group trail rides and pack trips. Children under six ride in arena. Fly-fishing with owner Patrick McCord, 1996 Orvis Guide of the Year. Fishing in the Roaring Fork and Fryingpan Rivers; the Fryingpan is a gold-medal stream which runs through the ranch. White-water rafting, four-wheel-drive trips, volleyball, hiking, horseshoes, mountain biking, and excursions to Aspen. Year-round whirlpool spa. Winter: cross-country skiing enthusiasts will enjoy some of the best skiing in Colorado. The ranch is an overnight stop on the Tenth Mountain Division Trail between Aspen and Vail. For downhill skiing, four world-class ski areas are just an hour away. Snowshoeing and snowmobile trails nearby. Ask about cross-country gear and snowmobiles.
Children's Programs: Children and families participate together. Supervised horse program for families. Child care available with advance notice (extra).
Dining: Western cuisine served family-style in the lodge dining room or at riverside cookouts. Wine and beer included with evening meals.
Entertainment: Movies, ranch rodeo, staff shows, campfires.
Summary: Year-round, friendly ranch for families, singles, and honeymoon couples, with excellent fly-fishing and horseback riding. Just an hour from the world-famous Victorian town of Aspen, Colorado. Ask about wine and food, jazz, comedy and film festivals in Aspen. Nearby: Hot springs pool in Glenwood Springs, town of Marble with nearby quarry.

See color photos, page 189.

Echo Canyon Guest Ranch
La Veta, Colorado

THE DUDE RANCHERS' ASSOCIATION

CDGRA

Echo Canyon Guest Ranch began in 1990. Today, owner Dave Brown of Phoenix, Arizona, and manager Bob Kennemer have created a guest ranch that offers a quality horse program coupled with scenic beauty and complete privacy. Echo Canyon offers one of the newest facilities and, as they say, "a unique Western adventure." As Brown says, "We're at the base of southwestern Colorado's 13,864-foot Spanish Peak and bordered on three sides by the San Isabel National Forest. The riding opportunities are varied from high-mountain trails and mountain creeks to the wide-open meadows of the sister Cucharas River Ranch where we grow hay and raise some livestock." Echo Canyon offers a family atmosphere with a program for those who wish to learn about horsemanship and to enjoy far-reaching vistas and riding through spectacular high country, unique rock formations, and open parks.

Address: P.O. Box 328, 12507 Echo Canyon Creek Road, La Veta, Colorado 81055
Telephone: (800) 341-6603, (719) 742-5524; fax: (719) 742-5525
E-Mail: echo@rmi.net
Internet: http://www.guestecho.com
Airport: Pueblo, 70 miles; Colorado Springs, 120 miles
Train: Amtrak station in Trinidad, 50 miles
Location: 20 miles southwest of Walsenburg, 120 miles southwest of Colorado Springs
Memberships: Colorado Dude and Guest Ranch Association, The Dude Ranchers' Association
Medical: Huerfano Medical Center
Conference: 30, fully-equipped, 1,300-square feet with equipment
Guest Capacity: 30
Accommodations: 12,800-square-foot mountain lodge and two-story four-bedroom cabins. The seven lodge rooms are spacious, with private baths and handmade aspen pole furnishings. Some feature two queen beds, some queen and twin beds. One room in the lodge is a honeymoon suite with its own fireplace, sitting area, and private deck. The cabins have four separate bedrooms, two baths, and a queen sofa sleeper for larger families and groups. These cabins are set off by themselves among the aspen and pine trees. There are two rooms above the conference center.
Rates: $$$. American Plan. Children's, seniors', and group rates available.
Credit Cards: VISA, MasterCard, American Express, Discover
Season: Late May to early October
Activities: Diversified riding program with solid riding instruction and weekly cattle work. Scenic riding on mountain trails, open meadows, and mesas. Four ranch ponds with 20" to 26" rainbow trout, and one mile along the Cucharas River. Ask about the great pack trips; hiking; jeep tours; trap-shooting, rifle, pistol, and archery instruction; volleyball; and horseshoes. Hot tub looks out to Echo Canyon. Grandote, an 18-hole championship golf course rated third best in the state, is just seven miles away.
Children's Programs: Children are welcome but are the responsibility of their parents. Riding program begins at age eight.
Dining: Family-style atmosphere where everyone dines together. Variety of ranch-style cuisine including beef, poultry, trout, Mexican, Italian and *real* Cajun dishes. Licensed cantina.
Entertainment: Weekly singing-cowboy cookouts, cowboy poetry, and mountain-man show. Instruction in proper roping techniques. Indoor game room includes a pool table, Ping-Pong, Foosball, video arcade games, a juke box, and board games.
Summary: A ranch known for a superb horse program. Every horse is owned and personally trained on the ranch. Extremely diverse riding opportunities on two separate, uniquely different ranch properties—guest-ranch and cattle-ranching combination. Because of the elevation, usually numerous wildlife sightings. Nearby: the Great Sand Dunes, Royal Gorge, white-water rafting, historic Trinidad, and Taos, New Mexico.

Drowsy Water Ranch
Granby, Colorado

THE DUDE RANCHERS' ASSOCIATION

CDGRA

Drowsy Water Ranch is exactly what you imagine a classic mountain dude ranch would be. This 600-acre ranch is in the beautiful Rocky Mountains, bordered by thousands of acres of backcountry and the Arapahoe National Forest. Situated in a private valley at 8,200 feet and surrounded by shimmering aspen and scented pine, Drowsy Water is genuine and offers its guests great Colorado hospitality. The remodeled log cabins are situated along Drowsy Water Creek, which meanders through the ranch. The Foshas are hosts and owners. Ken, Randy Sue, and their sons, Justin and Ryan, offer a quality horse program for experienced to beginning riders, and a full program for children of all ages. There's old-fashioned goodness to this ranch. It brings to mind another century, when people were less hurried and really cared about treating each other right.

Address: P.O. Box 147K, Granby, Colorado 80446
Telephone: (800) 845-2292, (970) 725-3456; fax: (970) 725-3611
E-Mail: dwrken@aol.com
Internet: http://www.dude-ranch.com/drowsy_water.html
Airport: Denver
Train: Amtrak to Granby, six miles
Location: 90 miles west of Denver, six miles west of Granby off U.S. 40
Memberships: The Dude Ranchers' Association, Colorado Dude and Guest Ranch Association
Medical: Granby Clinic, six miles
Conference: 40
Guest Capacity: 60
Accommodations: Guests enjoy comfortable, clean log cabins that are sheltered in stands of aspen and pine overlooking Drowsy Water Creek and the ranch ponds. Cabins have covered porches. The largest sleeps nine and looks out over the children's fishing pond. The cabins accommodate from two to nine persons. The sleeping lodge has another eight rooms, all with private baths.
Rates: • $$$. Full American Plan. Minimum one-week stay in high season, Sunday to Sunday. Family, children's, and off-season rates. Pack trips and river rafting extra.
Credit Cards: None. Cash, personal checks, or traveler's checks accepted.
Season: June to mid-September
Activities: 100 fine horses provide all the riding you could possibly want. Ken and Randy Sue have raised many of their own horses. Faster loping and slow ambling trail rides go out mornings and afternoons except Saturday afternoons, and all-day mountain rides travel to beautiful vistas at 10,500 feet. Weekly breakfast ride. Riding here will get you to some spectacular high country and views of the Continental Divide. Daily riding instruction available. River rafting on the Colorado River. Hayrides, fishing (equipment for beginners provided), heated pool, and whirlpool. Golf and tennis nearby. Two championship golf courses down the road, and alpine slide in Winter Park.
Children's Programs: This is one of the top children's ranch programs in the country. Parents may participate in kids' activities. Supervised children's program for ages six to 13 (Range Riders) with games and crafts. Children's riding program builds confident riders. Children under age five (Buckaroos) have a special program that includes horseback riding, games, crafts, and picnic hikes. Weekly kids' gymkhana.
Dining: Lots of home-cooked, hearty meals; salad bar. Special diets catered to. Families usually eat together. BYOB in cabins only.
Entertainment: Something different each night. Monday, square dancing; Tuesday, hayride for kids with marshmallow-toasting and adults-only dinner; Wednesday, country swing band; Thursday, carnival night; Friday, adults-only hayride; Saturday afternoon, family games.
Summary: Drowsy Water is one of the country's top family-owned and -operated ranches for parents with young children, also great for couples and singles. Lifelong friendships have formed here. Nearby: Rocky Mountain National Park.

Elk Mountain Ranch
Buena Vista, Colorado

THE DUDE RANCHERS' ASSOCIATION

CDGRA

Elk Mountain Ranch is a cozy hideaway, 9,535 feet high in the Colorado Rockies, dedicated to excellence, wonderful hospitality, and off-the-beaten-path charm. The ranch, 10 miles into the beautiful San Isabel National Forest, is surrounded by lush aspens, evergreen forests, and distant snowcapped peaks. It has been in operation since 1981. Hosts Tom and Sue Murphy and their young kids, Hunter and Tyler, take great pride in pampering their guests, and they do! Elk Mountain is a family-oriented ranch (great for couples and singles, too) with wonderful horseback rides and friendliness. Nature-lovers and photographers especially will appreciate all the deer, antelope, elk, and wildflowers. Everyone will take home fond memories and savor the peacefulness and relaxation. One family remarked, "We can't say enough about your staff, the food, and the beauty of the entire ranch. Your ranch is heaven on earth."

Address: P.O. Box 910K, Buena Vista, Colorado 81211
Telephone: (800) 432-8812, (719) 539-4430; call for fax
E-Mail: elkmtn@sni.net
Internet: http://www.elkmtn.com
Airport: Colorado Springs or Denver
Location: 120 miles southwest of Denver, 90 miles west of Colorado Springs, 20 miles southeast of Buena Vista; ranch will send you a detailed map.
Memberships: The Dude Ranchers' Association, Colorado Dude and Guest Ranch Association, America Outdoors
Awards: *Hideaway Report*
Medical: Buena Vista Medical Clinic, Salida Hospital
Conference: 25 (early June or late September for less than one week)
Guest Capacity: 32
Accommodations: The main lodge houses the dining room with fireplace, cowboy and mining artifacts, sitting room, library, sundeck, and the upstairs Elk guest suite. There are six one- and two-bedroom log cottages with private baths and queen- and king-size beds, as well as the Pioneer Lodge with three private rooms and baths, all tastefully furnished. Hot tub and large deck. Fresh fruit to each room. Sue loves flowers and has a colorful array hanging from cabin porches. The ranch generates its own electricity. Lights are out at 11 p.m.
Rates: • $$–$$$. American Plan with one-week minimum stay, Sunday to Sunday. Children's, off-season and non-riding rates available.
Credit Cards: VISA, MasterCard, American Express. Personal and traveler's checks accepted.
Season: June through September
Activities: Horseback riding is wonderful, with miles of trails and spectacular views of the distant Collegiate Peaks. Tom gives an excellent horse-orientation program. Overnight wilderness pack trips to Cow Gulch 12 miles away. Ask Sue about the weekly brunch trail ride overlooking Brown's Canyon. White-water rafting on the Arkansas River. Auto trips to Aspen for the views (Independence Pass at 12,095 feet) and shopping. Rifle marksmanship and trap-shooting (guns provided), trout fishing in two stocked ponds (some fishing gear is available at the ranch's trading post), archery, horseshoes, and volleyball.
Children's Programs: Full children's program for ages four to seven while parents are participating in activities. Riding for children eight years and older. Ranch encourages parents to interact with kids. Children eat with grown-ups.
Dining: Great, hearty ranch food. Freshly baked breads, desserts, evening hors d'oeuvres, BYOB. Weekly barbecues and Saturday candlelight dinners.
Entertainment: Old Western and kids' movies, library, chess, backgammon, tractor hayrides, square dances, campfires, hammered dulcimer concert.
Summary: Wonderful, remote, small, family-oriented ranch. Delightful, energetic hosts with young family and excellent staff who love what they do—and it shows. Riding is the main activity. Great for families, couples, and singles who enjoy outdoors and a remote wilderness setting. Great ranch store called the Trading Post. Nearby: Buena Vista (the white-water capital of Colorado), and the largest collection of peaks over 14,000 feet in the lower 48 states.

See color photos, page 190.

The Home Ranch
Clark, Colorado

THE DUDE RANCHERS' ASSOCIATION

As you drive up the gravel road to the ranch and see the hand-hewn log buildings set among shimmering aspens, two words come to mind: "paradise" and, maybe better yet, "heaven." The Home Ranch was the longtime dream of co-owner and builder Ken Jones and his wife, Cile. Ken grew up on horses and got most of his guest-ranch experience at the old Valley Ranch. While working there he met a guest who shared his enthusiasm. Ken and his partners, Steve and Ann Stranahan, have created a ranch so special that it boasts the highly coveted Relais and Chateaux membership. There's very little this ranch doesn't have for its guests. Best of all, it serves plenty of Old West rustic elegance and hospitality. The *Los Angeles Times* captured the essence when it said, "Here, guests commune with a world as fresh as a Rocky Mountain raindrop."

Address: Box 822K, Clark, Colorado 80428
Telephone: (970) 879-1780; fax: (970) 879-1795
E-Mail: hrclark@cmn.net
Internet: http://www.homeranch.com
Airport: Steamboat Springs via Denver
Location: 18 miles north of Steamboat Springs off Highway 129
Memberships: The Dude Ranchers' Association, Relais & Chateaux
Medical: Steamboat Springs Hospital
Conference: 30
Guest Capacity: 45
Accommodations: Each beautiful log cabin is wonderfully furnished and set in a grove of aspen trees, ensuring privacy. Each has its own hot tub on a covered deck, great for total relaxation at the end of a day's ride or for warming up after cross-country skiing. There are also rooms on both levels in the handsome main lodge. A wonderful 2,500-square-foot, two-floor, hand-hewn log cabin for large families is available as well. All rooms with nightly turn-down service, flowers, and robes. Full laundry service available (extra).
Rates: • $$$$. American Plan. Children's rates available.
Credit Cards: VISA, MasterCard, American Express. Personal checks accepted.
Season: Summer: June through mid-October. winter: mid-December through March. Open Christmas.
Activities: The ranch embraces the full Natural Horsemanship program that creates a willing partnership between horse and rider. Horsemanship is the center focus of the summer program. You're assigned your own horse for the duration of your stay. It's up to you how much you want to ride inside the adjoining one-million-acre Routt National Forest. Interested guests are taught how to saddle and bridle their horses. Rides go out in small groups each day accompanied by a wrangler. The ranch raises many of its own quarter horses; ask Ken about his quarter horse breeding program. Heated swimming pool, fishing and fly-casting in stocked pond or the Elk River, and an all-inclusive fly-fishing program with instruction available for all guests. Extensive hiking program with two full-time nature guides. The hike to Gilpin Lake is a favorite. Tennis and golf can be arranged nearby. Winter: see Cross-Country Skiing chapter.
Children's Programs: Kiddie wrangler. Complete children's program for ages six and up. Kids are completely looked after, breakfast to sunset. Riding starts at age six. While the ranch is very flexible, there's a strict policy that absolutely no children under age six are allowed.
Dining: Excellent, mouth-watering gourmet meals. Children usually eat dinner before adults. BYO wine and liquor (ranch will pick up with advance notice).
Entertainment: The Home Ranch features its own Western band, which has recorded an album in Nashville. Ranch and Steamboat Springs rodeos, barrel racing. Top local entertainers.
Summary: A world-class guest ranch in a world-class setting! Focus on Natural Horsemanship. Excellent kids' program. Ranch-raised quarter horses. Full winter program. Ask about horse workshops.

See color photos, page 191.

The Historic Pines Ranch
Westcliffe, Colorado

CDGRA

Driving to the Historic Pines Ranch, you come over Hardscrabble Pass down to Wet Mountain Valley with the majestic Sangre de Cristo Mountains looming to the west. The ranch, which celebrated its 100th birthday in 1993, was built by Englishman Regy Cusack, who ran it for 50 years. In 1984 the Rusks purchased the property, and today Dean Rusk (an authentic cowboy who grew up on his parents' ranch four miles away), his wife, Casey, and their daughter, Christy, are your hosts. The clean air (altitude 8,700 feet), breathtaking views, and down-home Western hospitality bring guests back again and again. "Our guests just can't believe how magnificent these mountains are," says Casey. "We really have a paradise, with tremendous views of Pikes Peak to the northeast and New Mexico to the south." Westcliffe and the Wet Mountain Valley comprise one of Colorado's oldest yet least-known vacation areas. When visiting the Pines, you'll enjoy one of the prettiest areas in the Rockies. Guests arrive as strangers but depart as members of the Rusk family.

Address: P.O. Box 311 K, Westcliffe, Colorado 81252
Telephone: (800) 446-9462, (719) 783-9261; fax: (719) 783-2977
E-Mail: pinernch@rmi.net
Internet: http://www.ranchweb.com/historicpines
Airport: Pueblo or Colorado Springs
Location: Eight miles northwest of Westcliffe off Highway 69 North, 70 miles west of Pueblo, 95 miles southwest of Colorado Springs
Memberships: Colorado Dude and Guest Ranch Association
Medical: Clinic, eight miles; St. Thomas More Hospital, 50 miles
Conference: 40
Guest Capacity: 40
Accommodations: The renovated 1890s lodge has four second-floor rooms and three large common areas on the main floor as well as two shared bathrooms. The lodge is furnished with Victorian antiques and is ideal for singles, couples, and small groups. The other four duplex cabins were all built in the 1980s. Each is decorated with its own theme—Western, Southwestern, country, and Victorian—with private baths, and living rooms with TVs and VCRs. Laundry facilities available.
Rates: • $$–$$$. American Plan. Children's and non-riding rates available. Two-, three-, five-, and seven-day packages.
Credit Cards: VISA, MasterCard, American Express, Discover
Season: May through October for ranch activities
Activities: The Pines offers a progressive but optional hands-on riding program specializing in high-country riding, team penning, and instruction. Many ranch-raised and trained horses. Guests may saddle their own horses. Half-day and all-day rides. Seven to ten people per ride with a pack trip into the high country on Tuesday nights. Riding at the Pines is especially scenic; it's all alpine riding through streams, meadows, and lush high-country areas. Fishing in the ranch's streams, stocked ponds, and in the mountain lakes. Raft trips can be arranged. Eight-person whirlpool, two saunas, and heated indoor pool.
Children's Programs: Children ages two to eight have many scheduled activities with their own counselors. Two playhouses. Baby-sitting available. Children are watched while parents are riding or rafting.
Dining: PRHC (Pines Ranch Home Cookin'): home-baked, home-cooked, served buffet-style. BYOB.
Entertainment: Square dancing, staff shows, sing-alongs, campfires, breakfast wagon rides, cookouts, Saturday guest rodeo at the ranch, and Westcliffe Stampede Rodeo in town during July. Ask about the Victorian tea room.
Summary: Delightful high-country Rocky Mountain ranch for families, couples, and singles. One of Colorado's most undiscovered regions! Progressive hands-on riding program (optional). Ranch at 8,700 feet. Pine Cone General Store. Nearby: Royal Gorge ("Little Grand Canyon") and Buckskin Joe.

King Mountain Ranch Resort
Granby, Colorado

CDGRA

King Mountain Ranch dates back to the 1940s. In the early 1960s the ranch was developed into one of America's finest private corporate hideaways. Today, King Mountain Ranch offers families one of the greatest guest ranch experiences, with its children's program, variety of amenities, and culinary excellence, all in a private setting. While the mountains and views are special, it is the extensive knowledge and ranching background of general manager Jim Rea that set the stage for fun, adventure, and camaraderie.

Address: P.O. Box 497, Granby, Colorado 80446
Telephone: (970) 887-2511, (800) 476-5464; fax: (970) 887-9511
E-Mail: hosts@kingranchresort.com
Internet: http://www.ranchweb.com/king
Airport: Denver
Location: 16 miles northwest of Granby off Highway 40, 95 miles northwest of Denver
Memberships: Colorado Dude and Guest Ranch Association
Medical: Granby Medical Center
Conference: 79, year-round
Guest Capacity: 79
Accommodations: Spacious rooms in two large three-story lodges, all with one king or two double beds. Rooms with a comfortable Western touch. Some family suites. Most rooms open to decks offering majestic views of the lake and mountain valley. Daily maid service and ice delivery.
Rates: • $$$. American Plan. Children's and off-season rates spring and fall. Three-night minimum mid-June to early September.
Credit Cards: VISA, MasterCard, American Express, Discover. Personal checks preferred.
Season: Year-round
Activities: Biggest draw here is that there are lots of activities—something for everyone, including horseback riding! Trail and meadow riding in the Arapaho Forest, spin- and fly-fishing for trout in 30-acre private lake, trap- and skeet-shooting on a range high above the lodge with a spectacular 360-degree view, large indoor heated pool, hot tub and sauna, two lighted tennis courts, bowling on two-lane bowling alley, and guided hiking. Nearby award-winning 18-hole golf course and white-water rafting. Plenty of winter activities on-site, including sleigh and snowcat rides, cross-country skiing, and snowshoeing. Nearby: Winter Park Ski Resort and Snowmobiling in Grand Lake.
Children's Programs: Summer: They call their very good, flexible children's program the Fox's Den. Four energetic college counselors create programs for kids ages four to 12 from 9 a.m. to 9 p.m., five days each week. Adventures include horseback riding, hiking, treasure hunts, campfires, arts, crafts, and more.
Dining: Creative Western and gourmet cuisine. Dining is really an experience here! Usually three to four entrées, appetizers, and scrumptious desserts. Western cookouts with a flair. Wine list and full bar. Kids may eat together or with parents.
Entertainment: Dining and relaxation are the evening activities. Time to relax, enjoy friends, and share the day's adventures. For those who wish, Ping-Pong, swimming, tennis, bowling, billiards, video library, occasional Western dances, singers, and nature talks.
Summary: Experienced and knowledgeable host and staff. A wide assortment of activities for everyone. Secluded mountain-valley location and diverse outdoor programs. Excellent for families, groups, and corporate meetings. Nearby: Rocky Mountain National Park.

See color photos, page 192.

La Garita Creek Ranch
Del Norte, Colorado

La Garita Creek Ranch, located at 8,100 feet, is located on the eastern slope of the San Juan Mountains and the Rio Grande National Forest in the high-desert, "Indian country" of southwestern Colorado. In the late 1970s and early 1980s, the ranch was known as the Balloon Ranch. Today La Garita Creek Ranch offers family members of all ages, couples and singles as well, a wide variety of ranch activities, including hot-air ballooning, technical rock climbing, cattle drives, white-water rafting, and llama treks, just to name a few. If you have your own plane, you may land on the 2,500-foot dirt airstrip and tie down for the week.

Address: 38145 County Road E-39, Drawer K, Del Norte, Colorado 81132
Telephone: (888) 838-3833, (719) 754-2533; fax: (719) 754-2666
E-Mail. krv@lagarita.com
Internet: http://www.lagarita.com
Airport: Colorado Springs, Alamosa, Durango. Ranch has 2,500-foot graded dirt airstrip for private single- and twin-engine planes.
Location: 200 miles southwest of Denver, 175 miles southwest of Colorado Springs, 125 miles east of Durango, 49 miles west of Alamosa
Memberships: Colorado Inn Keepers Association
Medical: Del Norte Medical Center, 10 miles; Life Helicopter service available.
Conference: 42 (off-season only)
Guest Capacity: 42
Accommodations: Six guest rooms on the upper level of the Stone Mountain Lodge have private baths and Southwestern decor. Two duplex cabins with two rooms each accommodate a total of 16 guests; the Cliff Dwelling Family Cabin is suitable for a family of up to eight persons. All cabins have fireplaces, and decks out front for relaxing.
Rates: \$–\$\$\$. American Plan. Includes all activities except hot-air balloon rides, llama treks, and fly-fishing instruction on the Rio Grande. Sunday to Saturday stays mid-May through September. Minimum three-night stay. Specials include singles' weeks, the "horse camp" experience for the entire family, and "Dirty Dudes" week (three days of working with the staff preparing for "the season," and three days of fun) for a 50-percent discount off the regular price. Children under age three are free; baby-sitting available.
Credit Cards: VISA, MasterCard, Discover, personal and traveler's checks.
Season: Summer: Early May through September. Winter: December to April, weather permitting.
Activities: Scheduled and diverse weekly activities program. Very hands-on riding program. Guests may care for their designated horse for the week if they wish. Activities include side-by-side and trail riding, fishing, skeet- and target-shooting, archery, hiking, mountain biking, swimming, jeep rides, and hayrides. A choice of white-water rafting, technical rock climbing, golfing, riding the Toltec-Cumbres Narrow Gauge Railroad or visiting the Great Sand Dunes and Alligator Farm. Hot air balloon rides and llama treks cost extra. Cattle drives are offered in the spring and fall with neighboring ranch. Winter activities include snow-mobiling, snowshoeing, alpine and cross-country skiing, and snowcat tours in the San Juan Mountains. Holiday activities and special weekly and weekend packages available.
Children's Programs: Excellent optional supervised children's program with counselors for ages three to five, six to 11, and teens. Nature hikes, picnics, fishing, exploring, swimming, treasure hunts, organized games, horseback riding, and crafts are just a few of the activities provided. One night a week children ages three and up head out for a supper campout, while the adults have a quiet candlelight dinner, Western dance, and creekside champagne breakfast the next morning.
Dining: Hearty ranch meals served buffet- or family-style. Cookouts, breakfast, and dinner rides. The Saddle Sore Saloon is open in the afternoon and evening.
Entertainment: Sing-alongs, Western movies (with popcorn), Western dance instruction, guest/wrangler talent show, hayrides, local history talks, team roping and penning, showdeo, awards night, and boot branding.
Summary: La Garita Creek Ranch offers a diverse activities program available both on and off the ranch. A small, friendly ranch that is ideal for families, couples, and singles. Great for family reunions. Friendly staff and children's counselors.

Lake Mancos Ranch
Mancos, Colorado

THE DUDE RANCHERS' ASSOCIATION

CDGRA

Lake Mancos Ranch, located at 8,000 feet looking out on the La Plata Mountain Range, has been owned and operated by the Sehnert family since the early 1950s. A favorite analogy used by founder Lloyd Sehnert when initiating new staff was, "Every guest should be treated like a precious piece of gold." This philosophy is still present as Kathy, Todd, and Robin open their ranch and year-round home to their guests. Through personal service, Lake Mancos Ranch has established a tradition of providing wonderful, heartwarming vacations to first-time guests and generations of returning families. You'll find all the necessary elements that make a guest-ranch vacation unique: horses, spectacular scenery, outdoor activity, comfortable cabins, hearty meals, and fun activities for children. Judging from comments made by longtime guests, it's the Sehnerts' Western hospitality and family "quality time" that keep them coming back to Lake Mancos Ranch, their "home in the mountains."

Address: 42688 CR-N, Dept. K, Mancos, Colorado 81328
Telephone: (800) 325-9462, (970) 533-7900; fax: (970) 533-7858
E-Mail: ranchlml@fone.net
Internet: http://www.lakemancosranch.com
Airport: Durango via Denver, Phoenix, or Albuquerque
Location: Five miles north of Mancos, 35 miles west of Durango
Memberships: The Dude Ranchers' Association, Colorado Dude and Guest Ranch Association
Medical: Cortez Hospital, 25 miles
Conference: 40
Guest Capacity: 55
Accommodations: There are 17 bright-red guest units with names like Spruce Mill, Golconda, and Bear Creek; cabins of various sizes; and four spacious units with private baths in the ranch house for couples and singles. All heated family cabins have comfortable living rooms and bedrooms, one or two bathrooms, private covered porches, king-size beds, refrigerators, and carpeting. Guest laundry available. Daily maid service.
Rates: • $$$. American Plan, Sunday to Sunday. Non-riding, children's, and off-season rates available. Three-day packages available.
Credit Cards: VISA, MasterCard, Discover. Personal checks accepted.
Season: Early June to October. September is adults-only.
Activities: Riding is the main activity at the ranch, with over 100 miles of scenic trails offering guests the opportunity to see some of Colorado's prettiest country. You'll explore shimmering aspen forests and lush mountain meadows. Children and adults usually ride separately. Family rides several times a week. Guests are assigned their own horses for their stay and riding instruction is available. Hiking, mountain biking, pond and stream fishing (rods and introductory fly-fishing instruction provided). Heated pool and hot tub. Four-wheel-drive and wildflower trips. Many like to visit Mesa Verde National Park, raft in Durango, golf in Cortez, or ride the spectacular Durango–Silverton narrow-gauge train, which was started in 1882.
Children's Programs: Supervised children's and teens' program for ages four and up during all daily adult activities. Hiking, gold-panning, arena activities, fishing pond, overnight camp-out, trail rides, lots to do. Children easily make friends here and initiate spontaneous actvities!
Dining: Home-style cooking. Two entrées each night. Weekly steak-fry. Creekside cookouts at Rendezvous Canyon. Bottomless cookie jar! Coffee, and lemonade always plentiful. BYOB. Children may eat at children's table or with their parents.
Entertainment: Cowboy poetry, hayrides, cookouts, skits, awards night, and fireside stories.
Summary: Lake Mancos is for down-to-earth families who enjoy vacationing together but appreciate some separate activities. The Sehnert family is one of the oldest guest-ranching families in Colorado. Riding is the main activity. Many singles and couples enjoy the camaraderie of the family summer season. Adults-only in September. Nearby: Old Durango and Silverton Railroad, Mesa Verde National Park.

See color photos, page 193.

Lane Guest Ranch
Estes Park, Colorado

Lane Guest Ranch celebrated its 46th year of continuous operation in 1998. Host and owner Lloyd Lane has developed one of the most successful summer resort ranch experiences in North America. His secret is best described by guests, who write, "The staff was wonderful, the food excellent, and there were plenty of activities! Staff, food, scenery were all top-notch—we've never been to a more loving resort." Lloyd's success has come about because he offers a wide choice of activities (besides horseback riding), such as hiking, swimming, fishing, white-water rafting, overnight pack trips—along with all-day child care for infants and up, comfortable accommodations, and an excellent chef, all in all one of the prettiest areas of Colorado—right next to Rocky Mountain National Park. Welcome to Lloyd Lane's famous "Colorado Vacation."

Address: P.O. Box 1766, Dept. K, Estes Park, Colorado 80517
Telephone: (415) 868 0300; call for fax
Internet: http://www.ranchweb.com/laneranch
Airport: Denver; shuttle available (extra)
Location: 67 miles northwest of Denver, 12 miles south of Estes Park off Highway 7
Memberships: American Hotel and Motel Association, Estes Park Chamber of Commerce
Medical: Estes Park Hospital, 11 miles
Guest Capacity: 85
Accommodations: Log-sided units accommodate from two to six. Twenty-six units are comfortably furnished with queen-size beds, private baths, patios, hammocks, TV/VCR, complimentary stocked refrigerators, and radios. Eighteen units have their own hot tubs. Early morning wake-up coffee served to your room when you wish. Ask about the Doctor's House for family reunions. One-day laundry service offered.
Rates: • $$$–$$$$. American Plan. Children's, seniors', weekly, and honeymoon/anniversary packages available.
Credit Cards: VISA, MasterCard
Season: June to early September
Activities: Daily ranch activity sign-up sheet with lots of programs. Horseback riding (except Sunday) in Rocky Mountain National Park and Roosevelt National Forest. Wine-and-cheese rides for adults; two overnight pack trips. Guided hikes, scenic photography class, and morning fishing trips are very popular. Landscape drawing and silversmith classes. Heated outdoor pool, sauna, and hot tub. White-water rafting about two hours away. Eighteen-hole golf at country club in Estes Park. Massage available (masseuse on staff).
Children's Programs: Extensive program with counselors; full child-care available for infants and older children during the day. Kiddie wrangler. Baby-sitting available in the evening (extra). Playground and children's activities.
Dining: Menu includes charcoal broiled steaks, seafood, broiled and poached chicken breasts and salmon, fresh trout, prime rib, pastas, excellent clam chowder, full salad bar, wonderful desserts, and homemade soups and rolls. California wines and mixed drinks (licensed bar), cappuccino and espresso, poolside café; special diets gladly accommodated. Complimentary house wine and beer.
Entertainment: Four nights of live entertainment. Shuffleboard, volleyball, horseshoes, well-stocked library, chess, table tennis, TV, over 600 video movies, and karaoke; Estes Park rodeos (July).
Summary: Lloyd Lane celebrated his 46th year of operation in 1998 and is proud of his over-90-percent occupancy rate. The ranch is in one of the prettiest areas in Colorado, with high mountain peaks and natural splendor. Come here to enjoy a wide variety of activities, food, and entertainment. If all you want to do is horseback ride, this is not the ranch for you. High staff-to-guest ratio (45 staff to 85 guests). Strong children's program for infants on up. Lots of families and couples. European-type concierge. Pets welcome. Advertised in the *Wall Street Journal* since the 1950s. Nearby: Estes Park for shopping.

See color photos, pages 194–197.

Laramie River Ranch
Glendevey, Colorado

THE DUDE RANCHERS' ASSOCIATION

CDGRA

The spirit of Bill and Krista Burleigh's Laramie River Ranch is captured by this recent guest quote: "Our family loves riding and fishing and we got to do plenty of both. With a mile and a half of river running through the property, there is plenty of opportunity for great fishing. Laramie River Ranch is blessed with exceptional scenery offering incredible horseback rides. The area is stunningly beautiful." The ranch is located in the Laramie River Valley of northern Colorado, not far from the Wyoming border. In 1995 Bill and Krista bought this historic ranch, which was homesteaded in the late 1800s and had entertained guests for over 50 years. Today they grow hay, graze cattle, and share their way of life in this remote valley. Here you will experience genuine Western hospitality, side-by-side horseback riding, private fishing, and a host of naturalist-led activities.

Address: The postal address is 25777 N. County Road 103, Drawer K, Jelm, Wyoming 82063
Telephone: (800) 551-5731, (970) 435-5716; fax: (970) 435-5731
E-Mail: vacationK@lrranch.com
Internet: http://www.lrranch.com/indexk.html
Airport: Laramie and Denver; free pickup from Laramie, Wyoming.
Location: 42 miles southwest of Laramie, Wyoming; 150 miles northwest of Denver, Colorado
Memberships: Colorado Dude and Guest Ranch Association, The Dude Ranchers' Association
Medical: Laramie Ivinson Memorial Hospital
Conference: 25
Guest Capacity: 25
Accommodations: The recently renovated lodge was built in the 1880s. A large stone fireplace in the great room, two open porches with rocking chairs, and a large enclosed porch overlooking the Laramie River provide guests with lots of room to relax. Seven guest rooms in the lodge have private baths. Five cozy log cabins sit along LaGarde Creek and the Laramie River. One guest wrote, "We loved being on the river listening to the sound of rushing water, windows wide open!" Homemade cookies and fresh flowers are just a few of the nice, friendly touches here. Daily maid service. Down pillows available. Smoke-free policy.
Rates: • $\$$–$\$\$$. All-inclusive American Plan. Children's, group, and off-season rates—Sunday to Sunday. Some three- and four-day stays available.
Credit Cards: Call for details. Personal and traveler's checks accepted.
Season: Early June through November
Activities: Morning, afternoon, cookout, and all-day rides are available for riders of all abilities, usually in small groups. There is an abundance of open terrain suitable for loping. Guests are welcome to help groom and saddle their own horses. Riding instruction available. Overnight pack trips. Fishing for wild brown and rainbow trout. Fly-fishing instruction provided, with guides and gear available. Other activities include tubing down the river, birding, hunting for wildflowers, roping a steer dummy, exploring beaver dams, animal-tracking, orienteering, volleyball, and horseshoes.
Children's Programs: Half-day program. Naturalist activities as well as learning about horses, wildlife, and more. Many activities are family-oriented so parents and children can explore the ranch together. Some baby-sitting is available.
Dining: Meals are served family-style. Scrumptious and varied entrées, warm homemade breads, and Nancy's famous desserts. Ask about the all-day Dagney ranch cookout ride! BYOB.
Entertainment: Cowboy poetry, Western music, and country dancing. Evening stargazing with a fascinating talk on the mythology of the constellations. Cowboy ranch show (kids' favorite), steer-roping demonstrations, local rodeos in July.
Summary: One family summed it up best—"The amount of activities was perfect for us, not too much, not too little, and we really appreciated the optional aspect. We had time for hiking, riding, reading, visiting, and napping." Bill and Krista Burleigh have created one of the excellent guest-ranch experiences in the Rockies.

See color photos, page 198.

Latigo Ranch
Kremmling, Colorado

THE DUDE RANCHERS' ASSOCIATION

CDGRA

At 9,000 feet, looking out to the spectacular Continental Divide, the air is crisp and the hospitality sincere. Nature lovers will enjoy the breathtaking scenery and the abundance of wildflowers and wildlife on thousands of acres. Latigo Ranch runs a four-season program, from hayrides in summer to cross-country skiing in winter. Here you can ride, hike, swim, fish, and interact with Salvadore or Pepe, the ranch llamas. Whether you and your family are at the ranch for Fourth of July or Christmas, you can be sure of one thing—many special memories. If you want to have some interesting conversations, just ask your hosts about their educational backgrounds. It's not uncommon for guests to engage in provocative discussions. Mostly, though, everyone takes in nature's beauty and serenity. As one guest wrote, "Between the depth of instruction in nature and riding, combined with the spirit of kindness that permeates the ranch, our experience was grand!"

Address: P.O. Box 237, Kremmling, Colorado 80459
Telephone: (800) 227-9655, (970) 724-9008; fax (970) 724-9009
E-Mail: latigo@compuserve.com
Internet: http://www.dude-ranch.com/latigo_ranch.html
Airport: Denver
Location: 130 miles northwest of Denver, 55 miles southeast of Steamboat Springs, 16 miles northwest of Kremmling
Memberships: Colorado Dude and Guest Ranch Association, The Dude Ranchers' Association
Medical: Kremmling Memorial Hospital
Conference: 38
Guest Capacity: 38
Accommodations: Guests stay in contemporary log duplexes nestled in the pine forest and one four-plex. Each is carpeted, with sitting room and fireplace or woodburning stove. All have refrigerators and homemade caramel corn.
Rates: • $$$–$$$$. American Plan, all-inclusive, no extras. Children's rates available. Rates vary depending on the season. Three- to six-night minimum stay. Overnight pack trip and river rafting included in price.
Credit Cards: VISA, MasterCard, American Express
Season: Late May to October (summer); mid-December to April (winter)
Activities: The main emphasis is on the horseback riding and the quality of the instruction for all levels on the trails, as well as in the arena. The ranch prides itself on a high wrangler-to-guest ratio so that ride groups are small and can be better tailored to fit guests' levels and interests. Rides include morning, afternoon, all-day, breakfast, sunset, and overnight pack trips to High Rock Creek. Riding at 9,000 feet with 360-degree views and serenity offers a genuine Rocky Mountain high. Heated swimming pool, fishing in streams and ranch pond. Jim Yost offers fly-fishing instruction, and day fishing trips. Hot tub available for sore muscles. Lots of hiking and rafting included nearby. Be sure to ask about weekly team cattle-penning! Winter: see Cross-Country Skiing section.
Children's Programs: Optional fully supervised program for children ages 3 to 13, while adults are riding. Families may ride exclusively together. Arts and crafts center. Kids under age 6 do not ride on the trail. Baby-sitting available.
Dining: Excellent food both summer and winter. Ranch fare with variety and gourmet touches. Weekly breakfast, lunch, and dinner cookouts. BYOB.
Entertainment: The three-story Social Club is a log-sided entertainment building where guests enjoy happy hour (BYOB), square/line dancing, piano, pool table, library, and hot tub.
Summary: Latigo Ranch is really known for three things: its hospitality (high staff-to-guest ratio), scenery, and horse program. The ranch is owned and operated by two families with interesting backgrounds. Open, expansive, high-mountain setting with excellent panoramic views. One guest commented, "You can't say enough about your views." Jim's geology and wildlife lectures. Be sure to see Jim Yost's movie on Ecuador, *Nomads of the Rain Forest*, a beautiful show seen on *Nova*. Fall cattle roundup in late September. (Also see write-up in Cross-Country Skiing section.)

See color photos, page 199.

Lazy H Guest Ranch
Allenspark, Colorado

THE DUDE RANCHERS' ASSOCIATION

CDGRA

Located on a mountain ridge near the base of Mt. Meeker, Longs Peak, and Rocky Mountain National Park, the Lazy H Guest Ranch focuses its activities on horseback riding and children's programs. Karen and Phil Olbert, along with their two daughters, Tami and Jenny, have created an atmosphere for families and children to enjoy themselves without a highly regimented schedule. One family wrote, "We came to Colorado expecting to ride and relax for a week. We never expected the warmth and friendliness we experienced here at Lazy H. The staff was wonderful and made us feel as if it were a pleasure to serve us, and not a job. Even though we took many pictures, we know they won't capture the beauty of the state, nor the spirit of Lazy H!"

Address: P.O. Box 248K, 15747 Highway 7, Allenspark, Colorado 80510
Telephone: (800) 578-3598, (303) 747-2532; call for fax number
E-Mail: lazyhranch@compuserve.com
Airport: Denver, 65 miles
Location: 65 miles northwest of Denver, 16 miles south of Estes Park on Highway 7
Memberships: The Dude Ranchers' Association, Colorado Dude and Guest Ranch Association
Medical: Estes Park Medical Center, 16 miles
Conference: 50
Guest Capacity: 50
Accommodations: The Navajo red and white-trimmed, 13,000-square-foot, log-sided and stone lodge was built in the 1930s. It's three stories look out across the valley. Each of the 11 guest rooms has its own individual charm. Rock Basin is the lovely honeymoon suite. There are three cabins; two are duplexes (Sundance and Cheyenne). All cabins and rooms have private baths and twin, double, king-size, queen-size, and bunk beds.
Rates: • $$$. American Plan. Children's and off-season rates. Three-day minimum stay. Rafting extra.
Credit Cards: VISA, MasterCard, Discover
Season: Year-round, including all holidays. Riding May to October.

Activities: The Olberts have put together a wonderful program of riding, children's activities, and evening entertainment. The length of the rides increases over the course of the week. Guests are assigned the same horse for their entire stay, usually eight guests per wrangler. Most is scenic trail riding; some loping for advanced riders. Ask about the Meadow Mountain all-day, Rock Creek breakfast, and Olive Ridge lunch rides. Below the ranch in a little valley is Rock Creek, where guests fish for browns and rainbows—all catch-and-release. Lots of hiking in Roosevelt National Forest. Heated swimming pool in front of the lodge. Rafting on the Poudre or Colorado River with local outfitters.
Children's Programs: Experienced counselors help create memories your kids will have for a lifetime. Terrific morning and afternoon programs for kids ages four and up. Crafts, picnics, nature hikes, swimming, and the star-studded petting corral. Overnight camp-out in tepee a favorite with kids ages eight and older. Beaver animal study.
Dining: Dining room looks out on Iron Clads and Meadow Mountain. Ranch-style, all-you-can-eat buffet and cookouts. Fully licensed bar. Wine available with dinner.
Entertainment: Marvelous Native American magic show, singing cowboy, mountain man, campfire sing-alongs, country line dancing. Rec room with Ping-Pong, pool table, and video games.
Summary: An integrated family vacation. Family-oriented, low-key ranch with plenty of riding, children's program, and nightly Western entertainment. Wonderful Native American show and mountain man talks. Ask about the mountain weddings and conference facilities. Nearby: Rocky Mountain National Park; Estes Park shopping; Boulder, Colorado.

See color photos, page 200.

Lost Valley Ranch
Deckers, Colorado

THE DUDE RANCHERS' ASSOCIATION

CDGRA

In the world of guest-ranching, Lost Valley Ranch is right at the top. The qualities that make the Foster family's ranch so unique are their superb staff, excellent accommodations, and fabulous children's/teen program. Everyone at the ranch exudes a caring and enthusiastic spirit, and guests quickly become friends. Lost Valley has been in the ranching business for more than 100 years and under the ownership of generations of Fosters for the past 39 years. This year-round cattle-and-horse ranch is a private island in the middle of 40,000 acres of the Pike National Forest. At Lost Valley, adventure is combined with fun. If the number of returning guests is any indication, the Fosters are doing everything right. Walt Disney stayed here years ago and told the Fosters, "If I had this place, I would do all that I could not to change its character." The Fosters took his advice. This is one of the best family ranches in the business.

Address: 29555 Goose Creek Road, Box K, Sedalia, Colorado 80135-9000
Telephone: (303) 647-2311; fax: (303) 647-2315
E-Mail: lostranch@aol.com
Internet: http://www.ranchweb.com/lost
Airport: Denver or Colorado Springs
Train: Amtrak to Denver
Location: Two hours southwest of Denver, 1½ hours northwest of Colorado Springs, 12 miles southwest of Deckers
Memberships: The Dude Ranchers' Association, Colorado Dude and Guest Ranch Association
Awards: AAA 4 Diamond; Mobil 3 Star
Medical: Langstaff-Brown Medical Clinic, one hour
Conference: 60, fall and spring only; largest room 1,600 square feet
Guest Capacity: 95
Accommodations: The 24 cabin suites (one, two, and three bedrooms) are some of the finest in the business. All have living rooms, fireplaces, refrigerators, covered porches with swings, full private tub/shower baths, and amenities such as daily maid service, oversized towels, coffeemakers, and delightful cowboy-hat amenities baskets. To ensure peace and quiet, the cabins are nicely spaced among the pines. No TVs or telephones. Laundry facilities are available.
Rates: • $$–$$$. American Plan, all inclusive packages. Children's and spring/fall rates available. During summer there is a seven-day minimum stay policy, Sunday arrival. Trap-shooting and Orvis fishing guides (extra).
Credit Cards: None. Personal checks accepted.
Season: March through November
Activities: All levels of Western riding. With 150 horses and 200 head of cattle, guests are encouraged to participate in ranch and cattle work. Quality fishing in Goose Creek, which runs through the ranch, or drive 20 minutes and wet your fly in the world-famous Cheasman Canyon on the South Platte River. Orvis fishing guides are available (extra). Heated outdoor swimming pool, two whirlpool spas, two plexi-paved tennis courts, trap-shooting (extra), and guided hiking. Ranch store. Seasonal cattle and horsemanship weeks.
Children's Programs: This is one of Lost Valley's strongest attractions. Children are supervised by a superb collegiate staff. This program provides tremendous fun for children, yet gives parents peace of mind knowing their children are safe and happy. The teens operate within a framework of freedom, friendship, and fun provided by the collegiate staff.
Dining: Mother Marion's recipes are famous. Down-home ranch cooking served buffet- and plate-style by friendly waitresses. Special diets accommodated. Nonsmoking dining room. BYOB cabins only.
Entertainment: Entertainment is second to none. Lost Valley's staff is talented. Enjoy musical entertainment, melodramas, square dancing, hayrides, campfires, and sing-alongs.
Summary: One of the top family guest ranches in North America. Excellent staff and superb children's and teens' programs. Year-round riding, cattle roundups, special horsemanship weeks. Great for family reunions and off-season conference groups. A true destination vacation.

LOST VALLEY RANCH
AAA

McNamara Ranch
Florissant, Colorado

McNamara Ranch takes only four guests, offers unlimited riding opportunities, and attracts mostly women who enjoy and can handle being in the saddle six hours a day. As owner Sheila says, "I feel a kinship with women and have developed my program for women (and some couples) of all ages to come, relax, and ride this magnificent country with me." And when it comes to riding, the sky's the limit. Sheila is quite a horsewoman—she spent 25 years in Maryland showing hunters and jumpers and fox-hunting. In fact, she still prefers an English saddle. As she says, "I've been riding for over 35 years!" If lots of undivided attention, a riding program tailored to your riding abilities, and delicious barbecued lamb chops (lamb is her specialty) sound like what you're looking for, read no further! Give Sheila a call.

Address: 4620 County Road 100, Florissant, Colorado 80816
Telephone: (719) 748-3466
Airport: Colorado Springs, 55 miles
Location: 55 miles west of Colorado Springs, 13 miles south of Florissant
Medical: St. Francis Hospital, Colorado Springs
Guest Capacity: Four
Accommodations: Two bedrooms in the main house, one with a double bed and loft, the other with a double bed. Both share one bath. Laundry room available for guests.
Rates: $$. American Plan. Side trips extra. No minimum stay (most guests stay about four days).
Credit Cards: None. Personal checks accepted; prefer traveler's checks or cash.
Season: June through October
Activities: Sheila gets up about 5:30 a.m. and hits the sack about 9 p.m. You're welcome to help tend the seven head of horses and the small flock of sheep. After morning chores are done, Sheila begins to think about riding. There are no set riding schedules; if you wish to ride to 12,000 feet and put seven hours in the saddle, you may. If you wish to ride bareback around the ranch, just ask Sheila. No nose-to-tail riding here. Just about the only thing you can't do here on horseback is ride on your own. With Sheila's knowledge of horses and the country, and her friendly, caring spirit, guests appreciate her riding, camaraderie, and commentary. Fly-fishing in stocked pond. Hiking and river rafting on the Arkansas River two hours away.
Children's Program: None. Best for older kids who really like to ride and love horses.
Dining: Sheila admits that riding is really her forte. She's a meat-and-potatoes chef. Enjoy hearty ranch cooking. Lamb is her specialty: steaks, chops, and leg of lamb. Sheila will ask what your preferences are, including beverages and wine. BYOL.
Entertainment: By day's end and after a big dinner, everyone is usually pretty tuckered out. Most enjoy the hot tub under the stars, looking out to Pikes Peak. Early to bed and early to rise is a good rule of thumb.
Summary: This is a small, intimate ranch for those who love horses and want personalized unlimited riding in the Colorado high country. Excellent for women who enjoy being in the saddle six hours a day. A very hands-on program of horsemanship, horse care, and all levels of riding. Sheila wants you to feel like you're visiting a friend in Colorado. Horses may sometimes be trailered out to take in other great rides. Sheila tailors a program for each guest. Ask about her lakeside tepee for overnight camping. Occasional cattle work on neighboring cattle ranch. Year-round riding, weather permitting.

Old Glendevey Ranch
Glendevey, Colorado

THE DUDE RANCHERS' ASSOCIATION

CDGRA

Garth and Olivia Peterson have traveled all over the world. Garth is a senior captain for a major airline and flies only international routes. At 35,000 feet, one has a chance to reflect and think about the important things in life. For Garth, that's the great outdoors and the Colorado backcountry. He was raised in the country and has always appreciated wildlife and the unspoiled wilderness. To fulfill his passion and his love for the outdoors, he began his wilderness pack-trip business in 1975. In 1985 Garth, Olivia, and son Matt bought Old Glendevey Ranch so they could share their love for the great outdoors with families and single people from around the world. Old Glendevey Ranch is special in that it combines ranch stays with wilderness pack trips. For those who want to get away from it all and experience nature at its best, the wilderness pack trip is a must. Old Glendevey is for those who would like a true wilderness experience and a ranch stay as well.

Address: Old Glendevey Ranch, Ltd., Glendevey Colorado Route, 3219 County Road 190, Drawer K, Jelm, Wyoming 82063
Telephone: (800) 807-1444, (970) 435-5701 (summer); (970) 490-1444 (winter); call for fax
E-Mail: glendevey@aol.com
Internet: http://www.duderanch.org/glendevey
Airport: Laramie, 55 miles; pickup available
Location: Approximately 100 miles northwest of Fort Collins, Colorado; 55 miles southwest of Laramie, Wyoming, off 3219 County Road 190
Memberships: The Dude Ranchers' Association, Colorado Dude and Guest Ranch Association, Colorado Outfitters Association, Rocky Mountain Elk Foundation
Medical: Ivinson Memorial Hospital, Laramie, 55 miles
Conference: 18 overnight
Guest Capacity: 18
Accommodations: The cozy, two-story lodge offers a dining room; lounging area with stone fireplace, library, and game room; and seven bedrooms upstairs, all carpeted, remodeled, and comfortable. Large, separate men's and women's bathroom facilities. Also guest porches for taking in the scenery and hot tub.
Rates: $$–$$$. American Plan. Children's, group, and non-rider rates. Minimum three-night stay.
Credit Cards: VISA, MasterCard. Personal checks and cash accepted.
Season: June through mid-September, October to mid-November (hunting), and December to April
Activities: Horseback riding, fishing, hiking, and relaxing are the main activities. The Petersons offer a flexible program. Many guests stay a few days at the ranch, then go off on a pack trip; some come specifically for pack trips while others prefer to stay at the ranch all week. Half-day morning and afternoon rides go to North Middle Mountain and around the ranch. All-day wilderness rides (eight hours) with lunch go out daily except Sunday. Fishing is challenging. Three miles of private McIntyre Creek run through the ranch. Also, guided fishing on the Laramie River offers some of the best wild brown trout in northern Colorado. Hikers can enjoy all kinds of hiking trails and old logging roads. Ask about winter activities.
Children's Programs: None. Children are welcome but must be supervised by parents. Usually kids under age 10 do not ride alone.
Dining: Family-style meals served in the dining room; traditional outdoor Western-style barbecues. Homemade soups, breads, and desserts. BYOB.
Entertainment: Very informal. Hayrides, wildlife viewing, and just plain relaxing by the fire with a good book from the library. Game room, horseshoes, volleyball, and occasional cowboy poetry and entertainment.
Summary: The Petersons' ranch offers a unique combination of wilderness pack trips and guest-ranch stays. Ask about their gourmet pack trips. In a relaxed Western style, the Petersons share with their guests the natural beauty of the Rawah Wilderness. Complete outfitting services offered in fall.

North Fork Ranch
Shawnee, Colorado

THE DUDE RANCHERS' ASSOCIATION

CDGRA

North Fork Ranch is located on the north fork of the South Platte River. This ranch is for families who like to spend their vacation together. Deana and Karen May and their children, Hayley and Tyler, are the hosts and owners of this delightful riverside ranch. Dean and Karen moved out West in the early 1980s. Today, North Fork offers families of all sizes a chance to ride, fish, hike, river-raft, swim, play, and have wholesome fun together. President Dwight Eisenhower made this part of the country famous when he came to fish and relax in this valley. North Fork is a 520-acre, turn-of-the-century property. The original homestead cabin dates back to the 1890s. One of North Fork's unique features is the beautiful estate built out of native rock, which looks out over the river and the ranch. Dean has a background in forestry and Karen in nursing; together they share with their guests an understanding of the land and a compassion for all those who travel through their ranch gates. What makes North Fork unique is that the Mays encourage children and their parents to spend quality time together. North Fork Ranch is wonderful for young and older families who love the outdoors and being together.

Address: P.O. Box B-K, Shawnee, Colorado 80475
Telephone: (800) 843-7895, (303) 838-9873; fax: (303) 838-1549
E-Mail: northforkranch@worldnet.att.net
Internet: http://www.northforkranch.com
Airport: Denver or Colorado Springs
Location: 50 miles southwest of Denver, six miles west of Bailey, 120 miles northwest of Colorado Springs
Memberships: The Dude Ranchers' Association, Colorado Dude and Guest Ranch Association
Medical: Conifer Mountain Medical Center, 20 miles. Karen May is a registered nurse.
Conference: 20, spring and fall
Guest Capacity: 43
Accommodations: The main lodge offers six rooms, each with private bath. The Homestead cabin offers accommodations for three families of four people; each unit has two bedrooms and a private bath. The Klondike cabin is a spacious duplex log cabin for families of four or six. Stonehenge, the three-story estate, offers several sleeping arrangements for families, couples, and singles. All accommodations are decorated in a unique style with antiques and Western art. Daily housekeeping service.
Rates: • $$–$$$. American Plan. Children's, off-season, and group rates available. Minimum one-week stay, Saturday to Saturday. Shorter stays in off-season.
Credit Cards: None. Personal checks accepted.
Season: May through September
Activities: Weekly program. Families enjoy riding together. Experienced wranglers guide groups of six to eight on half-day and all-day rides, champagne brunch rides, and overnight pack trips. White-water rafting on the Arkansas River with certified outfitters. Target- and trap-shooting (guns provided); fishing in the stocked pond or on the North Fork of the South Platte River. Sunday fly-fishing instruction. Private guided trips and fishing equipment available. Swimming in heated pool next to the river, or relaxing in the spa at Stonehenge.
Children's Programs: Counselors and baby-sitters are available from 9 a.m. to 4 p.m. for kids under age six so parents are able to participate in ranch activities. Fun-filled days are planned with pony rides, hiking, fishing, swimming, lunches in the tepee, and even a special kid's camp-out.
Dining: Everyone (guests and staff) dines together. Enjoy fresh breads, full turkey dinners. Buffalo barbecues and steak cookout. Ask about Dean's special Rocky Mountain oysters. Friday farewell dinner features fresh trout or quail. Special diets catered to with advance notice. BYOB.
Entertainment: Square dancing with live caller. Campfire sing-alongs, evening fishing, hayrides, and volleyball.
Summary: Great small family ranch for families who like to vacation with their children. Located in a beautiful valley along the river. Wonderful riverside setting, only 50 miles from Denver. North Fork was included on a *Good Morning America* segment and in *Good Housekeeping* magazine.

See color photos, page 201.

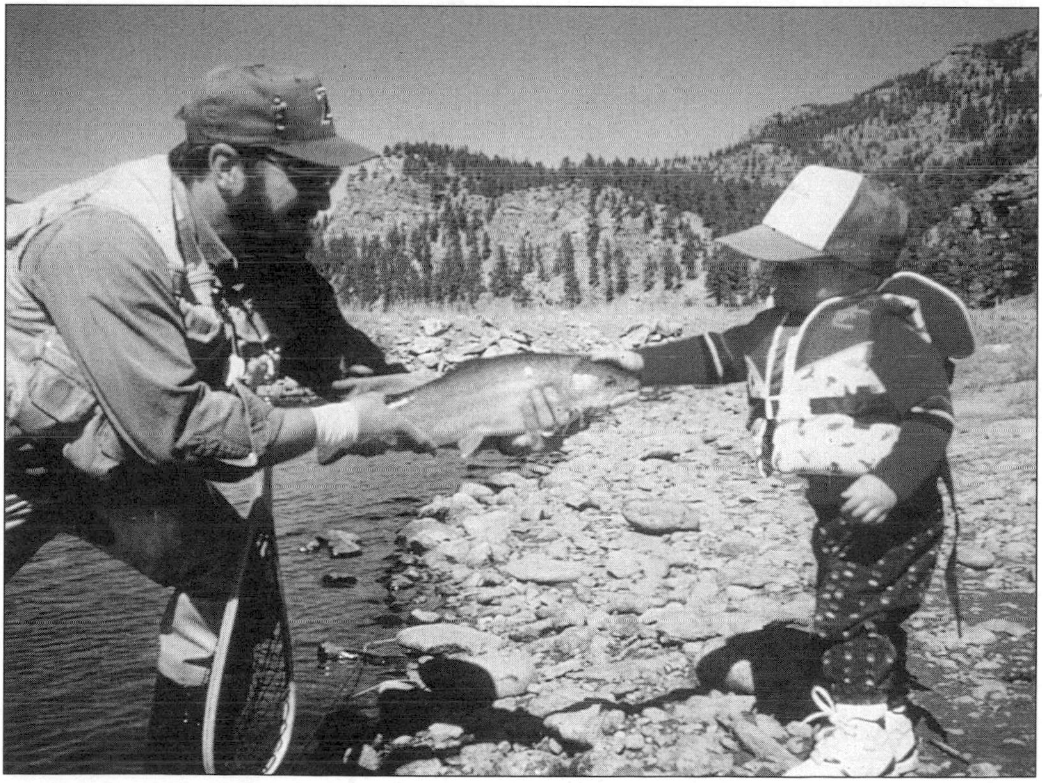

Peaceful Valley Ranch
Lyons, Colorado

CDGRA

Peaceful Valley Ranch is a ranch resort providing hospitality and personal attention in a Rocky Mountain setting. Near Rocky Mountain National Park and in the St. Vrain Canyon, Peaceful Valley offers wholesome family activities and fun for all. During summer, enjoy riding on scenic mountain trails. Hiking, llama treks, breakfast on the mountain, riverside picnics, and backcountry tours of ghost towns and gold mines display Colorado's beauty. During summer months the focus is on families, with lots to do and see for all. The spirit of the ranch is one of camaraderie, friendship, and diverse activities. Winter comes alive with weekend getaways, beautiful weddings, and group and corporate meetings.

Address: 475 Peaceful Valley Road, Drawer K, Lyons, Colorado 80540-8951
Telephone: (800) 955-6343, (303) 747-2881; fax: (303) 747-2167
E-Mail: howdy@peacefulvalley.com
Internet: http://www.peacefulvalley.com
Airport: Denver
Location: 65 miles northwest of Denver
Memberships: (Associate Member), Dude Ranchers' Association, Colorado Dude and Guest Ranch Association
Awards: AAA 3 Diamond; Mobil 3 Star
Medical: Longmont Community Hospital, 28 miles
Conference: Groups of eight to 100. Brochure available.
Guest Capacity: 100
Accommodations: 11 cabins and 42 lodge rooms. Moderate units are cozy and comfortable, most with queen beds and sitting areas, some are adjoining. Superior rooms and suites are roomy with full tub/shower bathrooms and sitting areas with views. The best rooms are appointed with whirlpool baths, private balconies, desks, and refrigerators. The best cabins have living rooms with stone fireplaces, private hot tubs, and refrigerators. Daily maid service and coin-operated laundry. Some rooms have telephones.
Rates: • $$–$$$. American Plan. Conference rates available. Children under age three are free (baby-sitting extra). Three-, four-, and seven-day packages available. Three-day minimum in summer. Off-season nightly rates available.
Credit Cards: VISA, MasterCard, American Express, Diners Club, Discover
Season: Open year-round. Riding mid-May through mid-October, Dude Ranch June through August.
Activities: Extensive riding with indoor arena. Beginning lessons to all-day trail rides. A good cross-section of riding. Usually eight guests per wrangler. Ask about all-day trip to Continental Divide and the Jamestown ride. Adults-only rides available. Hiking, indoor swimming pool, Jacuzzi, sauna, tennis, mountain biking, llama treks, and fly-fishing on St. Vrain River, which runs through the ranch. Golf and white-water rafting nearby. Winter: cross-country skiing, snowshoeing, and heated pool.
Children's Program: Extensive program for kids ages three through teens. Nursery and supervised children's program in summer. Strong teen program. Children's petting farm. Separate kids' dining area (optional).
Dining: Hearty ranch cuisine served family-style, special diets not a problem with advance notice. Beer, wine, and liquor available.
Entertainment: Line and square dancing, gymkhana (guest rodeo), hayrides, campfire sing-alongs, cowboy entertainment, talent show, happy hour each evening before dinner.
Summary: Wonderful ranch resort emphasizes personal service (two-to-one guest-to-staff ratio). Ideal for families, couples, and singles. Riding, hiking, and communing with the great outdoors. Lots for non-riders as well. Winter weekend getaways. Excellent for weddings—beautiful alpine chapel with views to the Continental Divide. Gift shop. Great for family reunions too. Rocky Mountain National Park nearby (elk, deer, and bighorn sheep sometimes seen). Video available.

See color photos, page 202.

Rawah Ranch
Glendevey, Colorado

THE DUDE RANCHERS' ASSOCIATION

CDGRA

Rawah (ray-wah) is Ute for "abundance," a word which fits Rawah Ranch today more than ever. At 8,400 feet, the ranch sits at the edge of the 76,000-acre Rawah Wilderness with the Laramie River steps from its door. Rawah is relaxed and nestled in a stunning, wildlife-rich valley 60 miles from town. It caters to folks who want unlimited riding, fine trout-fishing, and escape from the hectic pace of urban life to enjoy nature and wonderful hospitality. Rawah is owned and operated by the Kunz family, who have over 25 years of dude-ranch experience. You can also hike, photograph, pitch a few horseshoes, just loaf, or rock yourself to sleep in one of the rocking chairs on the front porch of the main lodge. Whatever you decide to do, you're in good hands at Rawah. It's one of the best.

Address: Glendevey, Colorado Route, Dept. K, 11447 North County Road 103, Jelm, Wyoming 82063 (summer); 1612 Adriel Cr., Dept. K, Fort Collins, Colorado 80524 (winter). (The ranch is in Colorado, but the nearest post office is in Wyoming.)
Telephone: (800) 820-3152; (970) 435-5715 (summer), summer fax (970) 435-5705; (970) 484-8288 (winter), winter fax (970) 407-0818
E-Mail: rawah@compuserve.com
Internet: http://www.rawah.com
Airport: Denver, with commuter air service to Laramie; free Laramie pickup
Location: 60 miles southwest of Laramie, Wyoming; 75 miles northwest of Fort Collins, Colorado
Memberships: The Dude Ranchers' Association, Colorado Dude and Guest Ranch Association
Medical: Laramie Ivinson Memorial Hospital; staff EMT
Conference: 32
Guest Capacity: 32
Accommodations: The log lodge is the hub of activity, with stone fireplaces in the living and dining rooms and a wonderful rocking-chair porch looking out at Middle Mountain. Five rooms with baths are in the lodge, and six single or duplex log cabins are scattered around the ranch. Cabins have fireplace, electricity, full baths. All rooms have choice of twin or king-size beds. Lodge rooms are carpeted, and cabins have the original wood floors.
Rates: • $$$. American Plan. Lower rates for kids ages six to nine. Off-season rates available. Sunday to Sunday.
Credit Cards: None. Personal checks, traveler's checks, and cash accepted.
Season: Mid-June through September. Adults-only in September.
Activities: Rawah goes out of its way to accommodate guests' riding preferences. Its wranglers help you enjoy mountain trail, breakfast, and loping rides, plus arena riding and instruction. Each riding day there are half-day rides every morning and afternoon, or all-day rides. High, low, fast, slow, short, long . . . it's your choice. Guests may saddle horses. Wild-trout fishing on the Laramie River, which runs through the ranch; the Poudre River nearby; more than 25 alpine lakes and the ranch's stocked pond. Some fishing equipment available. Each week includes an afternoon fly-fishing clinic with professional instruction. Great hiking (June Wheeler's "Trail Guide" provided). Lawn sports, skeet-shooting, rafting, and other notable excursions.
Children's Programs: A more "grown-up" ranch that kids love too. Children ages six and older are welcome to ride with their families or each other. No formal children's program. Fishing pond, playground equipment, separate recreation building.
Dining: Guests actually complain that Rawah's food is too good. Sunrise coffee, tea, or hot chocolate delivered to guest cabins. Special diets with advance notice. BYOB. Sunday evening welcome reception.
Entertainment: Cowboy singers, square dancing, geology presentation, "roll-o-roper," rec room, numerous games in lodge.
Summary: This ranch offers a terrific combination of riding, fishing, hiking, and Western hospitality. Here guests ride at their own pace in small groups. At least two weeks would be needed to cover the huge variety of terrain. One guest wrote, "Everything here is 'too'—too beautiful, too friendly, too delicious, too bountiful, riding that is too wonderful, too many choices, too little time." Video available.

See color photos, page 203.

Powderhorn Guest Ranch
Powderhorn, Colorado

THE DUDE RANCHERS' ASSOCIATION

CDGRA

Powderhorn Guest Ranch, with its picture-perfect setting in a narrow mountain valley, is a love story between two people who had a dream way back in high school. It took a while, but in 1984, Jim and Bonnie Cook bought the ranch and began a tradition along the banks of Cebolla (sa-VOY-a) Creek in southwestern Colorado. The Cooks fell in love with Powderhorn because of its riverside location (it used to be a fishing retreat) and its seclusion. Second only to riding, fishing is a popular activity. Jim is famous for his jeep trips describing the area's history, animals, and wildflowers. Powderhorn attracts a mixture of families, couples, and singles. One family from Cleveland, Ohio, summed it up best: "You are very special people to be able to bring such happiness to others. When we turn that curve and see the big red barn, we just know we're 'home' again."

Address: County Road 27, Drawer K, Powderhorn, Colorado 81243
Telephone: (800) 786-1220, (970) 641-0220
E-Mail: powguest@rmi.net
Internet: http://www.ranchweb.com/powderhorn; http://www.entertain.com/wedgwood/powder.html
Airport: Gunnison via Denver, complimentary pickup at Gunnison
Location: 38 miles southwest of Gunnison
Memberships: The Dude Ranchers' Association, Colorado Dude and Guest Ranch Association
Medical: Gunnison Valley Hospital
Conference: 35
Guest Capacity: 30
Accommodations: 13 individual log cabins with names like Snoopy, Peanuts, Prancer, Dancer, and Bashful. All have refrigerators and coffeemakers, as well as front porches with lawn chairs. All are carpeted and have private baths. Daily maid service is provided, with laundry facilities available.
Rates: • $$. American Plan. Children's and off-season rates. Five-day minimum stay, one week preferred. Sunday arrivals. No extra charge for singles.
Credit Cards: Personal checks and cash preferred. American Express accepted.
Season: Early June to mid-September
Activities: Horseback riding is the main activity, with emphasis on safety and pleasure. Caters more to beginning and intermediate riders. Guests may groom and saddle own horses. Instruction in the arena, weekly gymkhana, supper ride, all-day ride to East Fork with fresh fish caught for lunch. Groups are usually about six people, but rides will go out even if only one person signs up. Special attention given to children and novice riders. Fishing in the creek as well as two stocked ponds. Weekly fly-fishing clinic with guide. Equipment is provided, and licenses are available. Swimming in large heated pool. Twelve-person hot tub, hiking, four-wheel-drive trips. River raft trip is included. Golf available nearby.
Children's Programs: Kids must be six years old for the trail rides; little ones are happily led around in the arena. Here it's easy for parents to vacation with their children. No formal program. Kids enjoy participating in all activities.
Dining: Home-cooked meals are served family-style or buffet, all you can eat, and desserts with every meal. Several cookouts during the week on the picnic island. Everyone eats together, including the staff. Vegetarian and special diets are happily accommodated. BYOB, cabins only.
Entertainment: Something is planned each night. Classic Western movies (with popcorn), square dancing with a caller who teaches, campfire sing-alongs, weekly guest gymkhana, lodge with pool table, jukebox, table tennis, and Volleyball. Saturday night is Jim's special "Video of the Week" with the guests as the "stars."
Summary: Small, friendly, and fun! For down-home friendly guests in a beautiful river-valley setting. Family-owned and -operated guest ranch. Remote and peaceful, without a strictly regimented program. Families, couples, singles, and single parents quickly become one big family. Ask about adults-only week in September and family-reunion group rates.

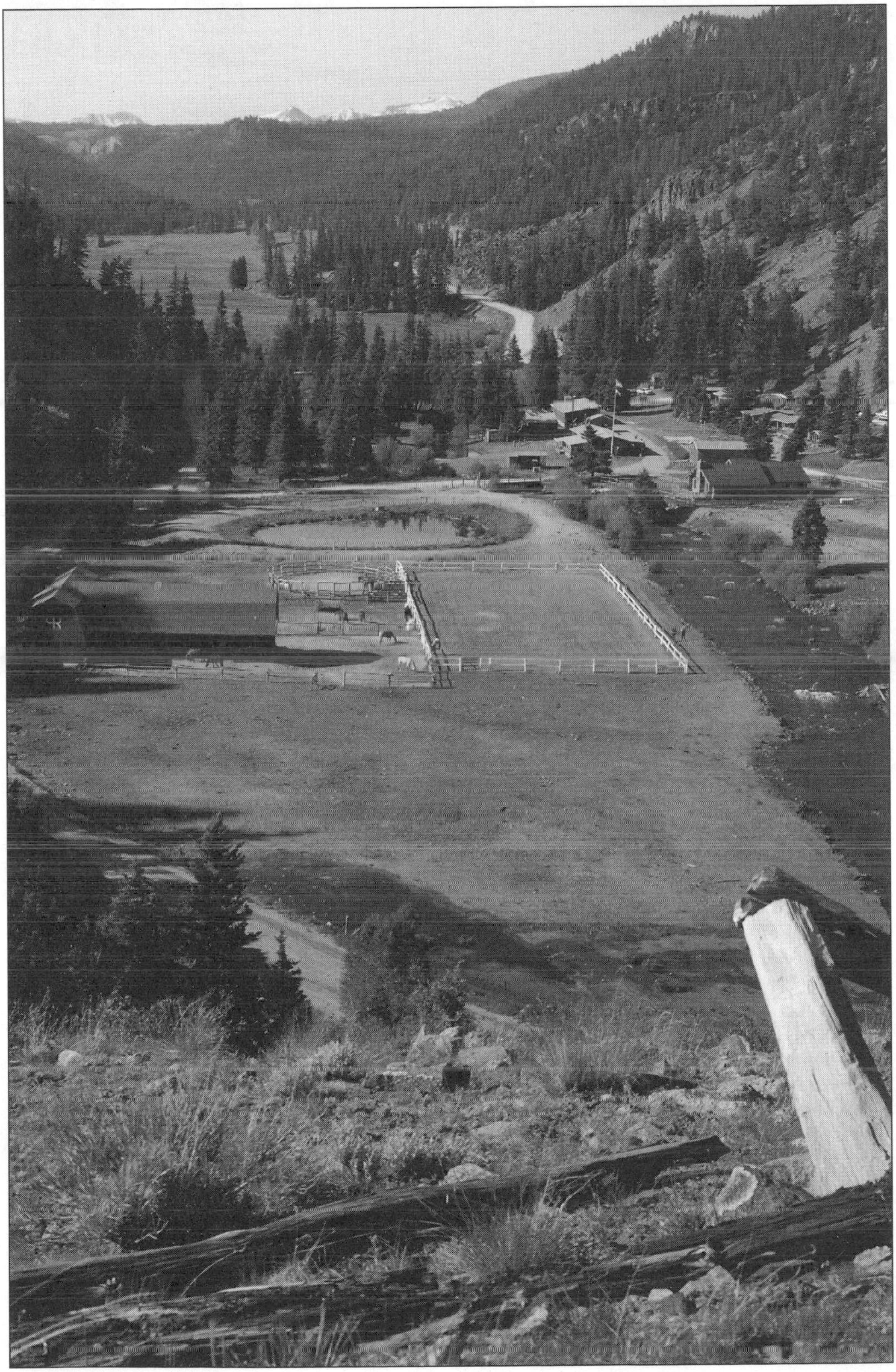

Rainbow Trout Ranch
Antonito, Colorado

THE DUDE RANCHERS' ASSOCIATION

CDGRA

Rainbow Trout Ranch was a sleeping giant, but no longer! In 1993 this marvelous paradise was reopened to the world by Doug, Linda, David, and Jane Van Berkum. Rainbow Trout was built back in the 1920s, and its 18,000-square-foot log lodge and cabins were used as an exclusive sportsman's retreat by fishermen and their families—thus its name. Today this great tradition is carried on in a number of ways. First and foremost, it's a haven for families who come to rejoice in natural beauty and in being together. Rainbow Trout serves up plenty of warm and friendly hospitality. When staff members say they're glad you came, they mean it. Guests can enjoy varied riding, visit Santa Fe or Taos, ride the Cumbres & Toltec Scenic Railroad, fish the Conejos River, or just savor all the family fun. At RTR you have the best of the Colorado Rockies and close proximity to New Mexico.

Address: 1484 FDR 250, Box 458K, Antonito, Colorado 81120
Telephone: (800) 633-3397, (719) 376-5659 (telephone and fax)
E-Mail: rainbow2@amigo.net
Internet: http://www.rainbow.com
Airport: Alamosa (available pickup extra); guests also fly into Albuquerque, Colorado Springs, and Denver
Location: Two miles off Highway 17 between Antonito, Colorado (22 miles), and Chama, New Mexico (29 miles), one hour southwest of Alamosa, Colorado
Memberships: The Dude Ranchers' Association, Colorado Dude and Guest Ranch Association
Medical: Regional hospital, La Jara; 45 minutes
Conference: 60, late May and September
Guest Capacity: 60
Accommodations: 15 old-time cabins with names like Deer, Birch, Cottonwood, and Cougar are situated above the main lodge and interspersed among the aspen and pines. They range in size from two bedrooms and one bath to three bedrooms and two baths. Larger cabins have living rooms and fireplaces. All have covered porches. Daily housekeeping. Laundry room.
Rates: • $$$. American Plan. Children's, off-season, and June rates. Sunday-to-Sunday stays June through August. Rafting, pack trips, trapshooting, and train rides extra.
Credit Cards: None. Personal checks, traveler's checks, and cash accepted.
Season: Late May through September
Activities: Horseback riding and fishing are the most popular ranch activities. You'll have your own horse for the week. Five to eight riders per ride, divided according to guests' wishes and abilities. Individual families can often ride together. Weekly overnight pack trip for teenagers and adults. The ranch's Conejos River and its tributaries are known for great fishing. Instruction and some gear available. Ask about the local professional guide service available for serious anglers. Heated swimming pool, hot tub, volleyball, basketball, and hiking. Ask about white-water rafting near Taos, New Mexico.
Children's Programs: Excellent supervised children's program for ages three to five, six to 11, and teens. Kids ages three to five take pony rides with a counselor; ages six to 11 have their own horse for the week and take trail rides. Crafts, hiking, swimming, and kids' cookouts also offered. Parents welcome to join in children's activities. Programs for children and teens not mandatory.
Dining: Hearty, home-cooked meals are served family-style in the lodge dining room. Lunch cookouts by the pool, chicken-and-steak barbecues at the picnic area, and candlelight dinner for adults are favorites. BYOB.
Entertainment: Something is planned most evenings. Weekly square dancing, Western dance, hayride, watching team roping, and sing-alongs. The lodge, with its huge wrap-around porch, is a great place to relax with a good book.
Summary: At Rainbow Trout you'll find the best of Colorado and proximity to some of New Mexico's most famous towns. Great for families who want to be together but enjoy different activities for varied interests and ages. Magnificent, historic lodge with views of the valley. Varied horseback riding and superb fishing in the Conejos River. Kids especially enjoy riding in Doug's century-old wagon. Located 2½ hours north of Santa Fe, 1½ hours northwest of Taos.

San Juan Guest Ranch
Ridgway, Colorado

THE DUDE RANCHERS' ASSOCIATION

CDGRA

San Juan Guest Ranch is surrounded by more 14,000-foot peaks than any other spot in the United States. The ranch is in southwestern Colorado's beautiful Uncompahgre Valley, "the Switzerland of America." It's also just four miles north of the quaint town of Ouray, which has been carefully preserved to keep its century-old charm, and the well-known town of Telluride, less than an hour away. The ranch caters to 30 guests and is big in hospitality, overseen by owners Pat MacTiernan and her son, Scott, and their fine college staff. In the Western tradition, San Juan Ranch excels in horseback riding with certified instruction. Be sure to ask about the wonderful overnight high-country pack trip to Parker's Place—one of the highlights of your stay. The special spirit of teaching and sharing passed down to Scott from his father makes San Juan one of the best.

Address: 2882 County Road 23, Dept. K, Ridgway, Colorado 81432
Telephone: (800) 331-3015, (970) 626-5360; fax: (970) 626-5015
E-Mail: sjgr@rmi.net
Internet: http://www.sjgr.com
Airport: Montrose or Telluride via Denver
Location: Five miles north of Ouray, 42 miles east of Telluride, six hours southwest of Denver by car
Memberships: Colorado Dude and Guest Ranch Association, The Dude Ranchers' Association
Medical: Ouray Clinic or Montrose Hospital, 30 miles; in-house EMT
Conference: 30, off-season only
Guest Capacity: 30
Accommodations: Guests stay in the comfortable, fully carpeted, two-story lodge. Nine individual apartments on both levels are decorated with lots of country charm, with common decks and views of the ranch and valley. Private baths and daily maid service. Queen-size, doubles, and bunk beds. Refrigerators and native wildflowers in rooms upon arrival.
Rates: • $$–$$$. American Plan. Children's, off-season, and group rates available. Six-day minimum stay, Sunday to Saturday. Winter: Stay one night or more bed-and-breakfast.
Credit Cards: VISA, MasterCard. Personal checks accepted.
Season: Summer: June through September; fall: adults-only, week stays; winter: bed-and-breakfast, open Christmas
Activities: Summer brings a full riding program with certified instruction available. Hourly, half-day, and full-day trail rides. Jeep trips to the wildflowers, ghost towns, and abandoned gold mines in the heart of the San Juan Mountains, and favorite Yankee Boy Basin. Fishing in the Uncompahgre River or private stocked ponds. Trap-shooting and rifle range (guns available). Hiking, eight-person hot tub, volleyball, horseshoes, and horse-drawn hay-wagon rides. Tennis and huge natural hot springs in Ouray. Balloon rides available (extra). Fall is a wonderful time to visit, as the aspens display a magnificent array of gold before the winter snows. To capture this beauty, Scott has created a photo adventure/workshop for adults only. Winter: sleigh rides, snowshoeing, tobogganing, and guided cross-country skiing. Downhill skiing at world-famous Telluride ski area, 45 minutes away.
Children's Programs: Excellent children's program! A child's paradise (ages six and older); activities include animal-feeding and petting zoo.
Dining: Hearty meals served family-style. Traditional turkey dinner starts each week. Lots of vegetables and salads. Fresh trout served weekly. Weekly cookouts and barbecues. Complimentary wine with dinner. BYOB.
Entertainment: Bonfire with cowboy singing and professional Western-dance instruction. Shopping in Ouray and Telluride. Scott's team-roping demonstrations are really exciting.
Summary: Picture perfect! Family-owned and -operated. Great for families, those without families, and single parents. Very strong children's program for kids ages six and older. Photography workshop. Be sure to ask about incredible historic and scenic train ride to ranch. Weekly cattle-moving. Certified riding instruction. Nearby: Victorian mining towns of Ouray and Telluride.

Seven Lakes Lodge
Meeker, Colorado

Seven Lakes is very special to me. Here, one beautiful September morning, I learned that I was to be a father. What a magical moment that was—and what an incredible place Seven Lakes is. Surrounded by quaking aspen, spring-fed lakes, and views as far as the eye can see, Seven Lakes is a masterpiece created by world-renowned businessman Henry Kravis and vice president Steve Cobb. Together with well-known sportsman and general manager Steve Herter, after years of planning and building, these men have combined one of the most exclusive and luxurious wilderness hideaways with one of the finest outdoor programs in the world. Sportsmen and -women alike come here to savor the beauty, ride, hike, fish, and shoot with the best. All who come relax, dine, rest, and recharge in this mountain paradise.

Address: 36843 County Rd. 17, Meeker, Colorado 81641
Telephone: (970) 878-4772; fax: (970) 878-3635
E-Mail: sevenlakes@cmm.net
Internet: http://www.sevenlakeslodge.com
Airport: Meeker, 25 miles for private airplanes and jets; Grand Junction, 120 miles; Steamboat Springs, 130 miles; Grand Junction, 130 miles; Aspen, 149 miles
Train: Glenwood Springs, 110 miles
Location: 25 miles east of Meeker, 260 west of Denver
Memberships: Trout Unlimited, Rocky Mountain Elk Foundation, National Sporting Clays Association
Medical: Pioneers Hospital, Meeker. Emergency helicopter service.
Conference: 22; executive telecommuting available. Cellular phones encouraged with restricted use in your private cabin or lodge room only.
Guest Capacity: 22
Accommodations: The 15,000-square-foot main lodge has a great room, reminiscent of the early days, with a giant moss-rock fireplace and adjoining bar and dining area. Guests can dine or relax on an outside, enclosed porch, with magnificent views in all directions and not another electric light to be seen for over a hundred miles. The second level has eight deluxe guest suites with full baths. The private, three-bedroom executive log cabin is a short walk from the main lodge, with views overlooking Cabin Lake.
Rates: • $$$$$. American Plan. Six-night packages.
Credit Cards: VISA, MasterCard, American Express; personal checks preferred.
Season: June through October
Activities: The entire activities program is tailored to individual guests' desires. Seven Lakes is your mountain hideaway and the staff will do all that they can to ensure you have one of the greatest experiences ever. All guiding is one-on-one with some of the best men and women guides in America. Extensive fly-fishing and sporting-clay programs. Horseback riding, hiking, and, for those inclined, a state-of-the-art exercise/fitness center. A good number may choose to sleep in late and enjoy the privacy and beauty . . . that's great too!
Children's Programs: Children ages 12 and older welcome. Children of all ages welcome when entire property is reserved.
Dining: One of the many highlights at Seven Lakes is the superb cuisine. Choose from a variety of entrées each evening. Trail and stream-side gourmet picnics and weekly barbecues cookouts with musical entertainment. Special diets not a problem. Fine wines available. Full bar.
Entertainment: Relax in the main lodge with your favorite beverage and hors d'oeuvres in front of a blazing fire while being serenaded by the legendary Lloyd Mabrey, and enjoy the sweeping views and sunsets from the terrace. Stimulating conversation and evening strolls.
Summary: In the world of true luxury guest ranches and sporting lodges, Seven Lakes is right at the top—world-class in every way. Fifty-five full-time employees insure all guests receive a truly world-class experience. One of Kilgore's best of the best . . . a shining star in North America.

Skyline Guest Ranch
Telluride, Colorado

THE DUDE RANCHERS' ASSOCIATION

CDGRA

When Dave and Sherry Farny bought Skyline Guest Ranch in 1968, their first concern was to preserve the natural beauty so that generations to come could enjoy this magnificent, breathtaking mountain paradise. They succeeded by deeding the property to the great wilderness protector, the Nature Conservancy. Thus the ambience and tranquility at Skyline will be savored for years to come. In the southwestern corner of the state, Skyline is nestled in the high meadows and aspen-rich peaks of the San Juan Mountains. The crisp air and the crystal-clear mountain water, not to mention the snowcapped 14,000-foot peaks, make this ranch one of the most beautiful. Mike and Sheila Farny, and young sons Luke and Andrew, preserve their "mountain joy" tradition, a spirit on which guest ranching was founded—honest and friendly hospitality. With postcard views all around, this is one of the best guest ranches in the West.

Address: Box 67K, Telluride, Colorado 81435
Telephone: (888) 754-1126, (970) 728-3757; fax: (970) 728-6728
E-Mail: skyline-ranch@toski.com
Internet: http://www.ranchweb.com/skyline
Airport: Telluride
Location: 15 minutes from Telluride
Memberships: The Dude Ranchers' Association, Colorado Dude and Guest Ranch Association
Medical: Telluride Clinic, eight miles
Conference: 35, new conference center
Guest Capacity: 35
Accommodations: Guests stay in 10 comfortable lodge rooms or six housekeeping cabins. All lodgings have magnificent views, private baths, and excellent beds with down comforters and sheepskin mattress covers. Awaken in the morning to sweet aromas from Skyline's famous kitchen. Laundry facility available. No smoking in buildings.
Rates: • $$$. American Plan. One-week minimum stay, Sunday to Sunday. Winter: see Cross-Country Skiing section.
Credit Cards: VISA, MasterCard, American Express. Personal and traveler's checks accepted.
Season: Summer: June to mid-October; winter: mid-December to April; open Christmas

Activities: Summer brings a full horse program with Mike's "natural horsemanship" instruction for all levels. Guests may become as involved as they wish—grooming, saddling, and riding. Usually six to eight per ride. Beginning, intermediate, and advanced rides. Be sure to ask about the Dunton Meadow, Lizard Head, and Wilson Mesa rides. Also ask the Farnys about their magnificent overnight to High Camp. Trout fishing is superb in the ranch's three mountain lakes and nearby streams. Lake swimming for the brave. Guided mountain biking, hiking, and four-wheel-drive trips over Ophir Pass and to the abandoned gold- and silver-mining camps of Tomboy and Alta. Tours of Mesa Verde National Park. Half-day and all-day white-water trips (extra). Hot tub and sauna. Massage available (extra). See Cross-Country Skiing section for winter activities.
Children's Programs: Really best for older children. No children's program, but kids can participate with parents. Kids under age six don't ride.
Dining: Skyline's cuisine is fresh and scrumptious. Vegetarian and special dietary requests are no problem. Breakfast rides and dinner cookouts are favorites. Complimentary beer and wine served with happy hour and dinner.
Entertainment: Dave plays a mean accordion. Sing-alongs, line dancing. Terrific library and cozy main lodge.
Summary: The Fabulous Farny Family and their spectacular mountain setting will hook you for life. Best for older children, singles, couples, and families who appreciate nature's best. Plenty of adventure here! Four-day pack trip for experienced riders in both June and September. Horsemanship clinics. Sheila's Outpost store. Ask about weekly video and new conference center. Nearby: Telluride—filled with museums, galleries, music, and shopping—just 15 minutes away.

See color photos, page 204.

T-Lazy-7 Ranch
Aspen, Colorado

Often readers of our books write to share special memories. Here's one I couldn't resist. "We spent a month at T-Lazy-7, a place we have enjoyed almost continuously over the past 30 years. Located on the outskirts of Aspen, T-Lazy-7 provides proximity to world-class music, lectures, art, and, of course, skiing and snowmobiling in the winter. Thus, it is a place of recreation, a place to 'be'; to attune with animals, flowers, grass, and water, magnificent red cliffs, and views of spectacular 14,000-foot peaks. It is at the end of the road, the last private property before entering the White River National Forest and Wilderness. Three miles of trout-filled Maroon Creek cascade through the spread, the sound commingling with that of more than 100 horses being driven from pasture to stable and back each day. Rick and Landon Deane are quality folk, caring and enthusiastic, talented and hard-working, committed to preserving and sharing a lifestyle fast disappearing from the American scene." Welcome to T-Lazy-7 Ranch, located in one of the most magical settings on earth!

Address: 3129 Maroon Creek Road, Drawer K, Aspen, Colorado 81611
Telephone: (888) T7LODGE (888-875-6343), (970) 925-7254 (lodging), (970) 925-4614; fax: (970) 925-5616
E-Mail: tlazy7@rof.net
Internet: http://www.aspen.com/tlazy7
Airport: Aspen (Sardy Field), six miles (10 minutes) from ranch
Location: Five miles from Aspen
Memberships: Colorado Outfitters Association
Medical: Aspen Valley Hospital, three miles
Conference: Specializing in private Western parties for up to 180
Guest Capacity: 75
Accommodations: The Deanes have made major investments to improve ranch accommodations, including a beautiful main log lodge with large vaulted main room and Western-style apartments. Without telephones or TVs, cabins have fully equipped kitchenettes, and fireplaces, or wood-burning stoves. Daily maid service with full linen change once a week. Laundry facilities.
Rates: \$–\$\$\$. Horseback riding and winter snowmobiling extra. Two-night minimum stay.
Credit Cards: VISA, MasterCard, Discover
Season: Summer: June through September; winter: end of November through March
Activities: The ranch is open to the public and is a base camp for a host of outdoor summer and winter activities. Tremendous hiking and varied scenic mountain trail riding. Private, family, and group rides available. Be sure to ask about the fall East Maroon Valley ride. Fly-fish in the stocked ponds or along three miles of private Maroon Creek for rainbow trout (catch and release); swim in the beautiful heated pool and Jacuzzi. Depending on the time of year, wildflowers and wildlife can be abundant. Winter: see Cross-Country Skiing chapter.
Children's Programs: No organized programs. Children's playground and lots of animals for the kids—reindeer, llamas, miniature horses, a burro, and a pet raccoon, to name a few. The ranch provides kids' fishing poles with hooks, bobbers, and bait. A children's heaven!
Dining: The ranch doesn't provide meals on a regular basis. Most guests cook in their cabins, each with a barbecue, or join in on some of the meal-oriented horse rides. Aspen is a 10-minute drive for elegant dining and all cuisines. During winter months, don't miss T-Lazy-7's famous sleigh ride dinner-dance.
Entertainment: Once a week there's a T-Lazy-7 guest-welcome hour with refreshments. Summer in Aspen blends culture with the outdoors, bringing the Music Festival, Food & Wine Classic, and many world-renowned sporting events to town. When the snow flies, Aspen's apres-ski and nightlife become the highlights. Groups, ask about private Western parties both summer and winter.
Summary: Family-owned since 1938. Near the world-famous town of Aspen, T-Lazy-7 offers sincere hospitality in the heart of some of the most famous scenery in North America. Easygoing, unstructured Western environment. Do your own cooking, or enjoy elegant dining in Aspen. Riding is open to the public.

See color photos, pages 206–207.

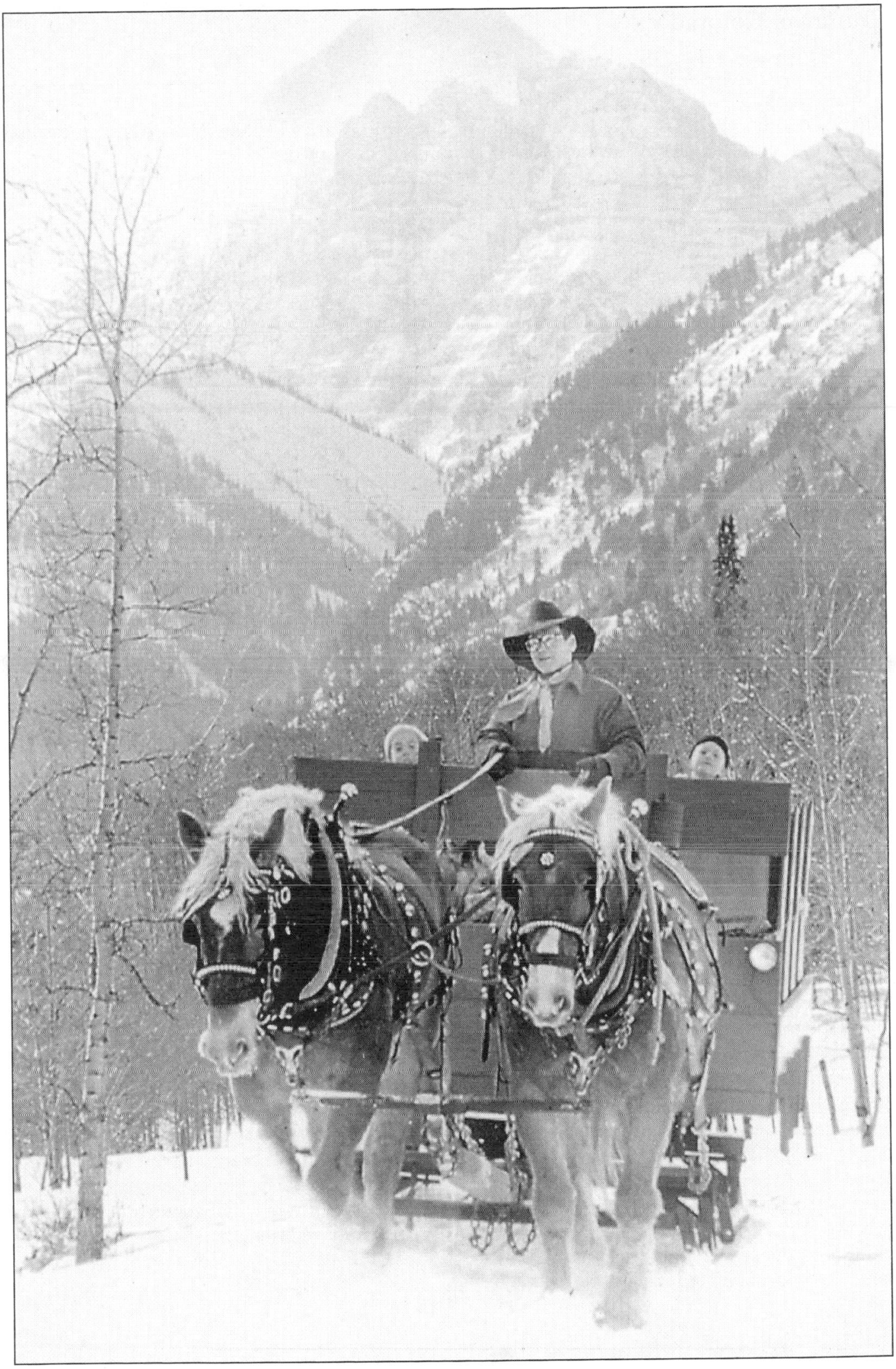

Tall Timber
Durango, Colorado

Throughout this guide I've exercised my "authorly" privilege of including a few extra-special properties that don't fit the exact mold of a ranch but do capture the spirit of adventure, wilderness, and luxury. This is one of them. Perched high in the splendor of the San Juan Mountains at 7,500 feet, Tall Timber is an exclusive hideaway. This Mobil 5-Star property is so secluded that guests arrive by the Durango–Silverton, one of the last narrow-gauge trains in the United States, or by helicopter. Dennis and Judy Beggrow discovered this remote spot in 1970 and today their son, Johnroy, oversees the operation. With no roads, no telephones, no stress, and no deadlines, Tall Timber equals seclusion, beauty, and, maybe most of all, a marriage of luxury and nature.

Address: Silverton Star Route K, Durango, Colorado 81301
Telephone: (970) 259-4813 (radiotelephone; be patient, there may be lots of static)
Internet: http://www.talltimberesort.com
Airport: Durango-La Plata; private planes to Animas Air Park with 5,000-foot paved runway
Location: 26 miles north of Durango
Awards: Mobil 5 Star
Medical: Mercy Medical Center, Durango; emergency helicopter available
Conference: 24
Guest Capacity: 24
Accommodations: All 10 wood-paneled condominium-style units are private and surrounded by quaking aspen. Each year the Beggrows and staff plant more than 65,000 petunias, pansies, and snapdragons. There are eight one-bedroom and two two-bedroom suites, each with its own living room, wet bar, floor-to-ceiling stone fireplace, and balcony. Turn-down service is provided each evening. Furnishings emphasize casual comfort. The main lodge is a massive three-story structure with wine cellar, wet bar, lounge, and dining room.
Rates: • $$$$$–$$$$$$. American Plan, includes transportation to and from Durango by train or helicopter (your choice). Four- and seven-day packages. Low season, children's, and helicopter rates. Four-day minimum stay.
Credit Cards: VISA, MasterCard. Personal checks accepted.
Season: Summer: Mid-May through October; winter: mid-December through mid-January
Activities: Most guests come in the summer to hike and take advantage of the incredible private helicopter excursions to mountaintops or even to Telluride for the day. Also available, heated pool (ask one of the staff to tell you how the pool arrived), three outdoor whirlpools (one overlooks the Animas River), sauna, putting green, driving range, nine-hole par-29 golf course, tennis court, fly-fishing with instruction. Jogging trails, plenty of hiking. All horse activities begin at a sister property a mile away. Guided horseback riding to high-mountain lakes, Silver Falls (a wonderful seasonal waterfall); morning, picnic, or afternoon rides; riding instruction available. Newly added white-water rafting, high-peak trekking, and massage. Winter: Christmas and New Year's are special. Call for details.
Children's Programs: Tall Timber is great for families who enjoy the outdoors together. Kids are the responsibility of their parents.
Dining: Food is not taken lightly. Each table in the dining room has its own picture window. Meals are served from a pre-selected menu and feature eggs Benedict, grilled salmon, beef Wellington, steak and trout, lots of fresh breads, and pastries. Many vegetables and herbs are fresh from the garden. (Ask about the extensive garden!) Dinners are candlelit with crystal and gold-rimmed china. Helicopter picnic lunch to Emerald Lake is a favorite. Stocked wine bar and extensive wines from around the world.
Entertainment: You're on your own. Extensive library.
Summary: Exclusive wilderness hideaway. Arrive by the exciting and historic Durango–Silverton narrow-gauge train or by private Tall Timber helicopters. Most come to hike, relax, savor the pristine beauty, and escape the pressures of the outside world. Helicopters are always available for private use of guests (extra). Special privileges for returning guests.

Wind River Ranch
Estes Park, Colorado

At 9,200 feet, the ranch looks out to the Rocky Mountain National Park's highest mountain—14, 255-foot Longs Peak. Wind River has been in operation for more than 60 years and has preserved the Old West with its rustic setting, antiques, and Indian artifacts. In 1996 Wind River began a new and exciting chapter in its history. Under the direction of the Ford family, it has created a program that touches hearts and souls, capturing the beauty of this magnificent mountain paradise and creating a platform for personal and spiritual enrichment. With numerous outdoor programs the ranch brings families, single parents, and couples together with highly motivated staff members and guest speakers in "the midst of God's creation." Ride, hike, golf, fly-fish, relax in a rocking chair, watch your kids laugh at the puppet show, or listen to a memorable message. As they say at Wind River, "It's a mountaintop experience" with a real mountain high.

Address: P.O. Box 3410 K, Estes Park, Colorado 80517
Telephone: (800) 523-4212, (970) 586-4212; fax: (970) 586-2255
E-Mail: jer2911@internetmci.com
Internet: http://www.windriverranch.com
Airport: Denver
Location: Seven miles south of Estes Park off Highway 7, 75 miles northwest of Denver
Memberships: Christian Camping International, Colorado Dude and Guest Ranch Association
Awards: Mobil 3 Star
Medical: Estes Park Hospital, seven miles
Conference: 56, early September
Guest Capacity: 56
Accommodations: 11 cabins (one, two, and three bedrooms) and four lodge rooms have modern comforts, including private baths, down comforters, individually controlled heat, and carpeting. Some have fireplaces or wood-burning stoves. All have a rustic Western feel. Each has a porch or patio with cypress rockers. Hanging baskets of flowers adorn the main lodge and pool. Daily maid service.
Rates: • $$$. American Plan. Children's and family-reunion rates available. Three-to-four-day and week-long stays.
Credit Cards: VISA, MasterCard, Discover
Season: Early June to mid-September
Activities: Do as much or as little as you wish. Ride, golf, fly-fish, hike, and more. Two-hour, half-day, and all-day rides, as well as breakfast rides. Unlimited instruction is available, as are weekly horsemanship clinics. Riding and hiking on miles of trails in Rocky Mountain National Park and Roosevelt National Forest. Swimming in the outdoor heated pool or hot tub. Fishing on and off the property (bring your own equipment). Ranch has its own stocked pond. Tennis, 18-hole golf course in Estes Park. Golfers, be sure to ask Randy about his PGA tour experience. River rafting nearby on the Cache La Poudre and Colorado Rivers.
Children's Program: Highly motivated college counselors create an organized program for children of all ages. Children under age six ride in an arena only. Fully fenced-in children's playground and fully equipped recreation hall. Counselors are excellent with kids
Dining: Families eat together. Grace before meals. Breathtaking upper-meadow cookout and wranglers breakfast, steak-dinner hay-wagon ride. Hearty and healthy meals.
Entertainment: For those who wish to relax, the ranch has an extensive library in the lovely, rustic, circa-1920 ranch house. Something is planned each evening: singing fireside program, uplifting and encouraging Christian speakers for all family members. Square dancing. Hayrides with Belgian draft-horse team. Ask about the Wind River Ranch playhouse.
Summary: Wind River Ranch is for families, single parents, and couples who want an exhilarating mountain guest-ranch experience and also wish to enjoy an uplifting, positive, Christian environment. Excellent children's program and wonderful speakers from around the country. Ride, golf, fly-fish, hike, rest, relax, and renew your spirit here. Wind River Ranch is a Rocky Mountain high. Nearby: Rocky Mountain and Roosevelt National Parks, town of Estes Park for shopping and many attractions.

See color photos, page 213.

Tarryall River Ranch
Lake George, Colorado

THE DUDE RANCHERS' ASSOCIATION

CDGRA

Once a cattle operation, Tarryall River Ranch developed into a dude ranch in the 1930s. Located at 8,600 feet in the central high-arid landscape of the Rockies and adjoining Lost Creek Wilderness (with Pikes Peak seen from the Monday orientation ride), the ranch is also near the famous gambling town of Cripple Creek. With tremendous Old West ambiance and under the direction of Jimmy and Jeannine Lahrman, Tarryall opened its gates once again in 1995. Together with a young and energetic staff, Jimmy and Jeannine bring a tremendous knowledge about the outdoors and education to their guests. In 1990 Jimmy, who is a world-class outdoorsman, hiked 2,200 miles of the Appalachian Trail over six months. He then went on to climb Mt. McKinley (20,320 feet). At Tarryall you'll have one great vacation plus the opportunity to better understand what the West is all about.

Address: 27001.5 County Road 77K, Lake George, Colorado 80827
Telephone: (800) 408-8407, (719) 748-1214; fax: (719) 748-1319
E-Mail: TarryallRR@aol.com
Internet: http://www.tarryallranch.com
Airport: Colorado Springs, 65 miles; Denver, 125 miles
Location: 60 miles southwest of Colorado Springs, 125 miles southwest of Denver
Memberships: Colorado Dude and Guest Ranch Association, The Dude Ranchers' Association
Medical: Langstaff-Brown Medical Clinic, 35 miles
Conference: 30
Guest Capacity: 30
Accommodations: Two single-family cabins, one duplex cabin (shared living room with fireplace), and four two-bedroom suites, each with a private bath. Tastefully decorated with many antiques. All cabins and rooms reflect the Western atmosphere of years gone by. None are equipped with telephones or TVs, and all cabins have covered porches. Daily housekeeping and guest laundry facilities provided.
Rates: • $$$. American Plan. Children's and group rates. Sunday-to-Sunday stays June through August. Rafting, pack trips, and off-ranch activities extra.
Credit Cards: None. Personal checks, traveler's checks, and cash accepted.
Season: Late May through September
Activities: The ranch offers a variety of organized activities. Adults and kids may ride together or separately. Riding terrain varies from rocky cliffs to open meadows, providing walking, trotting, and cantering rides. Ask about the Lizard Rock and Hankins Pass rides. Weekly overnight pack trip to a secluded high mountain meadow paradise. Fly- and spin-fishers enjoy the Tarryall River on the ranch and Gold Medal fishing at Spinney and Eleven Mile Reservoirs, about 30 minutes away by car. A full-day of white-water rafting on the Arkansas River is enjoyed by all. Hiking and scenic day trips. Trap-shooting and annual September cattle drives. Hikers and climbers, ask Jimmy to tell about his 30-day Mt. McKinley expedition.
Children's Programs: Full-time children's counselors for kids ages five and under. The ranch is small and intimate, so adults and children usually do things together. Kids ages six and older may trail-ride. Informal nature lessons and hikes. Kids love the Wednesday evening music program, weekly hayride, and petting zoo.
Dining: Family-style meals served in the lodge. All meals are home-cooked and waitresses provide full service. BYOB. Occasional wine and beer served.
Entertainment: Weekly evening hayride after Jimmy's famous chicken-and-ribs cookout. Square dancing. Country-Western sing-alongs.
Summary: Jimmy and Jeannine Lahrman have a tremendous knowledge about the land and go out of their way to share it. Young staff with a friendly, small, and very happy atmosphere. The ranch has that John Wayne–Old West feel to it; rustic, but not too rustic, with lots of heart and soul. Be sure to ask Jeannine about their ride across America.

See color photos, page 205.

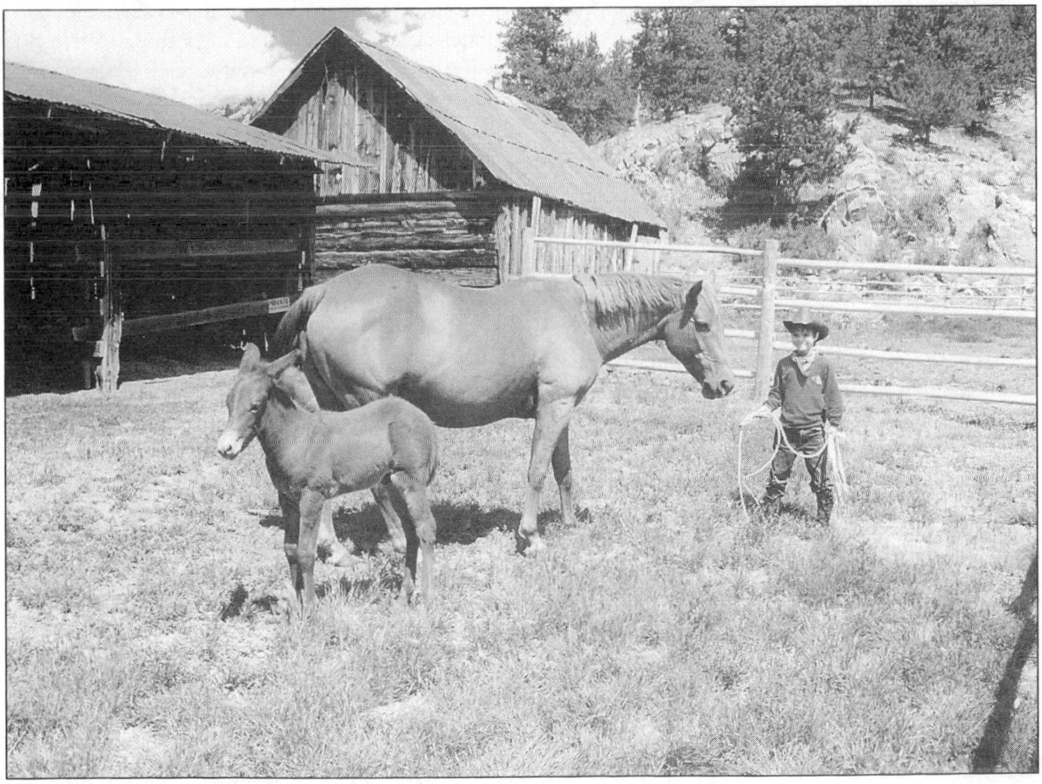

Tumbling River Ranch
Grant, Colorado

THE DUDE RANCHERS' ASSOCIATION

CDGRA

Tumbling River is the year-round home of Jim and Mary Dale Gordon, two very friendly Texans who serve Southern hospitality high in the Colorado Rockies. At 9,200 feet, the ranch is in Indian country on the banks of Geneva Creek and in the middle of Pike National Forest. This secluded spot is well known for the Ute Indians and trappers who once roamed these parts. The property is divided into an upper ranch (where most of the activities take place) built as a mountain retreat by a former mayor of Denver, and a lower ranch house, the Pueblo, built by Native Americans with carved beams and adobe walls for the daughter of Adolph Coors. You'll find a warm, informal atmosphere here and plenty of natural ambience and wildlife. Elk, deer, sheep, and mountain goats may be seen. One of the best features at Tumbling River is the children's program. One guest said, "A family can spend its vacation together and still get away from one another." Tumbling River Ranch, in one word, is terrific.

Address: P.O. Box 30K, Grant, Colorado 80448
Telephone: (800) 654-8770, (303) 838-5981; fax: (303) 838-5133
E-Mail: sdugan@purplemtn.com
Airport: Denver or Colorado Springs
Location: Four miles north of Grant, 62 miles southwest of Denver
Memberships: The Dude Ranchers' Association, Colorado Dude and Guest Ranch Association
Medical: Denver hospitals
Conference: 40, off-season only
Guest Capacity: 55
Accommodations: Accommodations are in two clusters: the upper ranch and the lower ranch, about a quarter-mile apart. Eight cabins (one is bi-level) have names like Indian Hogan, the Frenchman's Cabin, Big Horn, and Tomahawk. Most have fireplaces; twin, queen-size, or bunk beds for kids; and arching ceilings. Some are real log, some log-sided; all porches have swings and hanging geranium planters, and many bird-feeders are scattered about. There are also 14 rooms in the two upper and lower ranch lodges, each with its own fireplace.
Rates: • $$$$. American Plan. Children's, off-season, and group rates available. One-week minimum stay, Sunday to Sunday.
Credit Cards: None.
Season: Mid-May through September
Activities: The Gordons offer a wide variety of activities: riding with a string of 80 horses; half-day and all-day rides; overnight, family, adult, and kids' rides; pack trips (adults and kids ages 12 and older); and riding instruction. Four-wheel-drive trips and hiking to breathtaking 14,000-foot vistas. Fly-fishing with instruction in stocked ponds, streams, and mountain lakes; and weekly black-powder plus trap-shooting (guns and ammunition provided). The heated swimming pool has a full-length cabaña with tables and an eight-person hot tub with nearby old-time steam sauna. Weekly river-rafting on Arkansas River (extra).
Children's Programs: Excellent morning and afternoon supervised children's program for ages three through teens. Kiddie wrangler and programs for children three years old and up. Separate programs for children ages three to five, six to 11, and teens. Limited baby-sitting available for kids under age three. Children ages three to five ride with supervision. Ask about tepee overnight.
Dining: Complimentary coffee served in your cabin each morning. Every day except Wednesday there's a cookout. Favorite menus include apple pancakes with apple-cider syrup, and fajita lunch cookouts with homemade soup. Weekly "Gordon's hamburgers" poolside. Two adult candlelight dinners. Entrées include pork tenderloin with fettuccini Alfredo, beef tenderloin, and weekly Thanksgiving dinner. Pecan pies, too. BYOB.
Entertainment: Every night offers something different: hayrides, mountain campfires with hot chocolate, square dancing, ranch rodeos, talent shows. Old-fashioned farewell hootenanny.
Summary: Excellent family ranch with something for every family member. Lots of activities and outstanding children's program! Hosts and staff are tops! Wait until you see the old barn and marvelous old ranch trading post. Nearby: historic narrow-gauge train; the towns of Georgetown and Fairplay.

See color photos, page 208.

Vista Verde Ranch
Steamboat Springs, Colorado

THE DUDE RANCHERS' ASSOCIATION

CDGRA

In his business career, John Munn made a specialty of buying companies and making them better. When John and his wife, Suzanne, escaped the Midwest in 1991 to fulfill their dream, they took the same approach with Vista Verde. As John says, "The ranch was already a wonderful property. What we've done has simply made it better." And so they have. With a new lodge, upgraded cabins, a talented chef, and lots of energy, Vista Verde is indeed better than ever and one of the best year-round guest ranches in North America. Set in a secluded valley with hay meadows and mountain vistas, Vista Verde is not just a riding ranch. It offers tremendous diversity for those who want to do other things, like river rafting, fly-fishing, rock climbing, and hot-air ballooning. The Munns have kept their ranch small and charming—a hideaway to forget your worries and savor a piece of paradise that will be protected forever through the Nature Conservancy.

Address: Box 465K, Steamboat Springs, Colorado 80477
Telephone: (800) 526-7433, (970) 879-3858; fax: (970) 879-1413
E-Mail: 103573.3551@compuserve.com
Internet: http://www.vistaverde.com
Airport: The ranch is remote yet very accessible, with the Hayden Airport just 40 miles away. Ranch Suburbans meet you there.
Location: 25 miles north of Steamboat Springs, off Seed House Road
Memberships: The Dude Ranchers' Association, Colorado Dude and Guest Ranch Association
Awards: Mobil 4 Star
Medical: Steamboat Springs Hospital
Conference: 30
Guest Capacity: 36
Accommodations: Named after surrounding mountains, log cabins are nestled in aspens and pines. Handsomely furnished, they include woodstoves, full baths, and comfortable porches that overlook the meadows and forest. Most have private outdoor hot tubs and master suites for Mom and Dad. Three spacious rooms with splendid views are upstairs in the lodge. Wildflowers and welcome baskets are provided in each accommodation.
Rates: • $$$–$$$$. American Plan. Children's, low-season, and winter rates available. Hot-air balloon rides, and overnight pack trips (extra). One-week minimum, Sunday to Sunday.
Credit Cards: None. Personal or traveler's checks accepted.
Season: Summer: late May to September. Winter: Christmas to mid-March. (See Cross-Country Skiing section.)
Activities: Riding program includes in-depth arena instruction for all levels of experience. Numerous daily trail rides (such as Hole-in-the-Wall Canyon, The Cliffs, and Indian Hill) through the adjoining National Forest. Rock climbing with instruction provides a thrilling experience. Rafting on the Colorado, kayaking on the Yampa, professional and ranch rodeos, extensive hiking and nature program, mountain biking, guided fly-fishing and instruction, hot-air ballooning. Special theme weeks in June and September for cattle drives, fitness, photography, and fly-fishing.
Children's Program: Complete supervised program structured to provide some activities with parents (riding, rock climbing, rodeo, most meals) and apart (gold-panning, fire-engine rides, Indian lore, animal-feeding, and treasure hunts). Special tours and adventures for teens.
Dining: Award-winning chefs prepare gourmet meals with a touch of country. Home-grown vegetables; homemade, just-baked everything; hand-cranked ice cream. Special dietary needs accommodated. Wine and beer available.
Entertainment: Reception Sunday evenings hosted by the Munns. Something is planned each night: folk music, cowboy poetry, barn dancing, staff show, pro rodeo, and steer rodeo.
Summary: One of the top year-round ranches in North America, near the famous ski town of Steamboat Springs. With many on- and off-ranch activities, this isn't just a riding ranch. Lots of wilderness, lots of great food, and lots of good company. Ask about winter when it's Vista "Blanca."

See color photos, pages 210–211.

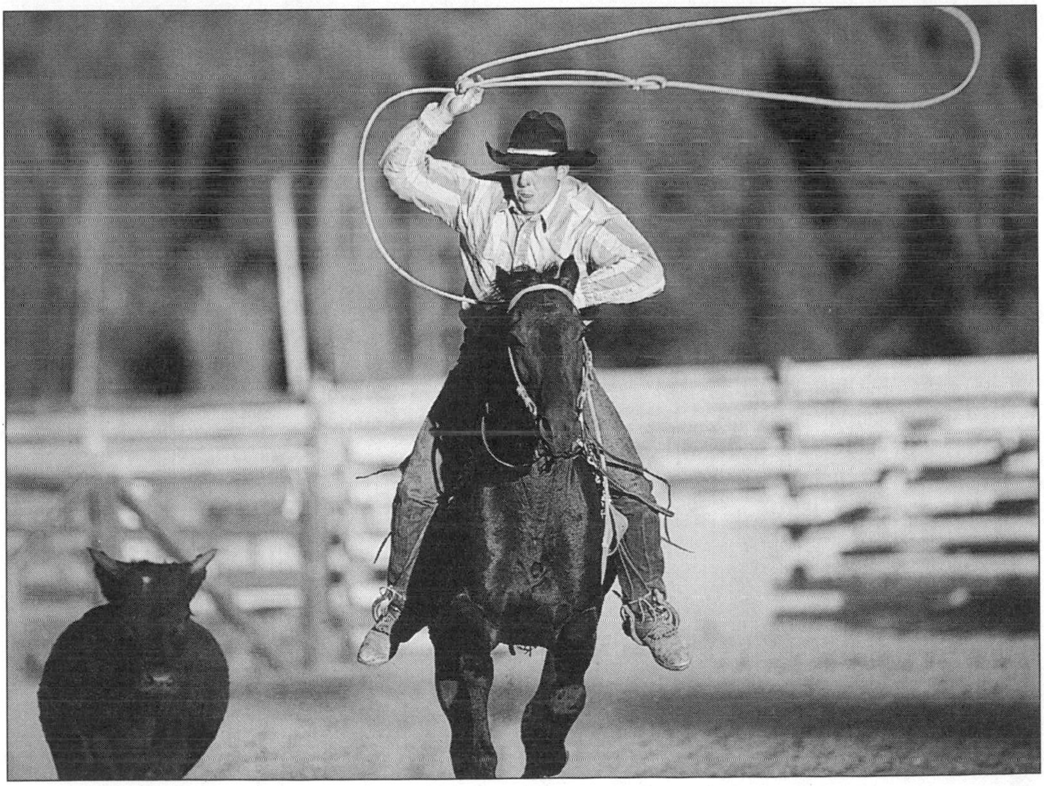

Waunita Hot Springs Ranch
Gunnison, Colorado

THE DUDE RANCHERS' ASSOCIATION

CDGRA

Since the early 1960s, the Pringles have hosted families, couples, and singles who are looking for an enriching Western experience. Near the Continental Divide at 8,946 feet, the ranch is adjacent to mountain meadows and Gunnison National Forest. Waunita was a noted health spa in the early 1900s; guests now enjoy colorful history and beautiful scenery along miles of riding trails or on four-wheel-drive trips. The swimming pool, fed by crystal-clear Waunita Hot Springs, is naturally soothing. The ranch has maintained the flavor of the Old West but is modern in all respects. Three generations of Pringles are actively involved with the ranch and its activities, seeking to provide a Western experience as well as a haven for their guests in a wholesome family atmosphere. One guest summed it up, "Thanks for the best week of the year."

Address: 8007 County Road 887, Dept. K, Gunnison, Colorado 81230
Telephone: (970) 641-1266; call for fax
E-Mail: rpringle@csn.net
Internet: http://www.waunita.com
Airport: Gunnison
Location: 27 miles east of Gunnison, 150 miles west of Colorado Springs off Highway 50
Memberships: The Dude Ranchers' Association, Colorado Dude and Guest Ranch Association
Medical: Gunnison, 27 miles
Conference: 35
Guest Capacity: 45
Accommodations: Two lodges are fashioned somewhat like old Western town buildings. Rooms are paneled and carpeted, with private baths and thermal heating. There are double, queen, and some bunk beds for kids. Laundry facilities available. Music hall/recreation center in top floor of the barn.
Rates: • $$–$$$. American Plan. Children's rates available. Summer: six-day stay. Early and late season discounts.
Credit Cards: None. Personal checks and cash accepted.
Season: June through September
Activities: Planned activities include daily horseback rides on a variety of trails, from flowered meadows to snowcapped mountain ridges. Guided rides are scheduled in small groups, and rides vary from beginners' walking rides to more advanced rides with some loping. Arena games for kids and cattle-penning for adults are scheduled one morning each week. The high ride to Stella Mountain's 12,500-foot summit, with lunch on its highest ridge, is unforgettable. Three cookout rides and an overnight at the forest camp on Canyon Creek are weekly highlights. Scenic four-wheel-drive trips. Gunnison River float and white-water trips, hayride, and marshmallow roast. Stocked pond and lake, with stream fishing available on Tomichi Creek and the Gunnison River.
Children's Programs: Best for children ages six and older. Children are welcome and included in most activities. Six-year-old children can begin riding by themselves. Special children's rides. Small-animal petting farm and arena games. The ranch is a natural playground. Part-time child care is available.
Dining: Wholesome meals served buffet-style, all you can eat. Fruit, coffee, tea, punch, and cookies always available. The no-alcohol policy complements the family atmosphere.
Entertainment: Cookouts at three different forest camps. Recreation room. Something special each night. The musically talented Pringle family features a night of Western music.
Summary: Waunita Hot Springs Ranch is a Christian, family-owned and -operated ranch featuring riding and activities for children and adults. Ranch emphasis is on families enjoying the ranch and activities together. Located at the site of a natural hot spring that provides thermal heat for buildings and water for the pool, it's historic yet modern. Late-season, adults-only weeks.

Whistling Acres Guest Ranch
Paonia, Colorado

THE DUDE RANCHERS' ASSOCIATION

CDGRA

Mt. Lamborn at 11,400 feet and Mt. Gunnison at 12,700 feet provide dramatic and scenic backdrops for Whistling Acres Guest Ranch in Colorado's Minnesota Creek Valley. These peaks border the Western Elk Wilderness area, enhancing guests' view of scenery and wildlife. Whistling Acres offers horseback riding, hayrides, cookouts, and many other activities. Guests can take an afternoon to explore the Black Canyon of the Gunnison National Monument, enjoy a float trip on the Gunnison River, or go in search of wildlife. Most families enjoy the riding, exploring, or just plain relaxing. Your stay at Whistling Acres can be as busy or as restful as you like. Hosts Bill and Bev Madison welcome friendly, easygoing families, couples, and singles who are young and the young-at-heart. Guests come here to enjoy the outdoors, explore the numerous activities available both on and off the ranch, and take part in the unstructured, low-key, friendly programs.

Address: 4397 "050" Drive, P.O. Box 88 K, Paonia, Colorado 81428
Telephone: (800) 346-1420, (970) 527-4560; fax: (970) 527-6397
E-Mail: wranch050@aol.com
Internet: www.whistlingacres.com
Airport: Montrose, 50 miles; Grand Junction, 70 miles; Denver, 240 miles
Location: 70 miles southwest from Glenwood Springs and Aspen
Memberships: Colorado Dude and Guest Ranch Association, The Dude Ranchers' Association, Colorado Hotel & Lodging Association
Medical: North Fork Medical Clinic, three miles
Conference: 33
Guest Capacity: 33
Accommodations: The spacious six-bedroom, five-bath, two-story house and two new log cabins provide comfortable lodging. Two stone fireplaces accent the two floors of the main ranch house. Multiple bed arrangements can satisfy any need whether it is single, double, or family requirements. The pavilion area is the center for all activities, such as nightly entertainment, horseshoes, volleyball, Ping-Pong or campfires. The sunroom, hot tub, and pool table provide year-around indoor activities.
Rates: $$$–$$$$ American Plan. Three- or six-day stays.
Credit Cards: VISA, MasterCard
Season: May to October
Activities: Meadow and mountain rides usually go out twice a day, lasting two to three hours. All-day and evening rides are available on request. Scenic walking and trotting, high-country trail riding, some loping in the meadows (depending upon your skill level). Hiking, jeep riding, and sightseeing are favorites of many guests. Trips to an authentic mountain-man fort, and the Grand Mesa (largest flattop mountain in the world) will make your trip memorable. At an additional cost, a two-day white-water rafting trip can be arranged.
Children's Programs: Bill and Bev encourage parents to spend quality time with their children. Programs available when adults are participating in activities include creative rock painting, making bead necklaces, games, and nature walks. Horseback riding in the pasture with kids' wranglers giving individual instructions while the adults are on a trail ride. Trail riding begins at age seven.
Dining: Hearty, home-cooked meals are served family-style in the ranch house or at the pavilion. Evening cookouts and breakfast rides are a big attraction for the guests. BYOB.
Entertainment: Evening campfires with sing-alongs, weekly mountain-man shows, Western singers, square and line dancing, games, and contests.
Summary: Bill and Bev are a wonderful Nebraska couple who grew up in the farming and ranching business. Whistling Acres offers a wholesome setting for adults and children wishing to ride and hike or explore surrounding areas by car. Seasonal cattle and hay work. Day trips include Black Canyon in Gunnison, and Grand Mesa and Fort Uncompahgre in Delta.

See color photos, page 209.

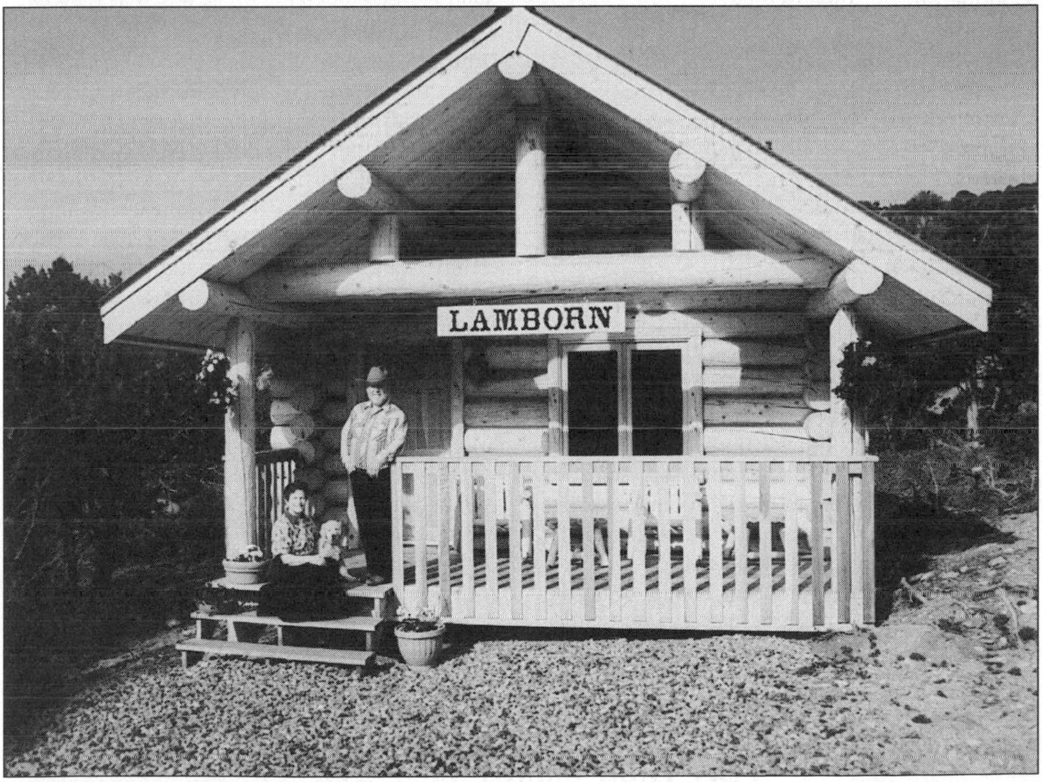
LAMBORN

Wilderness Trails Ranch
Durango, Colorado

THE DUDE RANCHERS' ASSOCIATION

CDGRA

A soaring eagle, the songs of coyotes, a deer bounding across the meadow, horses grazing in the pasture, and twinkling stars in the clear mountain skies—welcome to Wilderness Trails Ranch, "a blend of the past and present." Since 1970 the Roberts family has owned this lovely Colorado Rockies ranch. Today they offer one of the fine ranch-vacation experiences in the country. Wilderness Trails is snuggled next to the Piedra Wilderness in the Pine River Valley, not far from beautiful Vallecito Lake. The log lodge looks out over a picturesque meadow and on to the San Juan Mountains. Wilderness Trails offers a wonderful family-oriented, personalized wilderness experience you won't forget.

Address: 1766K County Road 302, Durango, Colorado 81301
Telephone: (800) 527-2624, (970) 247-0722; fax: (970) 247-1006
E-Mail: wtrk@wildernesstrails.com
Internet: http://www.wildernesstrails.com
Airport: La Plata Airport in Durango via Denver, Albuquerque, or Phoenix
Location: 35 miles northeast of Durango in southwest Colorado, 190 miles northwest of Albuquerque, New Mexico.
Memberships: The Dude Ranchers' Association, Colorado Dude and Guest Ranch Association
Awards: Mobil 3 Star, AAA 3 Diamond
Medical: Mercy Medical Center, Durango; 35 miles; local rescue service
Guest Capacity: 48
Accommodations: Comfortable, well-appointed, two-bedroom log cabins with porches, nestled among pines, spruce, and aspen. Lovely country furnishings; queen, king, or single beds; modern, private baths with shower/tub combinations; amenities packet; individually controlled heat. Three-bedroom, three-bath "cabin suites" feature wood-burning stoves in living rooms, separate room with minibar, coffeemaker, refrigerator, and robes. Laundry facilities available.
Rates: • $$$. American Plan. Family and children's rates. Discounts early June and September. Seven-night minimum stay in high season, Sunday arrival.
Credit Cards: VISA, MasterCard, Discover
Season: June through August for families; September, adults-only (six-night minimum)
Activities: Riding is the featured activity, with certified riding instructors and ranch-owned horses. Scheduled morning, afternoon, all-day, and weekly family rides into the San Juan Mountains. Ask about the Lake Lookout and Vista Grande rides. No more than eight to a ride, and rides are separated into "Sidekicks," "Trailhands," or "Trailblazers," depending upon ability. Weekly instruction by certified instructors. Boot rental available. Seventy-two-foot heated pool. Weekly jeep trip to Middle Mountain, tour to Mesa Verde cliff dwellings. River rafting, waterskiing, hiking, fishing, and hot tub. Historic Durango–Silverton Steam Train and overnight pack trip (extra).
Children's Programs: Exceptional programs for "never-bored kids" ages three to 17. Kids' wranglers, waterskiing, riding instruction, trail rides (helmets available), hayrides, and a variety of other activities keep the kids happy and entertained all day. Ask about the new foals and Indian "wild crafting." Parents do as much as they wish with their children.
Dining: Young children may eat with counselors, if parents desire. Weekly gourmet candlelight dinner with wine for adults. Hearty ranch cuisine plus vegetarian selections. BYOB—order in advance if you wish.
Entertainment: A variety of fun each evening—a hilarious staff show, intriguing magic show, country dancing, recreation room, and campfire sing-alongs. Horse-drawn hayrides.
Summary: Beautiful remote setting! Family-owned and -operated since 1970. Great hosts and staff attracting 95 percent families. Wide variety of activities and weekly adventure trips. Excellent kids' programs. Featured on *Good Morning America* and PBS in 1997. One guest summed it up: "Everyone of our clan, from little tykes on up, thought it was the best ever." September is "adults only" month and is perfect for singles and couples.

See color photos, page 212.

Wit's End Guest and Resort Ranch
Vallecito Lake (near Durango), Colorado

Wit's End Guest and Resort Ranch is the creation of Jim and Lynn Custer, located in the beautiful Vallecito Lake Valley just off County Road 500. Set amid thousands of aspens and pines, it offers guests a host of activities, all in a setting of luxury, charm, and quality. Wait until you see the beautifully restored, century-old main lodge. The craftsmanship and decor are exquisite. The ranch is surrounded by 12,000- to 14,000-foot mountains and looks out over its own Chain O'Lakes and meadows. At Wit's End you can do as much or as little as you wish. Unlike many guest ranches, Wit's End offers rustic elegance with all the freedoms that you might find at a resort. The theme is luxury at the edge of the wilderness. It's a wonderful haven for families, singles, couples, children of all ages, and groups.

Address: 254 CR 500 K Vallecito Lake, Durango, Colorado 81122
Telephone: (970) 884-4113; fax: (970) 884-3261
E-Mail: weranch@aol.com
Internet: http://www.ranchweb.com/witsend
Airport: Durango and La Plata
Location: 24 miles northeast of Durango, directly off County Road 500 and U.S. 160
Awards: 4 Stars by Star Rating Service; *Country Inns* magazine One of the 12 Best in America; Reeds Official Hotel Guide, Superior First-Class, voted America's Third Best Dude Ranch 1997.
Medical: Mercy Medical, Durango; local rescue service
Conference: 200
Guest Capacity: 226 in 37 cabins, 84 at main ranch, 142 streamside.
Accommodations: All of the one-, two-, three-, and four-bedroom log cabins are decorated for the most discriminating taste: knotty-pine interiors, native stone fireplaces, queen-size brass beds, down comforters, Berber carpets, balloon draperies, French doors, TVs, telephones, china dishes, attractive kitchens with separate dining areas, and swings and willow furniture on the porches.
Rates: • \$\$\$–\$\$\$\$. Full American Plan includes all ranch activities May through October. Three- and seven-day minimums. Nanny rates.
Credit Cards: American Express, VISA, MasterCard, Discover. Traveler's and personal checks accepted.
Season: May through October. Open holiday seasons and year-round for groups.
Activities: A host of outdoor activities for children, adults, and families. Lakeside and extensive mountain riding (one hour to all day), guided wilderness hikes, swimming in 50-foot heated pool or lake. Fishing in private ponds, half-mile private trout stream, or Vallecito Lake with 22 miles of shoreline; guided fly-fishing. Weekly arena activities in regulation rodeo arena; riding program includes beginning, intermediate, and selective advanced riding. Tennis, biking, hot tubs, mountaintop motor tours, hayrides, waterskiing, pontoon boat rides, and Fun in the Sun games with the staff. Massage and wilderness overnight trips. Nearby: white-water rafting, cattle drive, Indian ruins, golf, rodeos, and Durango–Silverton Train (additional charge). Winter: cross-country skiing with equipment included. Sleigh rides, guided mountain snowmobiling, and pond skating.
Children's Programs: Extensive summer program with counselors for kids ages four through 12, and teens too. Kids and teens each have own activity center and overnight campouts.
Dining: Dine in the exquisite, century-old lodge. Scrumptious meals served tableside, and wonderful desserts. Campfire cookouts and kids' meals. Room service, full bar, and extensive wine list.
Entertainment: Weekly seasonal live entertainment, cozy bar and lodge open before and after dinner. Dancing, singing, skits, roping, barrel racing, and karaoke.
Summary: World-class luxury ranch resort at the edge of the wilderness in Vallecito Lake Valley. Superb cuisine, wonderful accommodations, and kids' program. Excellent for special occasions. Resort spirit—do as much or as little as you please. Featured in "Great Country Inns" on PBS and the Learning Channel.

See color photos, pages 214–219.

Molokai Ranch
Maunaloa, Molokai, Hawaii

Molokai Ranch offers one of the most unique ranch and outdoor adventure programs in the world for individuals, couples and families who have a quest for adventure or simply wish to hide away to rest, relax, hike, horseback ride, swim and explore the beaches. Here on Molokai's southwest end, the ranch has created three distinct and separate camps with sweeping views of the Pacific Ocean. Kaupoa Beach Camp is situated oceanside. Kolo Cliffs Camp rises 100 feet from the shore looking out to the neighboring island of Lanai. Paniolo (Hawaiian for "cowboy") Camp has the highest perch, providing commanding views and horseback riding as part of the package. Molokai Ranch has created a base camp for a host of outdoor adventures using an upscale tent-camping concept that embraces the trade winds, the Aloha spirit, and all the magic Hawaii is famous for—with a little wildness thrown in. For those who have an adventurous spirit, or for people who simply wish to rest and recharge, Molokai Ranch is one of Kilgore's exciting new ranch adventures.

Address: P.O. Box 259 K, Maunaloa, Hawaii 96770
Telephone: (800) 254-8871, (808) 552-2791; toll free: 877-PANIOLO; fax: (808) 552-2773
E-Mail: info@molokai-ranch.com
Internet: http://www.molokai-ranch.com
Airport: Direct flights from Honolulu, Oahu, or Maui
Location: 54 miles from Honolulu
Medical: Molokai General Hospital, Kaunakakai
Conference: 160 in one camp. Excellent for corporate retreats, incentive programs, and meetings. Theater and professional rodeo arena available for customized corporate events.
Guest Capacity: 130 at Paniolo Camp, 40 at Kolo Cliffs, 160 at Kaupoa Beach Camp
Accommodations: Upscale one- and two-bedroom tents (called "tentalows"), elevated on private wooden platforms. Each unit is outfitted with queen-size beds, solar-powered lighting, ceiling fans, and private bathrooms with hot-water showers. Each tentalow features a deck which offers spectacular views of the Pacific Ocean, acres of pasturelands, and Molokai's scenic natural beauty, depending on the camp you select.
Rates: $$$–$$$$. Full American Plan including airport pickup on Molokai and all transportation at the ranch. Children's and group rates.
Credit Cards: VISA, MasterCard, American Express, JCB Card; traveler's and personal checks accepted
Season: Year-round; high season from December through March
Activities: A wide array of outdoor activities for children, couples, adults, and families. Horseback riding for those staying at Paniolo Camp, cattle herding and rodeo activities in the full-size rodeo arena. Guided cultural hikes, ocean kayaking, outrigger canoe surfing/sailing; mountain biking for all levels, with bikes, helmets, and guides provided. Shoreline fishing, archery, and beach activities too. Ask about seasonal catamaran sailing, whale-watching, surfing safaris, and snorkeling charters.
Children's Programs: Optional morning and afternoon programs for children ages four to 12. Activities include Hawaiian arts and crafts, nature walks, storytelling, and more. Horseback riding tailored to child's age and ability.
Dining: Each camp offers its own open-air dining pavilion with beautiful views where meals are served buffet-style. Picnic box-lunches available for adventurers upon request. Beer and wine available (extra).
Entertainment: Individual and group camp programs featuring an array of evening entertainment from music and Hawaiian arts and crafts to storytelling and stargazing.
Summary: Molokai Ranch is a 54,000-acre cattle ranch on the western side of Molokai. In 1996 the ranch started a new tradition by creating a base-camp activities program for travelers who wish to experience the beauty and ambiance of this magical Hawaiian paradise and who enjoy horseback riding, beach activities, ocean kayaking, mountain biking, snorkeling, and professional rodeo events. Those looking for a place to unwind and hide away will enjoy the beauty and tranquility of all the camps.

See color photos, pages 220–223.

Bar H Bar Ranch
Soda Springs, Idaho

The Bar H Bar Ranch, steeped in pioneer history, is one of the oldest ranches in southeastern Idaho and was homesteaded by the Mormon church. Their unique irrigation system is still used today by owners McGee and Janet Harris. The deep ruts of the Oregon Trail are visible as they follow the Bear River, which runs through the 9,000-acre ranch. Bar H Bar is located in the Bear River Range of the Wasatch Mountains and borders Caribou Cache National Forest. You'll see Idaho in all its beauty—hay meadows, a splendid variety of stately pine and shimmering aspen, cold streams, wildlife, and breathtaking panoramas of wildflowers in June and July. This is a real working cattle ranch that runs 2,000 head of beef cattle, pasturing most of them on private land. The Harris family keeps busy most of the year riding fence lines, doctoring cattle, and making sure the cattle are well fed. There's always plenty to do. The Harris motto is: "Come as a guest and leave as a friend. Enjoy our ranch and the spirit of cattle-ranching."

Address: 1501 Eight Mile Creek Road, Drawer K, Soda Springs, Idaho 83276
Telephone: (800) 743-9505, (208) 547-3082
E-Mail: barhbar@aol.com
Internet: http://www.barhbar.com
Airport: Salt Lake, 184 miles; Idaho Falls, 120 miles; Pocatello, 60 miles; Jackson, 100 miles
Location: 60 miles east of Pocatello off Highway 30 to Soda Springs
Medical: Caribou Memorial Hospital, eight miles
Guest Capacity: Four to eight
Accommodations: There are four rooms in an old-fashioned, rustic bunkhouse. Each room has a private entrance and is furnished with native lodgepole pine furniture with a sprinkling of antiques that reflect the early years of this pioneer ranch. From a full-length porch, you'll enjoy relaxing in comfortable rocking chairs and finding pleasure in the sights and sounds of nature.
Rates: • $$. American Plan. Family rates are available.
Credit Cards: None. Cashier's, traveler's, and personal checks accepted.
Season: Summer: May through October; Winter: December through March
Activities: Activities vary according to the season and include calving, branding, fence repair, and moving cattle to spring and summer ranges; also salting and doctoring cattle, irrigating and preparing cattle for market, and moving to winter range. Other activities include nature hikes (you may see a variety of wildlife), fishing on and off the ranch, and just relaxing. Winter: snowmobiling December through March.
Children's Programs: Children are welcome under the supervision of parents. Best for children over age 10.
Dining: You'll eat with the Harris family. Most meals are cooked and served family-style in the old ranch cookhouse. Three hearty meals a day in the tradition of the West, which may include homemade bread, pies, and other goodies, Dutch-oven cookouts, and steak-fries. The cookhouse is open to guests 24 hours a day for late-night snackers.
Entertainment: Everyone is usually pretty tired at the end of the day. Many go for an evening stroll, some retire early, others enjoy listening to the coyote serenades.
Summary: The Harrises have been in the cattle-ranching business for four generations. In 1993, they opened the ranch gates to the world to share their special love of the West and their way of life. If you're looking for a real hands-on working-ranch vacation with plenty of good food, savvy cow horses, and a wholesome time, give the Harrises a call. Because they take only four to eight guests there is plenty of flexibility for riding and other ranch activities. Featured in the 1995 *National Geographic Traveler* magazine guest ranch roundup.

Diamond D Ranch
Clayton, Idaho

Idaho Guest & Dude Ranch Association

The Diamond D is located in one of Idaho's hidden valleys. Many guests come by car and savor the long and winding gravel road up and over Loon Creek Summit that eventually switches back down into the rugged Salmon River mountain valley. This slow but scenic drive is breathtaking and gives everyone a chance to slow down and unwind to the pace that they will enjoy for their week or two, or more, at the ranch. The Diamond D is remote. On all sides it's bounded by millions of acres of wilderness and plenty of wildlife. Arriving at the ranch, you feel the same exhilaration the early gold-miners must have felt when they exclaimed, "Eureka! We have found it!" The Demorest family has been running this wonderful ranch since the 1950s. No telephones, no schedules, nothing but pure Idaho wilderness and friendly hospitality. If this strikes your fancy, write or call for their brochure, which is filled with color photographs.

Address: P.O. Box 35 K, Stanley, Idaho 83278 (summer); P.O. Box 1555K, Boise, Idaho 83701 (winter)
Telephone: (800) 222-1269; summer: radiotelephone (208) 756-4713 for emergencies only (The voice answering will probably say "McCall Air Taxi."); Winter: (208) 336-9772; fax: (208) 336-9772
E-Mail: DIADlld@aol.com
Airport: Boise, 45 minutes by charter plane, four hours by car. Air charter service available from Boise, Twin Falls, Idaho Falls, and Challis to the 2,800-foot dirt airstrip just four miles from the ranch. Private pilots: Do not attempt to fly in without contacting the Demorests for specifics.
Location: 75 miles north of Sun Valley off Highway 75. Ranch will send you a map.
Memberships: Idaho Guest & Dude Ranch Association
Medical: Emergency helicopter service available
Conference: 35; must book entire ranch
Guest Capacity: 35
Accommodations: Three comfortable two-bedroom cabins a short walk from the main lodge and near Loon Creek. One large four-bedroom cabin that sleeps 10. Several one-bedroom suites including the honeymoon/anniversary suite. Several upstairs lodge rooms. All rooms and cabins have electricity and modern bathrooms. Ranch is powered by a hydroelectric generator. Guest laundry.
Rates: • \$\$–\$\$\$. American Plan. Children's rates available.
Credit Cards: None. Personal checks and cash.
Season: Mid-June through October
Activities: No schedules, but lots of activities are available each day. Evening and morning sign-up sheets for horseback riding, hiking, and gold-panning (very popular and all supplies are provided). Ask about Rob's Hot Springs and Pinyon Peak (tremendous lookout point at 10,000 feet) rides. The Diamond D offers two- to seven-day pack trips to hot springs, mountain lakes, and historic ranches. Swimming in modern pool with adjacent hot tub. Ranch has its own lake with rowboats and fishing. Volleyball, badminton, and horseshoes on the green lawn in front of the lodge.
Children's Programs: Full supervision provided for children under age six. Kids under age six don't trail ride.
Dining: Wholesome ranch cooking. Special diets catered to with advance notice. Birthdays and anniversaries are always special. BYOB.
Entertainment: Campfire sing-alongs. Cards, games, video movies, and fireside conversation in the lodge.
Summary: Lovely remote ranch in the heart of some of Idaho's most pristine wilderness with all the comforts of home. Area full of Western lore, gold mines, and Indian stories. If you drive, you'll want to see the old mining town of Custer and the Yankee Fork gold dredge. Ask about the wonderful crafts program. Private pilots should call Tom or Linda for details.

See color photos, page 224.

Hidden Creek Ranch
Harrison, Idaho

THE DUDE RANCHERS' ASSOCIATION

Idaho Guest & Dude Ranch Association

Idaho, "The Gem State," is a nature-lover's paradise. Hidden Creek Ranch is one of Idaho's treasures. It has been created with great care by a couple who believe in love, respect, and understanding for nature. John Muir and Iris Behr searched the Rockies for a ranch where they could share their philosophy. As Iris says, "When we arrived at Hidden Creek, we felt the magic right away." In 1993, Hidden Creek Ranch opened its doors to the world with tremendous enthusiasm. In their private mountain valley, John and Iris bring to guest ranching a unique respect for nature and the environment. With European attention to detail, first-class accommodations, and a beautiful Idaho landscape, Hidden Creek Ranch is a true gem!

Address: 7600 East Blue Lake Road, Harrison, Idaho 83833
Telephone: (800) 446-3833, (208) 689-3209; fax: (208) 689-9115
E-Mail: hiddencreek@hiddencreek.com
Internet: http://www.hiddencreek.com
Airport: Spokane; private planes use Coeur d'Alene and St. Maries
Location: Five miles east of Harrison off Highway 97; 78 miles southeast of Spokane; 40 miles southeast of Coeur d'Alene
Memberships: The Dude Ranchers' Association, Idaho Guest & Dude Ranch Association, Audubon Society, Sierra Club, Windstar Foundation, Nature Conservancy
Medical: Kootenai Medical Center, Coeur d'Alene; 40 miles; members of Life Flight
Conference: 40; excellent for corporate retreats. Adventure Challenge course for team- and awareness-building.
Guest Capacity: 40
Accommodations: Authentic log cabins, comfortably appointed with private baths, overlooking the valley and timber-ridged mountains. The lodge is a spacious dining and meeting facility. Handicapped facilities.
Rates: • $$–$$$. American Plan. Children's, off-season, and group rates. Six-day stay Sunday through Saturday.
Credit Cards: VISA, MasterCard, and American Express. Personal checks preferred.
Season: Year-round.
Activities: Daily horseback riding: scenic, fast, challenging, all-day, lunch, champagne brunch, and dinner rides; hay wagon rides, Centered Riding® instruction, horse grooming and saddling lessons, cow herding games, barrel racing rodeo, fly-fishing, pond fishing, mountain hikes, nature walks, medicine-trail hike, mountain bike tours, archery and boat tours. The Body, Mind & Spirit Well-Being Program includes fitness hikes, jogging, yoga classes, stretching, breathing and relaxation training, meditation and visualization classes.
Children's Programs: Extensive program for children ages three to teens. Special activities include daily horseback riding, nature awareness, beading, and nature arts and crafts. Picnics, hiking and biking expeditions, campfires with Native American storytelling, a cookout followed by an overnight in Tepee Village, and more.
Dining: Iris and John believe that good food is one of the greater pleasures in life. Their chef offers an eclectic gourmet dining experience. Buffet lunches, four-course family-style dinners, and seven-course candlelight dinner. Complimentary cocktail hour with wine, beer, or soft drinks. Liquor available (extra).
Entertainment: Evening activities differ nightly and include a dinner ride, Western dance, campfire activities, roping lessons, Native American pipe and sweat-lodge ceremonies. Stay concludes with seven-course candlelight dinner, awards night, and quick-draw contest.
Summary: Hidden Creek Ranch is, indeed, one of Idaho's treasures, offering an outstanding children's program, a huge variety of activities with unparalleled Centered Riding® and Native American awareness program. You will find impeccable service with exceptional European attention to detail and gourmet cuisine. At Hidden Creek Ranch the emphasis is on environmental stewardship; and body, mind and spirit well-being achieved through a life in balance. Excellent video available! German spoken.

See color photos, pages 226–229.

Idaho Rocky Mountain Ranch
Stanley, Idaho

Idaho Guest & Dude Ranch Association

The Sawtooth and White Cloud Mountain Ranges of central Idaho are among the most spectacular regions of North America. Here lies the Idaho Rocky Mountain Ranch, a 1,000-acre paradise constructed in the 1930s. In 1951 the Bogert family acquired the ranch, and today it is operated under the guidance of their daughter, Rozalys Smith. Bill Leavell has been the ranch manager since 1988, and Sandra Beckwith is the lodge manager. The ranch is almost exactly as it was in the 1930s, right down to the monogrammed china. All furniture is handcrafted; period photographs and animal trophies grace the log walls. From the lodge front porch you look out to the bold, jagged, snowcapped peaks of the Sawtooth Mountains. At Idaho Rocky Mountain Ranch, you are surrounded by charm and incredible beauty.

Address: HC 64, Box 9934 K, Stanley, Idaho 83278
Telephone: (208) 774-3544; fax: (208) 774-3477
E-Mail: idrocky@cyberhighway.net
Airport: Boise, 130 miles; Sun Valley (Hailey), 65 miles; private grass airstrip in Stanley, 10 miles
Location: 50 miles north of Sun Valley/Ketchum
Memberships: Idaho Guest & Dude Ranch Association, Cross-Country Ski Areas Association, National Trust for Historic Preservation, Idaho Outfitters and Guides Association
Awards: National Register of Historic Places
Medical: Medical clinic in Stanley, nine miles; Moritz Hospital in Sun Valley, 50 miles
Conference: 42
Guest Capacity: 42
Accommodations: Beautifully preserved, 8,000-square-foot hand-hewn-log main lodge houses a large sitting room, dining room, and four rooms with queen beds and private baths. The lodge porch provides spectacular vistas of the valley below and mountains beyond, and the cane and hickory rockers are well-used throughout the summer. Nine duplex log cabins offer handcrafted furniture, stone fireplaces, private baths, and choice of twin or queen beds. Winter accommodations on the lower ranch include comfortable one- and three-bedroom cabins with woodstoves, private baths, kitchens, and great views.
Rates: $–$$. Modified American Plan (includes breakfast and dinner). Most activities are à la carte. Minimum three-night stay. Children's rates.
Credit Cards: VISA, MasterCard, Discover
Season: Summer: Early June through September; winter: December to April. Open Thanksgiving and Christmas.
Activities: On-site summer activities include a popular horseback-riding program; hot-springs swimming pool; fishing in the Salmon River and the private, stocked, catch-and-release ranch pond; mountain bike rentals; hiking trails; horseshoes; volleyball; sunset- and wildlife-viewing. Nearby activities include rafting on the Salmon and Payette Rivers, fishing in the Salmon River and numerous pristine mountain lakes, hiking, and mountain biking. Rock climbing, photography, nature study, ghost-town tours, and browsing in world-famous Sun Valley are other popular activities. Winter programs include ski touring on the ranch and nearby backcountry, hut-to-hut skiing, and wildlife-viewing.
Children's Programs: None. Lots of families. Kids are parents' responsibility.
Dining: Breakfast and dinner meals are included for guests. Breakfast features a continental buffet including homemade baked goods and a choice of hot breakfasts. Dinners include appetizer, soup, salad, choice of entree, and dessert. This is Idaho country cuisine, featuring fresh Idaho trout, steaks, lamb, pastas, and chef's specials. Vegetarian options are available. There are three special dinner events each week: a horse-drawn wagon ride to a Dutch-oven cookout, Western barbecue, and Idaho Night served family-style. Wine and beer bar.
Entertainment: Contemporary live Western music with local musicians. Library, games, and weekly nature talks and stargazing.
Summary: One of the most beautiful lodges in the country. Incredible log-and-iron architecture. Most activities are à la carte. Country cuisine. Spectacular views, individualized service, cultural events in Sun Valley area, hot springs swimming pool.

See color photos, page 225.

The Wild Horse Creek Ranch
Mackay, Idaho

You'll be surrounded by Western ranch elegance in the heart of Idaho's Central Rocky Mountains at the Wild Horse Creek Ranch. The ranch sits amidst the splendor of Copper Basin near Wild Horse Creek. It is backdropped by rugged ridges, pristine glacier lakes, and awesome backcountry trails—a place where the deer and antelope still play. If getting to know your family again is your vacation's priority (even if it's just the two of you), Wild Horse Creek will provide you a perfect venue. An 80-acre island in the wilderness, the ranch is small and intimate yet basks in the expanse of the outdoors. Guests can experience the charm, culture, and shopping opportunities offered in world-famous Sun Valley, just 20 miles west on a dirt road that travels over an inspiring pass. Resident manager and hostess extraordinaire Claire Casey's mission is to provide you with kind and gracious hospitality, assuring guests a warm and welcome respite.

Address: 4387 Wild Horse Creek Ranch Road, Drawer K, Mackay, Idaho 83251
Telephone: (208) 588-2575; call for fax number
Internet: http://www.scenicidaho/wildhorsecreekranch
Airport: Sun Valley, 35 miles; Idaho Falls, 105 miles; Twin Falls, 120 miles; nearby dirt strip for small planes (call for details)
Location: 20 miles east of Sun Valley
Memberships: Idaho Outfitters & Guides Association, Sun Valley-Ketchum Chamber of Commerce
Medical: Wood River Medical Center, Ketchum
Conference: 25
Guest Capacity: 28
Accommodations: Up to 28 guests in a variety of lodging options. The 6,000-square-foot main ranch house offers four rooms, including the King Fisher's Roost, the Otter's Slide, the Coyote's Yip, and the Red Fox Den, all with queen and twin beds. A separate building houses the honeymoon/anniversary suite, the Cougar's Perch, and the Bear's Lair, each with two bedrooms and one bath. Four more bedrooms are located in the Bunkhouse. Ask about our tepees. Pets accepted with deposit and the ranch is wheelchair accessible.
Rates: $$–$$$. American Plan. Fly-fishing and rafting extra. Riding is à la carte.
Credit Cards: VISA, MasterCard
Season: Summer: Memorial Day to November 15. Winter: Christmas to Easter for cross-country skiing, snowshoeing, snowmobiling, and corporate retreats.
Activities: Claire's goal is to meet your needs and your schedule. You can horseback ride or read a great novel, swim in the heated pool or lounge while soaking up the sun, hike or bike an endless offering of incredible trails, cast for fish or scope for birds, run raging rivers or canoe slow stretches just an hour away, golf or rock climb nearby. Soak in the hot tub and then try a night in one of their authentic tepees.
Children's Programs: Children are most welcome, although they are the responsibility of their parents. Keep them busy with swimming, horseback riding, playing pool, hanging out with the llamas, or just laying on their backs watching the clouds go by. Must be age five to trail ride.
Dining: Gourmet cuisine by chefs using some of Idaho's naturally grown food will please your palate. Eating outdoors in the clear Idaho air is the preference. Outdoor barbecues and firepits make evenings fun.
Entertainment: Get to know your family better; meet other guests and the occasional "local" around the recreation room's pool table, bar, or dart board; or lounge in front of a roaring fire in the Great Room. Head over the pass to Sun Valley for jazz, the symphony, ice shows, movies, or gallery walks.
Summary: An intimate, friendly retreat perfectly suited for week-long stays or for a two- or three-day respite from a summer of traveling between vacation spots in the incredible Northwest. Top-notch cuisine and seasonal mountain activities assure guests of enjoying a memorable outdoor experience. The one thing you will do is rest your soul and restore your spirits high in Idaho's mountains.

See color photos, pages 236–237.

Moose Creek Ranch
Victor, Idaho

THE DUDE RANCHERS' ASSOCIATION

Idaho Guest & Dude Ranch Association

Moose Creek Ranch is just an hour from Wyoming's famous Western town, Jackson. It's a beautiful drive over the mountain pass into Idaho from Wyoming. Kelly and Roxann Van Orden have lived in this beautiful part of the country, raising their five children, since 1971. Moose Creek offers a traditional dude-ranch experience with an emphasis on families and children. Surrounded by Targhee National Forest, with Moose Creek running through the ranch, guests are taught to groom and saddle their own horses, and how to ride properly in the high-mountain terrain. Besides the caring hospitality and children's program, the Van Ordens have one of the most incredible wild-horse programs in the country. Horses from the Adopt a Wild Mustang Program are trained and integrated into the remuda. Moose Creek Ranch offers sincere and wholesome Western hospitality for the entire family.

Address: P.O. Box 350, Victor, Idaho 83455
Telephone: (800) 676-0075, (208) 787-2784; fax: (208) 787-2284
E-Mail: moosecreekranch@pdt.net
Internet: http://www.webfactor.com/mooscrk/
Airport: Jackson Hole, 24 miles; Idaho Falls, 70 miles
Location: 18 miles west of Jackson Hole on the Idaho–Wyoming border
Memberships: The Dude Ranchers' Association, Idaho Guest & Dude Ranch Association, Idaho Outfitters and Guides Association
Medical: Hospital in Driggs, Idaho, 12 miles
Conference: 40 (off-season only)
Guest Capacity: 40
Accommodations: Four duplex cabins with covered porches and common walkways; three overlook Moose Creek. Each has a combination of queen- and twin-size beds, private baths with tub/shower combinations. The two-story ranch house has five bedrooms, three full bathrooms, kitchen, living room with fireplace, laundry room, and back deck overlooking the creek (usually booked with a six-person minimum). The main lodge has a large dining room, sitting area, fireplace, covered porch with large wooden swings, and the BYOB Wolf Trap Saloon. Indoor swimming pool area has hot tub and sauna. Guest laundry available.
Rates: • $$–$$$. American Plan. Seven-night minimum stay, Sunday to Sunday. Children's rates and discounted adults-only weeks in September. Bed-and-breakfast rates in winter.
Credit Cards: VISA, MasterCard, American Express, Discover. Checks preferred.
Season: Late May through September. Open November through April (lodging and meals only). Open Thanksgiving, Christmas, and Easter.
Activities: There are a variety of planned ranch and off-ranch activities weekly. Morning, afternoon, and all-day walking trail rides range from 45 minutes to seven hours. Rides go into Targhee National Forest. Be sure to ask about the 10,000-foot Oliver Peak ride overlooking the western side of the Tetons and the Idaho Mountain Valley. Ask about O.P. pack trip. Riding instruction in the arena. White-water trip on the Snake River included in weekly stay. Swimming in indoor heated pool.
Children's Programs: Roxann oversees the kids' program with tender loving care. While parents are enjoying their activities, the little ones are supervised by staff according to the theme (Indian, animal, mountain men) of the day. Flexible, caring program tailored to parents' desires.
Dining: Family-style Idaho ranch cooking. Will cater to special occasions and diets with advance notice. BYOB. Wine served for special occasions. Breakfast and dinner cookouts.
Entertainment: Square dancing, live midweek Western show or melodrama. Lots of stargazing and family enjoyment around the campfire.
Summary: Kelly and Roxann Van Orden have five children who all share their love and excitement. Great ranch for families and single parents. A wonderful "save the wild mustangs" program. Nearby: Jackson Hole, the Tetons, Yellowstone National Park, and the marvelous town of Victor.

See color photos, page 230.

Teton Ridge Ranch
Tetonia, Idaho

On the not-so-well-known west side of the Tetons is a paradise they call Teton Ridge Ranch. This luxurious guest ranch with splendidly designed log architecture overlooks the distant mighty Grand Tetons, rising some 13,775 feet. The ranch has hosted people from around the world, serving up warm, friendly, Idaho hospitality amidst this 4,000-acre pastoral paradise. If you're looking for lots of scheduled activities, read no further—this is not the ranch for you. Here the pace is slow: you can do as much or as little as you choose. You decide. At Teton Ridge Ranch, you'll relax, unwind, and savor exactly what you came here for . . . away from it all, on the other side of the Tetons.

Address: 200 Valley View Road, Drawer K, Tetonia, Idaho 83452
Telephone: (208) 456-2650; fax: (208) 456-2218
E-Mail: atilt@aol.com
Airport: Jackson Hole, 45 miles; Idaho Falls, 69 miles; small planes to Driggs Airport, 11 miles (7,200-foot paved and lighted airstrip). Extra charge for airport pickup at Jackson and Idaho Falls.
Location: 38 miles west of Jackson, Wyoming; 11 miles northeast of Driggs, Idaho
Awards: *Hideaway Report*
Medical: Teton Valley Hospital, 12 miles
Conference: 14 overnight, 32 for the day. Excellent for very small corporate retreats.
Guest Capacity: 14
Accommodations: The main 10,000-square-foot log lodge has a spacious living room; lower-level dining room; and five suites, each with balconies commanding views of the Tetons, woodstoves, and large bathrooms with Jacuzzi tubs. Separate 2,000-square-foot cottage with two bedrooms, large living room with fireplace, kitchenette, and 2½ baths. All accommodations have views of the Tetons and fine art.
Rates: • $$$–$$$$. American Plan. Low-season and corporate rates. One-week minimum stay July and August.
Credit Cards: None
Season: Summer: Late May through October; winter: mid-December through March.
Activities: Summer: no set program. Horseback riding, hiking, fishing, and plenty of R&R. Pack trips, white-water rafting, soaring, guided fly-fishing, sporting-clay shooting (the ranch has its own 16-station course) and trap-shooting are extra. Bird-hunting for Hungarian partridge, pheasant, and native grouse in the fall—guns, guides, and dogs provided. Ask about the Bechler River Hot Springs horseback ride in Yellowstone. Winter: see Cross-Country Skiing section. Many use the ranch as a home base to ski at Grand Targee, about 45 minutes away. Cross-country skiing from lodge on 25 kilometers of groomed trails.
Children's Programs: None. Well-behaved children over age 12 preferred.
Dining: Good food is an epicure's delight at Teton Ridge Ranch. Innovative American cuisine served nightly in candlelit dining room complete with two fireplaces, a view of the Teton Mountains, and good wine. Dinner might include mixed gathered greens with creamy lemon vinaigrette, cumin-roasted rack of lamb, grilled vegetables, Napoleons, and chocolate crème brûlée for dessert. Fresh bread served each night along with fresh vegetables, herbs, and greens grown in ranch garden during the summer. Special diets always accommodated.
Entertainment: You're on your own.
Summary: One of Kilgore's Best of the Best. Small, luxurious family and corporate retreat for those who appreciate and expect the finer things in life! No planned activities. You design your own program. Sporting-clay clinic and bird-hunting in September. Well-behaved pets allowed, kennel on property. Summer soaring at Driggs Airport. Shopping and art galleries in Jackson Hole.

See color photos, pages 232–233.

Twin Peaks Ranch
Salmon, Idaho

THE DUDE RANCHERS' ASSOCIATION

Idaho Guest & Dude Ranch Association

Little was left out when E. DuPont developed one of Idaho's first authentic dude ranches from a hay ranch dating back to 1923. After being closed for decades, this secluded private ranch, 18 miles south of Salmon, was opened to guests in the late 1980s by Allen and Lenabelle Davis. Its impressive setting, nestled in a mile-high valley in the shadow of surrounding peaks jutting up thousands of feet, has been described by guests as "unreal" and "hard to duplicate." The 2,900-acre ranch is wedged between the Salmon, the "River of No Return," and the Frank Church Wilderness. Its trails wind upward to a high-mountain camp at North Basin and to a fish camp at Williams Lake. Twin Peaks has it all—horseback riding, packing in to a tent camp, cattle drives, outboard and fly-fishing, shooting range, and overnight white-water rafting. A writer for *House and Garden* magazine wrote it was "the guest ranch of my imagination."

Address: P.O. Box 774, Dept. K, Salmon, Idaho 83467
Telephone: (800) 659-4899, (208) 894-2290; fax: (208) 894-2429
E-Mail: tpranch@earthlink.net
Internet: http://www.twinpeaksranch.com
Airport: Missoula, Montana, or Idaho Falls, Idaho. Complimentary transportation Sunday to and from Idaho Falls.
Location: 18 miles south of Salmon off Highway 93, three hours south of Missoula
Memberships: The Dude Ranchers' Association, Idaho Outfitters and Guides Association, Idaho Guest & Dude Ranch Association
Medical: Steele Memorial Hospital, Salmon; 18 miles; emergency helicopter service
Conference: 55, off-season only
Guest Capacity: 55
Accommodations: The original seven rustic cabins for two or four persons have their own three-quarter baths. Each deluxe cabin unit has two bedrooms with whirlpool tubs. The center room of the three-bedroom unit has a bath and game table. Six persons can be accommodated in these adjoining units. Ask about a suite in Salmon Run. The lodge adjoins a pool and hot tub with a sundeck and spectacular views.
Rates: • $$$$. American Plan. Children's, group, and off-season rates. June through September one-week minimum, Sunday to Sunday.
Credit Cards: VISA, MasterCard. Personal and traveler's checks accepted.
Season: April through November
Activities: Activities consume the entire week. Horseback riding takes in a wonderful variety of scenery from the Salmon River ride to the 9,000-foot North Basin overnight pack trip. White-water rafting to Ram's Head is a favorite highlight. Fishing, including fly-fishing, at two stocked ranch ponds, the Salmon River, or the fish camp at Williams Lake. Basic instruction is also provided.for archery, target- and trap-shooting. A Western cattle drive ending up at the regulation-size arena with team penning and barrel racing completes your week's stay.
Children's Programs: No set program. Kids begin riding at age six. Kids may eat together.
Dining: The view from the dining room is magnificent. Delicious Western cuisine is offered buffet-style with scrumptious desserts. Weekly breakfast cookout and dinner steak-fry barbecue served chuck-wagon style. BYOB, in cabins. Beer and wine are available in the lodge.
Entertainment: Line-dancing instruction and dancing to a country-Western band. Guest rodeo exhibitions. Nightly campfires, sing-alongs, marshmallow-roasting, and "s'mores."
Summary: The Davis family takes great pride in providing an unsurpassed variety of opportunities for you to have an exciting vacation that will beckon you back. Here you have the best of four worlds: working cattle, packing in to a tent camp, river-rafting, and outboard- and fly-fishing. Ideal for a family adventure!

See color photos, pages 234–235.

Western Pleasure Guest Ranch
Sandpoint, Idaho

Idaho Guest & Dude Ranch Association

On a cold winter day in 1939, Janice's grandpa packed up his family and left Colorado. Their destination was his beautiful dream ranch in northern Idaho. Many years and childhoods later, this ranch is now known as the Western Pleasure Guest Ranch. Since 1990, Roley and Janice Schoonover, and her parents, ranchers Jim and Virginia Wood, have transformed this third-generation family-owned and -operated cattle ranch into one of Idaho's quality guest ranches. Guests enjoy riding through the 960-acre cattle ranch or into the national forest. The ranch is located in Northern Idaho's scenic Panhandle region famous for Lake Pend Oreille, one of the largest freshwater lakes in the United States, and Schweitzer Mountain, a premier skiing destination for the Northwest. Hosts Roley and Janice share their love for their family ranch along with the rich history, beauty, and traditions of the area. Western Pleasure is for folks who appreciate sincere, real country hospitality, while enjoying beautiful new, handcrafted log accommodations.

Address: 1413 Upper Gold Creek Road, Drawer K, Sandpoint, Idaho 83864
Telephone: (208) 263-9066; fax: (208) 265-0138
E-Mail: rschoonover@nidlink.com
Internet: http://www.keokee.com/WPguestranch
Airport: Spokane, 90 miles
Location: 90 miles northeast of Spokane, Washington; 60 miles north of Coeur d'Alene, Idaho; 16 miles northeast of Sandpoint, Idaho
Memberships: Idaho Guest & Dude Ranch Association, Idaho Outfitters and Guides Association, Appaloosa Horse Association
Medical: Bonner General Hospital, 16 miles
Conference: 34
Guest Capacity: 34
Accommodations: Three log cabins and six lodge rooms. The newly built, handcrafted log cabins are secluded among tall pines to assure privacy. Each cabin can accommodate up to eight yet is cozy enough for two with one bedroom, loft, bathroom, and woodstoves for cool evenings. In 1996 the 10,000-square-foot log lodge was completed. The lodge provides six comfortable guest rooms with private baths. A large great room where guests gather features a big river-rock fireplace. In the downstairs rec room, relax while watching a favorite John Wayne movie.
Rates: $$. American Plan. June through September, three-day minimum stay. Off-season rates with shorter stays available.
Credit Cards: VISA, MasterCard
Season: Year-round
Activities: Horseback riding is the main activity, with varied terrain including ridges, forests, valleys, logging roads, and meadows. Slow, medium, and fast rides. Arena instruction. Two- to 2½-hour morning and afternoon rides plus weekly day rides. Ask about the Big Hill panorama, Grouse Creek Falls, and Gold Ridge scenic rides. Group wagon and private buggy rides too. An 18-hole golf course less than 10 miles from ranch. Winter: guests enjoy horse-drawn sleigh rides and cross-country skiing.
Children's Programs: Roley and Janice have two children who love to have other kids visit them. No formal children's program; kids and parents play together. The playground, with horseshoes, large log swing set, sandbox, tetherball, and volleyball, is a favorite.
Dining: Family-style meals served in the lodge. Homecooking and plenty to eat. Steaks and prime rib are specialties, ranch-raised all-natural beef. BYOB.
Entertainment: Old-fashioned sing-alongs around the campfire. Weekly country dancing.
Summary: Great for those who appreciate genuine country folks who love their family ranch and care about the land, their heritage, and Western traditions. Wonderful country spirit. Young, energetic, and friendly hosts—Janice was raised on the ranch. Beautiful northern Idaho scenery. Evening horse- and team-drawn buggy/wagon rides. Nearby: one of the country's largest freshwater lakes and Schweitzer Mountain.

See color photos, page 231.

Double JJ Resort Ranch
Rothbury, Michigan

Double JJ Resort Ranch encompasses 1,200 acres and is located 20 miles north of Muskegon, in west Michigan, on Big Wildcat and Carpenter Lakes, just 10 miles east of the Great Lakes. For over 60 years the Double JJ has entertained thousands of guests in a wonderful atmosphere complete with natural wooded areas for horseback riding and the Thoroughbred Golf Club, an 18-hole championship golf course designed by noted architect Arthur Hills. Today the Double JJ is owned and operated by Bob and Joan Lipsitz who have been involved in the outdoor recreation field since the early 1970s. Since its beginning in 1937, the Double JJ has grown to accommodate 300 guests. Said to be "America's Friendliest Resort" for the young and young-at-heart, guests can participate in activities from dawn 'til dusk. Horseback riding is offered for all ability levels on miles of wooded trails and countryside. Here the beauty of native Michigan comes alive, offering a host of recreational outdoor activities with a high percentage of returning guests year after year.

Address: Box 94 K, Rothbury, Michigan 49452
Telephone: (800) DOUBLEJJ (800-368-2535), (616) 894-4444; fax: (616) 893-5355
E-Mail: info@doublejj.com
Internet: http://www.doublejj.com
Airport: Muskegon, 20 miles; Grand Rapids, 45 miles; private airstrip on ranch
Location: 20 miles north of Muskegon off U.S. 31, 189 miles east of Chicago, 200 miles west of Detroit
Memberships: Appaloosa Horse Association, West Michigan Tourist Association
Medical: Muskegon General Hospital
Conference: 300; 20,000 square feet of conference space
Guest Capacity: 300
Accommodations: Double JJ Ranch—adult-exclusive bunkhouses and lodge rooms; The Back Forty Ranch—family cabins and kids-exclusive tepees, Conestoga wagons, and bunkhouses; and the Thoroughbred Golf Club—hotel and condominiums.
Rates: • $$–$$$. American Plan May through November. Horseback riding and golf packages available. Daily, weekend, midweek, and week packages. Conference and group rates. Holiday packages.
Credit Cards: VISA, MasterCard, Discover
Season: Year-round
Activities: Summer: Resort activities include daily riding with weekly breakfast and steak rides. Individual lessons and clinics. Rides are divided into small groups by experience levels. Rides vary from one to three hours and go out five times per day. Private lake with fishing and boating. Outdoor heated swimming pools, water slide, rope swings, hot tubs, four tennis courts, hiking, rifle and archery ranges, baseball, mini-golf, volleyball, hayrides, campfires, evening entertainment, and more. Eighteen-hole championship golf course. Winter: riding, sleigh rides, dogsledding, snowtubing, and cross-country skiing.
Children's Programs: Extensive children's programs. Ask about the Back Forty Ranch and full-time counselors.
Dining: Three meals per day. All you can eat. Weekly breakfast and steak rides. Full-service bar available.
Entertainment: All sorts of entertainment planned each day. Nightly entertainment, including live bands, DJ dances, staff shows, casinos, and staff-versus-guest volleyball. Professional rodeo each week with guest competitions and games. Hayrides, campfires, game and video room, theme weeks with costume parties.
Summary: Full-service resort ranch with adult, children, and family programs. This ranch will keep you entertained from morning until night. Singles, couples, families, and kids will always feel a part of the Double JJ family. Thoroughbred Golf Club rated 33rd in the nation by *Golf Digest*. Video available. Nearby: Lake Michigan, 10 miles; Silver Lake Sand Dunes, 15 miles; antique shops.

El Rancho Stevens
Gaylord, Michigan

El Rancho Stevens is in northern Michigan on Dixon Lake, known for its cool, refreshing waters and sandy beaches. This ranch was started by "Doc" and Candy Stevens in 1948. Doc had been an automotive engineer and bought the property with the intent of building a Michigan dude ranch. Today, this ranch/lake resort is run by Doc's son, Steve. It encompasses about 1,000 acres with good lakeside access, well-kept lawns, and open pastures. The Stevenses cater to couples and families. Those who enjoy water activities and horseback riding will enjoy El Rancho Stevens.

Address: P.O. Box 495 K, Gaylord, Michigan 49734
Telephone: (517) 732-5090
E-Mail: elrancho@freeway.net
Internet: http://www.elranchostevens.com
Airport: Traverse City, 60 miles; private planes to Gaylord, five miles
Location: 225 miles north of Detroit off I-75, 50 miles south of the famous Mackinaw Bridge, five miles southeast of Gaylord off McCoy Road
Memberships: West Michigan Tourist Association, Michigan Travel & Tourism, Gaylord Convention and Tourism Bureau
Medical: Otsego Memorial Hospital, six miles
Guest Capacity: 100
Accommodations: Two two-story lodges and two one-story lodges with 30 motel-style rooms. Each is comfortable, carpeted, with private bath and double beds. One two-bedroom suite has full bath and living room. No TVs or telephones in rooms.
Rates: • \$–\$\$. Modified American Plan (lunch extra). Children's, holiday, and off-season rates available. Two-night minimum stay.
Credit Cards: VISA, MasterCard, Discover
Season: June through September
Activities: Riding and hiking trails wander through the ranch and onto state lands with forested areas. All rides are on a per-hour basis and divided into beginner, intermediate, and advanced. All guests are guaranteed one ride each day. Rides usually go out on an hourly basis. Two breakfast rides each week. Large indoor riding arena. Heated swimming pool. Full lake activities including paddleboats and small sailboats, waterskiing, fishing, and canoeing. You may bring your own boat if you wish. Softball, archery, and volleyball. Gaylord has become the golf capital of northern Michigan, with many 18-hole golf courses nearby. Tractor hayrides and cookouts.
Children's Programs: Counselors and daily Junior Wrangler programs for kids ages two and up mornings and evenings. Riding, waterskiing, and other activities. Kids may eat with counselors at dinner. Evening entertainment after dinner for children. Kids have a great time with games and arts and crafts. They really love the independence, and so do their parents. Babysitters available (extra).
Dining: Buffet- and family-style. Soup and salad bar. Friendly waitresses tend to your needs. Cookouts and beach barbecues (chicken, ribs, and steaks) are ranch favorites. Breakfast rides. Licensed cocktail lounge in dining room and the Silver Dollar Saloon at the beach. Nonsmoking dining room.
Entertainment: Usually something every night: hayrides, country dancing, sing-alongs with marshmallow roasts. In Corral Capers, guests compete in games like egg-and-spoon races. Recreation room with video games, table tennis, and pool tables.
Summary: Affordable, friendly ranch resort on two-mile-long Dixon Lake. Run by the Stevens family since 1948. Great for families and single parents. Junior Wrangler program for children ages two and up. Some baby-sitting available for kids under age six. This ranch attracts families from lower Michigan, Ohio, Indiana, and Illinois. Indoor 8,500-square-foot riding arena. Nearby: Mackinaw Island and Bridge, Hartwick Pines State Park, canoeing down Ausable River.

Happy Hollow Ranch & Zeemering Farms Ltd.
Howell, Michigan

Ina (pronounced eena) Zeemering bought Happy Hollow Ranch in 1985 to fulfill a lifelong childhood dream. Born in the Netherlands and raised in Grand Rapids, Michigan, Ina went on to the University of Michigan, to law school, and became a judge. In creating Happy Hollow Ranch her desire has been to share her "paradise" with similarly situated professionals who appreciate the symbiotic relationship between people, animals, and nature. Her small, 110-acre retreat is the home to her Arabian breeding farm, her dog Portia (named after the blindfolded woman who holds the scales of justice), four cats, and 13 horses, and serves as a small dude ranch and conference center. It is privately owned and has five miles of riding trails that wander through woods, meadows, and wetlands. The ranch has conference capabilities of approximately 60, and has held seminars and workshops throughout the year. Guests can relax in the bunkhouse setting and walk, hike, ride, pick berries, watch birds, swim, fish, and paddleboat. There is a 120-by-80-foot indoor arena where people can take lessons, hone their riding skills, or just canter in a protected area. Horses are available for both riding and breeding purposes. As Ina says, "Guests can enjoy one of our horses, or bring their own equine companion for their stay."

Address: 4773-4441 Mack Rd., Drawer K, Howell, Michigan 48843
Telephone: (517) 546-3351; fax: (517) 545-5864
E-Mail: inaz@ismi.net
Internet: http://www.zfarms.com
Airport: Detroit Metropolitan, one hour; Lansing, 45 minutes; Flint, 30 minutes
Location: 55 miles northwest of Detroit, 35 miles north of Ann Arbor, 30 miles east of Lansing, 25 miles south of Flint
Memberships: International Arabian Horse Association, Michigan Arabian Horse Association
Medical: McPherson Hospital, seven miles; University of Michigan Hospital, 35 miles
Conference: 60 daily capacity
Guest Capacity: 14 overnight in bunkhouse, six in main house
Accommodations: Bunkhouse-style on second story of the indoor training arena with two full baths is best for groups up to 14. The 2,800-square-foot main house features two lofts with three queen-size beds and two full baths. Large fieldstone fireplace in great room.
Rates: $$. American Plan. Weekend and weekly rates, three-day minimum stay. Ask about horse boarding and training rates.
Credit Cards: None. Personal and traveler's checks accepted.
Season: April through October including Halloween, Christmas, New Year's, Valentine's Day. Special weekly/weekend rates for groups.
Activities: Riding and training. There are no set schedules. Riding program includes unlimited riding. Lessons available at additional cost. Swimming in the spring-fed two-acre lake, spin-fishing, hiking, berry picking (in season). Walking through five miles of trails, woods, pastures, and wetlands. Bird-watching galore. This is a working ranch and there are always things to be done. Ina does a lot of her own chores, and guests may help her or tend to their own horse, grooming and tacking up. Winter: riding and cross-country skiing.
Children's Programs: Best for older children who ride and love horses.
Dining: Breakfast consists of cereals, granola, fruit, bagels, and yogurt. Box lunch or other sandwiches. Dinners are catered by local restaurants and features salads, pastas, grilled meats, and lasagna. All meals included.
Entertainment: On your own. Reading, puzzles, cards, horse videos, TV, and evening strolls. Personal time includes a wide variety of mystery novels.
Summary: Happy Hollow Ranch is for horse enthusiasts seeking uninterrupted and tranquil time with or without horses. Your schedule is your own. Excellent environment for professional women and couples who appreciate beauty, intellectual discussions, and spirituality. Smoke-free environment.

Turkey Creek Ranch
Theodosia, Missouri

Overlooking Bull Shoals Lake in the heart of Ozark Mountain Country is the Edwards' Turkey Creek Ranch. Founded by Dick and Elda Edwards in 1953, it's run today by their oldest son and daughter-in-law, Robert and Loretta. This 700-acre working cattle ranch and lake resort offers affordable family fun with activities that appeal to all ages. Turkey Creek is a lakeside ranch resort geared to families having fun together. Some folks have been returning yearly since 1963.

Address: HC 3, Box 3180 K, Theodosia, Missouri 65761
Telephone: (417) 273-4362
Airport: Springfield, 85 miles
Location: 47 miles east of Branson; 47 miles northwest of Mountain Home, Arkansas
Memberships: Missouri Bull Shoals Lake Association, Ozark Mountain Region; Branson Chamber of Commerce
Awards: Mobil 2 Star
Medical: Baxter County Hospital, Mountain Home; 47 miles
Guest Capacity: 156
Accommodations: There are 24 standard or deluxe cabins and *casitas*. All cabins have kitchens complete with microwaves and full-size appliances, air-conditioning, color TV, carpeted bedrooms, daily newspaper delivered to each cabin in person by son Ryan, screened porch, picnic table, and barbecue grill. Cabin size varies from four- to 10-person capacity. Some cabins have wheelchair access.
Rates: • \$–\$\$. Riding and boat rentals extra. Meals not included.
Credit Cards: None. Personal checks accepted.
Season: Open year-round
Activities: No scheduled activities except daily guided trail rides, approximately one hour, going out several times each day. Hiking trails follow the bridle paths through the forest and along the lake. Lake activities include boating, fishing, waterskiing, and scuba diving. A variety of boats available. Fishing for many types of game and pan fish (bass, crappie, walleye, trout, sunfish, etc.). Resort activities include an indoor heated pool and whirlpool spa, outdoor pool with kiddie pool, tennis, shuffleboard, horseshoes, volleyball, and a golf putting area (golf courses nearby). Ranch activities vary according to time of year and guest experience. Turkey Creek has its own riding horses and herd of Angus/Simmental crossbred beef cattle. Occasionally guests may help with ranch work.
Children's Programs: No formal program. All kids welcomed by Ashley and Ryan (ages 12 and nine). Children are encouraged to participate in activities with their parents. Those too young for trail rides (under age eight) may be led on rides around the resort grounds. There's also a large playground area.
Dining: It is all up to you. Each cabin or *casita* has a fully equipped kitchen plus a picnic table and barbecue grill nearby. A variety of restaurants in the area. Catering for large groups with advance notice—talk to Loretta.
Entertainment: Take your pick—do a little or a lot. The 3,000-square-foot recreation building has two fireplaces, a piano and organ for sing-alongs, indoor heated pool and spa, pool tables, video games, shuffleboard, table tennis, air hockey, and much more. Turkey Creek has some of the best Ozark Mountain scenery to be found.
Summary: Family vacation ranch resort on Bull Shoals Lake in the heart of beautiful Ozark Mountain country, offering a wide selection of ranch and lake activities for all ages and abilities. Great for groups and family reunions. Fishermen, singles, and couples especially enjoy the spring and fall. Nearby: the famous country-music town of Branson, Missouri, with its wide variety of music shows; Silver Dollar City, Shepherd of the Hills, and White Water theme parks; Springfield, Missouri, with Bass Pro Shops Outdoor World Headquarters and Dickerson Park Zoo.

Turkey Creek Ranch, Missouri

63 Ranch
Livingston, Montana

THE DUDE RANCHERS' ASSOCIATION

One of the first dude ranches in the country to be chosen as a National Historic Site, the 63 Ranch is one of the oldest ranches in the business. It's still run by the same family that started it in 1930. At an altitude of 5,600 feet, you listen to the soothing sounds of Mission Creek as it tumbles down its rocky course through the ranch on its way to the Yellowstone River. The 63 offers guests an eye-opening view of what the early West was all about. Enjoy weekly cattle rides and fulfill your childhood dreams of being a cowboy. In July and August the 63 offers an overnight pack trip each week (limited to four guests) into the high country of the Absaroka-Beartooth Wilderness. There's also plenty of riding, fishing, hiking, and Indian lore. Sandra, Bud, their son, Jeff, and Sandra's mother, Jinnie (who founded the ranch with her husband, the late Paul Christensen), know the spirit of old-time dude ranching and welcome guests from all over the United States and many foreign countries.

Address: Box 979 K, Livingston, Montana 59047
Telephone: (406) 222-0570; call for fax
E-Mail: sixty3ranch@mcn.net
Internet: http://www.ranchweb.com/63ranch
Airport: Bozeman, 50 miles; or a small airstrip for private planes, six miles
Location: 12 miles southeast of Livingston
Memberships: The Dude Ranchers' Association, Montana Ranch Vacation Association, Gallatin Outfitters Association
Awards: National Register of Historic Places
Medical: Livingston Hospital, 20 minutes
Conference: Off-season available only by special arrangement
Guest Capacity: 30
Accommodations: Eight comfortable one- to four-bedroom cabins with wonderful log furniture, all different and unique. All have baths and showers; some are heated with gas, others with electricity. Double and twin beds. All arriving guests find in their cabin a cotton bandanna on their pillow, fresh seasonal wildflowers, and the 63 Ranch newspaper. Coin-operated laundry facilities. Pay telephone and soda machine.
Rates: • \$\$–\$\$\$. American Plan. Rates vary depending on the season. Children's and pack-trip rates. One-week minimum stay, Sunday-to-Sunday arrival.
Credit Cards: None. Personal checks, traveler's checks, cash accepted.
Season: Summer: mid-June to mid-September. Winter by special arrangement.
Activities: The 63 is known for its horses and excellent high-country scenic and open-meadow riding. Sidesaddle and Western lessons available. Lessons in arena each Monday for all guests. Picnic and barbecue rides. Blue Ribbon fly-fishing (ask Sandra for her "Montana's First Best Place for Fishing" pamphlet). Ranch pond also stocked with cutthroat trout for children and fly-casting practice. Swimming in a pond (for the courageous), hiking, Sandra's history lesson, homestead ride, and evening nature walk.
Children's Programs: No formal program. Best for children who enjoy riding. Each week is planned around the particular guests who are at the ranch, and children are always included. Recreation room, baby-sitter available. The ranch will teach four-year-olds to ride if they want to learn and go out on trail rides with families.
Dining: Beautiful dining room furnished with Molesworth furniture dating from the 1930s. Hearty ranch cooking with plenty of fresh fruits and vegetables. House specialties are prime rib and Mexican dinners. BYOB.
Entertainment: Sing-alongs, marshmallow roasts at Indian Tepee, square dancing and entertainment in the Ranch Pavilion with old-time cowboy music. Rodeo July 2–4 each year in town, or just peaceful reading and relaxing.
Summary: One of the greatest old-time ranches in North America. Wonderful, classic old-time, historic dude ranch with emphasis on riding. Great for the person who wants to enjoy good horses, scenery, and relaxing! Weekly cattle rides. Some guests stay for two or three weeks. First Montana dude ranch to be listed on the National Register of Historic Places. Fourth of July rodeo, museums. Nearby: historic town of Livingston, Yellowstone National Park, and world-class fly-fishing.

See color photos, page 238.

320 Guest Ranch
Big Sky, Montana

Located in the Gallatin Canyon, not far from the famous year-round resort of Big Sky, is the 320 Guest Ranch. It is situated on the Gallatin River adjacent to the U.S. 191 corridor from Bozeman to Yellowstone National Park and at the mouth of the Buffalo Horn Creek access—gateway to the million-acre Gallatin National Forest which joins Yellowstone. The ranch first hosted guests back in 1905. Today, the ranch is owned by David Brask, who notes, "The folks who truly enjoy the 320 Guest Ranch experience appreciate our proximity to some of Montana's finest natural wonders and our flexible resort ranch spirit. We go out of our way to make it easy for our guests to come and go as they please, fly-fishing, hiking, riding, or traveling to Yellowstone, Bozeman, or Big Sky. The diversity of accommodations—from one-room cabins to three-bedroom log homes—no minimum-stay requirement, and its size allows the ranch to cater to a wide variety of needs from corporate groups, to weddings, to families and couples."

Address: 205 Buffalo Horn Creek, Drawer K, Gallatin Gateway, Montana 59730
Telephone: (800) 243-0320, (406) 995-4283; fax: (406) 995-4694
E-Mail: 320ranch@montana.net
Internet: http://www.gomontana.com/320guestranch.html
Airport: Bozeman, 50 miles
Location: 12 miles south of Big Sky, 36 miles north of West Yellowstone off Highway 191
Memberships: Montana Guest Ranch Association
Awards: AAA 3 Diamond
Medical: Bozeman Hospital, 50 miles; doctor in Big Sky
Conference: Up to 150
Guest Capacity: 200
Accommodations: Accommodations have the creature comforts that you would expect in an upscale facility. Seven three-bedroom log homes, 12 riverfront two-bedroom cabins complete with kitchenettes and fireplaces, and 38 single cabins—some with fireplaces, some with kitchens. All have telephones and cable TV. Daily maid service.
Rates: • $$$. American Plan. Deluxe four- and seven-night Western packages includes everything. Basic ranch package includes lodging and meals. No minimum stay. Arrive any day. Wedding, group, corporate, and winter rates.
Credit Cards: VISA and MasterCard
Season: Summer: Late May to early October; winter: mid-November to mid-April
Activities: Summer: The two main activities are horseback riding and fly-fishing. Six different rides go out each day. One-hour to all-day rides best-suited for beginner to intermediate riders. Ask about the fly-fishing ride to Ramshorn Lake and the Cinnamon Mountain trail ride that offer views of the distant Tetons. The 75-by-200-foot indoor arena hosts rodeos, ropings, and lessons. Anglers enjoy the on-ranch guide service by Big Sky Outfitters for novice to advanced anglers. Fully equipped fly shop. Ask about the Gallatin, Madison, and Yellowstone Rivers for fishing. Hiking, river rafting with local outfitter, and day trips to Yellowstone Park. Winter: cross country and downhill skiing, snowmobiling, sleigh rides.
Children's Programs: Children are welcome. Trail riding begins at age eight. Baby-sitting available. Kids ages six and older are encouraged to participate with parents.
Dining: Full-service restaurant serving breakfast, lunch, and dinner. Western-style, hearty food served. Open to the public. Full bar.
Entertainment: Top local country bands entertain on Thursday nights. Weekly cowboy poet/folk singer. Special requests catered to with advance notice. Rodeos, ropings, and fly-casting demonstrations.
Summary: The 320 Ranch offers a unique resort ranch program with great flexibility. Proximity to top year-round recreational activities. Tremendous variety of upscale accommodations and summer and winter programs. Nearby: Yellowstone National Park and Big Sky Resort.

See color photos, page 239.

B Bar Guest Ranch
Emigrant, Montana

Montana Dude Ranch Association

Like conductors of the world's great symphony orchestras, Maryanne Mott and Herman Warsh have created a ranch that celebrates the wonderful things humans can do when inspiration and knowledge join hands in rich sensitivity. Here they provide each guest who passes through their gates a profound and personal sense of awe, a unique and lasting memory. Reflecting their lifelong interests in philanthropy, community, stewardship, and sustainability, at the B Bar you will find relationships of mutuality rather than exploitation, harmony rather than dominance, listening and looking, doing and learning. As you look to the awe-inspiring mountains, ride among the cattle or wildlife, or taste the fresh food, handpicked each day from the organic garden just outside the main lodge, you'll experience something here to be treasured. The B Bar Ranch can be summed up in one word—incredible!

Address: 818 Tom Miner Creek Road, Drawer K, Emigrant, Montana 59027
Telephone: (406) 848-7523; fax: (406) 848-7793
Airport: Bozeman
Location: 45 miles south of Livingston, 40 minutes from south entrance of Yellowstone National Park
Memberships: Montana Guest Ranch Association, Montana Dude Ranch Association
Conference: 34
Guest Capacity: 34
Accommodations: Six A-frame cabins with sleeping lofts. Each cabin has a covered porch with mountain views, pine furniture, flannel quilts, bathroom with shower, and an embossed surprise. Four rooms in the main lodge, in addition to a spacious living room with beautiful sculptures and paintings by regional artists. Log and leather furniture of the Molesworth tradition. Personal laundry service available.
Rates: $$$$$. American Plan. Seven-day package, Saturday to Saturday. Children's rates.
Credit Cards: None. Personal checks accepted.
Season: Summer: late May through September. Winter: mid-December through February.
Activities: Very flexible program with wide range of choices. This working cattle ranch offers guests the opportunity to observe real Western life. At 6,800 feet the ranch raises natural beef and encourages "work" rides to watch over the cattle herd as well as wildlife. Also tennis lessons, stream fishing, hiking, and outdoor hot tub. Winter: guided cross-country skiing and snowshoeing with instruction available. Some ranch work, including feeding livestock with team and sled. Full winter naturalist program.
Children's Programs: Supervised arena riding and instruction. Children ages eight to 12 must ride with parent; ages 13 and older ride with adults. Fly-fishing with instruction. For younger children there's a wading pool and sandbox in the B Bar's famous garden, books, games, puzzles, wildflower-pressing, and rubber-stamping. Nannies encouraged.
Dining: You won't find fresher food anywhere. The B Bar has an on-staff master organic gardener. Heirloom varieties of garden-grown and greenhouse produce. Ranch-raised natural beef. Home-baked breads and desserts. Campfire cookouts. Special diets and customized menus by request. BYOB.
Entertainment: Spectacular scenery, wildlife, and art—ask about the "The General." Wagon rides, books, video library, and player piano. Naturalist presentations and barn dances with live music.
Summary: One of the great ranches in North America, offering a blend of sophistication, natural wonder, recreation, agriculture, and environmental stewardship. Exclusive bookings available. Tremendous scenery, freshly grown food, comfort, and natural wonder. Special breeds of livestock raised. Smoke-free ranch.

Bear Creek Lodge
Victor, Montana

Roland and Elizabeth Turney's Bear Creek Lodge is a slice of heaven and a piece of paradise. In each edition of my guide I include a handful of properties that don't exactly fit the true ranch description but do serve up exceptional hospitality, beauty, and Western charm. This is one of them. In the majesty of the Bitterroot Mountains, Roland and Elizabeth share their private, intimate lodge with educated, gracious, caring travelers who wish to commune with nature without sacrificing the comforts of modern living. Bear Creek Lodge is exquisite and offers eight rooms for those who come to fly-fish, hike, explore, rest, relax, or maybe do a little horseback riding. Teachers by profession, Roland and Elizabeth have lived in New England; Argentina; Jackson Hole; and Santa Fe, New Mexico. As Elizabeth says, "Our parents taught us how to take care of others; our travels taught us how wonderful it is to be cared for by others." Roland and Elizabeth make dreams come true at Bear Creek Lodge.

Address: 1184 Bear Creek Trail, Drawer K, Victor, Montana 59875
Telephone: (406) 642-3750; fax: (406) 642-6847
E-Mail: info@bear-creek-lodge.com
Internet: http://www.bear-creek-lodge.com
Airport: Missoula; Hamilton for private aircraft
Location: 45 miles south of Missoula, 13 miles north of Hamilton, six miles west of Victor
Memberships: Independent Innkeepers Association, Trout Unlimited
Medical: Hospitals in Hamilton and Missoula
Conference: 16
Guest Capacity: 16
Accommodations: This choice three-story lodge was built in 1991—cozy comfort and rustic elegance describe it best. Eight guest rooms—three upstairs and five downstairs. Large common deck, lawn, lots of pine trees and privacy. Outdoor hot tub. Welcome flowers and daily fresh-baked treats. Exercise room, sauna, billiards table, extensive library.
Rates: • $$$. Includes lodging and all meals with complimentary beverages. Guided fishing and horseback riding extra.
Credit Cards: VISA, MasterCard, Discover
Season: March through December
Activities: Bear Creek Lodge is surrounded by beauty and all the adventure anyone could possibly want. You set your own pace. The Turneys' lodge is a base camp for a host of recreational opportunities in the Bitterroot River Valley. Many come to fly-fish at the lodge on Bear Creek or on the Bitterroot River. The Clark Fork, Rock Creek, Blackfoot, and Big Hole Rivers are also accessible as day trips. Guests enjoy horseback riding from the lodge with a neighboring outfitter. Hiking trails and lodge mountain bikes available.
Children's Programs: Families with children are welcome if they reserve the entire lodge.
Dining: Roland and Elizabeth eat with all the guests together around a large log table. Outstanding meals with great conversation. Elizabeth's cooking has been featured on a PBS special—"Country Inn Cooking." Dinner times are flexible to accommodate anglers. Picnics available for a day on the river or in the mountains. Fruit, cookies, coffee, tea, and cold drinks always available.
Entertainment: Cocktails, wine, and hors d'oeuvres nightly in front of the fire or on the deck. Extensive library with current editions and classic literature. Billiard table, hot tub, sauna, exercise room, satellite TV, and video library.
Summary: World-traveled, well read hosts. Western charm, superb cuisine, privacy. Exquisite hand-hewn log lodge in beautiful private setting with Bear Creek running by. Relaxed atmosphere with no set schedule. Best for adults unless families reserve entire lodge. Excellent for family reunions and business retreats. Fly-fishing, hiking, resting, some horseback riding, and mountain biking.

Beartooth Ranch and JLX
Nye, Montana

THE DUDE RANCHERS' ASSOCIATION

As you drive up Stillwater Canyon on your way to Beartooth Ranch, the magnificent Woodbine Falls signal your arrival, plummeting more than 1,000 feet before striking the river below. As you drive in the ranch gate you'll probably be greeted by Jim and Ellen Langston, your hosts at this wonderful, historic ranch. Jim, a native-born Montanan, is a past president of The Dude Ranchers' Association. Both Jim and Ellen exude the friendly, sincere spirit of the Old West and have friends from around the world who have come to savor and cherish their very special Montana hospitality and ranching goodness. Beartooth Ranch, one of the charter members of The Dude Ranchers' Association, began serving guests in 1904. At 5,061 feet, this 160-acre homesteaded ranch is four miles within the Custer National Forest boundary and adjacent to nearly one million acres of the Absaroka-Beartooth Wilderness Area. Jim and Ellen have been in the dude-ranch business since 1956. Here you'll live the history of Montana and savor the spirit of the Old West. With great fishing, scenic horseback riding, and down-home friendly hospitality, Beartooth Ranch is one of the best.

Address: HC 54, Box 350 K, Nye, Montana 59061
Telephone: (406) 328-6194 or (406) 328-6205; call for fax number
Airport: Billings Logan
Location: 23 miles west of Fishtail, 45 miles south of Columbus, 90 miles southwest of Billings
Memberships: The Dude Ranchers' Association, Montana Outfitters and Guides Association
Medical: Absarokee Medical Clinic, 30 miles; Stillwater Community Hospital, 45 miles; HELP helicopter from Billings, 90 miles
Guest Capacity: 20
Accommodations: 12 log-and-native-rock, heated cabins varying from one to four bedrooms, most with living rooms, some with fireplaces, and all with baths; one two-story lodge with 11 rooms, each with its own bath. Laundry facilities available. Daily maid service.
Rates: \$–\$\$. American Plan. Family and group rates available, one-week minimum stay, Sunday to Sunday.
Credit Cards: American Express, MasterCard, VISA
Season: June to September
Activities: Horseback riding is the main daily activity. Ask Jim and Ellen about their rides to Sioux Charley, Horseman Flat, and Nye Basin. Instruction available. Advanced riders occasionally may help wrangle horses. Excellent fly-fishing in the Stillwater River for rainbow, German brown, and brook trout. Fishing licenses available. Rental equipment available nearby. Pack trips, hiking, and swimming in the ranch pond. Horseshoe-pitching tournaments, volleyball, softball, badminton, table tennis, billiards, and bird-watching.
Children's Programs: Children's supervisors and wranglers arrange treasure hunts on horseback, melodramas, pageants, variety shows, lawn games, crafts, swimming, nature hikes, and trail rides. Children usually interact with families. Baby-sitting available (extra).
Dining: Breakfast is served short-order style. A buffet luncheon is ready at noon. Dinner, served family-style, begins at 6:30 p.m. Western ranch cooking. At 5:30 p.m., guests gather at Happy Hour Circle by the chuck wagon. BYOB. Luncheon rides and steak or hamburger barbecues at the riverside picnic area are held several times a week.
Entertainment: Campfires, singing, evenings in the lodge, and lots of outdoor activity.
Summary: Jim and Ellen Langston's Beartooth Ranch offers excellent sincere Montana hospitality, great fishing, scenic horseback riding, warmth, and kindness. Ask Ellen about the interesting geology here. Nearby: Rodeo of Champions and Festival of Nations in Red Lodge, and Western Days in Billings in mid-June.

Bonanza Creek Country
Martinsdale, Montana

THE DUDE RANCHERS' ASSOCIATION

Montana Dude Ranch Association

June and David Voldseth both grew up in ranch country—June in Wyoming and David right here in Martinsdale, where the Crazy and Castle Mountains reign supreme. David is a fourth-generation cowboy and landowner in this area. He and June bought a portion of David's uncle's ranch and began their own cattle business in 1975. They expanded their operation in 1994 to include guests and built a brand-new guest facility. Today, June and her staff run the guest operation; David and son Vance oversee the cattle business at the headquarters ranch, several miles away. What makes Bonanza Creek special is its riding program, which enables guests to feel the freedom of riding abreast; the small, intimate atmosphere; and the marvelous sweeping views over prime Montana ranch country to the distant, legendary Crazy Mountains. Come to Bonanza Creek to ride, relax, and occasionally work with the cattle.

Address: Lennep Route, Drawer K, Martinsdale, Montana 59053
Telephone: (800) 476-6045, (406) 572-3366; fax: (406) 572-3366
E-Mail: bonanza@3rivers.net
Internet: http://www.avicom.net/bonanza
Airport: Bozeman or Billings (pickup extra)
Location: 90 miles northeast of Bozeman, 130 miles northwest of Billings
Memberships: Montana Dude Ranch Association, The Dude Ranchers' Association
Medical: White Sulphur Springs Hospital, 40 miles
Guest Capacity: eight to 10
Accommodations: Three modern, cedar log cabins. Cowboy cabin sleeps eight (queen bed, single beds in loft, and sofa bed) with kitchen and living room. Indian cabin has queen-size bed, living room sofa bed, and covered porch. Duplex cabin has a bedroom and bath on each side with private entrances and porch. All have wood-burning stoves and bathrooms. Daily maid service.
Rates: • $$$. American Plan. Three- and six-night packages. Children's and off-season rates.
Credit Cards: VISA, MasterCard. Personal checks preferred.
Season: June to early September.
Activities: Riding is the main thing here. The Voldseths have been riding most of their lives—after all, cattle-ranching is their business. Usually two rides a day and an all-day ride once a week. Guests enjoy the wide-open riding opportunities. No head-to-tail riding here. Occasional cattle work, or more if guests request it. Fishing and swimming in two stocked ponds. Mountain bikes available.
Children's Programs: Kids welcome. Riding with groups begins at age six. Baby-sitting available (extra). Younger children not advised.
Dining: Good, hearty ranch cooking and plenty of it. Snacks and drinks always available. BYOB.
Entertainment: No formal entertainment. Evening visiting, stargazing. Listen to the howl of the coyotes. Campfires and evening strolls.
Summary: The Voldseths offer sincere ranch hospitality. Riding is not on trails but on open meadows, wooded hillsides, and mountain slopes. Advanced riders should ask June about opportunities. One couple wrote, "What a wonderful time we had—more stars than we've ever seen, good food, talk, and horses. We'll be back again!" Nearby: Bair Museum in Martinsdale, spa hot springs in White Sulphur Springs.

CB Cattle and Guest Ranch
Cameron, Montana

THE DUDE RANCHERS' ASSOCIATION

Montana Dude Ranch Association

This family-owned cattle ranch is in the famous Madison River Valley. Fly-fishers know this river for its trophy brown and rainbow trout. CB was established in 1971 by Mrs. Cynthia Boomhower of Palm Beach, Florida, who as a young girl fell in love with the West and dude ranching. Today her daughter, Sandy, and son-in-law, Chris, are the hosts. The ranch encompasses 21,000 acres and raises 200 head of Charolais crosses and a small herd of longhorn cattle. At 5,000 feet, the ranch lodge and cabins are situated where Indian Creek comes out of the Madison Range, which rises to 11,000 feet behind the property. You'll have a great feeling of Western nostalgia as you pass under the CB Ranch gate and experience the grandeur of Montana's Big Sky Country.

Address: P.O. Box 146 K, Cameron, Montana 59720 (summer); 4321 Orange Hill, Fallbrook, California 92028 (winter)
Telephone: (406) 682-4954 (summer); (760) 723-1932 (winter); call for fax
Internet: http://www.cbranch.com
Airport: West Yellowstone or Bozeman
Location: 20 miles southeast of Ennis off U.S. 287, 60 miles southwest of Bozeman
Memberships: The Dude Ranchers' Association, Montana Dude Ranch Association, International Women's Fishing Association (IWFA)
Medical: Ennis Hospital
Guest Capacity: 12 to 14
Accommodations: Three large, double log cabins, each with two double beds and a fold-out couch, with private entrances. All cabins have private baths and open fireplaces or one Franklin stove, with fire-starter in a little bucket. Furnished with real Navajo rugs, clip-on reading lights, candles, and fresh flowers. Additional electric heat and air-conditioning (seldom needed) in all cabins.
Rates: $$–$$$. American Plan. One-week minimum stay July and August, Sunday-to-Sunday arrival. Three-day minimum stay mid-June.
Credit Cards: None. Personal checks or cash accepted.
Season: Mid-June to early September
Activities: No planned activities at the CB Ranch. Traditionally, the men fished morning, noon, and night, and the ladies enjoyed horseback riding, walking, and reading. Today more women are fly-fishing, and so they should—fishing in this part of the country is superb. If you wish to float the famous Madison River, Sandy will put you in touch with one of the local guides (extra). You may also fish the waters of the Henry's Fork. Horseback riders are assigned their own horses for the length of their stay. Guided rides go out daily. Because the ranch is small, riding is flexible but always guided. Ask about the Indian Creek Waterfall ride. Weekly lunch ride with barbecue, weather permitting. White-water rafting can be arranged. Most of all, families usually do things together.
Children's Programs: Kiddie wrangler is available. Better for older children, ages 10 and up.
Dining: All meals are prepared fresh. There's always plenty of food. Sandy is proud of the fare—meat, potatoes, and fresh salads. Fresh berries, melons, vegetables, cakes, pies, and Sunday turkey dinner. Occasionally, wine served with dinner. BYOB.
Entertainment: The howls of coyotes at night. You may occasionally see deer, antelope, coyotes, elk, moose, and bear.
Summary: CB is very private, quiet, and relaxing. Here you'll truly feel a part of Montana's Big Sky Country. Many repeat guests. No planned activities. Most come to fly-fish the famous Madison River or the Henry's Fork, ride, or relax. Very occasional cattle work that guests can help with. If you need to be constantly entertained, ride on. Nearby: Yellowstone National Park, Virginia City, Lewis and Clark Caverns. Local rodeos in Ennis.

Boulder River Ranch
McLeod, Montana

THE DUDE RANCHERS' ASSOCIATION

In a rugged mountain valley at 5,050 feet, surrounded by the Absaroka Mountains, Boulder River Ranch is a neat old ranch on the banks of the beautiful Boulder River. This family-owned and -operated ranch is on one of the most productive trout streams in North America. Since 1918, the Aller family has played host to families from around the world who return year after year. Now run by third and fourth generations, Steve and Jeane, together with their children, Reed and Jordan, take only 30 guests at a time and specialize in superb fly-fishing and horseback riding. Experienced and novice anglers will enjoy tremendous fishing in the cold, crystal-clear waters of the Boulder River. Hardy swimmers love the river's natural pools. Riders savor the beautiful high-country and meadow trail rides to abandoned mines, homesteads, and the Indian caves. No matter which month you choose, fisherfolk and riders alike will enjoy every moment with the Allers.

Address: Box 210 K, McLeod, Montana 59052
Telephone: (406) 932-6406; fax: (406) 932-6411
E-Mail: boulderriver@mcn.net
Internet: http://www.boulderriverranch.com
Airport: Billings or Bozeman
Location: 110 miles southwest of Billings, 87 miles southeast of Bozeman, 28 miles south of Big Timber, off I-90 on Highway 298 South
Memberships: The Dude Ranchers' Association, Montana Ranch Vacation Association, American Quarter Horse Association, National Reining Horse Association
Medical: Certified EMT at ranch, emergency room in Big Timber
Conference: Up to 25
Guest Capacity: 30
Accommodations: Most of the 15 individual cabins are arranged in a semicircle around the front lawn just as they have been since 1918; each is comfortable, with fresh wildflowers, daily maid service private bath, and woodstove or fireplace for heat. Each looks to the Absaroka Mountains across the river. Happy hour at the end of the day brings guests onto the front lawn for tale-swapping. It's a nice family arrangement. Laundry facilities available. Cabin girls will do your laundry if you wish (extra).
Rates: • $$. American Plan. Children's and family rates available. Children under age three, free. One-week minimum stay, Sunday to Sunday.
Credit Cards: None. Personal checks and traveler's checks preferred.
Season: June to mid-September
Activities: Fly-fishing, horseback riding, and relaxing are the main activities here. The ranch raises and trains its own quarter horses. Half-day and all-day guided rides to Green Mountain, West Boulder Plateau, and Pruitt Park. Scenic walking, trotting, and some loping, depending on your level of experience. No riding on Sundays. Catch-and-release fly-fishing. Ask about the "Troutman." Boulder River is a haven for families who like to fish. Most fish on their own, but the Allers are always delighted to show novices the ropes. Guides are available (extra). Limited fishing gear available. Hiking. Swimming in the river.
Children's Programs: No structured children's program. Kids begin riding at age four. Kiddie wrangler; stocked pond for swimming and fishing. Baby-sitting on request.
Dining: Scrumptious family-style meals. Ranch-raised beef. Ranch chef will cook your freshly caught pond trout. Once-a-week breakfast rides with famous ranch "fry" bread and weekly steak barbecues. BYOB. Guests may bring their favorite bottle of wine to dinner.
Entertainment: Most guests like to retreat to the porches of their cabins and reminisce about their experiences of the day. There's no formal entertainment at the ranch.
Summary: Delightful, very relaxed, very informal family-owned and -operated ranch on two miles of the Boulder River; large percentage of return guests. Most come to fly-fish and ride. Singles' and couples' weeks. Fly-fishing clinics available on request. Be sure to ask about Jordan's rodeo career. Nearby: Yellowstone National Park, Big Timber Professional Rodeo in June. Nine-hole golf course in Big Timber.

Circle Bar Guest Ranch
Utica, Montana

THE DUDE RANCHERS' ASSOCIATION

Montana Dude Ranch Association

The Circle Bar is located in the heart of "Charlie Russell Country" in central Montana. In operation as a cattle ranch since 1890, the Circle Bar still provides an authentic Western experience, complete with spring and fall cattle drives and routine checking and moving of herds. In 1938 the ranch began accepting guests, and today it blends the Old West with modern conveniences. Situated in the foothills of the Little Belt Mountains and bordered on two sides by the Lewis & Clark National Forest, the terrain for horseback riding is ideal and varied from vast rolling hills to rugged mountain trails. The horses are suited to each individual's ability and chosen for their responsiveness and temperament. The Judith River, which runs through the ranch, provides excellent fishing for brook, cutthroat, brown, and rainbow trout.

Address: HCR 81, P.O. Box 61 K, Utica, Montana 59452
Telephone: (888) 570-0227, (406) 423-5454; fax: (406) 423-5686
E-Mail: cbr@circlebarranch.com
Internet: http://www.circlebarranch.com
Airport: Great Falls
Location: 90 miles south of Great Falls, 13 miles southwest of Utica near Route 87
Memberships: The Dude Ranchers' Association, Montana Dude Ranch Association, Montana Outfitters and Guides Association, Montana Ranch Vacation Association
Medical: All personnel first-aid certified; Central Montana Medical Center in Lewistown, 50 miles.
Conference: 30
Guest Capacity: 35
Accommodations: The nine log cabins all have private baths and are decorated in keeping with their names, such as the Eagles, Buffalo, or Trapper. Most have fireplaces or woodstoves, living rooms, and refrigerators. There are also four large well-appointed suites in the main lodge. The ambiance of the main lodge is Old West, with high ceilings, large oak handmade light fixtures which reflect the spaciousness of the Big Sky Country, and a native-stone fireplace separating the dining and living rooms. Daily maid service. Laundry facilities available.
Rates: $$$. American Plan. Conference, pack-trip, and off-season rates available. Three-night minimum stay. Arrivals any day.
Credit Cards: None. Personal checks or cash accepted.
Season: May to September
Activities: Your stay can be as relaxed and unhurried, or as structured and adventure-packed as you like. Flexible riding program for the accomplished rider or for those who have never ridden. Four-wheel-drive sight-seeing, Elk Refuge wildlife-viewing, and wildflower trips. Middle Fork pack trip with advance notice. Ask about Blackfoot Indian Cave, Hole-in-the-Ground, and Elk Refuge rides. Fishing on the Judith River (some equipment available). Hiking, photography, nature walks, horseshoes, outdoor heated pool, and indoor hot tub. Basketball and volleyball.
Children's Programs: All ages welcome. Unstructured children's activities. Family participation in all ranch happenings is encouraged.
Dining: A hearty breakfast of bacon and ranch-raised eggs, or lighter fare of yogurt, cereal, and fresh-baked cinnamon rolls starts the day. Lunch could include the Mountain Man sandwich and homemade soup. The evening meal can range from enormous rib steaks cooked over a wood fire and served outdoors, to a five-course gourmet meal featuring the chef's specialties of lemon-pepper cod, ranch-raised prime rib, or chicken cordon bleu.
Entertainment: Team-drawn wagon rides, square dances, campfire sing-alongs, pasture golf, horseshoes, basketball and volleyball, Ping-Pong, pool table, hiking, mountain biking (BYO bike), swimming, hot tub, extensive library, solitude.
Summary: Great for families, couples, singles, and groups. Flexible programs. Ask about the sister cattle ranch, R and S Angus, the spring and fall cattle drives in June and October, and the Charlie Russell ride.

Covered Wagon Ranch
Gallatin Gateway, Montana

Montana Dude Ranch Association

In 1982, Vic Benson, the patriarch of this old-time ranch, realized that he was getting on in years. A young fellow by the name of Will King worked at the ranch and expressed his desire to carry on what Vic's family had started. Vic and Will shared their ranch and way of life with guests from all over the United States and Europe, which Will King still carries on. It's a great story of devotion to the spirit of dude ranching and the memory of Vic Benson. Since 1925, the Covered Wagon Ranch has operated as a Western mountain ranch. The ranch is located just off the road in the Gallatin Canyon, three miles from the northwest corner of Yellowstone National Park between the Madison and Gallatin Ranges. Horseback riding is the principal activity. Fly-fishing is equally important to many, along with hiking and relaxing. Vic and Will operate their ranch as if they were entertaining personal guests. As Will says, "Our purpose is to welcome families as though they were our own." Covered Wagon Ranch offers old-time charm and hospitality.

Address: 34035 K Gallatin Road, Gallatin Gateway, Montana 59730
Telephone: (406) 995-4237; call for fax
E-Mail: coveredwagon@gomontana.com
Airport: Bozeman, 60 miles; West Yellowstone, 34 miles. Ranch vehicle will meet guests on arrival at either airport.
Location: 54 miles south of Bozeman and 34 miles north of West Yellowstone on Highway 191
Memberships: Montana Dude Ranch Association
Medical: Bozeman Deaconess Hospital, 54 miles
Conference: 24
Guest Capacity: 24
Accommodations: 10 one- and two-bedroom, nifty old-time log cabins, all with private baths and covered porches, sleep from two to six persons. Accommodations are rustic and very comfortable. A recreation lodge, with fireplace for gathering and relaxing.
Rates: • $$–$$$. Full American Plan. Children's, off-season, and non-riding rates available. Three-night minimum stay. Most stay a week.
Credit Cards: VISA, MasterCard, American Express. Personal checks preferred.
Season: Summer: May to October, winter: February to April
Activities: The program is very relaxed and informal. You set your own schedule. Guests enjoy horseback riding, fly- and spin-fishing, and hiking. Mountain bikes available. Nearby non-ranch activities include white-water rafting, golf, and tennis. In winter, the ranch is open to skiing guests; the upper Gallatin has the most reliable snow in the northern Rockies. Cross-country ski touring and downhill skiing are available nearby in West Yellowstone and Big Sky. Snowcoach trips into Yellowstone National Park by prior arrangement.
Children's Programs: No structured children's program. Children are treated as part of the family. Daily ranch program for kids old enough to ride.
Dining: Hearty ranch cuisine. Family-style meals served in the new 1997 log dining room. BYOB in cabins only.
Entertainment: Evenings include campfire visits to discuss the day's adventures and plans for the coming day. A guitar often encourages song. The recreation hall inspires action with table tennis, pool, and Foosball.
Summary: This is a wonderful little year-round ranch with the old-time dude-ranch spirit, rich in Western hospitality. Located along the Yellowstone Highway only three miles from the northwest corner of Yellowstone National Park and at the confluence of the Taylor Fork and Gallatin Rivers. A wonderful base camp for a host of outdoor adventures during summer and winter. Very small and unassuming.

Crazy Mountain Ranch
Deadrock, Montana

Montana Dude Ranch Association

The Old West comes alive at the one-and-only Crazy Mountain Ranch! Imagination coupled with architectural exactness and the dream of Glenn Patch have created one of the most authentic and unique Western town and guest ranches in North America. Built in 1995 and part of the 18,000-acre ranch, is the replication of an old-time Western town; located at the base of the Crazy Mountains near Livingston, Montana. Today this marvelous town comes alive, offering guests—families, couples, singles, and corporations—one of the most unique Old West experiences available in the United States. Crazy Mountain provides visitors complete privacy and rustic charm, along with myriad outdoor activities including riding, hiking, fishing, sporting clays, and the awesome Crazy Mountains. A trip to Deadrock is an Old West experience second to none.

Address: P.O. Box 343, Clyde Park, Montana 59018
Telephone: (888) 332-3762, (406) 686-4428; fax: (406) 686-4176
E-Mail: crazymount@aol.com
Internet: http://www.patchnet.com/deadrock
Airport: Bozeman, 50 miles; airport pickup available; 4,000-foot airstrip for private aircraft.
Location: 50 miles northeast of Bozeman; 20 miles northeast of Livingston
Memberships: American Quarter Horse Association, Montana Dude Ranch Association, Sporting Clays Association, American Paint Horse Association
Medical: Livingston Clinic, 20 miles
Conference: 40 to 75; conference facilities seat 250
Guest Capacity: 52 to 65
Accommodations: All rooms in the cabins and the three small Old West hotels are graciously appointed and each has a private bath with a combination twin-, queen-, or bunk bed. Everything you see is the "real thing," right down to the claw-foot tubs and antique doorknobs. You can soak all your saddle sores in the creekside hot tub under the stars.
Rates: $$$–$$$$$. American Plan. Children's and group rates available.
Credit Cards: VISA, MasterCard, American Express, Discover
Season: Year-round
Activities: Horseback riding with instruction. Rides vary from scenic trail and group rides to open meadow riding. Ask about the spring cattle drives and branding. Lake and stream fishing, canoeing, mountain biking, and sporting clays. Fall: ask about the pheasant-hunting programs. Winter: snowmobiling, cross-country skiing, ice fishing, sleigh rides, and sledding. Ask about the summer and winter Rendezvous Mountain Camp programs.
Children's Programs: Activities geared for children of all ages. Kids under age seven don't go on trail rides.
Dining: Excellent, wholesome cuisine that can accommodate most special diets. Ranch-raised beef, adults-only gourmet night, and weekly cookouts and lunch rides.
Entertainment: Nightly social hour. Entertainment depends on the season. Usually by special request.
Summary: One of the most unique Western towns/guest ranches in North America. A one-of-a-kind Old West experience second to none with spectacular views! Located on 18,000 private acres in the foothills of the beautiful Crazy Mountains. Great for families, couples, and singles, along with corporations and business groups who wish privacy and an authentic look at the Old West in a Western town setting. Year-round program. Ask about Rendezvous Mountain Camp. Nearby: Livingston, Bozeman, and Yellowstone.

See color photos, pages 240–241.

Diamond J Ranch
Ennis, Montana

THE DUDE RANCHERS' ASSOCIATION

The Diamond J was built in the 1930s as a traditional family-style guest ranch located in the Lee Medcalf Wilderness area overlooking the Madison River Valley, famous for cattle ranching and Blue Ribbon fly-fishing. In 1959 Peter and Jinny Combs were on their way to Alaska and stopped by as guests—the rest is history. Together with son Tim, the Combs family continues to carry on the Western and sporting traditions that have made this part of the country so famous. Today, as in years gone by, the ranch attracts well-traveled families and individuals who appreciate the old-style Montana guest ranch experience. Charlie Russell, one of Montana's most famous personalities once said, "You can get in a car to see what man has made, but you have to get on a horse to see what God has made." Come to ride, fly-fish, hike, wing-shoot, enjoy the camaraderie around a campfire—it's all still here at the Diamond J.

Address: P.O. Box 577 K, Ennis, Montana 59729
Telephone: (406) 682-4867; fax: (406) 682-4106
E-Mail: totalmgt@3rivers.net
Internet: http://www.ranchweb.com/diamondj
Airport: Bozeman, 60 miles; Ennis, 4,800-foot paved airstrip 12 miles away for light aircraft
Location: 14 miles east of Ennis off Highway 287, 60 miles south of Bozeman
Memberships: The Dude Ranchers' Association
Awards: Orvis-endorsed Fly-Fishing and Wing Shooting Lodge
Medical: Ennis Hospital, 12 miles
Conference: 36 (June, September, October)
Guest Capacity: 36
Accommodations: The 10 log cabins are constructed of lodgepole pine. Each has its own rock fireplace, hardwood floors, and hickory furniture and beds. Each cabin features a few Montana big-game trophies, a full bath with separate shower stall, and cast-iron tub. The bedroom-living rooms feature twin-, double-, and king-sized beds; writing desks; and covered front porches, each with a different railing design. No TVs or telephones in cabins.
Rates: • $$$–$$$$$$. American Plan. Children's and seasonal rates. Skeet- and trap-shooting, sporting clays, guided fly-fishing and wing-shooting/waterfowl packages available. July and August, one-week minimum stay, Sunday to Sunday.
Credit Cards: VISA, MasterCard, American Express
Season: June through October
Activities: Schedules are flexible. The ranch emphasizes a relaxed, unstructured atmosphere. Breakfast, half-day, and all-day rides. Ask about the Yellowstone National Park ride. Hiking. Excellent fly-fishing; the ranch is near some of the best Blue Ribbon streams in Montana: the Madison, Gallatin, Jefferson, Beaverhead, and Missouri. Ask about the scenic and white-water fly-fishing trips. Private two-acre lake with rainbow trout. Full-time guides are available. Indoor tennis, mountain-bike trails, heated swimming pool, hot tub. Massage available. Wing-shooting (guns provided) and 10 station sporting-clay course.
Children's Programs: Diamond J takes pride in their kids' horses. Kiddie wrangler and riding instruction. Usually children ride and eat lunches and dinners together. Baby-sitter available on request.
Dining: Meals served family-style in three rooms. At lunch and dinner, children and adults usually eat separately (not mandatory). House specialties: fruit pancakes, tostadas, ham loaf with honey mustard, and steak barbecue. Special diets catered to with advance notice. Cookouts. Prefer no smoking in dining room. A BYOB happy hour.
Entertainment: Square/line dancing, campfire, sing-alongs, games, and an excellent library (ranch subscribes to bestseller list).
Summary: One of the great Montana traditions. Lovely, unstructured, family owned and -operated guest, fly-fishing, and wing-shooting ranch. Very flexible programs; do as much or as little as you wish. Horses for novice and experienced riders, sporting-clay, trap and skeet courses, fly-fishing, scenic and white-water float trips (see write-up in Fly-Fishing section), indoor tennis and heated swimming pool. Fluent Spanish spoken. Orvis-endorsed. Nearby: Yellowstone National Park (70 miles), Museum of the Rockies in Bozeman, historic Virginia City.

See color photos, pages 242–243.

Elkhorn Ranch
Gallatin Gateway, Montana

THE DUDE RANCHERS' ASSOCIATION

Montana Dude Ranch Association

The Elkhorn Ranch is one of the old-time, no-nonsense dude ranches. A ranch steeped in history, it was started in the early 1920s by Ernest and Grace Miller. Located one mile from the northwest corner of Yellowstone Park, Elkhorn is at 7,000 feet in a beautiful valley surrounded by the Gallatin National Forest and the Lee Metcalf Wilderness. It's a gateway to incredible natural beauty, mountain scenery, and loads of wildlife. From ranch headquarters, rides go out in all directions. Since the early days, Elkhorn has been famous for its superb riding program and its dedication to preserving our Western heritage and to uniting families. Today, as in years gone by, the ranch combines old-fashioned Montana-style hospitality, rustic warmth, and natural beauty. At Elkhorn they still serve up the West that used to be.

Address: 33133 Gallatin Road, Drawer K, Gallatin Gateway, Montana 59730
Telephone: (406) 995-4291; call for fax number.
Airport: Bozeman and West Yellowstone
Location: 60 miles south of Bozeman off Highway 191, 30 miles north of the west entrance to Yellowstone Park
Memberships: The Dude Ranchers' Association, Montana Dude Ranch Association
Medical: Bozeman Deaconess Hospital, 60 miles
Conference: 30; June and September
Guest Capacity: 40
Accommodations: 15 original log cabins radiate old-time Western charm and the early spirit of dude ranching. Most were built in the 1930s. Each is set apart from the others and varies in size, sleeping one to eight persons. Most have colorful Hudson Bay foot blankets and comforters; some even have squeaky wooden floors. Most have electric heat in the bathrooms and woodstoves in the sitting areas. All have porches, most covered, and guests spend a good deal of time on them relaxing, reading, reflecting, and visiting. Nightly turn-down. Limited laundry facilities.
Rates: $$–$$$. American Plan. Children's rates available. One-week minimum stay, Sunday to Sunday, in July and August. Shorter stays available in June and September. Ask about the two-week package.
Credit Cards: None. Personal checks or traveler's checks accepted.
Season: Mid-June through September
Activities: This is a Western riding ranch. Beginners will feel just as much at home as do experienced riders. Great emphasis is placed on safety. Each morning at breakfast, guests are signed up individually for the day's riding, which starts at 10 a.m. Groups usually go out with six to eight people and two wranglers. All-day rides three times a week. Fishing rides twice a week. No riding on Sundays. Because there's such a diversity of riding, guests will seldom take the same ride twice. Fly-fishing enthusiasts will enjoy the Madison, Gallatin, and Yellowstone Rivers, all Blue Ribbon trout streams. Swimming in the ranch's spring-fed pond for the brave, and limited hiking. Keep an eye out: this is bear and wolf country.
Children's Program: Excellent all-day children's program. Peanut Butter Mother is with children ages six to 12 all day for dining, riding, and activities. Teenager "Jets," as they're called, ride and eat together. Baby-sitting available with advance notice.
Dining: Home-cooked meals served buffet-style in the main dining room of the central lodge. Children dine at their own table. Weekly breakfast, lunch, and dinner on the trail. BYOB (no liquor in dining room). Guests often have cocktails on their porches with other guests.
Entertainment: Weekly bonfires with singing and marshmallows, square dancing.
Summary: One of the classic, old-time dude ranches with lots of authentic Old Western charm! Emphasis on horseback riding for all ages. Excellent fly-fishing on nearby Blue Ribbon waters. Many guests happily stay two to three weeks.

See color photos, page 244.

G Bar M Ranch
Clyde Park, Montana

THE DUDE RANCHERS' ASSOCIATION

Sage-covered, rolling foothills of the Bridger Mountains are a part of Brackett Creek Valley, home to the G Bar M guest ranch. The Leffingwell family has operated this 3,200-acre cattle ranch since 1900 and has welcomed guests since the early 1930s. This part of the country was made famous by one of North America's early explorers and mountain men, Jim Bridger. The Leffingwells make no bones about it: "We have no golf, no pool, no tennis, and no structured entertainment." At the G Bar M, you can join in the daily activities that are part of this cattle/guest ranch or you can enjoy everything at your own pace. Part of the ranch has been designated as a game reserve; no hunting is allowed. George Leffingwell points out, "We here at the G Bar M think it is important to live in harmony with the land." Eagles, elk, deer, and even hummingbirds are part of the ranch family. While most guests come from the United States, some have come from as far away as Europe, Australia, and other parts of the world.

Address: Box 29, Dept. K, Clyde Park, Montana 59018
Telephone: (406) 686-4423; call for fax number
E-Mail: gbarm@imt.net
Internet: http://www.gbarm.com
Airport: Bozeman
Location: 26 miles northeast of Bozeman off State Highway 86
Memberships: The Dude Ranchers' Association
Medical: Deaconess Hospital in Bozeman, 26 miles
Guest Capacity: 15
Accommodations: Two rustic log cabins (one is actually a log house), both with full bathrooms and hot and cold running water. There are four rooms (three downstairs and one upstairs, called the Family Loft) in the ranch house, with private baths, double and twin beds, and carpeting.
Rates: $$. Full American Plan. Rates include everything, including pickup at airport. Children's rates available. Minimum stay is Sunday to Sunday.
Credit Cards: None. Personal checks accepted.
Season: May through September
Activities: Ranch raises and trains most of their own horses. Your horse is matched to your riding ability. Guests may participate in various kinds of cattle work, mostly herding, changing pastures, or ranch chores like checking fences or placing salt licks for the cattle. Because this is an operating cattle ranch (with around 200 head), you're expected to fit into the varied daily program unless you wish to entertain yourself by reading, hiking, or fishing for part or all of the day. Ranch fishing for rainbow trout in Brackett Creek. Limited fishing gear available.
Children's Programs: Children are parents' responsibility. Best for children ages four and older. Ranch is a wonderful learning experience. Kids may ride with adults.
Dining: Guests, ranch hands, and wranglers all eat together. Beef, pork and vegetables are all ranch-fresh. Mary Leffingwell cooked for years. Be sure to get copies of her *Sage Brush and Snow Drifts* cookbook and *Diamonds in the Snow*, an account of her life growing up in Montana.
Entertainment: No organized entertainment. Occasional colt training, on-the-ground roping, and horseshoeing, but the best is listening to George and Mary tell their "kitchen-table tales" (ranch stories). Once-a-week steak fry.
Summary: Small, working, family-run cattle and horse ranch, with wonderful old-time Montana hospitality. "The coffeepot is always on here," and you're welcomed into the family. Great for families as well as singles and couples. George insists on visiting with all new guests by telephone before they make a reservation, so give him a call. Ranch-raised horses. More open riding than trail riding. Nearby: Yellowstone National Park, 90 miles; Museum of the Rockies; Lewis and Clark Caverns. Ask about the family cookbook.

Flathead Lake Lodge
Bigfork, Montana

THE DUDE RANCHERS' ASSOCIATION

Montana Dude Ranch Association

Flathead Lake Lodge is on the shores of the largest freshwater lake in the West, encompassing 2,000 private acres that border national forest. Written up in *Better Homes & Gardens*, *Sunset*, and *Bon Appetit* magazines and a Mobil 4-Star property, this full-service dude ranch features the best of two worlds. For those who like water, there are all kinds of lake activities. If you'd rather be on horseback than on water skis or in a sailboat, there are plenty of horses and many scenic trails. In northwestern Montana, the lodge is 35 miles from one of nature's greatest wonders: Glacier National Park. Purchased in 1945 by Les Averill, a former airline pilot, and his wife, Ginny, the ranch has been operated by Doug and Maureen Averill, along with their children, since the early 1970s. Together with general manager Kevin Barrows, they make you feel at home. *Travel & Leisure* rated the ranch as the "best do-everything vacation in Montana."

Address: Box 248 K, Bigfork, Montana 59911
Telephone: (406) 837-4391; fax: (406) 837-6977
E-Mail: fll@digisys.net
Internet: http://www.averills.com
Airport: Kalispell
Train: Whitefish, 30 miles
Location: One mile south of Bigfork, 17 miles south of Kalispell
Memberships: The Dude Ranch Association, Montana Dude Ranch Association
Awards: Mobil 4 Star
Medical: Bigfork Medical Center, one mile
Conference: 90, with four meeting rooms. Conference packet and video available.
Guest Capacity: 120
Accommodations: The main lodge is a beauty, with a rock fireplace, dining facility, saloon, and three upper sleeping rooms. The south lodge has 15 rooms, and there are 13 two- and three-bedroom cottages/cabins and two larger deluxe cabins. Everything radiates warmth and charm.
Rates: • $$$–$$$$. American Plan. Children's, corporate, off-season, and convention rates. One-week minimum stay summer season, Sunday to Sunday.
Credit Cards: VISA, MasterCard, American Express. Personal checks preferred.
Season: May through October
Activities: Weekly horseback riding, instruction, and ranch rodeo. Breakfast, lunch, and dinner rides. Five guided hikes each week and wilderness hiking—ask about Jewel Basin. Heated pool right next to Flathead Lake. Four tennis courts. Extensive lake activities and private beach. Sailing (two classic 50-foot sloops), canoeing, lake cruising, waterskiing. Tremendous lake and river fishing for native trout. White-water rafting and float-fishing available.
Children's Programs: Tremendous college staff. Ages four to 12 participate in organized children's program. Baby-sitting for younger kids available. Nature program with arts and crafts. Complete recreation room and games. Kids' overnight camp. Trail rides for kids ages six and older. Kids do everything together. Kids rodeo with parent participation at end of week.
Dining: Social hour each evening in the Saddle Sore Saloon. Enjoy steak barbecues, fresh seafood, even pheasant and quail. Homemade breads and desserts. Kids usually eat together but are welcome to eat with parents.
Entertainment: Campfires with sing-alongs, Western barn dance, guest rodeo with various horse games, team roping with local cowboys, canoe and sailboat races. Evening cruises and volleyball games.
Summary: Fabulous location on 28-mile-long Flathead Lake with horse and children's programs and extensive lake activities. One of the most famous dude ranches in the country. Nearby: Glacier National Park, secluded Jewel Basin hiking area, National Bison Range, and Bigfork Summer Theatre (has featured such musicals as *Oklahoma!*). Be sure to have a huckleberry milkshake at the Dairy Queen. Golf available at 27-hole Eagle Bend Golf Course.

See color photos, page 245.

Hargrave Cattle and Guest Ranch
Marion, Montana

THE DUDE RANCHERS' ASSOCIATION

Montana Dude Ranch Association

I met Leo and Ellen Hargrave in 1989 on one of the most incredible Western events of our time—the Centennial Great Montana Cattle Drive. They were my hosts and ranch outfitters and gave me one of the most wonderful experiences of my life. Our friendship has grown and continues. Today they run a wonderful cattle ranch, offering guests from as far away as South Africa a rich, wholesome, and spirited experience that captures the imaginations of both the young and young-at-heart. Here the cowboy legend is alive—real cattle, real people, and a real sense of what this American way of life is all about. Come to savor the beauty of Montana and enjoy rich hospitality and friendship. Leo, Ellen, and The Hargrave Cattle Ranch are the real thing, with the right stuff!

Address: 300 Thompson River Valley, Dept. K, Marion, Montana 59925
Telephone: (406) 858-2284; fax: (406) 858-2444
E-Mail: hargrave@digisys.net
Internet: http://www.hargraveranch.com
Airport: Kalispell, 48 miles
Location: 40 miles west of Kalispell, off Highway 2 West
Memberships: The Dude Ranch Association, Montana Outfitters and Guides Association, National Cattlemen's Association, America Outdoors, Montana Dude Ranch Association
Medical: Kalispell Regional Hospital, 40 miles; emergency helicopter service available
Guest Capacity: 15
Accommodations: The Stable has a bedroom, loft, fireplace, kitchen, and bath and houses two to six guests. Rooms for two to six people in the main ranch house, Headquarters. Ask about the Chicken House and McGregor cabins, with down comforters on the beds and stained-glass windows. Ask about the 3,000-square-foot Pine Hill four-bedroom luxury home. Ellen likes color and usually plants red petunias and pansies in abundance.
Rates: • $$$. American Plan. Off-season rates. Wilderness pack trips additional. Six-night minimum stay in the summer, Sunday to Saturday.
Credit Cards: VISA, MasterCard. Personal checks preferred.
Season: Year-round, open all holidays
Activities: This is a working ranch where you can be up with the cowboys or sleep in. Spring: newborn calves everywhere. Horsemanship lessons and cattle herding opportunities mix with pleasure and scenic riding on 87,000 acres. The program here is flexible—do as much or as little as you wish. When not riding, guests enjoy hiking, canoeing, fly-fishing, early morning wildlife-viewing trips, roping, skeet- and target-shooting, or day trips to Glacier National Park. Overnight campout at Lost Lake. Ask about summer range riding and herd management. In May, Singles' and Women's Weeks. Spring cattle drives and fall roundups. Winter: call for details.
Children's Programs: Full program July to mid-August. As Ellen says, "We'll teach them about horses, the outdoors, and the Western spirit."
Dining: Western fare and plenty of it. Your hosts enjoy fine food: ranch-raised beef, local lamb and pork, fresh vegetables, and homemade desserts. Happy hours with creative hors d'oeuvres. Local microbrewery beer tasking. BYOB.
Entertainment: Relax in the horse barn over poker or challenge the wrangler to a game of pool. Sign up for massage; weekly cowboy guitarist fireside.
Summary: Leo and Ellen offer one of the truly great Western experiences in America. Small, friendly, real, and lots of personality—great folks sharing a way of life they love and cherish. Hands-on program—do as much or as little as you wish. Featured ranch on VISA television commercial. Nearby: Glacier National Park, National Bison Range.

See color photos, page 246.

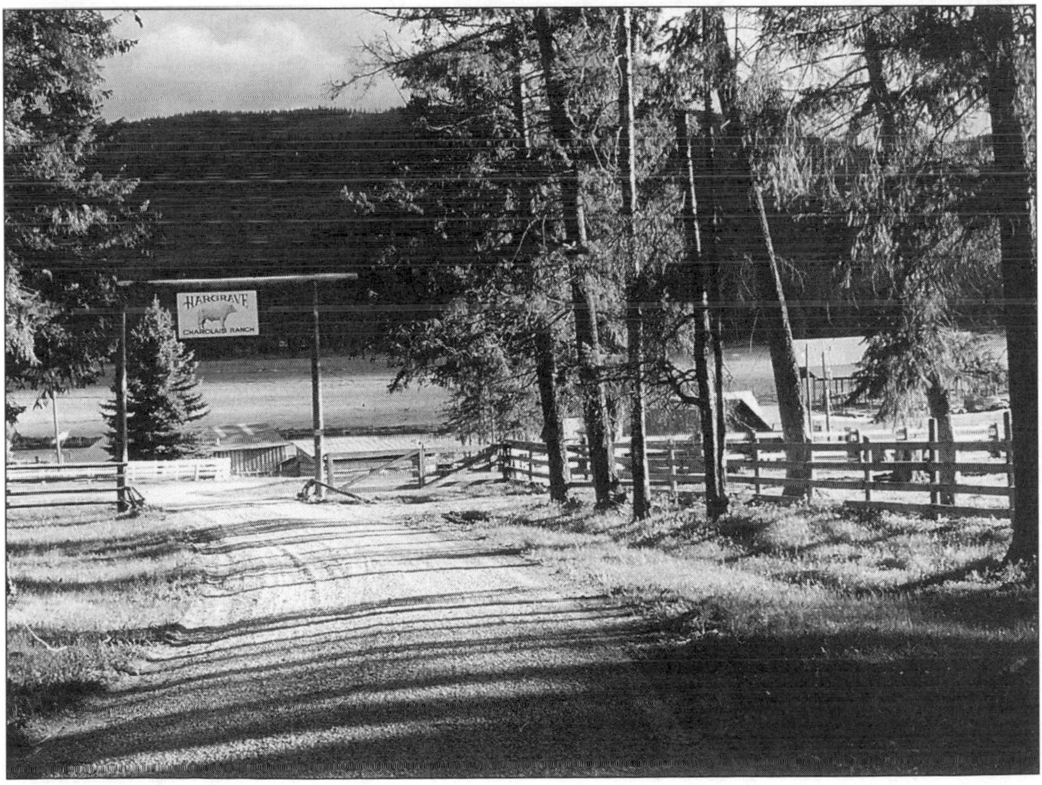
HARGRAVE
CHAROLAIS RANCH

Hawley Mountain Guest Ranch
McLeod, Montana

THE DUDE RANCHERS' ASSOCIATION

Montana Dude Ranch Association

Across the pasture gate you'll see the sawtooth-roofed lodge of Hawley Mountain Guest Ranch, perched on a rocky ledge. Here, surrounded by the beautiful Absaroka-Beartooth Wilderness and high above the cascading upper Boulder River, is a mountaintop retreat that boasts no crowds, no quick trips to tourist spots; just Old West hospitality and informal, relaxed living. Remote Hawley Mountain offers guests the opportunity to view ancient Indian pictographs, fish the Blue Ribbon waters of the upper Boulder River, explore the old ghost town of Independence by truck, or horseback ride to your heart's content. Guests who visit this wilderness hideaway appreciate the views, wildlife, and solitude. Hawley Mountain is relaxed, casual, private, and warmhearted. Be sure to ask about the locations used in the movie *A River Runs Through It*.

Address: P.O. Box 4 K, McLeod, Montana 59052
Telephone: (406) 932-5791; fax: (406) 932-5715 (summer only)
E-Mail: BBlewett@aol.com
Internet: http://www.hawleymountain.com
Airport: Bozeman, 100 miles; or Billings, 120 miles. Round-trip pickup available (extra).
Location: 42 miles south of Big Timber on Highway 298
Memberships: The Dude Ranchers' Association, Montana Dude Ranch Association, Rocky Mountain Elk Foundation
Medical: Pioneer Medical Clinic in Big Timber, 42 miles
Conference: 14
Guest Capacity: 20
Accommodations: Three rustic cabins and four lodge rooms. Absaroka and Beartooth cabins are set back in the pine trees for privacy with full baths, a bedroom with queen-size bed, sleeping loft, and comfortable living room with refrigerator and electric heat. In addition, the Absaroka cabin has a second-story screened-in sleeping porch accessible by ladder. All of the Eagle's Nest's A-frame lodge rooms have private baths with showers, bunk beds, double beds, refrigerators, and balconies overlooking the spectacular Boulder River Valley where the trout pond, horse pasture, and river disappear into the wilderness. Ask about the new Carbonate cabin overlooking the Boulder River with woodburning stove and kitchenette.
Rates: $$$. American Plan. Special June rates, Sunday to Sunday. Four-day minimum.
Credit Cards: None. Personal checks or traveler's checks accepted.
Season: June through September
Activities: As Ellen, the manager, says, "Because we take only 20 guests each week we really try to offer our guests a flexible program. Most come here to enjoy our scenic riding program, the superb fly-fishing (guide and equipment available), and our guided hiking." River rafting on the Yellowstone River and four-wheel-drive trips available too.
Children's Programs: None. Children join adults in all activities. Children should be at least six years old for horseback riding. Baby-sitting available by advance reservation. Fishing pond is a favorite. Be sure to ask Ellen about the kids' overnight stay in one of the authentic Crow Indian tepees.
Dining: Buffet in the lodge dining room offers hearty home-cooked meals with fruit and cookies for snacks. Special diets accommodated. BYOB.
Entertainment: Cookouts and campfires weekly with volleyball, horseshoes, and roping. Country-Western dance lessons weekly at the Road Kill Cafe (26 miles away) during summer months.
Summary: Hawley Mountain is a remote, rustic guest ranch surrounded by the wonders of nature. Great fishing, big views, scenic trail riding, a ghost town, and Indian artifacts. Ask about the Road Kill Cafe. September is adults-only month. Nearby: Yellowstone National Park.

J J J Wilderness Ranch
Augusta, Montana

THE DUDE RANCHERS' ASSOCIATION

Montana Dude Ranch Association

Small, intimate, friendly, and lots of wilderness. Welcome to the JJJ Wilderness Ranch in the heart of some of Montana's most spectacular country. For years the JJJ has welcomed guests from around the globe who not only wanted to get away from it all but also wanted down-home hospitality coupled with the magic of pristine wilderness. Today the JJJ is run by Ernie and Kim Barker, together with their young daughters. In the tradition that Ernie's folks began years ago, the ranch specializes in horseback riding, trout fishing, and hiking, and for those who wish, high-mountain pack trips into the famous Bob Marshall Wilderness—a vast stretch of unspoiled wilderness packed with wildlife and incredible beauty. With young children of their own, Ernie and Kim welcome a wide variety of guests and families with children. Those who have come over the years savor this family's, personal, friendly spirit and love for the great outdoors. In a valley at 5,500 feet in the Rocky Mountain Front Range of the Lewis & Clark National Forest, the JJJ is a slice of heaven and a piece of paradise.

Address: Box 310 K, Augusta, Montana 59410
Telephone: (406) 562-3653; fax: (406) 562-3836
Internet: http://www.triplejranch.com
Airport: Great Falls, 80 miles; free transportation, call for details.
Location: 80 miles west of Great Falls, 25 miles northwest of Augusta at the end of Sun River Canyon Road
Memberships: The Dude Ranchers' Association, Professional Wilderness Outfitters Association, Montana Dude Ranch Association
Medical: Teton Medical Center in Choteau, 45 miles; Great Falls, 80 miles; emergency helicopter available
Guest Capacity: 20
Accommodations: Six cozy cabins, with modern baths, private bedrooms or loft, and spacious living areas, randomly situated among the aspen and pine trees. The lodge lounging area is complete with dining area, fireplace, library, and piano.
Rates: • $$–$$$. American Plan. One-week minimum stay (Sunday to Sunday). Children's and pack-trip rates available.
Credit Cards: None. Personal checks and traveler's checks accepted.
Season: June through mid-September
Activities: The emphasis on horseback riding consists of horsemanship instruction followed by half-day and all-day rides on new trails each day. Also, there are hiking opportunities, guided nontechnical mountain-climbing, and nature hikes to learn to identify wildflowers, trees, and birds. Fly-fishing in the ranch trout ponds or nearby Gibson Lake and Sun River. Guides available. Ask about Mortimer Vista, four miles north of the ranch. Optional overnight pack trips. Also available are five- to eight-day pack trips that take in the incredible beauty and mystique of the Bob Marshall Wilderness. Wildlife includes mountain goats, bighorn sheep, elk, deer, and bear. Swimming in heated pool.
Children's Programs: A full-time kiddie wrangler supervises fun rides and games. Fishing in the stocked ranch ponds, swimming, playground, crafts, nature hikes, and inclusion in ranch chores keep youngsters busy. Horsemanship instruction.
Dining: Good food and plenty of it! Healthy and hearty home-style meals in the main lodge feature homemade goodies and traditional steak barbecues. Vegetarians very welcome. Coffeemaker, small refrigerator in each cabin. BYOB.
Entertainment: Evening outdoor campfires, occasional sing-alongs, tall-tale-telling, and cowboy poetry. Seasonal rodeos in Augusta, Choteau, and Great Falls.
Summary: The Triple J is a small, personal ranch that allows the Barkers to offer a variety of activity options. You'll discover new dimensions to life after spending a week or more. The ranch was included in the May 1985 issue of a *National Geographic* feature article on the Bob Marshall Wilderness. Nearby: Glacier National Park, Plains Indian Museum, Charles Russell Museum, and Lewis & Clark Interpretive Center.

Horse Prairie Ranch
Dillon, Montana

THE DUDE RANCHERS' ASSOCIATION

Montana Dude Ranch Association

The Horse Prairie Ranch is the oldest working cattle ranch in southwest Montana's historic Horse Prairie Valley. The ranch has nearly 7,000 acres and 20,000 acres of public leased range, and is nestled at the foot of the mountains of the Beaverhead National Forest. Owners Ken and Marie Duncan come from the software technology world and purchased the ranch in 1995. They have transformed it into a showplace of Western living and traditions. Their desire is to share with guests authentic ranch life and first-rate accommodations; sincere Western hospitality; and remote, beautiful scenery, including Montana's big-sky sunsets. Adventures include open range riding and working cattle nearly every day, and all the other activities typical of an authentic working cattle and guest ranch. Horse Prairie Ranch is truly a first-rate guest ranch in the last best place.

Address: 3300 Bachelor Mountain Road, Dept. K, Dillon, Montana 59725
Telephone: (888) RANCHLIFE (888-726-2454), (406) 681-3160; fax: (801) 221-7697
E-Mail: hpr@montana.com
Internet: http://www.netvoyage.com/hpr
Airport: Butte, 1½ hours (ranch shuttle service available); Idaho Falls, 2½ hours; Bozeman, 2½ hours
Location: 45 minutes southwest of Dillon, 2½ hours southwest of Bozeman
Memberships: The Dude Ranchers' Association, American Angus Association, American Braunvieh Association, Montana Dude Ranch Association
Medical: Barrett Memorial Hospital, Dillon
Conference: 16; executive telecommuting services
Guest Capacity: 24
Accommodations: Accommodations are excellent, upscale enough to feel pampered without taking away the authenticity of the ranch. Five log cabins include the Lake View with four bedrooms, two baths, large deck, and fireplace; Elk View with three bedrooms, two baths, and woodstove; Aspen View with two bedrooms, one bath, and woodstove; and the Lewis and Clark studio cabins, each with one bedroom and one bath. Cabins have fluffy down comforters and individual washers, dryers, and refrigerators.
Rates: $$$. American Plan. Three-, four- and seven-night stays available. Overnight pack trip included with one-week stays. Group rates available.
Credit Cards: VISA, MasterCard
Season: May through September
Activities: There is no limit to the activities—horseback riding, cattle herding, tending the herd's medical needs, practicing roping, and arena games. The ranch hands are very personable and really enjoy teaching and helping with wrangling skills. You can participate to whatever extent you desire. Canoeing and fly-casting on the ranch's 2½-acre lake (which is stocked with Montana's native west slope cutthroat trout), hiking, mountain biking, and skeet-shooting. For guests whose interests extend beyond the ranch, there is guided fishing nearby on the Blue Ribbon Beaverhead River, Big Hole River, and Clark Canyon Reservoir.
Children's Programs: All children are welcome. Best for kids ages eight and older. Kids are the full responsibility of their parents. Nanny rates available.
Dining: Dining at the Creekside Lodge. Well-presented, hearty, Western-style meals served family-style include ranch-raised natural beef, fresh vegetables, chicken, pasta, and delicious homemade breads and desserts. Breakfast wagon rides. Ask about the berry cobblers. BYOB.
Entertainment: Informal program. Folks are usually pretty tuckered out at the end of the day. Line dancing at the historic Old Red Barn, campfire Indian lore, and arena games.
Summary: Perhaps this best sums up the Horse Prairie Ranch experience: "The most beautiful, awe-inspiring, and magnificent scenery, and the most kind and hospitable people. Thanks for sharing this piece of heaven on earth." One of Montana's oldest cattle ranches is now also one of Montana's great working guest ranches. This ranch has it all—forest, sagebrush, lush meadows, mountains, cattle work, guest ranch activities, and nearby Blue Ribbon fly-fishing. Nearby: Ghost Town of Bannock and Lemhi Pass. History buffs: ask about Lewis and Clark.

See color photos, page 247.

Klick's K Bar L Ranch
Augusta, Montana

THE DUDE RANCHERS' ASSOCIATION

K Bar L is one of the only Western dude ranches that is truly "beyond all roads." To reach the ranch, you take a half-hour jet-boat up Gibson Lake or ride by saddle horse on a scenic mountain trail. If you arrive by jet-boat, you may be picked up in a mule-drawn surrey for a short ride to the ranch. The ranch was founded in 1927 and hosts Dick and Nancy Klick, along with their family, welcome you. The ranch is in a magnificent setting in the confluence of the North and South Forks of the Sun River. Fly-fishing is a stone's throw from your cabin. The ranch's backyard is the 1.5-million-acre Bob Marshall Wilderness Complex. The ranch is like "the hub of a huge wheel," with miles of mountain trails leading out in every direction. The wilderness is all scenic fish-and-game country. One of the highlights is the natural hot-springs pool with a year-round temperature of 86°F—great for total relaxation with stars and fireflies twinkling overhead at night.

Address: Box 287 K, Augusta, Montana 59410
Telephone: (406) 562-3551 (summer); (406) 562-3589 (winter)
Airport: Great Falls, 80 miles; ranch will pick you up (extra)
Location: 75 miles west of Great Falls, 35 miles west of Augusta. If you're driving, be sure to call Nancy or Dick for directions.
Memberships: The Dude Ranchers' Association, Montana Outfitters and Guides
Medical: Great Falls, 75 miles
Conference: 35
Guest Capacity: 35
Accommodations: The main lodge houses the kitchen, dining room, library, and Steinway piano in a comfortable fireside setting. The guest cabins are one, two, and three rooms with rustic furnishings, including Hudson Bay blankets and Navajo rugs, and water piped to your cabin door. A pitcher and washbasin are provided just like in the "good old days." Clean, separate cabins provide hot showers and modern toilet facilities. The ranch hydrosystem provides basic needs so you'll enjoy "roughing it."
Rates: $$–$$$. American Plan. Five-night, six-day minimum stays. Three-day, two-night minimum stay in June and September.
Credit Cards: None. Personal and traveler's checks accepted.
Season: June to mid-September
Activities: The Klick family has a history of great horsemanship and offers each guest his or her own personal saddle horse. As senior family member and founder Emil Klick (born in Montana in 1899) said, "I always broke and rode a good horse." And so the tradition continues. Good fishing starts a few feet from the cabins, or you may follow the stream on foot or horseback. Miles of streams around the ranch, including the North Fork, South Fork, and the Sun, as well as their tributaries. Pack trips are usually planned as loop excursions over trails leading to the Chinese Wall and the Continental Divide.
Children's Program: Children under age six not recommended.
Dining: Good, wholesome food served family-style. As Nancy Klick says, "Never had a complaint." Weekly barbecues. BYOB.
Entertainment: Your choice of horseshoes, sing-alongs, volleyball, and swimming.
Summary: A good piece of advice: reserve early. Others have discovered the Klicks' high-country hideaway. Remote ranch accessible only by saddle horse or jet-boat. Beautiful day rides to Slate Goat, Bear Lake, Pretty Prairie, and Elk Hill. Great for adventurous families, couples, or singles who love the outdoors. Dick and Nancy Klick were born into Western life and, together with their family, share this great Montana tradition. Saddle-horse and mule roundup in June. Nearby: Glacier and Yellowstone National Parks.

See color photos, pages 248–249.

Lake Upsata Guest Ranch
Ovando, Montana

Lake Upsata Guest Ranch overlooks a beautiful spring-fed mountain lake. Situated two hours south of Glacier National Park in the heart of Montana's Big Sky Country, Upsata specializes in wholesome family guest-ranch experiences, fun naturalist programs on wildlife, and Native American excursions. Host and owner Richard Howe grew up in Maine. His business career took him to many big U.S. cities, but in 1991 Richard heeded the call of the West. He wanted his two children, Chavon and Nicholas, to grow up with solid values and Montana's great outdoors in their backyard. The Lake Upsata program balances recreation and education with outdoor experiences in a magnificent lakeside setting. One family wrote, "Thanks for the great time—it was an adventure. Great setting, great staff, great host—we enjoyed it all."

Address: 135 Lake Upsata Road, Drawer K, Ovando, Montana 59854
Telephone: (800) 594-7687, (406) 793-5890; fax: (406) 793-5894
E-Mail: mail@upsata.com
Internet: http://www.upsata.com
Airport: Missoula, 50 miles
Location: 45 miles east of Missoula off Highway 200, north of Mile Marker 38
Memberships: various Chambers of Commerce
Medical: Missoula Hospital, 45 miles
Conference: 24
Guest Capacity: 30
Accommodations: Eight comfortable log cabins with covered porches and two tepees overlooking the lake. The cabins are along the lake among the aspen and evergreen trees. Each cabin has two full-size beds, toilet/shower, vanity, refrigerator, and porch.
Rates: • $$$. American Plan. Children's and off-season rates available. Group rates in spring and fall.
Credit Cards: None. Personal and traveler's checks accepted.
Season: May through September
Activities: A variety of activities include scenic trail-riding, fly-fishing, nature hikes, and mountain biking. The ranch is situated on a mile-long lake with canoe, paddleboat, rowboat, kayaks, dock, swimming beach, and six-person hot tub. Ask about the high-plains, game-range, and wilderness rides. Trips to the Blackfoot River for inner-tubing, Garnet (one of Montana's premier ghost towns), and the Flathead Indian Reservation (with a side trip to the National Bison Range and the People's Cultural Center).
Children's Programs: Half-day supervised programs designed for kids ages five to 15 with wildlife "circle of life" taught by trained naturalists. Crafts program creating "dream catchers" and wildflower-pressing. Kids wrangler. Children trail ride depending on age and ability. Kids' tree house and overnight tepee.
Dining: Hearty food served family-style in the lodge with views of Lake Upsata, Bob Marshall Wilderness, and Swan Range. Lakeside cookouts with steak and chicken. Complimentary beer and wine.
Entertainment: Informal. Wildlife talks or music. Lakeside campfire sing-alongs. Horseshoes, volleyball, and poker nights.
Summary: Family-oriented guest ranch with wonderful views overlooking Lake Upsata. Something for everyone. Variety of recreational activities and wildlife programs. Trips to ghost towns, bison range, and Flathead Indian Reservation. Great for parents who wish to share outdoor experiences with their kids. Nearby: Glacier National Park, National Bison Range, Blackfeet and Flathead Indian Reservations.

Laughing Water Ranch
Fortine, Montana

THE DUDE RANCHERS' ASSOCIATION

Montana Dude Ranch Association

If you're looking for a small, family-owned and -operated guest ranch in the forests of northwest Montana near North America's famous Glacier National Park, you've found it. Since 1988, the Mikitas' Laughing Water Ranch has offered singles, couples, and families a delightful personal ranch experience. You might be interested in knowing that the owners, Ted and Lucy Mikita, fly internationally as pilot and senior flight attendant for Northwest Airlines. As such they both have a keen eye for service, attention to detail, and hospitality. As you drive into their 220-acre ranch you'll pass the barn and a lovely meadow, and up on the rise you'll see the large main ranch house that's their lodge and headquarters. On the "back 40" is where you'll find the log cabins, "Fort Laramie" miniature stockade, and the "Kamp Kootenai" Indian tepee village. The ranch is bordered by the Kootenai National Forest in the Whitefish range of the Rocky Mountains and at one time was operated as a wild Christmas-tree ranch.

Address: P.O. Box 157 K, Deep Creek Road, Fortine, Montana 59918
Telephone: (406) 882-4680; fax: (406) 882-4880
E-Mail: 75604.3151@compuserve.com
Internet: http://www.ourworld.compuserve.com/homepages/lwr
Airport: Kalispell
Location: 50 miles north of Kalispell off Highway 93 near the Canadian border
Memberships: The Dude Ranchers' Association, Montana Dude Ranch Association
Medical: North Valley Hospital in Whitefish, 40 miles; emergency helicopter available
Guest Capacity: 32
Accommodations: Four two-room "suites" in the family's modern, one-story, log-sided, ranch-style house. Rooms vary, with comfortable furnishings, full baths, carpeting, and baseboard heating. Family-style dining room and open-beamed living room with parquet floors. Fully equipped recreation room with fireplace. Deck and Jacuzzi off living room. Four attractive duplex log cabins with single rooms, log furniture, private baths, and porches. Daily maid service.
Rates: • $$–$$$. American Plan. Children's, family, and off-season rates available. Four-day minimum stay.
Season: Summer: May through September
Activities: Two guided two- to four-hour horseback rides each day. Two all-day rides each week, and two-night pack trips during selected weeks. Riding instruction is tailored to individual skill level. Riding through scenic mountainous terrain. Loping in arena only. Fishing in two stocked trout ponds. Fishing gear (basic spinning equipment available), fly-casting, and off-ranch fishing can be arranged with prior notice. Weekly white-water rafting day trips to Glacier National Park and into nearby Canada to see the historic Canadian Mounted Police post.
Children's Programs: Morning activity program the Mikitas call Kamp Kootenai/Fort Laramie, with Native American/Western Cavalry themes. This program includes corral and pony rides, beaded crafts, nature walks, cookouts, Indian culture through sign language, and tepee campouts. At the Fort, kids enjoy guard duty, rifle and pistol practice, tack and horse care and feeding, along with scouting on horseback. Parents and children enjoy the Fort Laramie Pow-wow—a final day at the end of the week with gymkhana horse games, competitions, and dancing.
Dining: Wholesome, hearty ranch cooking. Menus include prime rib, trout fish-fry, huckleberry muffins, and pies. BYOB.
Entertainment: Something is planned each evening. Hayrides, square dances, mountain-man black-powder shoot and tomahawk throw, and volleyball games. Ping-Pong, pool table, game tables, and a large video library with a selection of Westerns, musicals, and classics.
Summary: Small, easygoing, very friendly, low-key, family-operated guest ranch 50 miles from Glacier National Park and 20 miles from the Canadian border. Kamp Kootenai/Fort Laramie for children ages four and up. Adults-only weeks. Ask the Mikitas about their beautiful Christmas wreaths.

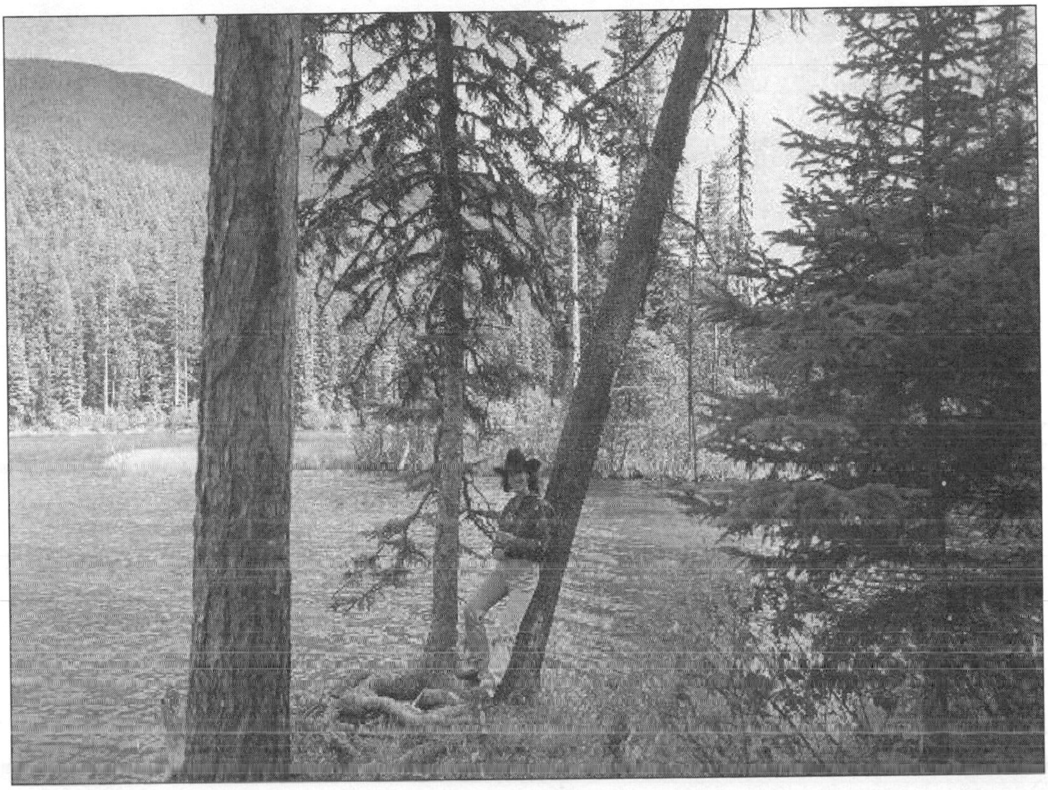

Lazy K Bar Ranch
Big Timber, Montana

THE DUDE RANCHERS' ASSOCIATION

In southern Montana, where the Crazy Mountains pierce blue sky at 11,178 feet, families have returned year after year to one of the West's oldest dude ranches—the Lazy K Bar. This historic ranch lies at the end of an unmarked mountain dirt road at 6,000 feet. For guests, the appeal is the chance to experience authentic old-time ranch life. Established by the Van Cleve family in 1880, the ranch became a founding member of The Dude Ranchers' Association back in 1926. The ranch is run today by Barbara Van Cleve, Tack, and Carol. Barbara's late husband, Spike, was a legendary horseman. Chairman of the board of directors of the Cowboy Hall of Fame, Spike was also a gifted writer and storyteller. Regarding horses, he used to say, "If God had meant man to walk, He would have given him four feet." For spectacular Big Sky scenery, riding on 42,000 private acres, and genuine Montana ranch hospitality, the Lazy K Bar and the Van Cleve family are, indeed, one of a kind.

Address: P.O. Box 550 K, Big Timber, Montana 59011
Telephone: (406) 537-4404; fax: (406) 537-4593
E-Mail: kirby@mcn.net
Internet: http://www.mcn.net/~kirby/lazykbar.htm
Airport: Bozeman or Billings; Big Timber Airport will accommodate small private jets.
Location: 25 miles northwest of Big Timber off U.S. 191 North, 85 miles northeast of Bozeman, 100 miles west of Billings
Memberships: The Dude Ranchers' Association, Montana Ranch Vacation Association
Medical: Big Timber Clinic, 25 miles
Guest Capacity: 35
Accommodations: 19 hand-hewn one- to four-bedroom log cabins built between 1922 and 1926 have rustic but cozy Western charm. Most have living rooms. All have fireplaces or woodstoves, views of the mountains, and names like Palmer, Miles, Ross-Lewin, and Stockade. Two are without baths. Wonderful old log main lodge with 1880 Brunswick billiards table. Personal laundry service and coin-operated machines available.
Rates: • \$–\$\$. American Plan. Rates vary with size and type of cabin and number of occupants. Special rates for children under age six. References required. One-week minimum stay. Arrival any day except Sunday.
Credit Cards: None. Personal checks always accepted.
Season: June 23 through Labor Day
Activities: Unlimited riding, usually at a leisurely pace (walking and jogging), through high alpine country or open rangeland. Morning, afternoon, and all-day rides every day except Sunday. Overnight rides on request. Guests may help with cattle and ranch work when it's there to be done. Mountain streams and lake fishing (kitchen will cook your catch), hiking, swimming pool (unheated but refreshing). No organized activities except Saturday night square dance, weekly campfire dinner, and Sunday morning campfire breakfast.
Children's Programs: Wrangler for children ages six to 12. Ranch requests parents to bring a nanny for children under age six.
Dining: Milk, cheese, butter, and meat are all fresh from the ranch. Children eat dinner with their wrangler. Guests may drink and entertain in their own cabins. Meals are served family-style.
Entertainment: Vintage 1880s grand piano, billiards table, extensive and unusual library, occasional slide and talent shows, local rodeos. Nearby cowboy poet gathering each August.
Summary: One of the country's most historic and oldest working dude ranches. Not open to the general public—references requested. This is one of the granddaddies of dude ranching. If you need a program director and an amenity basket, ride on! Ranch store. Nearby: Trips to Yellowstone Park, ghost towns, Indian reservation, Hutterite colony, Custer Battlefield, Lewis and Clark Caverns. Be sure to ask one of the Van Cleves about *A Day Late and A Dollar Short* and *Forty Years' Gatherin's*, books written by their late father, Spike Van Cleve.

Nine Quarter Circle Ranch
Gallatin Gateway, Montana

THE DUDE RANCHERS' ASSOCIATION

Montana Dude Ranch Association

Since 1946, from early June to mid-September, the Nine Quarter Circle Ranch has been doing what it does best—welcoming families. High in the Montana Rockies, in its own secluded mountain valley, the ranch is seven miles from the northwest corner of Yellowstone National Park. There's a five-mile drive up a winding, scenic, dirt road until the ranch is visible. Taylor Fork, a fly-fishing river, runs through the ranch, and most of the log structures overlook the green, grassy meadows with the striking mountain peaks in the distance. One of Montana's most famous, the ranch is run by Kim and Kelly Kelsey and their two young sons, Konnor and Kameron, and daughter, Kyleen. Kim and Kelly are the son and daughter-in-law of the founders, Howard and Martha Kelsey. As the Kelseys say, "Two things can never change or end, the goodness of nature and man's love for a friend." You'll find both here.

Address: 5000 Taylor Fork Road, Box K, Gallatin Gateway, Montana 59730
Telephone: (406) 995-4276
Internet: http://www.ninequartercircle.com
Airport: Bozeman or the ranch airstrip. Contact ranch for airstrip fact sheet.
Location: 60 miles south of Bozeman
Memberships: The Dude Ranchers' Association, Montana Dude Ranch Association
Medical: Bozeman Deaconess Hospital, 60 miles
Conference: 75; off-season only
Guest Capacity: 75
Accommodations: 20 one-bedroom to four-bedroom log cabins are furnished with log forest furniture and hand-sewn quilts made at the ranch. Woodstoves and porches. Most of the cabins are named after guests, for example, Hubbards' Cupboard and Wihtol's Wickiup. All cabins have private or family baths. The main lodge has a huge rock fireplace. The Kelseys have a clever "Medallion" award board for guests who have returned year after year; it's hanging in the dining room. Some guests have medals representing over 30 years. Guest laundry facilities.
Rates: • $$–$$$. American Plan. Children's and off-season rates available. Minimum one-week stay policy, usually Sunday to Sunday. Fall: three-night minimum stay.
Credit Cards: None. Personal or traveler's checks accepted.
Season: Mid-June through mid-September
Activities: Riding, fly-fishing, hiking, and wildlife viewing. Plenty of horses. The ranch raises and trains over 120 Appaloosas. Four or five rides, ranging from kiddie rides to advanced rides daily, go to vistas like Inspiration Point, Sunken Forest, and Alp Basin. Two all-day rides and an overnight pack trip go out weekly, including the Kelsey Killer "for those who want a real thrill." Great fly-fishing in the Gallatin River, east of Taylor Fork (which runs through the ranch), with the ranch fishing guide. Individualized instruction and local fishing trips available. Stocked trout-pond for casting and kids' catch-and-release fishing. Limited loaner fly-fishing rods and retail fishing shop on ranch. A spring-fed "swimming pool" for hardy swimmers.
Children's Programs: Full program for kids ages two to 10. Kiddie wrangler. Walking-led rides for kids ages five and under around ranch pasture. Playground and playroom. Weekly kids' picnic. Child supervision is provided during the morning and afternoon rides, as well as lunch and dinner. Kids love all the bunnies!
Dining: Children and teens eat early while parents enjoy happy hour. BYOB. Meals are home-cooked and family-style. Weekly barbecues and cookouts.
Entertainment: Square dancing, hayrides, weekly Western movies, volleyball, softball, and games on horseback (a big hit with the kids).
Summary: Wonderful family-run ranch for families throughout the summer. Adults-only in the fall. Great riding and fly-fishing. Ideal for young families with kids two to 15 and for grandparents, too. Appaloosas bred and trained on the ranch. Ask about the fall Bugle Rides! Private airstrip. Ranch store. Nearby: Yellowstone National Park, Museum of the Rockies in the Western college town of Bozeman.

See color photos, pages 254–255.

Lone Mountain Ranch
Big Sky, Montana

Montana Dude Ranch Association

Lone Mountain Ranch is one of the country's premier, year-round, family-run guest ranches with a unique and very strong naturalist program. What makes this ranch so special is that it offers people from around the world the opportunity to discover nature and enjoy first-rate guest-ranching in the summer, a world-class cross-country skiing program in the winter, and year-round fly-fishing. The ranch is in Montana's famous Gallatin Canyon, just down the road from Chet Huntley's Big Sky Ski and Summer Resort and Yellowstone National Park. Lone Mountain's naturalist program is one of the things that makes the ranch so famous. Throughout each week, naturalists lead hikes to teach visitors about the Yellowstone area's spectacular natural wonders. Activities are varied, including spotting soaring eagles, identifying wildflowers, banding birds, learning about geology or old Indian trails, taking early-morning trips to hear bugling elk, and visiting Yellowstone. Whether you're riding, hiking, fishing, skiing, or just daydreaming, the Lone Mountain crew will show you Montana's best.

Address: P.O. Box 160069 K, Big Sky, Montana 59716
Telephone: (800) 514-4644, (406) 995-4644; fax: (406) 995-4670
E-Mail: lmr@lmranch.com
Internet: http://www.lmranch.com
Airport: Bozeman
Location: 40 miles south of Bozeman off Highway 191
Memberships: Greater Yellowstone Coalition, Montana Dude Ranch Association, Cross-Country Ski Area Association.
Awards: *Hideaway Report, Family Circle, Snow Country*
Medical: Bozeman Deaconess Hospital, 40 miles
Conference: 50
Guest Capacity: 80
Accommodations: 24 well-maintained, fully insulated, one- and two-bedroom log cabins (each one sleeps two to nine) and luxury six-bedroom Ridge Top Lodge. Each features comfortable beds, electric heat, bathrooms with tub/shower, and a rock fireplace or woodstove. The cozy cabins are close to the clear mountain stream that winds through the property. All have front porches for relaxing.
Rates: • \$\$\$–\$\$\$\$. American Plan. Children under age two stay free (ask about nanny rates). Special package rates. Normally, minimum one-week stay, Sunday to Sunday.
Credit Cards: VISA, MasterCard, Discover
Season: Summer: late May to mid-October; winter: early December to early April
Activities: Naturalist programs, fly-fishing, riding, hiking, and relaxing are the main activities. Riding instruction, with usually fewer than eight on a ride. Exceptional fly-fishing (see Fly-Fishing section for special fishing packages). Tennis, swimming, white-water rafting, golf, rock-climbing, and scenic tram ride nearby. In winter, the ranch offers cross-country skiing vacations and exciting winter experiences (see Cross-Country Skiing section). Outdoor whirlpool and massage.
Children's Programs: Extensive program for ages four to 12 and teens focusing on nature, building confidence, adventure, and fun! Six experienced counselors from after-breakfast to after-dinner. Nannies encouraged for kids under age four.
Dining: Breakfast and lunch buffet-style. Dinner menu features seven entrées that change daily. Cookouts. Special diets catered to. Restaurant open to the public on a limited basis. Full bar. No smoking policy.
Entertainment: Informative and entertaining nightly programs.
Summary: Excellent, year-round guest ranch with world-class naturalist program and excellent children's program. Year-round fly-fishing with guides and instruction. Great for spring and fall conferences. Video of summer and winter programs available. September and October best for adults with kids back in school. Check the ranch's 100-page Internet site!

See color photos, pages 250–251.

Mountain Sky Guest Ranch
Bozeman, Montana

THE DUDE RANCHERS' ASSOCIATION

Montana Dude Ranch Association

Mountain Sky goes way back to the early days of dude ranching. Originally it was the famed Ox Yoke Ranch, run by an old Montana family. Today, under the ownership of Alan and Mary Brutger, the ranch has guests hailing from around the globe. Alan, who has owned and operated hotels in the past, has succeeded in blending the competence and service customarily expected in a fine hotel with the casualness and sincerity of a Western ranch. Mountain Sky Ranch has undergone extensive renovation and has emerged as a premier ranch. It's in the magnificent Paradise Valley, home of the famous Yellowstone River. Just as in the early days, great emphasis is placed on the family. The staff go out of their way to ensure that both young and the young-at-heart are happy and having one of the greatest experiences of their lives. Mountain Sky offers outstanding scenery; clean, fresh air; tranquility; lovely accommodations; and fine dining. At this ranch, the "Sky's" the limit.

Address: Box 1128 K, Bozeman, Montana 59715
Telephone: (800) 548-3392, (406) 587-1244; fax: (406) 587-3977
E-Mail: mountainsky@mcn.net
Internet: http://www.ranchweb.com/mountainsky
Airport: Bozeman
Location: 60 miles southeast of Bozeman, 30 miles south of Livingston
Memberships: The Dude Ranchers' Association, Montana Dude Ranch Association
Awards: AAA 4 Diamond
Medical: Livingston Clinic, 30 miles; Bozeman Deaconess Hospital, 60 miles
Conference: 75 (off-season only), conference package available
Guest Capacity: 75
Accommodations: 27 guest cabins, some that sleep up to seven, modern baths (with bathrobes), large picture windows, and sitting rooms. The older, more rustic cabins have been preserved, keeping the Old West charm with stone fireplaces or wood-burning stoves, pine furniture, and small front decks. All of the cabins have inviting front porches with hanging flower baskets. A bowl of fresh fruit is brought to each cabin daily. Yellowstone City, the main lodge, radiates warmth and comfort with three stone fireplaces, a hand-hewn-trussed ceiling, and braided rugs. It has a lounge, intimate bar, dining room, and for those who are musically inclined, a Yamaha grand piano.
Rates: • $$$–$$$$$. American Plan. Children's, corporate, and meeting rates. One-week minimum stay, Sunday to Sunday.
Credit Cards: VISA, MasterCard. Personal checks preferred.
Season: Mid-May to mid-October
Activities: Extensive riding program. Rides go out daily, except Sunday. Swimming in heated pool. Whirlpool and sauna. Guided nature hikes. Two tennis courts. Fishing on the Yellowstone River with guides available. Fishing on the ranch in a stocked trout-pond. Big Creek is minutes from your cabin door.
Children's Programs: Exceptional children's program. Kiddie wrangler, kids' cookouts and meals, hiking, swimming, fishing. Children can eat separately. Outstanding all-around program.
Dining: The food . . . wow! Gourmet, five-course dinners Tuesday and Saturday nights, featuring such favorites as poached salmon or rack of lamb, with fine wine. Hearty breakfasts; buffet-style lunch. Poolside barbecues. Children's meals with counselor are available. Special diets catered to. Full bar.
Entertainment: Evening country-Western dancing and folk-singing in front of the fire. Light, relaxing music with the twice-weekly gourmet dinners. Saturday ranch "shodeos." Volleyball, billiards. Monday night get-acquainted softball. Plenty of spots to curl up in and snooze or read a favorite book.
Summary: Excellent historic old-time ranch with superb children's program and fine dining. One of Kilgore's "Best of the Best." Excellent fly-fishing and horseback riding. River rafting on the Yellowstone River. Nearby: Yellowstone National Park, 30 miles.

See color photos, pages 252–253.

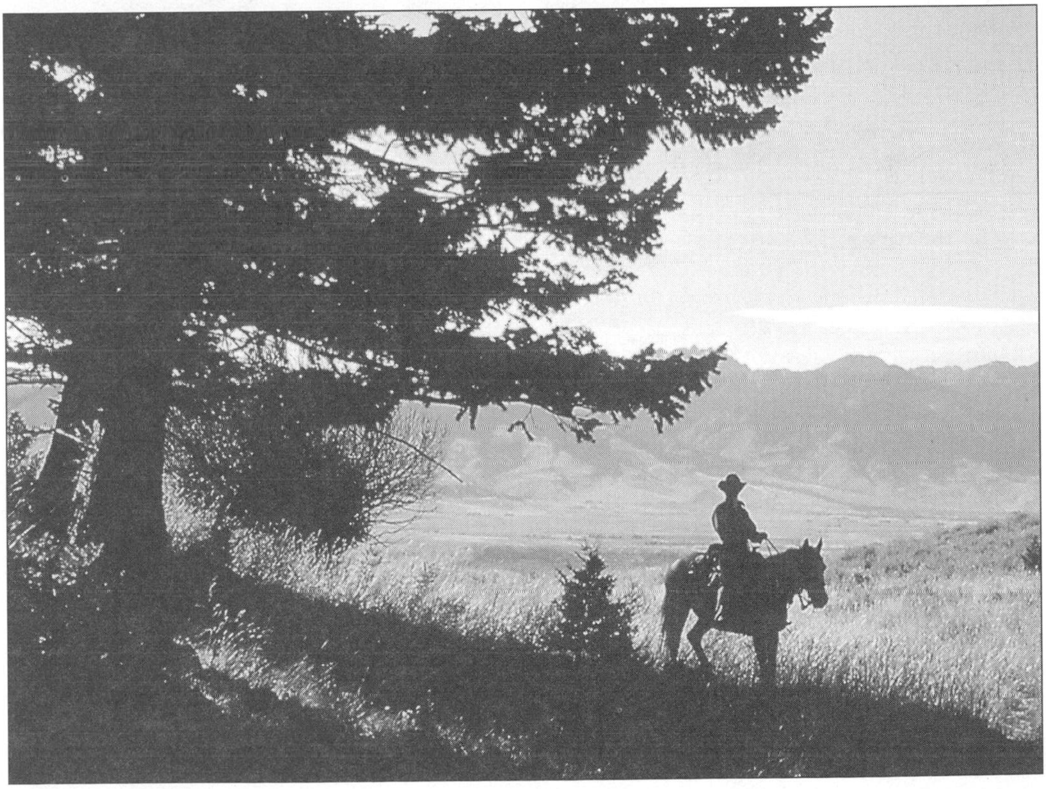

Parade Rest Ranch
West Yellowstone, Montana

Parade Rest Ranch is in the heart of some of North America's best fly-fishing. With Grayling Creek literally at the back door and Blue Ribbon trout streams surrounding it, Parade Rest offers a parade of outdoor activities, natural beauty, and, for those so inclined, lots of rest. There's no timetable or regimented activity list. Your time is your own, and you may do as much or as little as you wish. Life at Parade Rest is informal. The dress code is whatever's comfortable; for the most part, that means an old pair of jeans. Mornings and evenings are cool, with midday temperatures in the mid- to high 80s. Parade Rest Ranch is a small dude/fly-fishing ranch run the old-fashioned way.

Address: 7979 Grayling Creek Road, Drawer K, West Yellowstone, Montana 59758
Telephone: (800) 753-5934 (summer), (406) 646-7217; fax: (406) 646-7202
E-Mail: paraderest@wyellowstone.com
Internet: http://www.yellowstone-natl-park.com/parade.htm
Airport: West Yellowstone, or Gallatin Field at Bozeman; also, commuter flights from Salt Lake City to West Yellowstone
Location: Eight miles northwest of Yellowstone, 90 miles south of Bozeman off Highway 191
Medical: Yellowstone Medical Clinic
Conference: 60
Guest Capacity: 60
Accommodations: 15 turn-of-the-century log cabins with one to four bedrooms. All are named after famous fishing rivers nearby. Ask Pam about the Homestead cabin and her favorite Grayling single. All have porches, wood-burning stoves, full baths, and comfortable beds; the newest cabin is three-story Aspen North. Several are along Grayling Creek. Nightly turn-down service. The Gallatin Lodge is a happy gathering spot for reading, visiting, playing games, and listening to music.
Rates: • $$–$$. Full American Plan. Children's, corporate, off-season, and fly-fishing guide rates available.
Credit Cards: VISA, MasterCard
Season: Mid-May through September
Activities: Very few areas in the country offer such a diversity of fine fishing. Through the ranch flows 1½ miles of Grayling Creek, an excellent fly-fishing stream. Within minutes are the Madison, Gallatin, Firehole, and Gibbon. Full guide service is available. Just let Pam know what you'd like to do and she'll arrange it for you. Also, ask her about the three-day fly-fishing schools. Parade Rest is well known by all the local guides. Horseback riding is geared to your desires. Rides are accompanied by a wrangler and vary from an hour to all day. White-water and scenic raft trips. Six-person hot tub outside Gallatin Lodge overlooking Grayling Creek.
Children's Programs: No special programs. Children are welcome. Kids won't have enough time in the day to do everything they would like. Children are parents' responsibility.
Dining: Even if you're late from your fishing excursion, dinner will be waiting for you and your guide. The warm, friendly atmosphere is matched by great, hearty ranch cooking. Packed lunches are available to those wishing to ride, fish, raft, or explore all day. All meals are all-you-can-eat and served buffet-style in a central dining room. BYOB.
Entertainment: Nothing special. Many of the diehard fishermen eat dinner, then go back out for more fishing. Cookouts on Monday and Friday nights. Western cookouts are held Monday and Friday evenings. You may ride by horseback or on a horse-drawn wagon to the cookout site overlooking Hebgen Lake. Volleyball, basketball, horseshoes, and mountain bikes.
Summary: Great fishing, hearty food, a relaxed atmosphere. Sincere Western ranch hospitality. Nearby: Yellowstone National Park, 10 miles.

Pine Butte Guest Ranch
Choteau, Montana

THE DUDE RANCHERS' ASSOCIATION

Montana Dude Ranch Association

Pine Butte Guest Ranch is the former Circle 8 Guest Ranch that was privately owned before the Nature Conservancy took it over in 1978. The ranch is surrounded by wilderness—18,000 acres managed by the Conservancy and an additional 1-million-plus acres in the Bob Marshall Wilderness, one of the largest wilderness expanses in the continental United States. The Pine Butte Swamp, adjacent to the ranch, is one of the largest wetland complexes along the eastern slope of the Rockies. Also, it happens to be one of the last grizzly-bear strongholds in the lower 48 states. The ranch hosts a variety of nature adventures. Each spring and fall there are week-long custom nature tours and workshops led by regional experts. This is a ranch for those who love to hike and commune with nature. Pine Butte offers one of the finest naturalist programs of any guest ranch in North America.

Address: HC 58, Box 34C, Dept. K, Choteau, Montana 59422
Telephone: (406) 466-2158; fax: (406) 466-5462
E-Mail: pbuttegr@3rivers.net
Internet: http://www@tnc.org
Airport: Great Falls, 90 miles
Location: 90 miles northwest of Great Falls, 27 miles west of Choteau off Highway 89
Memberships: The Dude Ranchers' Association, Nature Conservancy, Montana Dude Ranch Association
Medical: Teton County Hospital, 27 miles
Conference: 24
Guest Capacity: 24
Accommodations: 10 rustic cabins and two lodge rooms. The cabins are set among the aspens, cottonwoods, and firs that line the South Fork of the Teton River. Built of native stone and wood, each cabin is complete with fireplace, private full bath, and hand-made hardwood furniture. The central lodge, with its huge fireplace and homey front porch, provides a perfect spot for guests to gather and get acquainted.
Rates: $$$. American Plan. Children's and off-season rates available. Group rates in spring and fall. One-week minimum stay, Sunday to Sunday. Two-night minimum stay in spring and fall.
Credit Cards: VISA, MasterCard, American Express
Season: May through September
Activities: At Pine Butte, a traditional Western guest-ranch atmosphere is combined with an in-depth natural-history program available to guests interested in furthering their knowledge of the outdoors. During summer, a full-time naturalist conducts daily treks that focus on local plants, animals, geology, and paleontology, including weekly visits to the Egg Mountain dinosaur site. Enjoy fishing and a heated outdoor swimming pool. Rides go out twice a day with a wrangler and last two to four hours. All-day rides, breakfast rides, and steak-fry rides go out weekly.
Children's Programs: None. Children under age eight not recommended. Ask about the summertime Schoolhouse Nature program for children.
Dining: Family-style meals served in the lodge dining room, featuring healthy food (homemade soups, breads, and pastries) presented with simple grace. BYOB.
Entertainment: Weekly square dance; slide shows and lectures four to five evenings, along with a weekly evening wildlife-watch.
Summary: Marvelous guest ranch for those who love to hike, commune with nature, and ride. Excellent natural-history tours with naturalists and workshops include birding, mammal-tracking, nature photography, paleontology (dinosaur dig), and wildflower identification. Ask about the spring and fall Montana grizzly-bear workshop. Nearby: Glacier National Park.

RJR Ranch
Eureka, Montana

Montana Dude Ranch Association

The RJR Ranch combines the best of three worlds in the northwest corner of Montana—fly-fishing, natural horsemanship, and platform tennis, and not necessarily in that order. In 1980 the ranch was built as an exclusive private family hideaway for entertaining family members, friends, and corporate colleagues. In 1993, Dick and Gail Reilly bought this 110-acre private mountain paradise and created the first Western guest ranch with platform tennis. As Dick says, "Why not? I've played this wonderful game most of my life and we've found that many of our fly-fishing guests who already have great hand-eye coordination, and tennis players who love the outdoors anyway, really enjoy the camaraderie and excitement here with our Big Sky Montana views." Dick (who has built platform tennis courts around the world) and Gail share their mountain magic with all kinds—from Davis Cup tennis players to those who simply share their love of the outdoors and adventure. Serve, cast, rest, hike, or ride—the Reilly's RJR Ranch is all about natural beauty and fun.

Address: 4005 Highway 93 South, Eureka, Montana 59917
Telephone: (888) 563-9012, (406) 889-3395; fax: (406) 889-3829
E-Mail: ranch@platformtennis.com
Internet: http://www.platformtennis.com/rjrranch.html
Airport: Kalispell, 65 miles
Location: 50 miles north of Whitefish, 65 miles north of Kalispell
Memberships: Montana Dude Ranch Association
Medical: Hospital in Whitefish, 50 miles
Guest Capacity: 16
Accommodations: Two bedrooms upstairs in the main lodge with shared bath. Connected to the lodge through an enclosed breezeway is a two-bedroom suite with livingroom, stone fireplace, sauna, and decks. A separate two-story cabin has two bedrooms upstairs and one downstairs. The Top Hand Cabin-home sleeps six with fireplaces, deck, and grass patio. The Chuck Wagon (down the hill) sleeps four.
Rates: $$-$$$. American Plan. Includes rafting in Glacier National Park and fly-fishing lessons.
Credit Cards: None. Personal checks accepted.
Season: Year-round
Activities: Dick comes from an incredible sports and recreation background and has created a program that reflects his love and understanding of the outdoors. Natural horsemanship; fly-fishing with instruction on the RJR trout pond containing five-pound rainbow trout; and Orvis guides available. Hiking and naturalist-guided trips into the mountains of the Kootenai National Forest; day trips to Glacier National Park for hiking, rafting, and sightseeing. Swimming in Glen Lake three miles away; and finally, platform tennis—three courts with instruction available.
Children's Programs: Kids of all ages welcome. Montana college students look after kids ages six and older during June, July, and August at parents' request. Sleeping in tepees, roping, horse care, arts and crafts, canoeing, hiking, and basketball.
Dining: Very nutrition-oriented in a tasty way. Special soups, salads, and healthy baked goodies. Chef prepares dinners served family-style. BYOB.
Entertainment: Professional weekly entertainment. Cowboy Doug, campfire sing-alongs, platform tennis, or casting in the trout pond.
Summary: The Dartmouth tradition of excellence, vision, passion, and the famous "Vox Clamatis in Deserto" live on here. The RJR specializes in natural horsemanship, fly-fishing, naturalist-guided hikes, healthful food, and platform tennis. Nearby are Glacier National Park and Fort Steele.

See color photos, page 256.

Seven Lazy P Ranch
Choteau, Montana

THE DUDE RANCHERS' ASSOCIATION

Montana Dude Ranch Association

Chuck and Sharon Blixrud have been in the guest-ranch and pack-trip business since the 1950s. What makes their operation special is that they combine their love for the great outdoors with a tremendous respect for nature and a thorough knowledge of the Bob Marshall Wilderness. Right against this 1.5-million-acre area that Montanans call "The Bob" are both of the Seven Lazy P ranches: the headquarters on the north fork of the Teton River at the base of Wind, Choteau, and Cave Mountains; and the lower ranch looking out on the Rocky Mountain front. Chuck grew up not far from Seven Lazy P headquarters. This part of Montana has some of the most spectacular, rugged geological formations in the country. The ranch combines an excellent riding, fishing, hiking, and pack-trip program with friendly ranch hospitality. Singles, couples, and families are all welcome.

Address: P.O. Box 178 K, Choteau, Montana 59422
Telephone: (406) 466-2044
Airport: Great Falls, 77 miles; paved and lighted runway for small planes in Choteau
Location: 27 miles west of Choteau off Highway 89, 77 miles northwest of Great Falls, 100 miles south of Glacier National Park
Memberships: The Dude Ranchers' Association, Professional Wilderness Outfitters Association, Montana Wilderness Association, Montana Dude Ranch Association
Awards: 1995 Montana Outfitter of the Year
Medical: Choteau, 30 miles
Conference: 20
Guest Capacity: 20
Accommodations: Four newly built, cozy log and frame cabins. Indian Head, Trap Line, and Aspen are duplex cabins with two bedrooms, each with a queen and twin beds, private bath, and porches. The Pine is a two-bedroom cabin with living room, wood-burning insert, private bath, kitchenette, and porch. All have electric heat. The spacious two-story lodge with three native stone fireplaces has sweeping views overlooking the Teton River Valley. An upper-level conference room with balcony is available for groups, workshops, and slide shows.
Rates: • $$–$$$. American Plan. Children's, off-season, and pack-trip rates. Three-day minimum stay.
Credit Cards: None. Personal checks, traveler's checks, and cash accepted.
Season: May through November
Activities: There are two fine programs at the Seven Lazy P. You may enjoy easygoing scenic mountain and meadow trail riding, taking in the breathtaking Rocky Mountain Front. If you wish to experience a spectacular high-country pack trip into the Bob Marshall Wilderness to view the Chinese Wall, you can do that too—it's your call. One thing for certain, you're in great hands. Fly-fishing for experienced anglers on the North Fork of the Teton River at the ranch or at the upper ranch, where the mountains soar overhead. Unlimited hiking; naturalist and Native American talks by retired Professor Shaw, who can hold an audience until the stars come out and then some. Wilderness fly fishing and pack-trip enthusiasts: ask about the Sun River and Alpine Lakes.
Children's Programs: No special programs. Kids ages six and up may trail ride. Children under age eight do not go on pack trips.
Dining: Hearty views and heart-healthy meals. Special diets catered to.
Entertainment: Library and wildlife movies, occasional volleyball and horseshoes. Most guests like to visit with each other, go for an evening walk, or drift off to sleep.
Summary: At the Seven Lazy P, you'll slow down, relax, and enjoy the sounds of nature. Superb family-owned and -operated guest ranch offering high-country and meadow trail rides and breathtaking mountain pack trips (selected 1995 Montana Outfitter of the Year), with more than 40 years of experience and tremendous Western hospitality. New guests and singles always feel like part of the family. If you expect to be constantly entertained, this is not the ranch for you. Many couples, singles, and older families. Ask about Laura and Hank's fly-fishing program, and Glacier National Park.

See color photos, page 257.

Sweet Grass Ranch
Big Timber, Montana

THE DUDE RANCHERS' ASSOCIATION

"We're a genuine old-time, working cattle-guest ranch, with unlimited riding as our main emphasis. Guests are welcome to take part in all pleasures of ranch life," say Sweet Grass hosts and owners Bill and Shelly Carroccia, who radiate warmth and sincere Western hospitality. The Sweet Grass Ranch is secluded in the Crazy Mountains 40 miles outside the small town of Big Timber. Cattle and dude ranching have been in the family since 1880. The Carroccias limit the number of guests so that everyone will actually feel like family. Families from all over have come to enjoy the beautiful open, rolling country; the foothills; and the magnificent high alpine country. Share in the ranch activities if you like, or do your own thing. Life is unstructured. Sweet Grass Ranch is a place where the whole family can enjoy the great outdoors, ride, fish, and savor the Old West.

Address: HC87, Box 2161K, Big Timber, Montana 59011
Telephone: (406) 537-4477 (telephone and fax)
E-Mail: sweetgrass@mcn.net
Internet: http://www.guestranches.com/sweet grass
Airport: Billings or Bozeman; pickup service available (extra).
Location: 120 miles northwest of Billings, 40 miles northwest of Big Timber. Driving directions will be sent to you.
Memberships: The Dude Ranchers' Association, Montana Ranch Vacation Association, National Register of Historic Places, National Cattlemen's Association
Medical: Clinic in Big Timber, 40 miles; advanced first-aid on ranch
Guest Capacity: 20
Accommodations: Guests are housed in six rustic log cabins (built between 1928 and 1935), or in four rooms on the second floor of the main house, some with living rooms and fireplaces. Lots of authentic old-time charm here. Private baths in six cabins; bath/shower house for two cabins. Coin-operated laundry facilities. In the main house there's a marvelous burl second-floor railing and banister.
Rates: • $$. American Plan. Children's rates available. One-week minimum stay. Many guests stay 10 days to two weeks. Most arrive and stay Sunday to Sunday.
Credit Cards: None. Traveler's checks and personal checks accepted.
Season: Mid-June through early September
Activities: Each morning one of the Carroccias' sons discusses ranch activities and options for the day. Every day is different. Those who wish to participate in ranch work may do so, like checking and salting livestock, trail-clearing, and doctoring cattle. In addition, half-day and excellent all-day rides go out every day except Sunday. These may be working or scenic walking, trotting, and loping rides. Bareback and dinner rides along with pack trips and cattle work are things you may enjoy, too. Riding instruction is available on request. Fishing in alpine lakes and on the Sweet Grass River, which runs through the ranch. Swimming in the creek for the hardy and brave; bird-watching. Photographers should bring lots of film.
Children's Programs: No special programs. Very flexible (old-time, ranch-style) riding for kids. Children are welcome and are included in all ranch activities. Baby-sitting can be arranged.
Dining: Meals and bread are home-cooked and served family-style in the circa-1925 main lodge. Ranch-raised Montana beef, fresh cream, and homemade ice cream. Weekly dinner ride. Sandwich pack lunches are served on all-day rides and trips.
Entertainment: As Shelly says, "Whatever guests would like to do." Some swap stories or go for an evening stroll. Both sons (Rocco and Tony) play guitar. Piano and pool table in lodge.
Summary: A wonderful, old-time Western Montana guest and cattle ranch. This rustic ranch serves up plenty of authentic Western spirit and genuine hospitality. Sweet Grass is a riding ranch. No set schedule; do as much or as little as you please. Cattle work. Most guests don't wish to leave the ranch. It's completely private, at the end of the road.

Triple Creek Ranch
Darby, Montana

Triple Creek Ranch is an exclusive mountain hideaway almost at the foot of beautiful Trapper Peak, just outside the tiny town of Darby. This modern "diamond in the rough" (adults-only property) was built in 1986 to create a wilderness retreat for those who yearned for nature's wildness but wanted to experience it with luxurious amenities. Triple Creek is managed by Wayne and Judy Kilpatrick; together with their wonderful staff, they have created a haven of rest, relaxation, and mountain splendor.

Address: 5551 West Fork Stage Route K, Darby, Montana 59829
Telephone: (406) 821-4600; fax: (406) 821-4666
E-Mail: tcrebiherroot.net
Internet: http://www.triplecreekranch.com
Airport: Missoula; private planes to Hamilton with 4,200-foot airstrip; helicopter pad at ranch. Airport pickup available.
Location: 12 miles south of Darby, 74 miles south of Missoula
Memberships: Relais & Chateaux
Awards: Relais & Chateaux; *Hideaway Report*, one of Six U.S. Hideaways of the Decade; Hospitality Award 1997
Medical: Marcus Daly Memorial Hospital, Hamilton; emergency helicopter service is available.
Conference: 36, executive telecommunicating facilities
Guest Capacity: 28 singles, 21 couples
Accommodations: Choose from cozy cedar to luxury log cabins. Each is tastefully furnished. Refrigerators are fully stocked with an array of beverages, and there's a full complimentary supply of liquor. For those who wish, there's satellite TV/VCR. The larger luxury cabins have massive handcrafted log king-size beds, double steam showers, and a private hot tub on the deck that looks out into the forest. Daily housekeeping and laundry service provided.
Rates: • $$$$–$$$$$$. American Plan. Single rates available. No minimum stay required.
Credit Cards: VISA, MasterCard, American Express, Discover
Season: Year-round, all holidays
Activities: Summer: an informal program that caters to each couple or individual. Horseback riding, hiking, fly-fishing (see Fly-Fishing section), white-water river rafting, helicopter tours, swimming in the outdoor heated pool. Tennis court and putting green. Bird- and wildlife-watching and photography. Serious golfers can drive to the Hamilton 18-hole golf course. In winter (see Cross-Country Skiing section), Triple Creek comes alive with the spirit of Christmas: hot buttered rum, sleigh rides with bells, and horseback riding in freshly fallen snow. Snowmobiling, wilderness cross-country skiing, downhill skiing, 28 miles away.
Children's Programs: Children under 16 are allowed only when entire ranch is reserved by a family or group.
Dining: All meals are varied and designed to tempt even the most finicky diners. Complimentary wine served. Special diets not a problem. Full room service available. Triple Creek will help you celebrate your birthday or anniversary. Open to public on very limited basis.
Entertainment: Planned evening entertainment. Lovely upstairs bar in the main lodge with occasional live music. Many go for a stroll under the stars or enjoy a glass of fine cognac in the hot tub.
Summary: One of Kilgore's "Best of the Best." World-class, luxurious, adults-only, mountaintop hideaway. Superb and friendly staff with personalized service second to none. Quiet, restful, intimate, romantic atmosphere (great for honeymoons), with gourmet cuisine and full room service. Triple Creek may be booked for family reunions and corporate retreats.

See color photos, pages 258–259.

White Tail Ranch
Ovando, Montana

Montana Dude Ranch Association

Montana's White Tail Ranch has been in business since the 1930s. Charm, personalized service, wilderness, and creekside settings are its hallmarks. In 1996 Bill and Diana Wellman became the proud new owners. Because of their passion for ranch life and their long careers in the corporate hospitality industry, they have created one of the most exceptional and caring guest-ranch programs in the country. As Diana says, "We understand the importance of planning, details, follow-through, and service—and we strive to do all this and more." In 1998 White Tail Ranch was featured in the Neiman Marcus distinguished *InCircle Club,* extolling the rustic ambiance and recreational opportunities that make the experience and people here so special. Ride into the high country, fish, hike, or snooze riverside. It's your choice. Welcome to White Tail Ranch.

Address: 82 K White Tail Ranch Road, Ovando, Montana 59854
Telephone: (888) 987-2624, (406) 793-5627; fax: (406) 793-5043
E-Mail: whitetail@montana.com
Internet: http://www.whitetailranch.com
Airport: Missoula or Helena; private aircraft into Lincoln
Location: 60 miles east of Missoula, 75 miles northwest of Helena, 25 miles west of Lincoln
Memberships: Montana Dude Ranch Association
Medical: St. Patrick's Hospital, Missoula; 60 miles
Conference: 25
Guest Capacity: 25
Accommodations: Nine original, red-trimmed cozy guest cabins with names like Skookum, Wapiti, Bear Trap, and Pine Cone, accommodate two to six people and are situated along Salmon Creek. Six have private baths, three use a common bathhouse. In winter, flannel sheets, down comforters, and electric blankets are provided. All cabins have electric heat and three have woodstoves. The main lodge houses the dining room and living room with a fireplace. Laundry services available.
Rates: $$–$$$$. Full American Plan. Children's, corporate, winter, off-season and non-riding rates available.
Credit Cards: None. Personal and traveler's checks accepted.
Season: May to mid-November, January to April
Activities: Summer: Extensive horseback riding for all levels, open-meadow to steep mountain trail riding. Ask about Windy Pass, Meadow Lake, and the Kleinschmidt Flats rides. Fly-fish on the famous Blackfoot River and its Northfork. Guiding, floating, and float-tubing available for an additional fee. Mountain biking, hiking, and relaxing. Salmon Creek runs through the ranch and past the cabins—a perfect spot for beginners to cast a line for native trout. Activities at nearby Coopers Lake. Winter: Dogsledding, guided and unguided snowmobiling, cross-country skiing, and snowshoeing. You may learn to drive your own dog team!
Children's Programs: Flexible children's program, two to four hours each day, includes educational nature exploration, outdoor games, arts and crafts, treasure hunts, hikes, and swimming. Trail riding begins at age eight. Children too young for trail rides may be led around the corral. Baby-sitting available with advanced notice.
Dining: Hearty ranch meals served buffet- or family-style, home-cooked and homemade! Lots of variety. Creekside cookouts and barbecues. Guests and staff dine together. Drinks, fresh-baked goodies, and fruit available throughout the day. Special diets accommodated. BYOB.
Entertainment: Cozy main lodge with piano, extensive library, games, and cards. Bonfires, stargazing, relaxing on the porch or in the hammocks. Wildlife viewing, horseshoes, volleyball, croquet, badminton, roping, and occasional primitive fire-building demonstrations. Local rodeos. Ask about educational Indian pow-wows.
Summary: One of the bright new stars in guest ranching. Old-time ranch with new spirit. Caring and personalized attention, creekside setting and lots of rustic charm! Small, intimate, and fully customized programs. Featured in Neiman Marcus, *InCircle Club*. Specialties include family reunions and weddings. Ask about photography workshops. Well-behaved pets welcomed. Video available.

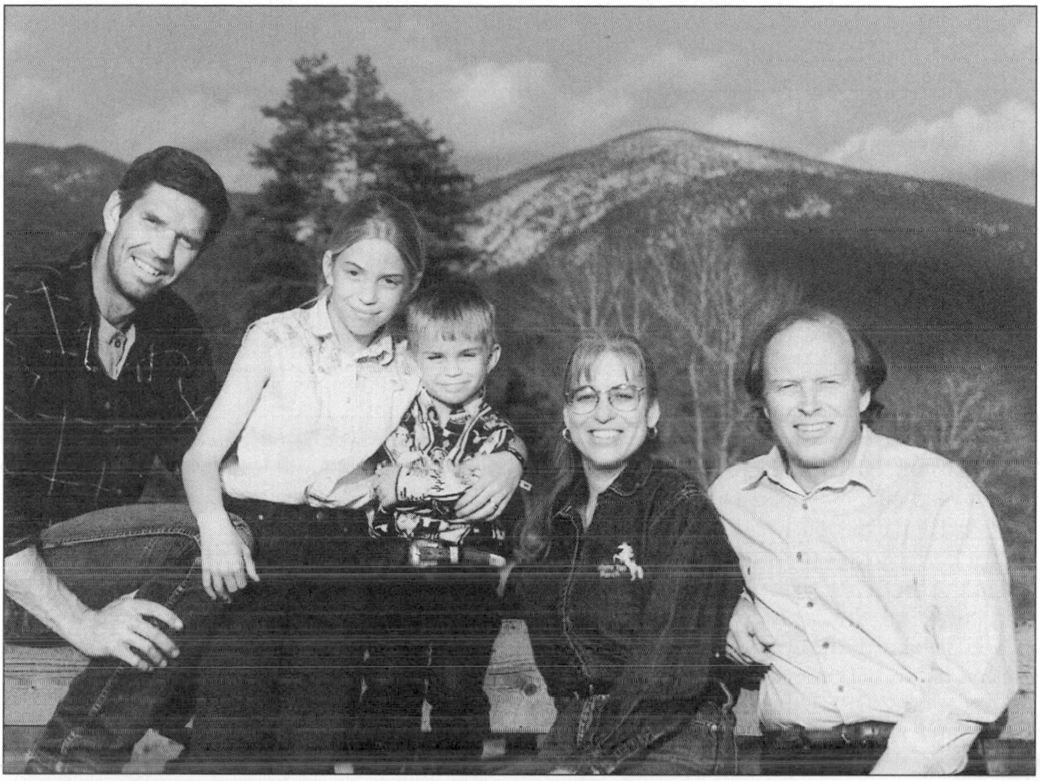

Cottonwood Ranch
Wells, Nevada

At 6,200 feet, the Cottonwood Ranch is in Nevada's high-desert country on Cottonwood Creek in the O'Neil Basin of Elko County, one of the largest cattle-producing counties in the United States. This working ranch runs 500 head of cows, calves, and bulls, as well as 80 head of horses over 2,000 acres. The fourth-generation Smith family leases more than 30,000 acres from the Forest Service and Bureau of Land Management. Horace Smith, his wife, Renie, and their adult children—Kim, Agee, and his wife, Vicki—go out of their way to ensure that each guest is well looked after. Cottonwood offers city folks a chance to get away from it all and experience life as it used to be. The Smiths have been in the cattle-ranching business and in this part of Nevada since the 1920s. Today their guests travel a good distance to experience their hospitality at this way-off-the-road paradise. Depending on the time of year, guests may (and are encouraged to) participate in a variety of ranch/cattle activities. The high-mountain cow camp is right in the middle of Nevada's summer home to hundreds of elk and mule deer. Here the air is so clean and it's so quiet that you may just think you've gone to heaven. Wilderness pack trips lasting almost a week take guests into the isolated and beautiful Jarbidge Wilderness, where they see dramatic views of mountain peaks, quaking aspens, willows, and meadows filled with sunflowers and lupine. The only sounds you'll hear in this country are those of nature.

Address: HC 62, Box 1300, Wells, Nevada 89835
Telephone: (702) 752-3604 (radiotelephone; you may have difficulty getting through); (702) 488-2355 (winter); (800) 341-5951
Airport: Elko or Twin Falls, both 120 miles
Location: 62 miles west of Jackpot, 120 miles northeast of Elko 120 miles south of Twin Falls, 75 miles northwest of Wells
Memberships: Nevada Outfitters and Guides Association, Nevada Cattleman's Association
Medical: Magic Valley Regional Medical Center, Twin Falls; 75 miles. Emergency helicopter service available.
Guest Capacity: 14; large groups can be accommodated with camping
Accommodations: Comfortable, rustic, five-bedroom, open-beam lodge with a deck offering panoramic views has two rooms with double beds, and three rooms with twin and bunk beds. Bathrooms are both private and shared. Once on the trail, the ranch provides all your gear, except sleeping bags and personal belongings. High-mountain cow camp—everything is provided except sleeping bag and personal gear. Check with the Smiths for exactly what you need.
Rates: • $$–$$$. American Plan. Pack-trip, cow-camp, children's, and group rates available. Two-day minimum stay at ranch.
Credit Cards: VISA, MasterCard, American Express
Season: May to September; lodge available to rent during off-season
Activities: For many years the Smiths have been known for their high-country pack trips. Today they welcome guests to participate in their weekly cattle-ranch activities. The Smiths and their expert guides will show you some of Nevada's magnificent backcountry. Seasonal cattle roundup and horse drive, trap-shooting at ranch. Seasonal big-game and bird hunting.
Children's Programs: Children welcome, but check with ranch. Kids begin trail riding at age seven.
Dining: Hearty, home-cooked, real ranch meals. BYOB. Cooking under the stars on pack trips. Wine served.
Entertainment: Hay-wagon and buggy rides, cookouts, occasional sing-alongs, cowboy poetry. Nature and wildlife are most of the entertainment here. The stars are forever.
Summary: One of Nevada's old-time ranching families. Authentic working cattle ranch serves up wonderful Western hospitality. The long drive in is worth every minute! Tremendous high-desert beauty, with the Jarbidge Mountains forming the backdrop. Cattle work, horse drives, wilderness pack trips, and high-mountain cow camp. Ask about Jarbidge Wilderness and the holistic cattle-ranching program.

Circle Z Ranch, Arizona

See ranch description on page 6.

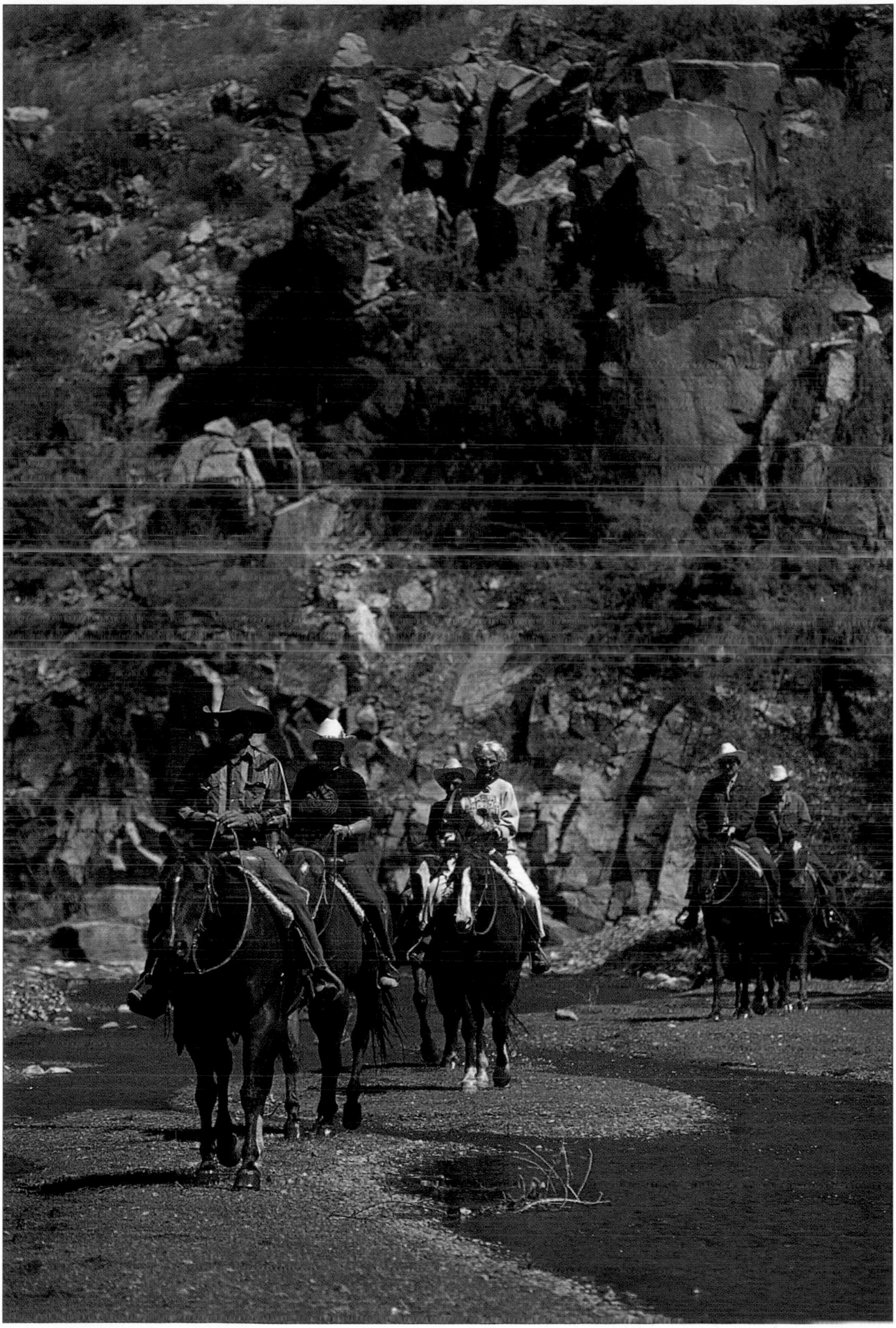

Flying E Ranch, Arizona

See ranch description on page 8.

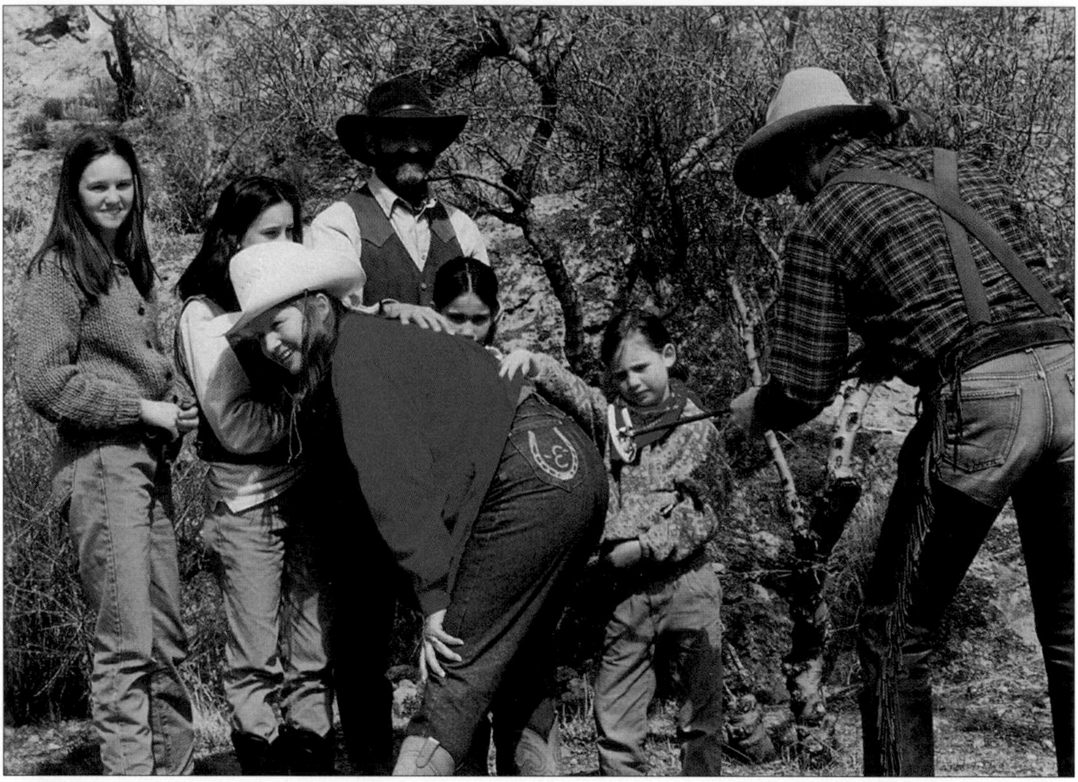

See ranch description on page 9.

The Horseshoe Ranch on Bloody Basin Road, Arizona

See ranch description on page 12.

Lazy K Bar Guest Ranch, Arizona

See ranch description on page 13.

Merv Griffin's Wickenburg Inn, Arizona

See ranch description on page 16.

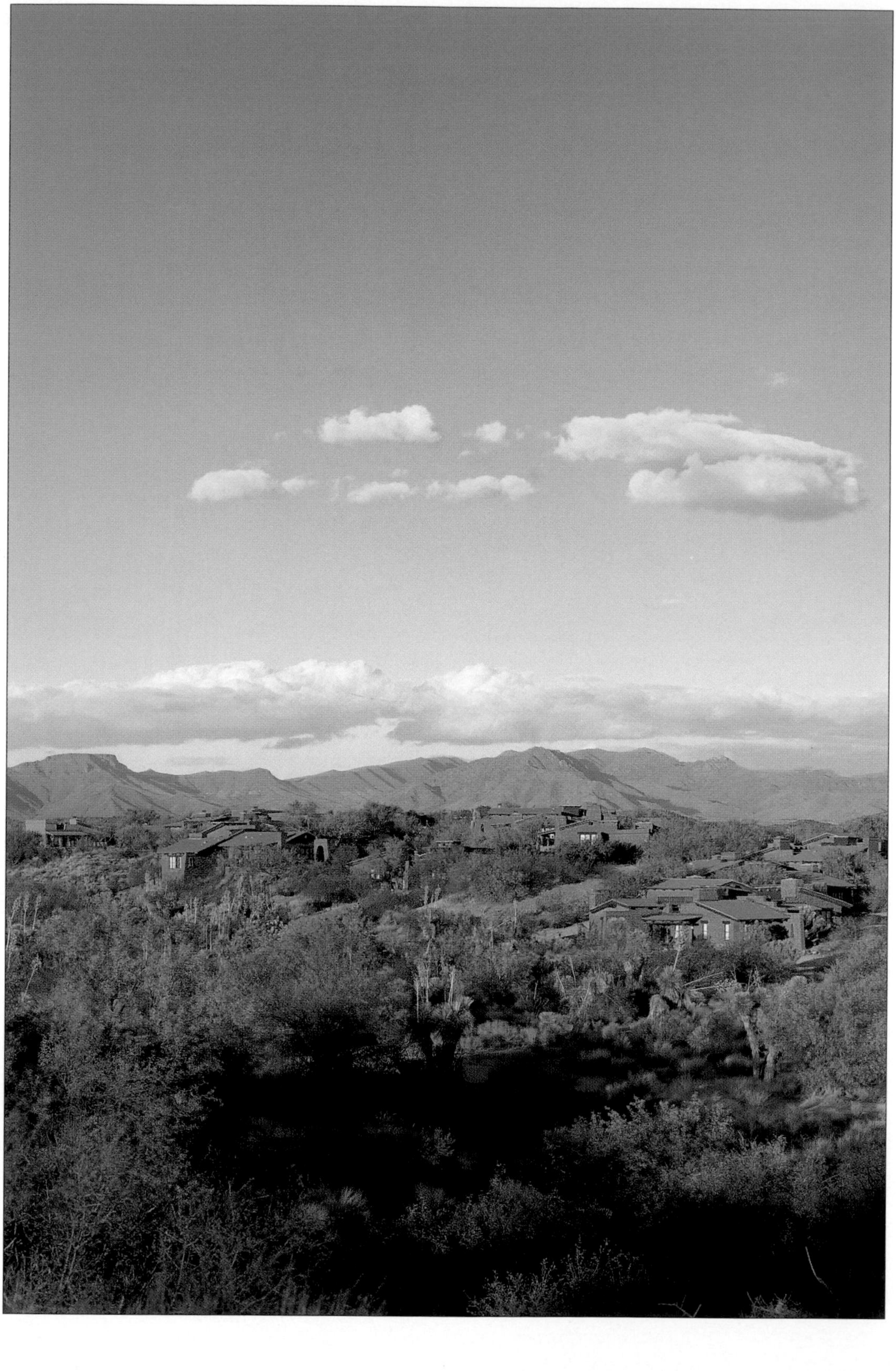

Merv Griffin's Wickenburg Inn, Arizona

See ranch description on page 16.

Rancho de los Caballeros, Arizona

See ranch description on page 20.

Rancho de los Caballeros, Arizona

See ranch description on page 20.

Rancho de la Osa, Arizona

See ranch description on page 19.

See ranch description on page 34.

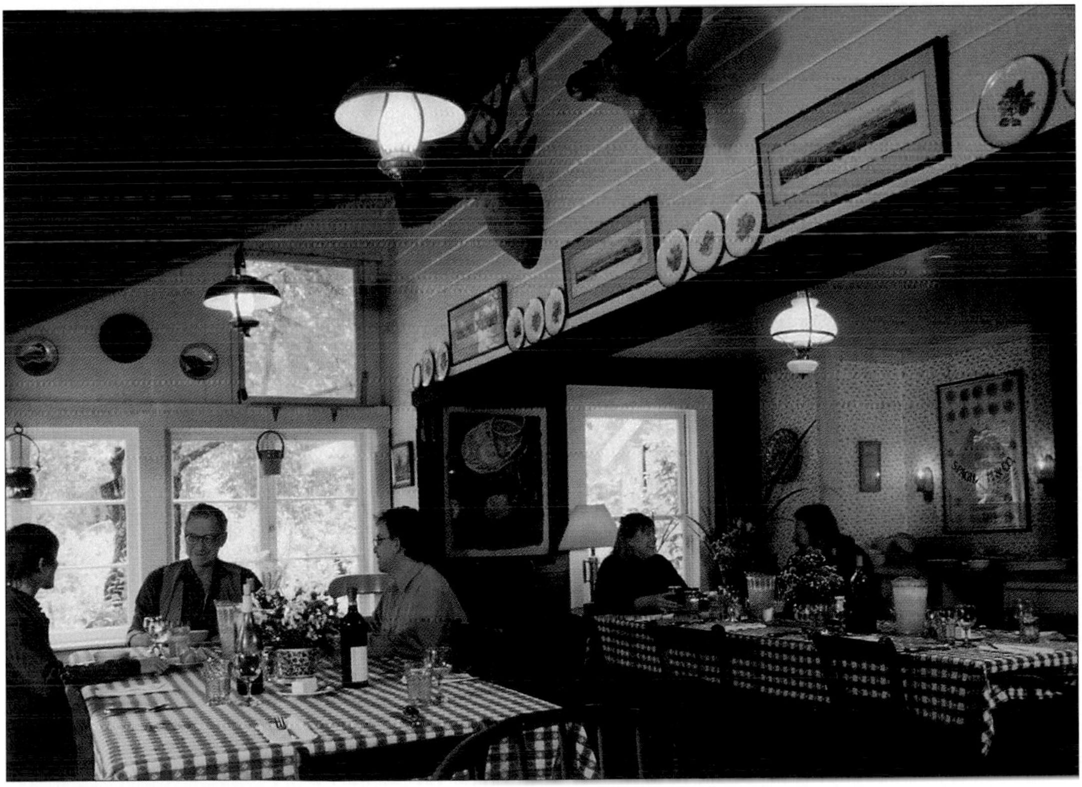

Alisal Guest Ranch, California

See ranch description on page 28.

See ranch description on page 28.

Hunewill Circle H Ranch, California

See ranch description on page 36.

Rankin Ranch, California

See ranch description on page 38.

Bar Lazy J Guest Ranch, Colorado

See ranch description on page 44.

C Lazy U Ranch, Colorado

See ranch description on pages 45 and 464.

Colorado Trails Ranch, Colorado

See ranch description on pages 46 and 445.

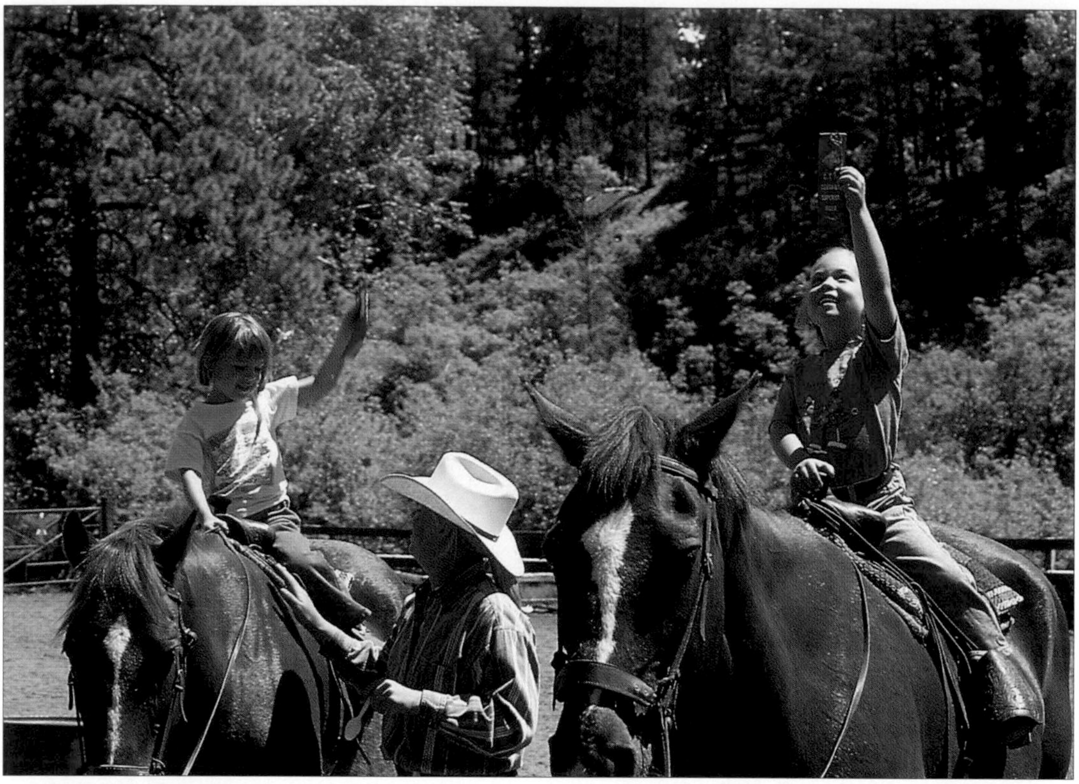

Colorado Trails Ranch, Colorado

See ranch description on pages 46 and 445.

Coulter Lake Guest Ranch, Colorado

See ranch description on page 48.

See ranch description on page 50.

Elk Mountain Ranch, Colorado

See ranch description on page 54.

The Home Ranch, Colorado

See ranch description on pages 55 and 465.

King Mountain Ranch Resort, Colorado

See ranch description on page 58.

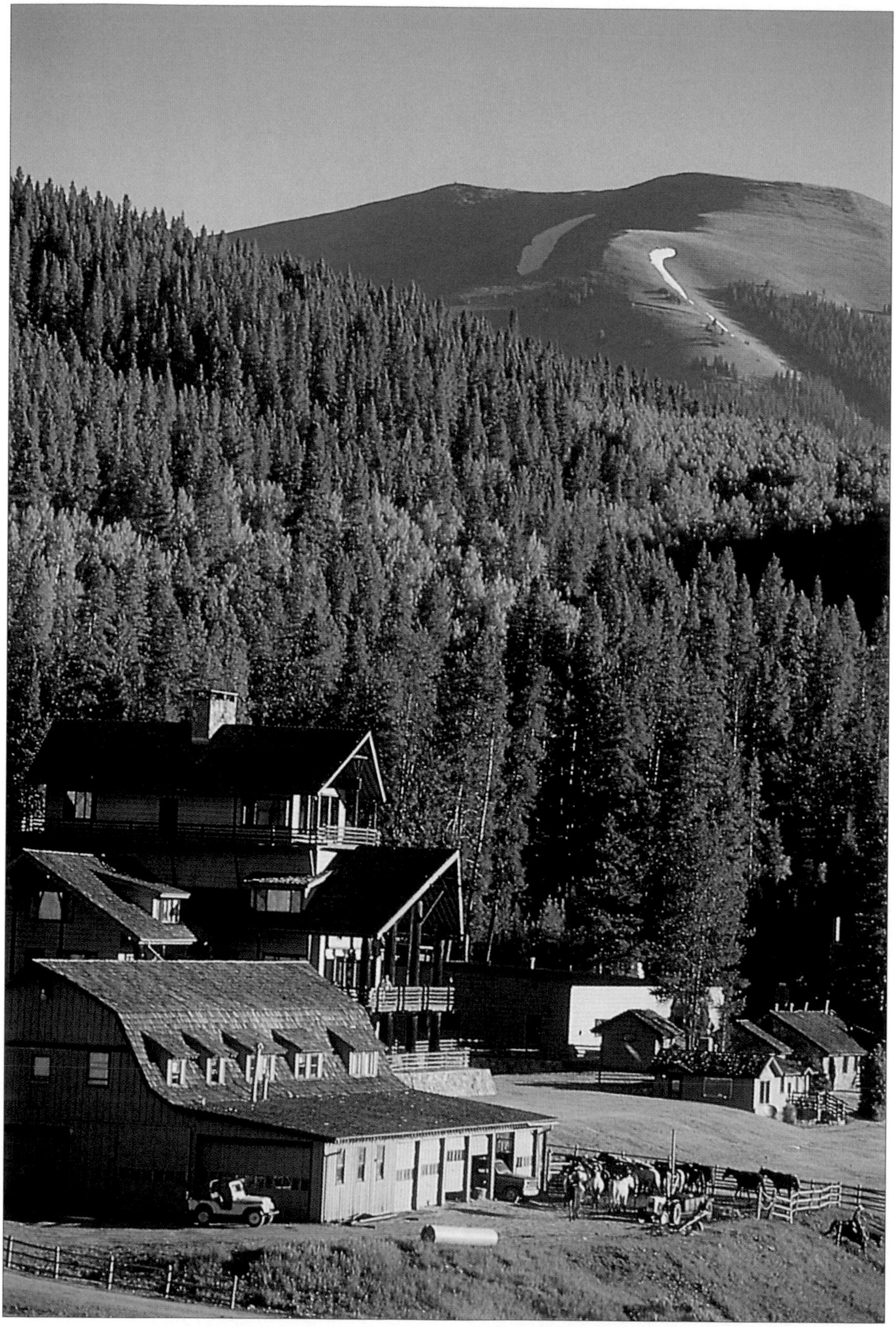

See ranch description on page 60.

Lane Guest Ranch, Colorado

See ranch description on page 61.

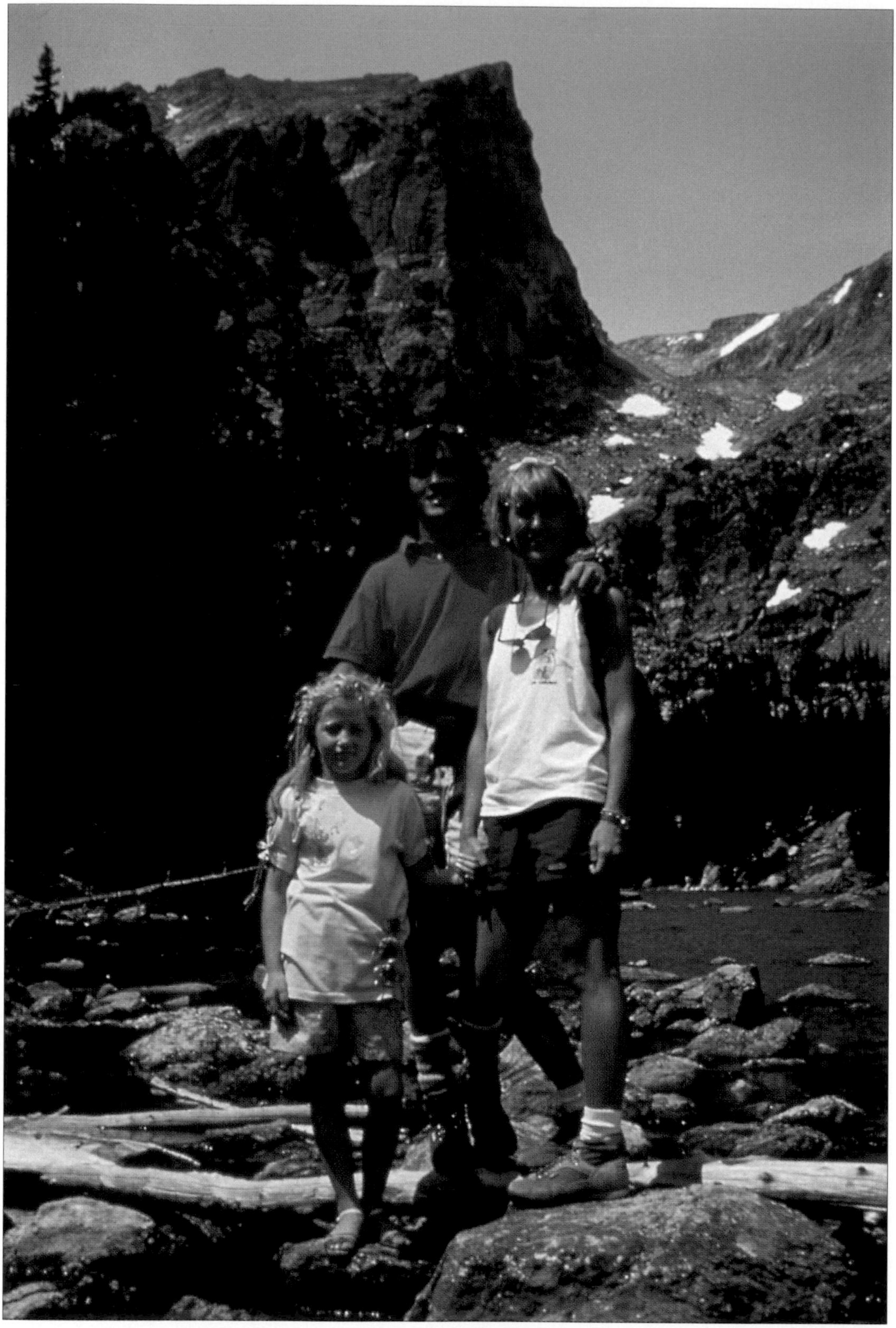

Lane Guest Ranch, Colorado

See ranch description on page 61.

Lane Guest Ranch, Colorado

See ranch description on page 61.

Lane Guest Ranch, Colorado

See ranch description on page 61.

Laramie River Ranch, Colorado

See ranch description on page 62.

Latigo Ranch, Colorado

See ranch description on pages 64 and 466.

Lazy H Guest Ranch, Colorado

See ranch description on page 65.

North Fork Ranch, Colorado

See ranch description on page 70.

Peaceful Valley Ranch, Colorado

See ranch description on page 72.

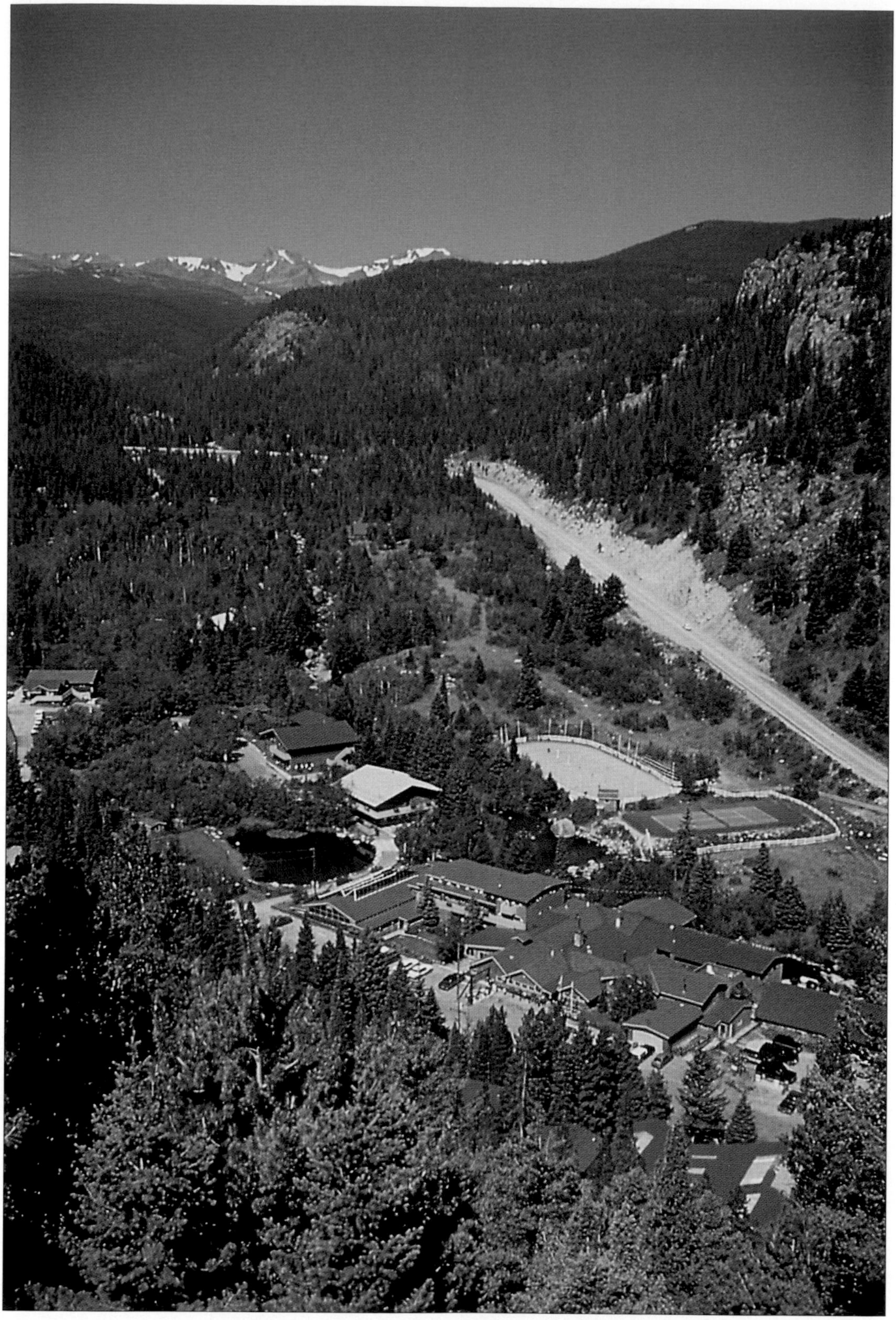

Rawah Ranch, Colorado

See ranch description on page 73.

Skyline Guest Ranch, Colorado

See ranch description on pages 82 and 467.

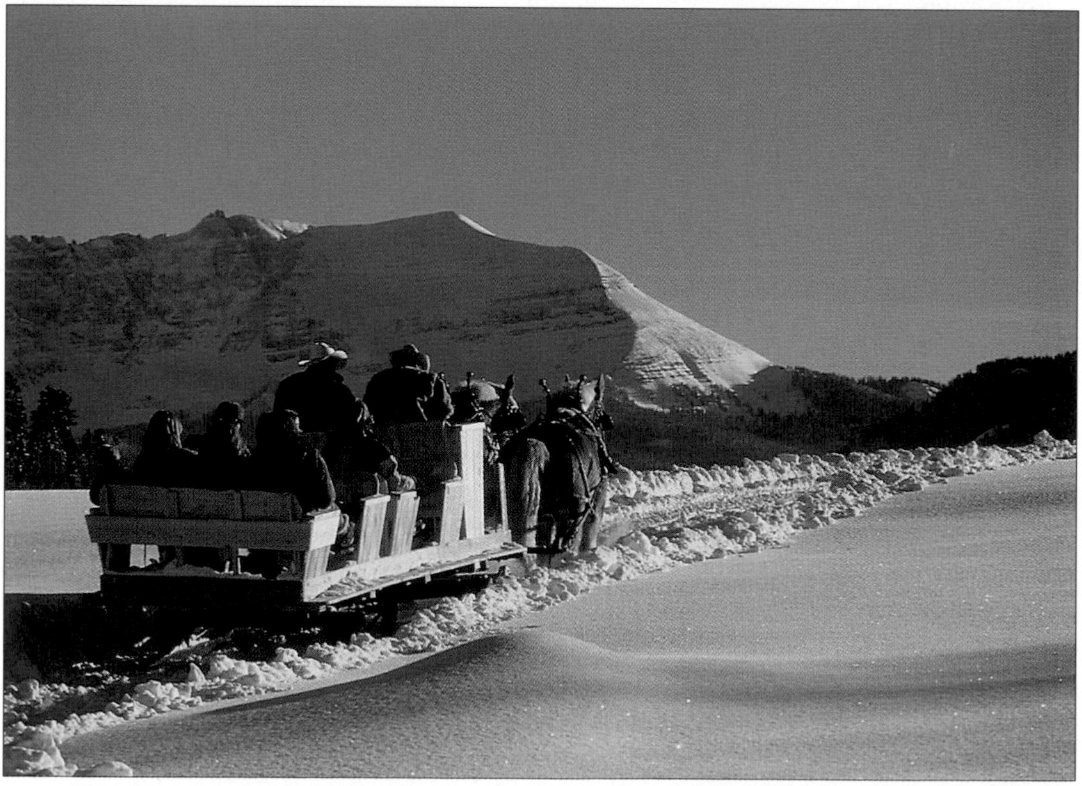

Tarryall River Ranch, Colorado

See ranch description on page 88.

T-Lazy-7 Ranch, Colorado

See ranch description on pages 84 and 470.

T-Lazy-7 Ranch, Colorado

See ranch description on pages 84 and 470.

Tumbling River Ranch, Colorado

See ranch description on page 90.

Whistling Acres Guest Ranch, Colorado

See ranch description on page 96.

Vista Verde Ranch, Colorado

See ranch description on pages 92 and 468.

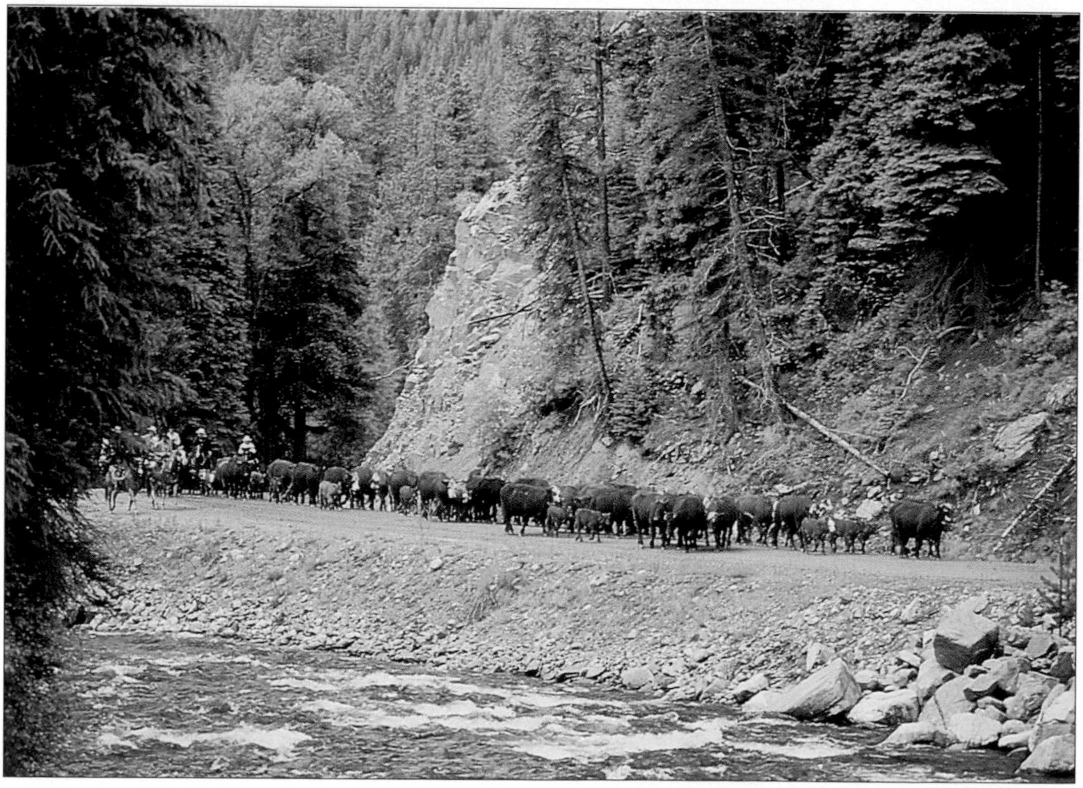

See ranch description on pages 92 and 468.

Wilderness Trails Ranch, Colorado

See ranch description on page 98.

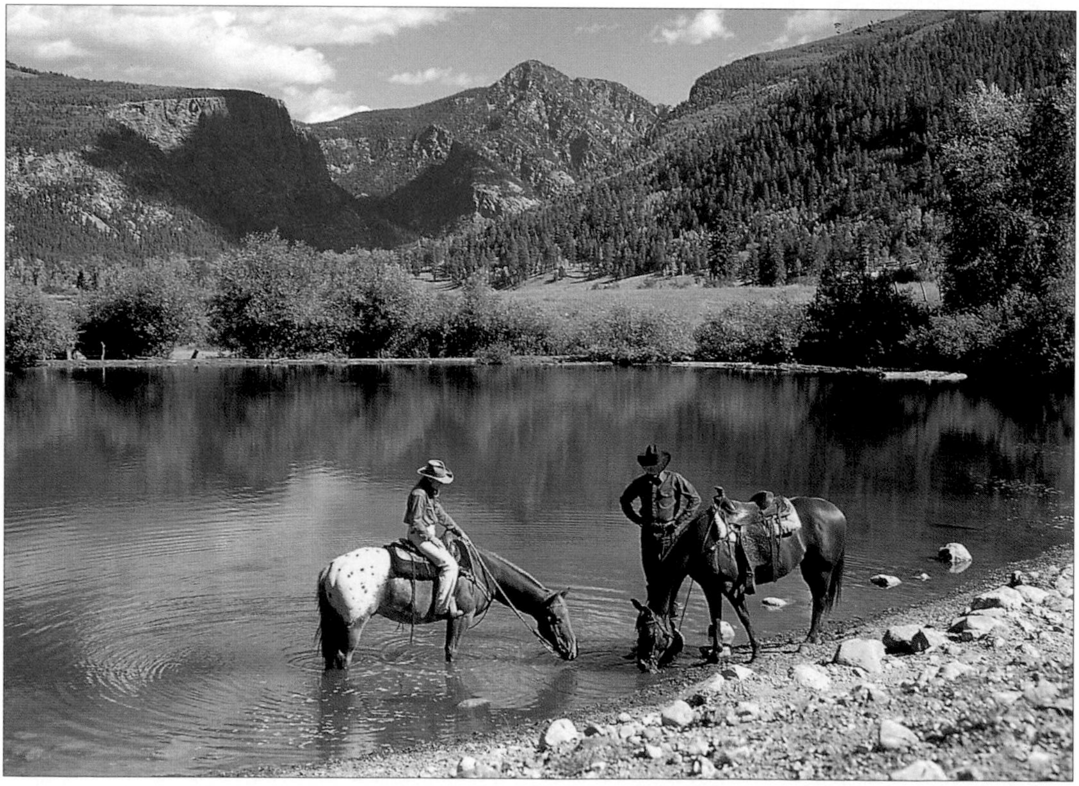

Wind River Ranch, Colorado

See ranch description on page 87.

Wit's End Guest and Resort Ranch, Colorado

See ranch description on page 100.

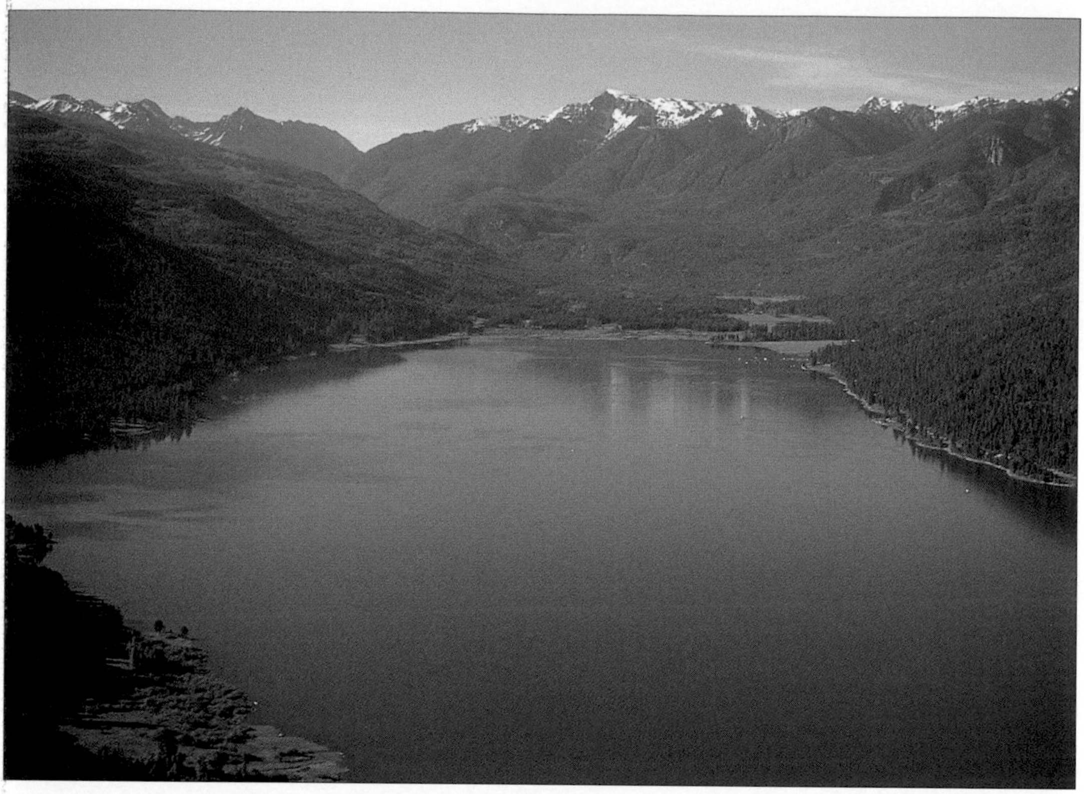

Wit's End Guest and Resort Ranch, Colorado

See ranch description on page 100.

Wit's End Guest and Resort Ranch, Colorado

See ranch description on page 100.

Wit's End Guest and Resort Ranch, Colorado

See ranch description on page 100.

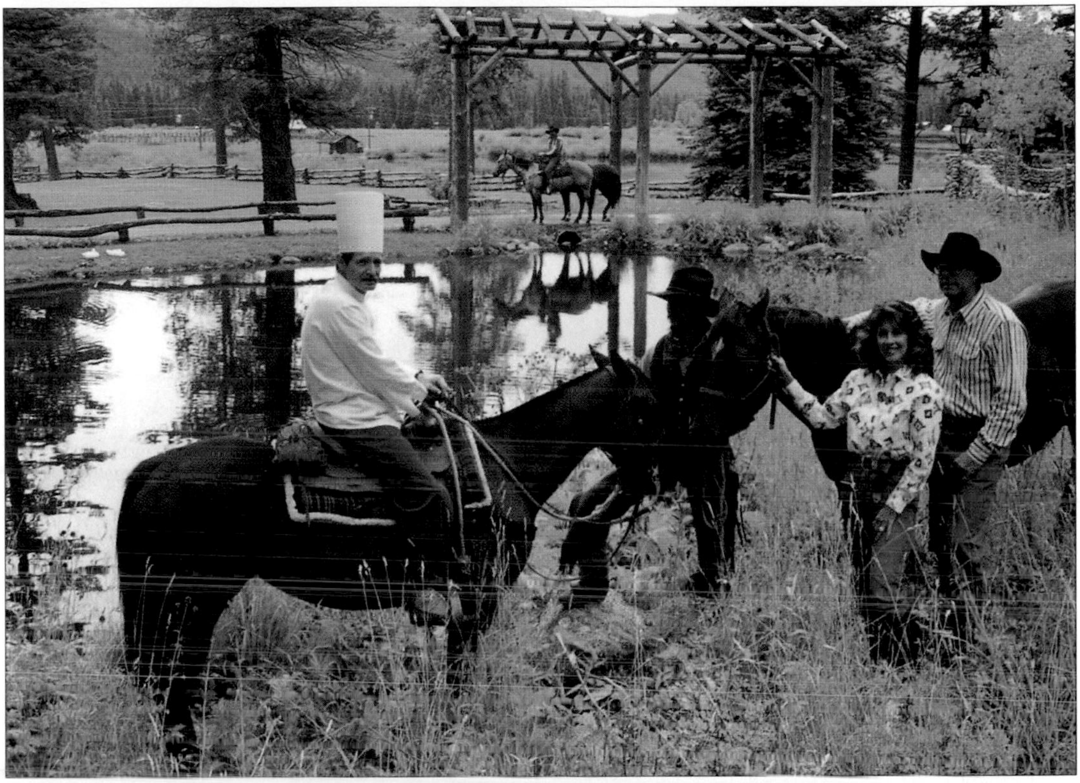

See ranch description on page 100.

Wit's End Guest and Resort Ranch, Colorado

See ranch description on page 100.

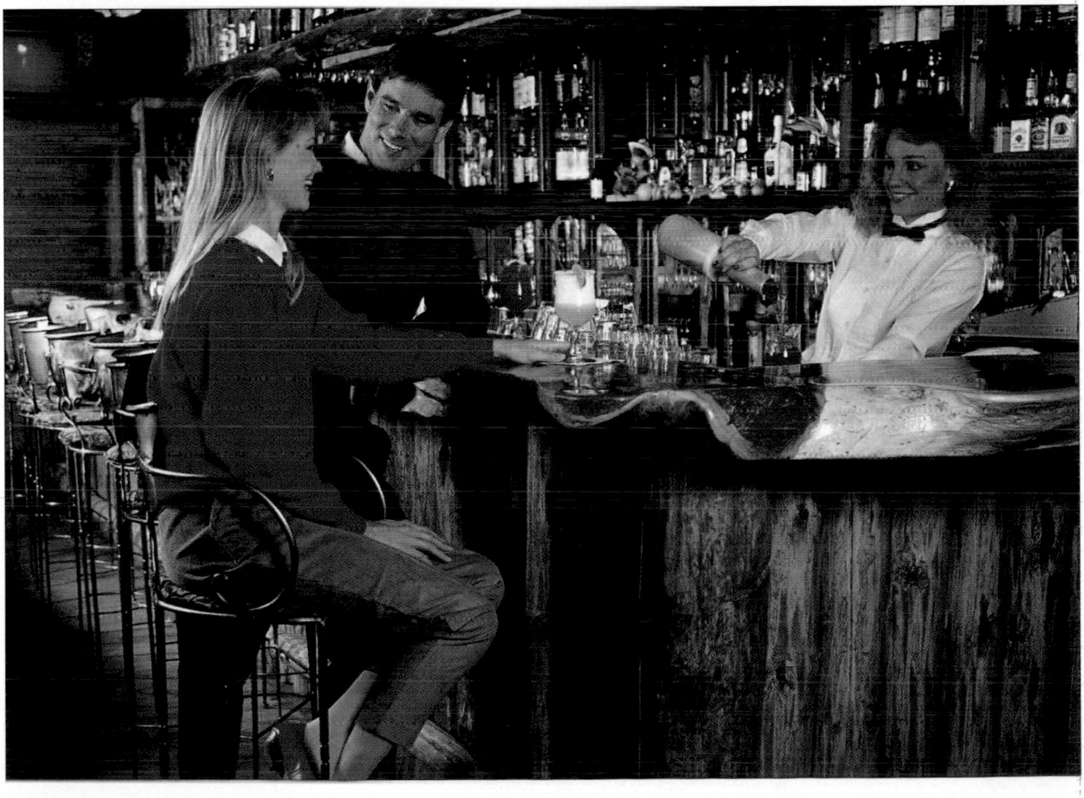

Molokai Ranch, Hawaii

See ranch description on page 102.

See ranch description on page 102.

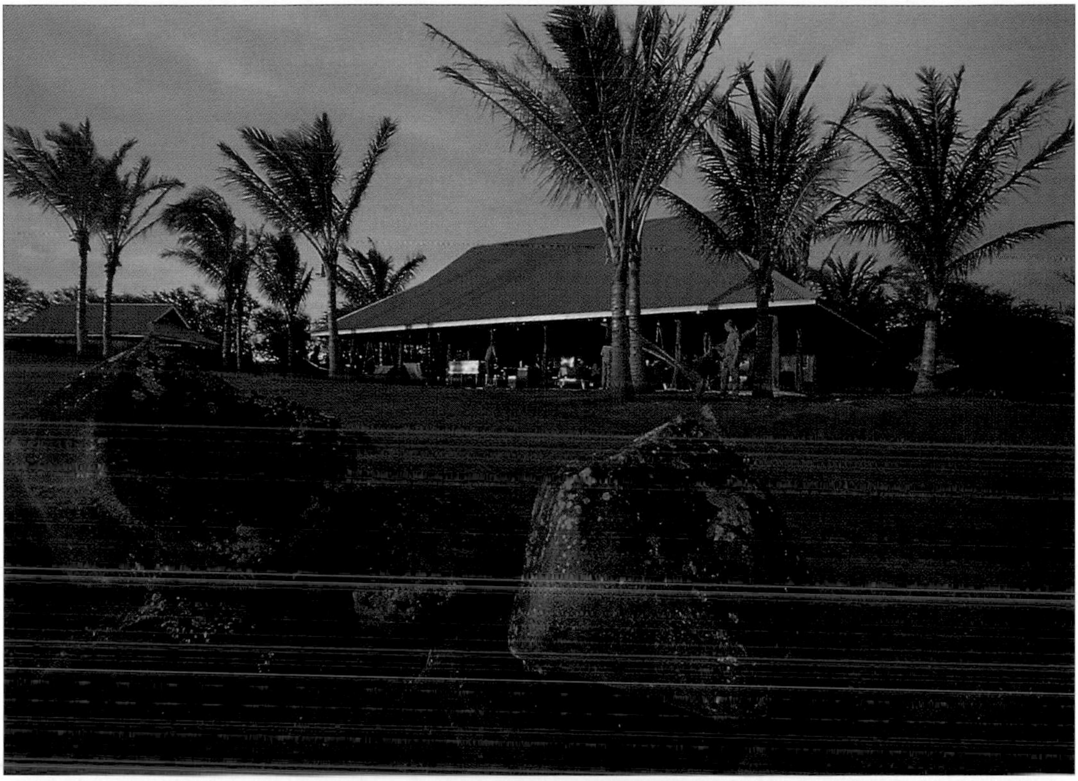

Molokai Ranch, Hawaii

See ranch description on page 102.

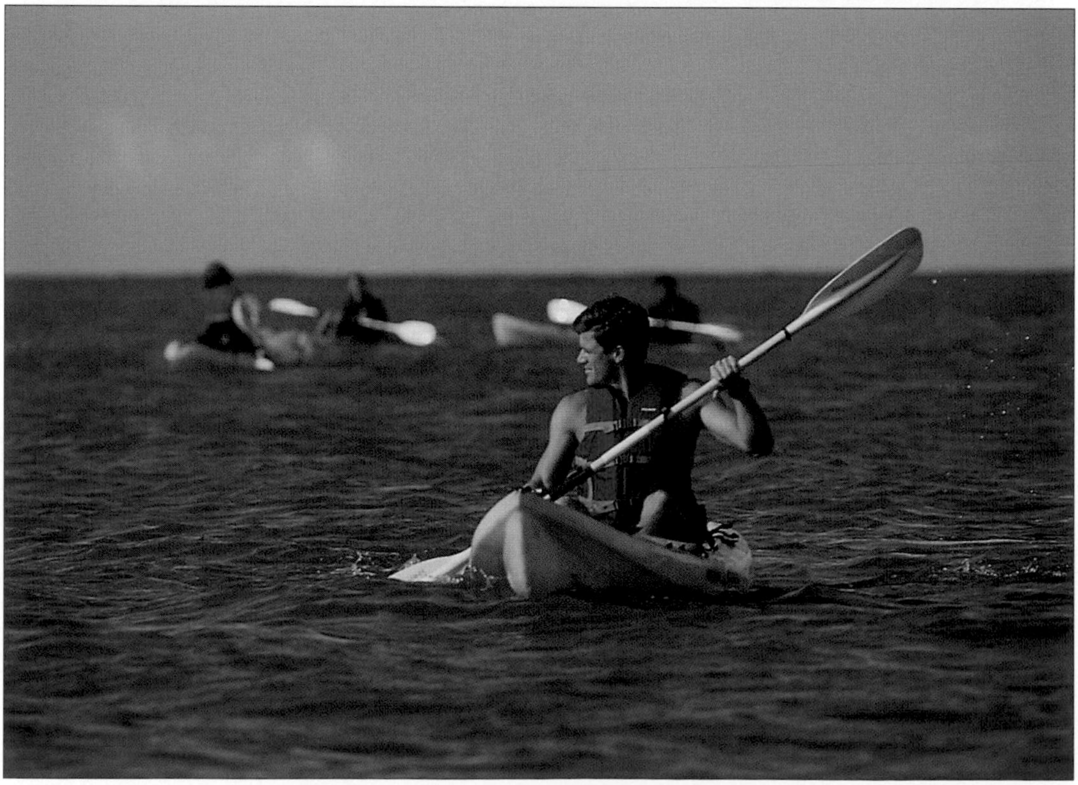

Molokai Ranch, Hawaii

See ranch description on page 102.

Diamond D Ranch, Idaho

See ranch description on page 105.

See ranch description on page 108.

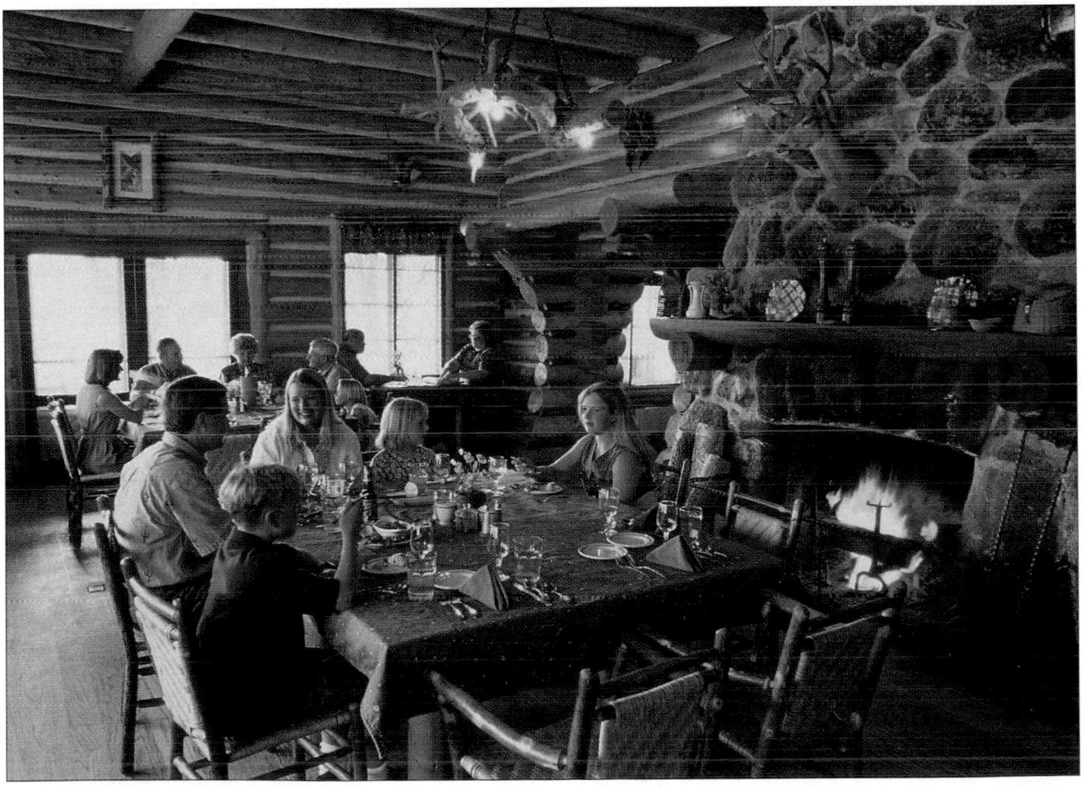

Hidden Creek Ranch, Idaho

See ranch description on page 106.

Hidden Creek Ranch, Idaho

See ranch description on page 106.

Hidden Creek Ranch, Idaho

See ranch description on page 106.

Hidden Creek Ranch, Idaho

See ranch description on page 106.

Moose Creek Ranch, Idaho

See ranch description on page 110.

See ranch description on page 116.

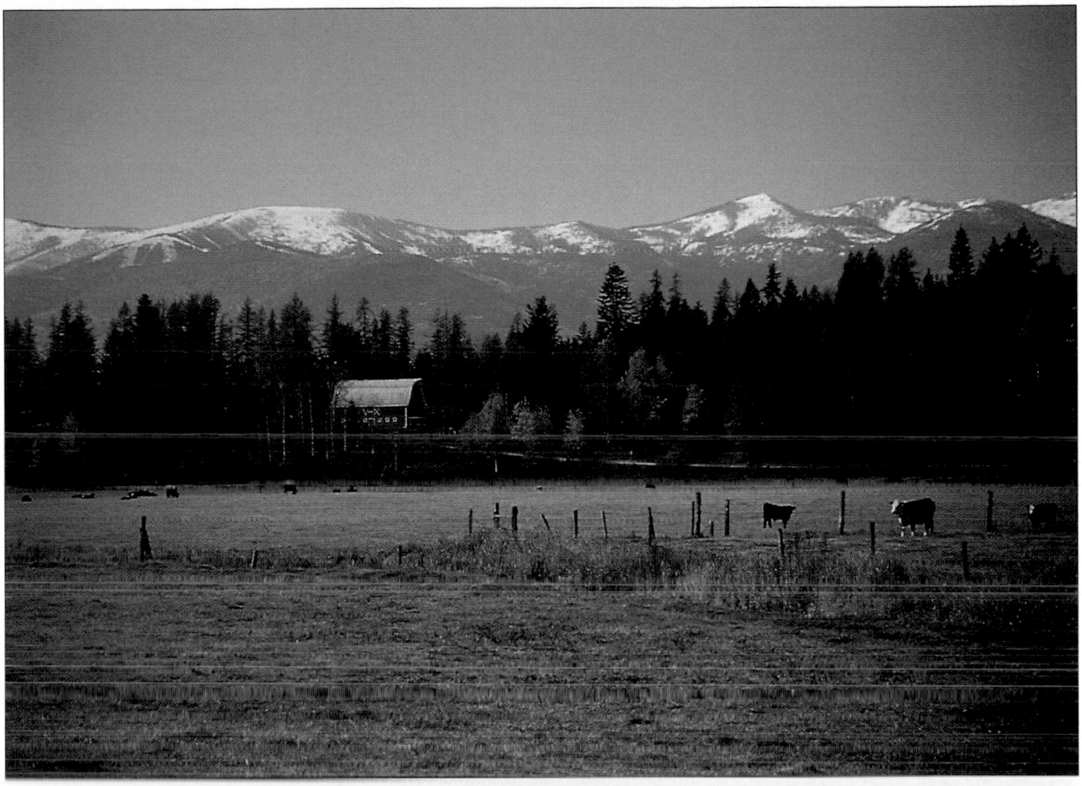

Teton Ridge Ranch, Idaho

See ranch description on pages 112 and 471.

Teton Ridge Ranch, Idaho

See ranch description on pages 112 and 471.

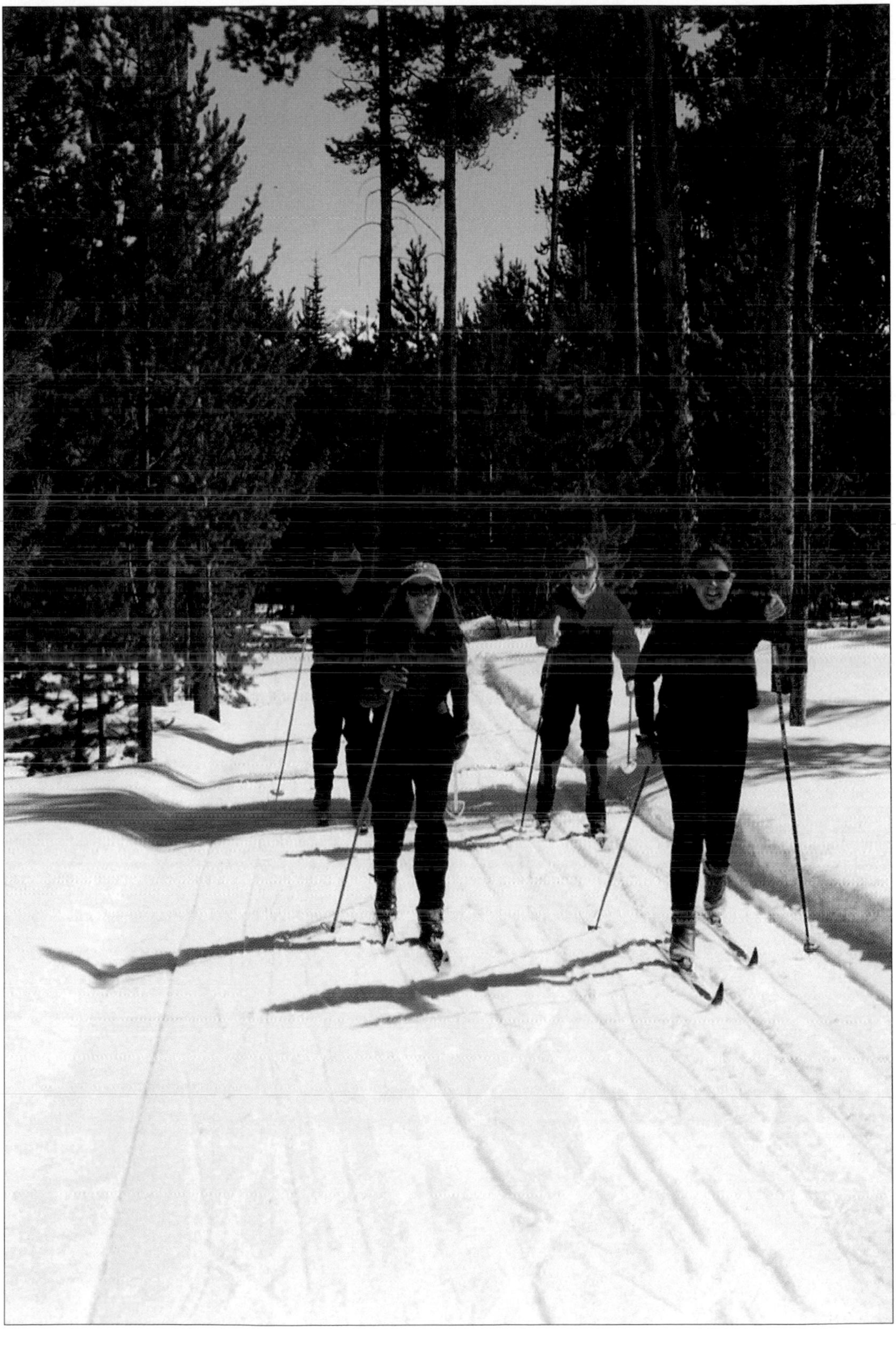

Twin Peaks Ranch, Idaho

See ranch description on page 114.

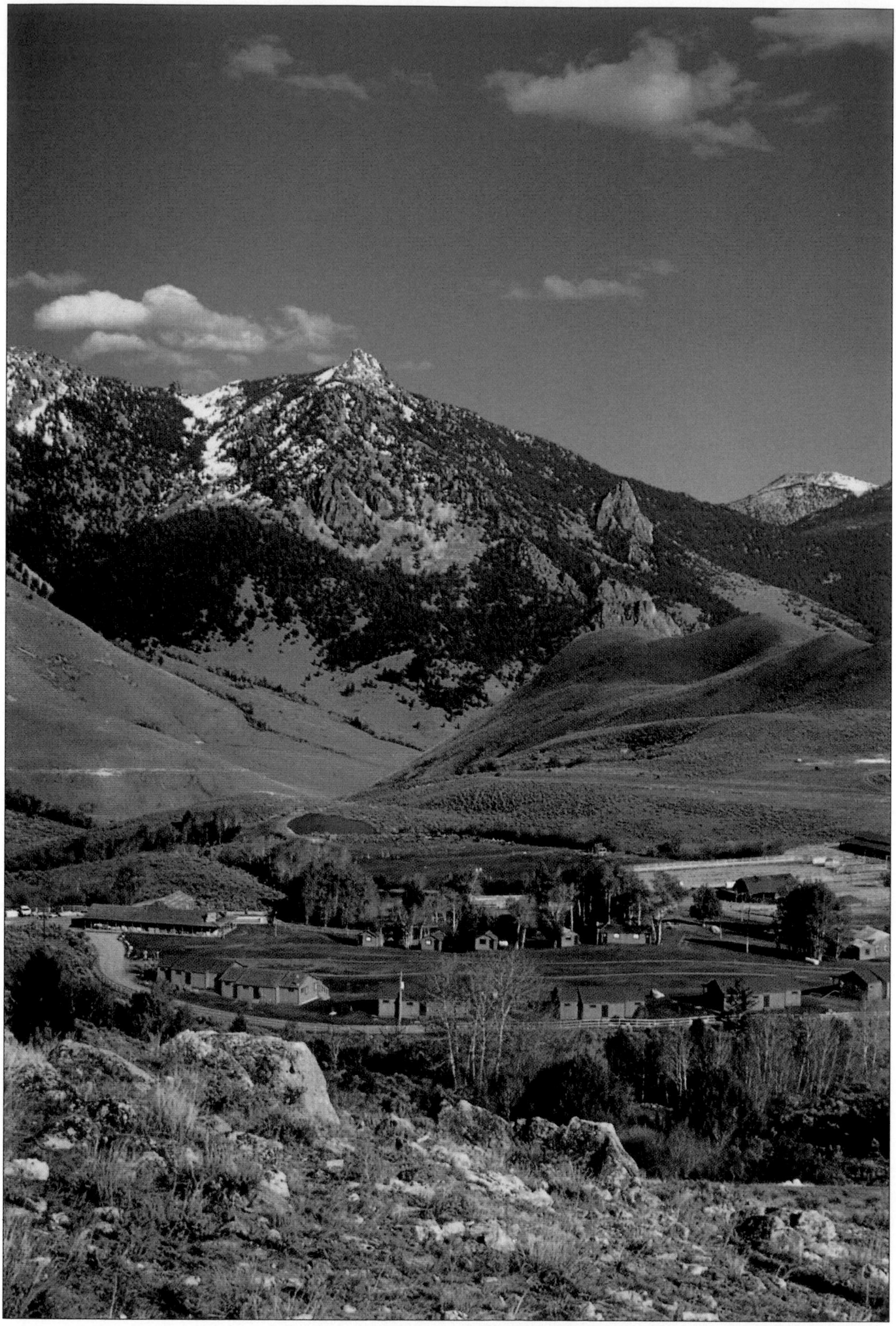

Twin Peaks Ranch, Idaho

See ranch description on page 114.

The Wild Horse Creek Ranch, Idaho

See ranch description on page 109.

The Wild Horse Creek Ranch, Idaho

See ranch description on page 109.

63 Ranch, Montana

See ranch description on page 124.

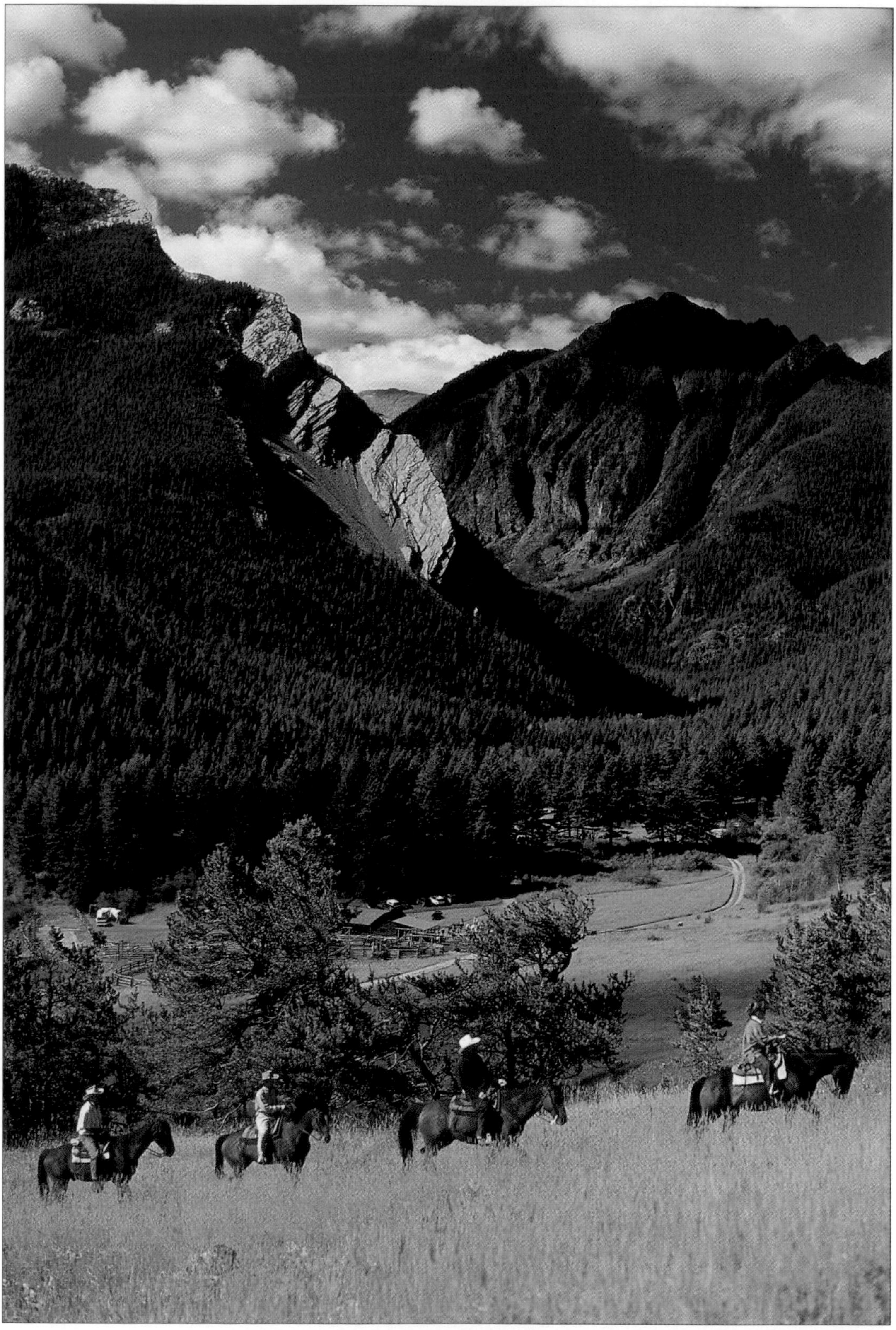

320 Guest Ranch, Montana

See ranch description on page 125.

Crazy Mountain Ranch, Montana

See ranch description on page 136.

See ranch description on page 136.

Diamond J Ranch, Montana

See ranch description on pages 137 and 448.

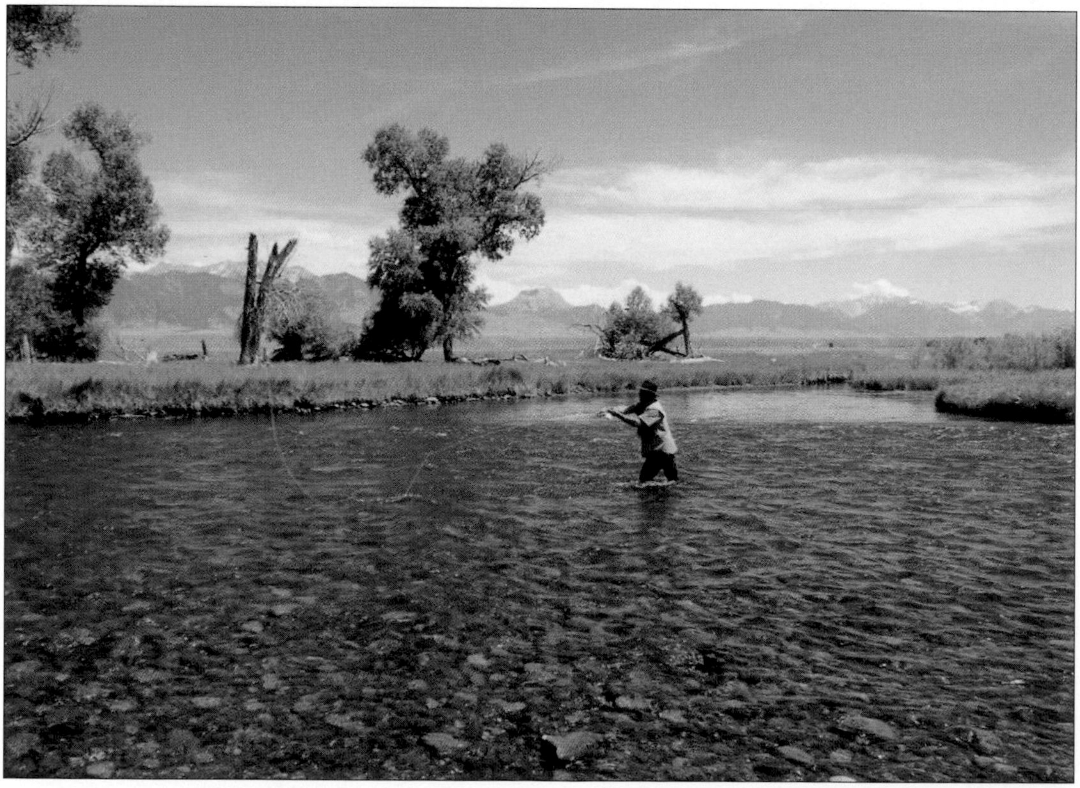

Diamond J Ranch, Montana

See ranch description on pages 137 and 448.

Elkhorn Ranch, Montana

See ranch description on page 138.

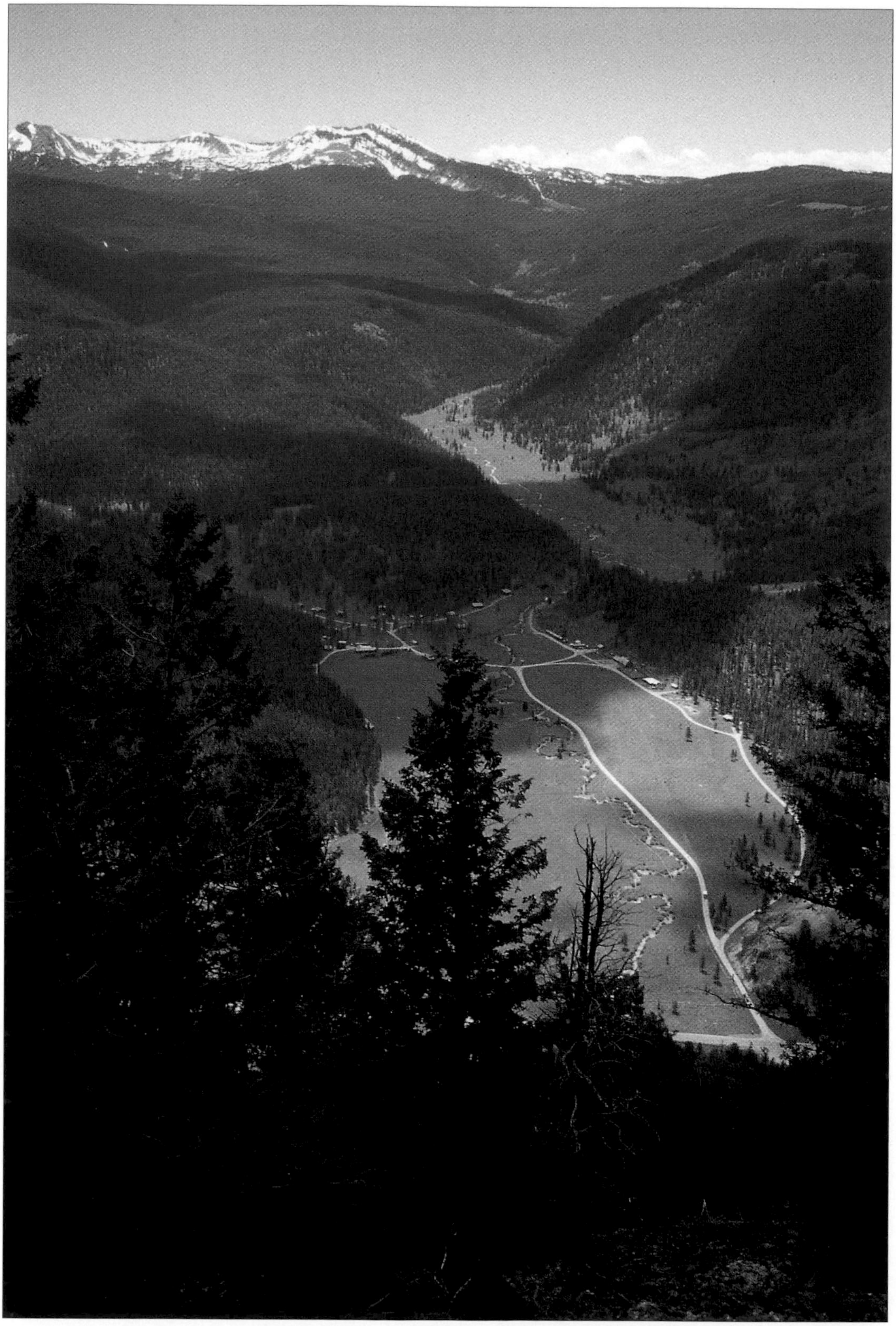

See ranch description on page 140.

Hargrave Cattle and Guest Ranch, Montana

See ranch description on page 142.

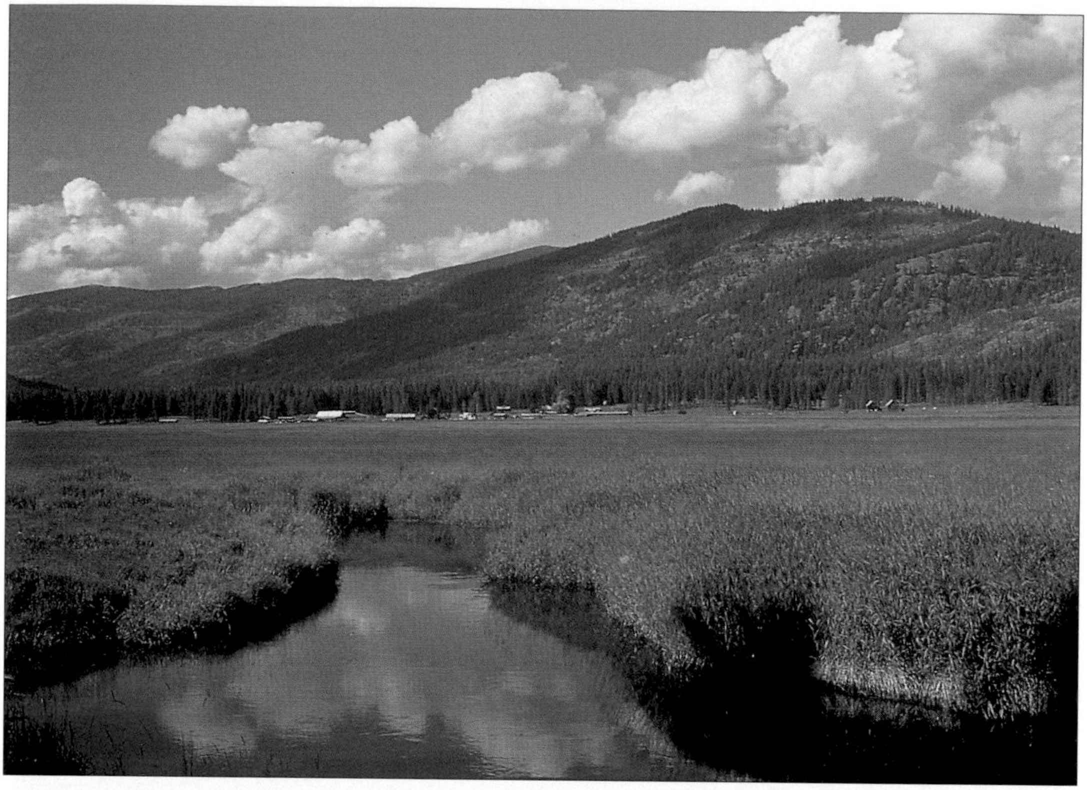

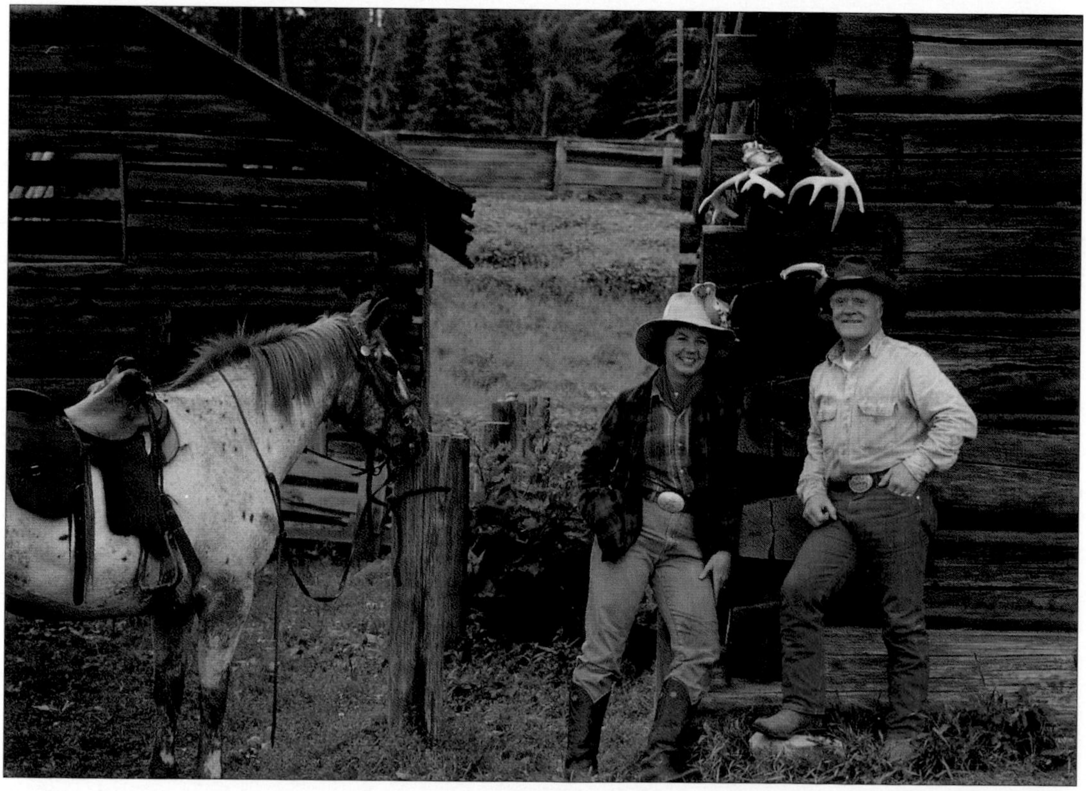

Horse Prairie Ranch, Montana

See ranch description on page 146.

Klick's K Bar L Ranch, Montana

See ranch description on page 148.

See ranch description on page 148.

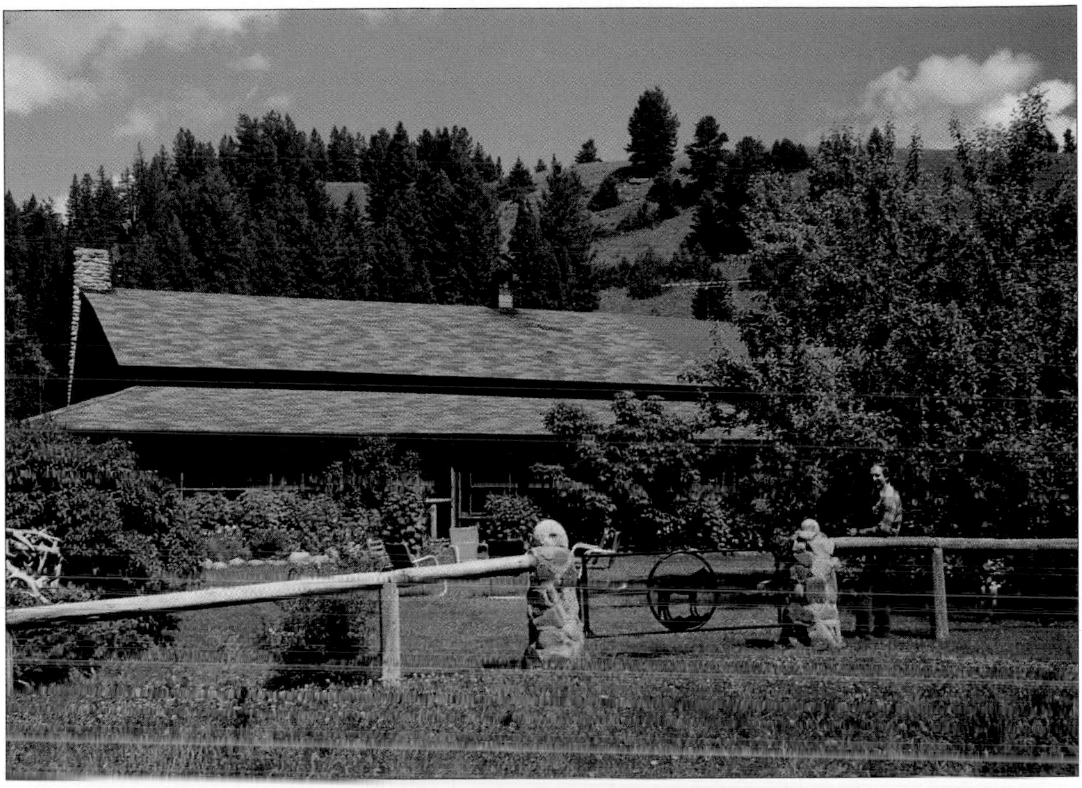

Lone Mountain Ranch, Montana

See ranch description on pages 154, 449, and 472.

Lone Mountain Ranch, Montana

See ranch description on pages 154, 449, and 472.

Mountain Sky Guest Ranch, Montana

See ranch description on page 156.

See ranch description on page 156.

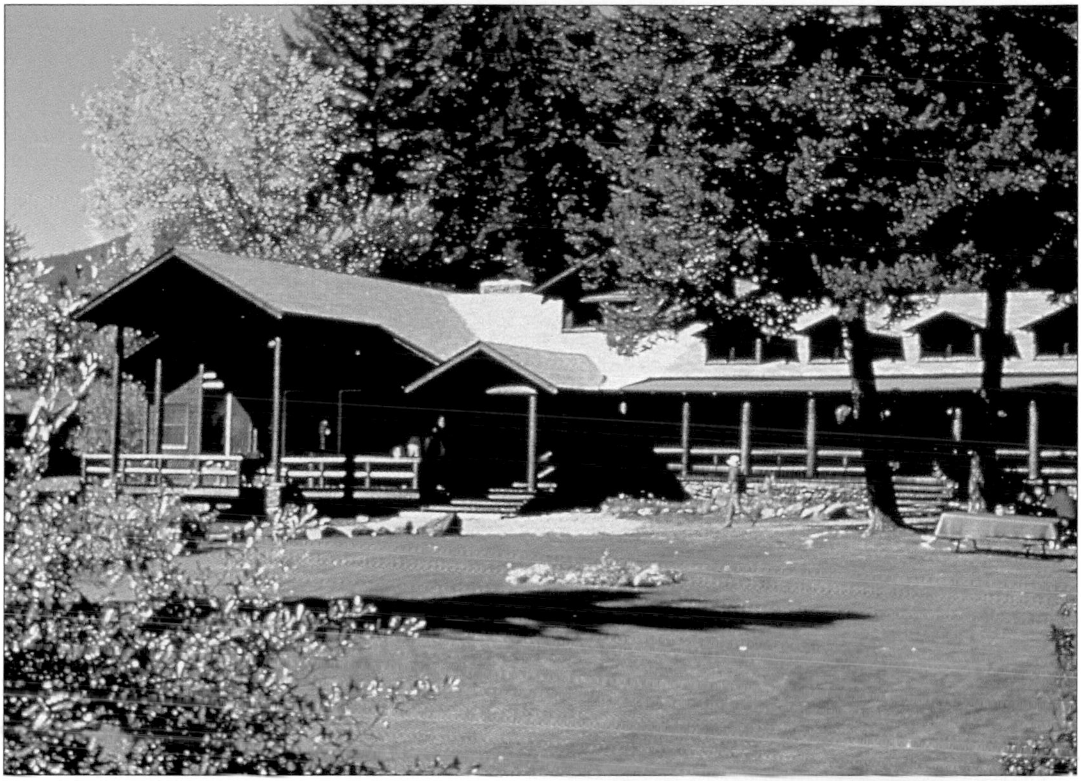

Nine Quarter Circle Ranch, Montana

See ranch description on page 153.

See ranch description on page 153.

RJR Ranch, Montana

See ranch description on page 160.

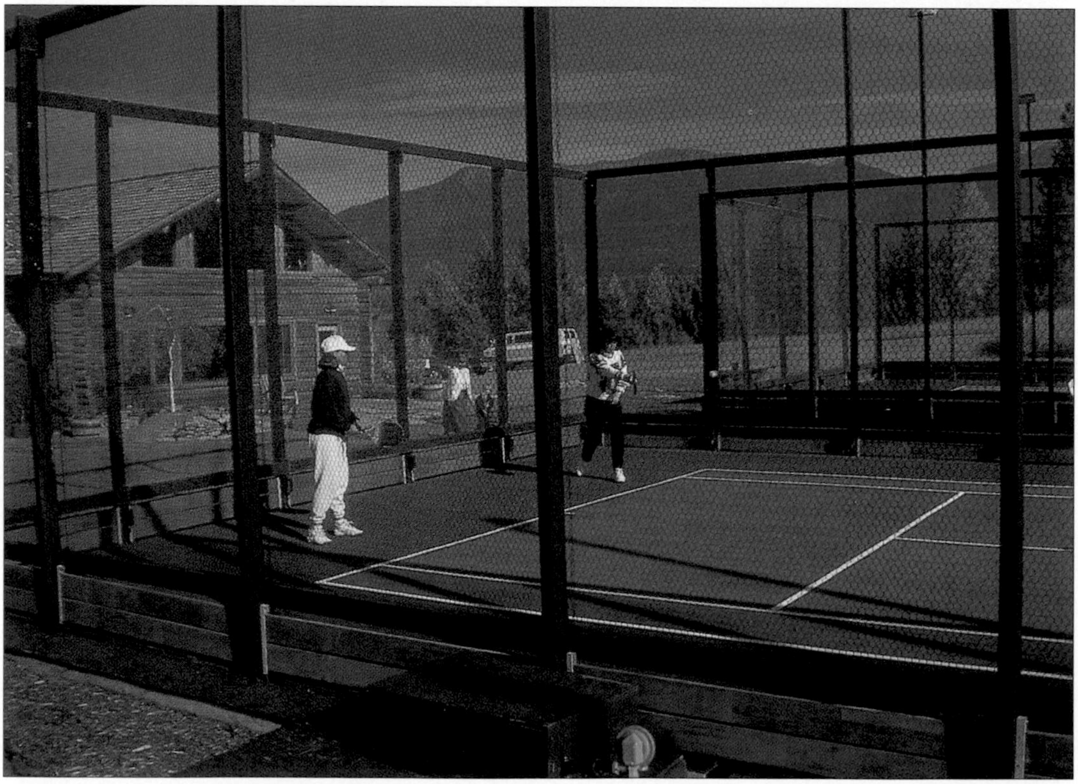

See ranch description on page 161.

Triple Creek Ranch, Montana

See ranch description on pages 164, 451, and 473.

Triple Creek Ranch, Montana

See ranch description on pages 164, 451, and 473.

The Lodge at Chama, New Mexico

See ranch description on pages 334 and 452.

See ranch description on pages 334 and 452.

Hartley Guest Ranch, New Mexico

See ranch description on page 333.

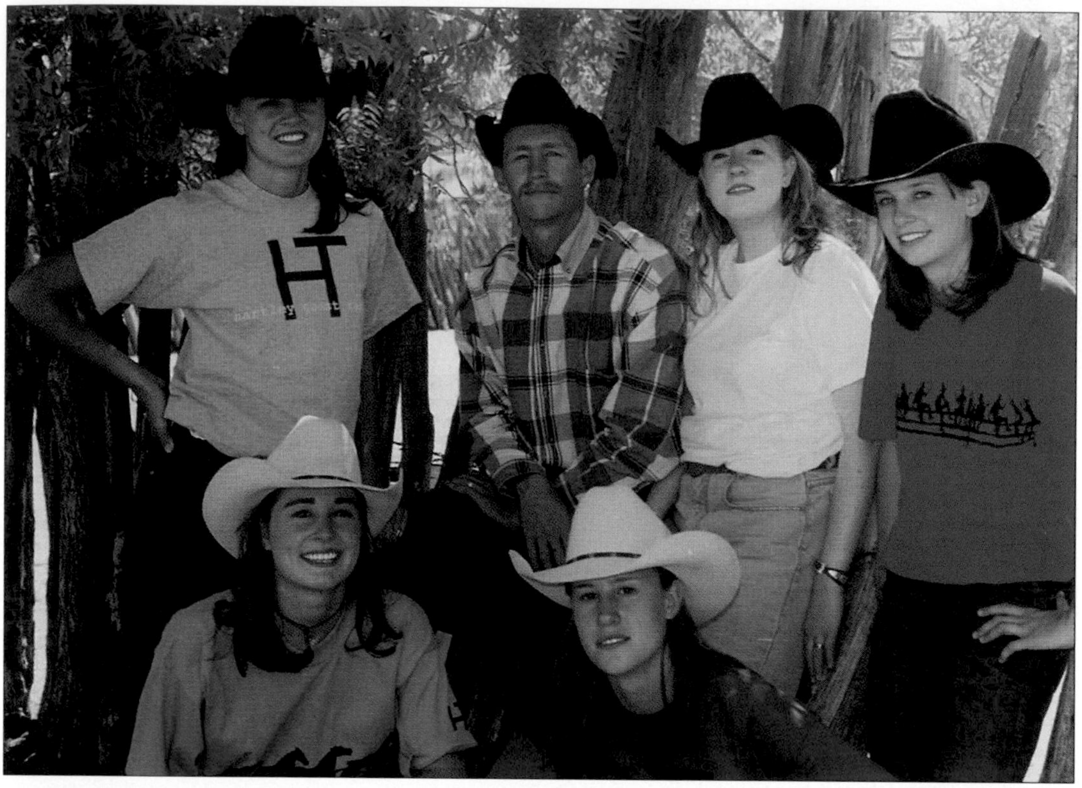

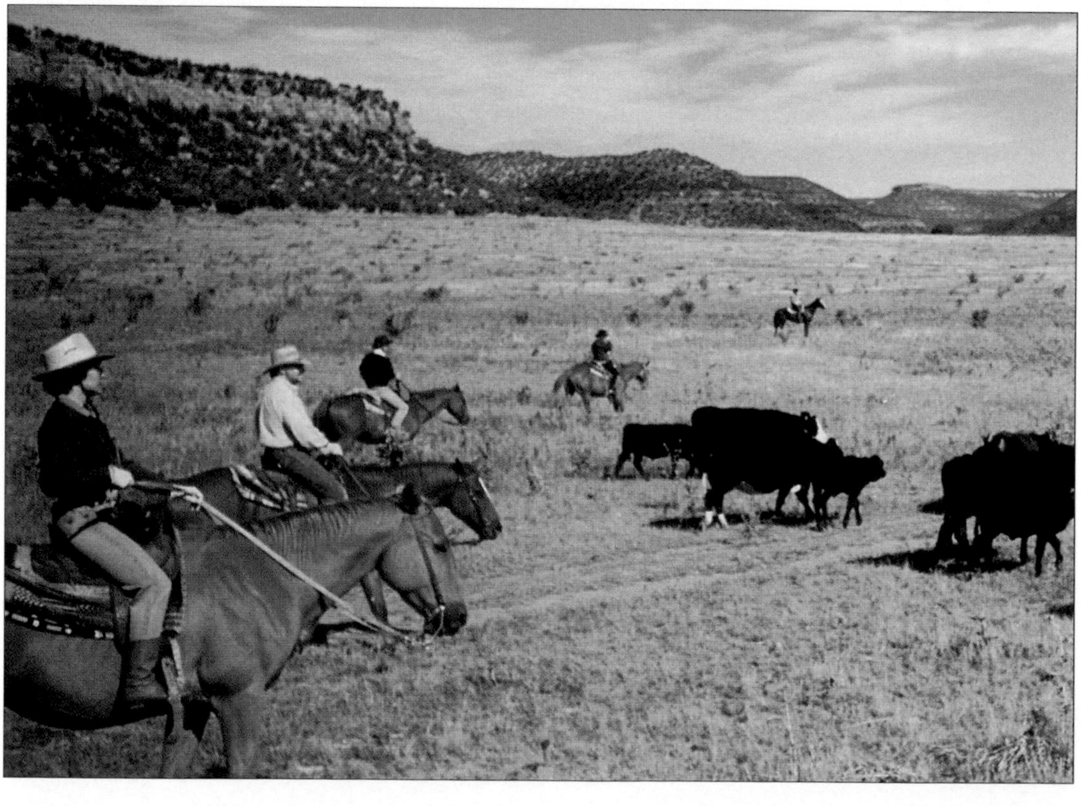

See ranch description on page 337.

Pinegrove Dude Ranch, New York

See ranch description on page 338.

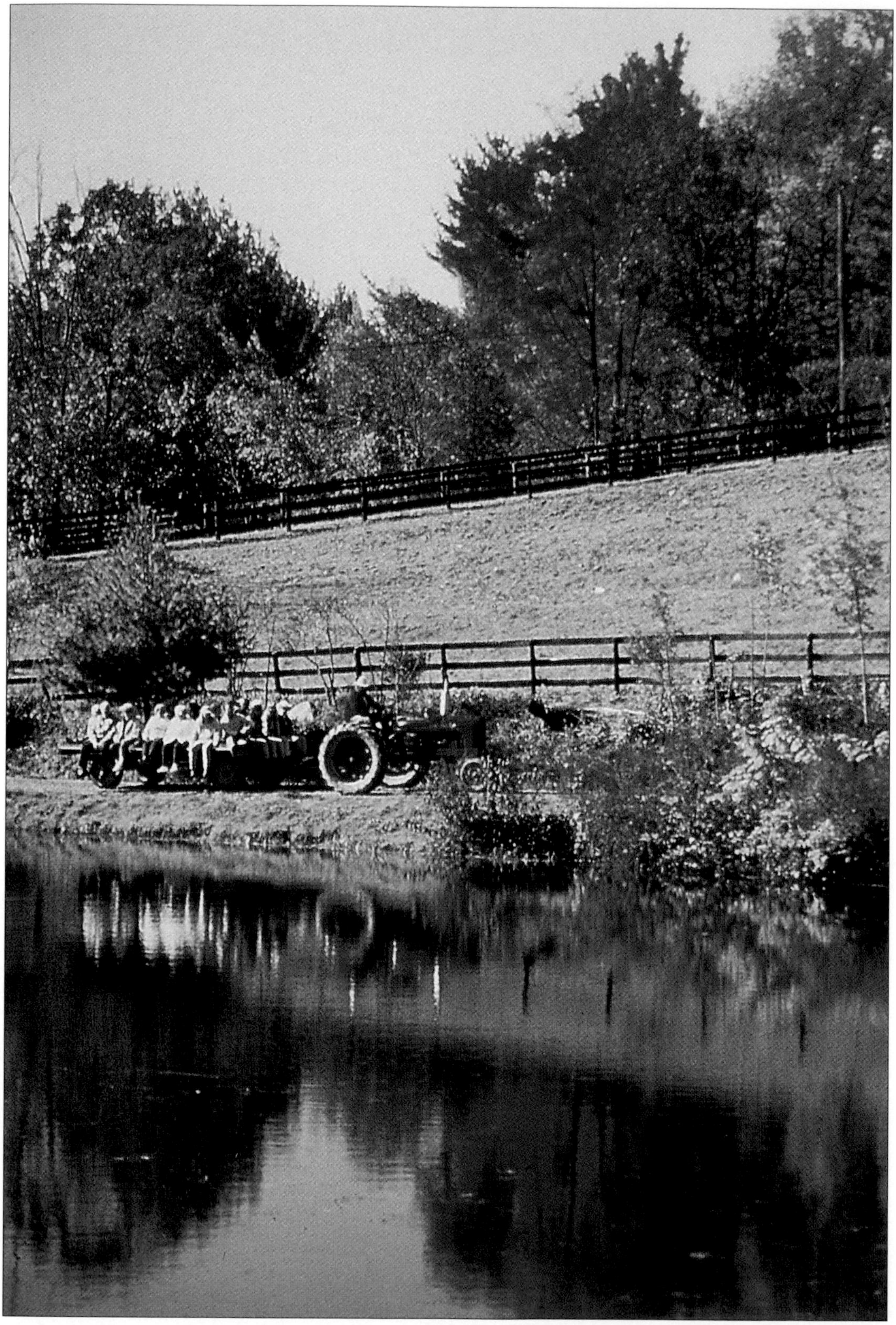

See ranch description on page 338.

Roaring Brook Ranch and Tennis Resort, New York

See ranch description on page 340.

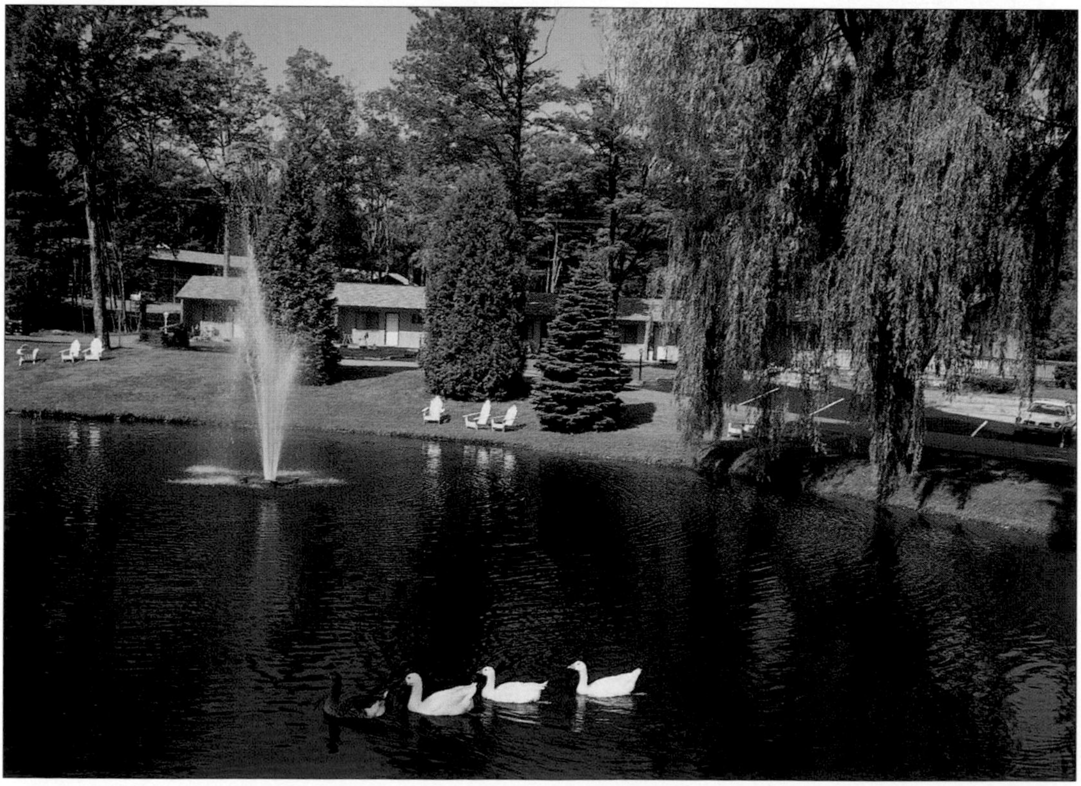

See ranch description on page 341.

Cataloochee Ranch, North Carolina

See ranch description on page 342.

See ranch description on page 343.

Earthshine Mountain Lodge, North Carolina

See ranch description on page 344.

See ranch description on page 345.

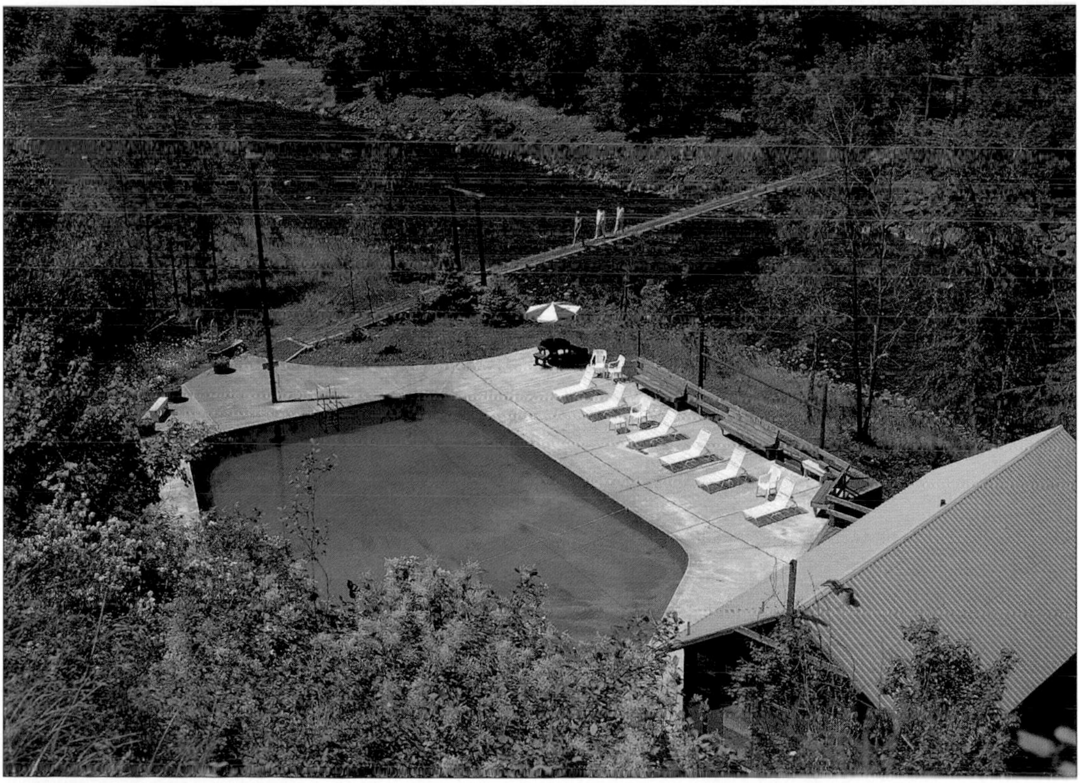

Aspen Ridge Resort, Oregon

See ranch description on page 346.

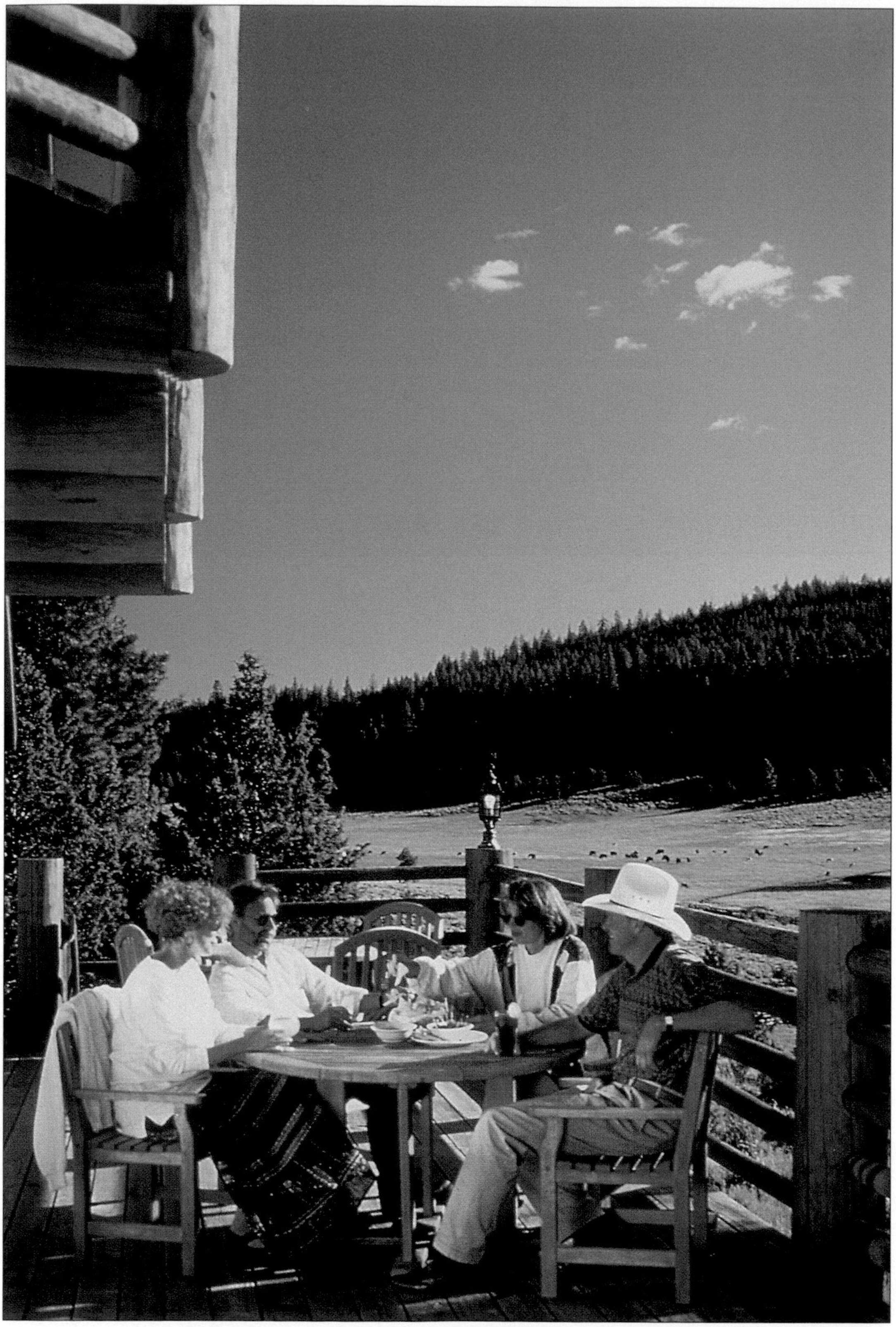

See ranch description on page 346.

Blue Bell Lodge & Resort, South Dakota

See ranch description on page 353.

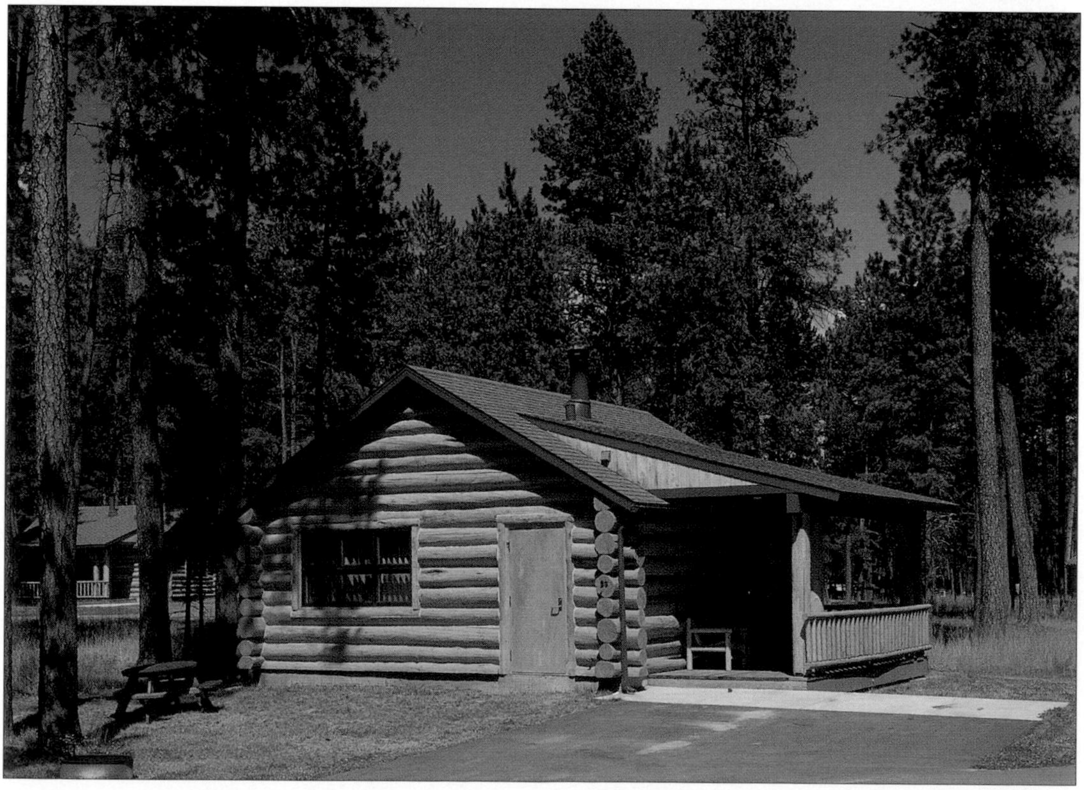

See ranch description on page 355.

Flying L Guest Ranch, Texas

See ranch description on page 357.

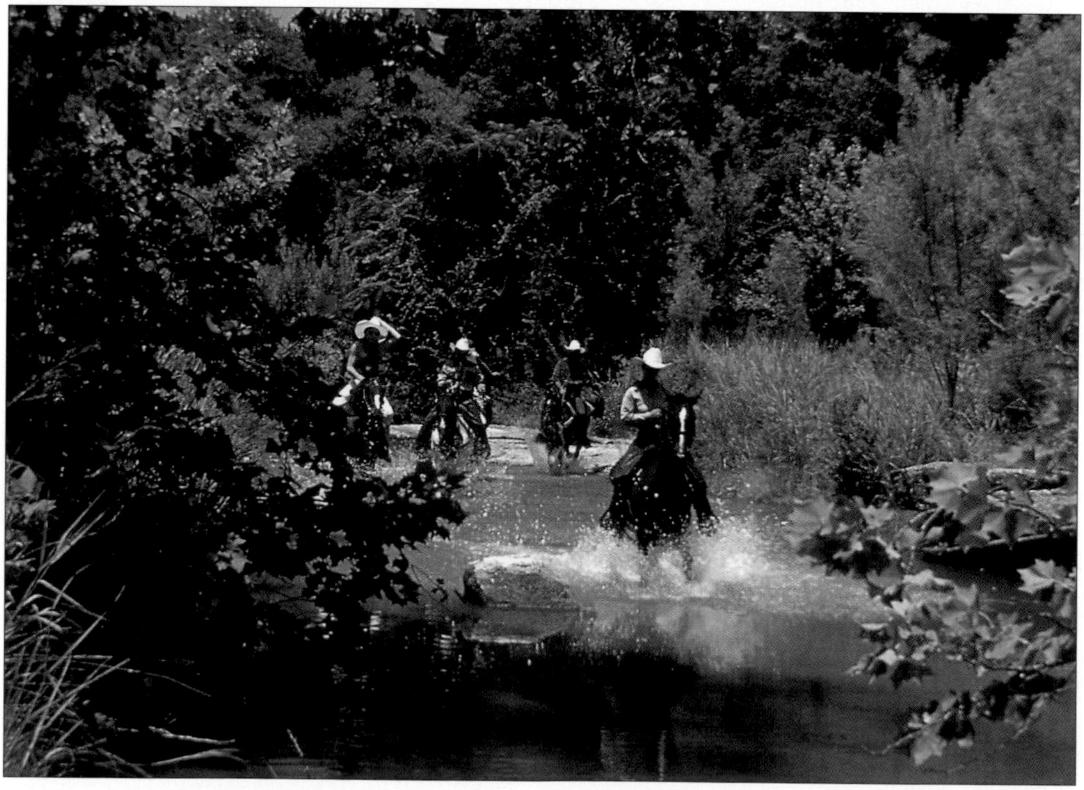

Reid Ranch, Utah

See ranch description on page 360.

Hidden Valley Guest Ranch, Washington

See ranch description on page 361.

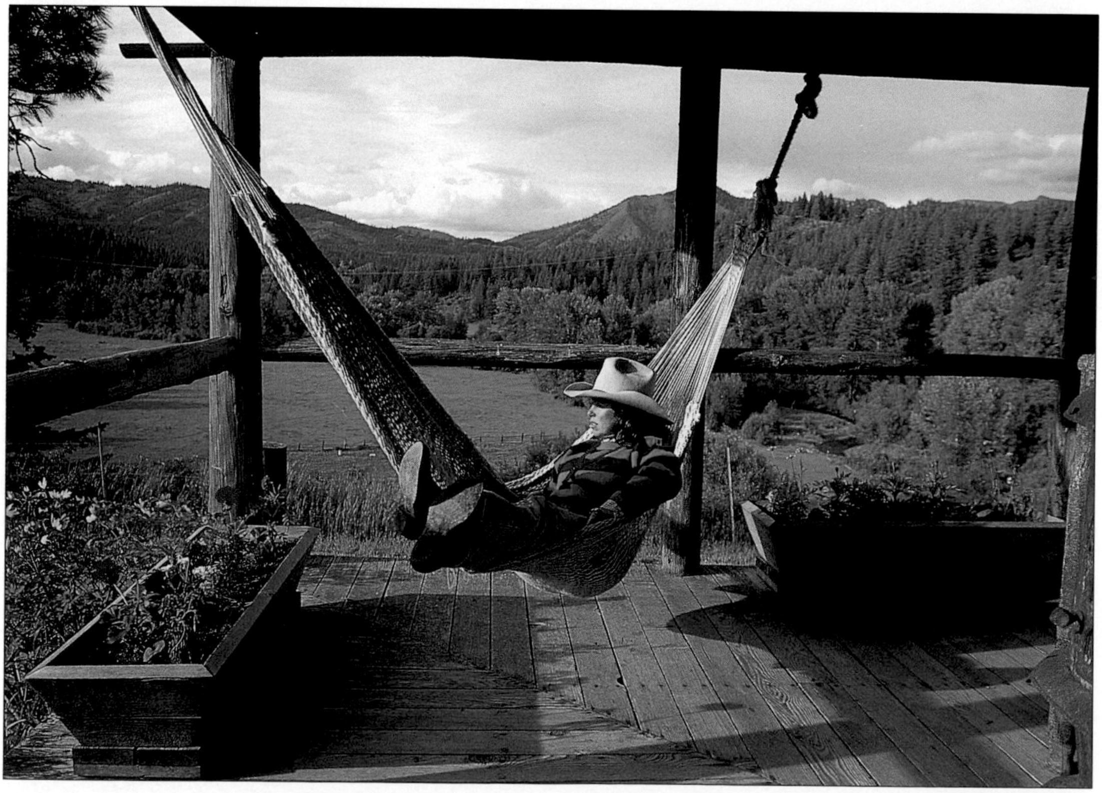

Bill Cody Ranch, Wyoming

See ranch description on page 365.

Bitterroot Ranch, Wyoming

See ranch description on page 366.

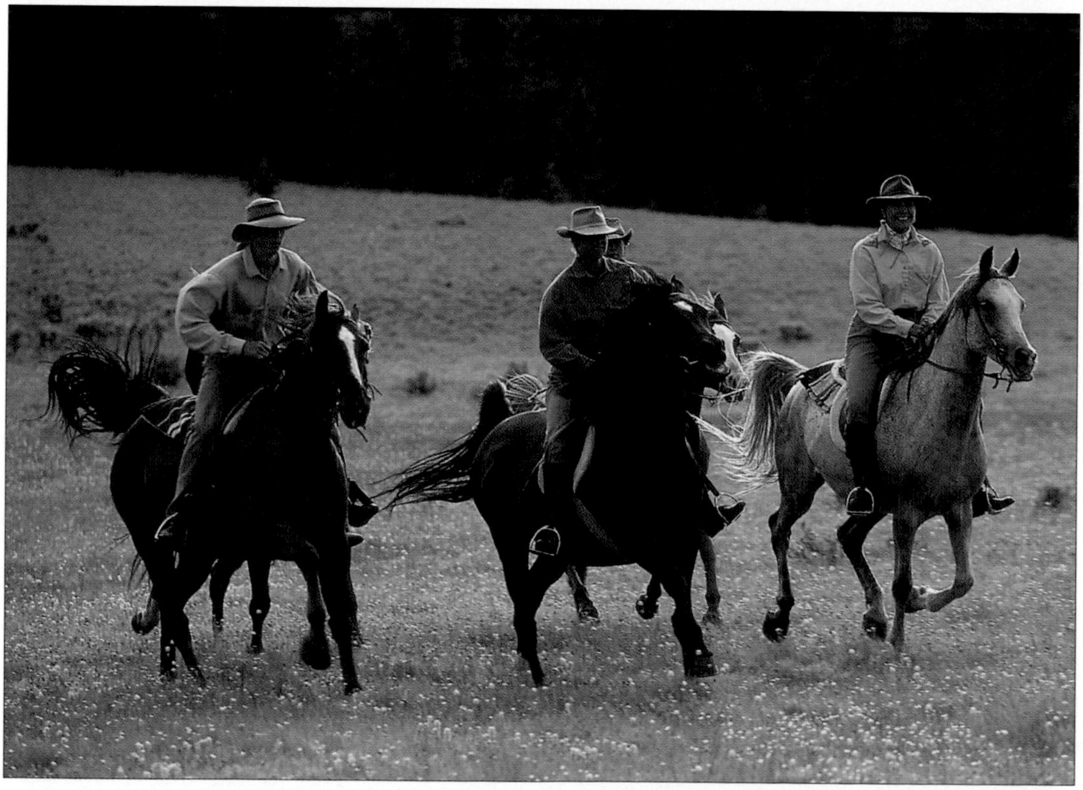

Brush Creek Ranch, Wyoming

See ranch description on pages 372, 453, and 475.

Brooks Lake Lodge, Wyoming

See ranch description on pages 370 and 474.

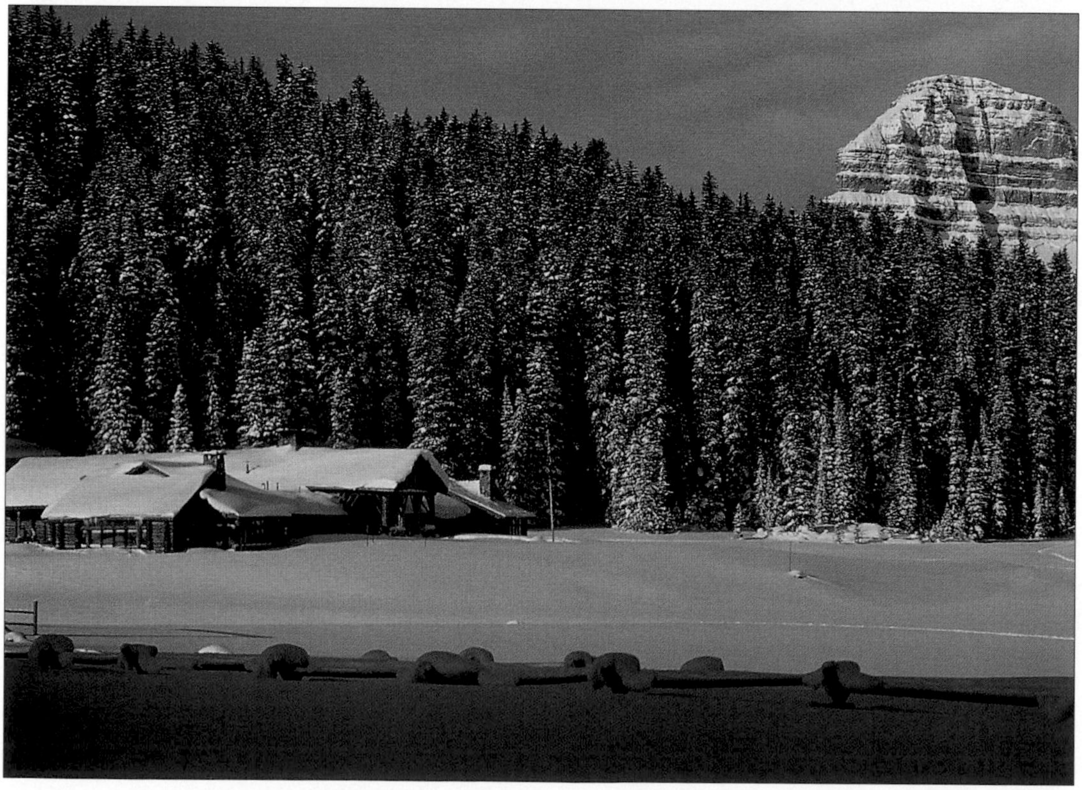

See ranch description on pages 370 and 474.

CM Ranch, Wyoming

See ranch description on page 374.

Canyon Ranch, Wyoming

See ranch description on page 454.

Crescent H Ranch, Wyoming

See ranch description on page 456.

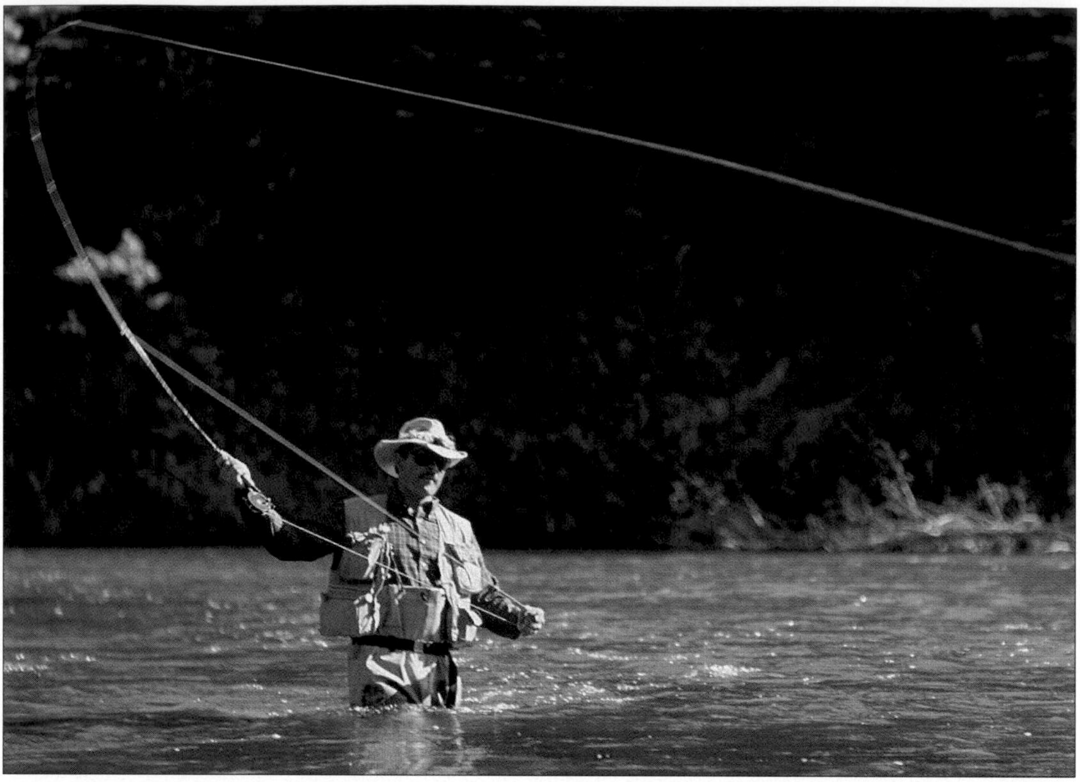

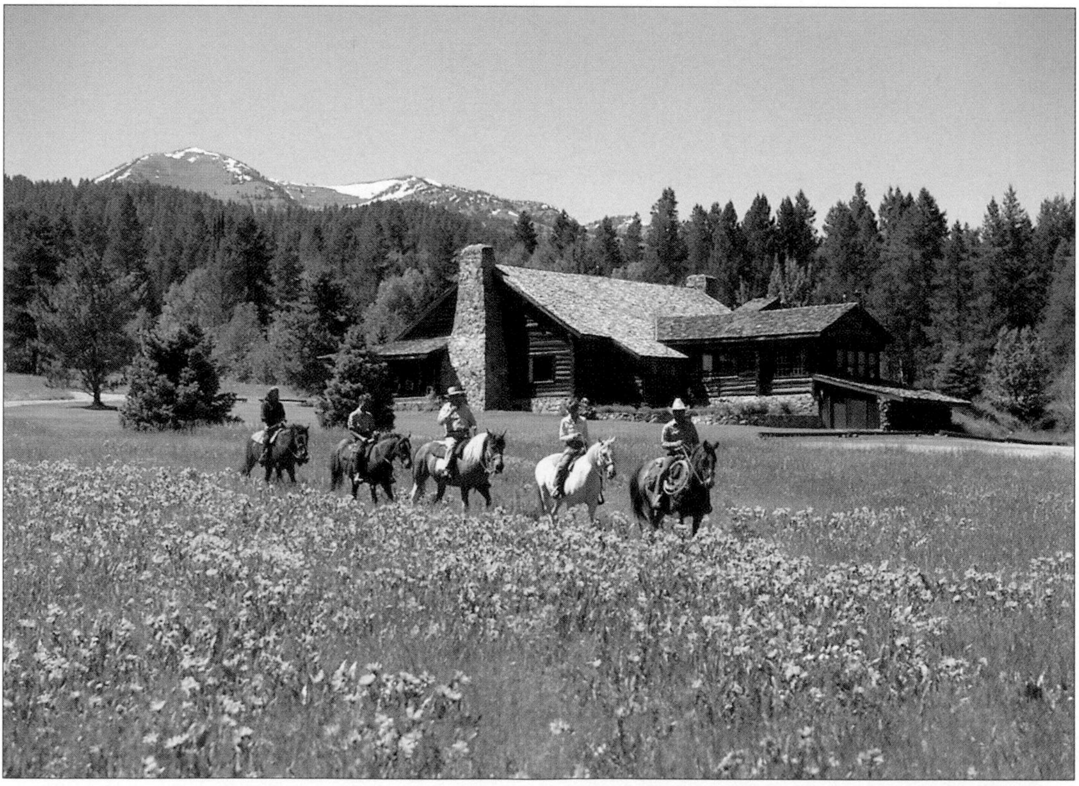

Crescent H Ranch, Wyoming

See ranch description on page 456.

Crossed Sabres Ranch, Wyoming

See ranch description on page 376.

See ranch description on page 376.

Double Diamond X Ranch, Wyoming

See ranch description on page 378.

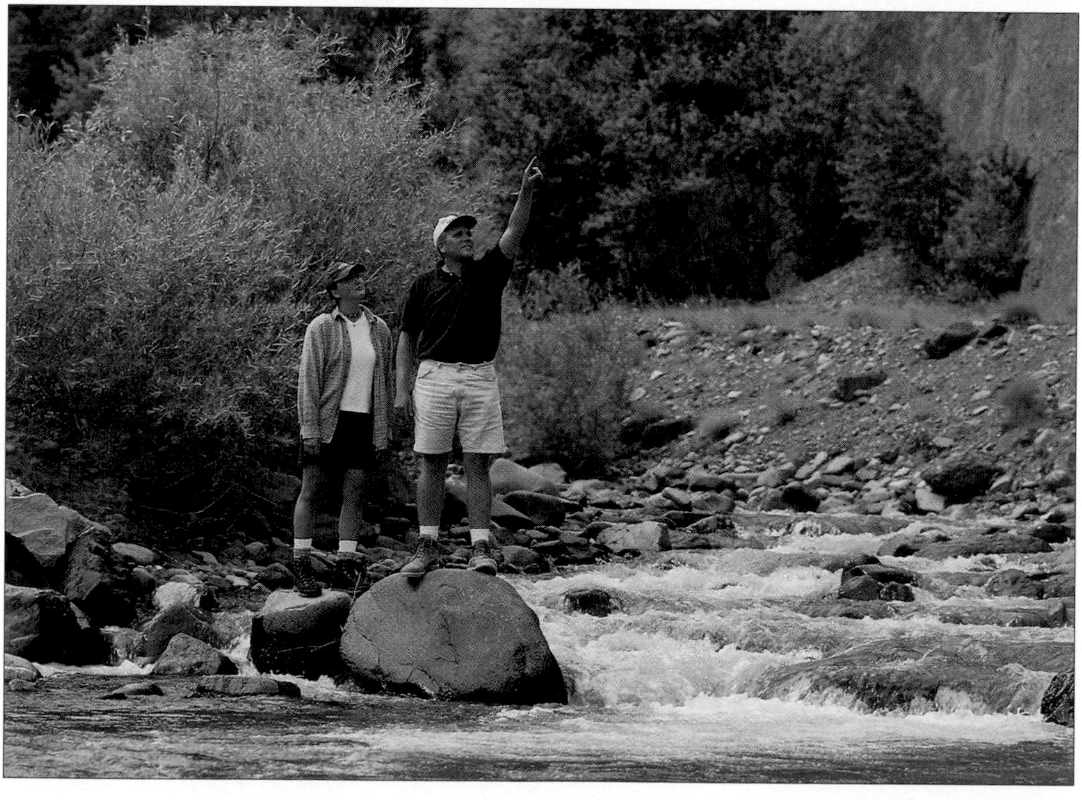

See ranch description on page 378.

Eatons' Ranch, Wyoming

See ranch description on page 375.

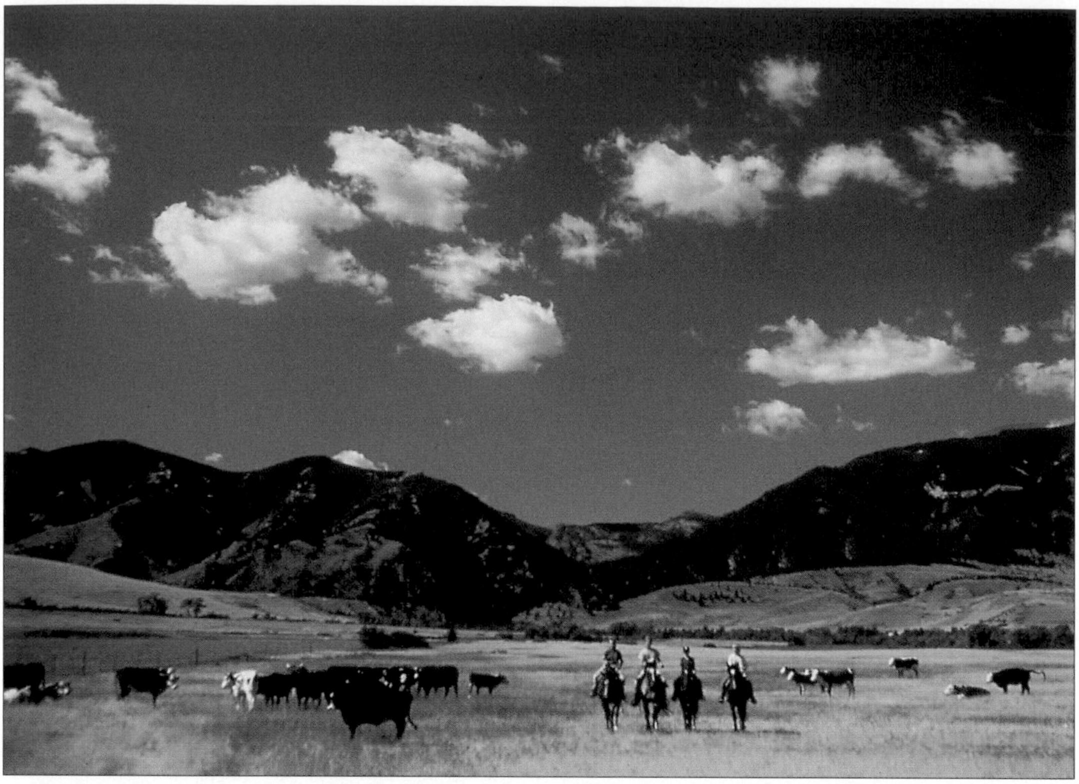

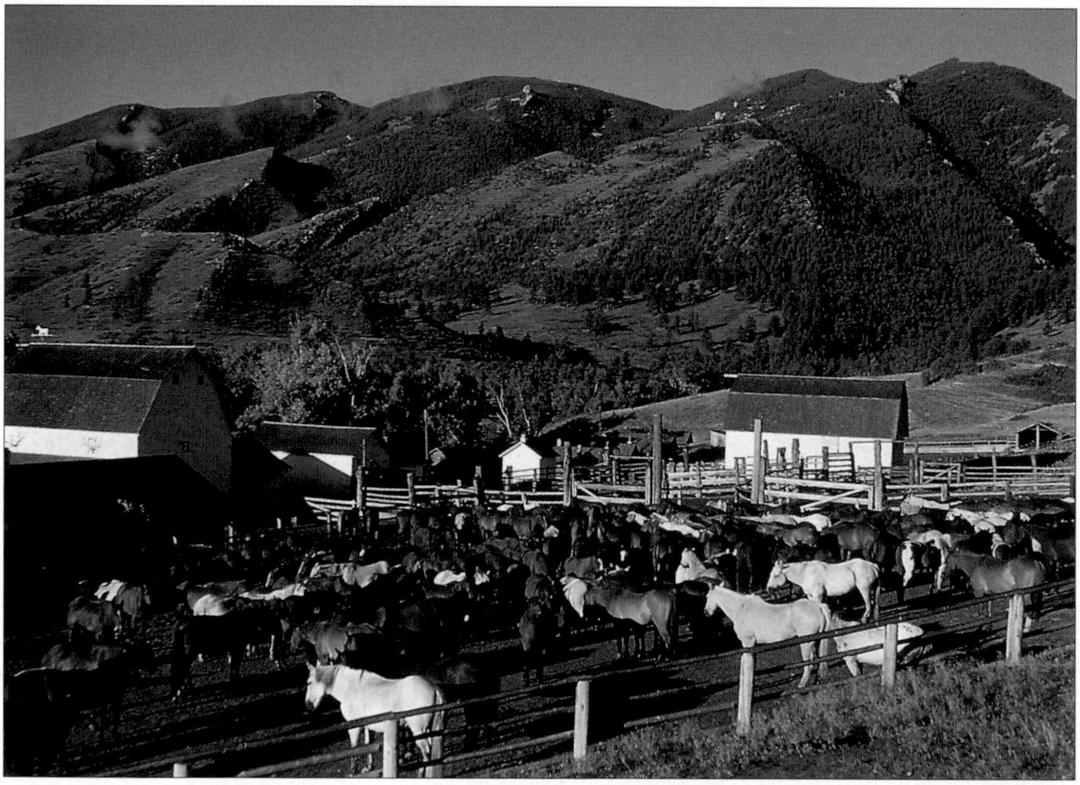

See ranch description on page 380.

Gros Ventre River Ranch, Wyoming

See ranch description on page 384.

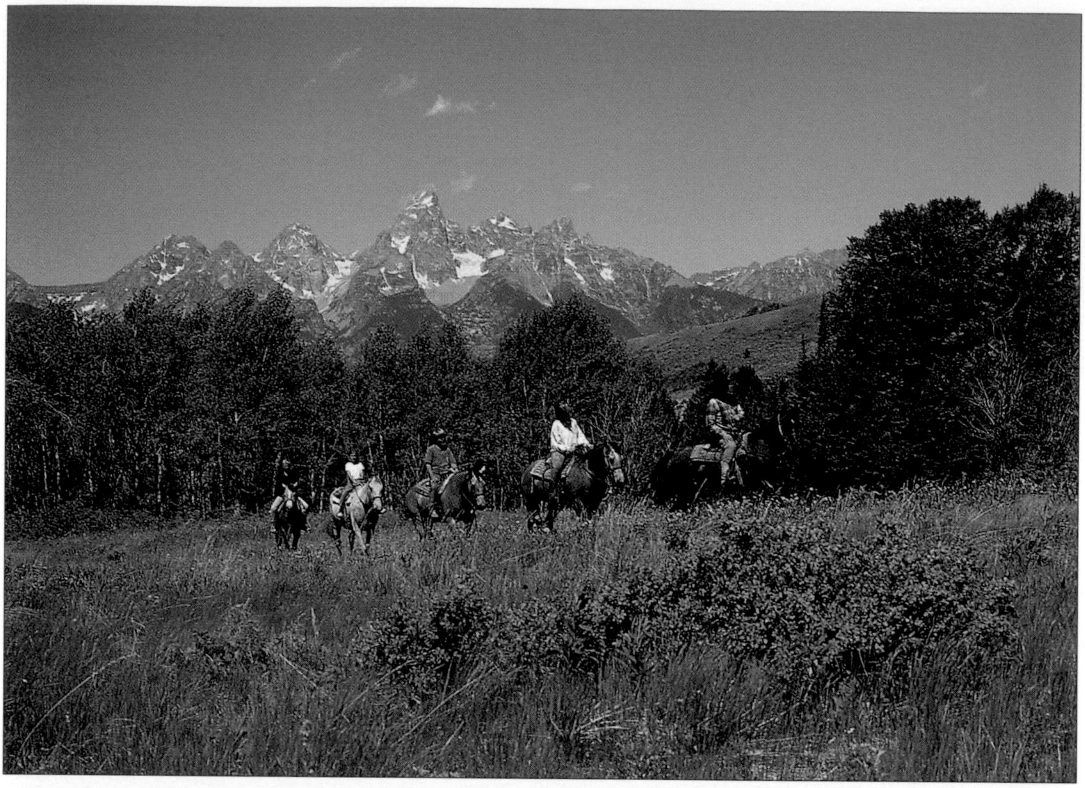

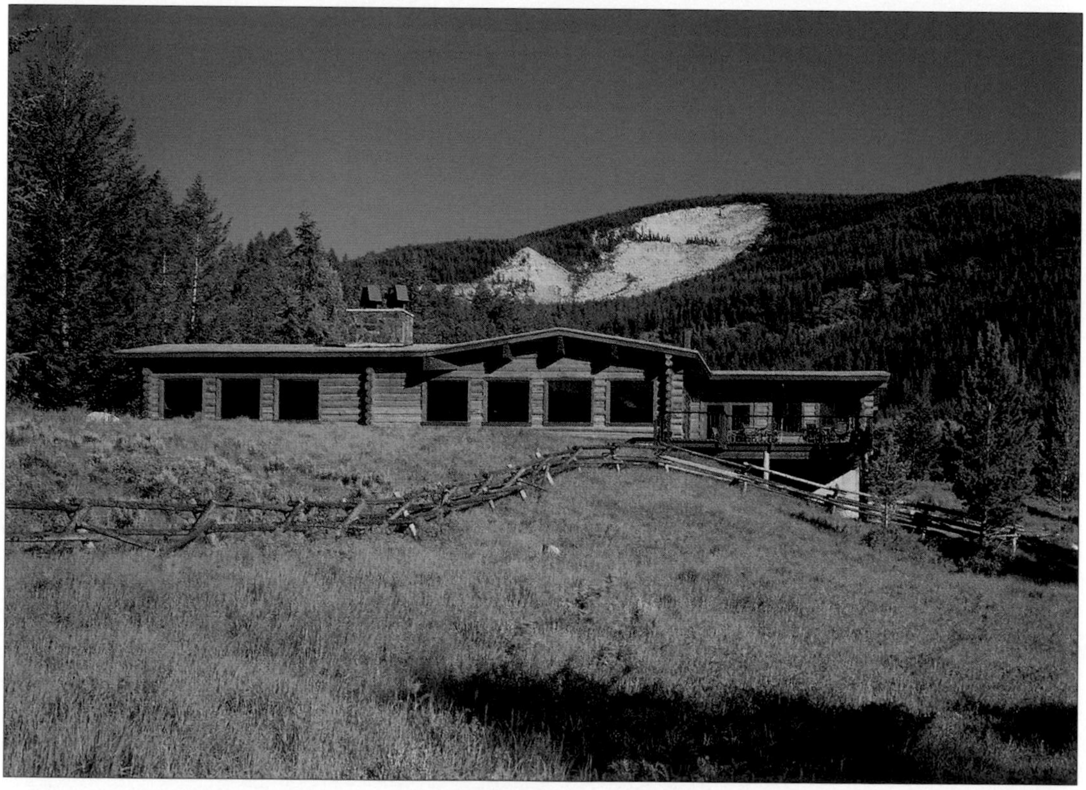

Gros Ventre River Ranch, Wyoming

See ranch description on page 384.

The Hideout at Flitner Ranch, Wyoming

See ranch description on page 390.

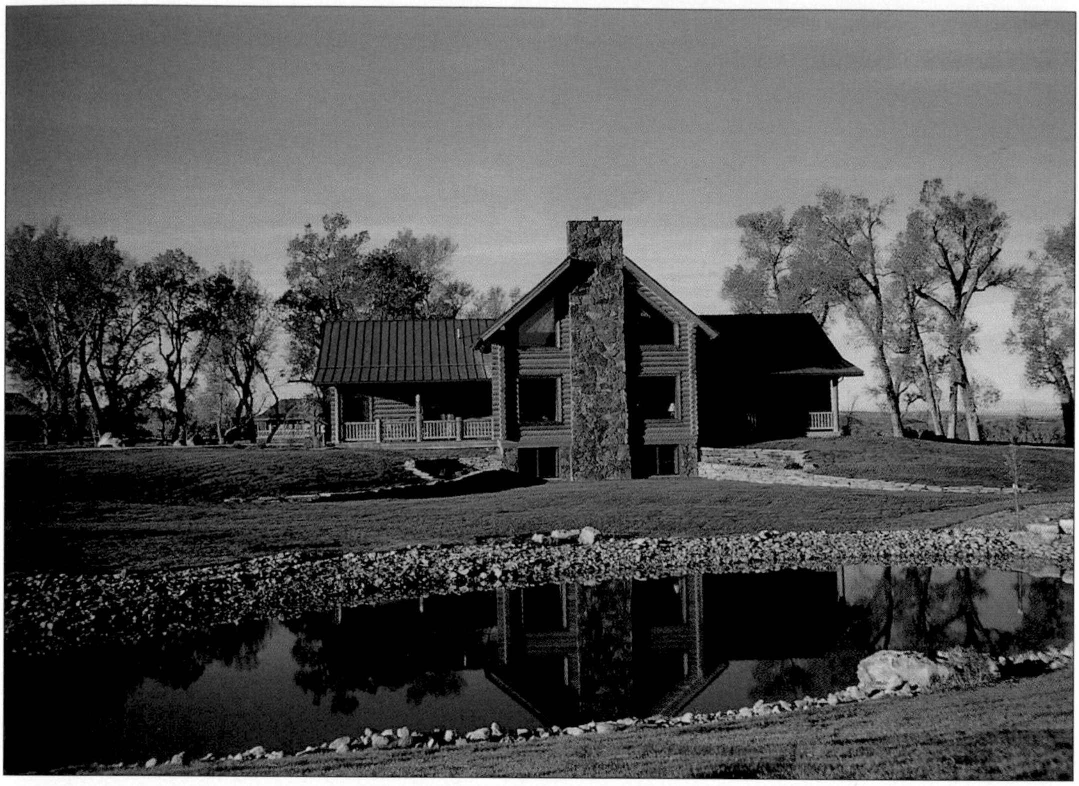

The Hideout at Flitner Ranch, Wyoming

See ranch description on page 390.

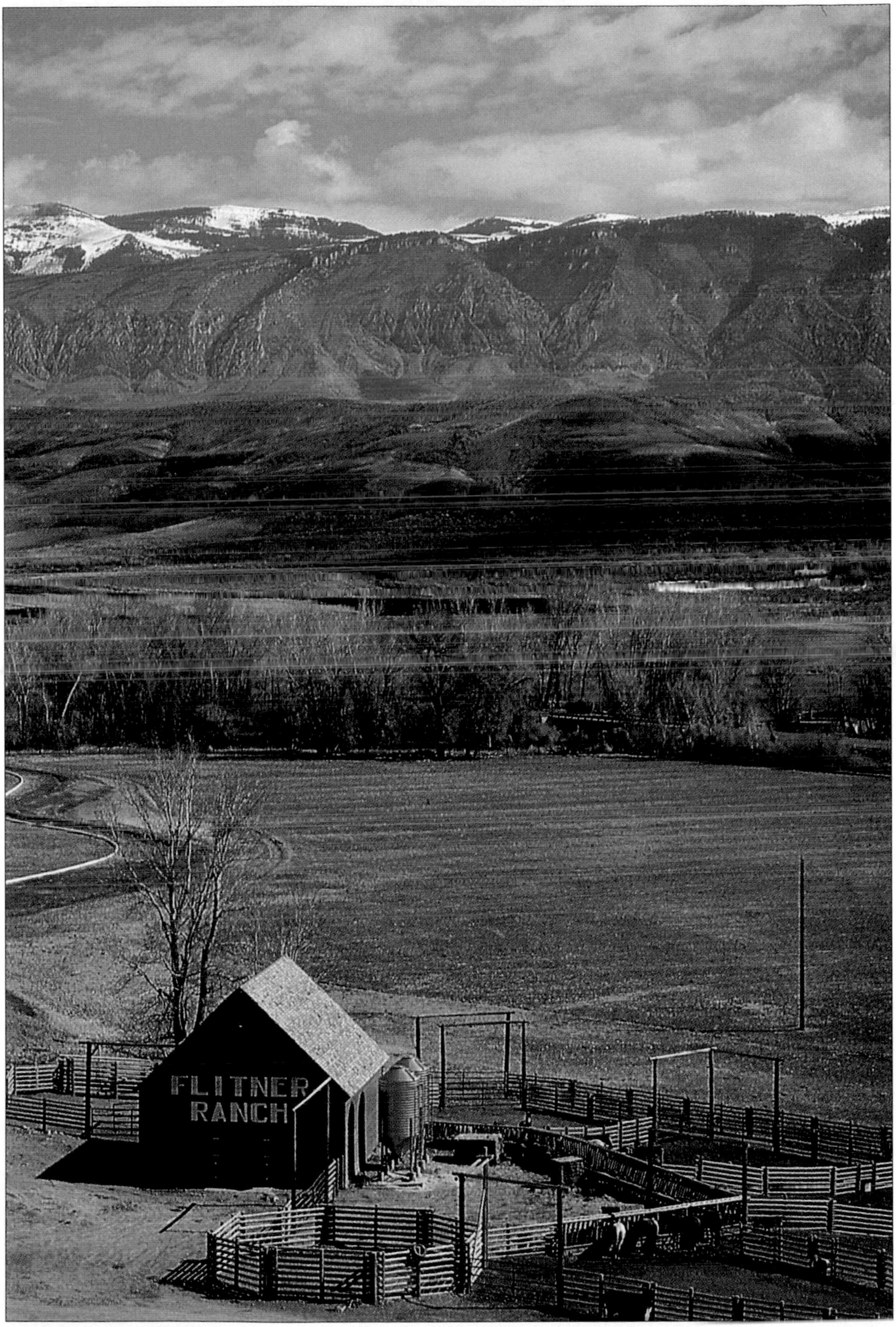

Lazy L & B Ranch, Wyoming

See ranch description on page 396.

Moose Head Ranch, Wyoming

See ranch description on page 391.

Lost Creek Ranch, Wyoming

See ranch description on page 398.

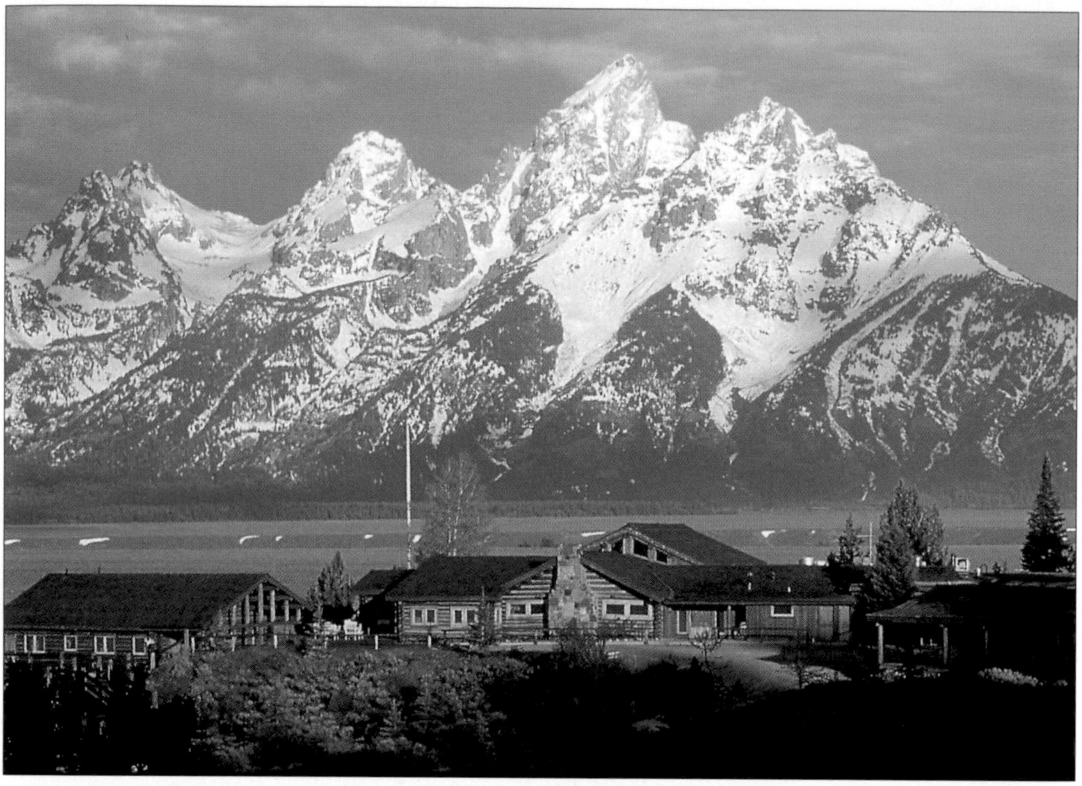

See ranch description on page 398.

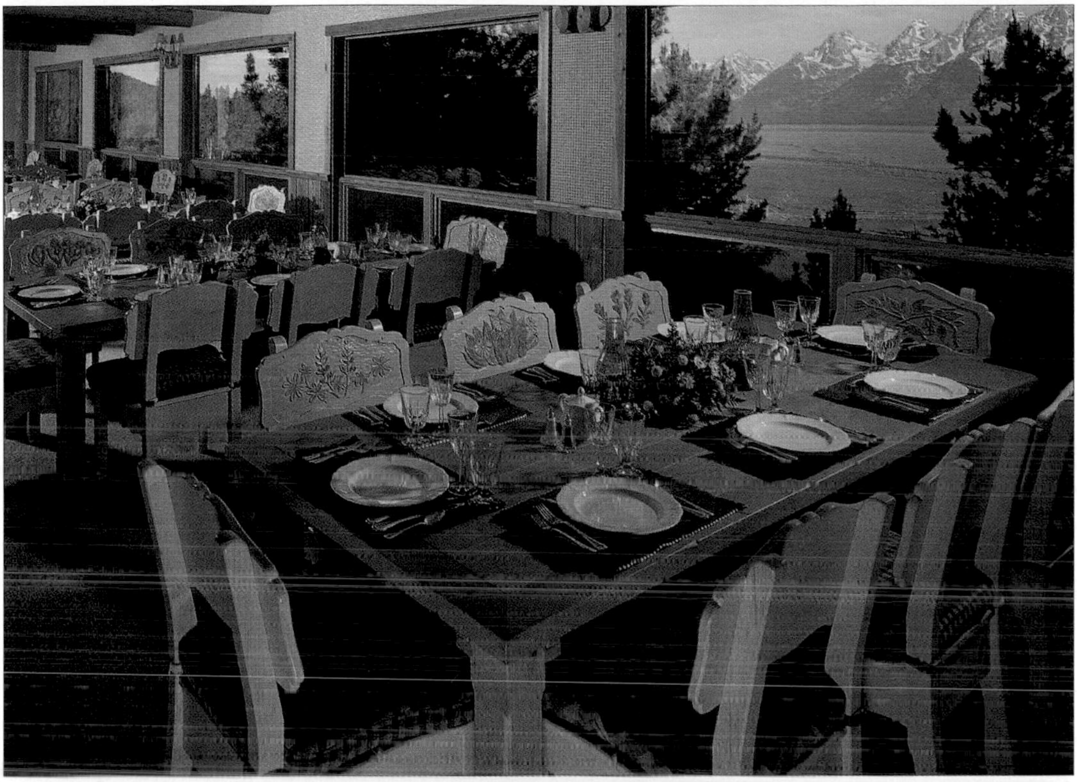

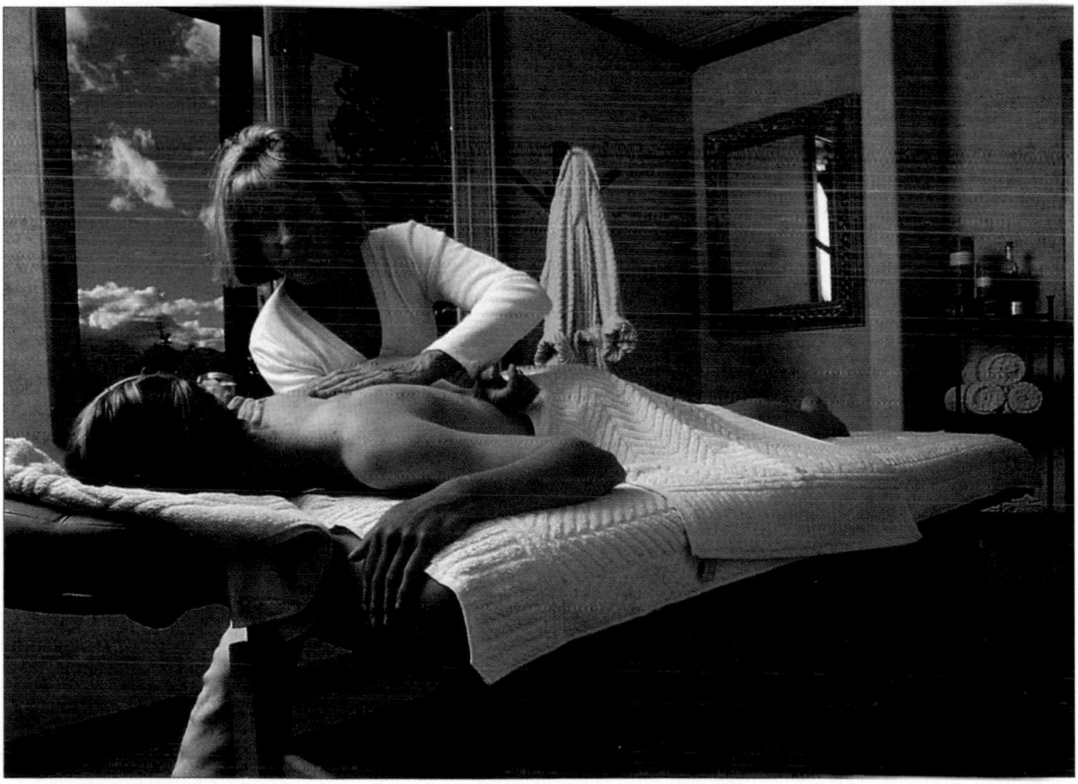

Paradise Guest Ranch, Wyoming

See ranch description on page 402.

Paradise Guest Ranch, Wyoming

See ranch description on page 402.

Red Rock Ranch, Wyoming

See ranch description on page 406.

Red Rock Ranch, Wyoming

See ranch description on page 406.

Seven D Ranch, Wyoming

See ranch description on page 410.

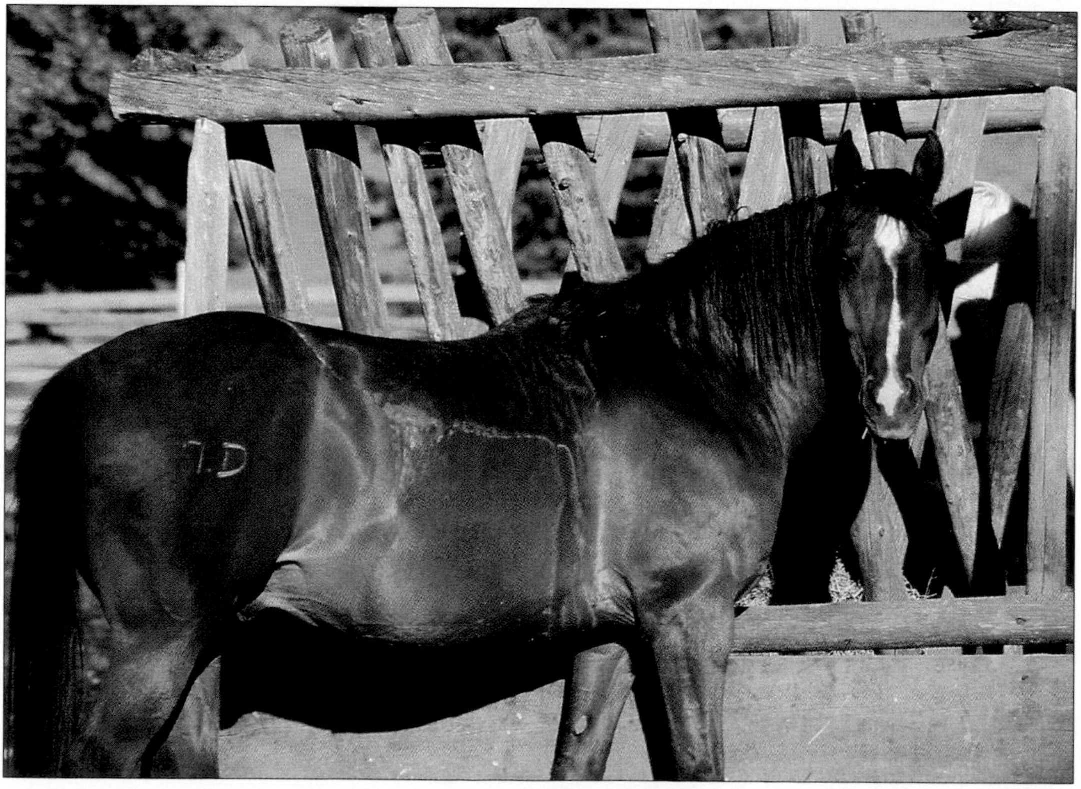

TA Guest Ranch, Wyoming

See ranch description on page 412.

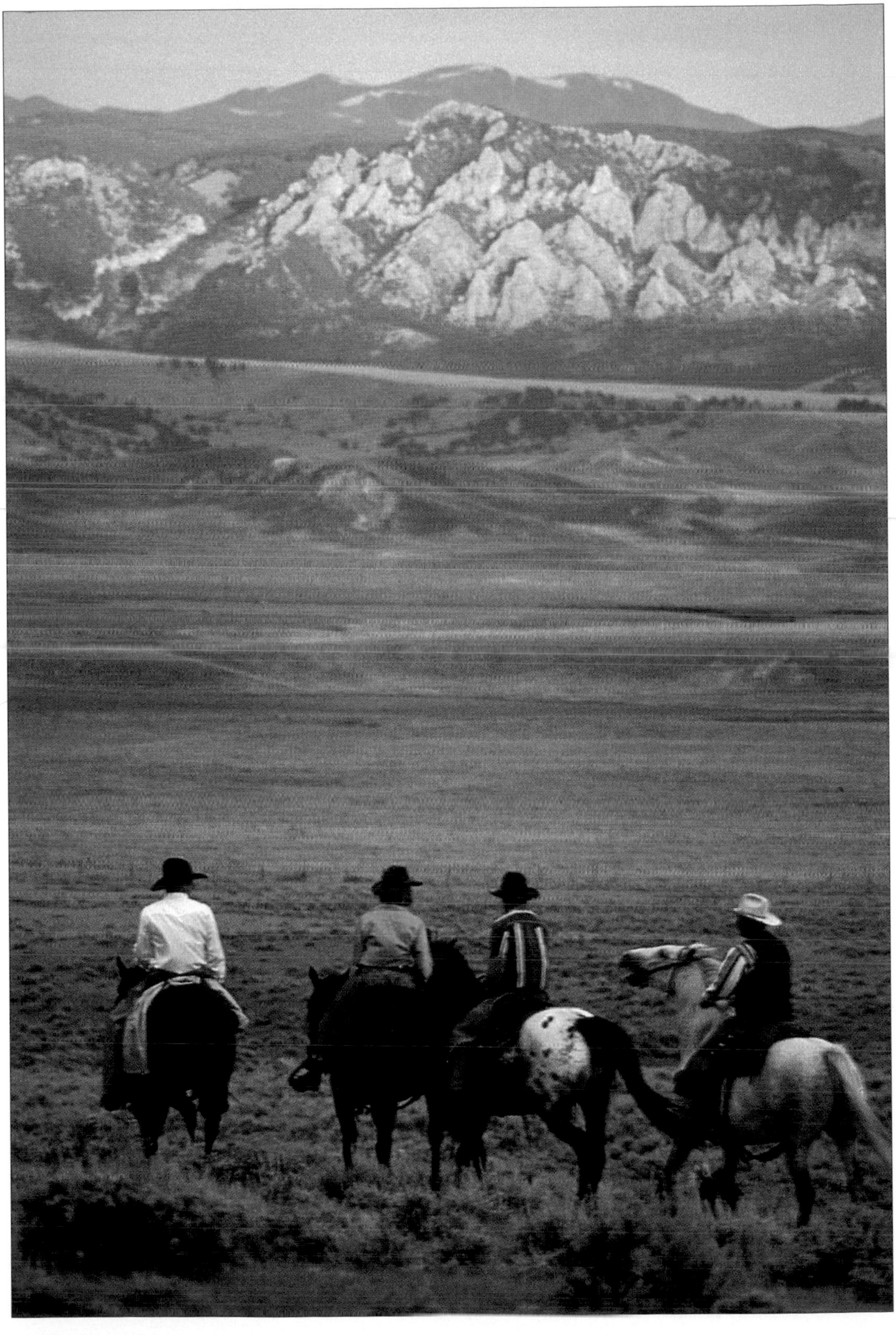

T-Cross Ranch, Wyoming

See ranch description on page 414.

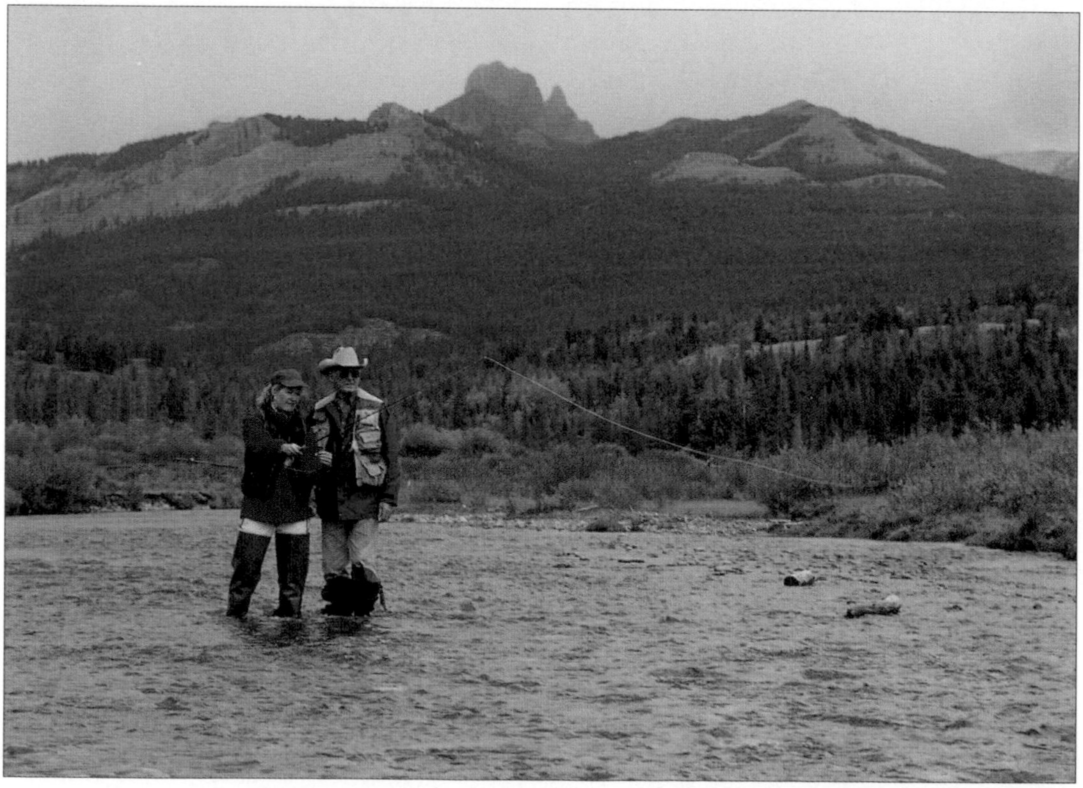

T-Cross Ranch, Wyoming

See ranch description on page 414.

Triangle C Ranch, Wyoming

See ranch description on page 418.

Triangle C Ranch, Wyoming

See ranch description on page 418.

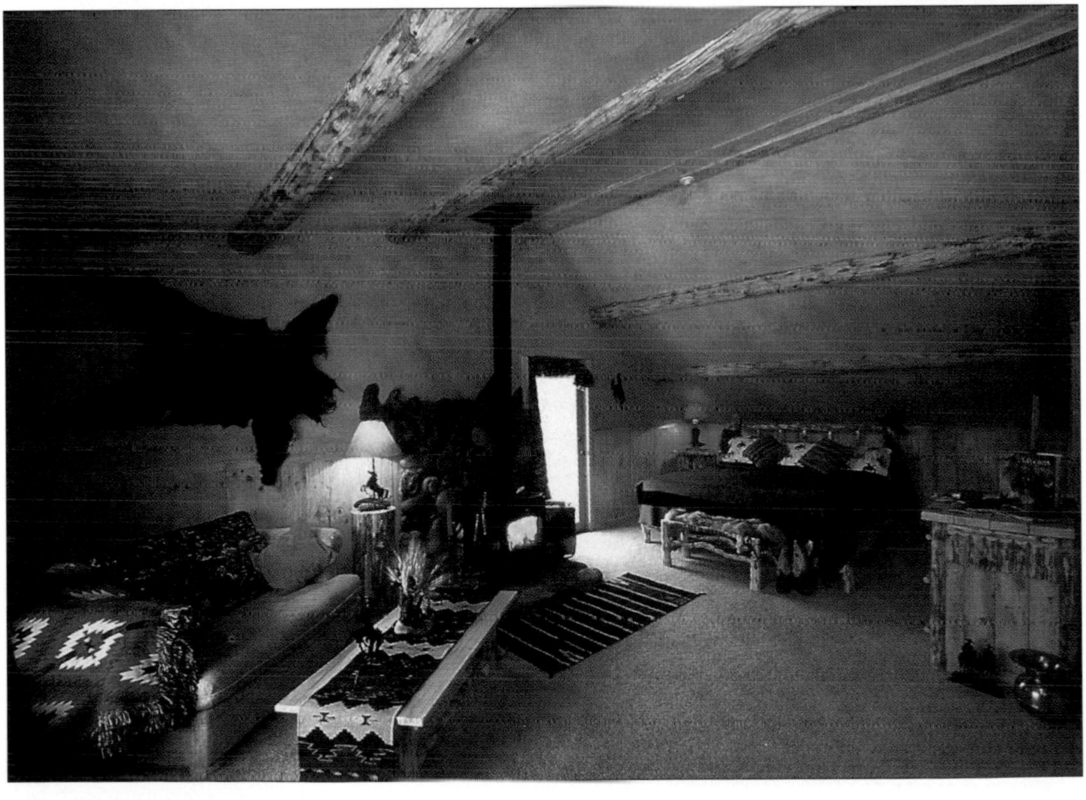

UXU Ranch, Wyoming

See ranch description on page 420.

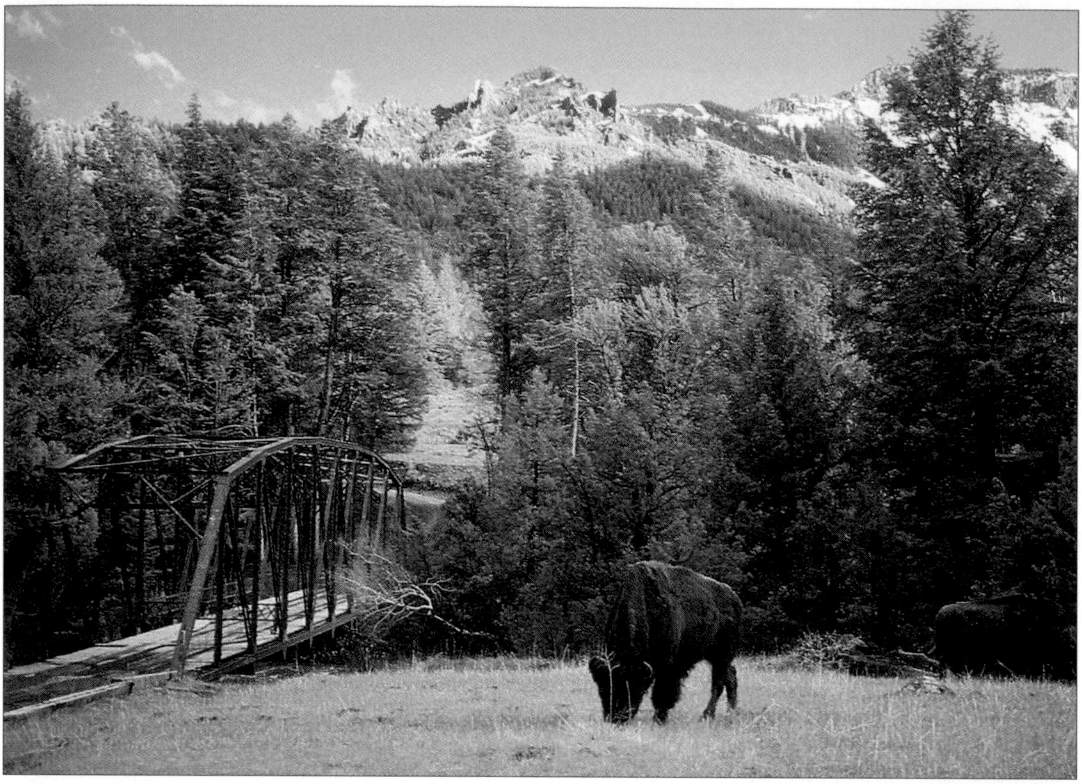

UXU Ranch, Wyoming

See ranch description on page 420.

Vee Bar Guest Ranch, Wyoming

See ranch description on page 422.

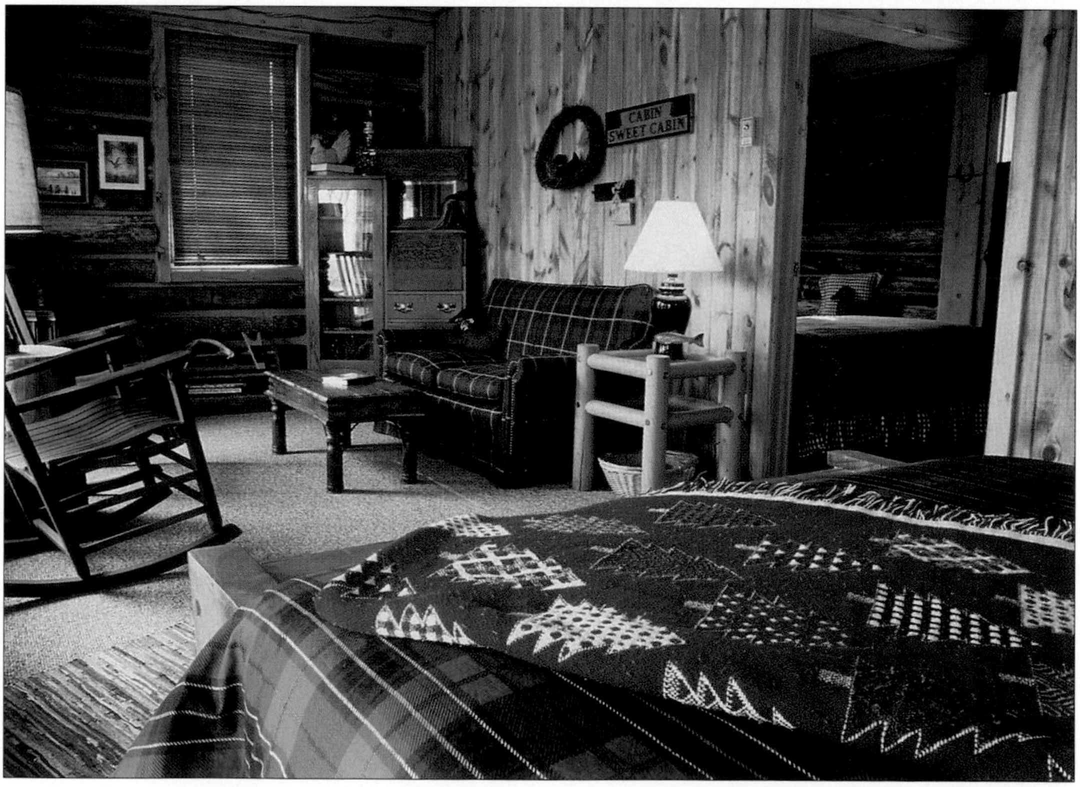

Vee Bar Guest Ranch, Wyoming

See ranch description on page 422.

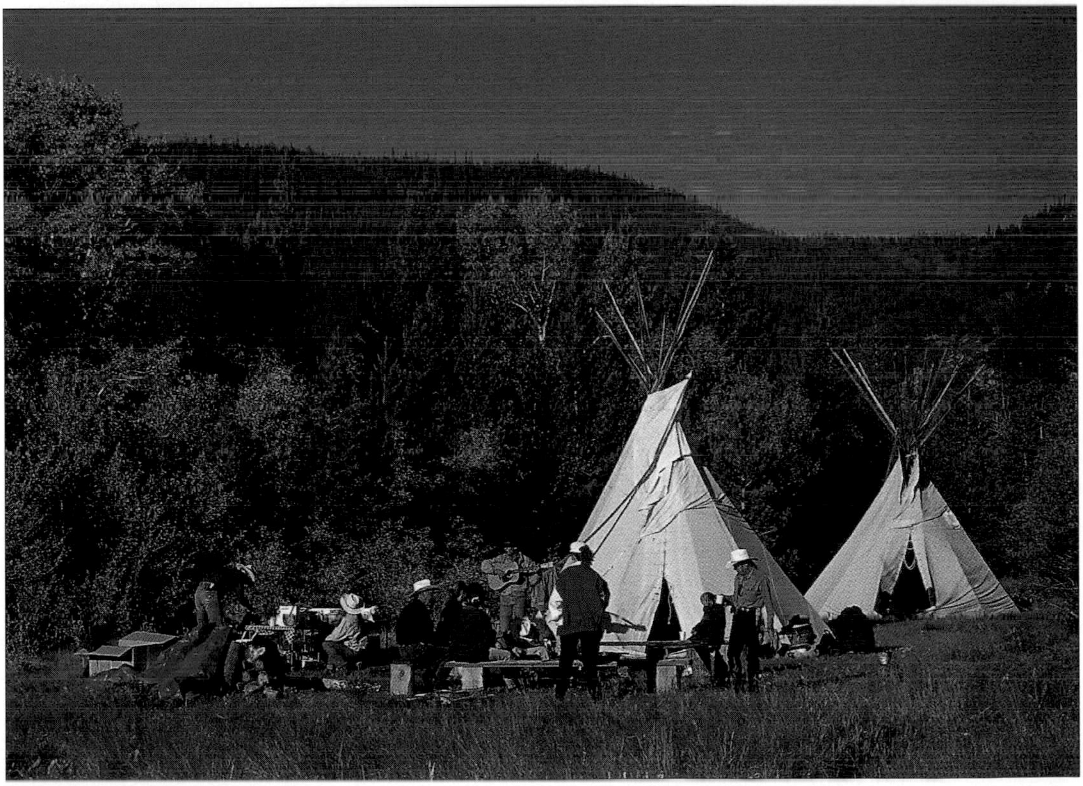

Trail Creek Ranch, Wyoming

See ranch description on page 416.

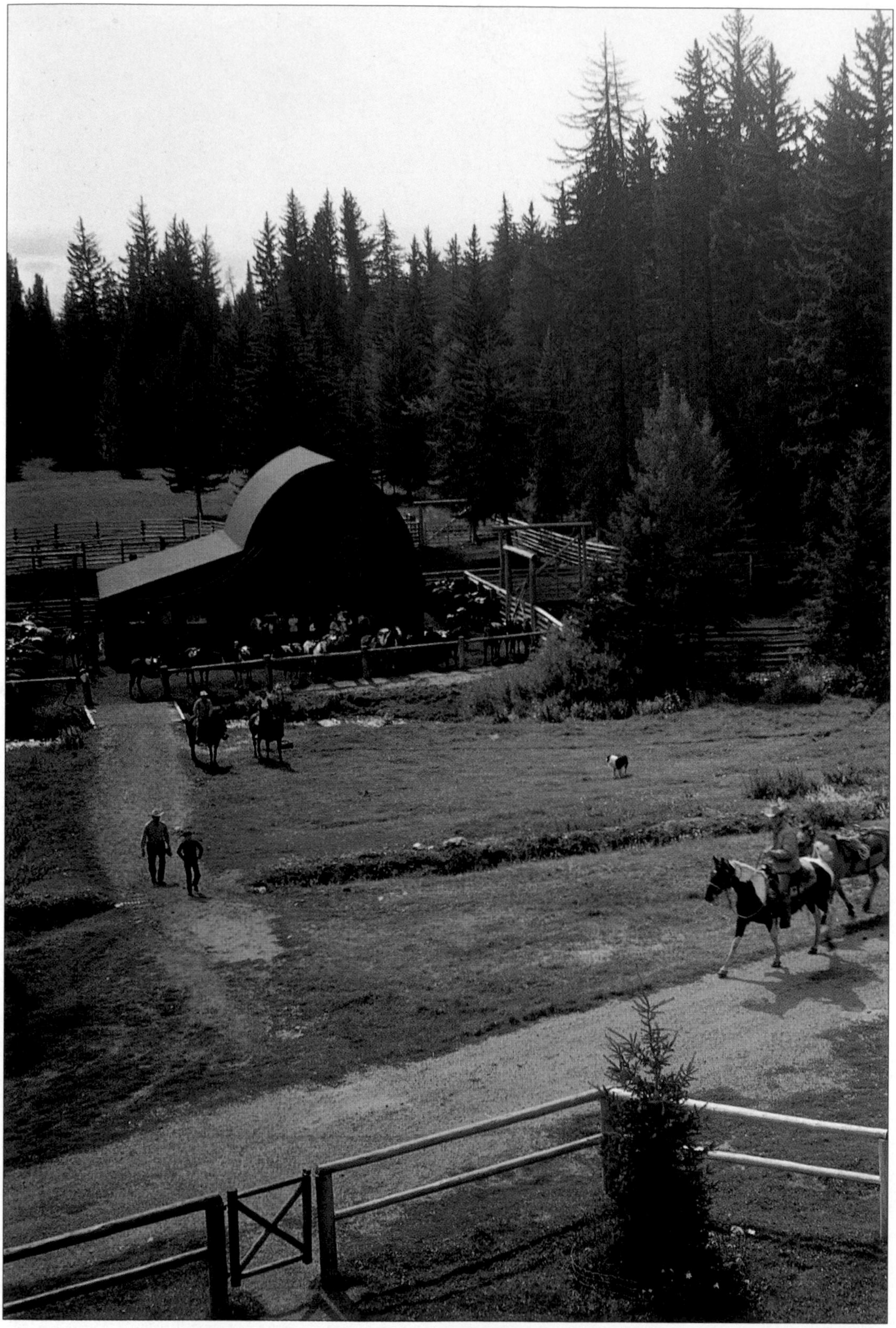

Three Bars Ranch, BC, Canada

See ranch description on page 437.

Echo Valley Guest Ranch, BC, Canada

See ranch description on page 430.

Echo Valley Guest Ranch, BC, Canada

See ranch description on page 430.

Echo Valley Guest Ranch, BC, Canada

See ranch description on page 430.

See ranch description on page 430.

Top of the World Guest Ranch, BC, Canada

See ranch description on page 440.

See ranch description on page 440.

Ranch Associations
in the United States and Canada

THE DUDE RANCHERS'
ASSOCIATION
P. O. Box 471
LaPorte, Colorado 80535
Tel: (970) 223-8440
Fax: (970) 223-0201

THE DUDE RANCHERS' ASSOCIATION

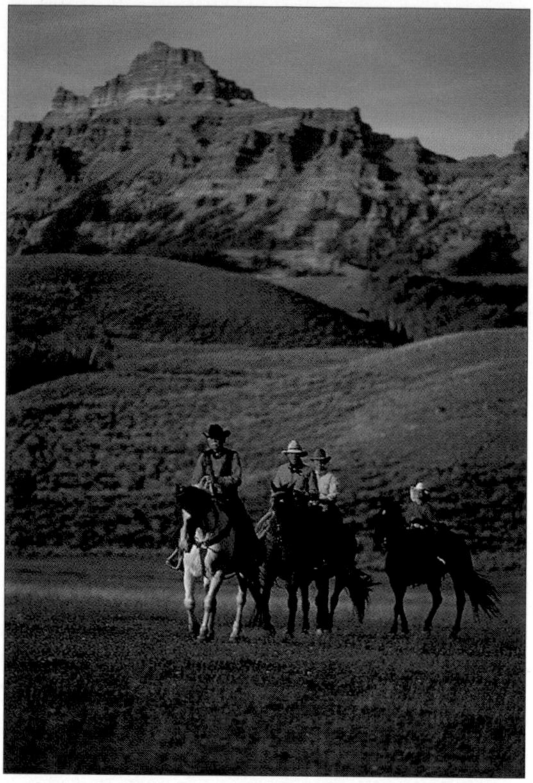

Since 1926 The Dude Ranchers' Association has been setting the standards for quality Western ranch vacations. We began with 35 members and today have more than 100. Members must go through a rigorous two-year screening process, including guest references, an appearance before the board of directors, and on-site inspections. Only those who meet the high standards of the association are accepted.

When you visit a DRA member ranch you'll find genuine Western hospitality, and while programs vary and accommodations range from rustic to upscale, the association requires that all ranch promotional material be accurate and honest. You'll get what's promised when you stay with a DRA member ranch.

For a list of the members, see page 498.
Look for our logo at the top of each member listing.

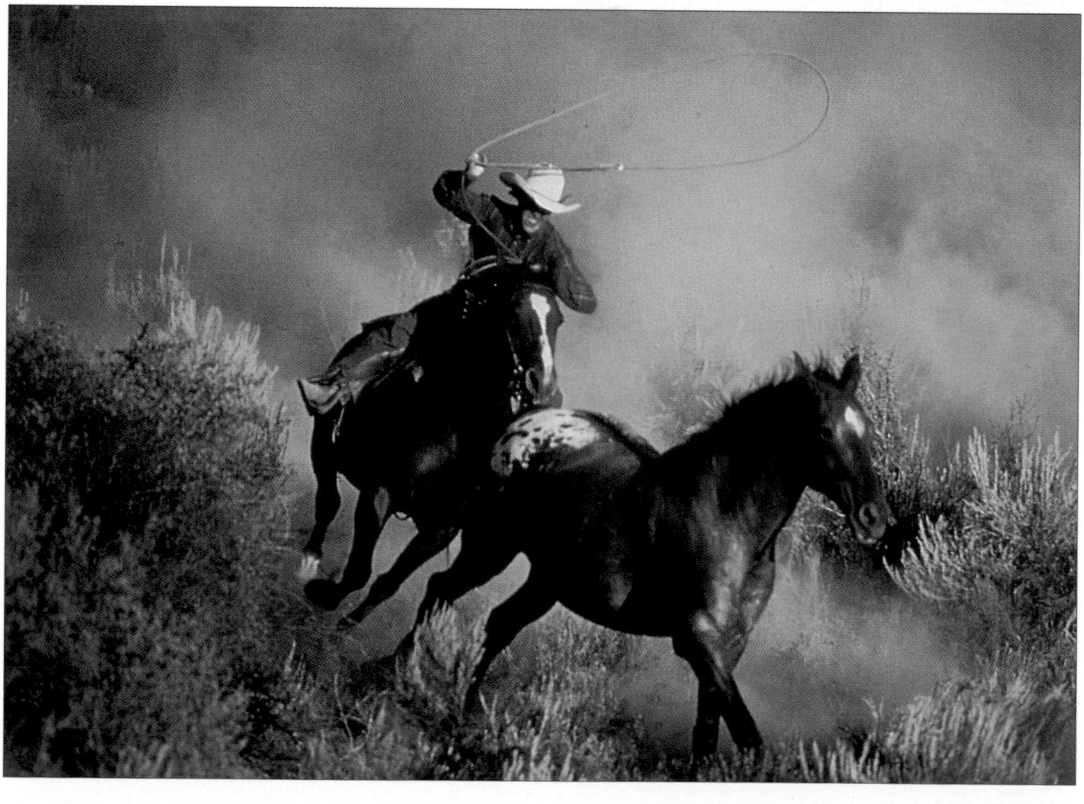

ARIZONA DUDE RANCH ASSOCIATION
P.O. Box 603
Cortaro, Arizona 85652
Tel: (520) 297-0252

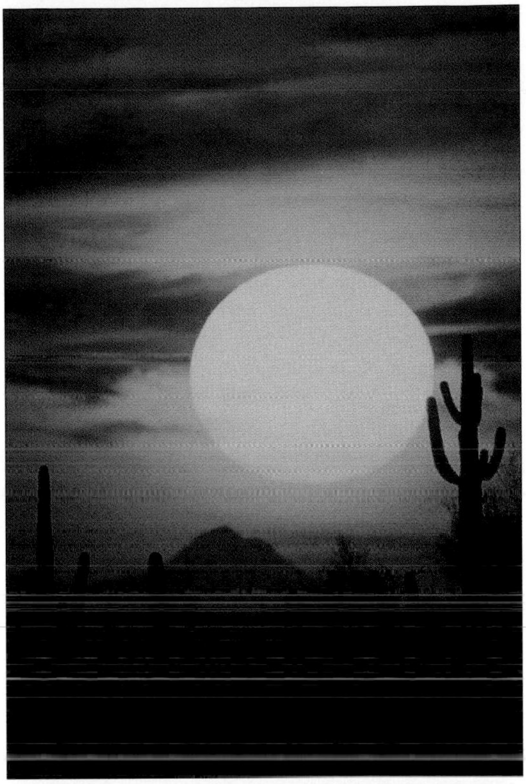

Welcome to Arizona, where our ranches are as diverse as our state. They range from smaller, rural ranches where riding and ranching are the primary focus, to larger resort-style ranches with all the amenities. Our guests—families, couples, and singles—come from every part of the country and the world. They share the desire to experience the Western lifestyle, to slow their pace, and to enjoy a vacation that is out of the ordinary. This wholesome environment also works wonders for corporate retreats and meetings, family reunions, and other groups who desire a more intimate atmosphere.

Each of our member ranches meet strict quality requirements as verified by association inspectors. All of our members are committed to preserving our valued tradition of Western hospitality.

For a list of the members, see page 498.
Look for our logo at the top of each member listing.

COLORADO DUDE AND GUEST RANCH ASSOCIATION
P.O. Box 2120
Granby, Colorado 80446
Tel: (970) 887-9248

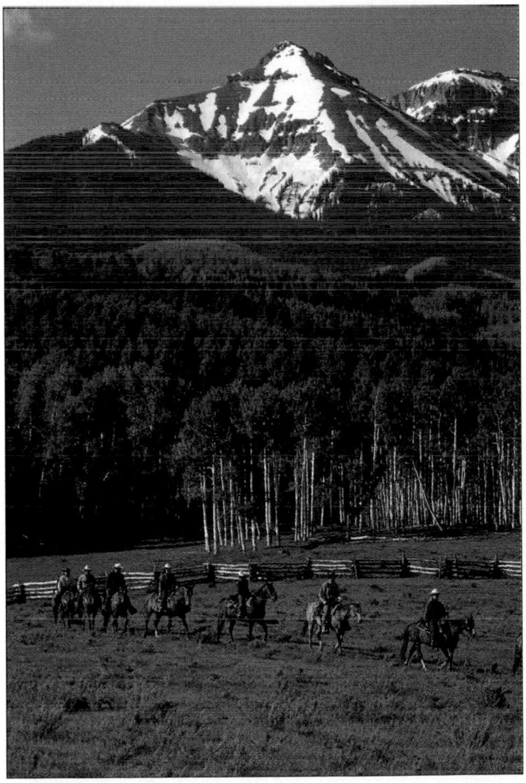

For over 60 years the Colorado Dude and Guest Ranch Association has maintained high standards and strict requirements for membership. Each member ranch is regularly inspected for cleanliness, facilities, hospitality, quality of riding programs, and honesty in their promotions, assuring you that your high expectations will be met. Our member ranches offer you America's best travel and vacation value. Base prices typically include nearly every cost for an entire ranch visit—all lodging and meals, riding and fishing, and a smorgasbord of ranch activities such as cookouts, hay rides, square dancing, and more. Your hosts and new lifelong friends provide you with virtually everything you'll need for your stay—at a price you can afford. Plus, you'll find wonderful hospitality and take away lifetime memories.

For a list of the members, see page 498.
Look for our logo at the top of each member listing.

IDAHO GUEST & DUDE RANCH ASSOCIATION
HC 72
Cascade, Idaho 83611
Tel: (208) 633-3217

Idaho Guest & Dude Ranch Association

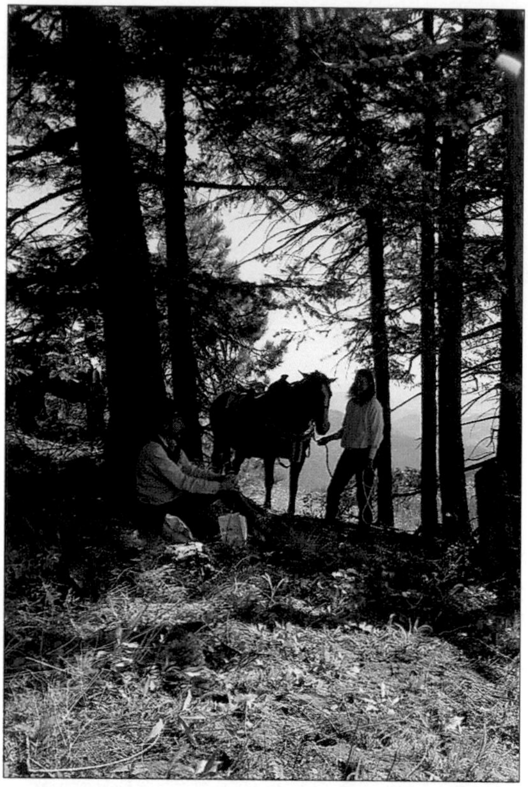

With their rugged individuality, remote locations, and variety of activities, our member ranches provide a wide variety of exciting Western vacations. These ranches range from large to small, accessible to remote, rugged to luxurious, on the open plains or near tree-topped mountain peaks. You'll find more of the Rockies than in any other state, the broadest wilderness system, and clean, free-flowing fishing and rafting streams. Traditions of the Old West still flourish in our untrammeled environment.

Legends still live strong in the heart of Idaho's ranches, and you can share in the rich traditions of Native Americans, mountain men, rough-riding cowboys, and sourdough prospectors. We invite you to experience for yourself the West's best-kept secret.

For a list of the members, see page 499.
Look for our logo at the top of each member listing.

MONTANA DUDE RANCH ASSOCIATION
300 Thompson River Road
Marion, Montana 59925
Tel: (406) 858-2284

Montana Dude Ranch Association

From Bigfork to Bridger and Marion to Martinsdale, the Montana Dude Ranch Association offers guests a chance to step right into the West. Our ranches offer a full range of activities from small intimate guest numbers to full children's programs. You can splash in a swimming pool or at the swimmin' hole in a crystal clear lake. You can ride to the tops of snowy ridges or herd cattle over prairies. Some of our ranches seat you around a Grandma's long table, while others offer gourmet dining from the buffet.

Ours is a territory with lots of real estate and few people, so it's important to keep in touch with each other. We find our greatest satisfaction and lots of old-fashioned pride in earning our neighbor's respect by doing a good job. Come join us in the honest hard-working lands of Montana.

For a list of the members, see page 499.
Look for our logo at the top of each member listing.

TEXAS GUEST RANCH ASSOCIATION
900 Congress Avenue, Suite 201
Austin, Texas 78701
Tel: (800) 375-9255
Fax: (830) 796-4481

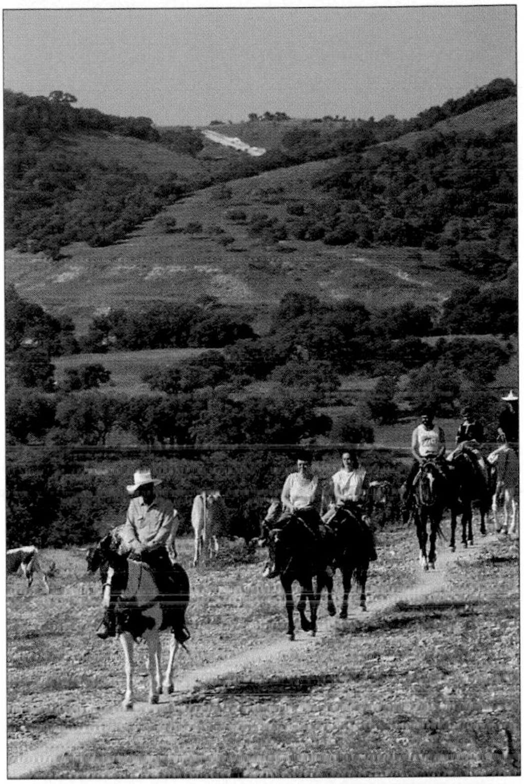

Texas is the birthplace of the American cowboy. All of the famous early cattle trails began in Texas and moved cattle out to many other parts of the country. No where else is the cowboy tradition and ranch living more alive today than in Texas.

When you visit a Texas Guest Ranch Association member ranch you are guaranteed to find friendly people, great hospitality, mounds of Texas barbecue, and more than a few authentic Texas cowboys. Our beautiful weather lets you enjoy a ranch vacation any time of the year. Our ranches vary from hill country to wide open spaces and from working cattle ranches to the finest resort ranches. When you treat yourself to a Texas-style ranch vacation, you can expect some really big fun.

For a list of the members, see page 499.
Look for our logo at the top of each member listing.

WYOMING DUDE RANCHER'S ASSOCIATION
P.O. Box 618
Dubois, Wyoming 82513
Tel: (307) 455-2584
Fax: (307) 455-2634
www.wilderwest.com/wyoming/wdrassoc/

Wyoming, the "Cowboy State," is home to the first Western dude ranch, and it is one of our members today. At each member ranch, Western hospitality, spectacular country, horses, wildlife, fishing, friendly people, and great family style meals are abundant. In Wyoming we live ranching, and we want to share the experience with you!

Each ranch has its own size, flavor, and programs. A week's stay is the norm, making you a part of the family and bringing you back again. We take pride in our association symbol, the bucking horse and rider. This symbol next to a ranch's name assures you that you will find the highest quality ranch and Western experience. See you in Wyoming!

For a list of the members, see page 499.
Look for our logo at the top of each member listing.

BRITISH COLUMBIA GUEST RANCHERS' ASSOCIATION
Box 3301
Kamloops, B.C. V2C 6B9
Tel: (250) 374-6836
Fax: (250) 374-6640
http://www.bcguestranches.com

SUPER, NATURAL BRITISH COLUMBIA®

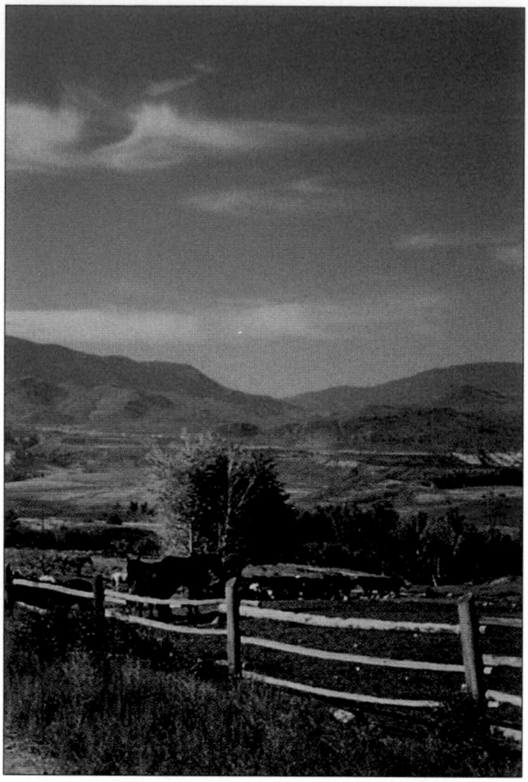

Unique in their settings, the ranches of the British Columbia Guest Ranchers' Association are committed to providing traditional Canadian hospitality. Our ranches offer a variety of experiences. Some are still working cattle operations where you can try your hand at cattle drives or branding. Others are remote lodges in pristine back country areas. Some are luxury resorts, complete with spa facilities and room service. Your British Columbia ranch stay can be a restful or active depending on your desires. Whichever you choose, you'll find yourself feeling like a guest of the family. We want you to enjoy comfortable accommodations and outstanding meals in a relaxed and friendly atmosphere.

For a list of the members, see page 500.
Look for our logo at the top of each member listing.

See member listing page 500.

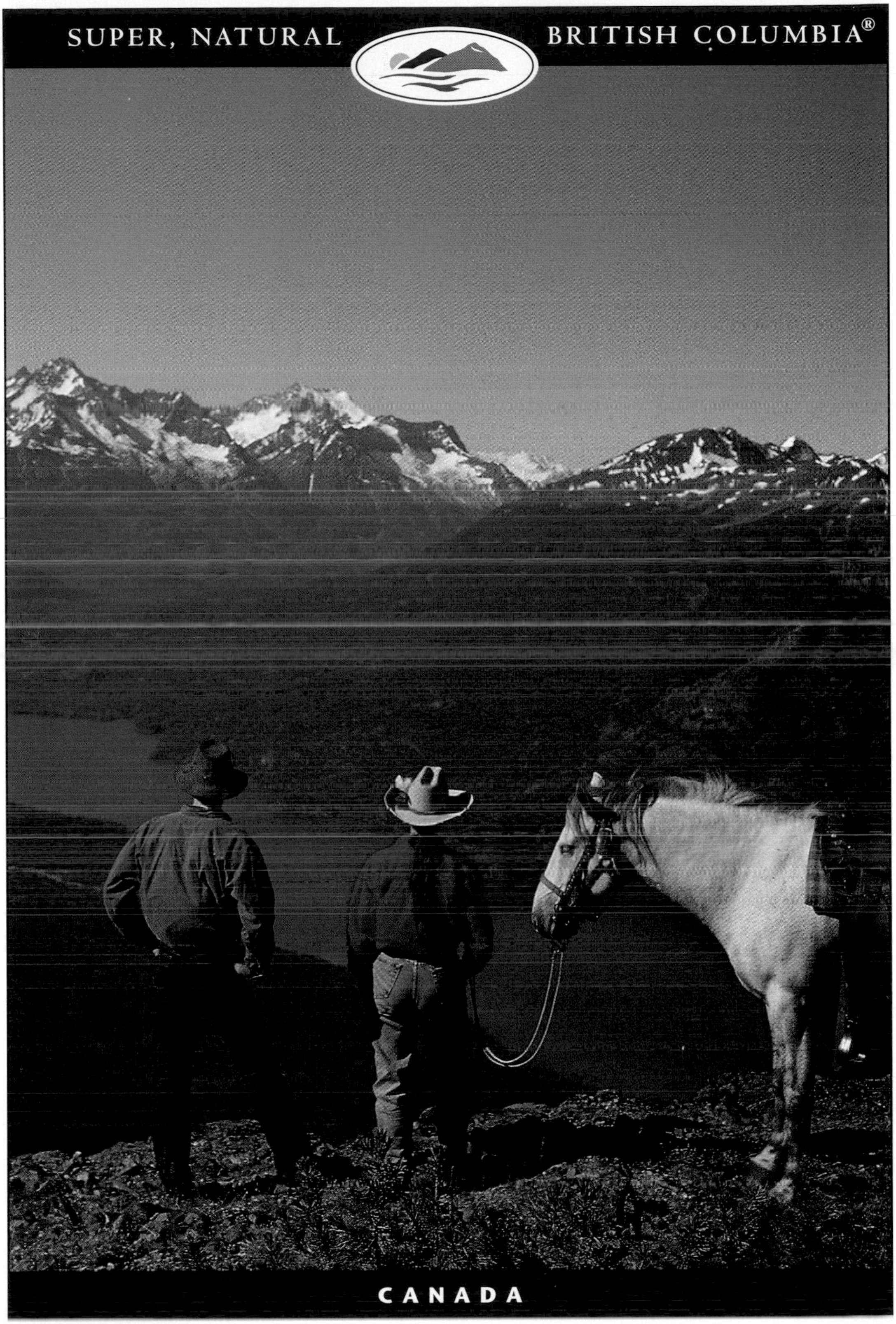

British Columbia Guest Ranchers' Association

See member listing page 500.

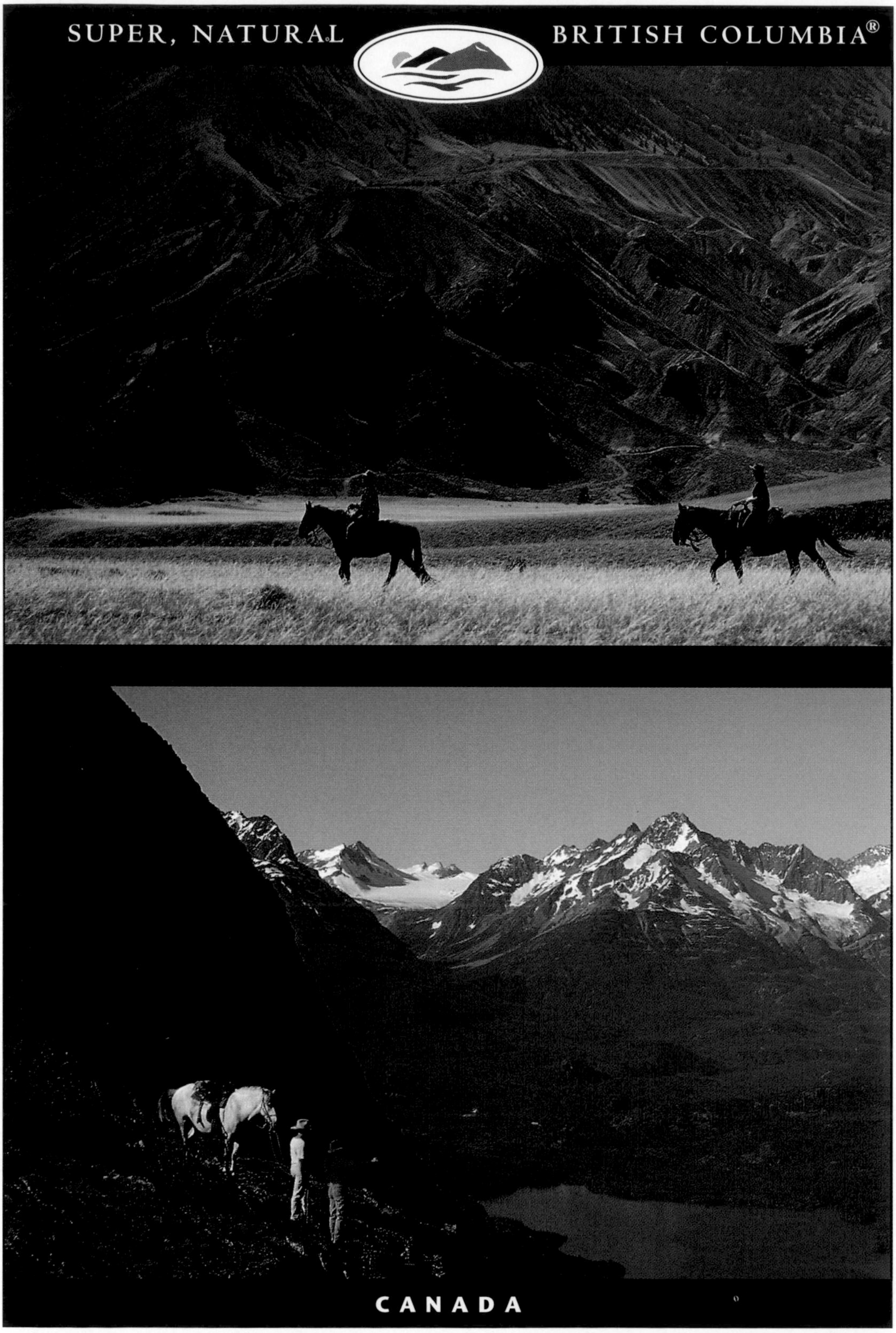

Hartley Guest Ranch
Roy, New Mexico

THE DUDE RANCHERS' ASSOCIATION

Hartley Guest Ranch is located in breathtaking northeastern New Mexico, the state called "The Land of Enchantment." The ranch is a family-owned and -operated working cattle ranch that has been in the Hartley family since the 1940s. With over 25,000 acres of private land, it varies in elevation from 4,800 to 6,000 feet. There are mesas, red-rock rims and canyons, and 200 miles of trails on high open plains and through forests of juniper, oak, and ponderosa pine. Guests come to enjoy the Hartley family spirit and all the various seasonal ranch activities which include riding, branding, looking for strays, roundups, and cattle drives. This ranch is secluded—the road ends here—and takes only 10 to 12 guests per week. Hartley Guest Ranch is all about family, ranching tradition, miles of New Mexico landscapes, and spectacular views.

Address: HCR 73, Box 55K, Roy, New Mexico 87743
Telephone: (800) OUR-DUDE (800-687-3833), (505) 673-2244; fax: (505) 673-2216
E-Mail: rhart@etsc.net
Internet: http://www.duderanch.org/hartley
Airport: Albuquerque, 220 miles
Location: 25 miles southwest of Roy, 220 miles northeast of Albuquerque (3½ to four hours driving), 160 miles northeast of Santa Fe
Memberships: The Dude Ranchers' Association, New Mexico Cattle Growers Association
Medical: Health Centers of Northern New Mexico at Roy, 25 miles. Northeastern Regional Hospital at Las Vegas, New Mexico; 100 miles.
Guest Capacity: 10 to 12
Accommodations: Six-bedroom, 2,200-square-foot guest house with living and dining rooms for reading or playing board games. Most rooms have queen-size beds and private baths; one with king-size bed and Jacuzzi tub. There is a shared kitchen for snacking and morning coffee, and a refrigerator full of soft drinks and juices. There are telephones in the rooms but no TVs. Laundry facility available. Smoke-free policy in building.
Rates: $$$. American Plan. Five-night stays minimum, June through August. Minimum three-night stays in off-season. Children's rates.
Credit Cards: None. Traveler's checks, personal checks, and cash accepted.
Season: April through mid-October
Activities: Do as much or as little as you wish. Authentic working cattle ranch with plenty of guided riding. Guests take part in gathering and driving cattle, looking for strays, and branding (May through July). The guests may also flank (throw and hold down) calves, vaccinate, or tag ears. All-day rides to move cattle to different pastures and shorter scenic rides for those who don't want to stay in the saddle all day. Once you're qualified by a wrangler, loping rides are available. Pack trips and overnight campouts. Fishing for bass, catfish, and perch. The stocked ponds are close to the main lodge. Hiking to dinosaur tracks, ancient Indian sites, petroglyphs, and incredible geological formations. White-water rafting on the Rio Grande near Taos. Basketball, volleyball, or relaxing in hot tub. Wildlife includes deer, roadrunners, coyotes, raccoons, turkeys, and the occasional mountain lion or bear sighting. Guided all-terrain-vehicle rides for everyone age 16 and older.
Children's Programs: Children are welcome, but no formal program. Best for ages nine and older. Riding usually begins at age five.
Dining: Generous home-cooked meals served family-style in the dining room or cooked outdoors over an open fire. Homemade breads and desserts. Guests join the Hartley family for all meals. BYOB.
Entertainment: Informal. Campfires, beautiful clear bright stars at night, and storytelling with the Hartleys and other guests. Outdoor hot tub.
Summary: As the Hartleys say, "Hartley Guest Ranch is for those who wish to experience the American West and fulfill the dream of being a real cowboy or cowgirl." Secluded with 25,000 acres. Featured on ESPN's "Men's Journal," and in *Sunset Magazine's* "Western Roundup of 50 Great Dude Ranches." Nearby: Santa Fe, three hours.

See color photos, page 262.

The Lodge at Chama
Chama, New Mexico

Welcome to the Lodge at Chama! Here, men and women come to enjoy privacy amid 32,000 acres of unspoiled mountain and forest scenery. The Lodge at Chama provides first-rate amenities and excellent service. Over the years, the Lodge has hosted many business and industry leaders. Because it takes only 24 people at any one time, guests quickly feel at home. Whether it's a high-level board meeting or plain old rest and relaxation, The Lodge at Chama has what it takes for groups or families who appreciate beauty, kindness, and a host of recreational opportunities. The Lodge's fine staff tailors everything to each group's preferences. (Be sure to see the Fly-Fishing section as well.)

Address: Box 127 K, Chama, New Mexico 87520
Telephone: (505) 756-2133; fax: (505) 756-2519
Internet: http://www.ranchweb.com/chama
Airport: Albuquerque; private jets to Pagosa Springs. Call regarding ranch airstrip.
Location: 100 miles north of Santa Fe, 90 miles west of Taos, 45 miles southeast of Pagosa Springs
Awards: *Hideaway Report* 1986 Fishing/Hunting Lodge of the Year; *Hideaway Report* 1990 Best Sporting Retreat
Medical: Local clinic; hospital in Española; emergency helicopter service available
Conference: 24 in boardroom, 50 for day meetings. Secretarial services, fax, speaker telephones, copy room. Ask for brochure.
Guest Capacity: 24
Accommodations: Vaulted ceilings, full animal mounts, and views of the Chama Valley beyond the well-kept lawns are the first thing you see as you enter the 13,500-square-foot main lodge. Just off the Great Room are 12 rooms, each with private bath and upscale amenities (bathrobes, hair dryers, and oversized towels), and two suites with fireplaces, TVs, and oversized baths with vanities. All rooms have telephones.
Rates: • $$$$$$. Full American Plan. Special rates for full lodge rental. Winter rates available. No minimum stay required. Average stay, three nights.
Credit Cards: VISA, MasterCard. Personal and corporate checks accepted.
Season: Year-round, all holidays
Activities: The Lodge will send you a detailed brochure and video outlining the activities. During summer, guests enjoy fly-fishing (see Fly-Fishing section), hiking, drives through the ranch property to view vistas and wild game (including one of the world's largest private elk herds and bison), horseback riding, wildlife photography, and sporting clays. Be sure to ask about the historic Cumbres & Toltec narrow-gauge railroad, North America's longest! Limited world-class hunting is offered September to December. Photographers will go through many rolls of film shooting the magnificent fall colors. Winter activities November to March include cross-country skiing (gear, guides, and instruction available), snowmobiling, sleigh rides to view wildlife, snowshoeing, snow tours, and ice fishing.
Children's Programs: Minimum age of 12 or by special arrangement
Dining: Gourmet ranch fare. Special requests and diets accommodated. Ask about Chama's delicious northern New Mexico dishes. Complimentary bar. Premium wines available.
Entertainment: Enjoy the spectacular sunsets, take an evening stroll, watch wide-screen TV, relax in front of the fire or in the huge indoor whirlpool and sauna, or read yourself to sleep. Customized entertainment and activities available on request with advance notice.
Summary: Where exclusivity, scenery, and wildlife reign supreme! Personalized service, delicious cuisine, and tremendous wildlife-viewing. Superb fly-fishing and hunting. One of North America's finest wildlife ranches! One of the world's largest private elk herds; large buffalo herd also.

See color photos, pages 260–261.

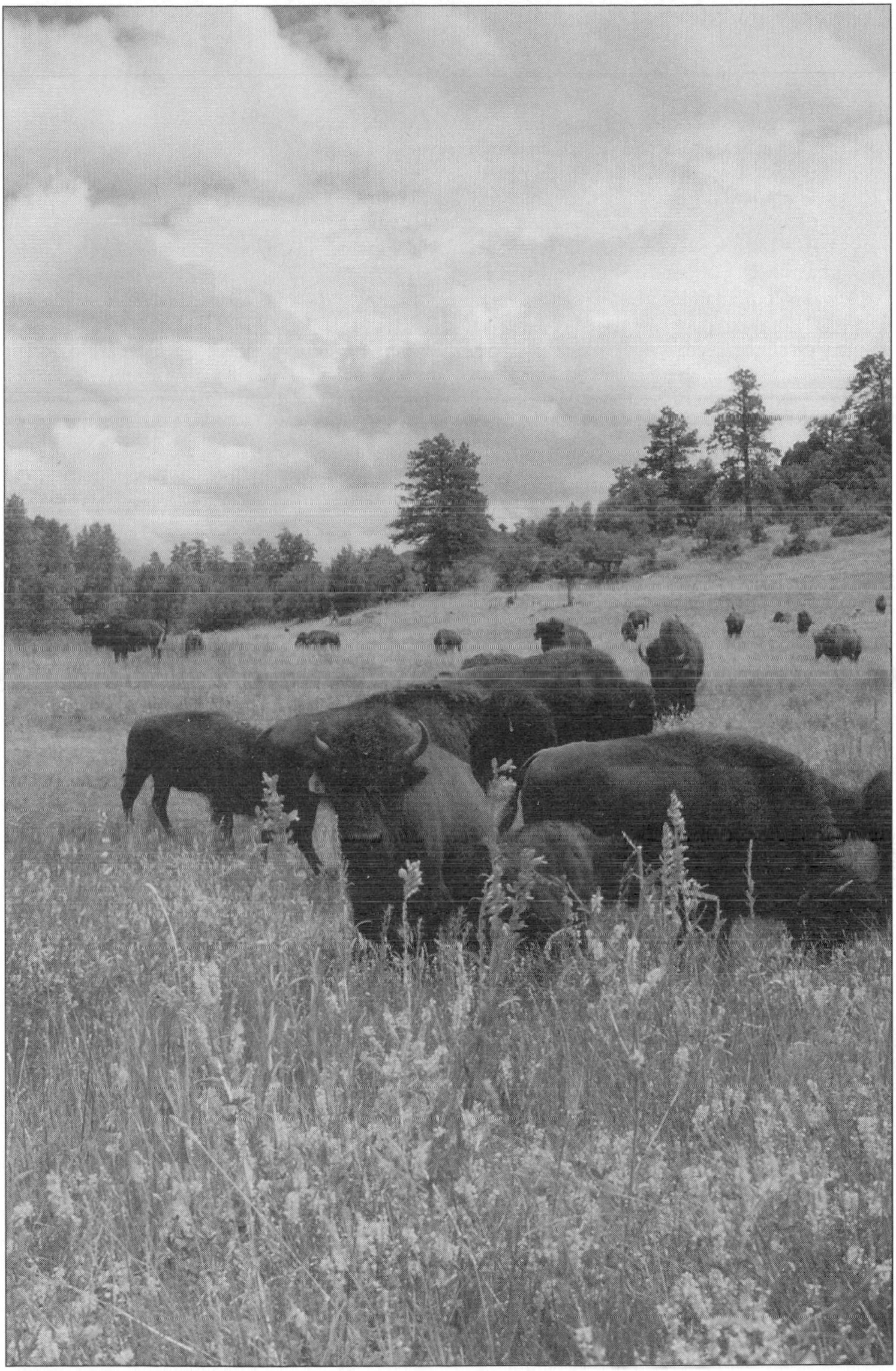

Los Pinos Ranch
Cowles, New Mexico

"Where the road ends and the trails begin" is how the McSweeneys describe Los Pinos Ranch. Originally the summer residence of the Amado Chaves family, this historic guest ranch has been in operation since the 1920s. Purchased in 1965 by architect Bill McSweeney, Los Pinos continues to be run by his family. Small and private, Los Pinos is located in the heart of the Sangre de Cristo Mountains. At an elevation of 8,500 feet, with a view of the Pecos-Baldy Wilderness Areas to the north, the ranch perches 500 feet above the wild and scenic Pecos River. Wildflowers and many birds abound in the area. Average summer temperature is 76 degrees at noon, dipping into the 40s at night. Limited to a dozen guests, Los Pinos recaptures the ambiance of an earlier, simpler time. Candlelit dinners in the main lodge are often followed by reading, music, or sharing tales of the day's adventures. Riding, fly-fishing, hiking, and birding are the order of the day.

Address: Route 3, Box 8 K, Tererro, New Mexico 87573 (summer–September); P.O. Box 24 K, Glorieta, New Mexico 87535-0024 (winter)
Telephone: (505) 757-6213 (summer); (505) 757-6679 (winter)
Airport: Albuquerque
Location: 45 miles northeast of Santa Fe off I-25. Map sent on request.
Medical: Medical clinic in Pecos, 23 miles
Guest Capacity: 12
Accommodations: Guests are housed in four original aspen-log cabins. Each cabin (three one-bedroom, one two-bedroom) is equipped with front porch, private bath (some with claw-foot tubs), and wood-burning stove. Plenty of warm blankets are provided for cool nights. The 1912-vintage lodge is a gathering place for guests. Its large screened-in porch offers a view of peaceful scenery and is a prime spot for a quiet read, games, or conversation. Inside are antique furnishings, fireplace, piano, paintings, and books.
Rates: $$. American Plan. Riding and guided fly-fishing are offered at an additional cost. Two-night minimum stay required.
Credit Cards: None. Personal checks or cash accepted.
Season: June to early September
Activities: Horseback riding is one of the main activities at Los Pinos. Guided half- and full-day rides wind through coniferous forest, aspen groves, and across spectacular high-mountain meadows of the Santa Fe National Forest. Beginning riders are welcome. The sparkling waters of the upper Pecos, the Mora, and their tributaries offer excellent fly-fishing. The "trophy" section of the Pecos begins just below the ranch. Guided full- and half-day fishing can be arranged. Trails for hiking are accessed from the ranch on nearby trailheads. Historic Santa Fe, with its museums, galleries, and fine restaurants, is an hour's drive by car. The towns of Pecos, Chimayo, and Taos, and various pueblos offer a diversity of cultures for the traveler.
Children's Programs: No children under six years of age except during family reunions. Children are parents' responsibility and participate with their families.
Dining: The staff takes pride and pleasure in the preparation and service of meals. Freshly-baked breads accompany most breakfasts and dinners. Lunches are packed for trail and streamside picnicking. Guests gather each evening for dinner in the lodge dining room. Cuisine offers a variety of flavorful, well-presented dishes throughout the week. BYOB.
Entertainment: A well-stocked library of local history and nature references; fireside conversation on cool evenings. Outside, nature provides its own array of sounds and sights—a chorus of coyotes, and excellent nighttime stargazing.
Summary: Lots of peace and quiet here. Rustic, cozy, and very friendly. If you like the outdoors and no planned activities, Los Pinos and the McSweeneys are terrific. Wonderful scenery, food, and fellowship. Nearby: Old Santa Fe Trail, Pecos National Historical Park, Indian pueblos, and Spanish villages.

Ridin-Hy Ranch Resort
Warrensburg, New York

Ridin-Hy is a year-round family resort ranch in the timberlands of Adirondack State Park and along the shores of beautiful spring-fed Sherman Lake. Did you know that Adirondack State Park is the largest park in the United States? Six million acres! The ranch is owned and operated by Andy and Susan Beadnell and their three sons. Since 1940, when the ranch was started by Susan's father, the property and guest accommodations have grown. Today the ranch hosts 195 guests who enjoy the privacy of the resort's 800 acres. Repeat guests make up three-quarters of the ranch's business. As one happy guest said, "There are not many resorts where you can trail ride, fish, swim, enjoy dinner, and square dance to your heart's content." All activities are complemented by a friendly staff. Here you'll enjoy the kind of care and service that comes from a family-owned and -operated resort ranch.

Address: Box 369K, Sherman Lake, Warrensburg, New York 12885
Telephone: (518) 494-2742; fax: (518) 494-7181
Airport: Albany
Location: 65 miles north of Albany, 15 miles north of Lake George off Route 87
Memberships: New York State Tourism Association
Medical: Glens Falls Hospital, 20 miles
Guest Capacity: 195
Accommodations: Rooms range from motel-style units and main lodge rooms overlooking the lake to private cottages for one to three families. All are comfortable, heated, with private baths. The main lodge, with a large stone fireplace that provides a warm and cozy atmosphere, is situated on the lake with views of the Adirondacks.
Rates: • $. American Plan. Summer riding and non-riding rates. Children's rates according to age. Winter rates and various ranch packages offered. Off-season rates. Two-night minimum stay.
Credit Cards: VISA, MasterCard, American Express, Discover. Personal checks accepted.
Season: Year-round, including Thanksgiving and Easter. Open Christmas week.
Activities: Horseback riding for the whole family, with pony rides for kids. Fast, slow, and intermediate mountain trail rides. Rides go out daily. A favorite ranch activity is the weekly guest "rodeo" and daily wagon rides. Riding during the fall colors is breathtaking. Free riding lessons available from experienced wranglers. Fishing for trout, pike, and small- and largemouth bass in two lakes and the Schroon River. Plenty of water sports on Sherman Lake, including paddleboats, rowboats, and swimming in Sherman Lake or heated indoor pool. Archery, two tennis courts, and whirlpool. Golf nearby. Full winter program including cross-country skiing, sleigh rides, snowshoeing, ice-skating, downhill skiing with instruction, snowmobiling, indoor pool, and horseback riding.
Children's Programs: Children's activities director. Organized activities year-round. Baby-sitting available. Under age seven ride in arena. The spirit here is for families to participate together.
Dining: The large country-style dining room looks out over Sherman Lake. Enjoy poolside steak barbecues and weekly smorgasbord dinners featuring ham and turkey roasts. Full weekly menu. Families eat together at assigned tables. Three meals daily from a choice of menus. Cash bar.
Entertainment: Nightly entertainment with social program year-round. The main lodge has a dance floor, cocktail lounge, TV, card tables, and complete game room. Jackpot rodeo at ranch with professional contestants, midweek mini-rodeo for guests. Hot-dog roasts, hayrides, pizza parties, and shows.
Summary: Wonderful year-round resort ranch run by the Beadnell family since 1940. Many repeat guests and a great family tradition. Eight hundred acres of privacy. One-stop, one-price vacation. Nearby: Lake George, Fort William Henry, Adirondack Museum, Stone Bridge Caves, Gore Mountain gondola, and Lake Placid.

See color photos, page 263.

Pinegrove Dude Ranch
Kerhonkson, New York

Pinegrove is nestled in the peaceful, gentle, rolling hills of upstate New York's Catskill Mountains, with miles of mountain trails for riding. Pinegrove is a year-round family-vacation wonderland that serves up Western hospitality. Dick and Debbie Tarantino started Pinegrove Dude Ranch in 1971. Today it is one of the most family-oriented resort ranches in the Northeast. In 1992 the ranch won the *Family Circle* Ranch of the Year award. At Pinegrove, all in one day, you can saddle up for a two-hour cattle drive, swim, hike, play tennis, and take an afternoon snooze before the evening entertainment begins. The ranch specializes in children's activities and the excellent full-time children's programs enable parents to enjoy themselves as well. At Pinegrove there is something to do for everyone, from toddlers to grandparents . . . morning, noon, and night.

Address: P.O. Box 209, Kerhonkson, New York 12446
Telephone: (914) 626-7345, (800) 346-4626; fax: (914) 626-7365
E-Mail: pinegrove@ulster.net
Internet: http://www.pinegrove-ranch.com
Airport: JFK, Newark, or Newburgh
Train: Poughkeepsie, 25 miles
Location: 100 miles northwest of New York City, one mile west of Kerhonkson off Route 209
Memberships: American Hotel and Motel Association, Association for Horsemanship Safety Education, Camp Horsemanship Association–certified wranglers
Awards: *Family Circle* Ranch of the Year 1992
Medical: Ellenville Hospital, six miles
Conference: Up to 300; 5,000 square feet of meeting space
Guest Capacity: 350
Accommodations: Guests sleep in comfortable, modern rooms with wall-to-wall carpeting, TVs, telephones, air-conditioning, and private baths. All 125 rooms are connected to the main lodge by air-conditioned/heated hallways.
Rates: • \$–\$\$. American plan. Children ages four to 16 half price. Kids under age four free. Single-parent, group, and senior discounts. Ask about family specials.
Credit Cards: VISA, MasterCard, American Express, Discover
Season: Year-round, all holidays
Activities: Nightly riding video and lecture for all newcomers. Daily riding instruction available. Ride over acres of picturesque rolling hills. Most trails are quite wide. You can go into the forest on secluded trails that cross streams and afford distant views. Most rides have 15 to 20 people. Rides go out on the hour, from 10 a.m. to 5 p.m. daily. Cattle-driving (call for information), bass-fishing in stocked lake, boating, hiking—all on the property. Indoor and outdoor facilities; tennis, swimming pools, miniature golf, bocci, archery, basketball, volleyball, paddle- and handball, table tennis, and shuffleboard. Complimentary 18-hole golf nearby. Winter: downhill skiing on two slopes, ice-skating, and nightly snow-tubing. All equipment and lessons included. Ranch has its own snowmaking equipment.
Children's Program: Full daycare program for kids ages three to 12. Nursery for ages three and under. Teen program too. Ask about Junior Wrangler instruction for ages four to seven. Lots of animals. Winter: great learn-to-ski-program.
Dining: Three all-you-can-eat meals daily from varied menu. Sunday barbecue in season. Parents eat with their kids. Complimentary snack bar 10 a.m. to midnight.
Entertainment: Hayride, nightclub with show, and cocktail lounge with live music plus square dancing. Western saloon with swinging doors and popcorn machine. Hitching Post pool bar. Game nights. Steer-roping and leather-carving demonstrations.
Summary: A great family-oriented, family-owned and -operated ranch resort. Terrific children's program. Complete, all-inclusive packages and plenty of activities. Program for all ages. Weekly cattle drives.

See color photos, pages 264–265.

Roaring Brook Ranch and Tennis Resort
Lake George, New York

Roaring Brook Ranch and Tennis Resort is one of the country's largest destination ranch resorts. Named after the creek which "roars" through the property in the spring, Roaring Brook is in Lake George township in New York's Adirondack Mountains. A resort area for vacationers since the turn of the century, this part of the country has historic significance. In fact, when President Thomas Jefferson first saw Lake George he called it "the queen of the American lakes," suggested by its purity and picturesque setting. The ranch has been under the continuous stewardship of one family since 1946 and is run today by George Greene. This picturesque 500-acre estate specializes in family, group, and corporate activities with accommodations for 300. The high percentage of repeat guests appreciate the all-inclusive vacation package. Although the ranch spirit prevails, tennis and poolside relaxation appeal to many. Roaring Brook has a large conference facility that can seat up to 1,000. The ranch draws most of its guests from metropolitan New York and New England.

Address: P.O. Box K, Lake George, New York 12845
Telephone: (518) 668-5767, (800) 882-7665 from New York and New England only; fax: (518) 668-4019
E-Mail: roaringb@adirondack.net
Internet: http://www.adirondack.net/tour/roaring
Airport: Albany, 60 miles
Location: two miles south of Lake George, one mile off Interstate 87, 60 miles north of Albany, 200 miles north of New York City
Memberships: New York State Hotel/Motel Association
Awards: Mobil 3 Star, AAA 3 Diamond
Medical: Glen Falls Hospital, seven miles
Conference: 300; a total of 17,000 square feet of conference space. Full audiovisual equipment available. On-staff conference coordinator.
Guest Capacity: 300
Accommodations: There are 140 motel-style rooms in nine buildings spread out around the property. All rooms have private baths, wall-to-wall carpeting, heat and air-conditioning, color TVs, and telephones. Most have deck areas. There are 17 two-room suites.
Rates: $–$$. Modified American Plan. Children's, riding, and conference rates available. Two-day minimum stay.
Credit Cards: VISA, MasterCard
Season: Mid-May to mid-October; conference year-round
Activities: The ranch recruits Montana wranglers to oversee the riding program. Four scheduled rides go out daily. All rides last about one hour. Groups of 25 to 30 go out at a time, split into experienced and inexperienced riders. New riders are encouraged, and group instruction is available. Five tennis courts, two lighted. The ranch tennis pro (who splits his tennis year between Boca Raton, Florida, and the ranch) offers all levels of tennis instruction with private lessons available. Three swimming pools (outdoor and indoor), badminton, archery, hiking, volleyball, table tennis, horseshoes, weight room.
Children's Programs: Children are parents' responsibility. Children's playground and counselor for children ages four to seven, morning and afternoons, summer season only. Pony rides, arts and crafts. Baby-sitting can be arranged.
Dining: Full-service, licensed dining room, and coffee shop; choose from varied menu. Full bar.
Entertainment: Two cocktail lounges with musical entertainment nightly in summer. Three or four family shows each week during July and August. Table tennis, billiards, movies.
Summary: Full-service destination ranch and tennis resort that appeals to families, couples, and conference groups. Singles enjoy the ranch as well, and it's also popular for family reunions. All-inclusive packages offered. Nearby: shoreline cruise on Lake George, Fort William Henry, National Museum of Racing, hot-air balloon festival, and dinner theater.

See color photos, page 266.

Rocking Horse Ranch
Highland, New York

Just 90 minutes north of New York City, Rocking Horse Ranch is one of the largest year-round resort ranches for the entire family and home to the ranch's award-winning six-horse Belgian team. Rocking Horse was started by Bucky and Toolie Turk, two brothers from Manhattan, who bought a small hotel and over the years created their resort ranch, complete with everything from three heated pools, giant and children's waterslide system, waterskiing, and boating in the summer—to skiing, giant snow-tube runs with lifts, and horse-drawn sleigh rides in the winter. Since 1958 the Turk family has operated this 500-acre ranch. Most guests come from New York, Pennsylvania, New Jersey, and Connecticut. With no hidden costs, the ranch recognizes that not everyone wants to ride, so there are plenty of options. For those who love Western activity, there are square dances, hayrides, horseshoes, bonfires, sing-alongs, marshmallow roasts, and lots of riding supervised by certified wranglers. Kids and parents will find a lot to do together and apart, at an affordable price.

Address: 600 Route 44-55, Dept. K, Highland, New York 12528
Telephone: (914) 691-2927, (800) 647-2624; fax: (914) 691-6434
Internet: http://www.rhranch.com
Airport: Stewart, JFK, Newark, or La Guardia
Train: Poughkeepsie
Bus: To New Paltz
Location: 75 miles north of New York City
Memberships: New York State Hotel Association
Awards: AAA 3 Diamond, Mobil 3 Star; *Family Circle* readers voted "My Favorite Ranch Resort" three years in a row
Medical: Vassar and St. Francis hospitals (Poughkeepsie), 6 miles
Conference: 250 in 2,800-square-foot auditorium
Guest Capacity: 400
Accommodations: 20 motel-style rooms and 100 rooms in main lodge, with two wings that sleep up to six people in each room. All rooms have TVs, telephones, air-conditioning, carpeting, double and king-size beds, private baths with showers, and daily maid service.
Rates: • $–$$. American Plan and Modified American Plan depending on season. Group rates available. Free children's specials (up to age 16).
Credit Cards: VISA, MasterCard, American Express, Discover
Season: Year-round, all holidays
Activities: Full-time activity director; over 100 horses give everyone the opportunity for plenty of rides. Riding instruction available. Safety always comes first, so guests are tested on their riding skills. Guided trail rides are divided into levels of experience. Several one-hour rides go out daily. Two outdoor and one indoor heated pools, giant and children's waterslide, paddleboats, beach volleyball, tennis, softball, basketball, rifle/archery range, mini-golf, fitness program with aerobics. Winter program includes skiing and giant snow-tube runs with two lifts, 100 percent snowmaking capability, horse-drawn sleigh rides, ice-skating, and of course, horseback riding. Quality equipment and instruction provided at ski area.
Children's Programs: Full program with counselors. Fully coordinated day camp and nursery program. Heated children's swimming pool with interactive fountains and waterslide.
Dining: Rotating menus, all you can eat, fresh fruit and dessert assortment. Licensed bar and nightclub.
Entertainment: Dances every night, band and disco; magic-comedy stage shows; square dancing; great talent shows; movies on big-screen TV; backgammon; cards; karaoke; activities social directors.
Summary: Year-round destination resort ranch. Large facility with wonderful spirit and service. The Turk family and their staff do a first-rate job for families of all ages. Great for family reunions. Be sure to see the award-winning Belgian draft-horse team. Outdoor group barbecues for up to 1,000. Nearby: oldest street in America, Kingston, Roosevelt's Hyde Park Mansion and Library, West Point Military Academy. Video available.

See color photos, page 267.

Cataloochee Ranch
Maggie Valley, North Carolina

In 1939 young forester Tom Alexander began the tradition and spirit of Cataloochee Ranch. A mile high in the Great Smoky Mountains of western North Carolina, Cataloochee (Cherokee for "wave upon wave") is a thousand-acre spread bordered by half a million acres of the Great Smoky Mountains National Park. Since 1939 the Alexander family has been sharing their Southern warmth and hospitality. This ranch looks out over the rolling hills of Maggie Valley, providing guests with a ringside seat for the four seasons as they unfold. Cataloochee offers an unhurried pace with the Smoky and Blue Ridge Mountains as a wonderful backdrop. Today your hosts are Alex (Tom's great-grandson) and his wife, Ashli Aumen, and general manager Tim Rice. For those who would rather not ride, the ranch is in the middle of western North Carolina's year-round recreational playground. In less than a day's drive, you can see everything from clogging to Appalachian folk art.

Address: 119 Ranch Drive, Maggie Valley, North Carolina 28751
Telephone: (800) 868-1401, (828) 926-1401; fax: (828) 926-9249
Internet: http://www.cataloochee-ranch.com
Airport: Asheville
Location: 35 miles west of Asheville, 150 miles northwest of Charlotte off Interstate 40 and U.S. 19, 185 miles north of Atlanta
Memberships: Friends of the Great Smoky Mountains National Park, Southeast Tourism Society, North Carolina Travel Council
Awards: Mobil 3 Star
Medical: Waynesville Hospital, 10 miles
Conference: 40
Guest Capacity: 88
Accommodations: Open fireplaces, handmade quilts, and antiques set the tone for each of the 12 cabins, some with kitchenettes. There is no air conditioning, as the mile-high elevation brings lots of cool mountain air. Guests enjoy electric heaters, midmorning fires, and warm summer days of about 75 degrees. Ask about the four newly built romance cabins. Silverbell Lodge has six units, two of which have full kitchens. The main lodge is the heart of the ranch, with an impressive stone fireplace and chandeliers made from ox yokes. There are a number of rooms on the second floor. Fresh wildflowers are provided in the rooms in the summer.
Rates: • $$–$$$. Modified American Plan. Horseback riding is extra. Children's and low- and high-season rates available. Group rates by request. Two-night minimum.
Credit Cards: VISA, MasterCard, American Express; personal checks accepted
Season: April through November; late December to March.
Activities: Slow, easygoing, scenic mountain horseback riding. Experienced riders can trot and lope; half-day and all-day rides, usually with eight to 10 guests to a ride. Ask about the Hemphill Bald and Swag rides. Riding instruction available. During the season the ranch offers backcountry pack trips. Fishing in ranch pond. Croquet, hiking, heated swim-spa, tennis, tractor-drawn wagon rides. Float and white-water rafting trips and six golf courses nearby. In winter, weather permitting, very casual cross-country skiing; downhill ski area one mile away.
Children's Programs: Children are welcome but no formal program. Kids must be age six to horseback ride.
Dining: Weekly outdoor barbecues, fresh garden vegetables (lettuce, broccoli, cabbage, squash, and spinach), fresh homemade jams and jellies, ribs, mountain trout, fall harvest game feast including venison and elk. Beer and wine available.
Entertainment: Nearby regional mountain music, clogging, folk/ballad singer. Horse-drawn carriage rides and tractor hayrides at ranch. Informal evening entertainment.
Summary: Family-oriented ranch with great Southern charm and beauty. Many professional families and family reunions. Off-season business seminars. Spectacular Southeastern scenery, moderate climate, backcountry pack trips. Nearby: Cherokee Indian Village, Biltmore Estate, Mountain Heritage Center, clogging, Blue Ridge Parkway, Great Smoky Mountain National Park.

See color photos, page 268.

Clear Creek Ranch
Burnsville, North Carolina

Clear Creek Ranch was born out of a longtime dream of owner Rex Frederick and his wife, Aileen, who have created their "Western ranch" in the mountains of North Carolina. Located in the Blue Ridge Mountains north of Asheville, the ranch was built in 1995. The views are glorious and the surrounding Pisgah National Forest provides 80,000 acres of riding and hiking trails. Hosts Rex and Aileen offer Southern hospitality in abundance, and have an enthusiastic staff of young people. While horseback riding is the most popular activity, tubing down the South Toe River is a close second! There is also a stocked trout pond, a heated pool, hot tub, and a high-quality mountain golf course within one mile of the ranch. The warm, friendly, relaxed atmosphere is a ranch trademark, and is a reflection of the hosts' own outgoing personalities and genuine friendliness. If returning guests are any indication, the folks at Clear Creek are doing it right!

Address: 100 Clear Creek Drive, Highway 80 South, Burnsville, North Carolina 28714
Telephone: (800) 651-4510, (828) 675-4510; fax: (828) 675-5452
E-Mail: ccrdude@prodigy.net
Internet: http://www.clearcreekranch.com
Airport: Asheville; pickup available at small additional charge
Location: 45 miles north of Asheville, North Carolina; three hours northeast of Knoxville, Tennessee; four hours north of Atlanta, Georgia
Memberships: High Country Hosts, The Dude Ranchers' Association (Associate Members)
Medical: Spruce Pine Hospital, 15 miles
Conference: 40
Guest Capacity: 50
Accommodations: Guest quarters are located in three separate buildings, all adjacent to the main lodge. There are cozy one-, two- and three- bedroom units, all with lodgepole pine beds, air-conditioning, heating, and carpeting. Big covered porches with an ample supply of rocking chairs provide beautiful views of the mountains. The main lodge offers a big porch and huge deck, dining room, and living room with a Carolina field stone fireplace where guests gather for cards or to tell stories about their day.
Rates: • $$–$$$ American Plan. Children's, off-season, and group rates available. Three-day minimum stay.
Credit Cards: VISA, MasterCard; personal checks preferred
Season: April to December; children's program June through August only
Activities: Horseback riding is available morning and afternoon, plus an all-day ride and picnic lunch on the Buncombe Horse Trail in the Pisgah National Forest. Wonderful rides through the spectacular, lush North Carolina Forests and across the crystal clear South Toe River—WOW! Tubing down the South Toe River is popular with children. Activity trips to local crafters, gem mines, hikes to Crab Tree and Linville waterfalls, fishing either in the pond or on the South Toe River for famous North Carolina mountain trout. Golf (five minutes away) and white-water rafting (45 minutes) are also options.
Children's Programs: During June, July, and August, there is an optional organized children's program for ages five through 12. This is supervised by the staff, and includes a Junior Wrangler Ride and picnic lunch, nature walks, and crafts.
Dining: Three hearty meals a day. Favorites include rib and chicken cookout, lasagna, Aileen's hot chicken salad, and the Sunday omelet bar. BYOB.
Entertainment: Evening activities include Rex leading karaoke singing, square dancing, local cloggers, marshmallow roasts, songs around the campfire, relaxing in front of the fire in the living room. Weekend highlight is the "Rodeo" on Saturday.
Summary: Southern hospitality, fabulous North Carolina scenery, the crystal-clear Toe River, and a relaxed, easygoing spirit are the hallmarks of Rex and Aileen Fredericks' Clear Creek Ranch! Completely surrounded by the Pisgah National Forest. Breathtaking fall colors, superb 18-hole mountain golf course (five minutes), and local arts and crafts famous to this part of the country. Nearby: Biltmore Estate, Grandfather Mountain, and the charming town of Blowing Rock.

See color photos, page 269.

Earthshine Mountain Lodge
Lake Toxaway, North Carolina

As the author, I've taken the liberty of including a few extra-special properties that don't fit the classical guest-ranch mold but do capture the spirit of adventure, nature, and hospitality. This is one of them. Earthshine Mountain Lodge is the dream and creation of two very gifted people: Marion Boatwright and his business partner, Kim Maurer. Here the magic of North Carolina's Blue Ridge Mountains, coupled with an energetic and caring staff, touch the hearts and souls of families, couples, and singles year-round. At Earthshine guests reconnect with things that really matter. Resting atop one of the grandest ridges in the Appalachians, the lodge looks out across some of North Carolina's most famous scenery. Built in 1990, Earthshine radiates old-fashioned goodness. If you're looking for a heartwarming experience for yourself, your family, or a small business group, give Marion or Kim a call. One couple said it best, "Earthshine attracts warm and friendly folks. It offers rustic luxury, warmth, and a wonderful variety of things to do." Earthshine is real mountain magic and the best of Blue Ridge Mountain hospitality.

Address: Route 1, Box 216-C, Dept. K, Golden Road, Lake Toxaway, North Carolina 28747
Telephone: (828) 862-4207
E-Mail: info@earthshinemtnlodge.com
Internet: http://www.earthshinemtnlodge.com
Airport: Asheville, 35 miles
Location: 50 miles south of Asheville off U.S. 64 between Brevard and Cashiers
Medical: Transylvania Community Hospital, 20 miles
Conference: 30
Guest Capacity: 30
Accommodations: Earthshine's 1½-story, hand-built, cedar-log lodge opens to one of the finest views in eastern America. Rock fireplaces, hand-made quilts, and log beds and rockers add to the mountain spirit. Eight guest rooms have a *Little House on the Prairie* feel with sleeping lofts that kids love. All 10 lodge rooms have private baths with tiled floors. Sunrise cottage is a mountain chalet for larger families or two families traveling together.
Rates: • $$. American Plan. Children's rates. Riding and roping instruction on an individual basis. Ask about exclusive family reunions and group opportunities.
Credit Cards: VISA, MasterCard, Discover
Season: Year-round, including all holidays
Activities: A wide variety of activities. Guided Western trail rides wind across mountaintop meadows and deep into forests. Three scheduled rides each day with only five guests per ride. Miles of hiking trails to a nearby 50-foot waterfall, West Fork of the French Broad River, and mountaintop views. Two unique features of Earthshine are the ropes course and a 30-foot climbing wall.
Children's Programs: This is one of the exceptional and exciting programs Earthshine has developed. Each morning talented staff members lead youngsters ages six to 12 on three-hour adventures. Kids go back in time to the 1800s to experience a pioneer homestead and visit a secret "Cherokee Village," learning and working as they go. Wilderness treks and creek hikes take the kids into the backcountry. In addition there are kids' cookouts weekly. Best of all for parents, Earthshine offers child care for younger kids so that parents are free to rest, relax, or explore!
Dining: A happy and healthy fresh-food experience, served Sunday-brunch–style, including vegetarian meals, fresh trout, and home-baked cookies in each room on check-in. BYOB.
Entertainment: Join-in entertainment. Mountain music, folk sing-alongs, Native American Cherokee games.
Summary: When asked what makes Earthshine so special, Marion Boatwright said, "When you look at a crescent moon and see the rest of its sphere lightly illuminated . . . that's Earthshine, a glimpse of wonder lit by a very special light." Wholesome goodness for singles, couples, families, and business retreats. One of the prettiest locations in the eastern United States and one of its greatest adventures!

See color photos, page 270.

Baker's Bar M Ranch
Adams, Oregon

THE DUDE RANCHERS' ASSOCIATION

Since the 1930s, the Baker family has operated this 2,500-acre ranch on the Umatilla River in the Blue Mountains of northeastern Oregon. Three generations of Bakers live and work this traditional guest ranch with emphasis on good family fun. The main lodge, built in 1864 as a stagecoach stop, is a vital part of the ranch. The notched, weathered logs were hewed while the Civil War raged. An old ledger shows that Teddy Roosevelt stayed here, and you will still find marks of the old stage road. There are five special things that bring guests back year after year—the Baker family; the riding; the excellent, hearty food; the peaceful river setting; and the geothermal warm-springs pool. The soothing water stays an almost constant 90 degrees; after a long day in the saddle, that pool is heaven. The Bar M is a family operation. When you walk in the front door you may be a stranger, but after just a day you feel like part of the family. Baker's Bar M is one of the best!

Address: 58840 Bar M Lane, Adams, Oregon 97810-3003
Telephone: (888) 824-3381, (541) 566-3381
Internet: http://www.ranchweb.com/barm
Airport: Pendleton, Oregon, and Pasco
Location: 31 miles east of Pendleton
Memberships: The Dude Ranchers' Association
Medical: Pendleton, 31 miles
Conference: Up to 45 people off-season only
Guest Capacity: 30
Accommodations: Guests stay in the old homestead with four two-room apartments; the circa-1864 ranch house with eight rooms in period furnishings (bathrooms down the hall); the two-bedroom Brookside cabin; or the three-bedroom Lakeside cabin with porches looking to the pine-studded hills. Queen-size beds in most rooms.
Rates: • $$. American Plan. Family and children's rates available. Usually six-night minimum stay mid-June through August. Arrivals noon Sundays.
Credit Cards: None. Cash or personal checks accepted.
Season: May through September; March, April, May, and September for conferences
Activities: No schedules except for mealtimes and riding. The emphasis is on family activities, horseback riding, warm-springs pool, and river swimming. Guests are assigned a horse for the week and are invited to saddle and groom it. Usually no more than 10 go out per ride. Two rides daily plus weekly all-day rides and occasional overnight trips to Little Bear Camp. Bareback riding, weekly horseback games, catch-and-release fishing for rainbow trout in the Umatilla River on ranch (some gear available), hiking trails, natural 40-by-60-foot warm-springs pool.
Children's Programs: Prefer no children under age six. There's no separate children's program, as the emphasis is on family activities. However, the ranch does allow them much freedom to play and explore.
Dining: The food is wonderful! Marvelous meals with Gene's famous raspberries, and Jerry's homemade bread. Ranch-raised beef and pork. Occasional Mexican fare. Always freshly baked cookies. No preservatives. BYOB.
Entertainment: Square dancing, basketball, and volleyball in the log recreation barn. Sing-alongs on the porch and evening swimming.
Summary: One of the great family-owned and -operated guest ranches for families, couples, and singles. It just doesn't get any better. Started in 1938 by the late Howard and Bonnie Baker, the ranch tradition is now carried on by their children, grandchildren, and great-grandchildren. Lots of friendly Oregon hospitality, rich in history. Nearby: Pendleton Roundup in mid-September. Spanish spoken.

See color photos, page 271.

Aspen Ridge Resort
Bly, Oregon

Aspen Ridge Resort offers guests a real ranch vacation. Set on the historic Fishhole Creek Ranch which was homesteaded in the mid-1800s, the resort overlooks a high-mountain meadow where cattle and sandhill cranes share the lush green expanse. Built in 1992, the ranch is rustically elegant with a handcrafted log lodge and cabins. The lodge features a wonderful restaurant, large rock fireplaces in the great room and lounge, beautiful antiques, and warm hospitality. Eighteen miles off the highway, this 14,000-acre ranch is surrounded by National Forest land. This is a working cattle ranch with a resort atmosphere, running a thousand head of cattle, where guests can ride horseback with the ranch cowboys to check, doctor, or move cattle. Guests set their own pace: riding, fishing, mountain biking, playing tennis, or simply relaxing in this beautiful setting. Steve and Karen Simmons, owners and hosts at Aspen Ridge, delight in sharing the pleasures of life on a working cattle ranch.

Address: P.O. Box 2 K, Bly, Oregon 97622
Telephone: (800) 393-3323 (outside Oregon), (541) 884-8685; call for fax number
E-Mail: aspenrr@cdsnet.net
Internet: http://www.aspenrr.com
Airport: Klamath Falls, or Reno; Lakeview, Oregon for private aircraft; 2,200-foot dirt strip on ranch
Location: Between Klamath Falls and Lakeview; 72 miles east of Klamath Falls; 18 miles southeast of Bly off Highway 140.
Memberships: Southern Oregon Visitors Association, Portland Oregon Visitors Association, National Cattlemen's Association
Medical: Sprague Valley Medical Clinic, Bly; 20 miles. Lake District Hospital, Lakeview; 50 miles.
Conference: 40
Guest Capacity: 40
Accommodations: Five 1,200-square-foot, handcrafted, custom two-story log homes and four hotel rooms in the lodge. Cabins are completely furnished and each has a fully-equipped kitchen, living room with woodstove, two bedrooms, loft, and bathroom. Maximum occupancy is six persons. Linens, housekeeping service, and firewood are provided. Lodge rooms vary in size and sleeping arrangements; all have private bathrooms. Ranch generates own power.
Rates: • $$–$$$$$. European Plan. Two-night minimum stay in cabins. Riding and fly-fishing are extra.
Credit Cards: None. Personal checks accepted.
Season: Year-round, except March
Activities: Horseback riding, as part of the cattle operation, is popular in late spring, summer, and fall. Guests are welcome to bring their own horses and participate in ranch activities. Special horse events include cutting, team roping, and roping schools, and offer great sport for spectators. Spin- and fly-fishing in nearby lakes and streams, catch-and-release fly-fishing only for trophy trout on the ranch. A tennis court, swimming lake, and miles of trails for mountain biking, jogging, and hiking are available. Seasonal wildlife-viewing and wildflower gathering. Winter: Christmas and New Year's celebrations. Snowmobiling and cross-country skiing begin right at the door.
Children's Programs: No special programs. The ranch is family-oriented and encourages parents and children to participate in activities together.
Dining: The lodge restaurant serves breakfast, lunch, and dinner daily in an atmosphere of relaxed elegance. Guests order from a menu that features country breakfasts, homemade desserts, and excellent mesquite-barbecued beef, ribs, chicken, and trout. The Buffalo Saloon with full bar service is open daily. Restaurant open to the public.
Entertainment: Appearing nightly outdoors, a sky full of stars and a chorus of coyotes. Occasional cowboy poetry and live music.
Summary: One of Kilgore's bright new stars in the West. A beautiful 14,000-acre cattle ranch nestled among towering pines overlooking a high-mountain meadow and run with a resort feel. Steven and Karen Simmons have been in the cattle business for years and, together with daughters Ann and Lynn, run one of the West's exciting new year-round guest and cattle ranches with new accommodations. Excellent riding opportunities, fly-fishing, hiking, and winter snowmobiling. Ask about the barbecued beef and Carmel connection.

See color photos, pages 272–273.

Flying M Ranch
Yamhill, Oregon

It's not called the Flying M for nothing. In Oregon's beautiful northwest corner, in the heart of wine country, the Mitchell family ranch has its own 2,135-foot private turf airstrip. Many private pilots and guests savor this grass landing strip that makes travel to the ranch so convenient. The center of the ranch is the hand-hewn log lodge built in 1985. The lodge rests at the edge of a meadow where the North Yamhill River and Hanna Creek join under alder and maple trees cloaked with moss. A bar in the lodge was handmade from a six-ton Douglas fir log. Some of the lounge tables surrounding the dance floor are made from cross-cuts of myrtle, cedar, walnut, and maple. Hanging from the Sawtooth Room ceiling is a Mitchell surrey, which came from the early homestead. While most guests come from surrounding counties, the Flying M has had visitors from as far away as South Africa and Australia.

Address: 23029 N.W. Flying M Road, Dept. K, Yamhill, Oregon 97148
Telephone: (503) 662-3222; fax: (503) 662-3202
E-Mail: flyingm@bigplanet.com
Internet: http://www.flying-m-ranch.com
Airport: Portland, 45 miles; 2,135-foot turf airstrip at ranch
Location: 45 miles southwest of Portland off Highway 47
Memberships: Oregon Guides and Packers, Unique Northwest Country Inns, Portland Oregon Visitors Association
Medical: McMinnville Hospital, 15 miles; Life Flight helicopter available
Conference: 150
Guest Capacity: 150
Accommodations: Eight cabins with kitchens; 24 rooms in the "bunkhouse" motel. These rooms vary considerably: some have queen-size beds; all have full baths and electric heat. The cabins have wood-burning stoves and electric heat. The tiny honeymoon cabin is wonderful with fireplace, queen-size bed, two-person indoor bath/whirlpool, TV, carpeting, and a wonderful private deck overlooking the North Yamhill River. Ask about the overnight to weekly camping facilities. Many guests bring their own horses and camp. If this interests you, ask about Big, Little, and Old Horse camps.
Rates: • $–$$$. Meals and horseback riding extra. Family and group rates. Daily picnic rates, too. Two-night minimum stay in cabins, April–September.
Credit Cards: VISA, MasterCard, American Express, Discover, Diners Club
Season: Year-round, including Thanksgiving and Easter. Closed for Christmas, December 24 and 25.
Activities: Horses rented by the hour. Overnight trail rides to Trask Mountain cabin usually once a month. Trout fishing in the North Yamhill River, lighted blacktop tennis court, and pond for swimming. Seasonal elk and deer hunting. In winter the ranch doesn't get much snow and there's no specific program. Most people come to enjoy the fine dining, visit wineries, listen to country music, and ride horses.
Children's Programs: Ask about the kids' horse camp. Great environment and outdoor experience. Kids are the responsibility of parents except during the horse camp.
Dining: Ranch cooking ordered from a menu, homemade desserts, weekly steak-fries and cookouts, and seafood. Wonderful selection of local wines; mixed drinks available. Dining room seats 180, open to the public. Monthly brunch. Winter dinners at Elk Camp (rain or shine) along the river.
Entertainment: Tractor-drawn hayrides. Live music on weekends for dancing.
Summary: A wonderful setting in Oregon's beautiful northwest corner. The property has been in the Mitchell family since the early 1930s. Charming cabins and magnificent log lodge. Great for singles, couples, families, and groups. Bring your own horse. Horse-camping and boarding facilities available. Dining open to public, private airstrip, and trout fishing. Nearby: local wineries, the Gallery Players of Oregon theater company, horse shows and bull riding in the DeLashmutt Equestrian Center.

Obstinate J Ranch
Trail, Oregon

"Hook a dream on the Rogue River." Welcome to southern Oregon's landmark Obstinate J Ranch, located in a beautiful river valley with 600 acres right on the world-famous Rogue River, just off Highway 62. Since the 1960s, sisters Bunny and Pat and their families have been offering a wonderful independent ranch, fishing, and horseback-riding experience to families, groups, and couples. Today Pat's daughter, Martha, and son, Fraser, offer guests great fishing for trout, steelhead, and salmon, as well as horseback riding, rafting, or sightseeing some of Oregon's colorful artistic festivals and natural wonders. Here you set your own schedule and enjoy your own cooking. The Obstinate J is a home away from home.

Address: 29680 Highway 62, Dept. K, Trail, Oregon 97541
Telephone: (541) 878-2718; call for fax number
Airport: Medford, 27 miles
Location: 27 miles northeast of Medford on Highway 62, six hours south of Portland, eight hours north of San Francisco
Memberships: Oregon Lodging Association
Medical: Providence Hospital & Medical Center, 30 miles; medical clinics nearby.
Conference: 20 (August–April)
Guest Capacity: 20
Accommodations: Three comfortable guest houses overlook the river. Two-bedroom Steelhead has large covered and screened-in porch. Duplex Yankee Acorn/Rebel Oaks sleeps seven and is great for extended families. East End sleeps eight with washer/dryer and dishwasher. All have fireplaces, baths, twin and queen-size beds, along with fully equipped kitchens. No TV or telephones—just the marvelous sounds of the river.
Rates: • $–$$. Lodging/guest-house rental only. Meals not included. Guided fishing and horseback-riding packages available. Two-night minimum. Week and weekend rates.
Credit Cards: None. Personal checks, traveler's checks, and cash accepted.
Season: Year-round
Activities: Most come to enjoy the abundant fishing, trail and arena horseback riding, and the relaxing sound of the river rushing by. Fly-fishing and spinning-reel enthusiasts fish for seasonal trout, steelhead, and salmon. Local guide service can be arranged for drift-boat and wade fishing. Guests can bring their own gear or equip themselves at the professional tackle shop just down the road from the ranch. Martha offers a horse program for the novice as well as the experienced rider—both English and Western. A competition English rider and instructor, she tailors her program to the guest's level of experience. Ask about the fall cattle roundup. Swimming pool, sauna, tennis court, and recreation room are also available to guests. River-raft rental and rafting excursions available in Shady Cove.
Children's Programs: A great family place for kids to roam and play under parental supervision. No organized activities. Baby-sitting by prior arrangement. Generally kids ages seven and up go on trail rides.
Dining: As Martha says, "Everyone who comes enjoys cooking for themselves. Here we provide our guests with the freedom to do as they wish on their vacation." Full kitchens in all guest houses. Guests may also choose from a variety of restaurants nearby.
Entertainment: Informal weekly potluck barbecues. Complimentary barbecues are also held on major holidays.
Summary: A wonderful place to fish, ride, relax, and take in the sounds of Oregon's famous Rogue River. As Martha says, "We appeal to guests who want to have their own house for a vacation and who appreciate the independence of cooking their own meals." The Obstinate J provides wonderful, quality time for families and friends. Nearby: Ashland Shakespearean Festival, scenic Crater Lake, and historic Jacksonville.

Rock Springs Guest Ranch
Bend, Oregon

THE DUDE RANCHERS' ASSOCIATION

Just outside Bend in the foothills of the Cascade Mountains, Rock Springs Guest Ranch was founded by the late Donna Gill. A schoolteacher, Donna developed an early love for young people, their parents, and the great outdoors. Her spirit and the tradition she inspired are carried on by her nephew, John Gill, his wife, Eva, and young daughter Hannah, along with their fine staff. "Our goal is to provide the highest quality vacation experience for each of our guests, with an emphasis on the family," says John. Rock Springs attracts guests from all over the world. With the snowcapped peaks of the Three Sisters Mountains in the distance, Rock Springs provides trappings of the West as well as modern conveniences. It is one of the best guest ranches in the West for families. The ranch is radiant with hospitality, cozy with warmth, and as for activities—you name it, they've got it. Rock Springs is also popular for business meetings and retreats during non-summer months.

Address: 64201 Tyler Road, Drawer K, Bend, Oregon 97701
Telephone: (541) 382-1957, (800) 225-3833; fax: (541) 382-7774
E-Mail: info@rocksprings.com
Internet: http://www.rocksprings.com
Airport: Redmond/Bend, 19 miles
Location: nine miles northwest of Bend, 180 miles southeast of Portland
Memberships: The Dude Ranchers' Association, Meeting Professionals International, Resort and Commercial Recreation Association, America Outdoors
Medical: St. Charles Hospital, Bend; 9 miles
Conference: 50; ask for the detailed conference information packet
Guest Capacity: 50
Accommodations: Individual cabins and duplex-triplex units nestled in ponderosa pines. Rooms are finished in knotty pine with private baths. All cabins have decks, and most have fireplaces and refrigerators.
Rates: • $$–$$$. Full American Plan in summer. One-week minimum stay, Saturday to Saturday. Modified American Plan for Thanksgiving. Corporate meeting packages available.
Credit Cards: VISA, MasterCard, Diners Club, American Express, Discover
Season: Late June through August and Thanksgiving. All other times are dedicated to corporate conferences, retreats, and seminars.
Activities: Horseback riding is the ranch's summer specialty. Scenic trail riding with views of Cascade Mountain Range. Six usually go out per ride. Two rides daily, at 10 a.m. and 2 p.m. Weekly luncheon rides. Heated, hourglass-shaped swimming pool; two tennis courts, with tennis pro in July. World-class fly-fishing in nearby Metolius and Deschutes Rivers and in lakes. Local guide service available. Hiking and self-guided nature walks. Everyone enjoys relaxing in the huge free-form whirlpool overlooking the pond. Golf and white-water rafting nearby. Billiards, table tennis, volleyball, and basketball.
Children's Programs: Terrific children's program with counselors. Adults are free to do their own thing if they wish. Children ages three to five and six to 12 enjoy a variety of activities and adventures. Lunch and dinner are available in a separate dining room. Counselors on duty from 9 a.m. to 8:30 p.m. Children under age six do not take trail rides. Special infant and nanny rates available. Ask about kids' overnight campout and hayride.
Dining: Buffet-style meals are a highlight of the Rock Springs experience, including a wide variety of cuisine from traditional prime rib and fresh Northwest seafood to vegetarian and health-conscious choices. Special diets catered to. Fresh fruit and home-baked cookies available between meals. Local beers and Northwest wines available.
Entertainment: Scheduled nightly activities. Volleyball, Western dancing, pool table, table tennis, and a variety of games.
Summary: One of the premier guest ranches for families. Superb corporate-meeting ranch offering exclusive use of all facilities for each group. Nearby: two-dozen championship golf courses, High Desert Museum (wildlife and cultural museum).

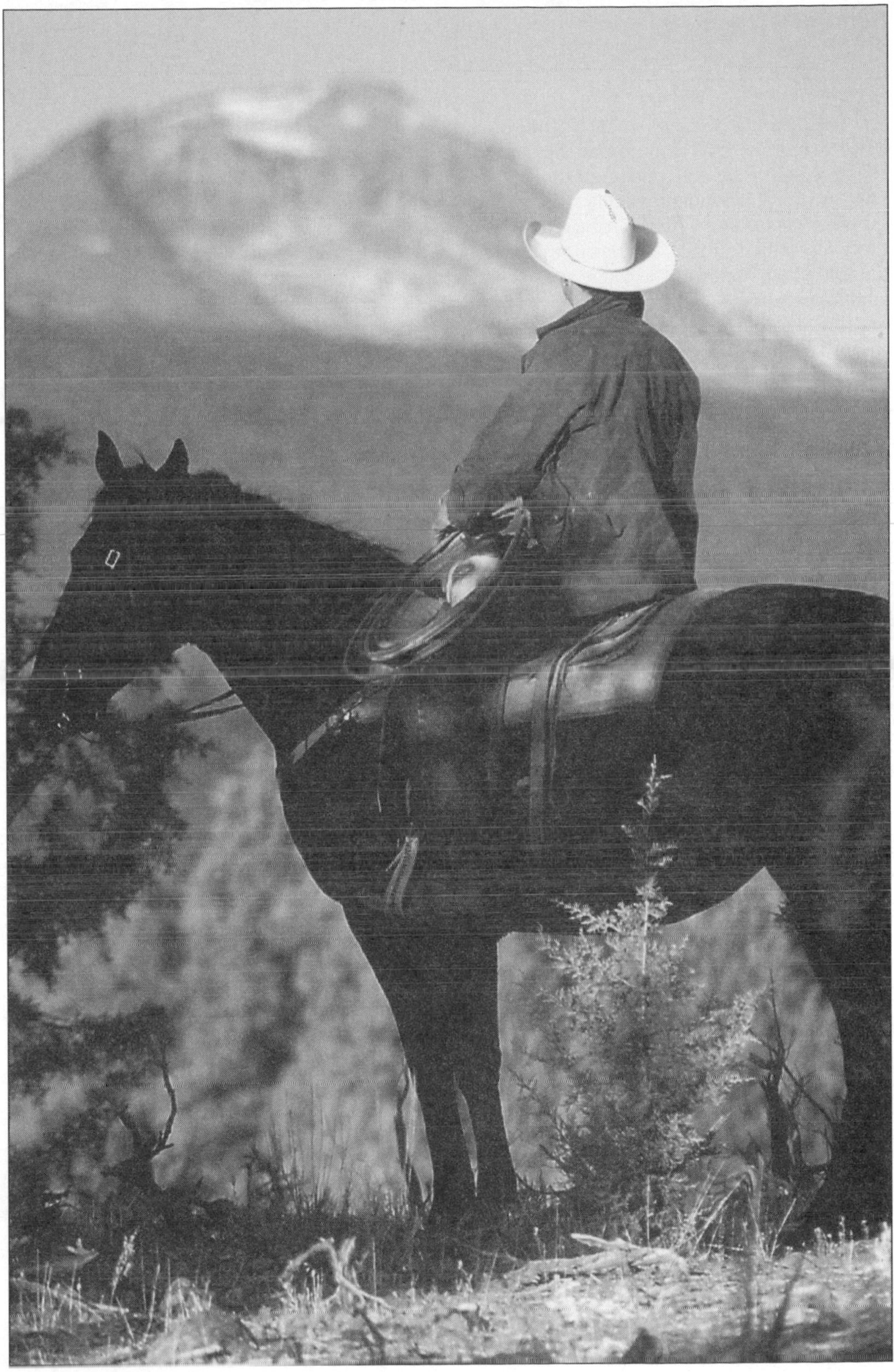

Ponderosa Cattle Company and Guest Ranch
Seneca, Oregon

The 120,000-acre Ponderosa Ranch is one of the most beautiful and historic ranches in the Northwest. The lush mountain meadows, bubbling streams, abundant wildlife, and snow-capped peaks, along with the scattered herds of cattle, combine to make this ranch a picture of the Old West. In 1988 the Oren and Fleming families purchased this beautiful ranch. Soon, out of a desire to share a part of the vanishing western lifestyle, Izzy and Nancy Oren added a new guest-ranch facility to the existing ranch operation. Their goal was to allow guests to participate in the daily operation of caring for the 3,000 head of cattle that comprise the Ponderosa herd. Izzy and Nancy bring a lifetime of hospitality, business experience, and love of a Western heritage to the ranch. The cowboys and supporting staff are native to the area, many of whom are descendants of homesteading families who immigrated to the area by way of the nearby Oregon Trail. The program at the Ponderosa gives every guest a chance to spend five to six hours in the saddle each day, learning and participating in the "job for the day." And as Izzy, who was raised in Europe, says, "We offer an incredible adult experience that is balanced between the guest's riding experience and the ranch job scheduled for the day." Since the cowboy program is limited to 20 guests each week, guests get a "hands-on" experience that will be remembered for a lifetime.

Address: P.O. Box 190 K, Seneca, Oregon 97873
Telephone: (541) 542-2403; fax: (541) 542-2713
E-Mail: seeyou@PonderosaGuestRanch.com
Internet: http://www.PonderosaGuestRanch.com
Airport: Redmond or Boise; private 4,000-foot airstrip on ranch with private air-taxi service available
Location: 35 miles northeast of Burns, 35 miles southwest of John Day, 160 miles east of Redmond, 320 miles southeast of Portland, 240 miles west of Boise
Medical: Blue Mountain Hospital, 35 miles; Air Life Helicopter
Conference: 48
Guest Capacity: 48

Accommodations: The eight triplex log cabins are arranged in the pines behind and to the west of the lodge, with valley views. Each has common covered porches, individual entrances, two double beds, wood floors, a country motif, individual baths/showers. No TVs or telephones in rooms. The 7,000-square-foot main log lodge with the beautiful hand-carved front door has a dining room, cozy living room with stone fireplace, bar, and gift shop. The covered veranda overlooks the picturesque Silvies Valley.
Rates: • $$$$. American Plan. Corporate and group rates. Special holiday packages.
Credit Cards: VISA, MasterCard
Season: May to mid-October cowboy program. Special programs available at other times of the year.
Activities: Summer activities at the Ponderosa are regular ranch activities. They change daily and can include cattle work such as sorting, gathering, scattering, roundup, roping, and riding fences. With 60 different pastures, there's always something to do. All riding is geared to ability levels, and previous riding is recommended but not required. You may, depending on your ability, participate in all ranch activities. Fishing in creeks and on the Silvies River. Seasonal deer-, elk-, antelope-, goose-, and duck-hunting. Skeet-shooting and .22-caliber rifle range available.
Children's Programs: None. Must be 18 years or older.
Dining: Hearty family-style ranch cooking. Chuck-wagon lunches on the trail. Full bar and fine Oregon wines.
Entertainment: Jukebox music, pool table, and TV in lodge. Occasional line dancing, live music, and mountain-man storytelling.
Summary: Historic 120,000-acre cattle ranch. Guest ranch built in 1993. Located in a magnificent eastern Oregon valley. Unlimited riding and cattle experiences, depending on your abilities. No children under age 18. Featured in *Western Horseman,* February 1998 issue. German, French, and Spanish spoken.

Blue Bell Lodge & Resort
Custer, South Dakota

South Dakota drew a lot of attention after Kevin Costner's film *Dances with Wolves*. The state is rich in early American history and diverse in its stunning landscape. Blue Bell Lodge, in the heart of 73,000-acre Custer State Park, is owned and operated by Phil and Sue Lampert. Blue Bell was built back in the 1920s and offers travelers a home base for a diverse combination of recreational activities. The lodge, along with its old and new cabins, offers families and couples a place to be on their own in the midst of panhandling wild burros, the world's largest state buffalo herd, and scenic drives. At Blue Bell you are, for the most part, on your own and free to roam as you wish. One of the unique things about this lodge is the horse-camping program. For those traveling through South Dakota by car or RV, Blue Bell offers rustic and modern comfort in the heart of magnificent Custer State Park.

Address: HCR 83, Box 63K, Custer, South Dakota 57730
Telephone: (605) 255-4531, (800) 658-3530 (telephone will be answered "Custer State Park Resort Company"; ask for Blue Bell); fax: (605) 255-4706
E-Mail: email@custerresorts.com
Internet: http://www.custerresorts.com
Airport: Rapid City, 50 miles
Location: South on Highway 87 toward Wind Cave National Park and Hot Springs, 44 miles southwest of Rapid City off Highway 36
Memberships: South Dakota Outfitters and Guides Association, National Tour Association, AAA, Mobil Travel Guide, American Bus Association
Medical: Custer General Hospital, 11 miles
Conference: 90; very large gatherings as well
Guest Capacity: 72 to 148
Accommodations: Blue Bell has 29 cabins, 11 of which were built in the 1920s. All of the older cabins have one main room with kitchenette, a modern bathroom, and electric heat. The 16 new log cabins are very spacious—one large room with two beds and sitting areas, modern bathrooms, refrigerators, microwaves, coffeemakers, and fireplaces. All cabins have outdoor fire grates and picnic tables.
Rates: $. Food and activities à la carte, no minimum stay
Credit Cards: VISA, MasterCard, American Express, Discover
Season: May through September (some cabins are kept open during the winter months, but most activities are closed)
Activities: Guided, scenic horseback trail rides throughout the day, offering one-hour, two-hour, half-day, and all-day rides. Breakfast and dinner rides and overnight pack trips can be scheduled with advance notice. Trout fishing in French Creek or one of the nearby lakes. Swimming beaches also at nearby lakes. Paddleboats and rowboat rentals available nearby, or you can rent a mountain bike. Excellent hiking throughout the park. The Park Service offers interpretive programs. Ask about the Buffalo Safari jeep rides.
Children's Programs: Children of all ages are welcome, and many come. No special programs.
Dining: The rustic Buffalo Dining Room and Buffalo Wallow Lounge are popular gathering places. Home-cooked meals, served family-style. Buffalo, fresh trout, chicken, and beefsteaks are specialties. Ask about the hay wagon rides in the wildlife area. Full bar.
Entertainment: Old-fashioned hayride and chuck-wagon cookout, with sing-along entertainment scheduled most evenings.
Summary: A wonderful 73,000-acre destination with lots of history, wildlife, and recreation opportunities. Located in the heart of Custer State Park. Rustic and modern cabins. Phil and Sue Lampert were both born and raised in South Dakota and know the history very well. Very informal program—you're on your own with lots to do. Depending on the time of year, there are lots of buffalo and elk. Horse-camping available. Very popular for family reunions.

See color photos, page 274.

Triple R Ranch
Keystone, South Dakota

THE DUDE RANCHERS' ASSOCIATION

Jack and Cherrylee Bradt have been in the guest-ranch business since 1977. One of last year's guests said, "I've been to five other dude ranches and the Triple R is the only one I am coming back to." When Jack says, "Come back and see us," in his big, robust, friendly way, you know he means it! Today the Triple R shares a special kind of hospitality and unique proximity to two of the wonders of the world: Mt. Rushmore's and Crazy Horse Memorial's huge mountain carvings. In the heart of the Black Hills National Forest and surrounded by the Norbeck Wildlife Preserve, the ranch offers travelers and vacationers a home to explore a part of the West Kevin Costner made famous in *Dances with Wolves*. In 1995, Jack and Cherrylee began a new program (unique in North America), opening their ranch to wheelchair-bound individuals and their families. Son-in-law Andy, injured in an accident, opened their eyes to the need for a ranch that offers outdoor recreational enjoyment for all. The Triple R is a diamond in the rough, offering an informal, low-key, wonderful ranch/country atmosphere surrounded by nature—the greatest healer of all.

Address: P.O. Box 124 K, Keystone, South Dakota 57751-0124
Telephone: (888) RRRANCH (777-2624, evenings only), (605) 666-4605. If Jack and Cherrylee are not in, Slim always answers the phone.
Airport: Rapid City, 25 miles
Location: 25 miles southwest of Rapid City off Highway 16A
Memberships: The Dude Ranchers' Association, Black Hills, Badlands & Lakes Association
Medical: Rapid City Regional Hospital, 25 miles
Guest Capacity: 10
Accommodations: Small, simple, wood-sided, carpeted cabins, with private baths. Each cabin is modestly decorated. The ranch house has accommodations upstairs for two or more persons.
Rates: • $$. American Plan. Six-day stay is usual with arrival on Sunday. Four-day minimum. Special off-season rates and programs.
Credit Cards: VISA, MasterCard. Personal checks and cash accepted.
Season: Year-round
Activities: Guests enjoy the informally planned activities at the ranch or driving to see the wonders of Mt. Rushmore and Crazy Horse Mountain. Most guests come here to ride. Rides to old mines and ghost towns. Half-day, all-day, and breakfast rides. This is rugged country, so most riding is done at a walk. Call Jack and Cherrylee for details. Horse-drawn wagon rides and hiking trails abound.
Children's Programs: No children's program. Ranch activities are suited to children ages seven and older.
Dining: Home-cooked meals, family-style. Ranch specialties are barbecued ribs and South Dakota steaks. Meals are served in a "sit down, pass around, down-home" manner. All meals are hearty and wholesome. BYOL.
Entertainment: Cowboy chuck-wagon supper and musical show. Mt. Rushmore lighting ceremony and day trip to Crazy Horse Memorial. Jack's cowboy poetry about actual events and guests. Many guests join in on Talent Night with their own talent or poetry.
Summary: Jack and Cherrylee offer tremendous hospitality in a low-key atmosphere near world-famous Mt. Rushmore. Ranch great for couples and families and wheelchair-bound individuals. Both the Norbeck Wildlife Preserve and the Black Elk Wilderness Area are abundant with wildlife and vegetation. Trips to the historic town of Deadwood, now with legal gambling, available at extra charge. Ask about the Save the Ranch and cattle-drive programs.

Cibolo Creek Ranch
Shafter, Texas

TGRA Texas Guest Ranch Association

Luxurious, authentic, historical, beautiful. It is hard to describe Cibolo Creek Ranch, but this is a beginning. With the same vision and passion that brought Milton Faver, ranching pioneer, to West Texas and the Chinati Mountains back in 1857, Faver's three crumbling old forts have been restored to world-class luxury and historical accuracy, right to the last square nail and peach tree. Milton Faver is often referred to as the "mystery man of the Big Bend," and the current owner has also elected to avoid the spotlight. But the result of his and his team's work is apparent in the three National Historic Site designations and five Texas State Historical Markers that the ranch has been awarded. This magnificent property was rediscovered in 1988, and the seemingly impossible restoration task was begun soon afterward. Fueled with energy and vision second to none, a team of archaeologists, architects, builders, and ranch hands set out to prove what Walt Disney said years ago, "All our dreams can come true if we have the courage to pursue them." This dream came true! In 1993, the ranch gates were opened to the world. If you have ever read Tom Peter's book *In Search of Excellence,* this is what it is all about.

Address: P.O. Box 44 K, Shafter, Texas 79850
Telephone: (915) 229-3737; fax: (915) 229-3653
E-Mail: www.cibolocreekranch.com
Internet: http://www.cibolocreekranch.com
Airport: Midland, 212 miles; El Paso, 224 miles; Alpine, 60 miles. Private 5,300-foot full lighted and paved airstrip on ranch. Air charters from nearby airports direct to the ranch.
Location: Off Texas Highway 67, 200 miles southwest of Midland, 32 miles south of Marfa, five miles north of Shafter
Memberships: Texas Guest Ranch Association
Medical: Big Bend Medical Center, 60 miles
Conference: 35
Guest Capacity: 35 total at Cibolo Creek Ranch, La Cienega, and La Morita
Accommodations: Three separate guest areas. All rooms are furnished with authentic Mexican and Spanish antiques. Ceilings with traditional *vigas* and *latillas*. Each bedroom has all the amenities of a luxury hotel—down pillows, fluffy towels, most with fireplaces.
Rates: \$\$\$–\$\$\$\$\$. Activities à la carte, no minimum stay.
Credit Cards: VISA, MasterCard, American Express, Discover and Diners Club
Season: Year-round
Activities: Touring the forts, walking, horseback riding, and wildlife-viewing are the main activities. Tremendous riding potential for all levels. More challenging rides through remote and rugged areas of the Chinati Mountains. Mountain wildlife and birds are plentiful. Buffalo, elk, longhorns, and Hi Jolly, the camel, can be watched from the deluxe vehicles. Many Indian shelters in the area, heated swimming pools, and Jacuzzis at each fort. Off-ranch activities include visits to McDonald Observatory, Fort Davis National Monument, Fort Leaton, Big Bend National Park, Big Bend Ranch State Natural Area, rafting through the Rio Grand Rapids, the ghost town of Shafter, and shopping across the border in Mexico, 25 miles away.
Children's Program: None. Children are the responsibility of parents. Better for children ages six and older. Nannies welcome.
Dining: Superb! Served at the forts, at the Hacienda, and on the trail. Flexibility in menus arranged for groups. Excellent wine cellar. Cross-cultural cuisine with Southwestern and Mexican influences.
Entertainment: Stimulating conversation. Historical and contemporary library, customized entertainment, game room with music and video library.
Summary: This 25,000-acre ranch/fort/hacienda is world-class in every way. One of Kilgore's "Best of the Best." For those who appreciate beauty, privacy, history, and excellence. Superb for couples and individuals. Small corporate retreats, boards of directors' meetings, and family reunions. Average ranch elevation of 5,000 feet and low humidity result in a comfortable year-round climate. Massage nearby.

See color photos, page 275.

Dixie Dude Ranch
Bandera, Texas

Texas Guest Ranch Association

Five generations of the same family have operated this nostalgic working ranch since 1901. The ranch was co-founded by Dee and Billie Crowell and her father, William Wallace Whitley, and today is run by Billie's grandson, Clay Conoly, and his wife, Diane. A dude ranch since 1937, the Dixie Dude captures the authentic Old West. Over 725 acres make up the setting for scenic horseback rides through the Texas Hill Country. Hearty Texas cuisine is served daily in the family-style dining room, occasionally on the range, or poolside. Dixie Dude is a great place for rest and relaxation or taking part in daily planned activities. No one remains a stranger long. Folks gather in the Round-Up Room, play games, dance, or just get acquainted by the fireplace. Guests return year after year for the family atmosphere, food, and scenic hill-country rides.

Address: P.O. Box 548K, Bandera, Texas 78003
Telephone: (800) 375-9255, (830) 796-7771; fax: (830) 796-4481
E-Mail: cccdixie@hctc.net
Internet: http://www.tourtexas.com/dixiedude ranch
Airport: San Antonio
Location: nine miles southwest of Bandera
Memberships: Texas Guest Ranch Association, Texas Hotel & Motel Association, Texas Longhorn Breeders Association
Medical: Bandera Medical Clinic and Sid Peterson Hospital, Kerrville; 34 miles
Conference: 50
Guest Capacity: 70
Accommodations: Guests stay in comfortable motel-like rooms in the main lodge and in individual rustic and modern duplex log and stone cabins, many of early-Texas architecture. All complete with air-conditioning and vented heat; some with TV but no telephone. Mostly double beds, all with private baths and tiled floors.
Rates: • $. American Plan. Children's, weekly, and group rates available.
Credit Cards: VISA, MasterCard, American Express, Discover
Season: Year-round except Christmas Day
Activities: Each guest is entitled to two supervised morning and afternoon rides each day. There are trails on over 1,500 acres. Usually you'll see the ranch longhorns and sometimes native wildlife such as whitetail deer. This is rocky hill country, so most riding is done at a walk. Outdoor heated pool, hayrides, bonfires, cookouts, river-tubing in Medina River in Bandera, hiking, volleyball, table tennis, tetherball, basketball, horseshoe-pitching, and fishing for catfish in stocked pond. Winter program is the same, weather permitting. Bandera Gun Club for skeet-shooting. Shotguns can be rented.
Children's Programs: Children are parents' responsibility. Riding instruction and baby-sitting available but extra. Children under age six ride with adult or parent. Shallow children's pool. Large ranch playground. Weekly piñata party.
Dining: Family-style and buffet. Texas ranch-style meals served, briskets and pork rib barbecues, and Dixie Dude Ranch's famous fried-chicken dinners. Weekly breakfast rides. Hamburgers and hot dogs poolside. BYOB.
Entertainment: Old-ranch-tractor hayrides through hill country. Cowboy poetry and guitar-playing cowboys around the bonfire. Bandera rodeos and country-Western dance lessons. Will Rogers–type trick roping show.
Summary: Old-time Western stock ranch turned guest ranch with Old West charm. Best for families who wish to introduce their children to the Old West and a simpler way of life. Couples and singles will enjoy Dixie Dude as well. Century-old barn and Range War Cemetery. Be sure to get a copy of Dixie Dude Ranch's cookbook. Fluent Spanish spoken. Nearby: Frontier Times Museum, Cowboy Artists of America Museum, Sea World of Texas, and Fiesta Texas in San Antonio.

Flying L Guest Ranch
Bandera, Texas

TGRA Texas Guest Ranch Association

The Flying L Guest Ranch, a beautiful Texas Hill Country resort and conference center offers warm Southern hospitality as well as the modern comforts you would expect at a resort. This 542-acre ranch in "The Cowboy Capital of the World" is known for limestone cliffs and live oak and mesquite trees. Winters are mild and brief, which attracts many visitors from the north. The Flying L continues a wonderful tradition of treating every guest—kids and adults alike—as a star. All ages will enjoy walking along the scenic roads and manicured lawns. Moms and dads treat themselves to tennis under the lights, or a suite with whirlpool. Kids are free to roam and explore, ride horses, swim, play basketball, or watch an old-fashioned Western shootout. As one guest wrote, "We enjoyed the facility, the food, and especially the kindness of your staff." When they say, "Y'all come back," people do!

Address: P.O. Box 1959 K, Bandera, Texas 78003
Telephone: (800) 292-5134, (830) 460-3001; fax: (830) 796-8455
E-Mail: sales@flyingl.com
Internet: http://www.flyingl.com
Airport: San Antonio, 45 miles
Location: 45 miles northwest of San Antonio, one mile south of Bandera
Memberships: Texas Tourism Council, Meeting Planners International, Texas Society of Association Executives, Texas Guest Ranch Association
Awards: AAA 3 Diamond
Medical: University of Texas Medical Center, 35 minutes
Conference: 140 capacity; three conference rooms, 2,800-square-foot meeting space; full conference packet/meeting planner kits available. Audiovisual equipment available.
Guest Capacity: 140
Accommodations: All of the guest rooms are comfortable, spacious guest houses that sleep four to six, with living rooms, one or two bedrooms, and private baths. All rooms have cable TVs, telephones, refrigerators, microwaves, and complimentary coffee. Some with whirlpool and covered patio or deck. General store available.
Rates: • $$. Modified American Plan, includes breakfast, dinner, horseback rides, discounted green fees, children's activities, nightly entertainment, and use of all amenities. Special rates for children, groups, seniors, military. Children under age three stay free. AAA discounts.
Credit Cards: VISA, MasterCard, American Express, Discover
Season: Year-round, all holidays
Activities: Guided rides for ages six to adult along scenic trails, over hills, and through the creek. Separate rides for children ages three to five. Riding lessons and private family rides in the Hill Country State Natural Area are extra. One ride per person per day is guaranteed (second upon availability). Enjoy the Texas-size pool. Year-round fishing in San Julian Creek and Medina Lake. Seventy-two–par championship golf course, driving range, pro shop, and clubhouse on ranch. Discounted golf green fees included (cart rental extra). Private lessons available (extra). Two lighted tennis courts and basketball court. Horseshoes, shuffleboard, volleyball, table tennis, softball, and water volleyball. Tubing on nearby river (extra).
Children's Programs: Full children's program for ages three to 12 during summer, spring break, and holidays. Playground and supervised activities include pony rides, petting corral, storytelling, fishing, arts and crafts, and peewee Olympics. Parents responsible during all meals. Baby-sitting available.
Dining: Food is a big thing! Breakfast is served creekside three mornings a week. Weekly Mexican fare and "grande" barbecues with beef brisket and chicken, cole slaw, potato salad, corn on the cob, beans, and homemade cobbler. Steak night and home-cookin' night. Fully licensed Branding Iron Saloon.
Entertainment: Nightly program with a variety of entertainment. Summer rodeo, hayrides, campfire and marshmallow roasts, sing-alongs, and trick roping.
Summary: Resort ranch attracts guests from all over the country. Famous for warm hospitality, children's program, family and corporate cuisine, entertainment and 18-hole golf. A guest ranch and resort all in one. Excellent for corporate meetings and family reunions.

See color photos, page 276.

Garrett Creek Ranch
Paradise, Texas

TGRA Texas Guest Ranch Association

Garrett Creek Ranch is, without a doubt, one of the top executive-conference ranches. Veteran meeting-planner Leslie Schultz came up with the idea after years of conference work. Her goal was to create an environment where executives and business groups could meet away from city life—one that would lend itself to creative thinking and team-building and would foster positive intellectual interaction with the very best in professional service and amenities. Today the ranch is superbly run by general managers Burl and LaNelle Kirkland and resident manager Tara Pettiet. Along with their staff, they host leading companies from around the country. Just off the foyer is a wall that's filled with letters of praise from company heads and meeting planners. This ranch is exclusively for business and professional groups. The information that the ranch sends to prospective groups is extremely thorough and well thought out, including a detailed planning guide, description of facilities, price and billing information, and a well-illustrated color brochure. Perhaps the ranch motto says it best: "Paradise is closer than you think." With a tranquil setting, winding walking paths, rocking chairs, and first-class amenities, Garrett Creek offers one of the leading corporate retreats in North America.

Address: Route 2, Box 235, Paradise, Texas 76073
Telephone: (940) 433-2055 (ranch); fax: (940) 433-8767
E-Mail: Paradise@ntws.net
Internet: http://www.gcrnet.com
Airport: Dallas-Ft. Worth, 45 miles; helipad on ranch
Location: 45 miles northwest of Dallas-Ft. Worth
Memberships: International Association of Conference Centers, Meeting Planners International, Texas Society of Association Executives, Texas Guest Ranch Association
Medical: Decatur Hospital, 14 miles; emergency helicopter and helipad available
Conference: 100
Guest Capacity: 96
Conference: The ranch tries to book one large group or several small groups at a time, and is designed to provide a wide range of meeting formats. Six conference rooms seat 10 to 100 comfortably. Standard audiovisual equipment and comfortable padded, swivel-reclining meeting chairs.
Accommodations: Six clustered log cabins with four to six rooms per cabin, covered porches, and rocking chairs. Each is first-class and individually decorated with high ceilings, hardwood floors, business telephones, and color TVs. Adjacent is the Old West town called Paradise Junction, with 16 rooms and a parlor. The ranch has a total of 48 guest rooms and three studios.
Rates: • $$$. Full American Plan, complete meeting package. One-night minimum stay.
Credit Cards: VISA, MasterCard, American Express, Discover; Master billing preferred
Season: Year-round, closed Christmas through New Year's
Activities: Excellent team-building/ropes course facility. Swimming, jogging, par course, volleyball, basketball, bicycles, two paddle-tennis courts, and driving range.
Children's Programs: None. Adults only.
Dining: Delicious food and a variety of menus. Breakfast and lunch buffets and sit-down dinners. Ask about the special menus, which include South of the Border Mexican Fiesta, Paradise Luau, Cattle Baron's Steak, and Bunkhouse Spread. Full bar.
Entertainment: Ranch will arrange any entertainment you desire. Theme nights, campfires, and cowboy singers.
Summary: One of the top conference ranches in the United States for corporate groups, meetings, and retreats. Designed by a meeting-planner for business and professional groups. Excellent team-building facilities. Day meetings also available. Excellent conference packet available on request.

Lazy Hills Guest Ranch
Ingram, Texas

Since 1959 Bob and Carol Steinruck and their family have been welcoming folks from around the world to their 750-acre guest ranch in the heart of the beautiful Texas Hill Country. Lazy Hills is family-oriented and has earned the reputation as "The Family Ranch for Folks of All Ages." The ranch is the perfect setting for family reunions, corporate, church, or school retreats, seminars and workshops. The Round-up Room is great for meetings and will seat 150 comfortably. The ranch also offers a low-elements, team-building challenge course. The mild climate and low humidity help make Lazy Hills a year-round haven for fun and relaxation. The countryside is tranquil, the pace slow. Listen to nature's peace or watch deer or an occasional armadillo. As the folks at Lazy Hills say, "Come on out and enjoy our 'brand' of fun."

Address: Box K, Ingram, Texas 78025
Telephone: (800) 880-0632, (830) 367-5600; fax: (830) 367-5667
E-Mail: lhills@ktc.com
Internet: http://www.lazyhills.com
Airport: San Antonio, 70 miles
Location: 70 miles northwest of San Antonio off Interstate 10, 105 miles southwest of Austin
Memberships: Texas Guest Ranch Association, Texas Hotel & Motel Association
Medical: Sid Peterson Memorial Hospital, Kerrville; 10 miles
Conference: 150
Guest Capacity: 100
Accommodations: Lazy Hills offers 26 guest rooms, all with electric heat, air conditioning, private baths with showers, and pleasant porches. Some rooms also have wood-burning fireplaces. Rooms are furnished with twin or queen beds and will sleep four to six people. Daily maid service and bath linens are provided. Ask about the inspirational book on Praise.
Rates: • $–$$. American Plan. Group rates available. Summer, weekends, and holidays, three-night minimum stay.
Credit Cards: VISA, MasterCard, Discover
Season: Year-round
Activities: One-hour scenic trail rides are always guided and go out four times a day. More than 30 miles of wooded hiking for nature lovers. You will also find a junior-Olympic swimming pool, children's wading pool, hot tub, volleyball, basketball, two lighted tennis courts, game room with billiards, ping-pong and Foosball. There is also shuffleboard and horseshoes, three spring-fed stocked (bass and catfish) fishing ponds, and hayrides.
Children's Programs: There is a great deal to keep children busy. During the summer months, scheduled children's activities in morning and afternoon. There is also a playground with a merry-go-round, sandbox, and treehouse. Baby-sitting is extra.
Dining: Family-style or buffet, three hearty Texas meals are served daily in spacious dining room. Guests enjoy chicken-fried steak or Mexican fiestas. Barbecue is served outdoors at the cookout grounds. Hotdogs and hamburgers are served poolside. Homemade rolls and desserts. Picnic lunches always available.
Entertainment: Family-oriented entertainment is planned each night during the summer. Bonfires with s'mores, piiata parties, hay wagon rides pulled by team of draft horses or ranch truck.
Summary: A family-owned and -operated guest ranch in the Texas Hill Country. The guests who come and return year after year have high family values, the majority from Texas and surrounding states. Also ideal for small and large groups and family reunions. RV hook-ups available. Group barbecues. Off-season bed and breakfast. Spanish spoken. Nearby: golf, Cowboy Artists of America Museum, Kerrville, Fredericksburg, LBJ Ranch and National Park, Fiesta Texas, Sea World, San Antonio River Walk.

Reid Ranch
Salt Lake City, Utah

The Reid Ranch sits at 7,800 feet on the slopes of the Uinta Mountains, once home to the Uinta Ouray Indians. Homesteaded in the late 1800s, the property is abundant with Western folklore and history, from Chief Tabby to Butch Cassidy and the Sundance Kid. Today the ranch is owned by Mervin and Ethna Reid, both Ph.D.s, and managed by their son, Gardner. Only two hours east of Salt Lake City, the ranch owns 400 acres and is surrounded by state and federal forest land. The Reids, all from Utah, have a very successful Reading Center that attracts people nationwide. They bought the ranch to host groups and families from around the world and to establish a learning environment where individuals, teachers, students, and professionals could have fun in nature's setting. It's ideal for business-executive meetings, and relaxing vacations. The ranch offers lodge facilities for seminars, family reunions, and group retreats.

Address: 3310 South 2700 East K, Salt Lake City, Utah 84109
Telephone: (800) 468-3274, (801) 848-5776 (summer); (801) 486-5083 (winter); fax: (801) 485-0561
E-Mail: ereid@xmission.com
Airport: Salt Lake City, 100 miles
Location: 50 miles east of Heber City off I-40, 100 miles east of Salt Lake City
Memberships: International Reading Association
Awards: United States Department of Education, Nationally Validated Reading and Computer programs
Medical: Heber City Hospital, 50 miles
Conference: 110; two 2,000-square-foot meeting/dining rooms
Guest Capacity: 110
Accommodations: Two modern lodges and two guest homes. One lodge, The Bunkhouse, has two rooms that sleep 26 each in bunk beds and a 2,000-square-foot dining/meeting room. The main three-story lodge has seven large bedrooms that sleep up to seven adults each. The 24-foot cathedral ceilings, spacious entry, library with adults' and children's books, large dining area, and decks provide a wonderful atmosphere.
Rates: • $$. American Plan. Children's rates available; children ages two and younger free. Family, corporate, and group rates available. No minimum stay.
Credit Cards: VISA, MasterCard, American Express
Season: June through September
Activities: Adults and children can participate in activities such as horseback riding (half-hour and hour rides). Riding sign-up sheets for one-hour to all-day rides on the ranch's limited number of horses. Rides are mostly walking, guided trail rides. Lake activities include fishing, canoeing, and paddleboating. Hiking; fossil-hunting; swimming in two of the heated pools and whirlpool spa; one light sports court for tennis, sand volleyball court, and basketball. Photography, archery, and four-wheel-drive trips.
Children's Programs: Excellent setting for family reunions. Kids are the complete responsibility of their parents. Reading Camp program each summer with teachers and counselors.
Dining: Buffet breakfast and lunch. Barbecues, special meals on request, weekly cookouts. Groups should contact ranch in advance. BYOB.
Entertainment: Campfires, tractor hayrides, occasional forest ranger talks.
Summary: Excellent group/conference ranch facility. Great for business groups, large family reunions, and church retreats. Special seminars for teachers on teaching methods and leadership workshops for administrators, reading/computer camp for students; English and reading classes taught as a second language for adults. Nearby: largest piñon-and-juniper forest in the world, Dinosaur National Monument. Spanish spoken fluently.

See color photos, page 277.

Hidden Valley Guest Ranch
Cle Elum, Washington

Hidden Valley Guest Ranch is a shining star. With charm, character, and lots of personality and hospitality, this ranch is terrific. It offers a year-round getaway in a relaxing atmosphere. The ranch is nestled in the Swauk Valley of eastern Washington, in the foothills of the Wenatchee Mountains, at 2,500 feet. On 750 acres of canyon and rolling range, the ranch has been continuously operated as a guest ranch since 1947, when Hollywood cowboy and entertainer Tom Whited carved Hidden Valley from an old homestead dating to 1887. Many original buildings, including the homestead cabin, form the nucleus of the lodging facilities. Today Hidden Valley is owned and operated by the Coe family. Come to relax, visit, and enjoy the old-time charm and serenity.

Address: 3942 Hidden Valley Road, Cle Elum, Washington 98922
Telephone: (800) 5-COWBOY (800-526-9269), (509) 857-2322; fax: (509) 857-2130
E-Mail: brucecoe@televar.com
Internet: http://www.ranchweb.com/hiddenvalley
Airport: Commuter flights via Seattle to Yakima; private planes use DeVere Field, six miles
Location: eight miles northeast of Cle Elum off Highway 970, 85 miles east of Seattle
Awards: Northwest Best Places 2 Stars
Medical: Kittitas Valley Community Hospital, 20 miles
Conference: 25
Guest Capacity: 40
Accommodations: One- and two-bedroom cabins and two fourplex cabins, each with its own personality and a name like Cedar, Aspen, Apple Tree, Spruce, or Elkhorn. The cabins are wonderful! All are fully furnished with private baths and entries, gas heat, some fireplaces, and private porches.
Rates: • $$. American Plan. Riding is an additional charge. Off-season and bed-and-breakfast rates. Two-night minimum stay during summer and major holidays.
Credit Cards: VISA, MasterCard
Season: Year-round, including all holidays except Christmas Day
Activities: The activities program here is informal and flexible. The ranch offers a host of different recreation opportunities: swimming in the heated pool, 10-person hot tub, hiking, chuck-wagon barbecues, breakfast rides, fishing in Swauk Creek, wildflowers, and bird-watching. Great mountain biking. Lighted sports court for paddle tennis, volleyball, and basketball. Be sure to ask about the unique "vacation with your own horse" program. Twice-a-day leisurely scenic rides are geared for the beginning and intermediate rider. Riding program is run separately by Bruce's brother and sister-in-law, Matt and Julie Coe (509-857-2087). In winter, cross-country skiing, sledding, and snowshoeing. Bring your own gear.
Children's Programs: Family participation in all activities is encouraged. No organized children's program. Children under age six do not go on trail rides, however pony rides are available.
Dining: Family-style dining served buffet-style for breakfast and lunch. Table service with choice of light entrées in evening. Ranch specialties include Hidden Valley pork chops, barbecue, and Bruce's Mexican dishes. Vegetarian fare provided cheerfully on request. BYOB.
Entertainment: Recreation lounge overlooks the pool and resembles a hunting lodge with fireplace, pool table, honky-tonk piano, and loads of atmosphere.
Summary: The Coes' Hidden Valley Guest Ranch is a diamond in the rough! Lots of Old West charm, warmth, and hospitality. Great setting and views. Excellent for two-day, three-day, and week-long ranch getaways and retreats. Optional riding program is run separately from the guest ranch operation by Bruce's brother, Matt. Ask about "vacation with your own horse" program.

See color photos, page 278.

Woodside Ranch
Mauston, Wisconsin

The 1,300-acre Woodside Ranch is open year-round and offers plenty of country-style activities for families. This is one of the few guest ranches in the country with a small buffalo herd. Woodside sits in the upper Dells on a high, wooded hillside with views of the Lemonweir Valley. Woodside is a family-run guest ranch started in 1914 by William Feldmann as a family farm. Soon the Feldmanns and their half-dozen children had friends wanting to be part of their fun. Grandpa Feldmann started charging guests $10 a week and they still kept coming, so in 1926 he put an ad in the *Chicago Tribune*; the rest is history. Each year the ranch grew, until there were 21 cabins with fireplaces and a lodge. It's managed today by the Feldmanns' youngest daughter, Lucille Nichols, and their grandson, Rick Feldmann.

Address: W4015, Highway 82, Box K, Mauston, Wisconsin 53948
Telephone: (608) 847-4275, (800) 626-4275
Internet: http://www.mwt.net/~woodside
Airport: Madison, 70 miles; small private airport in Mauston-New Lisbon, 11 miles
Train: Wisconsin Dells, 20 miles (free pickup)
Bus: Greyhound to Mauston, four miles (free pickup)
Location: 20 miles northwest of Wisconsin Dells, 70 miles north of Madison, 220 miles north of Chicago, 200 miles south of Minneapolis on Interstate 90/94.
Memberships: Wisconsin Innkeepers Association
Awards: Mobil 2 Star—Ranch Category
Medical: Hess Memorial Hospital, six miles
Conference: 100
Guest Capacity: 150
Accommodations: Woodside offers rustic, informal accommodations. There are 21 one-, two-, and three-bedroom cabins with fireplaces, of which half are authentic log cabins. The main house has rooms with private baths that accommodate up to four people. All rooms have thermostatically controlled heat and air conditioning. You must bring your own towels.
Rates: $–$$. American Plan. Three-day, six-day, and weekly rates available. Minimum three-day, two-night stay. Children's rates. Pet owners: ask about pet rates.
Credit Cards: VISA, MasterCard, Discover
Season: Year-round, except Thanksgiving and Christmas Eve
Activities: Summer recreation director on staff. Eight one-hour rides go out daily for novice to experienced riders. Daily breakfast rides, covered wagon and hayrides. Fourteen to 18 guests go out on trail rides. Ask about the advanced ride and the Saddle Club (must pass corral riding test). Two tennis courts, new swimming pool, miniature golf, volleyball, large sauna. Fishing in five-acre stocked lake. Paddle- and rowboats available, canoeing nearby. Several loaner poles, but you have to dig your own worms. Horseshoes, outdoor heated pool, and softball. Winter: beginner alpine skiing with rope tow, night skiing, extensive cross-country skiing with 12 miles of tracked trails. Horseback riding, sleigh rides, ice-skating, ice fishing.
Children's Programs: Free supervised day-care 9 a.m. to noon and 1 to 4:30 p.m. for infants through age seven. Pony rides in ring for children of all ages. Evening baby-sitting available at extra cost.
Dining: Barbecues, buffalo cookouts, and chicken dinners; family-style, all-you-can-eat meals with everyone assigned to a table. Traditional country-style, like going to Grandma's house.
Entertainment: Square dancing and line dancing, polkas, 1950s music, sing-alongs, evening hayrides, and campfires with marshmallow roasts. Amateur-night talent shows and guest rodeos. Trading Post Cocktail Bar with snacks, souvenirs, and game room.
Summary: Family-owned and -operated ranch resort for families, featuring log cabins with fireplaces, year-round horseback riding, horse-drawn wagon rides, and sleigh rides. Free summer children's day-care for infants through age seven. If you need to get dressed up for dinner or have TV or telephones in your room, Woodside is not for you. Open seven days a week in summer, weekends the rest of the year. Winter weekend program. Small buffalo herd. Adults-only week at end of August.

Absaroka Ranch
Dubois, Wyoming

THE DUDE RANCHERS' ASSOCIATION

Wyoming Dude Rancher's Association

Absaroka Ranch is at the base of the spectacular Absaroka Mountains, just 25 minutes from the town of Dubois and just 1½ hours from the world-famous valley of Jackson Hole. The dirt road to the ranch offers exhilarating mountain views. The ranch hosts only 18 guests at a time. Budd and Emi Betts, their young children Lindsay and Robert, and their staff specialize in the personal touch. At 8,000 feet, the ranch is big on outdoor space, with thousands of acres and miles of trails, mountain streams, and valleys. Wildlife abounds; it's not uncommon to see elk, moose, deer, eagles, and even occasional bear and wolves. The valley is surrounded by the Shoshone National Forest and wilderness, offering all the elements conducive to total rest and relaxation. If this catches your fancy, better get on the telephone—Budd and Emi book up quickly. Absaroka (named after the Crow Indians) is a very special place and attracts people who want a very personalized and secluded old-time guest-ranch experience. Guests come from around the country, and most who travel through Budd and Emi's gates are families.

Address: P.O. Box 929-K, Dubois, Wyoming 82513
Telephone: (307) 455-2275; call for fax number
E-Mail: absaroka@wyoming.com
Internet: http://www.wyoming.com/~dte/guest-ranch/absaroka/
Airport: Jackson or Riverton via Denver or Salt Lake City
Location: 75 miles east of Jackson Airport, 16 miles northwest of Dubois off U.S. 26/287
Memberships: The Dude Ranchers' Association; Wyoming Dude Rancher's Association
Awards: *Hideaway Report* 1990 Family Guest Ranch of the Year
Medical: Emergency Clinic in Dubois, 16 miles
Guest Capacity: 18
Accommodations: Four cabins (Delta Whiskey, Six Point, Five Mile, and Detimore) are snug and heated, with two bedrooms and adjoining baths, comforters, and full carpeting. One cabin has a fireplace; all have covered porches with views of the Wind River Mountains and the manicured lawn in front where kids and families gather.
Rates: • $$$. American Plan. Group, family, and children's rates available. Special rates for return guests, June and September.
Credit Cards: None. Personal checks accepted.
Season: Mid-June to mid-September
Activities: Activities center around guided scenic mountain horseback riding, guided hiking, and guided fly-fishing. Morning, afternoon, and weekly all-day, breakfast, and evening cookout rides. All levels of riding. Ask about Six Mile Overlook, Jackson Nob, and the beaver-pond rides. For those not inclined to ride, hikes go out as requested to the Continental Divide and to Jade Lake with picnic lunches. Experienced fishermen should talk to Budd about his all-day off-ranch fishing trips. The trout streams in this area are challenging and productive. Limited fishing gear available. The ranch chef will gladly cook your fish for you. Float trips in Jackson Hole can be arranged. Ask about walking and horse pack trips (the ranch has a brochure on these). Swimming in crystal-clear but very chilly streams and lakes. Many guests like to warm up in the redwood sauna at the end of the day.
Children's Programs: No organized children's program. The Gold Pinch Palace recreation room has a Foosball table, jukebox, and pop machine. Children's games, instructional horseback and game rides. Baby-sitting can be arranged.
Dining: Creative meals served family-style. Grilled beef tenderloin and creative pasta dishes are ranch specialties. Complimentary wine with dinner. BYOB.
Entertainment: Something is usually planned every evening. Cowboy magic, campfire sing-alongs, horseshoes, campfires, slide shows, weekly rodeos in Jackson.
Summary: Small, rustic, secluded, very personal and family-oriented dude ranch, right at the base of the Absaroka Mountains. Walking and horse pack trips (ask for brochure), float trips. Saturday night in the Western town of Dubois. Nearby: Yellowstone National Park, Grand Teton National Park.

Allen's Diamond 4 Ranch
Lander, Wyoming

Wyoming Dude Rancher's Association

A rugged, high-mountain ranch, a necklace of mountain lakes, and two salt-of-the-earth people: that's what makes this ranch sparkle. Jim and Mary Allen and their wonderful and caring staff will welcome you to Diamond 4 Ranch, which is remote, pristine—and close to heaven. The Allens' paradise is located in Wyoming's highest and most rugged range, the Wind River Mountains. These mountains boast the largest active glaciers in the lower 48 states, with scores of alpine lakes teeming with trout, abundant wildlife, and world-class mountain-climbing. The ranch is best-suited for families, groups, and individuals who are adventuresome and love to fish, hike, and ride. Go with an open mind so you may fill it to the brim with beauty and images you'll savor all your life. Jim and Mary, famous for their wilderness pack trips, have guided some of the country's top brass. They also share their ranch with those who choose not to go on pack trips. For many years Jim ran the horse program for the National Outdoor Leadership School, and loves to share his knowledge of the wilderness. The Diamond 4 Ranch is an incredible lifetime experience for those who want the ultimate wilderness experience.

Address: P.O. Box 243-K, Lander, Wyoming 82520
Telephone: (307) 330-8625 (summer cellular), (307) 332-2995 (fall, winter, spring); fax: (307) 332-7902
E-Mail: Diamond4@wyoming.com
Internet: http://www.wyoming.com/~dmndfour
Airport: Riverton, 50 miles
Location: 35 miles west of Lander, 120 miles southeast of Yellowstone off Highway 287
Memberships: Wyoming Dude Rancher's Association; Wyoming Outfitters Association
Awards: Shoshone National Forest's 1997 Outfitter of the Year
Medical: Lander Valley Medical Center
Conference: 10
Guest Capacity: 10 to 15
Accommodations: Three log cabins with beds and bunks. Each cabin has propane lights (no electricity on ranch), woodstove, rustic furniture, and covered porches with marvelous burl poles. Each is nestled among the lodgepole pines. The main lodge is the gathering place for visiting and home-style meals. Central shower house and lavatory has hot and cold water.
Rates: • $$$. American Plan. Children's rates. Three-night minimum ranch stay. Four-day, three-night minimum pack trips.
Credit Cards: None. Personal and traveler's checks accepted.
Season: June through September
Activities: Those who prefer to stay at the ranch become members of the family, riding, hiking, and fishing in the magnificent high-alpine country. Pack trips are great for groups or families of four or more. As Jim says, "Our wilderness pack trips are best-suited for folks with a hearty sense of adventure. There's no finer vacation than a classic wilderness horse pack trip here, deep in the Wind River Mountains of Wyoming."
Children's Programs: Mary and Jim welcome children. Children are encouraged to participate with parents in daily activities. Ask about kids on pack trips.
Dining: Hearty family-style meals served in main lodge. Staff and guests dine together. Meals always include meat, fresh salads and vegetables, home-baked breads, biscuits, and desserts—all you can eat. Special diets by advance request. Coffee and cookies always available. BYOB.
Entertainment: Visit at the main lodge, relax on the porch of your cabin, listen to the wilderness and the horse bells. Here, it's wilderness, wilderness, wilderness.
Summary: Jim and Mary Allen offer the same wonderful, sincere hospitality that Jim's grandfather did in the 1920s. One of North America's premier wilderness ranch and pack trip experiences. 1997 Outfitter of the Year award for outstanding public service, land stewardship, and wildland ethic. The Allens have hosted some of the world's top VIPs, who come to experience Wyoming's Wind River Mountains. Ask about youth two-week pack trip with wilderness skills program for kids ages 9 to 15.

Bill Cody Ranch
Cody, Wyoming

Right in the middle of what Teddy Roosevelt called "the most scenic 52 miles in all of America" lies Bill Cody Ranch, just 30 minutes from the east entrance to Yellowstone National Park and the famous Western town of Cody, Wyoming. This small, friendly property gives you the freedom to plan your own guest-ranch vacation with no minimum-stay requirement and a very flexible rate structure, à la carte activities program, and lots of value. There is a ride here for everyone, as the ranch utilizes 16 trailheads, on and off the ranch, in the 2.5 million acres of the Shoshone National Forest. Due to the rugged, mountainous terrain, all the rides are done at a walk. No matter how much or how little you are looking to do, John and Jamie are proud to share their Wyoming heritage and home with you and will create a package that is tailored to fit your family's adventure vacation.

Address: 2604 Yellowstone Highway, Dept. K, Cody, Wyoming 82414
Telephone: (307) 587-6271, (307) 587-2097; fax: (307) 587-6272
E-Mail: billcody@cody.wtp.net
Internet: http://www.wtp.net/BillCody
Airport: Cody or Billings
Location: 26 miles west of Cody just off U.S. Highway 14/16/20
Awards: AAA 3-Diamond
Memberships: Cody Chamber of Commerce
Medical: West Park Hospital, Cody; 26 miles
Conference: 30
Guest Capacity: 65
Accommodations: Historic lodge built in 1925 and previously owned by the grandson of Buffalo Bill. Facilities are nestled off the Northfork Highway that leads to the park in a valley shaded by pines and aspen. Fourteen one- and two-bedroom cabins with large private baths are log-sided with Western interiors. All are spotless and comfortable. No TVs or telephones. All cabins are smoke-free. All have handmade Western furniture and covered porches.
Rates: $$-$$$. À la carte to all-inclusive American Plan packages. Cabin-only and off-season rates.
Credit Cards: VISA, MasterCard, Discover
Season: May to September
Activities: Scheduled and unscheduled riding is the main activity at the ranch. Rides go out morning, noon, and evenings. Rides either leave from the ranch or are trailered to points near Yellowstone National Park to provide a variety of mountain terrain. On these rides, wranglers cook your lunch over an open fire. Many of the wranglers are accomplished mountain guides who return each year. One is even an author of mountain guide books and Western tales. Rides go out in small groups of no more than 10 per ride. Riding open to the public. Guided fishing trips, pack trips, and white-water float trips available. Enclosed hot tub, basketball court, horseshoe pitching; practice roping skills on the dummy roping steers.
Children's Programs: Children ages six and older ride their own horses. Baby-sitting available for children under age six while parents ride. Children can join in most ranch activities but are their parents' responsibility.
Dining: Hearty, ranch-style breakfast served each day in the dining room. Steaks, trout, and nightly specials served with homemade breads, soup, and salad. Wednesday- and Saturday-night creekside barbecues feature steaks, ribs, chicken. Licensed full-service bar and dining open to public. Lunches provided for excursions.
Entertainment: Weekly musical entertainment could be a Western singer or a guest with a guitar. Forest Service slide show and interpreter's program three evenings a week. Nightly trail rides. Rodeo in Cody every night, June through August (30 minutes away).
Summary: A friendly ranch that attracts traveling families and couples who want to experience a guest ranch and have a home base while exploring Yellowstone National Park and Cody. Most come for three days, some stay for a week or longer. As Jamie says, "Here you can truly pick your desired vacation package." Nearby: Buffalo Bill Historical Center, Old Trail Town, Yellowstone National Park.

See color photos, page 279.

Bitterroot Ranch
Dubois, Wyoming

Wyoming Dude Rancher's Association

Bitterroot Ranch offers one of the premier riding experiences in North America for advanced and intermediate riders, as well as novices who are very motivated to learn how to ride. It's bordered by the Shoshone National Forest to the north, the Wind River Indian Reservation to the east, and a 50,000-acre game habitat area to the south and west. The ranch is owned and operated by Bayard and Mel Fox. Bayard is a Yale graduate who lived for many years in Europe, the Middle East, and the South Pacific. Mel was brought up on a farm at the foot of Mt. Kilimanjaro and spent several years working with wildlife in one of Africa's famous game parks. The Foxes place a strong emphasis on their riding program and provide at least three horses per guest, splitting rides into small groups according to ability. They provide both English (for experienced riders) and Western tack, offer a jumping course for advanced riders, and give formal instruction twice per week. They raise and train their purebred Arabian horses exclusively for the use of their guests. The riding terrain is extremely varied. Sagebrush plains, grassy meadows, and colorful rocky gorges give way to forested mountains and alpine clearings. Because of their international backgrounds and strong equestrian program, Mel and Bayard get many European guests. When you request their brochure, you can also learn about their sister company, Equitour, which runs riding tours in 28 countries around the world.

Address: Box 807 K, Dubois, Wyoming 82513
Telephone: (800) 545-0019 (nationwide); (307) 455-2778; fax: (307) 455-2354
E-Mail: equitour@wyoming.com
Internet: http://www.ridingtours.com/Bitterroot
Airport: Riverton or Jackson
Location: 26 miles northeast of Dubois, 80 miles west of Riverton, 100 miles east of Jackson off Routes 287 and 26
Memberships: Wyoming Dude Rancher's Association
Medical: Clinic in Dubois; Riverton Hospital, 80 miles
Guest Capacity: 32
Accommodations: 12 cabins; many are old-time rustic log cabins. Most have wood-burning stoves; all have electric heat, full bathrooms. The main lodge offers a big stone fireplace, piano, library, card room, and small bar (BYOL). Laundry facilities.
Rates: • $$$. American Plan. Group and children's rates available. One-week minimum stay, Sunday to Sunday.
Credit Cards: VISA, Mastercard, Discover. Personal checks and traveler's checks accepted.
Season: Last weekend in May through last week in September
Activities: Full riding program and optional videotaped instruction. Opportunity to work cattle in national forest. Cattle drive in June and September. Overnight pack trips offered (extra). Bayard is a keen fly-fisherman. There's good catch-and-release fly-fishing on the ranch in the East Fork of the Wind River, which is full of cutthroat trout. Two stocked trout ponds plus other excellent fishing opportunities nearby. Hiking or soaking in outdoor hot tub at the end of the day.
Children's Programs: No special programs. Children are welcome and enjoy all the animals: chickens, geese, guinea fowl, peacocks, foals, sheep, cats, dogs, and calves. Baby-sitting available.
Dining: Many guests are European, so the standards for the cuisine are high. Complimentary French, Italian, California, and Chilean wines with dinner.
Entertainment: Informal cocktail hour before dinner, hosted by Bayard and Mel. Piano and extensive video library in main lodge; pool table.
Summary: Bitterroot is a rider's ranch offering excellent programs with both English and Western tack. Riding groups are kept small. Expert instruction. Ranch-raised Arabians. Many guests are experienced riders. Great fly-fishing, regular cattle work and team sorting. Unstructured and remote (16 miles into the ranch from the highway.) Its sister company, Equitour, organizes exciting riding holidays in 28 countries for riders of almost all abilities. Many single people, couples, and Europeans. Fluent German and French spoken.

See color photos, page 280.

Cheyenne River Ranch
Douglas, Wyoming

Cheyenne River Ranch is in the wide-open prairie country of eastern Wyoming, where sagebrush and prickly-pear cactus dot the landscape. The wind blows the tumbleweeds, and you can see forever. For many, this is the Old West—the way it was and still is. Don and Betty Pellatz have been in the ranching business since 1953 and, along with their son Chuck, have welcomed guests to their 8,000-acre cattle-and-sheep ranch since the 1970s, usually only one family or couple at a time to ensure a real hands-on experience. Here the aroma of country cooking and the land are surpassed only by the warm, sincere Western hospitality that the Pellatz family shares. There's nothing fancy at all about Cheyenne River Ranch, but then that's one of the reasons guests return. Don was raised in this part of the country. Betty, his wife and partner for over 40 years, came originally from Illinois. Together they've raised five children, devoting their lives to each other and the ranching tradition of the West. As Betty says, "It does get warm and the wind does blow, but we think this is God's country. When you ride the prairie you get the whole view of the landscape. The air is clean and the smell of the sage—it's wonderful." Here you'll put things in perspective and share the rhythm of ranch life with a family that cares. When you stay with the Pellatz family, their home is your home!

Address: 1031 Steinle Road, Dept. K, Douglas, Wyoming 82633
Telephone: (307) 358-2380; fax: (307) 358-5796
E-Mail: cheyenneriverranch@juno.com
Airport: Casper, 100 miles
Location: 50 miles northeast of Douglas, off Highway 59 and County Road 40
Memberships: WHOA-Bed and Breakfast and Ranch Recreation Establishments of Wyoming, Wyoming Stock Growers and Wool Growers Association
Medical: Converse County Memorial Hospital, 50 miles
Guest Capacity: 12 (usually only one family/couple at a time)
Accommodations: Bunkhouses have two bunk beds and a full queen bed with private baths. Three bedrooms are in the ranch house, two with full beds, one with twin beds; two have shared baths. All are immaculate, with quilts on the beds. There's a sheep wagon for those who want to experience the real West.
Rates: • $$$. American Plan. Children's, family, bed-and-breakfast, and cattle-drive rates. Three-day minimum stay. Most guests arrive Sunday and leave Saturday.
Credit Cards: None. Personal checks and cash accepted.
Season: May to October
Activities: The rooster lets you know the day has begun. This is a working cattle-and-sheep ranch. April is calving and sheep-shearing time. June is branding and lambing. May through October there are three cattle drives, moving cattle from winter pasture to summer range. The program here depends completely on what you wish to do and what ranch work must be done. Chuck will teach you about horses. There's swimming in an aboveground pool.
Children's Programs: No organized program. Occasional bottle-feeding of lambs three times a day, gathering eggs, and swimming. Young children may ride.
Dining: Ranch cooking. Lasagna, barbecue steaks, pork chops, and casseroles. If you like lamb, let Betty know. Cookouts at Red Hills. The Pellatzes are nonsmokers and nondrinkers.
Entertainment: Lots of visiting, lots of rock- and fossil-hunting. Tours of one of the largest U.S. open pit coal mines. Stargazing. Learn to rope.
Summary: This is an 8,000-acre working cattle-and-sheep ranch in the wide-open eastern Wyoming prairie. Usually one family/couple at a time. Warm, friendly, sincere ranch hospitality! Just like visiting your favorite grandparents. Cattle and sheep work, cattle drives. Nearby: Mt. Rushmore, Devils Tower.

Breteche Creek Ranch
Cody, Wyoming

Breteche Creek is a unique, nonprofit, educational ranch just east of Yellowstone National Park, located on the edge of the Shoshone National Forest and the 18-million-acre wilderness system that encompasses Yellowstone. The area is dramatically rugged, has a very remote feeling, and teems with wildlife, including grizzly bear, eagles, and elk. Breteche Creek combines the recreation of a guest ranch with educational programs in areas ranging from ornithology and astronomy to painting and photography. Various activities, workshops, and educational rides and hikes are offered weekly. Riding is available almost every day of the week, often with education in natural history. Guests may choose between the day's activities or hiking, fishing, or exploring on their own. Breteche Creek Ranch is a 7,000-acre working cattle-and-horse ranch, so there are frequent opportunities to move cattle. Anyone who can sit on a walking horse can usually help move cattle—it's horse-wrangling that requires much more experience. As co-founder Chase Reynolds, says, "Breteche Creek is a remarkably beautiful, untrammeled area, and in keeping with its pristine nature we direct our guests' attention to the natural world around us. In creating a camp-like atmosphere, we sacrifice certain conveniences, such as electricity (we do have hot showers, propane lighting, flannel sheets, and gourmet meals)." The Breteche Creek Ranch experience is like going on a high-country pack trip with the comforts of a mountain-based, ranch-camp retreat. Here the marvelous Outward Bound spirit prevails.

Address: P.O. Box 596 K, Cody, Wyoming 82414
Telephone: (307) 587-3844; fax: (307) 527-7032
E-Mail: breteche@wavecom.net
Airport: Cody or Billings; pickup service available from Cody.
Location: 18 miles west of Cody, 30 miles east of Yellowstone Park, off the Yellowstone Highway 14/16/20
Memberships: Nature Conservancy, Cornell Laboratory of Ornithology
Medical: West Park Hospital, 18 miles
Conference: 16; ask about Westin Cabin
Guest Capacity: 20
Accommodations: Nine "tent cabins" (wooden frame buildings with canvas roofs, some heated with woodstoves) are scattered along the creek, each one tucked among aspens for privacy. Each accommodates from one person to a family of four. A central lodge of native lodgepole and aspen houses the dining room. Comfortable washrooms have hot and cold running water. Ask about the lounge tent and wood-fired hot tubs.
Rates: • $$–$$$. American Plan. Children's and group rates available. Three-night minimum stay.
Credit Cards: None. Personal checks, traveler's checks, and cash accepted.
Season: June through September.
Activities: Traditional dude-ranch activities: riding, hiking, fly-fishing, swimming, horsemanship, and cattle work. Educational programs are offered in such subjects as ornithology, ecology, botany, astronomy, wildlife tracking, Plains Indian mythology, photography, and nature writing. Naturalist-guided day tours of Yellowstone Park. Self-guided hiking trail. Call for details.
Children's Programs: None. Children over age six are welcome to ride. If you wish to bring younger kids, best to ask the ranch for details.
Dining: Gourmet Western cuisine. BYOB.
Entertainment: Cowboy poetry and songs. Mountain-man storytelling. On-ranch rodeo exhibitions and famous Cody Nite Rodeo.
Summary: "This is not a place for those who need to blow-dry their hair every morning." This is a place for those who want to try something totally different from the traditional guest ranch, who love (or would like to learn more about) the outdoors, and who want to be in a place that gets more traffic from wildlife than it does from vehicles.

Brooks Lake Lodge
Dubois, Wyoming

THE DUDE RANCHERS' ASSOCIATION

Wyoming Dude Rancher's Association

Brooks Lake Lodge is in a world of its own. Recent guests have described the ambience in the following terms: enchantment, splendor, the greatest place in North America, a spiritual place, heaven on earth. It's all of these! Built in 1922, the lodge was an overnight stop for bus travelers on their way to Yellowstone National Park. It later became a dude ranch, known as the Diamond G Ranch. In 1988, the Carlsberg family discovered what Bryant B. Brooks had written about in 1889: "Among the pines glistened a lake . . . what a sight! Tracks of elk and bear. Where I sat on my horse stretched a broad, peaceful valley. I stood closer that day to nature's heart than ever before." The lodge's new doors opened in 1989. This is a very special place. I think you'll agree!

Address: 458 Brooks Lake Road, Drawer K, Dubois, Wyoming 82513
Telephone: (307) 455-2121; fax: (307) 455-2121 (call first)
Internet: http://www.brookslake.com
Airport: Jackson, 60 miles
Location: 60 miles northeast of Jackson off Highway 287/26, 23 miles west of Dubois off Highway 287/26
Memberships: The Dude Ranchers' Association, Wyoming Dude Rancher's Association, Association of Historic Hotels of the Rocky Mountain West
Medical: Jackson, 60 miles
Conference: 30 (overnight); 125 (day only)
Guest Capacity: 30
Accommodations: Six comfortable lodge rooms with a distinctive motif and exquisite handcrafted lodgepole furnishings. Six cabins nestle in the spruce behind the lodge, with wood-burning stoves, electric heat, and private baths with bathrobes. Several have wonderful old clawfoot bathtubs. The massive log lodge is furnished with wicker, antiques, and handcrafted works by Wyoming artists. No telephones or TVs. The Great Hall houses a collection of game mounts from throughout the world. The front lobby, with its large stone fireplace, serves as a gathering spot for afternoon tea and evening entertainment. A separate spa cabin provides welcome relief after a hard day of riding, hiking, or in winter, snowmobiling and cross-country skiing.
Rates: • $$$. American Plan. Children's, group, and winter rates available. Three-day minimum stay in summer. Liquor extra.
Credit Cards: VISA, MasterCard, American Express
Season: Summer: Mid-June to mid-September; winter: late December to mid-April
Activities: In summer, an unstructured, informal program of daily horseback rides. The lush green meadows with abundant wildflowers lure the hiker, while Brooks Lake and nearby lakes and streams offer enjoyable fly-fishing. Canoes, fly-fishing rods, and tackle available. See the Cross-Country Skiing section for winter activities.
Children's Programs: None. Children must be age seven or older to ride horses. Families are encouraged to vacation together. Nannies are welcome.
Dining: Hearty regional Western cuisine and health-conscious meals. High tea is served at 4:30 p.m. in the front lobby, including English finger sandwiches, cookies, banana bread, or other baked pastries.
Entertainment: Before or after dinner, the Diamond G Saloon offers a full bar (open at 6 p.m.) with hors d'oeuvres, pool, darts, or perhaps a video. Forest Service naturalists provide evening talks weekly. Campfire cookouts with cowboy poetry and singing.
Summary: This ranch is in a world of its own. The spectacular scenery and warm hospitality leave guests with memories they treasure for years. Superb hiking and mountain trail riding. A great adventure back in time, offering rustic luxury. Listed on the National Register of Historic Places. Summer and winter programs. Be sure to ask about the old Yellowstone touring bus.

See color photos, pages 282–283.

Brush Creek Ranch
Saratoga, Wyoming

THE DUDE RANCHERS' ASSOCIATION

Wyoming Dude Rancher's Association

Brush Creek Ranch serves up the best of the Old West. Nestled in dramatic granite outcroppings in the southeast portion of Wyoming, Brush Creek Ranch was home to generations of Western families like the Uihleins and, most recently, the Caldwell family, who spent the summer here. Mr. Uihlein built the main lodge in the early 1900s and consolidated several cow camps into the 6,000-acre Brush Creek Ranch as it is today. When the Caldwells took over in the mid-1950s, they used it as a private family retreat and continued the cattle operations. In 1991 they opened their ranch gates to guests from around the world. Brush Creek Ranch is managed today by family members Kinta and Gibb Blumenthal, who grew up on the ranch. For those who love to ride, fly-fish, and hike, or simply wish to rest, reflect, and enjoy the majesty of the Saratoga Platte Valley, the Brush Creek Ranch experience is old-time, real, and authentic.

Address: Star Route, Box 10, Saratoga, Wyoming 82331
Telephone: (800) RANCH-WY (800-726-2499), (307) 327-5241; fax: (307) 327-5384
E-Mail: kblumen@csn.net
Iternet: http://www.dudranch.org/brush_creek
Airport: Denver, 195 miles; Laramie, 65 miles. Airport pickup is extra.
Location: 65 miles west of Laramie off the Snowy Range Road, Wyoming 130; 16 miles northeast of Saratoga off Wyoming 130
Memberships: The Dude Rancher's Association, Wyoming Dude Rancher's Association
Awards: Orvis-endorsed Lodge
Medical: Clinic in Saratoga Lodge, 16 miles
Conference: 24
Guest Capacity: 24
Accommodations: White-sided, green-trimmed, 1900s-style, three-story lodge or rustic cabins. The lodge is fronted by a small fountain, cascading rock garden, and pine trees planted by the homesteaders. The lodge features a native stone fireplace in the library and Western murals in the first-floor dining room. Sleeping accommodations are on the second and third floors. Each room is unique, with a turn-of-the-century feel. All have private baths and entrances; some have private, screened porches. Two cabin duplexes, located near the main lodge, were originally the cowboy bunkhouse and icehouse. Each has been completely remodeled with Western, rustic charm; private bathrooms; and queen-size beds.
Rates: • $$$. Full American Plan for three-day minimum stay. Children's, group, and off-season rates. Horseback riding and fly-fishing combined packages.
Credit Cards: VISA, MasterCard. Personal checks or cash accepted.
Season: Year-round; closed Thanksgiving and Easter
Activities: The ranch offers superb riding and fly-fishing. This is a working cattle operation with over 500 head of cattle. Guests may help move cattle or enjoy magnificent, wide-open riding country with big views. Daily morning and afternoon rides. Scheduled all-day rides, sunrise and sunset rides on request. Ask about Francis Draw, Homestead Cabin, and Barrett Ridge rides. The ranch is an Orvis-endorsed Lodge and offers guided and non-guided fly-fishing on three miles of Brush Creek or on the nearby North Platte and Encampment Rivers. Hiking and mountain biking. Also available in the area are golf, tennis, float trips, and a natural hot springs. Winter: cross-country skiing, snowmobiling, and dog sledding.
Children's Programs: Half-day programs planned five times a week. Local baby-sitting available on request.
Dining: Western-style food with a gourmet flair. BYOB.
Entertainment: Barn dances in the hayloft of the old log barn. Campfire sing-alongs. Horse-drawn hayrides, breakfast rides, creekside barbecues, and pitching horseshoes. Fly-casting and -tying demonstrations.
Summary: Wonderful ranch for those who want authentic Western charm. This is wide-open cattle country. The real down-home ranch goodness and Old West charm make Brush Creek Ranch a winner—for riding, fly-fishing, and easygoing hospitality.

See color photos, page 281.

CM Ranch
Dubois, Wyoming

In 1997 the Kemmerers, a family with Wyoming roots dating back 100 years, became the proud new owners of the historic and famous CM Ranch—a ranch they had visited as guests since the 1950s. The family is dedicated to carrying on the rich tradition. Life is simple on the CM Ranch, but then that's what makes ranch life so wonderful. The ranch's objective is to provide a charming and comfortable headquarters where guests can relax and enjoy informal, outdoor pleasures in the magnificent mountain country of the West. This classic ranch is one of the oldest dude ranches in the United States, with a fine reputation. The ranch, which borders the Fitzpatrick Wilderness area, is listed in the National Register of Historic Places.

Address: P.O. Box 217 K, Dubois, Wyoming 82513
Telephone: (307) 455-2331, (307) 455-3012; fax: (307) 455-3984
E-Mail: cmranch@wyoming.com
Airport: Jackson or Riverton; private, surfaced airstrip 10 miles outside Dubois, 10 miles from ranch (large enough for small private jets)
Location: Six miles southwest of Dubois
Medical: Clinic in Dubois, hospital in Jackson
Conference: 25, small business groups
Guest Capacity: 60
Accommodations: Large, well-kept lawns, aspen, and cottonwoods surround 14 log cabins along Jakey's Fork, a branch of the Wind River. The green-roofed cabins have one, two, and three bedrooms; rustic wood furniture; wood-burning stoves; and comfortable porches with views of the creek, meadows, or Badlands. Three beautifully decorated log houses with full amenities sleep up to six—East House, West House, and Meadow House. The CM employs a baby-sitter and laundress for guests' convenience (extra). Daily maid service for cabins and houses.
Rates: • $$–$$$. American Plan. Reduced rate for children under age 12. One-week minimum stay, Sunday to Sunday arrival. Non-riding rates.
Credit Cards: None. Personal or traveler's checks accepted.
Season: Mid-June to end of mid-September.
Activities: You can ride, fish, hike, swim in the outdoor pool (parents must supervise their children at the pool), picnic, or relax with a book. Horses are matched to your ability. Usually six guests on each ride. Rides go out twice a day except Sunday. Weekly all-day picnic rides to Whiskey Mountain, which is home to the largest herd of bighorn sheep in North America. Four miles of stream run through the property, so anglers can fish privately for brook, rainbow, and brown trout. Fishing guide and tackle shop. Fishing at Torrey, Ring, and Trail Lakes is a short drive away. Tennis and golf nearby.
Children's Programs: No set program. Children of all ages are welcome. Kids start riding at age five. Full-time kiddie wrangler and baby-sitter available on the premises.
Dining: Dining room decorated with Native American treasures. Menu includes meals that are carefully planned, well balanced, light, and healthy, such as Cornish game hens, poached salmon, lots of vegetables, and salads. Picnic lunches always available for special outings. Homemade breads and vegetarian dishes. BYOB. Welcome cocktail gatherings Monday evenings.
Entertainment: The recreation building has rooms for reading and games, two pianos, Ping-Pong, geology room, and small library. Weekly square dancing in town, volleyball and softball with guests and crew. Weekly music and cowboy poetry.
Summary: One of the most beautiful, really old-time historic ranches in North America. Tremendous warmth and personality. Second, third, and fourth generations come to the CM each summer. Great for families and large family reunions. The 7,000-foot altitude results in a predominantly dry and sunny summer climate. Rock hounds and geology buffs will be fascinated by the extraordinary red sandstone and geological displays.

See color photos, page 284.

Eatons' Ranch
Wolf, Wyoming

THE DUDE RANCHERS' ASSOCIATION

Wyoming Dude Rancher's Association

Eatons' Ranch is the granddaddy of dude ranches. Started in 1879 in North Dakota by brothers Howard, Willis, and Alden, the ranch relocated to its present site 18 miles west of Sheridan in 1904 to provide "more suitable and varied riding." Run now by the fourth and fifth generations, this 7,000-acre working cattle/guest ranch has over 200 head of horses with daily rides for every type of rider. There's no end to the varied riding ter rain. You can hike or ride through open rangeland and wildflower-studded trails that traverse the intricate Big Horn Mountains just west of the ranch. One guest said, "What makes the Eatons' ranch such a success is that it has just enough structure to draw a family together but enough beautiful wide-open spaces to give us our reins."

Address: P.O. Box K, Wolf, Wyoming 82844
Telephone: (800) 210-1049, (307) 655-9285, (307) 655-9552; fax: (307) 655-9269
E-Mail: jeffway@eatonsranch.com
Internet: http://www.eatonsranch.com
Airport: Sheridan, 18 miles
Location: 18 miles west of Sheridan. Ask for a map if you have any questions.
Memberships: The Dude Ranchers' Association, Wyoming Dude Rancher's Association
Medical: Sheridan Memorial Hospital, 18 miles
Conference: 65 (June, late August, and September)
Guest Capacity: 125
Accommodations: One-, two-, and three-bedroom cabins suitable for large and small families, couples, and singles. Most have twin beds; all have private baths. Several have living rooms with fireplaces and real old-fashioned outdoor iceboxes, stocked and delivered the way they always have been with big blocks of ice onboard a '20s-vintage Model A pickup. Most of the original cabins were built by and named after early guests. Laundry facilities available.
Rates: $$$. American Plan. Children's rates; children ages two and under free. Late June through early September, one-week minimum stay. You may arrive any day of the week.
Credit Cards: VISA, MasterCard, Discover. Personal checks preferred.
Season: June to October
Activities: Eatons' Ranch is one of just a handful of ranches left in the country that allow you to ride on your own (if you wish), only after the corral boss is confident that you're ready. Daily rides go out twice a day, except Sunday. Pack trips, picnics, and riding instruction available. Fishing in Wolf Creek, hiking, bird-watching, and swimming in the heated outdoor pool. Golfers will enjoy the nine-hole course at a neighboring ranch or three courses in Sheridan.
Children's Programs: Children enjoy a variety of ranch activities. Kids go to Howard Hall for crafts, games, and treasure hunts. Kids must be six years old to go on trail rides. Nannies are encouraged for younger children.
Dining: Large dining room. Hearty Western ranch cooking, barbecues, noon cookouts. At your first meal, look for your personalized wooden napkin ring marking your place. BYOB in cabins.
Entertainment: Weekly cocktail party hosted by Eaton/Ferguson families on Tuesday evenings. Team roping. Bingo, weekly country-Western dancing at Howard Hall, the ranch's recreation building. Staff-versus-guests softball games. Occasional rodeos in town. Books available in the main ranch house.
Summary: One of the most famous dude ranches in North America! The ranch exudes history and intrigue. Many multigeneration families return the same week each summer, year after year. Wonderful ranch store and post office. Ride on your own. Ask about the fall and spring horse drives, for experienced riders only. Nearby: King's Saddlery and Museum; Little Big Horn Battlefield; Fort Phil Kearney; polo tournaments and Bradford Brinton Museum in Big Horn, 20 miles away.

See color photos, page 292.

Crossed Sabres Ranch
Wapiti, Wyoming

THE DUDE RANCHERS' ASSOCIATION

Wyoming Dude Rancher's Association

Crossed Sabres Ranch was established in 1898 by Tex Holm as a stagecoach stop. As you walk around this historic ranch, you can imagine the old stage with a team of six stout horses chomping at the bit as they wait for passengers. Crossed Sabres exudes life and rugged character the minute you lay eyes on the place. Besides the "years gone by" ambiance, the ranch has a special feature: it's built alongside a wonderful stream that serenades all the cabins as it meanders and tumbles down the mountain. Fred could well have been a Western movie star with his blue eyes and mustache. Today, as before, families come to savor the spirit of the West and share one another's joy and excitement. Many love to sit in the rocking chairs on the porch of the main house, listening, watching, and remembering. Welcome to Crossed Sabres Ranch.

Address: P.O. Box K, Wapiti, Wyoming 82450
Telephone: (307) 587-3750
Internet: http://www.ranchweb.com/csabres
Airport: Cody or Billings
Location: 43 miles west of Cody off U.S. Highway 14/16/20
Memberships: The Dude Ranchers' Association, Wyoming Dude Rancher's Association, Wyoming Outfitters Association
Medical: Cody Hospital, 43 miles
Guest Capacity: 45
Accommodations: All 17 cabins, half of which are along Libby Creek, have names like Red Cloud, Yellow Hand, Indian Echo, and Rides on Clouds. Each is rustic but comfortable and heated, with double and single beds, log furniture, and wooden floors. Hand-hewn pine rocking chairs sit on each porch.
Rates: • $$–$$$. American Plan. Children's rates; children under age two free. Everything included. One-week minimum stay, Sunday to Sunday. Don't arrive before 3 p.m.
Credit Cards: None. Personal or traveler's checks accepted.
Season: Late May to October
Activities: A weekly program that gives guests a chance to relive history and to see what makes this part of Wyoming so famous. Sunday evening, after the welcome beef-and-pork barbecue dinner, Fred discusses the week's calendar of events, which includes daily horseback riding (mostly slow and easy scenic riding), a day in Cody, an overnight pack trip into the Shoshone National Forest, and an all-day guided trip to Yellowstone National Park. This is really special because Fred is one of the few men alive who really knows the history of the park—in the late 1800s his great-uncle was the park's second supervisor. Also included are river rafting on the Shoshone River, fishing in nearby streams, and relaxing.
Children's Programs: No special program. Geared around families being on vacation together. Everyone rides and eats together. Younger children may ride with parents.
Dining: Wholesome family meals in the beautiful authentic Old Western main lodge, built in 1898 with unique burl posts and beams. As Fred says, "Our food is just good. I eat it all the time. Nothing fancy, just hearty ranch cooking." BYOB in cabins only.
Entertainment: Cody rodeo, square dancing, movies, and sing-alongs. Game room.
Summary: One of the most historic dude ranches in the country. Tremendous Old West charm. Fred is an old-time Westerner and cattle-rancher with a heart of gold. Fred is a cowboy through and through. His famous Yellowstone Park tour is an absolute must. Weekly ranch program with on- and off-ranch activities.

See color photos, pages 288–289.

25 · RED CLOUD

Double Diamond X Ranch
Cody, Wyoming

THE DUDE RANCHERS' ASSOCIATION

The Double Diamond X Ranch makes its home along the banks of the South Fork of the Shoshone River, 34 miles southwest of the famous Western town of Cody, Wyoming. The ranch is surrounded by the rugged Absaroka Mountain Range, the Washakie Wilderness, and the Shoshone National Forest. Summer months usually bring mountain breezes, cool nights, and warm daytime temperatures. The ranch was homesteaded in 1914 by the Ray Siggins family, whose descendants are still prominent in the Cody area. The guest-ranch operation began in the early 1930s and has operated continuously, first by Ray's children and grandchildren, and since 1988 by Patsy and Russ Fraser. The Double Diamond X offers a traditional Western vacation year-round, with seasonal wildlife-viewing and a customized family holiday program during Christmas and Thanksgiving. Extensive travel and Western backgrounds enabled the Frasers to design a ranch with a special emphasis on quality, personal service, and living and learning about the West. Russ's experience as Director and CEO of several major financial institutions means that groups, seminars, and retreats are at home here.

Address: 3453 Southfork Road, Dept. K, Cody, Wyoming 82414
Telephone: (307) 527-6276, (800) 833-7262; fax: (307) 587-2708
E-Mail: ddx@cody.wtp.net
Internet: http://www.ddxranch.com
Airport: Cody, 34 miles
Location: 34 miles southwest of Cody off Southfork Road
Memberships: The Dude Rancher's Association, American Outdoors, Wyoming Outfitters
Medical: West Park Hospital in Cody, 34 miles
Conference: 38
Guest Capacity: 38
Accommodations: Five log cabins and the Trail House Lodge are arranged around the main lodge that houses the living room with fireplace, library, dining room with fireplace, kitchen, gift shop, office, and original Western art. The cabins sleep from four to seven in two bedrooms, each with one or two baths. The Trail House is made up of six units and one suite, all with private baths. Two handicapped units. The main lodge, cabins, and Trail House all have covered porches and rockers.
Rates: • $$$. American Plan. Children's and group rates. One-week minimum stay Saturday to Saturday from mid-June to mid-September. Shorter stays available other months.
Credit Cards: VISA, MasterCard
Season: Year-round, including all holidays. Ask about custom Christmas package.
Activities: Western trail riding with safety instruction weekly. Two rides daily. Weekly all-day ride and an optional overnight ride. Riding is geared wonderfully for families and beginning and intermediate riders. Ask about Slide Mountain, South Fork Trail, Boulder overnight, and the School House River Trail. Fly- and spin-fishing on the Shoshone River and stocked pond. Swimming in the indoor heated pool, hiking, wildlife-viewing, and photography. River rafting and Yellowstone Park trips available.
Children's Programs: Extensive morning and afternoon program for children ages one to 12. The children's program is topic-oriented; topics are explored through activities including arts and crafts, music, stories, and lots of educational materials. Riding opportunities depend on child's ability. Baby-sitters and nannies welcome.
Dining: Varied ranch cuisine. Special diets and children catered to. Fresh fruit and home-baked cookies available between meals. Your catch-of-the-day is happily prepared. BYOB.
Entertainment: Something planned each evening. Includes sharp-shooting, singing, storytelling, square dancing with a live caller. Ask about weekly trip to Cody that includes rodeo, Old Trail Town, and Buffalo Bill Historical Center.
Summary: A year-round Western guest-ranch experience with an excellent program for kids ages one to 12. The Double Diamond X shares incredible views, history, talent, and fun. Great for groups, family reunions, weddings, and custom holiday packages. Professional entertainment, indoor heated pool, team-drawn wagon and surrey rides. Nearby: Western town of Cody, Yellowstone National Park.

See color photos, pages 290–291.

Flying A Guest Ranch
Pinedale, Wyoming

THE DUDE RANCHERS' ASSOCIATION

Wyoming Dude Rancher's Association

In 1965 Lowell Hansen went to Wyoming on a hunting trip. He returned with the Flying A Guest Ranch. Today Hansen's daughter, Debbie, and her husband, Keith, offer discerning adults a distinctive Western vacation. Located just 50 miles southeast of Jackson Hole at 8,200 feet, the Flying A is near the Gros Ventre Mountains in a magnificent, wide-open meadow with 360-degree views. The drive is slow and beautiful through neighboring cattle ranches. The ranch offers an unstructured, casual Western atmosphere. You can ride through the quiet seclusion of groves of aspens and pines; fish in the abundant ponds and mountain streams; and enjoy the wonder of moose, deer, and elk in their natural habitat and spectacular sunsets on the distant peaks. Built in the early 1930s, the Flying A has been tastefully restored and offers exquisitely comfortable facilities. It hosts adults from across the United States and abroad.

Address: 771 Flying A Ranch Road, Drawer K, Pinedale, Wyoming 82941-9313
Telephone: Summer, (307) 367-2385, call for fax; winter, (800) 678-6543. Don't be surprised if someone answers "Jack Rabbit Charters"; it's owned by the Hansen family.
E-Mail: flyinga@wyoming.com
Internet: http://www.flyinga.com
Airport: Jackson, 50 miles; airport for private planes in Pinedale
Location: 50 miles southeast of Jackson off Highway 191, 27 miles north of Pinedale
Memberships: The Dude Ranchers' Association, Wyoming Dude Rancher's Association
Medical: St. John's Hospital in Jackson, medical center in Pinedale, helicopter service available
Guest Capacity: 14
Accommodations: Six cabins, named after the colorful characters who settled in the valley. All have that exquisite Ralph Lauren feel. Original hand-carved native pine furniture blends beautifully with new oak floors, tasteful art, and cozy flannel sheets and comforters. Cabins have living rooms, modern bathrooms with a shower or shower/tub combination, full-sized kitchens and bedrooms. All cabins have electric heat, and most have a fireplace or wood-burning stove. Kitchens contain everything from coffeemakers to wineglasses. Each cabin also has one or two private covered porches overlooking the little stream and grassy meadow where wildlife come to graze.
Rates: • $$$. American Plan. One-week minimum stay, Sunday to Sunday.
Credit Cards: None. Personal and traveler's checks accepted.
Season: June to October
Activities: Very relaxed and unstructured. Debbie, Keith, and their staff offer a customized program. Guests are encouraged to set their own schedules around the ranch activities offered each day. Trout fishing on ranch property or mountain streams. Keith is a superb fly-fisherman and offers fly-casting instruction and guiding. Unlimited horseback riding or guided hiking to explore the high country. The riding program is tailored to ranch guests. Ask Debbie about her favorite rides to Jack Creek, Rock Creek, and Bartlett Canyon. Mountain bikes also available. Hot tub. Overlooks Wind River Range and Hay Meadows.
Children's Programs: Must be age 16 and older. Adults-only unless entire ranch is reserved by one family.
Dining: Three meals served with a casual yet gourmet flair. For that added touch, china is used at dinner. Weekly barbecues with smoked-trout appetizer. Each evening the ranch serves appetizers in the Gilded Moose Saloon, which overlooks the ranch pond and the Wind River and Gros Ventre Mountain Ranges. BYOB.
Entertainment: Visiting with other guests, lots of R&R, video library, horseshoes, volleyball, and croquet. Evening team-drawn hayride and cards.
Summary: One of the prettiest guest ranches in America! Small, adults-only. Magnificent, peaceful, remote, private setting. Do exactly as you like, no structured program. Warm, cozy accommodations with lovely interior touches. Tremendous wildflowers in June and July; the beautiful colors of changing aspen trees and abundance of wildlife in fall. Nearby: Yellowstone National Park, the Tetons.

See color photos, page 293.

Flying S Ranch
Saratoga, Wyoming

The Flying S is one of Wyoming's real gems! A hideaway that provides a wonderful Western atmosphere for those seeking privacy and independence with no set schedule. Located at the foot of Pennock Mountain in the Medicine Bow Mountain Range, the Flying S is a historic cattle ranch homesteaded in the 1890s. Its hand-hewn log buildings are set along a creek that flows through the middle of the ranch. Bob and Jane Shiley, both well-traveled corporate and legal professionals, have created a level of accommodations desired by discerning guests, while retaining the aura that the Shileys fell in love with the first time they saw the ranch. The Flying S offers a bed-and-breakfast atmosphere with completely renovated log cabins, wonderful breakfasts, and opportunities to hike and explore the ranch and surrounding mountains. A guest recently expressed the essence of the ranch: "These past days at the Flying S Ranch constitute one of the most memorable and pleasant vacations we have known. While providing us with every modern convenience, you have not intruded upon the natural beauty and mystique of the West. As lovers of Wyoming we will return to the warmth and beauty of the Flying S." Because of its size, guests consider the Flying S Ranch their own private piece of paradise, enjoying independence, privacy, and a completely unregimented stay in a magnificent old-West tradition.

Address: P.O. Box 1070 K, Saratoga , Wyoming 82331
Telephone: (307) 326-8600; fax: (307) 326-5894
Airport: Denver, 250 miles; Saratoga for small planes and private jets
Location: 10 miles northeast of Saratoga
Memberships: Aircraft Owners and Pilots Association
Medical: Clinic in Saratoga, 10 miles; hospital 50 miles
Guest Capacity: Four to six
Accommodations: Each of the two very private log cabins has a cozy living room, bedroom with king-size bed, full bath with shower, deck with hot tub, and mountain views. The larger cabin has a fireplace, accommodations for an extra guest in the living room, and an additional half-bath. All buildings are non-smoking.
Rates: $. European Plan.
Credit Cards: VISA, MasterCard
Season: May through October
Activities: Explore the 1,300-acre ranch and the million-acre adjacent Medicine Bow National Forest. An all-day hike can take you to the top of 10,043-foot Pennock Mountain for lunch. Read or relax in the yard swing, screened porch, or library in the ranch house. Soak in your own hot tub. Horseback riding, world-class trout fishing, white-water rafting, and scenic dinner float trips through local outfitters. Bob is a certified flight instructor and offers spectacular mountain flights for guests.
Children's Programs: The ranch is limited to adults-only.
Dining: Breakfast is served at the large dining room table on antique china with offerings of lighter (fresh fruit, yogurt, cereal), and heavier (meat, eggs, sweets) fare. Western breakfast cookouts are frequently held on a high ridge with a 100-mile view. Box lunches available (extra). Very good restaurants in Saratoga (15-minute drive), provide several options for dinner.
Entertainment: Stars, coyotes, deer, antelope, a soothing creek, rustling aspen leaves, and wide-open spaces.
Summary: Superb! The Flying S is an historic cattle ranch offering sophisticated adult guests solitude, expansive vistas, excellent hiking, great fly-fishing, and horseback riding (through an outfitter), and fine accommodations. Guests have a choice of restaurants for lunches and evening dining in Saratoga, a genuine Wyoming ranch town. Enjoy the Shiley's Western paradise for a night, a week, or longer. Perhaps this guest's comment says it all, "Everything about your operation is first-class—the hospitality, the ranch, the feeling of great peace and new friendships." Be sure to ask Bob about the incredibly scenic mountain flying opportunities.

Gros Ventre River Ranch
Moose, Wyoming

THE DUDE RANCHERS' ASSOCIATION

Wyoming Dude Rancher's Association

At 7,000 feet, Gros Ventre River Ranch is a great place to savor the mighty Tetons, take quiet walks, fish, ride, explore, or just relax and enjoy this year-round paradise. This old ranch has been in the guest-ranching business since the early 1950s but was bought by Karl and Tina Weber in 1987. They've given the place a real face-lift without diminishing the Old West charm. In fact, the Webers and their fine staff have enhanced what was there and created a world-class guest ranch. Guests will enjoy the lodge, with views that capture the splendor of the Tetons, magnificent wilderness scenery, and the rushing Gros Ventre River. While preserving the past, the Webers and general managers Chuck and Buzzie Smith have made it possible for people from around the world to settle in and enjoy rustic elegance and nature at its best.

Address: P.O. Box 151 K, Moose, Wyoming 83012
Telephone: (307) 733-4138; fax: (307) 733-4272
Internet: http://www.ranchweb.com/grosventre
Airport: Jackson, 18 miles
Location: 18 miles northeast of Jackson. You'll be sent a map with your confirmation.
Memberships: The Dude Ranchers' Association, Wyoming Dude Rancher's Association
Medical: St. John's Hospital in Jackson, 18 miles
Conference: 34; May to June, mid-September to October
Guest Capacity: 34
Accommodations: Nine log cabins, all winterized. Four cabins have 10-foot ceilings, fireplaces, sliding glass doors that open to decks with magnificent views of the Tetons, and kitchenettes. Beds are turned down each evening. Laundry facilities available. The handsome lodge could well be on the cover of *Architectural Digest*; it features original art, two decks overlooking the Gros Ventre River with views of the distant Tetons, and a lovely dining room, living room, and bar area. On the lower level is a rec/conference room that opens out to a landscaped area overlooking the river.
Rates: $$$–$$$$. American Plan. Children's and off-peak rates. Weekly minimum stay mid-June to early September, Sunday-to-Sunday arrivals.
Credit Cards: None. Cash, personal checks, and traveler's checks accepted.
Season: May through October; December through March, cabin rentals through Christmas
Activities: Summer: horseback riding with slow to fast half-day, all-day, and lunch rides. Fly-fishing in the legendary Snake River, Crystal Creek, or Gros Ventre River, which runs through the ranch (fishing gear available). The stocked beaver ponds provide a sure catch for fishermen and are enjoyed by all. Ranch swimming hole, canoeing in Slide Lake, hiking, mountain biking at ranch. (Bikes available.) Golf and tennis 10 miles away. Winter: cross-country skiing (bring your own gear), snowmobiling, and alpine skiing in Jackson.
Children's Programs: No set programs. Children under age seven don't go on trail rides. Occasional baby-sitting available at an extra charge. If child care is a must, BYON (bring your own nanny).
Dining: Excellent cuisine. Rack of lamb, baked trout, barbecued chicken, ribs, and steaks grilled to order. Complimentary wine with dinner. BYOB happy hour with hors d'oeuvres.
Entertainment: Cards or quiet music. Weekly rodeos in Jackson, campfires and marshmallow roasts, weekly cookouts with country-Western singing by local entertainers. Naturalist program.
Summary: World-class guest ranch with magnificent views of the Tetons and Gros Ventre River. Emphasis on horseback riding, fly-fishing, and relaxation. Excellent for families, couples, singles, and small corporate groups. Nearby: adjacent Yellowstone National Park, National Elk Refuge, the town of Jackson, Gros Ventre Slide (largest landslide in the United States). Bordered by Grand Teton National Park.

See color photos, pages 294–295.

GROS VENTRE RIVER RANCH

H F Bar Ranch
Saddlestring, Wyoming

The H F Bar Ranch, one of the great old dude ranches in America, has preserved that old-ranch feeling. Since the late 1920s, this 10,000-acre ranch has received distinguished guests from around the world. The ranch is owned and run today by Margi Schroth and her young children, Lily, Brianna, Cara, Turner, and Gus. The H F Bar's horse corrals, barns, and ranch headquarters haven't changed much over the years, nor have the surrounding pastures, with native grasses rising to meet the timbered hills leading into the Big Horn Mountains. Margi has tried to keep things as they always have been, and guests keep returning. As Margi says, "I've made a tremendous effort to maintain our Old Western traditions and keep things very, very simple here." Don't be surprised if you find out from Margi that they are booked months in advance.

Address: 1301 Rock Creek Road K, Saddlestring, Wyoming 82840
Telephone: (307) 684-2487; fax: (307) 684-7144
E-Mail: mschroth@wyoming.com
Airport: Sheridan, 35 miles
Location: 12 miles northwest of Buffalo, 35 miles southwest of Sheridan
Medical: Family Medical Center, Buffalo
Conference: 95, audiovidual equipment available
Guest Capacity: 95
Accommodations: 26 older rustic cabins built from local timber. Each has its own charm, with names like Brookside, Meadowlark, and Round-Up. Each has a living room, fireplace, one to seven bedrooms and one to two full bathrooms. Ten are heated with propane or electricity. Most have that days-gone-by feeling. The ranch stream sings outside many of the cabins. A horse-drawn wagon delivers old-fashioned blocks of ice to your cabin each morning, as well as any items you request from town or the ranch general store, an old H F Bar tradition.
Rates: • $$–$$$. American Plan. Children's rates. The ranch encourages families to BYO nannies and offers a 50-percent discount for them. One-week minimum stay, no set arrival day.
Credit Cards: None. Personal or traveler's checks accepted.
Season: Mid-June to mid-September
Activities: It's a relaxed atmosphere, and guests can do as they please. With 200 horses and 10,000 acres, there's plenty of riding for beginners as well as experienced horsemen, who can ride unsupervised only after their riding ability has been checked out by the wranglers. Half-day and all-day rides, pack trips, and riding instruction available. All rides customized to families or individuals. Excellent catch-and-release fly-fishing in the North and South Forks of Rock Creek, which runs through the ranch. Ask about fishing guides and day trips to Big Horn River. Swimming in heated pool, hiking, and sporting-clay shooting. Guns available (extra).
Children's Programs: Kids of all ages welcome—no formal program per se. Margi says, "We are extremely child-friendly." Staff baby-sitters for hire with advance notice. Margi encourages you to bring your own nanny for very small kids. Hayrides, craft days, hamburger cookouts. Trail riding begins at age five.
Dining: Each family is assigned its own table. Children may eat earlier and have their own menu. Hearty country fare; everything baked and cooked from scratch. BYOB. Wine picked up with advance notice.
Entertainment: Weekly country dancing to live music; roping, and occasional bronc riding at the ranch; family hayrides, softball games, storytelling; rodeos in town.
Summary: A great ranch for the entire family and children of all ages. Lots of family time here. Many second- and third-generation families return year after year. First-time families receive a hearty welcome. Staff of 60 college students. Fascinating geology; Indian sites on ranch. Nearby: Big Horn Equestrian Center, King's Saddlery and Museum.

High Island Ranch and Cattle Company
Hamilton Dome, Wyoming

THE DUDE RANCHERS' ASSOCIATION

Wyoming Dude Rancher's Association

In 1994, Frank and Karen Robbins sold the family company and bought High Island Ranch, a 45,000-acre cattle ranch in the wide-open spaces of Wyoming. Ranching is not new to the Robbins. For many years they owned other cattle ranches in Montana and Alabama. Because of its size and all the country it encompasses, High Island offers individuals, couples, families, and small corporate groups the freedom to really be cowboys. With their Southern hospitality and Western heritage, Frank, his wife, Karen, and their two children share their Wyoming paradise and their cowboy way of life with those who want to experience ranch life for a week or more. Here you'll see a tremendous diversity of terrain, from the 6,000-foot prairie to 11,000-foot mountains. This working cattle ranch is rugged, remote, large, and beautiful. Here the traditions of the Old West live on.

Address: 346 Amoretti, Thermopolis, Wyoming 83427
Telephone: (307) 867-2374; fax: (307) 867-2314
E-Mail: highis1994@aol.com
Internet: http://www.gorp.com/highisland/
Airport: Cody, 75 miles
Location: 35 miles north of Thermopolis, 75 miles south of Cody
Memberships: Wyoming Dude Rancher's Association, The Dude Ranchers' Association
Medical: Hot Springs Memorial Hospital, Thermopolis
Conference: 25 (rustic)
Guest Capacity: 25
Accommodations: The main lodge, located at 6,000 feet on Cottonwood Creek, has 12 rooms, den area, large dining area, and gift shop, all in Western decor. Also, two private log cabins, four-wall canvas tents, separate men's and women's shower houses. The upper lodge on Rock Creek, at 9,000 feet, has eight rooms furnished with log beds, blanket rugs, and wood-burning stoves. Powered by propane, it features a comfortable seating and dining area accented by prints and numerous animal mounts. Here also are 12 four-wall canvas tents, one private cabin, and two tepees; men's and women's shower houses and outhouses. Bring your own sleeping bag, towel, soap, and toiletries.
Rates: • $$$. American Plan. Children's rates available.
Credit Cards: VISA, MasterCard
Season: End of May to early September
Activities: Branding week: guests get to participate in all the cattle work, including branding and doctoring calves. Spring and fall cattle drives move 200 head of cows and calves 45 miles to new pastures. This is the real thing. For those who want to experience long days in the saddle, bedrolls, and hearty ranch food cooked over the campfire on the trail, this is an adventure you'll never forget. Unlimited riding available weekly. Private fishing for cutthroat trout in high mountain streams. Ask about the special family fishing and riding weeks.
Children's Programs: Children age 16 and older go on cattle drives. Children age 12 and older are welcome on roundup weeks. Children should be experienced riders. Ask about special family weeks which accommodate younger children.
Dining: On the trail, an old-fashioned chuck wagon pulled by two stout draft horses follows with plenty of hearty food, including fresh fruit, vegetables, cold drinks, and cowboy coffee or tea. Almost everything is cooked on an open fire. Standard Western fare at the upper and lower lodges. A nonsmoking, non-alcohol environment is promoted.
Entertainment: Listening to the call of the coyotes or cows calling for their young. Original cowboy music. Campfire sing-alongs. Grand Finale Western barbecue.
Summary: Authentic working cattle ranch with old-fashioned cattle drives. Bring your own sleeping gear. Groups and corporations may rent ranch for entire week. Ask about private fly-fishing and family weeks in August.

Heart Six Ranch and Buffalo Valley Cabins
Moran, Wyoming

THE DUDE RANCHERS' ASSOCIATION

Wyoming Dude Rancher's Association

Heart Six Ranch looks out over the lush Buffalo River Valley and on to the magnificent Tetons. The ranch has a long history of Western hospitality and over the years has entertained guests from around the world. With lots of Old West charm, the ranch is owned by Brian and Millie Harris and is managed today by Joe and Karen Dowdy. Parents and children love the personal attention and proximity to Jackson and nearby national parks. Heart Six is a ranch where families come to catch the spirit of the West. Here children can run free, play hard, and laugh with other kids, while parents enjoy the majesty of nature, the Tetons, good food, and great company.

Address: P.O. Box 70 K, Moran, Wyoming 83013
Telephone: (888) 543-2477, (307) 543-2477; fax: (307) 543-0918
E-Mail: heartsix@wyoming.com
Internet: http://www.heartsix.com
Airport: Jackson, 35 miles
Location: 35 miles northeast of Jackson off Highway 26
Memberships: The Dude Ranchers' Association, Wyoming Dude Rancher's Association
Medical: St. John's Hospital in Jackson
Conference: 50
Guest Capacity: 50
Accommodations: Comfortable red-roofed log cabins with Western decor. Several duplexes. One-, two-, and three-bedrooms can sleep up to 12. Many have woodstoves or fireplaces, and twin and double beds. Cozy main lodge with large fireplace and picture windows looking out over the Buffalo Fork Valley. Laundry facilities.
Rates: • $$–$$$. American Plan. Group, children's, and off-season rates. Six-day minimum stay during the summer with arrivals on Monday, departures on Sunday. Winter and snowmobile rates on request.
Credit Cards: MasterCard, VISA
Season: Year-round, open Christmas and New Year's.
Activities: Summer: scenic mountain-trail horseback riding in the Bridger-Teton National Forest, from two-hour to all-day rides, morning and afternoon. Instruction and arena riding available. Don't miss the chance to float the Snake River through Grand Teton National Park. There's a good chance you'll see local wildlife (buffalo, moose, elk, bear, eagles). Learn about local geology and wildflowers on hikes and trail rides with a Forest Service naturalist each week. Fishing, hiking, canoeing, and mountain biking. Overnight pack trips and one-day wilderness fishing trips by reservation. Winter: snowmobiling in Yellowstone and across the Continental Divide. One-day and overnight guided snowmobile tours offered, as well as lodging and meals. Ask about snowmobiling, cross-country skiing, and snowshoeing.
Children's Programs: Excellent, fully-supervised program with counselors, available during meals. Kids of all ages are entertained during the day. Horseback rides, arts and crafts, organized games, hiking, swimming, fishing, and canoeing. Evening baby-sitting available at an extra charge by off-ranch personnel.
Dining: Ranch cuisine. Enjoy three hearty meals a day, including fresh-baked breads, cakes, and cookies. Breakfast and dinner rides. BYOB.
Entertainment: Each evening you're entertained on the ranch or in Jackson. One night is Jackson Hole rodeo night. Two-stepping and line dancing at the Western Dance Party. Sunset rides. Weekly cowboy singing and poetry, and occasional Native American dancing
Summary: Great ranch for families catering to kids of all ages. Excellent children's program with lots of planned activities, or rest and relax—you decide. Incredible view of valley and Tetons. Horseback riding, relaxing, sightseeing, and wilderness fly-fishing pack trips are the main pastimes here. Wedding parties welcome. Winter: Experience the beauty of Wyoming on a snowmobile. Nearby: Grand Teton and Yellowstone National Parks, and the Snake River.

Heart Six Ranch and Buffalo Valley Cabins, Wyoming

The Hideout at Flitner Ranch
Greybull, Wyoming

THE DUDE RANCHERS' ASSOCIATION

Wyoming Dude Rancher's Association

Wyoming's Flitner family ranch was founded in 1906. Today David and Paula, along with their grown children and families continue a tradition of excellence in ranching and farming. For many years they have hosted guests from all over to come and experience their Western lifestyle. In the early 1990s they built new facilities to accommodate their discerning clientele. David's college days at Dartmouth, along with Paula's European upbringing and the family's extensive travel, gave them the sensitivity and understanding to create a first-rate guest-ranch program, with rugged days in the saddle, incredible views, and grace and comfort at day's end. Here old-time ranching combines with modern-day luxuries to offer one of the country's best working-ranch experiences geared to adventurous riders.

Address: P.O. Box 206, Drawer K, Shell, Wyoming 82441
Telephone: (800) 354-8637, (307) 765-2080; fax: (307) 765-2681
E-Mail: hideout@tctwest.net
Internet: http://www.thehideout.com
Airport: Cody, 69 miles; Billings, 145 miles; private 6,000-foot paved airstrip nearby and helicopter service available.
Location: 18 miles northeast of Greybull off Highway 14 East; 69 miles east of Cody
Memberships: The Dude Rancher's Association, Wyoming Dude Rancher's Association
Medical: 25 miles to clinic. Hospital in Cody, 69 miles.
Conference: 25
Guest Capacity: 32
Accommodations: Lower Hideout—Built in 1994, the first-class main lodge and cabins look out to the Bighorn Mountains. The 5,000-square-foot main lodge has three levels, a spacious great room with wood-burning fireplace, dining area, cozy family room with large-screen satellite TV, and a loft for small business meetings or relaxing. All rooms have private baths; two are in the main building and the others in the log cabins surrounding the lodge. Each cabin has its own porch with willow rocking chairs. Hot tub available. Upper Hideout—A half-day ride away is the ranch's mountain retreat. Three log cabins and a cookhouse nestle among the trees at 8,000 feet. Cowboy tepees are available too.
Rates: • $$$–$$$$. American Plan. June through October: three-day minimum stay. Off-season and winter rates.
Credit Cards: VISA, MasterCard, American Express
Season: Year-round. Working cowboy adventures March through November.
Activities: Summer: ranch and cowboy adventure programs offer all kinds of riding and cowboy opportunities. The large cattle herd requires lots of work—do as much or as little as you please. Enjoy the incredible geology of internationally known Sheep Mountain and the recently discovered dinosaur tracks. Take an airboat tour of the Bighorn River, or fly-fish on four private miles of Shell Creek. Winter: call for details.
Children's Programs: Recommended age for children riding is age 12 and up, or experienced younger children.
Dining: Hearty gourmet ranch cuisine. Grilled steaks, homemade chicken and noodles, pot roasts, barbecued ribs, and ranch-family recipes. Complimentary soda, beer, and wine available. BYOL.
Entertainment: Roping competitions, arena horseback games, and chuck-wagon cookouts on the banks of Shell Creek. Satellite TV and card games. Volleyball, skeet-shooting, horseshoes, and Western dancing.
Summary: Historic family-owned cattle ranch with beautiful first-class guest accommodations. Sophistication, old-time ranching, and European roots go hand in hand here. Ranch work. Large cattle herd, good horses, airboat rides, and panoramic views of incredible geologic formations. Contrasting climates, with warm days and cool nights. Nearby: many sightseeing opportunities, from active dinosaur digs to Little Big Horn Battlefield and Yellowstone National Park.

See color photos, pages 296–297.

Moose Head Ranch
Moose, Wyoming

THE DUDE RANCHERS' ASSOCIATION

Wyoming Dude Rancher's Association

Moose Head Ranch is a gem nestled completely within the boundaries of Grand Teton National Park. It offers guests a wonderful panoramic view of the majestic, spectacular Teton Range. Centrally located in the Jackson Hole Valley, Moose Head provides a feeling of seclusion and solitude, yet abundant activities on and off the ranch are easily accessible. While the ranch was originally homesteaded in 1923, it has been owned by the Mettler family since 1967. Louise Mettler Davenport and her husband, Kit, run the ranch with a personal approach. Louise sits down with every family on their first day to point out hikes or excursions that shouldn't be overlooked. A trip to Yellowstone, white-water rafting, and scenic drives fill any time you don't feel like being in the saddle. The college-age Moose Head staff is equally friendly, filled with polite manners and Southern charm—great role models for your kids! Guests leave feeling a part of the Moose Head family, usually return, and always tell their friends.

Address: P.O. Box 214 K, Moose, Wyoming 83012

Telephone: (307) 733-3141, fax: (307) 739-9097 (summer); (850) 877-1431, fax: (850) 878-7577 (winter)

Airport: Jackson, 26 miles

Location: 26 miles north of Jackson

Memberships: Wyoming Dude Rancher's Association, The Dude Ranchers' Association

Medical: St. John's Hospital in Jackson, 26 miles

Guest Capacity: 40

Accommodations: Log cabins scattered among the aspen, cottonwoods, spruce, and pines by trout ponds or along streams. Each of the 14 cabins offers privacy and comfort for couples and families (seven with adjoining living rooms). All have private baths with shower and tub, electric heating, and porches. Coffeemakers and refrigerators in cabins. Daily maid service. Ice is brought to your cabin each day. The spacious lodge has an incredible deck on the west side with comfortable chairs, and planters overflowing with perennials—a great way to relax and catch your breath after a ride or before a meal. Half a dozen hummingbird feeders provide bird-watching up close!

Rates: $$$–$$$$. American Plan. Rates for children age six and under. Five-night minimum stay, arrivals any day.

Credit Cards: None. Personal checks accepted.

Season: Mid-June to late August

Activities: Supervised horseback rides twice daily. Weekly all-day rides. The Davenports believe in promoting family togetherness, so you ride and eat with your children rather than separately. Always small groups, usually one family per wrangler. Don't come here to do a lot of fast riding, but do if you want to see lots of wildlife (elk, buffalo, mule deer, antelope, moose, coyotes). There is dry fly-fishing (catch-and-release) on the property in a series of several excellent, well-stocked trout ponds with cutthroat trout up to 28 inches. Kit Davenport loves to teach the art of the cast, making converts and enthusiasts of all ages. Many fish off the property on the Snake River and other streams. Fishing flies and equipment available. Tennis and golf can be arranged at local clubs, as can scenic and white-water float trips on the Snake River. (A must!)

Children's Programs: Children of all ages welcome, but no set children's program per se. Limited baby-sitting available. No organized activities.

Dining: Louise feels that good food is just as important as good riding. Outstanding gourmet chefs serve breakfast to order, buffet lunches, and two-entrée dinners that the whole family will enjoy. Abundant picnics provided when you need to miss a meal. Don't plan on dieting! Sunday night cookout. BYOB.

Entertainment: Informal, pre-dinner cocktails and hors d'oeuvres each evening where most guests gather and visit. After dinner, most do their own thing. Others enjoy volleyball, Ping-Pong, croquet, softball, horseshoes, and fly-fishing.

Summary: One of the great family ranches in North America with incredible views, family riding, superb Southern college staff, outstanding food—wait until you see the trout.

See color photos, page 299.

Hunter Peak Ranch
Cody, Wyoming

Off Chief Joseph Highway, Hunter Peak Ranch is located on the banks of the Clarks Fork River, Wyoming's only designated Wild and Scenic River. The river divides the property with 20 acres on one side, home to the buildings and pastures, and 100 acres on the other side for pastures and irrigated hay meadows. A hand-powered trolley provides transportation across the river. Homesteaded in 1907, the ranch has evolved into a relaxing, family-oriented ranch. The hand-hewn log ranch house offers a warm and cozy atmosphere for guests. The house is appointed with Indian rugs; a beautiful cinnamon-bear rug; head mounts of elk, deer, and antelope; tack; and antique tools. Hunter Peak is situated near the spectacular Sunlight Basin, Beartooth Plateau, and Yellowstone Park. The ranch is within the Shoshone National Forest and adjacent to the North Absaroka and Beartooth Wilderness Areas. Pack trips into these areas are truly a highlight. In addition, the ranch offers week-long active educational programs that allow guests to follow the trail of the Nez Perce Indians and learn about the local history, nature, and traditions of the area. Louis Cary is the third generation to be running the ranch, with his wife, Shelley. Guests appreciate Louis' lifelong knowledge of the area and enjoy his tales and stories. A unique feature of Hunter Peak is the flexible cooking and meal program. Hunter Peak is for more-independent travelers who like the freedom to do as they please.

Address: Box 1731 K, Painter Route, Cody, Wyoming 82414
Telephone: (307) 587-3711
Internet: http://www.nezperce.com/ranchhp.html
Airport: Cody or Billings
Location: 60 miles northwest of Cody, 120 miles southwest of Billings
Medical: West Park County Hospital, 60 miles
Conference: 25
Guest Capacity: 40
Accommodations: The 40-year-old cabins—one log, the other framed and finished in wood paneling—are wood-heated and close to the river. The log cabin sleeps two; the framed cabin sleeps four in two bedrooms. The main sleeping lodge, built in 1972, has six rooms sleeping four to 12, with carpeting and steam heat. All accommodations but one have kitchens. No TV or telephone. Laundry facilities available. Limited smoking area.
Rates: \$–\$\$ European Plan for ranch stays and pack trips. \$\$–\$\$\$ American Plan for Educational programs.
Credit Cards: VISA, American Express. Personal checks are accepted for deposit.
Season: Year-round
Activities: Do as much or as little as you please. Activities are very flexible. Shelley and Louis are helpful in planning your activities: hiking; scenic four-wheel-drive trips; hourly, half-day, or all-day horseback rides; pack trips; and fishing for rainbow, cutthroat, brook, and golden trout. Winter: cross-country skiing, snowshoeing, snowmobiling, and ice fishing. Year-round photography and wildlife-viewing a favorite.
Children's Programs: None. Children welcome.
Dining: Enjoy a wonderful variety of home-cooked ranch food with Shelley and Louis, or cook for yourself in your own cabin. BYOB.
Entertainment: Small library and table tennis in recreation room. Outdoor volleyball, badminton, croquet, horseshoe-pitching, baseball.
Summary: Small, family-run ranch with flexible cooking, meal, and activities programs located just off the Chief Joseph Highway. Provides an ideal ranch setting for the independent-minded traveler in incredible mountain country: 1999 marks the ranch's 50th anniversary! Very low-key, independent atmosphere. Nearby: Sunlight Basin, Beartooth Plateau, Daisy and Lulu mining area, Yellowstone National Park, Buffalo Bill Historical Center, nightly rodeos in Cody.

Kedesh Ranch
Shell, Wyoming

THE DUDE RANCHERS' ASSOCIATION

Wyoming Dude Rancher's Association

Imagine Indians riding across a windswept landscape of pastel colors and red-rock formations shaped with time; the breeze and the warmth of the hot summer sun; cottonwood trees along Shell Creek, water fights, fishing, the Big Horn Canyon (third-largest in the United States), dinosaur digs, and natural geologic formations. Welcome to Kedesh Guest Ranch and the Shell Valley. Kedesh is Hebrew for "sanctuary," and in a way that's exactly what the Lander family (Chuck, Gail, Dana, and Bill) offer. Now, don't misunderstand. This is not a hideaway protected by rocky cliffs. It is hidden by cottonwood trees and located off the road that joins Sheridan and Cody, Wyoming. The Kedesh Ranch concept is simple: provide a friendly, low-key, family-oriented environment for the young and young-at-heart to ride, fish, hike, and explore. Chuck is a geologist by training and spent many years in oil and gas exploration. His knowledge of the area and its geologic formations is tremendous. Gail's roots are in Montana, and she has a great love and understanding for the Native American culture. One guest wrote, "It's awesome country. You can't describe it. It's a spiritual place as well."

Address: 1940 Highway 14, Dept. K, Shell, Wyoming 82441
Telephone: (800) 845-3320, (307) 765-2791; call for fax number
E-Mail: kedeshranch@tctwest.net
Airport: Cody, 70 miles; Billings, 140 miles
Location: 70 miles east of Cody, 20 miles east of Greybull off Highway 14
Memberships: The Dude Ranchers' Association, Wyoming Dude Rancher's Association, Wyoming Outfitters Association
Medical: Big Horn Clinic, 20 miles; Coe Medical Center, 70 miles
Conference: 32
Guest Capacity: 24
Accommodations: Six green-roofed cabins arranged in a circle. One fourplex cabin has four rooms and one long deck on the front, facing the horse pasture. The back common porch with dividing bamboo screens overlooks Shell Creek. Each has two queen-size beds and private baths. The five other duplex cabins with common screened-in porches have queen-size beds and private baths. All are carpeted. Daily maid service available.
Rates: • $$. American Plan. Children's, group, and off-season rates. Five-night minimum stay. Saturday-to-Saturday stays preferred.
Credit Cards: VISA, MasterCard accepted with handling fee. Personal checks preferred. Traveler's checks and cash accepted.
Season: June to end of September
Activities: Each day a little something different is planned. Riding usually in the morning and evening each day, tailored to avoid the warmth of the day. Dana oversees the horseback program. Beginner riders will feel at home with other levels of riding. Occasional cattle work and team penning. Fishing and tubing in Shell Creek, fossil- and arrowhead-hunting. Each week is usually filled with many optional off-ranch outings, including white-water rafting and day trip to Big Horn Mountain, Indian petroglyphs, Shell Falls, Medicine Wheel, Cody, and dinosaur digs.
Children's Programs: Kids are responsibility of parents. Weekly dudeo. Kids ages five and up may trail ride. Families interact together.
Dining: You'll never be hungry at Kedesh. Home-cooked meals become the main event, served family-style. Weekly cookouts. BYOB with discretion.
Entertainment: Something usually planned each evening. Trips to Cody Rodeo and Buffalo Bill Historical Center. Evening rides, campfire folklore, and line dancing. Ask about the hayride and the game called "Sticks."
Summary: Located on Shell Creek in the heart of magnificent Shell Canyon and its incredible geologic formations. A low-key, very laid-back family ranch for families, couples, and singles. Many off-ranch activities offered. Be sure to ask about the mustang horses.

Lazy L & B Ranch
Dubois, Wyoming

THE DUDE RANCHERS' ASSOCIATION

Wyoming Dude Rancher's Association

An enthusiastic woman called my office all the way from Manhattan to tell me, "You were absolutely right. The Lazy L & B was fantastic—super and varied riding, tremendous spirit, great scenery. I just can't say enough. Thank you!" The Lazy L & B has been in the guest-ranching business for many years. Today it's owned and operated by Bob and Lee Naylon, a terrific young couple. Together with their young daughter, Piper Alison, they've touched a lot of hearts. Their experience comes from over 25 years of horse-packing, hiking, and working in the ski industry. Located in a secluded river valley of cottonwoods with contrasting red-clay cliffs, the ranch adjoins the Wind River Indian Reservation. With the 50,000-acre elk refuge, Wind River for fishing, rolling prairie, badlands, alpine meadows, deep river gorges, and high-mountain forests, the Lazy L & B offers incredible riding diversity and fun for all!

Address: 1072 East Fork Road, Drawer K, Dubois, Wyoming 82513
Telephone: (800) 453-9488, (307) 455-2839; fax: (307) 455-2634.
Internet: http://www.ranchweb.com/lazyl&b
Airport: Jackson or Riverton; private planes may land on 5,000-foot lighted and paved airstrip in Dubois.
Location: 70 miles east of Jackson, 22 miles northeast of Dubois
Memberships: The Dude Rancher's Association, Wyoming Dude Rancher's Association
Medical: Doctor in Dubois, hospital in Lander
Guest Capacity: 35
Accommodations: Parts of the lodge, cabins, and corrals are the original 1890s sheep-and-cattle-ranch buildings. A newer addition to the lodge provides two cozy fireplaces, a library, and game tables where guests enjoy cowboy songs and poetry. Comfortable log cabins are arranged around a central courtyard. Two are located along the river. All have private baths or showers, electric heat, and small refrigerators. Some porches have views of the distant Absaroka and Wind River Ranges. Some have wood-burning stoves.
Rates: • $$$. American Plan. Children's, large-family, and group rates available. Minimal charge for nannies/baby-sitters.
Credit Cards: VISA. Personal checks preferred.
Season: End of May through August. Adults-only in September.
Activities: Most guests come here to ride. Riding groups consist of no more than seven divided by skill level; 2½- to 3½-hour rides in the morning and afternoon. Wednesday and Thursday are all-day rides in the high country. Although most guests wish to ride daily, other activities include hiking, mountain biking, rifle range, a leather-tooling and bead shop, and game room for the kids. Anglers enjoy fishing in the ranch's stocked ponds, the East Fork River, or neighboring Wiggins Fork, Bear Creek, and Wind River. Swim in the solar-heated pool or relax in the Jacuzzi by the river.
Children's Programs: Supervised riding program for children age five years and older with riding and safety instruction. Three nights a week, children dine early with wranglers, one night having their own hayride barbecue. They enjoy feeding the horses, petting zoo animals, and playing corral kick-ball games.
Dining: Hearty ranch cooking with fresh vegetables and fruits along with ranch-baked breads and desserts daily. Family-style meals, buffet breakfasts, picnic lunches and barbecues on the trail. BYOB happy hour each evening.
Entertainment: Campfires, cowboy poetry and music, horseshoes, and children's hayride and game room. Dubois offers square dancing, museum, and the National Big Horn Sheep Center.
Summary: Beautiful setting and wonderful family-oriented riding ranch with great hosts Bob, Lee, and daughter Piper. Excellent for families, singles, and adults. Surrounded by 50,000-acre Elk Refuge, Indian reservation, and national forest. Spectacular variety of riding terrain and back-country trips. September, adults-only. Nearby: Grand Teton and Yellowstone National Parks.

See color photos, page 298.

Lost Creek Ranch
Moose, Wyoming

Lost Creek Ranch is magnificent. Breathtaking views of the mighty Tetons and superb cuisine make Lost Creek what it is today—a world-class showplace owned and operated by the Halpin family! Located on the eastern slope of the Jackson Hole Valley at 7,000 feet, the ranch is situated on a rise with commanding views of the entire Teton mountain range and the valley. This privately owned ranch and spa is bordered by Grand Teton National Park and Bridger-Teton National Forest. The beautiful lodge and cabins are furnished with high-quality decor featuring custom-made furniture and original artwork. The cabin amenities, superb service, and tremendous outdoor opportunities make Lost Creek ideal for families, individuals, and corporate groups who appreciate excellence. Ride horses, float the Snake River, hike, enjoy a Dutch-oven cookout on Shadow Mountain, or relax on the expansive lodge deck and watch the sun set behind the Tetons. You can do it all at Lost Creek Ranch.

Address: P.O. Box 95 K, Moose, Wyoming 83012
Telephone: (307) 733-3435; fax: (307) 733-1954
E-Mail: ranch@lostcreek.com
Internet: http://www.LostCreek.com
Airport: Jackson via Denver or Salt Lake City
Location: 20 miles north of Jackson
Awards: Mobil 4 Star
Medical: First-aid office at ranch; St. John's Hospital in Jackson, 20 miles
Conference: 55
Guest Capacity: 55
Accommodations: Luxury two-bedroom, two-bath (with tub and shower) cabins with queen and single beds in all bedrooms. All cabins have refrigerators with ice-makers, coffee and hot chocolate, and electric heat. The living-room cabins have queen sleeper sofas, full kitchenettes, and free-standing gas log fireplaces. Beds are turned down each evening, and the "mint fairy" always leaves a surprise. Maid service twice daily. Courtesy laundry service.
Rates: $$$$$. Full American Plan. One-week minimum stay, Sunday to Sunday. Off-season nightly, corporate, and group rates. No charge for children age five and under.
Credit Cards: American Express. Personal checks accepted.
Season: Late May through mid-October
Activities: Full riding program with instruction. Very flexible and personalized. Beginner, intermediate, and advanced rides. No more than eight to a ride. Ask about Chips Bluff, Snake River, and Cunningham's Overlook; and about the new full-service health spa: The Spa at Lost Creek. Heated swimming pool and giant hot tub, tennis court, Snake River scenic float trips, cookouts, guided hiking, skeet-shooting on request. Many guests enjoy the Yellowstone and Grand Teton National Parks tours. Guided fishing and golf nearby (extra).
Children's Programs: Supervised kids' program (ages six to 13). Ask for details about the children's program. Children under age six do not trail ride. Game room and youth cookout. Families are encouraged to bring nannies.
Dining: Outstanding cuisine with two entrées served nightly. Wine list available. Optional dinner hour for children. Special diets served by prior arrangement.
Entertainment: Weekly cookouts, campfire sing-alongs, video programs, Western swing dance, weekly gymkhana, weekly rodeo in Jackson, and impromptu programs.
Summary: One of Kilgore's Best of the Best luxury resort-spa ranches! Superb personal service, and all you need for instant indulgence in a secluded mountain-resort setting. Excellent for family vacations and corporate retreats. Ask about ranch and spa packages. Afternoon and evening children's program. Language interpreters available. Nearby: historic Western town of Jackson (art galleries; shopping; Western events such as shootouts, theater groups, stagecoach rides; and white-water rafting), Yellowstone and Grand Teton National Parks, National Elk Refuge.

See color photos, pages 300–301.

Lozier's Box R Ranch
Cora, Wyoming

THE DUDE RANCHERS' ASSOCIATION

Since the turn of the last century, when the ranch was first homesteaded, the Lozier family has operated this backcountry working cattle ranch. As in days gone by, the Box R maintains many traditions of the Old West. Sublette County is famous for cattle ranching and its beauty. I know this firsthand because I cowboyed on a neighboring ranch in the late 1970s. Today the Lozier family oversees 300 head of cattle and 100 head of horses and mules. On all vacations offered, horseback riding is the main activity. Bordering the Bridger Wilderness, the Loziers offer short pack trips into the Wind River Mountains, and longer custom horseback trips for wilderness enthusiasts. If you'd like to spend a week or more with an old-time ranching family in beautiful accommodations, give the Lozier family a call today.

Address: Box 100-K, Cora, Wyoming 82925
Telephone: (307) 367-4868 (inquiries), (800) 822-8466 (reservations); fax: (307) 367-6260
E-Mail: boxr@wyoming.com
Internet: http://www.boxr.com
Airport: Jackson or Pinedale for private airplanes; free pickup on Sunday and Wednesday
Location: 60 miles southeast of Jackson, 10 miles north of Pinedale via State Highway 352
Memberships: The Dude Ranchers' Association, Wyoming Outfitters Association, Rocky Mountain Elk Foundation
Medical: Jackson Hospital, 60 miles; clinic in Pinedale
Guest Capacity: 18 adults, 22 family/group
Accommodations: One-, two-, and three-bedroom log cabins with private baths and daily maid service. Rooms range from single "Honeymoon Suite" cabins to family-style cabins for up to five. Social and recreational rooms adjoin several of the lodge rooms.
Rates: • $$$. American Plan, Sunday to Sunday, Sunday to Wednesday, and Wednesday to Sunday. Ask about cattle drives, pack-trips, spot packs, and adults-only weeks.
Credit Cards: VISA, MasterCard and Discover for reservation deposits. Cash or personal/certified checks preferred for balance.
Season: Late May to mid-September
Activities: You'll be assigned your own personal horse and tack for the week, and depending on your ability, you may help with the early morning wrangling of the horse "cavy." You may also lend a hand in doctoring, locating, salting, and working the ranch cattle on the open range. With owners' approval, competent adult riders may have the opportunity to ride on their own. Authentic spring cattle drives and full roundups are popular. Choose a ranch-based cattle drive or spend part of your week camping in the mountains with the cattle. Access to excellent trout fishing on the ranch's streams, 11 trout ponds, and several large nearby lakes and rivers.
Children's Programs: No program per se. The ranch is best-suited for children age eight and over. Older children may ride separately or with adults. Swing set, pool table, darts, horseshoes, roping and fishing with parental supervision.
Dining: Family-style meals specializing in ranch beef, turkey, chicken, salads, homemade breads, pastries, and soups. Drinks, fruit, and cookies are available throughout the day, with evening hors d'oeuvres and social hour in BYOB bar.
Entertainment: Informal. Horseshoes, rope Oscar the steer, spacious social room, library, and BYOB bar. Recreation room with pool table, darts, games, and TV/VCR for educational/informational/meeting purposes. You're free to do as you please after dinner or sit on the porch and watch the sun go down.
Summary: The Lozier's Box R Ranch is a true working cattle/horse ranch in the heart of Wyoming's cattle ranching country, run today by fourth-generation family. Great for active, outdoor folks, both adults and older children, wanting to enjoy the peace and tranquility of this remote ranch on the wilderness boundary, with separate adult and family weeks throughout the summer. Ask about cattle drives and roundups, pack trips to Bridger Wilderness, "spot" packs/gear drops, and ranch-based vacations. Nearby: Jackson Hole, Yellowstone and Teton National Parks.

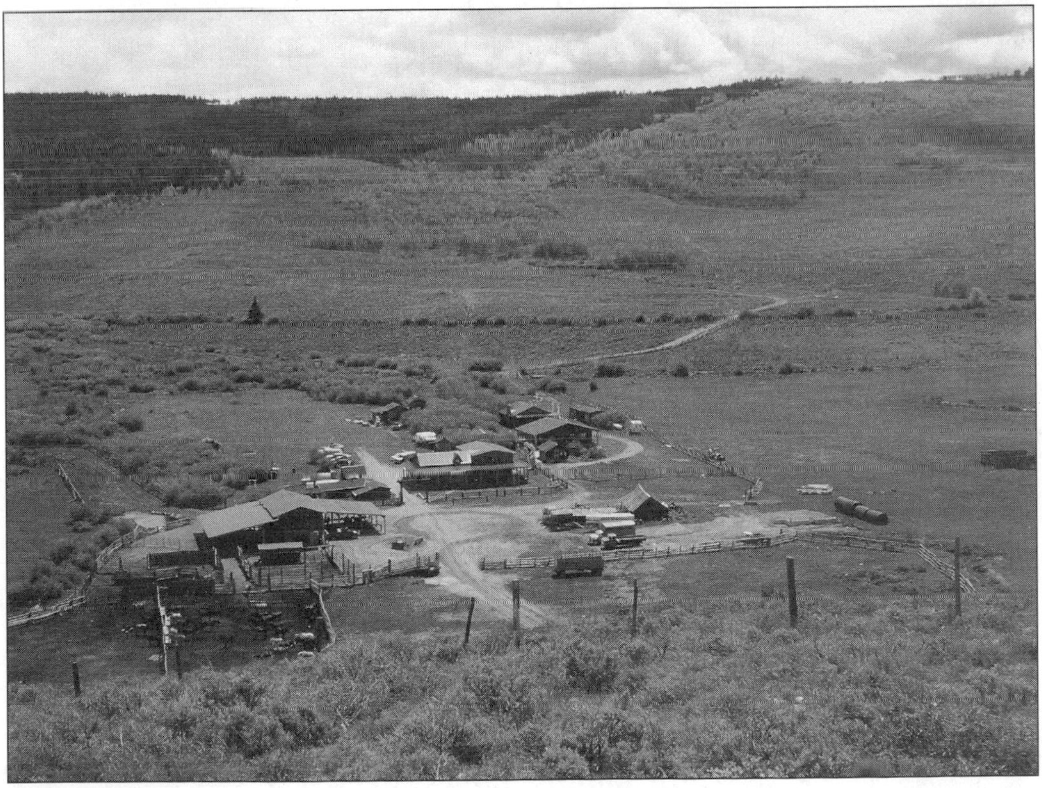

Paradise Guest Ranch
Buffalo, Wyoming

THE DUDE RANCHERS' ASSOCIATION

Wyoming Dude Rancher's Association

Paradise Guest Ranch is one of the leading family guest ranches in North America offering traditional dude-ranch activities with lots of riding and fishing. Along with this, Jim says, "We keep an ear to the ground as to what modern-day guests need and expect." Dude ranches reflect the personality of the owners and hosts. Jim and Leah Anderson love what they do, and it shows. Once the prized hunting ground for the Sioux, Crow, and Cheyenne Indians, the ranch rests in a mountain valley next to French and Three Rivers Creeks, surrounded by tall forests of evergreens. The peace and tranquility are only occasionally interrupted by the calls of wildlife or the exuberant sounds of families having fun. It's little wonder that the ranch brand is "FUN." In the 1980s the ranch underwent extensive renovation. It lives up to the name "Paradise" for good reason, as it offers the rustic flavor of the Old West along with many modern conveniences.

Address: P.O. Box 790 K, Buffalo, Wyoming 82834
Telephone: (307) 684-7876; fax: (307) 684-9054
Internet: http://www.paradiseranch.com
Airport: Sheridan or Casper
Location: 46 miles south of Sheridan off Hunter Creek Road, 110 miles north of Casper, 176 miles south of Billings
Memberships: The Dude Ranchers' Association, Wyoming Dude Rancher's Association
Medical: Johnson County Memorial Hospital in Buffalo, 16 miles
Conference: 50; 2,400-square-foot meeting space off-season only
Guest Capacity: 70
Accommodations: 18 luxury one-, two-, and three-bedroom log homes, each with living room, kitchenette, fireplace, central heat, and deck overlooking pine-covered mountains, Fan Rock, and French Creek. Each day your hot chocolate, tea, and coffee basket will be filled.
Rates: • $$–$$$. American Plan. Children's and pack-trip rates. One-week minimum stay, Sunday to Sunday.
Credit Cards: None. Personal checks accepted.
Season: Late May to October
Activities: Riding is the main activity, with one wrangler to a maximum of seven guests. Nine to 12 separate rides each day. Guests can choose walking, trotting, or loping rides. Beginners can learn all three if they wish and are able. Adults and children may ride together or separately. Also offered are bag-lunch rides or occasionally Jim's special cooked-on-the-trail lunch rides. His mules pack all the grub, and the wranglers do all the cookin'. Ask about rides to Seven Brothers and Sherd Lakes and the cattle-ranch-country ride through spectacular Cougar, Red, and Sales Canyons. Selective cattle-moving. Instruction available on one of 130 horses. Full fishing program for kids and adults. Heated outdoor swimming pool and indoor whirlpool spa.
Children's Programs: Excellent children's program, activities counselor for kids, toddlers to teens. Kids' rodeo in arena with gymkhana events. Kids and parents may interact as much or as little as they like. Ask about teen social and teen overnight pack trip campout.
Dining: All you can eat, three meals a day, family-style. Real mule-drawn chuck-wagon dinner and cookouts, home-baked breads. Wine available. Stocked saloon.
Entertainment: Square dancing, talent night, sing-alongs, and recreation center. Thursday is parents' night off, as kids are camping out.
Summary: Jim and Leah's Paradise Ranch is one of the very best guest ranches in the business. Traditional dude-ranch values with first-rate accommodations. Lots of family reunions. Ask about kids' and adults' naturalist hiking program. September adults-only program followed by fall conferences. Video available.

See color photos, pages 302–303.

R Lazy S Ranch
Teton Village, Wyoming

THE DUDE RANCHERS' ASSOCIATION

Wyoming Dude Rancher's Association

Magnificent scenery, a friendly staff, and Western hospitality make the R Lazy S one of the great guest ranches. Since 1947 the McConaughy family has operated this wonderful ranch almost at the foot of the majestic Tetons, bordering Grand Teton National Park. In 1975, Howard and Cara Stirn purchased the McConaughys' interest. Since then, both the Stirns and the McConaughys have hosted families from all over the country. While it's close to Jackson and the world-class ski resort at Teton Village, the ranch still maintains its privacy and solitude. Being so close and yet so far gives guests many options for activities and excursions. By the end of one week, you'll only have begun. It's difficult to enjoy all of the Jackson Hole area's activities during a typical week-long stay, which is why the ranch enjoys a high repeat clientele. Regardless of how long you stay, you'll enjoy the friendly spirit and the magnificent mountain scenery.

Address: Box 308 K, Teton Village, Wyoming 83025 (summer); 1902 West 1575 North, St. George, Utah 84770 (winter)
Telephone: (307) 733-2655, fax: (307) 734-1120 (summer); (435) 628-6546 (telephone and fax) (winter)
Airport: Jackson, 13 miles
Location: 13 miles northwest of the town of Jackson, one mile north of Teton Village
Memberships: The Dude Ranchers' Association, Wyoming Dude Rancher's Association
Medical: St. John's Hospital, 13 miles
Guest Capacity: 45
Accommodations: 14 beautifully modernized one-, two-, and three-bedroom log cabins, all with electric blankets and fabulous views, scattered around the ranch property among the aspen trees. All have one or two bathrooms, depending on size; some have living or sitting rooms; all have electric heaters, fireplaces, or wood-burning stoves, and lovely hanging baskets with colorful flowers. One teen dorm (boys' or girls') with bathroom sleeps four in bunk beds. The main lodge is a favorite gathering place at day's end. Laundry facilities available.
Rates: $$–$$$. American Plan. Minimum one-week stay, Sunday to Sunday.
Credit Cards: None. Personal checks accepted.
Season: Mid-June through September, adults-only month of September
Activities: The nearby Snake River (a mile from ranch buildings) and neighboring Teton Mountain trails offer many activities. The ranch offers a full riding program. Half-day and all-day rides with picnic lunches. No riding on Sunday. Pack trips and riding instruction available. Extensive fly-fishing program. Claire and Bob's daughter and son-in-law are partners in Westbank Anglers, a first-rate guide and fly-fishing shop three miles from the ranch. Fishing in Snake, South Fork, Green, and North Fork Rivers, and streams, lakes, and stocked ranch pond. Weekly fishing clinic. Hiking, swimming in ranch swimming hole, or tubing. River rafting, tennis, and golf can be arranged nearby. Waterskiing or scenic boat rides once a week on Jackson Lake.
Children's Programs: The ranch cannot accommodate children under seven years of age. Kiddie wranglers with programs for kids and teenagers. Children eat together in own dining room. Gymkhanas.
Dining: The lovely dining room looks out to the meadows and the Tetons beyond. Family- and buffet-style food. Ranch hosts Sunday welcome happy hour. Weekly cookouts. BYOB.
Entertainment: Kids' marshmallow roasts, hayrides, and cookouts around the ranch. Jackson Rodeo, volleyball, softball, and horseshoes. Evening Western square dancing. Nature walk and fly-fishing clinic.
Summary: Spectacular setting, looking to the Tetons. Adults-only in September for peak fly-fishing season. R Lazy S is great for families or single parents and their children (age seven and over). Ask about the R Lazy S cookbook. Nearby: shopping, rodeo, and melodrama in town of Jackson; Teton Village with its mountain tram; Yellowstone National Park.

Savery Creek Thoroughbred Ranch
Savery, Wyoming

Joyce Saer's Savery Creek Thoroughbred Ranch is best suited for advanced/intermediate English and Western riders who can handle very good horses and are not looking for plush accommodations. Her ranch borders the family's historic old dude ranch, the Boyer YL Ranch, which has been turned out to pasture. Savery Creek offers unique and highly personalized riding opportunities for advanced riders. Joyce spent much of her life in Europe, particularly in Spain, and is an outstanding horsewoman. She was the first woman racehorse-trainer in Spanish history and won their Gran Premio in 1958. Joyce fox-hunts each year in Colorado and Ireland and is a lifetime member of the USCTA. Guests stay in the ranch house. The countryside is beautiful and varied, and the ranch is in one of the last unspoiled, un-touristy areas in Wyoming. The name "Wyoming," an Indian word meaning "mountains and valleys alternating," could have originated in the Savery Valley. There are deer, antelope, elk, coyotes, eagles, and other wildlife. Savery Creek Thoroughbred Ranch is for those who wish focused riding opportunities and who savor the West in low-key Western comfort.

Address: Box 24 K, Savery, Wyoming 82332
Telephone: (307) 383-7840; call for fax number
Airport: Hayden, paved landing field at Dixon, 11 miles
Location: Nine miles north of Savery; 70 miles south of Rawlins; 60 miles north of Craig; 280 miles from Denver
Medical: Steamboat Hospital, two hours; clinic at Baggs, 20 miles
Guest Capacity: No more than four
Accommodations: The eclectic ranch house is beside Savery Creek in cottonwood trees and has three guest bedrooms. One overlooks the creek and has a private bath. The other two bedrooms are small, have queen-size beds, and share a bathroom. Most guests don't spend much time in their rooms except, as Joyce says, "to crash" at the end of a busy day. For the adventurous, there are two covered, early-day sheep wagons.
Rates: • $$$. American Plan. Three- to four-day minimum stay.
Credit Cards: Personal and traveler's checks accepted.
Season: Mid-June to October
Activities: This is a riding ranch where each guest has the opportunity to ride several different horses. The horses are exceptional, many of competition and show quality. It's possible to ride in three directions without seeing another person. Good riders may help wrangle and drive cattle out of the pastures. Savery Creek caters to experts and those wishing to improve their skills. Western and English saddles, jumping and dressage lessons available. Cross-country course in the woods and a jumping area across the creek. Fly-fishing on Savery Creek, the Little Snake, or on Hog Park Reservoir. Tennis, swimming in Savery Creek, hiking, and badminton.
Children's Programs: Best for older children who are horse crazy and can ride.
Dining: Ranch specialties include garden vegetables, beef, lamb, and fruit. Wine served. Guests usually bring their own spirits for cocktails and conversation before dinner. Many cookouts and picnics, especially on the rim of the Red Desert.
Entertainment: Cowboys practice team roping once a week at Dixon Arena. Bring your favorite book; most guests are pooped at the end of the day. Evening conversation and bridge; selection of books, music, *Wall Street Journal*, and *The New Yorker*.
Summary: Small, rustic ranch catering to enthusiastic and sophisticated expert riders (both English and Western) and a limited number of urbane guests who have a passion for horses. Nearby towns of Saratoga and Steamboat Springs offer day trips; as does the Red Desert with its fossils, interesting formations, antelope and "real" wild horses. Spanish and limited French spoken.

Red Rock Ranch
Kelly, Wyoming

THE DUDE RANCHERS' ASSOCIATION

Wyoming Dude Rancher's Association

Nestled in a secluded valley high (7,200 feet) on the eastern slope of Jackson Hole's spectacular mountain country is Red Rock Ranch, named for the Indian-red cliffs and rock formations you see while driving up from the little one-horse town of Kelly, some 15 miles from the ranch gates. This operating old-time cattle ranch, homesteaded in 1890, offers some of the best guest-ranching in the business. Since 1972 it has been owned by the MacKenzie family. With a first-rate string of horses, wranglers will take you through spectacular country. Fly-fishers will enjoy the stocked ranch pond and Crystal Creek, a two-mile catch-and-release fly-fishing stream which runs through the ranch. RRR is one of the best!

Address: P.O. Box 38 K, Kelly, Wyoming 83011
Telephone: (307) 733-6288; fax: (307) 733-6287
E-Mail: redrockranch@blissnet.com
Internet:http://www.ranchweb.com/redrock; http://www.blissnet.com/~redrockranch
Airport: Jackson, 30 miles
Location: 30 miles northeast of Jackson
Memberships: The Dude Ranchers' Association, Wyoming Dude Rancher's Association
Medical: St. John's Hospital, Jackson, 30 miles
Conference: 30, early June and September
Guest Capacity: 30
Accommodations: Nine authentic log cabins named after Native American tribes, such as Apache, Navajo, Sioux, and Cheyenne. Built in the early 1950s, cabins are one- and two-bedrooms with private baths for each bedroom. All have twin or queen-size beds, adjoining living rooms, electric heat, woodstoves, small refrigerators, and carpeting. They're tastefully decorated in Western style. Each cabin has a small porch with a chair or bench. A comfortable lodge, dining room and deck (with wonderful views), and adult pool hall/bar are available to guests. Activities room is for square dancing, Western swing, and a children's recreation room. Laundry facilities are available.
Rates: $$$. American Plan, includes all activities except river trips and pickup at airport. Off-season rates.
Credit Cards: None. Personal checks or cash accepted.
Season: June through September
Activities: Here you can enjoy some of the most beautiful riding in the country. Morning, afternoon, and all-day rides offered. You may ride in smaller groups if you wish. Monday morning orientation rides in the arena acquaint guests with their horse for the week. Ask about the White Canyon and Grizzly Lake rides. Swimming in a heated pool that overlooks the incredible Gros Ventre Mountain Valley, an eight-person hot tub, hiking, and plenty of relaxing. Scenic river trips can be arranged down the Snake River—a must!
Children's Programs: Children are looked after only during riding and adult dinner hour. Wranglers take kids on day rides. One night a week they take an overnight pack trip. Age limit for riding is age six and older. Children's recreation room and weekly gymkhana. Nannies are encouraged for young children.
Dining: Professionally trained chefs serve up a variety of Western ranch cooking. Weekly cookouts for breakfast and on Sunday evening; special diets catered with advance notice. Children eat evening meal before adults three nights a week (teens optional). BYOB.
Entertainment: Hors d'oeuvres and drinks (BYOB) before dinner. Sing-alongs, weekly rodeo in Jackson, pickle ball (mini-tennis) court, dancing in the Dance Hall.
Summary: One of the best! A fun, family-oriented guest ranch with lots of camaraderie and Old West spirit. Unspoiled wilderness, plenty of horseback riding. Return guests rarely leave the ranch once they arrive. Laid-back, relaxing atmosphere. *New York Times* fax to read each morning with your breakfast. Working cattle ranch, horse-drawn surrey rides. Adults-only weeks.

See color photos, pages 304–305.

Rimrock Ranch
Cody, Wyoming

THE DUDE RANCHERS' ASSOCIATION

Rimrock Ranch is named after the rock formations surrounding the property. It's just 26 miles from Yellowstone National Park's east entrance and at the edge of the Shoshone National Forest. Your hosts, Gary and Dede Fales, are continuing the great family tradition of receiving guests that was begun in 1956 by Glenn and Alice Fales. Gary grew up on the ranch and met Dede there back in 1964. This family-owned and operated ranch is located on Canyon Creek, and looks out across Wapiti Valley to the Absaroka Range of the Rocky Mountains. Today, as before, Rimrock offers its guests one of the great dude-ranching experiences. Here families, couples, and singles enjoy excellent trail riding, taking in spectacular vistas in the old-time Western spirit.

Address: 2728 Northfork Road, Dept. K, Cody, Wyoming 82414
Telephone: (307) 587-3970; fax: (307) 527-5014
E-Mail: rimrock@wyoming.com
Internet: http://www.rimrockranch.com
Airport: Cody or Billings
Location: 26 miles west of Cody
Memberships: The Dude Ranchers' Association, Wyoming Outfitters Association
Medical: Cody Hospital, 26 miles
Guest Capacity: 32
Accommodations: Cabins are located on both sides of Canyon Creek. Comfortable, simple, and homey, each of the nine log cabins (two of which can accommodate seven to 10 people) is furnished with Western decor. Some have stone fireplaces. All have private baths with hot and cold running water. Each has a porch; all but one have carpeting. Heated with gas. Laundry facilities on premises.
Rates: • \$\$–\$\$\$. American Plan. Ask about sliding-scale rates for families. One-week minimum stay, Sunday to Sunday. Pack-trip rates.
Credit Cards: VISA, MasterCard. Personal checks accepted.
Season: Last week in May through September
Activities: All-day and half-day trail rides. Gary says, "Guests should learn how to ride at three gaits: walk, trot, and canter." Terrain lends itself to spectacular views and an easygoing pace. Some loping and challenging rides for those riders who can handle it. Ask about the Table Mountain Ride; breakfast ride to Green, Lost, and Holy City Creeks. Guests get their own horse for the week. Experienced wranglers. As many as three separate rides in different directions and at different paces go out at one time. Fishing in the ranch pond and weekly river rafting in the North Fork of the Shoshone River. Tour of Yellowstone National Park. Separate from ranch activities are horse pack trips into Yellowstone Park, Bridger-Teton, and Shoshone National Forests. Heated swimming pool.
Children's Programs: Children and parents participate in activities together. Children's fishing pond. Riding available for kids ages six and older. Very young children not advised.
Dining: Meals are served family-style, buffet, and barbecues. On or off the trail, hearty ranch cooking. Alice's famous prime rib is a specialty. BYOB.
Entertainment: Dede and Gary host an "introduction party" every Sunday evening. Cookouts and singing cowboys. Table tennis, cards, and billiards in the recreation room with lots of memorabilia. Heated swimming pool. Cody Nightly Rodeo.
Summary: Gary and Dede exemplify the true meaning and down-to-earth spirit of dude-ranching. Wonderful, low-key ranch that has hosted people from around the world since 1956. Excellent trail riding and wilderness pack trips and beautiful pool with incredible views and cabins along river. Ask about winter snowmobile tours of Yellowstone Park and famous tour of Yellowstone Park. Nearby: Buffalo Bill Historical Center, July Fourth Cody Stampede.

Seven D Ranch
Cody, Wyoming

THE DUDE RANCHERS' ASSOCIATION

Wyoming Dude Rancher's Association

The Seven D Ranch is a cozy haven in the midst of a magnificent wilderness, bought in the late 1950s by Dewey and Lee Dominick, a surgeon and his wife. Today the family tradition continues under their grandson Ward and his wife, Nikki. The ranch is in the remote and beautiful Sunlight Basin, deep within the Shoshone National Forest. Surrounded by the Absaroka Mountains, it has vast pastures where the horses are turned out each night to graze and where you'll find a small herd of registered Black Angus cattle. The Seven D appeals to all ages. For those who wish to relax, the ranch offers the peace of a mountain hideaway. The more-energetic may want to take a leisurely morning or afternoon ride, cast for trout, or hike into the Absaroka Wilderness. And folks with even more get-up-and-go may enjoy a full day of riding or fishing, or a wilderness pack trip into Yellowstone Park. Most of all, there's a wonderful atmosphere of history, camaraderie, laughter, and energetic participation. If you've ever wondered where Marlboro Country is, many of the ad photographs were taken right here at the Seven D.

Address: P.O. Box 100, Cody, Wyoming 82414
Telephone: (307) 587-3997 (ranch), (307) 587-9885 (office and fax)
E-Mail: ranch7d@wyoming.com
Internet: http://www.nezperce.com/ranch7d.html; http://www.7dranch.com
Airport: Cody or Billings
Location: 50 miles northwest of Cody via Chief Joseph Scenic Highway (Highway 296) and Sunlight Basin Road, a beautiful drive
Memberships: The Dude Ranchers' Association, Wyoming Dude Rancher's Association
Medical: Cody Hospital, 50 miles
Conference: 32
Guest Capacity: 32
Accommodations: A clear mountain-spring creek winds near 11 rustic log cabins that are nestled in a beautiful aspen grove and have names like Trapper, Aspen, Big Buffalo, Waldorf, and The Fireplace. Cabins vary from one to four bedrooms each, with private baths, woodstoves, and fresh wildflowers. Guests enjoy using the woodstoves during delightfully cool summer evenings. Daily maid service. Laundry facilities available.
Rates: • $$$. American Plan. Children's and off-season rates. Minimum one-week stay, Sunday to Sunday. Pack-trip rates available.
Credit Cards: None. Personal and traveler's checks accepted.
Season: Mid-June through mid-September
Activities: Rides every day except Sunday. Your choice of scenic, half-day, or all-day rides. Riders are accompanied by experienced wranglers on beautiful and varied trails. Five to eight riders go out per ride. Ask about Big Skyline, Memorial and the "Oh My God" rides with views into Montana. Instruction available and encouraged. Two- to 10-day horse pack trips with advance arrangement into the North Absaroka Wilderness and Yellowstone Park for groups of six or less. This has been the trip of a lifetime for many. Superb fishing on and off the property. Seven D hosts a full-time fly-fishing guide as well as a private mile-long stretch of the Sunlight River. Limited fishing gear available. Many fishing opportunities for the young and the young-at-heart. Mountain biking, hiking, and wildflower walks, soccer, and softball. Float trips available in Cody.
Children's Programs: Counselors for children ages six through 12 during adult daytime activities. Kids are entertained with horseback rides, arts and crafts, organized games, and hiking to the Indian caves. Pony rides for children under age five.
Dining: Excellent food! Beautiful old ranch dining room, weekly brunch rides and barbecue. Ask about Uncle Marshall's famous barbecued Chilean lamb—wow! Ranch-raised beef. Special diets catered to with advance notice. BYOB.
Entertainment: Books in the marvelous old main lodge. Recreation hall with piano, table tennis, billiards, square dancing with live caller. Gymkhanas, horseshoes. Marvelous naturalist talks.
Summary: The Seven D is one of the old-time greats! The Dominick family members exude warmth and plenty of Western hospitality. Lots of family reunions. Excellent wilderness pack trips. Adults-only weeks in September.

See color photos, page 306.

Spear-O-Wigwam Ranch
Sheridan, Wyoming

THE DUDE RANCHERS' ASSOCIATION

Wyoming Dude Rancher's Association

As you peer through the log-framed entrance supporting the oversized cast-iron ranch brand, it may seem that you're on a dirt runway and about to take off into the wild blue yonder. Fear not. It's only the dirt road leading straight to the ranch. As your car rumbles over the cattle guard, be prepared. You're about to take off on a tremendous experience with ranch managers and the Riehm family, who have owned the ranch since 1973. Spear-O-Wigwam was established in the early 1920s by the Willis Spear family, who entertained many Eastern friends. An early guest was Ernest Hemingway who, in 1928, completed *A Farewell to Arms* at the ranch. Hemingway was overheard saying one day, "There are two places I love, Africa and Wyoming." The ranch is in the Big Horn National Forest. At 8,300 feet, the air is clear, the mountain water pure, the summer days cool, and the scenery spectacular.

Address: Box 1081 K, Sheridan, Wyoming 82801
Telephone: (888) 818-3833, (307) 674-4496 (summer); (307) 672-0002 (winter); fax: (307) 655-3951
E-Mail: spearo@wavecom.net
Internet: http://www.spear-o-wigwam.com
Airport: Sheridan or Billings
Location: 30 miles southwest of Sheridan
Medical: Sheridan Memorial Hospital, 30 miles
Memberships: The Dude Rancher's Association, Wyoming Dude Rancher's Association, America Outdoors
Conference: 30
Guest Capacity: 30
Accommodations: Seven beautiful old-fashioned log cabins, one to four bedrooms each, all with private baths, heat, and Western decor. Cabins have such names as Hemingway, Porcupine, Chipmunk, and Bears Den. The main lodge has a huge fireplace, library, bar, and dining room. Laundry facilities available. Daily maid service and nightly turn-down service. The ranch generates its own electricity, and the generator works around the clock.
Rates: $$. American Plan. Children's, group, and off-season rates available. Three-night minimum stay, arrival any day.
Credit Cards: None. Personal checks accepted.
Season: Mid-June to mid-September
Activities: Informal program. Riding and relaxing are the two main activities. Riding every day—your choice of half-day or all-day rides. Guests put together their own riding groups and select their own rides. Because of the mountain terrain and high altitude, there's little opportunity for fast rides. The emphasis here is on the scenery and wildlife. Pack trips through breathtaking country to remote Beaver Lake (extra), where there's a permanent tent camp. Trout fishing in streams or lakes (river guide available), kiddie pond, excellent hiking and nature photography, breakfast cookouts, and evening barbecues. Swimming and boating on nearby park reservoir, hot tub.
Children's Programs: No separate program. Families are encouraged to participate together. Some families bring their own baby-sitters. Nannies welcome—ask about special nanny rates. Cribs available. Varied riding program for young kids. Here younger children can ride. Call for details.
Dining: Meals served family-style at one long table seating 30. Western cuisine features prime rib, fried chicken, steaks, home-baked breads, and desserts. Complimentary wine served occasionally with dinner. BYOB.
Entertainment: Happy hour each evening. Rodeos in Sheridan and Buffalo; weekly polo in Big Horn, 20 miles away. Recreation room with pool table, table tennis, and cards. Staff members often entertain with cowboy songs and poetry.
Summary: Informal, relaxed atmosphere. As Barbara says, "We just sort of let things happen, and you don't have to do anything if you don't want to." The ranch has a magnificent setting. Riding and relaxing are the two main activities. Many couples and families return year after year. Abundant wildlife and wildflowers of the Big Horn Mountains. Pets are allowed, but arrangements must be made in advance.

TA Guest Ranch
Buffalo, Wyoming

Wyoming Dude Rancher's Association

Earl Madsen grew up in the Big Horn Mountains of Wyoming. Though his career as an environmental lawyer took him around the United States, throughout his travels and practice his heart was in Wyoming. In 1991, together with his wife, Barbara, he fulfilled his lifelong dream by purchasing one of the most historic ranches in the western United States. After three years of intensive restoration, the TA Ranch opened its gates once again. Earl and Barbara offer the discriminating traveler a glimpse of history and heartwarming experiences of hospitality, cuisine (great beef), and cattle-ranch activities. Guests enjoy being able to ride side-by-side across the thousands of acres of open range, creek bottoms, and rolling hills of the Old West. The vistas in this part of the country are spectacular and immense. When temperatures warm up during midsummer, guests enjoy relaxing after lunch with an iced tea out on the veranda in the marvelous cottonwood groves. The TA Ranch, indeed, captures the true authentic spirit of the West.

Address: P.O. Box 313K, Buffalo, Wyoming 82834
Telephone: (800) 368-7398, (307) 684-5833; fax: (307) 684-5663.
E-Mail: taranch@trib.com
Internet: http://www.taranch.com
Airport: Sheridan, 45 miles; Casper, 100 miles
Location: 13 miles south of Buffalo on Wyoming 196 (old Highway 87)
Memberships: National Cattleman's Association, Wyoming Dude Rancher's Association
Awards: National Historic Register, State of Wyoming Historic Preservation
Medical: Buffalo Medical Center, 13 miles
Conference: 32 to 75 (day)
Guest Capacity: 32
Accommodations: Five historic beautifully renovated buildings set in a cottonwood grove on Crazy Woman Creek. The old ranch house and cookhouse are furnished with Victorian antiques, providing an elegant yet comfortable setting. The bunkhouse is cozy with hardwood floors and a complete kitchen. The ranch house offers spacious lounging on a 65-by-12-foot covered porch in the shade of the cottonwoods. There's also a living room with wet bar and a study. Ask about the granary and milk barn!
Rates: • $$$. American Plan. Children's rates for age 12 and under. Kids under age three free. Three-day minimum stay.
Credit Cards: VISA, MasterCard
Season: May through mid-October
Activities: The main activities are horseback riding, fishing, hiking, and touring historic sites. A working cattle-and-horse ranch since 1882, the ranch can accommodate all riding levels. Rides go out twice a day with a wrangler. Everyone is invited to participate in the work activities, including herding cattle, cutting pairs, and overseeing care of the herd, depending on the time of year. Trout fishing in Crazy Woman Creek and private reservoir is excellent for experienced and novice anglers. Ask about the native brown trout and guided fishing program on the Big Horn River. Hiking and trail riding in the Big Horn Mountains. The TA is a perfect base for touring nearby historic sites, including Ft. Phil Kearney, the "Hole-in-the-Wall outlaw hideout," Little Big Horn, and the Oregon Trail.
Children's Programs: None. Children are welcome but are the complete responsibility of their parents; under age eight are not recommended. Kids should typically be old enough to enjoy riding. Nannies encouraged (nanny rates available).
Dining: Family-style meals feature Western menus including excellent natural TA lean beef, home-grown trout, wild game, and specialty Basque cuisine. Ranch can cater to food preferences. Complimentary wine and beer served.
Entertainment: Volleyball, horseshoes, roping, games such as backgammon and cribbage. VCR presentations, local living-history programs, wildlife- and bird-watching. Western history library. Local rodeos.
Summary: One of Wyoming's most beautiful and historic guest and conference ranches! Completely restored historic property is on National Historic Register. Open-meadow range riding—not nose-to-tail. Excellent fishing opportunities. Guided tours to Custer Battlefield. Eighteen-hole golf nearby.

See color photos, page 307.

Triangle X Ranch
Moose, Wyoming

THE DUDE RANCHERS' ASSOCIATION

Wyoming Dude Rancher's Association

Known for its old-time traditions, beauty, hospitality, and caring spirit, Triangle X has just about everything one could ask for in old-time dude ranching, including a million-dollar view: located just outside Moose in the world-famous Jackson Hole Valley, Triangle X has panoramic views of the awesome Teton Range and Snake River Valley. The ranch was established in 1926 by John Turner, Sr., as a cattle-and-hunting ranch. The Turner family runs a first-rate operation. Their repeat business (some guests have been returning for over 40 years) proves it. Among the ranch's unique features are its year-round summer and winter programs, its superb location, an exciting wilderness pack trip, river-rafting programs, and its well-supervised Little Wrangler riding program for kids ages five through 12. This program makes the Triangle X a wonderful family experience.

Address: Star Route Box 120K, Moose, Wyoming 83012
Telephone: (307) 733-2183; fax: (307) 733-8685
E-Mail: johnturner@blissnet.com
Internet: http://www.trianglex.com
Airport: Jackson, 25 miles
Location: 25 miles north of Jackson
Memberships: The Dude Rancher's Association, Wyoming Outfitters Association, Wyoming Dude Rancher's Association, America Outdoors
Medical: St. John's Hospital in Jackson, 25 miles
Conference: 50, off-season only
Guest Capacity: 75
Accommodations: One-, two-, or three-bedroom log cabins with private baths, warm wool blankets, and covered porches. Cabins are very clean (with polished wood floors), comfortable, and ranch-cozy. Laundry facilities available. Small ranch gift shop with hats, shirts, nature books, and river-rafting reception area.
Rates: • $$–$$$. American Plan. One-week minimum stay, Sunday to Sunday. Off-season, pack-trip, and winter rates available.
Credit Cards: None. Personal or traveler's checks.
Season: Summer: May to November; winter: mid-December to April
Activities: Summer: Triangle X is predominantly a riding ranch. Riders enjoy a variety of trails to the tops of timbered mountains, through wildflower meadows, over sagebrush, and along the Snake River, always with the magnificent Teton Mountain Range as a backdrop. Breakfast rides and weekly Dutch-oven suppers. Scenic, medium, and faster trail rides. Weekly nature ride by Forest Service personnel. Hiking and extensive Triangle X scenic Snake River rafting program. Trout fishing on the famous Snake River or in Yellowstone National Park for either the expert or the beginner who wants to learn. In-house fishing guides who are well-versed on fly- or spin-fishing. Triangle X offers the ultimate wilderness experience in the form of four-day to two week pack trips into the Teton Wilderness and southern Yellowstone areas. Winter: snowmobiling along the Continental Divide snowmobile trail and cross-country skiing in Grand Teton National Park adjacent to the ranch (where snowmobiling is not allowed).
Children's Programs: Children ages five through 12 have their own kiddie wrangler who supervises riding lessons, rafting, and museum trips. Children under age five don't ride. Kids are their parents' responsibility when not riding. Parents may ride with kids.
Dining: Meals are hearty and delicious, served family-style in a wonderful dining room with commanding views overlooking the Tetons. Sunday ranch cookout; Wednesday evening cookout ride; Friday morning breakfast ride. Children dine separately at all meals except cookouts. Parents can eat with kids, but kids can't eat with parents. BYOB.
Entertainment: Monday evening social. Campfires with old-fashioned sing-alongs, Western guitar music, square dancing, rodeos in Jackson, weekly slide shows of local history. Forest Service nature talks.
Summary: Triangle X and the Turner family are old-time greats in the dude-ranch business. Besides its location, million-dollar views of the Tetons, and Old West dude ranch atmosphere, Triangle X is known for its riding, river rafting, and superb four-day to two-week pack trips and an exciting winter snowmobiling and cross-country program. Located in Grand Teton, 32 miles from Yellowstone National Park.

T-Cross Ranch
Dubois, Wyoming

THE DUDE RANCHERS' ASSOCIATION

Wyoming Dude Rancher's Association

When you pass through the gates of the T-Cross Ranch, the outside world is all but forgotten. This old-time authentic dude ranch has been in business since the 1920s. Today, as in years gone by, the spirit, informality, and relaxed Western atmosphere offer guests an experience of a lifetime. Located 15 miles north of the small Western town of Dubois, the ranch is situated in a private valley surrounded by the Shoshone National Forest. The ranch is owned and managed by Ken and Garey Neal. Ken has worked ranches and horses since he can remember. To his guests and friends he is the real Marlboro Man! He and I go way back; in fact, we began our guest-ranching careers at the same ranch. The remote T-Cross Ranch in every way captures old-time guest ranching at its best.

Address: P.O. Box 638 K, Dubois, Wyoming 82513
Telephone: (307) 455-2206; fax: (307) 455-2720
Internet: http://www.ranchweb.com/tcross
Airport: Jackson or Riverton. Surfaced airstrip three miles west of Dubois for private jets and planes. Free pickup from Dubois.
Location: 15 miles north of Dubois off Highway 26/287, 85 miles east of Jackson Airport
Memberships: The Dude Ranchers' Association, Wyoming Dude Rancher's Association, Nature Conservancy
Medical: Dubois Clinic, 15 miles; Riverton Hospital and Jackson Hospital
Conference: 24 (June and September)
Guest Capacity: 24
Accommodations: Eight wonderful, cozy log cabins tucked in the pines truly capture the old spirit of the West, with Indian rugs, incredible handcrafted log furniture, down quilts, woodstoves or fireplaces, hot showers, and individual porches. The main lodge is filled with Western memorabilia and charm. Laundry facilities available.
Rates: • $$$. American Plan. Off-season, group, and nanny rates available. Sunday-to-Sunday arrival in July and August. Four-night minimum June, September, and October.
Credit Cards: None. Personal checks, traveler's checks, and cash accepted.
Season: Early June to late October
Activities: The main activities are riding, hiking, fly-fishing, and relaxing. Guests are assigned a horse for the duration of their stay. Morning and afternoon rides go out daily except Sunday. All-day rides go out at least twice a week with a pack mule carrying lunch and fishing gear. Ask about rides to Five Pockets, Ramshorn Basin, Deacon Lake, and Twilight Falls. Depending on ability, guests take walking, trotting, and loping rides, and Ken's rugged ride. Fly-fishers enjoy Horse Creek, which runs through the ranch. Another favorite is the Wiggins Fork of the Wind River. There are also high-mountain lakes, climbing opportunities, bird-watching, wildflowers, relaxing on the porch, or soaking in the hot tub at the end of the day. Bring your art supplies along.
Children's Programs: Children ages six and older ride, hike, and tube-float the river with a youth wrangler. They enjoy games, crafts, and treasure hunts. Ask about overnight tepee campouts. Friday morning gymkhanas. Nannies are encouraged for younger children.
Dining: Ranch cooking. Cook will prepare your freshly caught fish. Breakfast, lunch, and dinner cookouts. Happy hour each evening in the lodge. BYOB.
Entertainment: Weekly Western singing by local groups, cowboy poetry by our cowboy wrangler, square dancing, campfires, volleyball, and horseshoes.
Summary: One of the greatest old-time authentic guest ranches in North America. Here the spirit is rich in tradition and hearty in hospitality. Superb scenic horseback riding, fly-fishing, hiking, and relaxing. Perfect for family reunions. Adults-only September and October. You may bring your own horse. Featured in *National Geographic Traveler* magazine, *New York Times*, *Boston Globe*, *London Financial Times*, and *Town & Country*.

See color photos, pages 308–309.

Trail Creek Ranch
Wilson, Wyoming

THE DUDE RANCHERS' ASSOCIATION

Trail Creek Ranch is very special to me—it's the ranch where my parents took me as a young child. It's here that a seed was planted, which blossomed into my love for this incredible way of life. I'm proud to say that Trail Creek Ranch is responsible, to a large extent, for this guidebook. Back in the 1940s, a young Olympic skier named Elizabeth Woolsey bought a rundown ranch at the foot of Teton Pass, 10 miles from Jackson. With her tenacity and tremendous spirit, Betty transformed the ranch into one of the prettiest family-oriented ranches in the country, offering sincere Western hospitality. To the east the property consists of lush, green hay meadows; the rest is timbered, with many bridle trails and Trail Creek, which runs through the ranch. Trail Creek Ranch is a working ranch, raising hay that supports a fine string of horses and pack mules. Daily riding and pack trips are the main activities. Betty touched many lives over the years. In 1997 Betty passed on and left the ranch to her longtime friend and colleague Muggs Schultz (who has worked at Trail Creek since the 1950s) and the Jackson Hole Land Trust. Today Muggs, Alex, and their staff continue to greet guests and make new friends.

Address: P.O. Box 10 K, Wilson, Wyoming 83014
Telephone: (307) 733-2610
Airport: Jackson via Salt Lake City or Denver
Location: two miles west of Wilson, 10 miles west of Jackson
Memberships: The Dude Ranchers' Association
Medical: St. John's Hospital, Jackson
Guest Capacity: 25 (summer); 10 (winter)
Accommodations: The Main Lodge, with the living room, library, dining rooms, and sun deck, is the heartbeat of Trail Creek. Two family cabins and cabins made up of several bedrooms with private baths comfortably house the guests. Cabins overlook the hay meadows and beyond to the Sleeping Indian, a beautiful mountain in the Gros Ventre Range. There are also several rooms in the Main Lodge and separate boys' and girls' bunkhouses for teenagers.
Rates: $$. American Plan. Everything included except pack trips. Some guests stay 10 days to two weeks.
Credit Cards: None. Personal checks accepted.
Season: Mid-June to mid-September (summer); February and March (winter)
Activities: In summer, riding is the main activity. All rides go out in groups of five to six twice a day; also all-day luncheon rides to Ski Lake and Grand Teton Park (more experienced riders). Pack trips, with families or groups, go out for two- to seven-day trips into the high country (arranged in advance). Fishing in the Snake River, nearby lakes, and ranch pond. Hiking; swimming in heated pool. River rafting with local outfitter. In winter, the ranch takes no more than 10 guests who enjoy cross-country skiing on the ranch and nearby downhill skiing, both in the backcountry and at Jackson Hole and Grand Targhee Ski Resorts.
Children's Programs: No formal program, but kids have the time of their lives. Kids six and older may ride together if they wish. Parents with young children are encouraged to bring their own baby-sitter or nanny.
Dining: The ranch garden supplies some of the lettuce, asparagus, and herbs for family meals of roast beef, pork chops, baked ham, roasted chicken, fish, soups, and salads. BYOB. Informal cocktail hour before dinner daily.
Entertainment: No formal evening program. Many go to the Stagecoach Bar in Wilson for country-Western dancing or into Jackson. Jackson rodeo twice a week.
Summary: One of the all-time great small guest ranches with a lovely setting near world-famous Jackson, Wyoming. Nearby: the Tetons, Yellowstone National Park, Jackson, National Elk Refuge. Be sure to buy a copy of Betty's *Off the Beaten Track*.

See color photos, page 316.

Triangle C Ranch
Dubois, Wyoming

THE DUDE RANCHERS' ASSOCIATION

The Garnicks are one of the most colorful dude-ranch families in the Jackson Hole area. Over the past 30 years the family has been involved in dude ranching and entertainment. Son Cameron, who has a wonderful family himself with eight children, has 17 movies to his credit and owns the Jackson Hole Playhouse—a must to visit while you are in Jackson. If you've ever wondered what the real Marlboro Man looks like, wait until you meet him. In 1994, the Garnicks bought Triangle C Ranch just over Togwotee Pass—a ranch with a colorful past and nominated for the National Register of Historic Places. What attracted Cameron and his great old folks, Billie and Bill, to this ranch was a combination of things: big views, old-time charm, and proximity to Jackson Hole and Dubois, two of Wyoming's most famous Western towns. Like the other ranches they have owned or managed before, the Garnicks have infused their magical Western spirit into the Triangle C. The Garnicks know what Western hospitality is all about and, coupled with their knowledge and love for people and children, that makes the Triangle C experience one of the best!

Address: 3737 Highway 26, Drawer K, Dubois, Wyoming 82513
Telephone: (307) 455-2225, (800) 661-4928; fax: (307) 455-2031
E-Mail: info@trianglec.com
Internet: http://www.trianglec.com
Airport: Jackson
Location: 50 minutes northeast of Jackson, off Highway 26
Memberships: The Dude Ranchers' Association
Medical: Hospital in Jackson
Conference: 40
Guest Capacity: 40
Accommodations: The main lodge is perched on a bluff overlooking the Wind River and out across to the Absaroka Mountains. The eight old, rustic, green-roofed, "tiehack" log cabins were built back in the 1920s and radiate that Old West charm. Each has its own bath with hot and cold running water. The Pinnacle Cabins, built in 1997, bring a new definition of luxury to the ranch.
Rates: • $$$. American Plan. Three-night minimum stay. Most take the six-night package, arriving Monday, departing Sunday. Children's, group, and off-season rates.
Credit Cards: VISA, MasterCard. Personal checks preferred.
Season: Year-round. Summer: May through mid-September. Winter: mid-December through March.
Activities: As Billie says, "Do as much or as little as you like." Weekly programs with riding, hiking, and fishing; for the brave, join the Polar Bear Club and swim in the Wind River. Ask about the Pelham Lake and Shoshone Wilderness rides, Cameron's famous six-day John Coulter ride with pack mules, the sunset rides, and the "cowboy up" program. Don't miss the scenic float trip on the Snake River.
Children's Programs: The Garnicks have one of the most famous children's programs in the country for kids ages five to 15. Your youngsters are always in good company with Cameron's eight ranch-raised youngsters. Wonderfully fun naturalist program with awards. Kids love learning about wildlife, setting animal traps, learning about horse care. Ask about the tepee-village overnight.
Dining: Hearty ranch fare, with special diets catered to. Ranch-baked bread, prime rib, barbecued ribs, and trout amandine. The weekly steak-and-chicken barbecue cookout ride is a favorite as are the breakfast rides. Saloon.
Entertainment: Get-acquainted campfire on Monday nights. Hardies, forest ranger talks. Weekly ranch rodeo and gymkhana. Jackson Hole rodeo and Cameron's theater night in Jackson. Family square dancing in Dubois.
Summary: One of Kilgore's Best of the Best. One of the greatest dude-ranching families. Wonderful children's program—Cameron Garnick has eight children, so your kids are always in great company. Old-time ranch with a great Western spirit, 85 years of storytelling, and rich Western hospitality. Ask about winter programs into Yellowstone National Park.

See color photos, pages 310–311.

UXU Ranch
Cody, Wyoming

Wyoming Dude Rancher's Association

The UXU Ranch captures the spirit of the Old West. It has an interesting history and a wonderful river that rushes by. In 1996, the ranch began a new tradition of guest-ranching. Owner and host Hamilton Bryan grew up in the San Francisco Bay area. A huge part of his childhood was spent on his family's cattle ranch. Ham (as his friends call him) has traveled the world for business and pleasure and always had ranching in his heart. In 1995, he began his search for a ranch to call his own. He had three requirements: a river, proximity to a beautiful national park, and Old West charm. The UXU has all three and more. When Ham drove across the ranch bridge, he knew this was it! Today, under his direction, guests come to enjoy good company, breathtaking views, delicious gourmet food, the Shoshone River, and a wide variety of outdoor activities. Just 17 miles from Yellowstone National Park.

Address: 1710 Yellowstone Highway, Wapiti, Wyoming 82450
Telephone: (800) 373-9027, (307) 587-2143; fax summer: (307) 587-8307; fax winter: (415) 781-8447
E-Mail: uxuranch@aol.com
Internet: http://www.uxuranch.com
Airport: Cody, 35 miles (served by Delta and United)
Location: 35 miles west of Cody; 17 miles east of Yellowstone National Park
Memberships: (Associate Member) The Dude Ranchers' Association, Wyoming Dude Rancher's Association
Medical: Cody Hospital, 35 miles
Conference: 12 to 24
Guest Capacity: 36
Accommodations: 12 one- to three-bedroom log cabins, with remodeled private baths, down comforters and pillows, some with fireplaces or gas stoves, each with a sitting porch. All cabins are carpeted and include bathrobes, oversized towels, and bathroom amenities. Ask about the two cabins overlooking the river. Hot tub by the lodge with views of the Absaroka Mountains. Laundry available.
Rates: • $$–$$$. American Plan. Minimum four-day stay; one-week preferred, Saturday to Saturday. Children's and nanny rates available.
Credit Cards: VISA and MasterCard. Personal checks accepted.
Season: June to October
Activities: Guests come to horseback ride, fly-fish, hike, white-water raft, and visit Yellowstone National Park. Favorite rides include June Ridge, Clayton Mountain, and Elks Fork all-day ride and barbecue. Mountain bikes available. There's also golfing and sporting clays in Cody and windsurfing and waterskiing on Buffalo Bill Reservoir, 15 miles away. Be sure to ask about pack trips into surrounding wilderness.
Children's Programs: Some organized activities for children ages six and older. Children ages six and older may trail ride. The ranch creek provides hours of fun! Archery and riflery, too. Nannies are encouraged for younger children. Baby-sitting can be arranged with prior notice.
Dining: Ham has traveled the world and appreciates fine food. Wonderful cuisine includes roast salmon with basil aioli, lamb chops with grilled polenta, and citrus-berry meringue tarts. Over 30 California wines featured. Children usually eat dinner together prior to adults. Special diets can be arranged with prior notice.
Entertainment: Cocktails and hors d'oeuvres each evening. Cookouts, weekly local entertainment; Cody rodeo barbecue features Ham's famous butterflied leg of lamb. Weekly trips to the famous Buffalo Bill Historical Center. Main lodge has a fully stocked honor bar and cigar selection. Piano and billiards.
Summary: Superb ranch for those who enjoy some of the finer things in life. Big mountain views, the North Fork of the Shoshone River, dramatic rock outcroppings, delicious food, fine wine, Old West charm and comfort. The UXU captures the spirit of the West and serves up a variety of outdoor adventure and hospitality. Ham's UXU is a great place for families, couples, singles, and family reunions! Many repeat guests. Ask about photography and cooking courses. Nearby: historic Western town of Cody, Yellowstone National Park.

See color photos, pages 312–313.

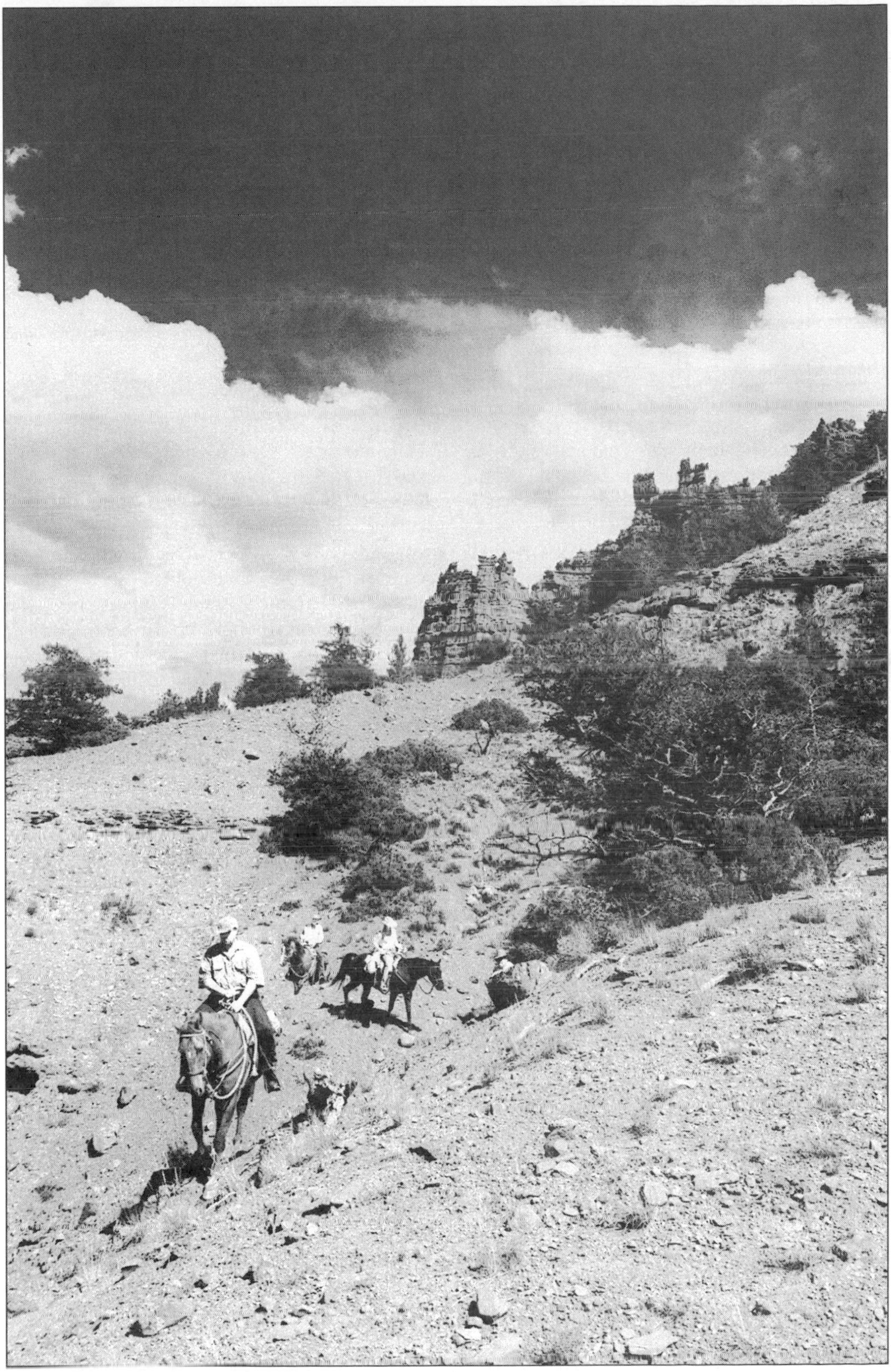

Vee Bar Guest Ranch
Laramie, Wyoming

Wyoming Dude Rancher's Association

Listed on the National Register of Historic Places, the Vee Bar Guest Ranch is located in the Centennial Valley near the 12,000-foot Snowy Range Mountains, part of the magnificent Medicine Bow National Forest. The August 1995 edition of *Wyoming Wildlife* described the Snowies as southeast Wyoming's answer to the Tetons, only without the crowds. A showplace of Western charm, this old cattle ranch was once a stopover for stagecoaches traveling west on the Overland Trail. Since 1912, the ranch has had a colorful history taking in guests, running cattle and buffalo, and welcoming travelers on Wyoming's Scenic Railroad. What makes the Vee Bar special over and above the hospitality is the varied riding program and the Little Laramie River that traverses the ranch's 800 acres. Guests may ride in the wide-open meadows surrounding the ranch or explore the owners' other beautiful 5,000-acre cattle ranch just up the valley, bordering the national forest. The Cole family serves up one of the greatest guest-ranch experiences in the country!

Address: 2091 State Highway 130, Laramie, Wyoming 82070
Telephone: (800) 483-3227, (307) 745-7036; fax: (307) 745-7433
E-Mail: veebar@lariat.org
Internet: http://www.vee-bar.com
Airport: Laramie. Courtesy shuttle available.
Location: 20 miles west of Laramie off Highway 130
Memberships: National Register of Historic Places, (Associate Member) The Dude Ranchers' Association, Wyoming Stock Growers' Association, Wyoming Dude Rancher's Associaiton
Medical: Ivinson Memorial Hospital, Laramie
Conference: 40
Guest Capacity: 38
Accommodations: The lodge and cabins reflect quality and comfort that characterize the Vee Bar. Guests appreciate the magnificent two- or three-bedroom cabins and duplex suites along the Little Laramie River. All have sitting areas with fireplaces, refrigerators, and amenities such as coffee, tea, and hot chocolate. Many of the cabins have the added convenience of built-in washers (soap provided) and dryers. Cabins have river and mountain views and all are within walking distance of the lodge. Daily maid service.
Rates: • $$$–$$$$ Summer: American Plan. Three-day minimum stay. Special rate for booking entire ranch. Winter: Bed-and-breakfast rates. Corporate and group rates.
Credit Cards: VISA, MasterCard. Personal and traveler's checks accepted.
Season: Year-round. Guest ranch early June through early September. Bed-and-breakfast, conferences, weddings, and special groups remainder of the year.
Activities: Scheduled activities program with flexibility. Varied riding and terrain for all levels and ages includes wide-open meadow and mountain riding. Weekly Deerwood Ranch campout. Summer cattle drives with overnight. Fishing on the Little Laramie, guided hiking into the Snowies, and river-tubing for the brave. Archery and trap-shooting. Winter: nearby cross-country and alpine skiing, and snowmobiling.
Children's Programs: No special programs. Children age six and older take part in all ranch activities. Wonderful Western environment for parents and children. Baby-sitting available for kids under age six.
Dining: Vee Bar welcome roundup on Sunday evenings. Family-style dining with an elegant gourmet touch. The ranch chef will accommodate special diets with advance notice. Wine, beer, and liquor available.
Entertainment: Musical, historical, and educational presentations. Team-drawn hay-wagon rides. Old West Saloon with honor bar, pool table, and player piano. Friday gymkhana and Awards Night.
Summary: Historic Western ranch with rich Western charm. Jim and Carla Cole are two of the very best! Wonderful service, fantastic spirit, great hospitality, and excellent wide open riding. Tremendous environment for families, couples, singles, and corporate groups. Private fishing on the Little Laramie River. Cattle drives and overnight campouts on owners' 5,000-acre cattle ranch. Adults-only weeks. Video available.

See color photos, pages 314–315.

Guest and Resort Ranches
in Canada

Brewster's Kananaskis Guest Ranch
Banff, Alberta, Canada

The Kananaskis Guest Ranch is the Brewster family's original homestead. Established in 1923 by Missy Brewster, it is owned and operated by fifth-generation Brewsters. The ranch is an hour west of Calgary in spectacular Kananaskis country on the edge of the Bow River and at the end of Banff's mountain corridor. The movies *River of No Return* and *Legends of the Fall* were both filmed in this area. The modern lodge and several of the cabins overlook the Bow River.

Address: P.O. Box 964, Banff, Alberta, Canada T0L 0C0
Telephone: (800) 691-5085, (403) 673-3737; fax: (403) 673-2100
E-Mail: kgr@brewsteradventures.com
Internet: http://www.brewsteradventures.com
Airport: Calgary, 60 miles
Location: 28 miles east of Banff, 45 minutes west of Calgary off the Trans-Canada Highway
Memberships: Alberta Hotel Association, Banff/Lake Louise Tourism Bureau, Calgary Convention and Visitors Bureau
Medical: Canmore Hospital, 15 minutes
Conference: 60; Lyster seminar building; Brewster Donut Tent for barbecues and special events accommodates up to 1,000
Guest Capacity: 60
Accommodations: 33 cabins and chalet accommodations. One or two-bedroom units feature cedar interiors with antique dressers and night stands, wall-to-wall carpeting, double and single beds, full shower and bath. Some cabins are original Brewster family dwellings. The main lodge houses the X Bar X cocktail lounge and a fully licensed dining room.
Rates: • $–$$. American Plan. Includes half-day of horseback riding per day. Group, barbecue rates and seminar packages available. No minimum stay. Ask about Brewster's Mountain Lodge in Banff.
Credit Cards: VISA, MasterCard, American Express. Traveler's checks accepted.
Season: June through September
Activities: Half-day and all-day rides. A favorite is riding to the ridge on Yamnuska Mountain. Ask about the ride, voyageur canoe trips, and rafting packages from the ranch. Hiking and fly-fishing are also popular activities. Overnight pack trips to the historic Brewster Company ranch with rustic log cabin accommodations in the Devil's Head Mountain area. Riding is also available at the family's Lake Louise Stables (in Banff National Park), where you can ride to spectacular Lake Agnes or Plain of Six Glacier. Four golf courses lie within 30 minutes of the ranch. Indoor heated whirlpool. For groups of 100 or more the ranch will organize on-site rodeos with local cowboys.
Children's Programs: No organized programs. Children are the responsibility of parents, and must be at least four feet and seven inches tall or seven years old to ride.
Dining: Open to the public, overlooking the Bow River. Enjoy a wide variety of dishes including charbroiled steaks, fish, and vegetarian options. Western barbecues, the family specialty, are available weekly featuring a hip of beef with all the trimmings and a roaring bonfire in the famed Donut Tent.
Entertainment: The lounge just off the dining room features a pool table, country music, piano, and TV. Hardwood floors, small bar, and stone fireplace make for a cozy atmosphere.
Summary: Brewster's Kananaskis Guest Ranch is a division of Brewster's Rocky Mountain Adventures, based in Banff. The ranch offers guests freedom to do whatever they want. There are no schedules—your time is your own. This is a very independent place where you can do as much or as little as you wish on an à la carte basis. Many stop over here on their way to Banff, Lake Louise, or Calgary. This family-run company offers a host of activities and tours in the Kananaskis, Banff, and Lake Louise areas. If you are planning a trip from the ranch to Banff and Jasper, these are the folks to talk to. Be sure to ask about their new hotel in Banff: Brewster Mountain Lodge. Groups and corporations should ask the Brewsters about their famous Donut Tent for barbecues. In 1998 the ranch celebrated its 75th anniversary.

Chilcotin Holidays Guest Ranch
Gold Bridge, British Columbia, Canada

SUPER, NATURAL BRITISH COLUMBIA®

Snowcapped mountains, 360-degree views of breathtaking scenery, crystal-clear water, alpine wildflowers, Douglas fir forest, bighorn sheep, moose, deer, mountain goats, grizzly, black bear, and even wolves. Here you'll follow game trails, cross rivers and glaciers, and enjoy some of the world's best views. Chilcotin Holidays is famous for its four-season customized wilderness adventures with guiding and outfitting rights to one of the largest territories in British Columbia, covering over 2,000 square miles. Kevan comes from a Cariboo-Chilcotin pioneer ranching family and Sylvia has a graduate degree in tourism and resource management. Together with an outstanding caliber of licensed guides and their sure-footed mountain Cayuse horses, they offer customized adventures and learning experiences in the great western Canadian wilderness. Whether you come for a leisurely vacation on the ranch or a wilderness trip into the high country, one thing is for certain—you will have an experience of a lifetime. Kevan and Sylvia will make sure that your group is well-matched according to similar interests, abilities, and even ages.

Address: Gun Creek Road, Gold Bridge, British Columbia, Canada V0K 1P0
Telephone: (250) 238-2274; fax: (250) 238-2274
E-Mail: chilcotin_holidays@bc.sympatico.ca
Internet: http://www.chilcotinholidays.com
Airport: Vancouver
Location: 4½ hours north of Vancouver, two hours north of Whistler Resort. Ask about their "Chilcotin Express" between the ranch and Vancouver.
Memberships: British Columbia Guest Ranchers' Association, Cariboo Tourism Association, B.C. Fishing Resort and Outfitters Association
Medical: Squamish Hospital, 1½-hour drive. Emergency helicopter available.
Conference: 18
Guest Capacity: 18
Accommodations: Surrounded by mountains and wilderness, the two-story ranch house looks to the Bendor Mountain Range and features fireplace, sunroom, and large central dining room. There are nine rooms with queen- or twin-beds, feather duvets, and shared baths. Daily maid service. The permanent alpine base camps have log and tent cabins with heaters and hot showers. All camps have radiotelephones.
Rates: $$. All-inclusive packages with guides from dawn to dusk and much more. Every detail is taken care of. Organizers who bring six or more guests come at no charge (i.e., families or groups).
Credit Cards: MasterCard. Traveler's checks and cash accepted.
Season: Year-round including holidays and special Christmas events
Activities: The Chilcotin Mountains are known for sunny skies and dry climate (a bug-free environment). The biodiversity of the area gives rise to an abundance of wildflowers that bloom May through September. While riding old Indian trails, you will have a chance to explore ancient seabeds studded with fossils. Remember, if you put your own group together, organizers that bring six or more guests come at no charge.
Children's Programs: Riding lessons, gold-panning, horse sports. Able children included with parents in all riding.
Dining: Healthy country cooking served family-style. Creative vegetarian dishes. Ask about the wonderful salmon Indian meal. Fresh fruit, vegetables, and lots of homemade fresh baking.
Entertainment: Campfires, biathlon target practice, bareback lessons, gymkhanas, horse logging and horseshoeing demonstrations; learn to pack a horse; visit mining towns, museums, and pioneer log cabins.
Summary: A wilderness adventure for all levels of enthusiasts! As Kevan and Sylvia say, "We give our guests five-star wilderness experiences." One of the truly great ranch-wilderness adventures in North America for small groups of six to eight. Larger groups by special arrangement. Seven distinct adventure packages—guest-ranch stays, wildlife-viewing pack trips, wilderness guide training, alpine fly-in fishing, wilderness hiking retreats, and mountain biking clinics. Winter: snowmobile and ski adventures. Whistler Ski Resort, two hours away.

Echo Valley Guest Ranch
Clinton, British Columbia, Canada

SUPER, NATURAL BRITISH COLUMBIA®

At Norm Dove's Echo Valley Guest Ranch you'll discover a great Canadian Wilderness paradise, with a colorful gold-rush past, that offers contrast, textures, wildlife and more simple delights with the abundance of nature. Located in historic ranch country, adjacent to the mighty Fraser River, Echo Valley Ranch Resort is one of North America's finest destinations for adventures in horseback riding, hiking, river rafting, and native culture. Norm Dove is one of the most incredible men I've ever met, with a passion for excellence and life second to none. As Norm says, "At Echo Valley, you'll find adventure, beauty, cleansing spring waters, and ranch-grown organic produce—fresh air unattainable in any urban center and night skies undimmed by city lights." Norm and Nan Dove blend Western tradition, modern comforts and quality. They say Echo Valley is "the best of everything in the great Canadian wilderness." And so it is!

Address: Echo Valley Ranch, P.O. Box 16 K, Clinton, Jesmond, British Columbia, Canada V0K1K0
Telephone: (800) 253-8831 (reservations), (250) 459-2386; fax: (250) 459-0086
E-Mail: evranch@uniserve.com
Internet: http://www.evranch.com
Airport: Private 3,900-foot grass airstrip at ranch or Kamloops for scheduled flights
Location: 270 miles north of Vancouver, 30 miles from Clinton, 100 miles from Kamloops
Memberships: British Columbia Guest Ranchers' Association, Cariboo Tourism Association, Vancouver Tourism Association, API
Medical: Ashcroft Hospital in Ashcroft
Conference: Up to 40; 650 square feet; audiovisual equipment available
Guest Capacity: Up to 40; groups of 20 or more can "book the ranch"
Accommodations: The Dove Lodge is of log construction with six guest bedrooms, all with private baths and spectacular views. All guests dine in Dove Lodge. Games room, sauna, and outdoor hot tub. The Lookout Lodge has nine large bedrooms with private baths. Seven of the bedrooms have outside balconies. Two cabins each have private bedroom, bathroom, sitting area with gas fireplace, loft and private deck. One log cabin with four-poster bed, fireplace, tastefully furnished sitting area, private deck with its own outdoor Jacuzzi hot tub. Spa: Two full-time aestheticians qualified to perform complete beauty and health-spa services.
Rates: • $$–$$$. American Plan. Ask about "Booking the Ranch" program.
Credit Cards: VISA; personal and traveler's checks accepted
Season: Year-round
Activities: The ranch offers a great selection of activities. They include—horseback riding; hiking; white-water rafting; overnight stays in tepees at the High Bar Indian Reserve; gold panning; bird-watching with resident naturalist, features falcon-training; and trout-fishing in prestine mountain lakes, air transportation is available if necessary. Thai and Western massage, facials, pedicure, manicure, available. Occasional cattle moving. Winter: cross-country skiing, snowshoeing, sleigh-riding, and ice-fishing, weather permitting.
Children's Programs: Adult-oriented with a minimum age requirement of 13 years. Exceptions apply if you "book the ranch." Great for family reunions.
Dining: Meals created by a professional chef. Hearty gourmet food prepared from fresh farm meat and vegetables. Buffet-style breakfast and lunch. Dinner served at the table. Complimentary beer and wine with dinner. Special diets accommodated.
Entertainment: Satellite TV, karaoke, sing-alongs, line dancing, billiards, shuffleboard, darts, board games, or feeding the animals. Check out the stars—at 3,650 feet with no light or air pollution, you will be astonished at how many stars you see!
Summary: Norm Dove is one of a kind—what a spirit and what a ranch! One guest summed it up, "Rarely have I seen a place look better than it does in its brochure, but it is the case with Echo Valley (and if you have seen their brochure, you know this is no small compliment!)" An incredible adventure and the best of everything in the great Canadian wilderness.

See color photos, pages 318–321.

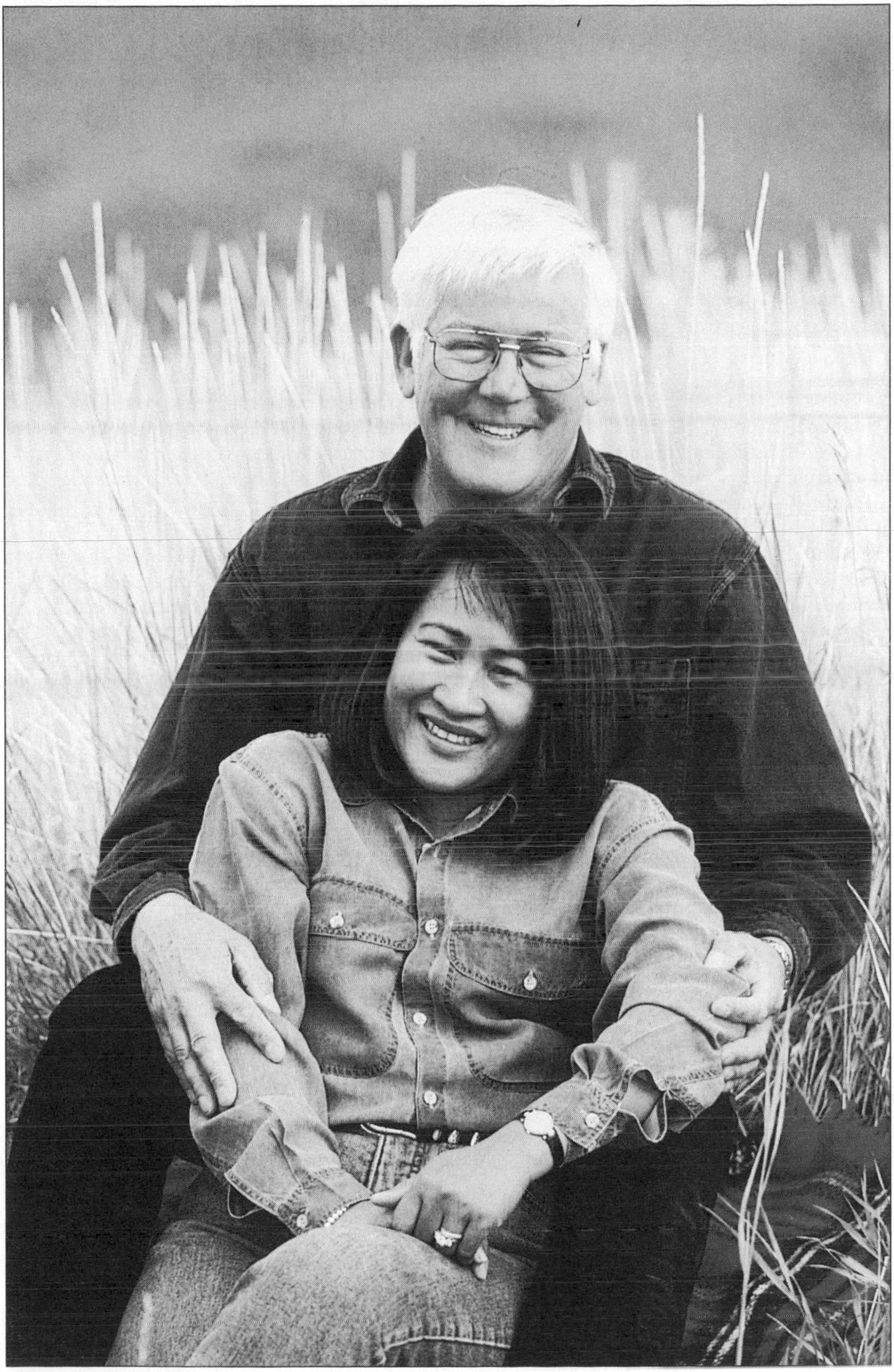

The Hills Health and Guest Ranch
108 Mile Ranch, British Columbia, Canada

SUPER, NATURAL BRITISH COLUMBIA®

In 1984, Pat and Juanita Corbett created the Hills Health and Guest Ranch. The Hills offers extensive indoor and outdoor wilderness programs and an adventure spa, in addition to comfort, independence, and a range of horseback activities. Here fitness, wellness, spa treatments, and guest ranching go hand in hand. At The Hills you may ride, hike, take a variety of fitness classes or be pampered with massages, facials, or herbal wraps.

Address: Box 26, 108 Mile Ranch, British Columbia, Canada V0K 2Z0
Telephone: (250) 791-5225; fax: (250) 791-6384
E-Mail: thehills@bcinternet.net
Internet: http://www.grt-net.com/thehills
Airport: Williams Lake via Vancouver Inter-National
Location: Eight miles north of 100 Mile House off Highway 97, 295 miles north of Vancouver
Memberships: British Columbia Guest Ranchers' Association, Cross-Country Division of the Canadian West Ski Areas Association, British Columbia Hotel Association, International Spa and Fitness Association
Medical: 100 Mile House, eight miles
Conference: 150; four separate meeting rooms
Guest Capacity: 150
Accommodations: The Hills is perched on one of the Cariboo hilltops. As you drive up you encounter three ranch lodge structures. Around the bend on either side of the ridge are 20 A-frame, two-level modern chalets, with kitchens and two decks. These comfortable chalets are on either side of a road, with the "sunrise" cabins on the left and the "sunset" cabins on the right. Each cabin looks out over Cariboo ranch country. Also 26 lodge rooms. You may rent a chalet and cook your own meals or take part in the full American plan. Laundry service available.
Rates: • $\$\$$–$\$\$\$$. American Plan and Bed and Breakfast Plan. Many packages available, including spa-wellness package. Children's and group rates. No minimum stay.
Credit Cards: VISA, MasterCard, American Express
Season: Year-round, open all holidays
Activities: A combination of spa, horseback riding, and hiking are the main activities in the summer. Half-day horseback riding with cowboy breakfast served at Willy's Wigwam. One- to two-hour and all-day "mountaintop" rides with lunch. Indoor 20-by-40-foot heated pool, two Jacuzzis, and two saunas open to public members as well as guests. Daily programs include aerobics, weights, massage, facials, wraps, waxing, reflexology, and wellness workshops. Superb fitness, nutritional, and kinesiology counselors on staff. Fishing at nearby lakes for rainbow, Eastern brook, and lake trout. Guided hiking. PGA par-72 golf course and five tennis courts nearby. Winter: Cross-country skiing, downhill skiing and snowboard park, snow tubing, skating rink, snowmaking, dogsledding, and ski shops.
Children's Programs: Children of all ages are welcome and are parents' responsibility. In winter, kids' ski school. Baby-sitting available.
Dining: The Hills' fine restaurant, Trail's End, is overseen by member chefs of the Canadian Federation of Chefs de Cuisine, featuring traditional ranch food, low-fat spa cuisine, and weekly outdoor barbecues.
Entertainment: Wellness workshops, horse-drawn hayrides, two TVs in each chalet, singalongs in Willy's Wigwam (a tepee in the woods), some of Canada's best live country music in dining room three nights with wonderful local singer Bob Dalrymple. Line dancing.
Summary: Voted by industry peers and sponsored by *Spa Management Magazine* International Specialty Spa of the year 1993, 1995, 1996, and 1997. Guest ranch and spa combination makes The Hills very unique in North America. An affordable family guest ranch as well as an affordable award-winning adventure spa. Wonderful musical entertainment. Numerous lakes, historic gold mining, Cariboo Trail, Williams Lake Stampede Fourth of July, Anaheim Lake Stampede in early July. French and German spoken.

Homeplace Guest Ranch
Priddis, Alberta, Canada

THE DUDE RANCHERS' ASSOCIATION

The Homeplace Ranch is a small, year-round, very personable guest ranch in the Canadian Rocky Mountain foothills, 30 miles southwest of Calgary. The ranch is bordered by several beautiful ranches and the Kananaskis Forest Reserve. Mac Makenny, his wife, Jayne, and their daughter, Jessi, offer guests a way of life for which southern Alberta is known. As Mac says, "We really enjoy folks who appreciate and respect horses and want a hands-on experience!" Guests come to share the traditions, heritage, recreation, and natural beauty that constitute this unique lifestyle. There is seasonal wildlife and native mountain flowers. Camera buffs and artists ought to bring their gear. At Homeplace the staff–guest ratio is high, as is the horse-to-guest ratio. The Makenny family welcomes you to their home and makes every effort to see that you are well looked after. If you are from another country, Mac may raise your flag to welcome you.

Address: Site 2, Box 6, RR1, Dept. K, Priddis, Alberta, Canada T0L 1W0
Telephone: (877) 931-3245, (403) 931-3245; fax: (403) 931-3245
E-Mail: homeplace@cadvision.com
Internet: http://www.cadvision.com/homeplace-ranch/
Airport: Calgary
Location: 30 miles west of Calgary off Route 22, 50 miles east of Banff off Route 22
Memberships: The Dude Ranchers' Association, Alberta Outfitters Association, Travel Alberta, Convention and Calgary/Visitors Bureau
Medical: Foothills Hospital in Calgary, 30 miles
Conference: 12, winter only; Alberta barbecue for 150
Guest Capacity: 14
Accommodations: Guests are comfortable staying in the lodge's eight small private rooms. All rooms are finished in cedar. Guest bedrooms are on both levels of the two-story lodge. All have private baths, some with twin futon beds, others with four-posters. Decks off main lodge. A hot tub is outside on the back lower deck of the lodge. There's also a one-bedroom, 1912 log cabin about 200 yards away, shower and bath in main lodge. This is a great place for couples and honeymooners.
Rates: • $$. Full American Plan. Rates vary depending on the season. Ask about the three-, four-, and seven-day packages, particularly the Rocky Mountain Ranch Rodeo Holiday. Three-day minimum.
Credit Cards: VISA. Personal checks preferred.
Season: Year-round, open all holidays
Activities: Very hands-on horse/guest program. Guests may groom their horses. Excellent horses, from gentle to spirited polo ponies for really advanced riders. Wonderful all-day and half-day rides. Ask about the Hog-Back, Kananaskis, and Fish Creek Run rides, and the Homeplace Cow Camp. Weekly, Mac takes guests down to the neighboring Harvey Ranch to check on their cattle—some cattle-moving. Pack trips, riding instruction available (many come from Calgary for daily instruction in the off-season), fishing, and hiking. Golf and tennis nearby. Winter: cross-country skiing, sleigh rides, and dogsledding.
Children's Programs: No planned program. Children over age seven may ride. Mac usually takes the kids aside and asks them about their riding desires, and he sure does hear some exciting stuff. As Mac says, "Kids tell it like it is!" Daughter Jessi welcomes all kids.
Dining: There is lots of homemade everything here, from applesauce muffins to fresh blackberry pie and big beef barbecues. Vegetarian meals prepared on request. Beer is always in the refrigerator. BYOL.
Entertainment: Nothing formal is planned. Occasional hay-wagon rides, dances, and exhibition polo in Calgary.
Summary: Very small and intimate guest ranch run by the Makenny family. Warm hospitality. Great for people who really appreciate or want to learn about horses. Your horse is yours for the week! Ask Mac about Spruce Meadows, the Bar U Historic Ride, and the cow camp. Near Calgary. Branding weekends end of May, Calgary Stampede early July. Polo three times a week, June to September. Nature-from-the-Saddle workshops.

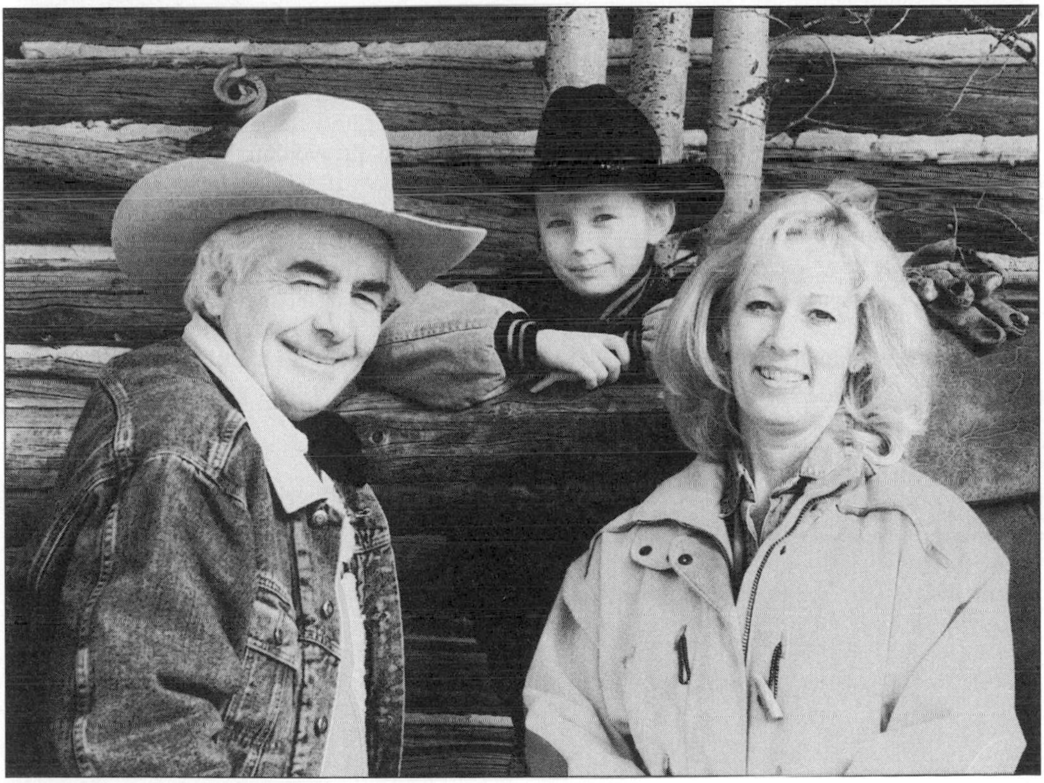

Springhouse Trails Ranch
Williams Lake, British Columbia, Canada

SUPER, NATURAL BRITISH COLUMBIA®

Springhouse Trails Ranch is the home of Werner and Susi Moessner, two very kind and friendly people who moved to British Columbia from Stuttgart in 1978. Werner grew up on a farm. As a young man he started a construction firm, which is still run by his son. In the late 1970s, the Moessners flew to British Columbia, rented an RV, and began looking at ranches. They found Springhouse Trails, and Werner spent two years rebuilding the ranch. In 1980, they received their first guests. Today the ranch is run with the help of the Moessner's daughter, Eve, her husband, Herbert, and their young daughter, Sabrina. At 3,000 feet, the property overlooks a small lake, grass-covered rolling hills, and open meadows. They grow many of their own vegetables and serve fresh eggs from their 30-plus chickens. At Springhouse Trails they pretty much let you do as you please. Many of the guests are Europeans who enjoy the fact that the Moessners are bilingual. In fact, they like it so much, they stay for three to six weeks at a time. In traditional German fashion, the property and accommodations are immaculate, the food hearty, and yes, they serve great German beer, too.

Address: Box 2 K, Springhouse Trails R.R. 1, Williams Lake, British Columbia, Canada V2G 2P1
Telephone: (250) 392-4780; fax: (250) 392-4701
E-Mail: springhouse@skybridge.bc.ca
Internet: http:/skybridge.bc.ca/springhouse
Airport: Williams Lake via Vancouver International; private planes to Springhouse airport
Location: 11 miles southwest of Williams Lake on Dog Creek Road, six hours northeast of Vancouver by car
Memberships: Cariboo Tourist Association
Medical: Williams Lake Hospital
Guest Capacity: 42
Accommodations: Guests stay in four log cabins with full kitchens and two large, one-story complexes. One is a dorm building that has a common hallway with eight rooms and two end apartments with full kitchen facilities for those making extended visits. The second building has individual units with separate entrances. Daily maid service. Also available are 12 RV hook-ups, with shower and laundry facilities.
Rates: • $–$$. American Plan. European Plan, RV, tenting, children's rates, and five-day packages available. No minimum stay.
Credit Cards: VISA, MasterCard
Season: May to September
Activities: Informal program. Ride, hike, walk, canoe, or just relax as you wish. All guests ride with a wrangler or other guests. Guided riding is available. Werner and Herbert assign horses according to riders' abilities, with hour rides, all-day picnic rides, and night rides. Ask about river rafting.
Children's Programs: No children's programs, but kids are welcome. If a two-year-old wants to sit on a horse or can ride, Werner will put him or her on a horse. Kids' playground and trampoline. Baby-sitting available.
Dining: The ranch has a large, separate, fully licensed restaurant with views and a fireplace in the center. Hearty ranch food, including favorites such as German schnitzel and barbecues twice a week. Excellent German beer. Wine (mostly Canadian) and liquor are served. Special coffees (Spanish, Swiss, Irish, Monte Cristo, and Rudesheimer iced coffee). Full bar.
Entertainment: Nothing formal. Guests usually make their own.
Summary: Lovely, small, easygoing, family-owned and -operated guest ranch surrounded by trees, overlooking meadow and pond. German hosts with a good many European guests. Many guests stay three weeks and longer. Ask about the bird sanctuary. RV hook-ups. Nearby: Indian arts and crafts, Indian rodeos, Williams Lake Rodeo, tennis, golf and mini-golf for the kids.

Three Bars Ranch
Cranbrook, British Columbia, Canada

THE DUDE RANCHERS' ASSOCIATION

SUPER, NATURAL BRITISH COLUMBIA®

When it comes to deluxe guest-ranching, the Three Bars Cattle and Guest Ranch is at the top. This magnificent ranch couples old guest- and cattle-ranch tradition with deluxe, modern-day comforts you would expect from a resort hideaway. The Old West charm has been carefully crafted with log architecture. The hospitality is under the direction of Jeff and April Beckley, a young couple who grew up in the cattle- and guest-ranch business. When they say the welcome mat is out and the coffee pot is on, they mean it!

Address: S.S. 3, Site 19-62 K, Cranbrook, British Columbia, Canada V1C 6H3
Telephone: (250) 426-5230, (877) 426-5230; fax: (250) 426-8240
E-Mail: threebarsranch@cyberlink.bc.ca
Internet: http://www.threebarsranch.com
Airport: International airports in Calgary, Edmonton, and Vancouver link regular scheduled flights to Cranbrook.
Location: Six miles north of Cranbrook off Highway 95A in southeastern British Columbia
Memberships: The Dude Ranchers' Association, British Columbia Guest Ranchers' Association
Medical: Cranbrook Regional Hospital, nine miles
Conference: 40
Guest Capacity: 40
Accommodations: 10 hand-hewn log duplex cabins provide 20 units. Three of the duplexes are adjoining for families. Each unit has one queen or two double beds, private full bath, handmade furniture, hardwood floor adorned with Navajo-pattern rugs, porches, and gardens all set within a landscaped yard and connected by wooden boardwalks. In the ranch's 5,000-square-foot log lodge are the dining room, fireplace lounge, library, and bar, complete with pool table and conference room.
Rate: • $$$. Full American Plan. Children's and group rates. Three-night minimum stay May to October. No minimum stay in winter.
Credit Cards: VISA, MasterCard
Season: May through September riding program; October through May conferences and groups. Christmas ranch program.

Activities: Three Bars offers a host of summer, fall, and winter activities. Jeff is a professional reining horse trainer. Consequently there is a tremendous amount of emphasis on and opportunities for horsemanship, instruction, and personal improvement at all levels. Guests are invited to join the cattle drives or ride with the cowboys to check on the ranch's cattle herd when work is being done. This doesn't happen every day or every week; ask April about the schedule. Progressive trail-riding program. Morning, afternoon, and two all-day rides each week. Guided hikes into the mountains.

Fly-fishing on the St. Mary's River—catch-and-release only. Guide service available on request (extra). Weekly river float trips (July and August). The tennis court, indoor heated swimming pool, outdoor Jacuzzi, horseshoe pit, children's play area, petting zoo, mountain bikes, and archery available.
Children's Programs: Children's riding program begins at age six. Kids are looked after only when they're horseback riding. Kids under age six don't ride. Parents are responsible for kids when they're not riding. Baby-sitting available.
Dining: Cocktails and appetizers before dinner. Wonderful ranch cooking with Western flair. Saturday night farewell barbecue. Special diets easily accommodated.
Entertainment: Something planned each evening, including trading anecdotes on the day's riding activities in the "old-time" saloon while shooting a game of pool, or relaxing around the fireplace. Staff/guest volleyball, weekly Fort Steele Theatre, casino night, archery, fly-casting lessons, and cowboy music.
Summary: Three Bars Guest Ranch is a top gun! Deluxe Western accommodations coupled with full guest- and cattle-ranch activities. Superb professional reining horse instruction and horsemanship, cattle-penning, and 11,000-square-foot indoor riding arena. Beautiful lodge, and indoor heated swimming pool. Historic Fort Steele 30 minutes away—a must! Delicious seasonal raspberries. Horsemanship clinics. Video available on request.

See color photos, page 317.

Wild Rose Ranch

Kimberley, British Columbia, Canada

THE DUDE RANCHERS' ASSOCIATION

SUPER, NATURAL BRITISH COLUMBIA®

Wild Rose Ranch is situated in the heart of British Columbia's Kootenay region, famous for spectacular mountain scenery and broad river valleys. In 1993 Barry Rogers and Shannon Langley, both with extensive outdoor and recreation careers in Canada, discovered their private paradise tucked in a valley along Wolf Creek at the base of 7,000-foot Teepee Mountain. Today, along with their five-year-old son, Nikolas, they offer a guest ranch experience that reflects their love and understanding of the great outdoors and their appreciation for the heritage of Western Canada. Cattle, horses, magnificent river overlooks, open grasslands, and pine forests capture the Wild Rose Ranch experience. As Shannon says, "Because we take only 12 guests at a time, we are able to share our appreciation and desire to help folks worldwide understand the precious resources and natural beauty in this part of Canada." Those who want an intimate experience, personal family attention, and a program designed for adults and older children will cherish the Wild Rose Ranch adventure.

Address: P.O. Box 181 K, Kimberley, British Columbia, Canada V1A 2Y6
Telephone: (800) 324-6188 (U.S. and Canada), (250) 422-3403; fax: (250) 422-3149
E-Mail: wildrose@cyberlink.bc.ca.
Internet: www.ranchweb.com/wildrose
Airport: Cranbrook and Vancouver, Calgary, or Spokane
Location: 30 miles north of Kimberley; 30 miles north of Cranbrook and 163 miles west of Banff; 209 miles north of Spokane
Memberships: British Columbia Guest Ranchers' Association, British Columbia Fresh Water Resorts and Outfitters Association, The Dude Ranchers' Association
Medical: Cranbrook Hospital, 30 miles
Guest Capacity: 12
Accommodations: Three rooms in the main lodge, which houses six people. A newly constructed duplex cedar log cabin, with two suites, houses six guests as well. All rooms have private baths, with queen- or queen/single-bed combinations. Both the deck of the main lodge and the veranda of the cabin look out to Teepee Mountain and Wolf Creek.
Rates: $$–$$$. American Plan. Rates very with dates and length of stay.
Credit Cards: VISA, MasterCard
Season: May to November
Activities: The ranch lies on the "warm, sunny side of the Canadian Rockies" adjacent to Premier Ridge, a protected wintering ground for elk, deer, and bighorn sheep. The ranch offers a relaxed, personalized vacation that features a variety of activities in a region often referred to as the "Serengeti of North America." In addition to riding, canoeing, or white-water rafting, special programs are offered for wildlife-viewing/bird-watching and nature photography. On warm summer afternoons, many cool off with a dip in Wasa Lake (five miles away). Fly-fishermen test their mettle against "west slope" cutthroat trout.
Children's Programs: No organized children's programs. Children are the responsibility of their parents at all times. Children under age 12 have limited riding. Children under age eight ride in the pastures with supervision. All children (age 12 and under) must wear a helmet.
Dining: Home-cooked meals using fresh garden vegetables and fruit in season. Count on a Saturday night barbecue. Special requests are welcome. If you have a specialty dish that you love to share with others, you may become a "celebrity chef." Daily adventures are shared around the cocktail table before dinner. Wine is served with dinner.
Entertainment: Evening campfires, local rodeos, Fort Steele Historic Park, local entertainment.
Summary: Small ranch with warm hospitality and spectacular views to Teepee Mountain. Horseback riding on 7,230 acres, and all-day fly-fishing trips to streams, rivers, and lakes within a 40-mile radius. Most come for a five-night stay. Best for older families, couples, and singles who are looking for a family adult atmosphere. Ask about Premier Ridge designated wildlife viewing area. Nearby: Fort Steele.

Top of the World Guest Ranch
Fort Steele, British Columbia, Canada

SUPER, NATURAL BRITISH COLUMBIA®

Top of the World Ranch has been in the guest ranching and cattle business for many years. In 1995 the Sadler family became the proud new owners and brought their lifelong love for the West and their tireless enthusiasm to one of Canada's most successful guest ranches. Today, the 40,000-acre ranch offers Canadians, Americans, and a good number of Europeans the opportunity to ride, hike, and mountain bike in the spectacular Canadian Rockies. Many particularly enjoy the ranch's proximity to white-water rafting and historic Fort Steele, one of the most fascinating completely restored fort towns in North America. Top of the World offers families, couples, and singles exposure to nature, the mountains, horseback riding, a wholesome environment, and a well-rounded holiday.

Address: Box 29 K, Fort Steele, British Columbia, Canada V0B 1N0
Telephone: (888) 996-6306, (250) 426-6306; fax: (250) 426-6377
E-Mail: tow@cyberlink.bc.ca
Internet: http://www.cyberlink.bc.ca/~tow
Airport: Cranbrook, via Calgary or Vancouver, complimentary pickup
Location: 16 miles north of Cranbrook off Highway 93/95, 135 miles south of Banff, 200 miles southwest of Calgary, 180 miles north of Spokane
Memberships: British Columbia Guest Ranchers' Association
Medical: Cranbrook Hospital, 16 miles
Conference: 35, October through March
Guest Capacity: 35
Accommodations: The complete lodge, upstairs guests rooms, and cabins were totally renovated in 1996. They feature log furniture in guest rooms and cabins, leather furniture with hand-carved tables in the lodge. All rooms have private baths. Each of the log cabins has a covered porch with log rocking chairs and tables. The main lodge has large decks where guests relax, enjoy the beautiful views, lounge in the brand new 10-person hot tub, or watch the many hummingbirds.
Rates: $$. Full American Plan. Children's, large family, and group discounts. May to October. three-, four- and seven-night packages. Ask about both ranch and the new multisport packages.
Credit Cards: VISA, MasterCard. Personal checks preferred.
Season: May through October
Activities: Riding is the main focus for the ranch package. They offer both trail and open riding. Morning, afternoon, and all-day rides offer incredible views of the Purcells and Canadian Rockies. The ranch has a 400- to 500-head cattle operation as well, and offers cattle-work opportunities. Riding, hiking, mountain biking, and nearby white-water rafting are the main ranch activities. Of the property's many lakes, Loon Lake is a favorite for canoes and rowboats. Some like to swim in Lake Wasa, five miles away. Several golf courses are nearby. Ask about the new multisport package which includes five activities. Guests are treated to a theatrical performance at historic Fort Steele during its season.
Children's Programs: There is a wonderful play area with a complete playground, children's wrangler, and activity director. Kids age six and older may trail ride. Baby-sitting available upon request.
Dining: T-bone steak barbecue every Friday night, roast turkey, grilled salmon, and eggs benedict are just a few of the ranch specialties, along with a good variety of vegetables, fruits, and homemade breads. Special diets catered to with advance notice. Wine and beer available.
Entertainment: Occasional pony chuck-wagon races, barrel racing and rodeos in nearby towns, piano in lodge, sing-alongs, recreation room with pool table, Foosball, shuffleboard, and darts. Outside games include volleyball, croquet, badminton, horseshoes. Once-a-week trip to the Wild Horse Theater in Fort Steele Heritage Town included in weekly package during theater season.
Summary: Riding, big Canadian Rocky Mountain views, and wholesome family atmosphere. Special kids' rates! Guest ranch/working cattle ranch on 40,000 acres. Program allows for exciting day trips like white-water rafting and visiting historic Fort Steele (a must!). Guests come from United States, Canada, and Europe.

See color photos, pages 322–323.

Fly-Fishing Ranches
in the United States and Canada

Introduction

This fly-fishing chapter was designed for the novice as well as the expert angler. If you've never had a fly rod in your hands, don't worry about it. Many of the people who visit these lodges are just like you. They've dreamed about fly-fishing but for one reason or another have never taken the time to try it. Others may be intermediate-to-expert anglers. Regardless of your level of skill or aptitude, you'll have a fun and exciting time. Those who are experts will be challenged. The ranches and lodges listed here are doing what they do for one reason: they love to fish. They're running their operations for you and will do everything possible (within reason, of course) to ensure that your time with them is as pleasurable as it is exhilarating.

Fly-fishing is booming. If you doubt my words, look at the major outdoor wear/sporting goods companies and mail-order catalogs. You'll see complete sections, sometimes entire catalogs, devoted to water, fish, and all the exciting equipment that goes with them. Fly-fishing, like golf, has become a very exacting sport, and to become an expert takes a tremendous amount of skill, patience, and dedication. Those unfamiliar with the sport might wonder why anyone would put on a pair of waders that come up to your Adam's apple and stand in the middle of a cold, whirling stream whipping a long, colored line through the air. But people around the world have found that once they try it, they're likely to get hooked. Besides the marvelous array of equipment and the thrill of hooking and landing a trophy-size (or even a small) fish, fly-fishing offers men, women, and children a chance to get out into nature and away from the pressures of daily living. Realizing the demand for quality fly-fishing retreats where people can receive guidance and instruction, not to mention camaraderie, I've included some of the top fly-fishing lodges in the United States. While many of the ranches in this guide offer fly-fishing and are located on or near superb trout waters, this chapter is also devoted to those that offer instruction and guide service.

In selecting a facility, you must first decide where in North America you would like to go. Read the descriptions and write or call for a brochure. As with all ranches in this guide, remember that each is unique and represents the personality of the host. Ask for references and find out if the level of instruction is sufficient to help you achieve your expectations.

Even though it's an exacting sport, the basics of fly-fishing are not difficult to master. A tremendous amount of information is available in books and videos. I strongly recommend that you contact a fly-fishing school before embarking on a fly-fishing vacation. Most of the sport's leading instructors would agree that if you can master, or at least become familiar with, the techniques of fly-casting before you leave, your overall experience will be much more enjoyable and fulfilling. The easiest way to find out about these schools is to contact your local fly-fishing store/outfitter.

Before buying any equipment, check with the lodge to see what you'll need to bring. Many have their own shops and can take care of most of your needs. Don't be afraid to ask questions. The more you learn about this sport, the more fun you'll have.

Colorado Trails Ranch
Durango, Colorado

THE DUDE RANCHERS' ASSOCIATION

CDGRA

Since 1960 Colorado Trails Ranch has been known for its outstanding horse program. It is now proud to add a comprehensive fly-fishing program of equal quality to the long-established riding program. With professional guides on staff, a well-stocked tackle shop and four miles of private water, Colorado Trails Ranch is a fisherman's paradise. During the summer the ranch offers an excellent family-oriented program. This enables the fishing enthusiast to enjoy his/her sport while the other members of the family enjoy participating in their favorite ranch activities. The fishing opportunities begin in June and are at their peak during the months of September and October, a glorious time to be in the Rockies. Colorado Trails Ranch boasts a wide range of fishing experiences, from stocked ponds where beginners gain confidence in casting techniques to the wide-open freestoners of the Florida and Piedra Rivers. There is something for all levels of experience. For the avid angler, the ranch even offers float and wade trips on the world-famous San Juan River.

Address: 12161 County Road 240, Durango, Colorado 81301
Telephone: (800) 323-3833, (970) 247-5055; fax: (970) 385-7372
E-Mail: CoTRanch@aol.com
Internet: http://www.colotrails.com
Airport: La Plata County, 18 miles from ranch
Location: 12 miles northeast of Durango on County Road 240; 200 miles north of Albuquerque; 350 miles southwest of Denver
Memberships: Trout Unlimited, The Dude Ranchers' Association, Colorado Dude and Guest Ranch Association, American Quarter Horse Association, American Humane Association, American Riding Instructions Association
Awards: *Family Circle* 1990 and 1991 Family Resort of the Year, 1988 American Humane Association's outstanding service in the field of humane education (Rosemary Ames Award)
Medical: Mercy Medical Center, Durango
Conference: 60, three different room setups, 4,800-square-feet
Guest Capacity: 65 (33 rooms)
Accommodations: Guests can stay in four types of comfortably furnished cabins. All rooms have private bathrooms, carpeting, electric baseboard heat, and porches. Laundry facilities available.
Rates: $$$. All-inclusive American Plan. Family, off-season and nanny rates.
Credit Cards: VISA, MasterCard, American Express, Discover, Diners Club
Season: Late May to October; conferences: mid-May, late September and October
Activities: Full guest-ranch activities as highlighted in Guest Ranch portion of book. Fly-fishing program includes two ponds and a mile of challenging mountain stream on the ranch. Private Florida River fishing sites are available within a four-mile radius of the ranch. Private Piedra River fishing is 30 minutes from the ranch, and the San Juan River is an hour away for world-class float and wade excursions. Colorado fishing licenses available at the ranch. Ask about special fall fly-fishing clinics.
Children's Programs: Full ranch program for kids and teens. Fly-fishing instruction available for older children who enjoy or seriously want to learn to fly-fish.
Dining: The dining room overlooks scenic Shearer Creek Valley and Eagle Ridge. Hearty ranch food and plenty of it. No bar. Drinking permitted in cabins only.
Entertainment: A program every evening, hayrides, cookouts, ice-cream socials, dances; professional rodeos and melodrama in Durango.
Summary: One of the leading guest ranches in America. Outstanding ranch for families, children, and teens with an extensive kids' program. Caring and personable staff. Full Western riding and fly-fishing programs. Ask about adults-only weeks, family reunions, and the exciting trip to Mesa Verde Indian Cliff Dwellings. Nearby: the famous Durango–Silverton Narrow Gauge train.

See color photos, pages 186–187.

Big Hole River Outfitters
Wise River, Montana

Craig Fellin may not tell you this, but his operation is considered one of the finest in North America. Craig is modest in his demeanor, soft-spoken, and very low-key. He is, in fact, a giant in his knowledge and fly-fishing expertise. What makes his operation unique is the size, personal attention, superb guides, and proximity to diverse unpressured fishery waters in southwestern Montana. In 1983, Craig set about finding a wilderness setting that would offer discriminating guests a superb fishing vacation as well as an enriching experience savoring the beauty and splendor of the American West. And that's exactly what he did. In addition to being near some of Montana's great trout-fishing waters, his lodge is in the heart of Montana's ranch country and close to one of the most historic Indian battlefields. Craig's philosophy is simple: "Take only 10 guests and give them one of the greatest fishing experiences of their life." And that's exactly what he does! Big Hole River Outfitters offers great fishing, genuine Western camaraderie, hearty laughter, and fun for all. Fellin's outfit is first-class.

Address: c/o Frontiers International Travel, P.O. Box 959, Wexford, Pennsylvania 15090
Telephone: (800) 245-1950, (724) 935-1577, (406) 832-3252 (ranch); fax: (724) 935-5388
E-Mail: mikejr@frontierstrvl.com
Airport: Butte via Salt Lake City or Bozeman
Location: Wise River, 50 miles southwest of Butte in southwestern Montana
Memberships: Montana Trout Foundation, Trout Unlimited, Fishing Outfitters of Montana, Big Hole Foundation, Big Hole and Beaverhead Outfitters & Guides Association
Medical: St. James Hospital, Butte
Guest Capacity: 10
Accommodations: Large cedar cabin with two bedrooms, a duplex cabin, or a two-bedroom log cabin along the Wise River. All have electric heat and private bathrooms with shower and bathtubs. Two of the cabins have woodstoves, kitchens, living rooms, and open, screened porches.
Rates: • $$$$$. American Plan. Six-night and five-day packages only. Saturday to Friday.
Credit Cards: VISA, MasterCard. Personal checks accepted.
Season: Early June to mid-October
Activities: The fly-fishing program is tailored to guests' level of experience. Personal, patient instruction for beginners is one of Craig's specialties. Here beginners will learn, have fun, and catch fish. Advanced anglers will have the opportunity to cast over trophy fish. One guide to a maximum of two guests. Guided float or wading trips on the Big Hole, Beaverhead, and Wise Rivers. Be sure to ask Craig about his private-water trophy trout-fishing opportunities. Other accessible rivers include the Upper Clark Fork, Jefferson, and Deep Creek, as well as other well-kept-secret streams. Horseback trips to a mountain lake can be arranged by a local outfitter. Rental equipment available on a limited basis; however, Craig has a very well-stocked fly shop with Winston rods. On those days you don't care to fish, your fishing guide can take you on a wonderful sightseeing trip. A trained naturalist is also available for picnic-lunch hikes. Golfers will appreciate the new championship "Old Works" Jack Nicklaus golf course nearby.
Children's Programs: Craig encourages teens to learn about fly-fishing. Ask Craig about his special father/son and father/daughter weeks.
Dining: Country family-style meals. Lunches are served streamside with cloth napkins and tablecloths. Happy hour before dinner. Fine dining by candlelight with soft music in the lodge. Wines served with dinner.
Entertainment: After a relaxing dinner, guests are pleasantly tired and ready to drift off to sleep.
Summary: Fly-fishing just doesn't get any better than the Craig Fellin experience! Wonderful scenery; sincere, caring, personalized hospitality and service. Only 10 guests. Craig has been featured on the *Today Show*, ESPN's *Fly-Fishing the World*, and in *Condé Nast Traveler*. Ask about special novice and family weeks.

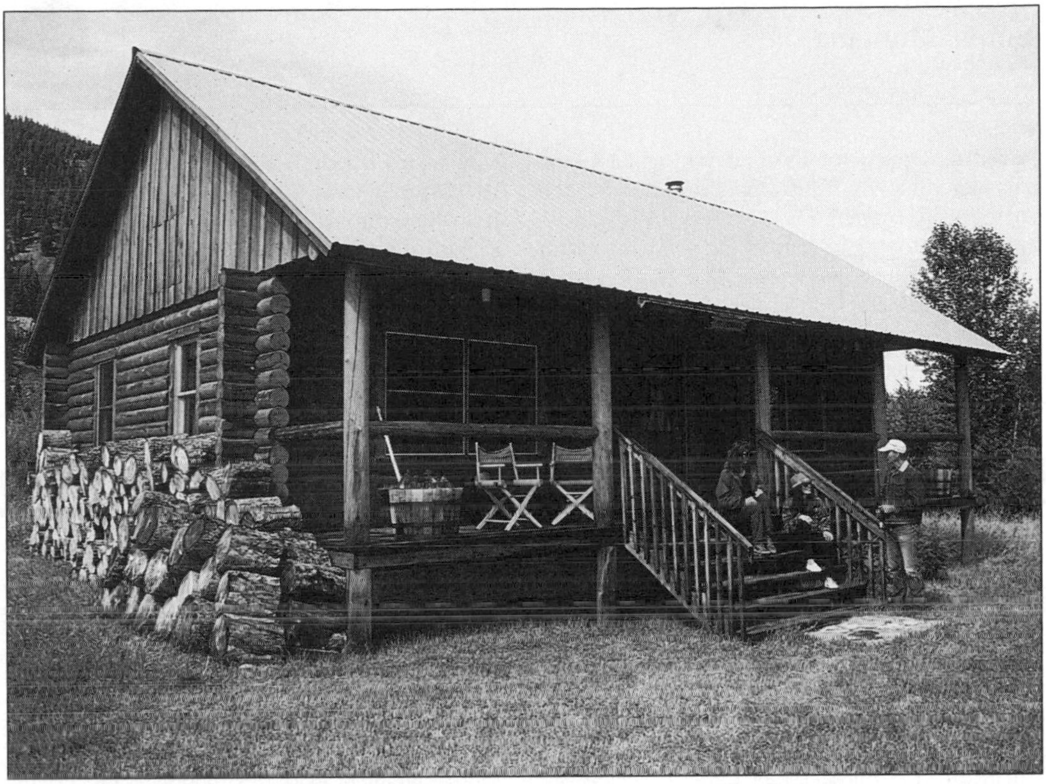

Diamond J Ranch
Ennis, Montana

THE DUDE RANCHERS' ASSOCIATION

World-renowned for its trout fishing, Montana has incredible fly-fishing opportunities for the adventurous angler. The Madison River Valley's famous Diamond J Ranch is surrounded (within a 70-mile radius) with seven Blue Ribbon trout rivers, spring creeks, the Bear Trap Wilderness Area, and numerous high-mountain lakes. What makes the Diamond J Ranch fly-fishing experience so special is that it not only caters to experienced and novice anglers, but also provides a wonderful environment for non-anglers with a host of outdoor activities from June to October. This marvelous Orvis-endorsed ranch has been in operation since 1930 and is run today by owners Peter, Jinny, and Tim Combs.

Address: P.O. Box 577 K, Ennis, Montana 59729
Telephone: (406) 682-4867; fax: (406) 682-4106
E-Mail: totalmgt@3rivers.net
Internet: http://www.ranchweb.com/diamondj
Airport: Bozeman
Location: 14 miles east of Ennis off Highway 287, 60 miles south of Bozeman
Memberships: The Dude Ranchers' Association
Awards: Orvis-endorsed Fly-Fishing and Wing Shooting Lodge
Medical: Ennis Hospital, 14 miles
Conference: 36 (June, September, October)
Guest Capacity: 36
Accommodations: 10 cozy log cabins, each with hardwood floors, a rock fireplace, and hickory furniture and beds. Each has a full bath with separate shower stalls and a cast-iron tub. Cabins have writing desks and porches.
Rates: • $$$–$$$$$$. American Plan. Call for fly-fishing and wing-shooting packages.
Credit Cards: VISA, MasterCard, American Express
Season: June through October
Activities: The ranch is in the Madison River valley and very close to its crown jewel, the Madison River. Many take side trips to fish the Beaverhead, Big Hole, Missouri, Jefferson, Gallatin, and Yellowstone Park waters (Firehole and Gibbon). The ranch has its own little stream (called Jack Ass Creek) and private, two-acre Jinny Lake. Be sure to ask about Bear Trap Wilderness white-water trophy-trout trips. Most fishing takes place from June through November with wet flies and salmon fly hatches in June. Dry-fly–fishing July and August and streamer fishing for spawning browns in September. Available trips include wading, floating, and belly tubes on Ennis, Quake, and Hebgen Lakes and on mountain lakes, rivers, and springs. Full guide service available. Usually one guide per two guests. Full Orvis tackle shop in Ennis. All trips are tailored individually to each guest. Non-fishing members of the family will enjoy full horseback riding, tennis, swimming, hot tub spa, scenic float trips, and hiking. Do as much or as little as you wish. Bird-hunters: be sure to talk with the ranch about their superb wing-shooting program. Wild birds include Hungarian and chukar partridge, pheasant, mountain grouse, ducks, and geese.
Children's Programs: No set program. Kids can spin-fish or fly-fish, depending on their age. Kiddie wrangler with instruction. Kids usually ride together. Baby-sitting available upon request.
Dining: Barbecue and sack lunches on shore for all those who fish. Anglers on overnight float trips get to experience the log "chalet." Back at the ranch, family-style hearty dining in three (they prefer no smoking) dining rooms. BYOB happy hour.
Entertainment: Informal evening programs. Campfires, sing-alongs, naturalist talks and a great library. The Combses subscribe to the best-seller list.
Summary: Orvis-endorsed fly-fishing and wing-shooting ranch for all levels of experience—the young and the young-at-heart. Excellent also for those who like to ride, hike, relax, and enjoy the family environment. Fishing opportunities include Blue Ribbon rivers, high-mountain lakes, and the Bear Trap Wilderness white-water trophy-trout expedition. Superb upland bird and waterfowl hunting on 30,000-acre ranch. See summer writeup in main section of book.

See color photos, pages 242–243.

Lone Mountain Ranch
Big Sky, Montana

Montana
Dude
Ranch
Association

Lone Mountain Ranch is one of the great year-round guest ranches in North America. Besides offering wonderful summer and winter programs, the ranch also specializes in a superb fishing program for those who wish to learn the art, the science, and more about the fun of fly-fishing. Under the direction of Gary Lewis (a native Montanan who has been fishing for as long as he can remember) and his talented staff, Lone Mountain offers one of the only year-round fly-fishing programs. As Gary says, "We encourage people to have fun when fly-fishing. Our program is not about catching big fish and lots of fish, it's really showing all ages the total fly-fishing experience with a strong teaching emphasis. We encourage children 12 years and older to come along with adults and enjoy our streams and rivers, the mountains, nature, wading through swirling waters, watching eagles soar overhead, and perhaps even spotting a bear or a mountain sheep. We show folks the best possible experience with lots of hands-on teaching." Lone Mountain offers family vacations for anglers, giving them access to some of the country's best Blue Ribbon trout-fishing, while non-fishing members of the family can enjoy horseback riding, naturalist activities, and full children's program, along with the numerous other ranch activities Lone Mountain Ranch is a winner!

Address: P.O. Box 160069 K, Big Sky, Montana 59716
Telephone: (800) 514-4644, (406) 995-4644; fax: (406) 995-4670
E-Mail: lmr@lmranch.com
Internet: http://www.lmranch.com
Airport: Bozeman
Location: 40 miles south of Bozeman off Highway 191
Memberships: Greater Yellowstone Coalition, Orvis-endorsed Fly-Fishing Lodge, Montana Dude Ranch Association
Awards: *Hideaway Report*, *Family Circle* Top Ranch Award
Medical: Bozeman Deaconess Hospital, 40 miles
Conference: 50
Guest Capacity: 80
Accommodations: 24 fully insulated one- and two-bedroom cozy log cabins that sleep two to nine; and the luxury, six-bedroom Ridge Top Lodge. Each features comfortable beds, electric heat, bathrooms with tub/shower, and a rock fireplace or woodstove. Cabins are close to the clear mountain stream that winds through the property. All have front porches for relaxing.
Rates: • $$$–$$$$. American Plan. Children under age two stay free (nanny rates available). Special package rates. Normally, minimum one-week stay, Sunday to Sunday.
Credit Cards: VISA, MasterCard, Discover
Season: Late May to mid-October (summer); early December to early April (winter)
Activities: The fly-fishing program is best for guests ages 12 and older. In addition to the Gallatin River, a short drive from the ranch, there are numerous streams and spring creeks as well as high alpine lakes and the waters of Yellowstone Park which offer a variety of exceptional fishing adventures. July is prime time for dry flies, with the salmon fly-hatch in full swing on most of the major rivers. Mid-September through October finds water conditions excellent and few crowds, with the scenery and wildlife-viewing at their peak. Fishing in the winter is a unique experience! Ask about cross-country skiing.
Children's Programs: Extensive ranch program for kids ages four and older.
Dining: Ranch cooking with a gourmet flair. Special diets catered to. Restaurant open to the public on a limited basis. Full bar. No smoking.
Entertainment: Informative and entertaining nightly programs.
Summary: Lone Mountain Guest Ranch offers year-round fly-fishing opportunities for adults and children over age 12. Each of the four seasons brings exciting fly-fishing coupled with full ranch activities. Fly-fishing shop, excellent restaurant, and year-round guest ranch activities for the entire family. Nearby: Big Sky Ski Resort and Yellowstone National Park.

See color photos, pages 250–251.

Parade Rest Ranch
West Yellowstone, Montana

Parade Rest Ranch is in the heart of some of North America's best fly-fishing and just 10 miles from Yellowstone National Park. With Grayling Creek literally at the back door and Blue Ribbon trout streams surrounding it, Parade Rest is a parade of outdoor activities, natural beauty, and, for those so inclined, lots of rest. Here there's no timetable or regimented activity list. Your time is your own. The Seely family has been in the guest-ranching business since the late 1970s, and today, with managers Jim and Pam Feaster, they run a delightful operation. Life at PR is informal; the dress code is whatever's comfortable, and, for the most part, that means an old pair of jeans. Mornings and evenings are cool, with midday temperatures in the mid- to high 80s. Parade Rest is a ranch run the old-fashioned way.

Address: 7979 Grayling Creek Road, Drawer K, West Yellowstone, Montana 59758
Telephone: (800) 758-5934 (summer), (406) 646-7217; fax: (406) 646-7202
E-Mail: paraderest@wyellowstone.com
Internet: http://www.yellowstone-natl-park.com/parade.htm
Airport: West Yellowstone, or Gallatin Field at Bozeman; also, commuter flights from Salt Lake City to West Yellowstone
Location: Eight miles northwest of Yellowstone, 90 miles south of Bozeman off Highway 191
Medical: Yellowstone Medical Clinic
Conference: 35
Guest Capacity: 60
Accommodations: 15 turn-of-the-century log cabins with one to four bedrooms each radiate Western warmth and are cheerfully furnished. All are named after famous nearby fishing rivers. Ask about the Homestead cabin and a favorite Grayling single. All have porches, wood-burning stoves, full baths, and comfortable beds; the newest cabin is three-story Aspen North. Several are along Grayling Creek. Nightly turn-down service. The Gallatin Lodge is a happy gathering spot for reading, visiting, playing games, and listening to music.
Rates: • \$–\$\$. Full American Plan. Children's, corporate, off-season, and fly-fishing guide rates available.
Credit Cards: VISA, MasterCard
Season: Mid-May through September
Activities: Very few areas in the country offer such a diversity of fine fishing. One-and -one-half miles of Grayling Creek flows through the ranch, an excellent fly-fishing stream. Within minutes are the Madison, Gallatin, Firehole, and Gibbon. Full guide service is available. Just let Pam know what you'd like to do and she'll arrange it for you. Also, ask her about the three-day fly-fishing schools. Parade Rest is well known by local guides. Horseback riding is geared to your desires. Rides are accompanied by a wrangler and vary from an hour to all day. White-water and scenic raft trips. Six-person hot tub outside Gallatin Lodge overlooking Grayling Creek.
Children's Programs: No special programs. Children are welcome. Kids won't have enough time in the day to do everything they would like. Children are parents' responsibility.
Dining: Even if you're late from your fishing excursion, dinner will be waiting for you and your guide. The warm, friendly atmosphere is matched by great, hearty ranch cooking. Packed lunches are available to those wishing to ride, fish, raft, or explore all day. All meals are served all-you-can-eat, buffet-style in a central dining room. BYOB.
Entertainment: Nothing special. Many of the diehard fishermen eat dinner, then go back out for more fishing. Cookouts on Monday and Friday nights. Volleyball, basketball, horseshoes, and mountain bikes.
Summary: Great fishing, hearty food, a relaxed atmosphere. Sincere Western ranch hospitality. Nearby: Yellowstone National Park for short day trips.

Triple Creek Ranch
Darby, Montana

For those who wish to combine luxury, personal service (second to none), and fly-fishing in an incredible vacation package, welcome to Triple Creek Ranch. Just one mile from the West Fork of Montana's Bitterroot River, Triple Creek is situated ideally for anglers and non-anglers alike. Fish from sunrise to sunset, relax poolside, or unwind in Montana's high country with an afternoon massage. This mountain hideaway offers superb fly-fishing guides who will take you wade- or float-fishing or in a helicopter to experience some of the best fishing in Montana. In addition, a full luxury program offers horseback riding, white-water rafting, gourmet dining, hiking, and wildlife viewing. In the world of luxury hideaways, general managers Wayne and Judy Kilpatrick and their superb staff have taken Triple Creek right to the top.

Address: 5551 West Fork Road K, Darby, Montana 59829
Telephone: (406) 821-4600; fax: (406) 821-4666
E-Mail: triplecreekinfo@graphcom.com
Internet: http://www.triplecreekranch.com
Airport: Missoula, 74 miles. Private planes to Hamilton with 4,200-foot runway. Helicopter pad at ranch. Airport pickup available.
Location: 12 miles south of Darby, 74 miles south of Missoula
Memberships: Relais & Chateaux
Awards: Relais & Chateaux, *Hideaway Report* Top 10 U.S. Resort Hideaways 1997 Hospitality Award
Medical: Marcus Daly Memorial Hospital, Hamilton. Emergency medical helicopter service available.
Conference: 36. Executive telecommuting facilities.
Guest Capacity: 28 singles, 21 couples
Accommodations: 18 cozy-to-luxurious cedar log cabins. All have fireplaces and refrigerators stocked with complimentary beverages and a full supply of liquor. Each cabin has satellite TV/VCR. Larger luxury cabins have handsome, handcrafted, king-size log beds; double steam showers; and private decks with hot tubs overlooking the forest. Daily housekeeping and laundry services.
Rates: • \$\$\$\$–\$\$\$\$\$\$. American Plan. No minimum stay. Single rates. All fine wine and liquor complimentary.
Credit Cards: VISA, MasterCard, American Express, Discover
Season: Year-round, open all holidays
Activities: A complete luxury experience, with horseback riding, hiking, and scenic drives through Montana's wild backcountry. For those who especially want to fly-fish, Triple Creek offers a customized guided program. Tell the ranch what you'd like to experience (be reasonable, now), and they'll do everything possible to make your fishing dreams come true. Experienced anglers: be sure to ask about the skwala, salmon, green drakes, and caddis hatches from mid-March to October. Outdoor heated pool and Jacuzzis.
Children's Programs: Children under age 16 allowed only when entire ranch is reserved by a family or group.
Dining: Excellent! Gourmet meals with menus featuring Montana beef, seafood flown in from the coast, and wild game. Special diets never a problem. Full room service available. Extensive wine list and full bar. Open to public on very limited basis.
Entertainment: Wonderful Sunday campfire sing-along with your favorite brandy. Main lodge has book and video library and fabulous complimentary bar upstairs.
Summary: In the world of luxury and service, Triple Creek is second to none. Adults only (children over age 16 welcome). Excellent fly-fishing program with guides, superb cuisine, luxury amenities. Private and secluded. Service is the hallmark here. Executive telecommuting available—you can work a little and relax too! Ask about the world-class Elk Meadow Executive Center.

See color photos, pages 258–259.

The Lodge at Chama
Chama, New Mexico

The unspoiled, picturesque San Juan Mountains of northern New Mexico are home to the 32,000-acre Lodge at Chama ranch. Since 1950 the ranch has maintained the highest standards of excellence in fly-fishing, wildlife-viewing, and lodging amenities. Today, guests enjoy an atmosphere of luxury and exclusivity. Both lake and stream fly-fishing are the highlights of guest activities from June to October. Rainbow, brown, brook, and cutthroat trout thrive in this pristine environment of isolated, high-country lakes and miles of crystal-clear streams. Heavy-bodied fish from 16 to 25 inches will test your fishing skills. Your guide will put you where the fish are, share some fishing secrets, and help to give you a fly-fishing experience of a lifetime.

Address: Box 127K, Chama, New Mexico 87520
Telephone: (505) 756-2133; fax: (505) 756-2519
Internet: http://www.ranchweb.com/chama
Airport: Albuquerque; private jets to Pagosa Springs. Call regarding ranch airstrip.
Location: 100 miles north of Santa Fe, 90 miles west of Taos
Awards: *Hideaway Report* 1986 Fishing/Hunting Lodge of the Year; *Hideaway Report* 1990 Best Sporting Retreat
Medical: Hospital in Española; emergency helicopter service available
Conference: 24 in board meeting room
Guest Capacity: 24
Accommodations: The 13,500-square-foot lodge offers panoramic views of the beautiful Chama Valley and snowcapped Colorado peaks from its 12 rooms. The huge living room is dominated by a 20-foot-wide rock fireplace, original Western art, sculptures, and fish and wildlife mounts. The 12 rooms have private baths, sitting/desk areas, lofty ceilings, large closets, and upscale amenities. Two spacious junior suites, named Roadrunner and Bear, have fireplaces, vanity baths, TVs, and lounging areas.
Rates: • $$$$$$. Full American Plan. No minimum stay. Lodge and ranch may be booked exclusively if desired.
Credit Cards: VISA, MasterCard. Personal and corporate checks.
Season: May to October for fishing; mid-September to January for hunting; conferences and wildlife-viewing year-round
Activities: Private lake and stream fishing. Some waters reserved for catch-and-release only. Fishing equipment available; however, most people bring their own gear. Self-guided nature trail from lodge. Hiking, picnics, wildlife tours, photography trips. Guided ranch trail rides. Non-fishing spouses enjoy off-ranch activities, including narrow-gauge train rides, shopping tours to Taos or Santa Fe, and white-water rafting. After a full day of outdoor activities, you may relax in a 10-person, indoor, hydrotherapy whirlpool or enjoy a sauna. Superb fall elk-hunting on limited basis.
Children's Programs: Minimum age of 12 unless by special arrangement.
Dining: Gourmet ranch cuisine. Trail lunches and fishermen's special shore lunches. Excellent varied cuisine for all three daily meals. Ranch specialties include steaks, chops, buffalo, trout, and fowl as well as New Mexican specialties made with wonderful chilis grown in New Mexico. Home-baked bread, rolls, desserts, and pastries. Complimentary bar. Premium wines available.
Entertainment: Wide-screen TV offers network programs, VCR movies. Fishing and wildlife videos.
Summary: World-class fly-fishing and wildlife-viewing. One of North America's most exclusive ranch retreats. Elk and deer are frequent sundown visitors to the lodge grounds. One of the world's largest private elk herds. Ranch buffalo herd.

See color photos, pages 260–261.

Brush Creek Ranch
Saratoga, Wyoming

THE DUDE RANCHERS' ASSOCIATION

Wyoming Dude Rancher's Association

At the foot of southern Wyoming's Snowy Range Mountains and in the upper North Platte Valley, Brush Creek Ranch, a 6,000-acre working cattle-and-guest ranch, offers fly-fishing guests the combination of a guest ranch and a superb array of fly-fishing opportunities, both on and off the ranch. Three miles of private Brush Creek, along with the 140 miles of Blue Ribbon freestone waters of the Upper North Platte and Encamp-p ment Rivers (regarded by many as some of the finest and least-discovered fly-fishing opportunities in the West), offer guests wonderful fishing adventures. Whether you're fly-fishing, hiking, horseback riding, savoring the beauty of this scenic valley, or enjoying the towns of Encampment or Saratoga, Kinta and Gibb Blumenthall offer guests a rich and heartwarming adventure.

Address: Star Route, Box 10, Saratoga, Wyoming 82331
Telephone: (800) RANCH-WY (726-2499), (307) 327-5241; fax: (307) 327-5384
E-Mail: kblumen@csn.net
Internet: http://www.duderanch.org/brush-creek
Airport: Denver, 195 miles; Laramie, 65 miles. Airport pickup is extra.
Location: 65 miles west of Laramie off the Snowy Range Road, Wyoming 130; 16 miles northeast of Saratoga off Wyoming 130
Memberships: The Dude Ranchers' Association, Wyoming Dude Rancher's Association
Awards: Orvis-endorsed Lodge
Medical: Clinic in Saratoga, 16 miles
Conference: 24
Guest Capacity: 24
Accommodations: Vintage 1900s-style, white-sided, green-trimmed three-story lodge or rustic cabins. The lodge features a native stone fireplace in the library and Western murals in the dining room on the first floor. Sleeping accommodations are on the second and third floors. Each room is unique. All have private baths and entrances; some have private, screened porches. These rooms have a turn-of-the-century feel. The two cabin duplexes, located near the main lodge, were originally the cowboy bunkhouse and icehouse. Each has been completely remodeled with Western, rustic charm; private bathrooms; and queen-sized beds.
Rates: • $$$. Full American Plan. Children's, group, and off-season rates. Three-day minimum stay.
Credit Cards: VISA, MasterCard. Personal checks or cash accepted.
Season: Year-round; closed Thanksgiving
Activities: In addition to fishing three miles of Brush Creek on the ranch property and the trout pond, guests enjoy the Upper North Platte and Encampment Rivers, two of Wyoming's premier trout streams. These Blue Ribbon waters boast wild and aggressive trout, including browns, rainbows and cutthroats, ranging from 10 to 26 inches and averaging 13 to 17 inches. These rivers provide over 140 miles of classic Western trout waters. In addition, two tailwater sections at the "miracle mile" and gray reef on the Platte offer guests a chance to catch large browns and rainbows year-round. Guests also enjoy high-mountain lakes and streams of the Snowy Range and Sierra Madre Mountains, fishing for brookies, browns, cutthroat, rainbows, splake, and golden trout.
Children's Programs: Half-day programs planned five times a week. Local baby sitting available on request.
Dining: Western-style food with a gourmet flair. Breakfast rides, creekside barbecues. BYOB.
Entertainment: Barn dances in the hayloft of the historic log barn. Campfire music. Horse-drawn wagon rides, and pitching horseshoes. Fly-tying demonstrations and fly-casting lessons.
Summary: Brush Creek Ranch offers families, couples, and individuals the opportunity to fish one of the least-known Blue Ribbon trout rivers in Wyoming, in addition to enjoying a full guest-ranch program. Six thousand acres of old-time Western charm and a full guest-ranch/fly-fishing program. Nearby: Snowy Range Mountains and the Old West towns of Encampment and Saratoga.

See color photos, page 281.

Canyon Ranch
Sheridan, Wyoming

Canyon Ranch has been in the Wallop family since the late 1880s. Originally cattle-and-horse ranchers, the Wallops welcome executives, individual families, and very small corporate groups who come to take in the magnificent views, intimate friendly hospitality, and superb mountain fishing. Today the ranch is owned by former U.S. Senator Malcolm Wallop and run by his son, Paul. Canyon Ranch specializes in "fly-fishing the way fly-fishing used to be." This is not trophy-fish country, but what makes it so special is that you won't run into lots of people and you will catch lots of fish. What Paul's guests enjoy is the total fishing experience. Paul loves the great outdoors; sharing his appreciation for wildlife, the mountains, and the old-time easy-going spirit of the West brings guests back year after year. As a British Ambassador said, "I've been to a lot of places where I caught bigger fish, but this is the best fishing I've ever had."

Address: P.O. Box 11 K, Big Horn, Wyoming 82833
Telephone: (307) 674-6239; fax: (307) 672-2264
E-Mail: pwallop@wavecom.net
Airport: Sheridan
Location: At the mouth of Little Goose Canyon, 13 miles south of Sheridan
Medical: Sheridan County Memorial Hospital
Guest Capacity: 16
Accommodations: Two private rooms and a large loft with six beds and four full baths in the lodge (built in 1993), including laundry facilities, fax machine, two telephone lines, TV, VCR, and views of Lion's Head and Little Goose Canyon. Hot tub, too. The remote and private family cabin, about 20 minutes from the main ranch up on the mountain, sleeps six with two bedrooms and a loft, one bath, kitchen, living/dining area, and front porch. Gas water heater, range, and refrigerator, but no electricity or telephone. Guests cook and clean for themselves, and need a four-wheel-drive vehicle to reach the cabin. All bedding is provided.
Rates: • $$$–$$$$. Weekend and weekly packages, four-night minimum stay, arrival any day.
Credit Cards: VISA, MasterCard. Personal checks preferred.
Season: Mid-June through September
Activities: Fly-fishing is the main activity. Experienced guides take you to quality, uncrowded waters throughout the Big Horn mountains. A variety of waters are available: private streams and lakes, secluded mountain streams, and wilderness lakes. It's rare to find other fishermen around these private and public waters. All trips are walk–wade. The fishing will challenge and encourage everyone from novice to expert. As Paul says, "This is fishing the way it used to be." For non-fishing friends or family there are excellent opportunities for a variety of hikes, from all-day outings to evening strolls. Horseback riding available. Wildlife-viewing is superb; ranch-management goal has always been to enhance wildlife habitat and diversity. Almost all of the traditional Western wildlife species inhabit the ranch. Fifteen-station sporting-clays course.
Children's Programs: Best for older children who love to fish. Ask Paul about the father/son and mother/daughter fishing trips.
Dining: Excellent seasonal fare and a varied menu for all three meals. Special diets catered to. Fishing lunches served streamside. Complimentary beer and wine. BYOB.
Entertainment: Paul will arrange for tickets to local events if guests wish. Videos available, or just sit and watch the sunset from the front porch.
Summary: One of Kilgore's "Best of the Best": an exclusive, intimate, private hideaway with superb service and privacy! A 3,800-acre private ranch in the Big Horn Mountains that has been in the Wallop family since the 1880s. Today it caters to families, executives, individual families, friends, or small groups. Paul Wallop works closely with guests before they arrive to insure that their expectations are met. Excellent private and public mountain-stream and lake fly-fishing, privacy, and excellent and fresh food. Ask about the private bird-hunting opportunities, and Paul's "Cast and Blast" program.

See color photos, page 285.

Crescent H Ranch
Wilson, Wyoming

Located just eight miles from Jackson Hole, the 1,300-acre Crescent H Ranch is a world-class fly-fishing destination. Nestled at the base of the Grand Teton mountain range, the ranch was recognized for its international fly-fishing reputation when it was christened as the original Orvis-endorsed Fishing Lodge in 1986. Here you'll experience rustic elegance, gourmet cuisine, excellent fly-fishing with experienced guides, proximity to the world-famous Western town of Jackson Hole, and the beauty of the Tetons. In 1997, investor and sportsman John Thornton became the proud new owner of this magnificent property. He and his staff are committed to continuing the tradition of excellence in superb guest and fly-fishing vacations.

Address: Box 347 K, Wilson, Wyoming 83014
Telephone: (888) TETONS1 (888-838-6671), (307) 733-3674; fax: (307) 733-8475
E-Mail: info@crescenth.com
Internet: http://www.crescenth.com
Airport: Jackson, 8 miles
Location: 8 miles west of Jackson outside the little town of Wilson on Fall Creek Road
Memberships: Trout Unlimited, Jackson Chamber of Commerce
Awards: Original Orvis-endorsed Lodge in North America, *Hideaway Report*
Medical: St. John's Hospital, Jackson
Conference: 25
Guest Capacity: 25
Accommodations: The 15 log buildings on the ranch are all in harmony with the surroundings. Ten charming log cabins sit in a large semicircle on a gentle slope above the main lodge, each with superb views of the ranch and valley. Cabins have one, two, or three bedrooms, all decorated in hunter green and comfortably furnished. Each has a shower, marble-topped bedside tables, carpeting, brass beds, and baskets of fresh fruit for new arrivals. The handsome 70-year-old lodge reflects the elegant rustic spirit here, with 30-foot ceilings, two stone fireplaces, wagon-wheel lamps, original Western art, and bronze sculptures.
Rates: • $$$$–$$$$$. American Plan. Group, corporate, and fly-fishing packages and schools available. Four-night minimum in June and September. Seven-night minimum stay July and August, Saturday to Saturday.
Credit Cards: None. Personal checks accepted.
Season: Early June through September
Activities: Patty Reilly, a noted world-class fisher, directs the outstanding fly-fishing program. Experienced guides will show you the unmatched quality and tremendous variety of fishing opportunities in the Jackson Hole area. Guests may also experience and enjoy fly-fishing for native cutthroat trout in several miles of private spring creeks; float the Snake River through Grand Teton National Park, or fish for large browns and rainbows in the Green River. Additionally, guests can fish the nearby South Fork (in Idaho) and the Firehole and Yellowstone Rivers in Yellowstone National Park. Guided horseback rides go out in the mornings and afternoons. Weekly breakfast cookout rides. Hiking, guided nature walks, scenic and white-water float trips, and two championship golf courses nearby make this a destination vacation to suit everyone.
Children's Programs: Ranch is oriented to adults and children ages 12 and over.
Dining: Elegant cuisine! Specialty game, fresh fish, two nightly entrées, and mouth-watering desserts. Fine wine and liquor served (included). Weekly Grand Barbecue overlooking the Snake River includes cowboy music.
Entertainment: Hosted cocktail hour each evening. Some enjoy the nightlife in Jackson or the charming town of Wilson. Others prefer to savor the ambiance and casual evening program with fly-tying demonstrations, slide shows, or evening strolls.
Summary: One of Kilgore's "Best of the Best." Premier guest ranch with superb fly-fishing. Excellent cuisine and rustic elegance. First Orvis-endorsed Lodge. Orvis fly-fishing schools and equipment. Nearby: Jackson, Teton Village, Yellowstone and Grand Teton National Parks.

See color photos, page 286.

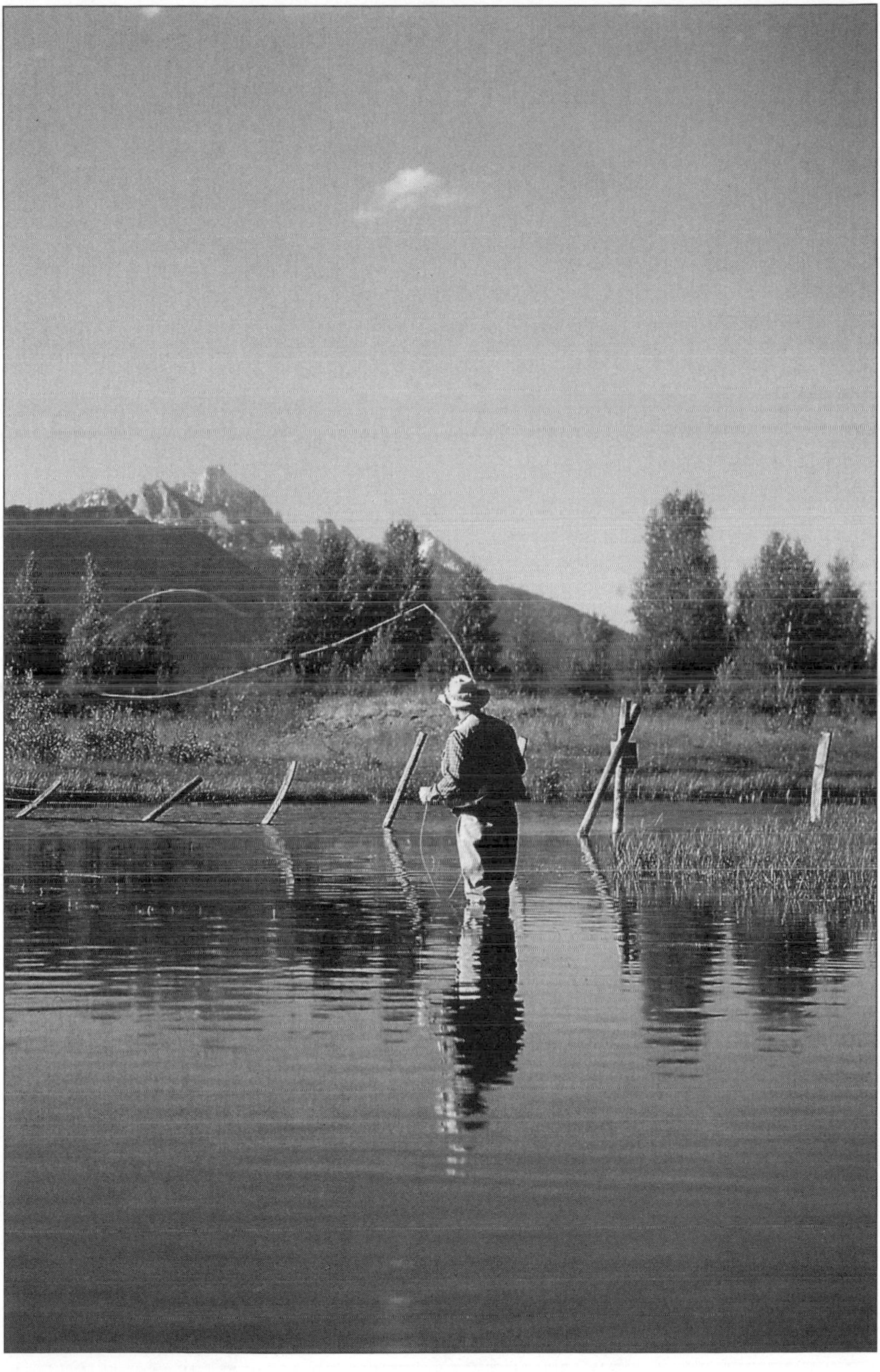

Cross-Country Skiing Ranches
in the United States and Canada

Introduction

Unlike Scandinavians, for whom cross-country skiing is a way of life, most North Americans have discovered the sport only in the last two decades. Many of us used to think of Nordic skiing (or "skinny-skiing," as it's sometimes called) not as recreation but largely as an occupational necessity. It was one of those things done by mountain-climbers, snowbound villagers, and *National Geographic* crews working on stories in the Antarctic.

Now cross-country skiing, along with snowshoeing, snowmobiling, and even dogsledding, has become a wonderful part of the winter activities at many ranches. It combines natural splendor, camaraderie, and winter magic.

Skinny-skiing is friendly and fun. It's so well suited for the whole family that almost half the adults out on the trails have children under age 18. The best way to start is with a skiing professional on machine groomed trails, learning not just how to travel across the flats but also the whole gamut of descent techniques (more kinds of turns than in downhill skiing). When you can stay on the tracks, try "skating," graduate to backcountry touring, telemark on lift-served slopes, enjoy hut-to-hut trips, or ski to wilderness *yurts* (circular, domed tents).

Author and friend Jonathan Wiesel explains, "Machine-set tracks guide skis forward so your ankles don't have the chance to splay out to the side. This transforms 'walking on skis' into gliding, helping you out-think your feet. Groomed trails open the grace and beauty of winter not just to super-athletes but to anyone at any pace, giving you the thrill of speed with confident control. Best of all, cross-country consumes enough calories that two hours on skis justifies a second dessert."

Equipment has evolved at a dizzying pace. There are track and skating skis, wider boards for breaking your own trail (bushwhacking), and metal-edged gear for telemarking. The latest innovation is the "micro ski," which is three-fourths the length of the older models. They look like toy poodles when you think you need St. Bernards, but they make turning and learning a breeze on packed snow, and falls are reduced by 50 percent.

In this guide we've included facilities that offer unique winter opportunities. Each property has its own character, programs, and beauty. Here are some questions to ask.

How many miles of machine-groomed track are there? Are there skating lanes as well?

What is the altitude? (If it's above 6,000 feet and you're coming from sea level, plan to take it easy for at least the first day.)

What kids' programs and facilities are available: day care or baby-sitting, special narrow-track setting, snow-play area, ski equipment, special trails?

What kinds of equipment are available: track, touring, telemarking, micro skis? Do they have modern boot-binding "systems"?

Is instruction included in the package? What about guide service?

What other recreation is available on-site? Is there a downhill ski area nearby?

Winter ranches are famous for hospitality, diverse entertainment, and culinary excellence. Regardless of whether you're a single person, couple, or family, you can use these wonderful winter properties to visit, snowshoe, ice-skate, take a ride by sleigh or horse, sit in the Jacuzzi enjoying splendid mountain views, or relax in front of a blazing fire. Welcome to ranch country in winter.

Aspen Lodge Ranch Resort
Estes Park, Colorado

CDGRA

High in the beautiful Rocky Mountains just outside Estes Park is a resort ranch that offers outstanding scenery, wonderful cross-country skiing, sleigh rides drawn by Belgian draft horses, winter horseback riding, snowmobiling, and great conference facilities. Aspen Lodge provides a unique environment for the winter enthusiast. Away from the hustle and bustle of the big ski resorts, this small, uncrowded resort offers an excellent environment for corporate, group, and professional meetings. The lodge, over 30,000 square feet, is one of the largest log structures in North America. It features 36 guest rooms, a massive moss-rock fireplace, and meeting rooms. Its comfortably appointed cabins are cozy, making them perfect for singles, couples, and families. Featuring 15 kilometers of cross-country trails, with many acres of untracked trails in Rocky Mountain National Park, Aspen Lodge at Estes Park is suited for both beginner and expert. Finally, between Estes Park and the lodge there are incredible herds of elk to be seen!

Address: 6120 Highway 7, Estes Park, Colorado 80517
Telephone: (970) 586-8133, (800) 332-6867; fax: (970) 586-8133
E-Mail: aspen@aspenlodge.com
Internet: http://www.aspenlodge.com
Airport: Denver, 65 miles
Location: 65 miles northwest of Denver off Highway 25, seven miles south of Estes Park
Memberships: Colorado Dude and Guest Ranch Association
Awards: AAA 3 Diamond, Delta Dream Vacation, Official Hotel Guide: *Best Dude Ranch 1996*
Medical: Full hospital, seven miles
Conference: 150, with excellent conference facilities; five meeting rooms, some with fireplaces and decks, all with windows offering superb views of Longs Peak
Guest Capacity: 150
Accommodations: The lodge features several hospitality suites and can accommodate up to 150 guests. Choose from 36 lodge rooms or 23 multiroom cabins with porches. Each is designed with comfort in mind. Cozy motif ensures a pleasurable stay.
Rates: • \$–\$\$. American plan and à la carte. Special group and holiday packages. Sleigh rides and horseback riding extra. Special Christmas package available.
Credit Cards: VISA, MasterCard, American Express, Diners Club, Discover
Season: Year-round
Activities: Cross-country skiing with rentals and instruction available. Snowshoeing and ice-skating. Intermediate and expert skiers will enjoy guided tours to Wild Basin of Rocky Mountain National Park. Sleigh rides, tobogganing, racquetball, sauna, hot tub, weight and exercise room in Sports Center.
Children's Programs: Available for groups on request.
Dining: The dining lodge looks out to Longs Peak and offers meals served in the casual dining room. Varied menu. Children's menu also available.
Entertainment: No regularly scheduled entertainment. Special Christmas and Easter programs with children's activities available.
Summary: One of the largest log structures in North America. Winter lodge resort with extensive winter activities and conference facilities catering to groups of five to 150. Sports Center and Western bar; great wildlife-viewing, ask about the elk. Wonderful Christmas program.

C Lazy U Ranch
Granby, Colorado

THE DUDE RANCHERS' ASSOCIATION

CDGRA

C Lazy U offers a wonderful winter riding and cross-country skiing program. The ranch invites families with children (and what a program it is for kids). The ranch caters to families who wish to savor the magic, splendor, peace, and beauty of this winter wonderland. Cross-country skiers enjoy over 25 kilometers of machine-groomed trails, in addition to hundreds of acres of wild, untracked skiing possibilities. Full instruction, guide service, and equipment are available. Imagine horseback riding all bundled up through the fresh snow. Well, you can do that too. The Christmas program brings out all the joy of the holidays with tree-trimming, caroling, filled stockings, Christmas trees for guests' rooms, turkey dinner, and, of course, Santa arriving on his sleigh all the way from the North Pole. The C Lazy U winter adventure is one you'll cherish a lifetime.

Address: P.O. Box 379, Granby, Colorado 80446
Telephone: (970) 887-3344; fax: (970) 887-3917
E-Mail: ranch@clazyu.com
Internet: http://www.clazyu.com
Airport: Denver
Train: Granby
Location: Six miles northwest of Granby, off Highway 125; 90 miles west of Denver
Memberships: Colorado Dude and Guest Ranch Association, The Dude Ranchers' Association, Cross-Country Ski Association
Awards: Mobil 5 Star, AAA 5 Diamond
Medical: Granby Medical Clinic, six miles
Conference: 70
Guest Capacity: 110
Accommodations: 18 fully insulated, comfortable units. Suites vary from one- to three-room family units with baths and carpeting. Some have fireplaces and Jacuzzi bathtubs. Daily fresh fruit; fireplace restocked every day. Hair dryers, nightly turn-down, bathrobes, and coffeemakers with everything you need.
Rates: • $$$–$$$$. American Plan. Everything but the bar tab and trap-shooting is included. Ask about the five-night winter packages and week-long stays during Christmas and New Year's. Special children's rates January to March.
Credit Cards: None. Personal checks accepted.
Season: Mid-December through March
Activities: 25 kilometers of groomed trails, ice-skating, sledding, inner-tubing, horse-drawn sleigh rides, and trap-shooting. Indoor health spa with whirlpool and sauna. Racquetball court. Downhill skiing nearby at Silver Creek and Winter Park, transportation provided. Morning and afternoon horseback riding on winter trails or in enclosed arena. All cross-country skiing, skating, and racquetball equipment provided. Fully equipped exercise room with fitness machines in the patio house.
Children's Programs: Full children's program all winter. Ice-skating, sledding, snowmobile tubing, and horseback riding.
Dining: Excellent cuisine, including homemade soups, rack of lamb, Christmas turkey dinner, and ice-cream pie. Full service bar. Extensive wine list. Kids eat before adults.
Entertainment: Christmas and New Year's programs. Game room, country-Western singing, ice-skating party with bonfire and schnapps, weekly nighttime cross-country skiing along a torch-lit trail to the awaiting bonfire and goodies.
Summary: World-class, year-round destination ranch with wonderful winter riding and holiday programs for families. Excellent Christmas and New Year's program. Superb children's program morning, noon, and night. Full winter activities. Spanish, French, and German spoken.

See color photos, page 185.

The Home Ranch
Clark, Colorado

THE DUDE RANCHERS' ASSOCIATION

The Home Ranch is one of the premier winter settings in North America. Host-owner Ken Jones and his wife, Cile, along with a very competent and friendly staff, combine the best of two worlds—rustic elegance and winter adventure. Guests from around the world gather here to enjoy what the Home Ranch has to offer. In the beautiful Elk River valley near the small town of Clark, not far from Steamboat Springs, this ranch provides a gracious combination of Western warmth, downhill and cross-country skiing, and snowshoeing. The ski trails that radiate from the property give skiers varied terrain, rolling valleys, and glistening forests. If that's not enough, a short drive to Steamboat will put you on downhill slopes that will challenge even the most advanced skier.

Address: P.O. Box 822 K, Clark, Colorado 80428
Telephone: (970) 879-1780; fax: (970) 879-1795
E-Mail: hrclark@cmn.net
Internet: http://www.homeranch.com
Airport: Steamboat Springs and Hayden
Location: 18 miles north of Steamboat Springs
Memberships: The Dude Ranchers' Association, Relais & Chateaux
Medical: Routt Memorial Hospital
Conference: 30
Guest Capacity: 40
Accommodations: Eight secluded cabins and six beautiful lodge rooms, furnished with antiques, Indian rugs, original artwork, down comforters, and robes. Each cabin has its own woodstove and a private enclosed outdoor whirlpool. Large families may elect to stay in the 2,500-square-foot, hand-hewn, spacious, beautifully trimmed log cabin.
Rates: • $$$–$$$$. American Plan. Three-night minimum stay.
Credit Cards: VISA, MasterCard, American Express
Season: Late December to late March, including Christmas
Activities: The main focus of the winter program is the excellent downhill skiing/cross-country outdoor adventure package. The ranch offers twice daily shuttles to Steamboat Springs for downhill skiing. In addition, there are more than 50 kilometers of tracked trails throughout the valley, 20 kilometers of which are groomed for telemark skiing. The instructor-guides are qualified to teach all levels of cross-country skiing. One of the more popular excursions is lunch at the lamasery. Guests ski or take the sleigh about one mile up to the mountain cabin, have a lunch of gourmet Western fare, and return to the main lodge. Heated outdoor swimming, snowshoeing, and sauna. Equipment is available for both adults and children at Slim Boards Ski Shop.
Children's Programs: Best for kids who want to ski. During winter there are usually not many children here. Children under age six not allowed.
Dining: Excellent meals with many Home Ranch specialties, such as breast of duck, fresh fish, filet mignon, European dishes, praline cheesecake. BYO wine and liquor (ranch will pick up with advance notice).
Entertainment: Well-stocked library; grand piano; recreation hall, Home Ranch band, The Ranch Hand Band, performs once a week. Ask Ken about his "Family Tree Album."
Summary: One of Kilgore's Best of the Best. One of the prettiest ranches in North America. Great for people who like to ski hard and eat well, and for those who don't like to ski—that's OK too. Famous ski town of Steamboat Springs nearby. French and German spoken.

See color photos, page 191.

Latigo Ranch
Kremmling, Colorado

THE DUDE RANCHERS' ASSOCIATION

CDGRA

Guests who keep returning to Latigo Ranch are drawn by the relaxed atmosphere, spectacular scenery, cuisine, and warm hospitality of the owners. Latigo is tucked in a corner of Arapaho and Routt National Forests, on the side of Kasdorf Mountain. With 100-mile views to the distant high mountain peaks of the Continental Divide and 250,000 acres of national forest bordering it, Latigo Ranch offers a spectacular winter wonderland of scenery, skiing, and snowshoeing. Since the ranch lies at 9,000 feet on top of Colorado's Gore Range, snow conditions are hard to beat. For most of the winter, several feet of dry powder make it just perfect for all kinds of winter activities. Hosts Kathie Yost and Lisa George have both been schoolteachers (music and English). Randy George has a degree in engineering and an M.B.A.; Jim Yost has a Ph.D. in anthropology and has taught anthropology and linguistics at the University of Colorado. A stay at Latigo is not only a recreational heaven but also a stimulating intellectual experience. Above all, Latigo offers a low-key, relaxing ambiance. People leave here feeling like they've been visiting family at their private winter retreat.

Address: Box 237K, Kremmling, Colorado 80459
Telephone: (800) 227-9655, (970) 724-9008; fax: (970) 724-9009
E-Mail: latigo@compuserve.com
Internet: http://www.dude-ranch.com/latigo_ranch.html
Airport: Steamboat Springs or Denver
Location: 16 miles northwest of Kremmling, 55 miles southeast of Steamboat Springs, 130 miles west of Denver. Ranch will send detailed map.
Memberships: Colorado Dude and Guest Ranch Association, Colorado Cross-Country Ski Areas Association, The Dude Ranchers' Association, Cross-Country Ski Areas of America
Medical: Kremmling Memorial Hospital, 16 miles
Conference: 25 if staying overnight
Guest Capacity: 25
Accommodations: Three log duplex cabins, three bedrooms on each side with sitting room, electric heat, and wood-burning stove. A fourplex consists of four single bedrooms with two queen beds and two with double beds, all with fireplaces in the bedrooms.
Rates: • $$. American Plan, all inclusive except equipment rental. Group rates available.
Credit Cards: VISA, MasterCard, American Express
Season: Mid-December to early April. Open Christmas.
Activities: Do as much as you wish. Latigo machine-grooms and packs over 35 miles of track for classic and skate-skiing and snowshoeing. There's also unlimited backcountry and telemark skiing for the more adventurous. Daily lessons are provided for beginning and advanced skiers on both cross-country and telemark techniques. Be sure to ask Randy or Jim about their packed telemark slope and moonlight fondue ski tours. Tubing and sledding are also enjoyed by many. Bring your own ski gear, or rentals are available en route to Latigo.
Children's Programs: No special program. Children's lessons available. Baby-sitting by prior arrangement. Talk to Kathie about the options for your children.
Dining: Full breakfast. You order what you want. Hot lunch (sack lunch by arrangement), family-style dinner. Can cater to special diets. BYOB.
Entertainment: VHS player available, pool table, Ping-Pong, and Foosball. Guests enjoy lively discussions and the cozy library.
Summary: The Latigo winter experience is best for those who appreciate the majesty of the mountains and value the solitude and serenity of this remote location. Excellent private trail system. Warm, friendly family hospitality. Ask about the dogsled rides and Jim's movie on Ecuador, *Nomads of the Rain Forest*. Spanish spoken.

See color photos, page 199.

Skyline Guest Ranch
Telluride, Colorado

THE DUDE RANCHERS' ASSOCIATION

CDGRA

Do you yearn for a classic ski lodge, where you can sit around the potbellied stove, sip hot cider, and eat freshly made cookies after a fabulous day of skiing with your host, former U.S. Ski Team member and world-class skier Mike Farny and his family? You'll find that experience at Skyline. The beauty of the mountains will set you aglow. Skyline Guest Ranch is just five miles from Telluride Ski Resort, where you'll find incredible terrain for alpine and Nordic skiing. The resort has 10 lifts, one of which is used for Nordic access to the mountaintop, with its 30 kilometers of groomed and set trails. If you want to ski at the ranch, there are marked backcountry trails. Ask Sheila about skiing back to the ranch from the ski area—an exciting and adventurous trip. Skyline is noted for its spectacular setting: you can see three 14,000-foot peaks from the front porch. Skyline feels secluded enough, yet it's only eight miles from the wonderful historic mining ski town of Telluride, 15 minutes away.

Address: Box 67 K, Telluride, Colorado 81435
Telephone: (888) 754-1126, (970) 728-3757; fax: (970) 728-6728
E-Mail: skyline-ranch@toski.com
Internet: http://www.ranchweb.com/skyline
Airport: Telluride, eight miles
Location: Eight miles from Telluride
Memberships: The Dude Ranchers' Association, Colorado Dude and Guest Ranch Association
Medical: Telluride Medical Center, eight miles
Conference: 35
Guest Capacity: 35
Accommodations: Each of the 10 lodge rooms has its own comfortable log bed with down comforter and sheepskin bed cover, its own thermostat control, and a private bath. Attached to the lodge is a log addition with two apartments equipped with kitchenettes. There are four housekeeping cabins, each with a kitchenette; each accommodates from two to six skiers. No smoking in any building.
Rates: • \$–\$\$. European Plan. Breakfast included. No minimum stay.
Credit Cards: VISA, MasterCard, American Express. Personal checks and traveler's checks accepted.
Season: Early December to early April. Open Christmas.
Activities: Alpine and Nordic skiing; machine-groomed, single-track trails. Afternoon and evening horse-drawn sleigh rides. Snow-shoeing and cross-country equipment available. Snowmobiling from Skyline up to old mining ghost town can be arranged (extra). Small retail store: Sheila's Outpost. Wonderful outdoor hot tub and sauna available.
Children's Programs: Children are welcome but are the responsibility of parents. Baby-sitting available (extra). Excellent ski program at Telluride ski area for kids. Cribs and high chairs available.
Dining: The kitchen cooks a hearty skier's breakfast with a special each morning. You're on your own for lunch—most eat at the ski area. Wonderful après-ski delicacies and hot cider. Dinners with fine wines are prepared nightly for guests, except on Monday, when the dining room is closed. Ask about the dinner sleigh rides open to the public.
Entertainment: Cozy evening fires at the ranch and local entertainment in Telluride. Be sure to ask about moonlight cross-country ski tours and boot hockey on the pond.
Summary: Host Mike Farny is a world class championship skier whose small, friendly, classic ski lodge offers excellent food, hospitality, and ski opportunities close to the famous ski town of Telluride. Skyline is a marvelous base camp for winter fun in and around Telluride. Incredible setting surrounded by 14,000-foot mountain peaks with lots of sunshine and mountain joy. Great for both cross-country and downhill skiing. Mike has been known to ski with guests—lots of fun and excitement!

See color photos, page 204.

Vista Verde Ranch
Steamboat Springs, Colorado

THE DUDE RANCHERS' ASSOCIATION

CDGRA

With blue Colorado sky overhead and lots of powdery snow on the ground, this secluded ranch looks like Vista Blanca; it captivated new owners John and Suzanne Munn. Following their purchase in 1991, they have continued to develop Vista Verde into a top-notch winter wonderland. The characteristics of the summer guest-ranch carry over with a limited number of winter guests: handsomely furnished, cozy log cabins and lodge rooms; fine dining; and a wide variety of activities. It's both a working ranch where you can help feed the animals and a relaxing ranch, whether you're soaking in the outdoor hot tubs or simply reading by the fire. Holidays are traditional and special, with horse-drawn sleighs and caroling. Winter at Vista Verde is a happy, heartwarming time and brings exhilarating outdoor winter fun. If you are looking for great food, romance, and lots of snow fun, give Vista Verde a call.

Address: P.O. Box 465K, Steamboat Springs, Colorado 80477
Telephone: (800) 526-7433, (970) 879-3858; fax: (970) 879-1413
E-Mail: 103573.3551@compuserve.com
Internet: http://www.vistaverde.com
Airport: Special winter service to Hayden via major carriers or direct service from Denver. Ranch Suburbans will pick you up.
Location: 25 miles north of Steamboat Springs
Memberships: Cross-Country Ski Areas of America, Professional Ski Instructors of America, Colorado Dude and Guest Ranch Association, The Dude Ranchers' Association
Awards: Mobil 4 Star
Medical: Steamboat Springs Hospital
Conference: 30
Guest Capacity: 36
Accommodations: Authentic log cabins are nestled among the aspens and pines overlooking the snow-covered meadows and forest. Handsomely furnished, they include woodstoves, full baths, down comforters, antiques, artwork, and most have private outdoor hot tubs. New lodge rooms offer splendid views and convenience.
Rates: • $$$–$$$$. American Plan. Children's, post-holiday, and package rates available. Ski rental, snowmobiling, dogsledding, and ice climbing extra. Minimum stays: call for details.
Credit Cards: None. Personal checks or traveler's checks accepted.
Season: Christmas to mid-March
Activities: There are about 20 miles of groomed trails with double tracks and skating lanes, telemark hills, and unlimited backcountry opportunities in the surrounding national forest; professional instruction; complimentary guided ski tours; and first-class rental equipment. Ski instructors meet each morning at breakfast to organize activities with guests. Many guests like to go off and ski on their own; others enjoy being guided. Variety of other activities include snowshoeing, sleigh rides, horseback riding, ski-in lunches at the lodge or old homestead cabin, moonlight skiing, dogsledding, ice climbing, off-ranch snowmobiling, and even fly-fishing. Spa building with outdoor hot tubs, sauna, exercise equipment. Masseuse available. Daily transportation provided to nearby Steamboat Ski Area for downhill diehards.
Children's Programs: Other than at holidays, there are few children—they're in school. Fun-in-the-snow activities at the sledding hill, snow cave, and igloo; feeding the animals; and indoor games at Sweethearts Parlor.
Dining: Dining is a major part of Vista Verde's winter experience. Candlelight dinners overlooking the snow-laden meadows; lunches on the sun deck; and hearty, scrumptious breakfasts. Special diets catered to. Beer and wine available.
Entertainment: Each evening may include light folk music, fireside chats with local personalities, occasional dancing, and moonlight skiing.
Summary: A real romantic winter getaway. Candlelight dining, great food, and lots of snow and winter activities. Perfect for honeymoons, couples, and good friends. Downhill skiing too!

See color photos, pages 210–211.

T-Lazy-7 Ranch
Aspen, Colorado

Winter in Aspen, Colorado draws celebrities and guests from around the world each year. World-class downhill skiing, coupled with the charm of the old mining town of Aspen and its incredible nightlife, are only five miles away from T-Lazy-7. Located at the base of the world-famous Maroon Bell Mountains, this winter hideaway offers guests incredible value along with the opportunity to enjoy a host of winter activities, including snowmobiling, some cross-country skiing, and proximity to Aspen. Rick and Landon Deane carry on the tradition that Rick's parents began in 1938. Winters in this part of the country are really spectacular and offer something for everyone. T-Lazy-7 offers a relaxed environment, warm hospitality, and winter magic!

Address: 3129 Maroon Creek Road, Drawer K, Aspen, Colorado 81611
Telephone: (888) T7LODGE (888-875-6343), (970) 925-7254 (lodging), (970) 925-4614 (snowmobiles); fax: (970) 925-5616
Airport: Aspen (Sardy Field), six miles (10 minutes from ranch)
Location: Five miles from Aspen
Memberships: Colorado Outfitters Association
Medical: Aspen Valley Hospital, three miles
Conference: Specializing in private Western parties for up to 150
Guest Capacity: 75
Accommodations: Ranch accommodations, including a beautiful main log lodge with large vaulted main room and Western-style apartments. Without telephones or TVs, cabins have fully equipped kitchenettes, fireplaces, or wood-burning stoves. Daily maid service with full linen change once a week. Laundry facilities available.
Rates: $–$$$. Snowmobiling extra. Two-night minimum stay.
Credit Cards: VISA, MasterCard, Discover
Season: Winter: end of November through March. Summer: late May through September.
Activities: The activities program is open to the public and serves up a variety of sleigh rides, snowmobile tours, Western sleigh rides, and dinner nights. Cross-country skiing, ice-skating, outdoor swimming in the heated pool and Jacuzzi, and nearby alpine skiing at four world-class ski areas within a 20-mile radius. Be sure to ask about the Western party nights, and moonlight sleigh rides.
Children's Programs: No organized programs. Most kids are in the excellent ski-school programs in Aspen or Snowmass.
Dining: Ranch does not provide meals on a regular basis. Most guests cook in their cabins or join in on some of the meal-oriented snowmobile tours. Aspen is a 10-minute drive for elegant dining and world-class cuisine. Don't miss T-Lazy-7's famous sleigh ride dinner-dance.
Entertainment: As Landon says, "For an evening of organized chaos and wholesome fun, nothing beats our Western party night." It's a full evening of entertainment with sleigh rides, hearty Western steak dinner, and dancing to live country-Western band.
Summary: The Deane family was one of the original founders of Aspen. T-Lazy-7 Ranch offers one of the great winter experiences for folks who enjoy snowmobiling to the world-famous Maroon Bells, sleigh rides, Western party nights, and proximity to internationally famous Aspen and its downhill skiing and evening nightlife.

See color photos, pages 206–207.

Teton Ridge Ranch
Tetonia, Idaho

"Teton Ridge is a gem on the other side of the Tetons." Five miles from the nearest paved road, the 4,000-acre ranch offers gracious hospitality, excellent food, elegant accommodations (Jacuzzi, steam shower, and woodstove in each bedroom suite), and superb cross-country skiing. The delightful 10,000-square-foot log lodge and separate two-bedroom cottage accommodates only 14 guests at a time. The upper floor is largely devoted to a living room with cathedral ceiling, opening onto a deck with a stunning profile of the almost-14,000-foot Grand Tetons. The ranch is part of the largest intact ecosystem in the lower 48 states. Guests seem to acclimate quickly to the 6,800-foot altitude, which is a good thing, since 20 miles of snowcat-groomed striding and skating trails take off a dozen yards from the door. This is "ego skiing" at its height—gentle uphills and descents winding through meadows, aspens, and conifers, with views of both the Tetons and the Big Holes. It's the only trail system in North America that moves between two states, starting in Idaho and winding east into Wyoming. The ranch is, indeed, one of Kilgore's "Best of the Best."

Address: 200 Valley View Road, Drawer K, Tetonia, Idaho 83452
Telephone: (208) 456-2650; fax: (208) 456-2218
E-Mail: atilt@aol.com
Airport: Jackson, 45 miles; Idaho Falls, 69 miles; small planes to Driggs Airport, 11 miles (7,200-foot paved and lighted airstrip). Extra charge for pickup at Jackson and Idaho Falls.
Location: 38 miles west of Jackson; 11 miles northeast of Driggs
Memberships: Cross-Country Ski Areas Association, Idaho Guest & Dude Ranch Association
Awards: *Hideaway Report*
Medical: Teton Valley Hospital, 12 miles
Conference: 14 overnight, 32 for the day. Excellent for very small corporate retreats.
Guest Capacity: 14
Accommodations: The main 10,000-square-foot log lodge has a spacious living room, lower-level dining room, and five suites, each with balconies commanding views of the Teton Range, woodstoves, and large bathrooms with Jacuzzi tubs. Separate 2,000-square-foot cottage.
Rates: • $$$. American Plan. No minimum stay, but most come for four to five days.
Credit Cards: None
Season: Mid-December through March
Activities: The region is famous for its snow depth and quality (the high country receives over 40 feet of powder annually). Ask about the "snorkel skiing" in the Teton backcountry if you wish. You can also arrange an overnight ski to a wilderness *yurt* (domed tent). Visitors often alpine ski at Grand Targhee, or head over Teton Pass to Jackson Hole for more downhilling, shopping, and a sleigh ride in the National Elk Refuge. Other options include horse-drawn sleigh rides, dogsledding, a snowmobile trip into Yellowstone National Park, and sporting clays on the ranch. Bring your own cross-country equipment, or rent top gear at Skinny Skis in Jackson Hole or Yostmark in Driggs.
Children's Programs: Winter wonderland. Parents are responsible for children. Best for older children.
Dining: Good food is an epicure's delight at Teton Ridge Ranch. Innovative American cuisine served nightly in candlelit dining room complete with two fireplaces, a view of the Teton Mountains, and good wine. Dinner might include mixed gathered greens with creamy lemon vinaigrette, cumin-roasted rack of lamb, grilled vegetables, Napoleons, and chocolate crème brûlée for dessert. Fresh bread served each night along with fresh vegetables, herbs, and greens grown in ranch garden during the summer. Special diets always accommodated.
Entertainment: You're on your own. Most read, relax, or enjoy fireside chats and a glass of brandy. Usually "high tea" after skiing.
Summary: One of Kilgore's Best of the Best. Teton Ridge is ideal for couples or small groups who enjoy privacy, a pristine setting, luxury, and stellar cross-country and alpine skiing. Nearby: skiing, shopping, and art galleries in Jackson Hole.

See color photos, pages 232–233.

Lone Mountain Ranch
Big Sky, Montana

Montana Dude Ranch Association

Lone Mountain Ranch is a wonderful destination for both cross-country and downhill skiers. It offers a variety of cross-country skiing opportunities right from each cabin's doorstep. The double-wide, machine-tilled, and tracked trail system winds 40 miles through meadows, across ridges, and up deep Rocky Mountain valleys. In addition, miles of ungroomed trails lead guests to spots where they can ski and carve telemark turns in untracked powder. Every effort has been made to design a trail system to please every level of skier. Many of the guests participate in optional all-day naturalist-guided ski trips into the Yellowstone or Spanish Peaks backcountry that surround the ranch. All trips are led by guides who are knowledgeable about skiing, the winter environment, and the area's natural wonders. One of the more popular trips leads skiers to the interior of Yellowstone by snowcoach. Guests then disembark for backcountry skiing through the geyser basins, viewing wintering elk and grazing buffalo. The ranch recommends that all beginners take lessons from their Professional Ski Instructors Association–certified instructors to help develop the skills needed to maximize the enjoyment of this lifetime activity.

Address: P.O. Box 160069 K, Big Sky, Montana 59716
Telephone: (800) 514-4644, (406) 995-4644; fax: (406) 995-4670
E-Mail: lmr@lmranch.com
Internet: http://www.lmranch.com
Airport: Bozeman, 40 miles
Location: 40 miles south of Bozeman
Memberships: Greater Yellowstone Coalition, Montana Dude Ranch Association, Cross-Country Ski Area Association, Professional Ski Instructors of America (PSIA)
Awards: Various *Snow Country Magazine* Awards
Medical: Bozeman Deaconess Hospital
Conference: 50
Guest Capacity: 60
Accommodations: 24 fully insulated one- and two-bedroom cozy cabins with comfortable beds, electric heat, bathrooms with tub/shower, and rock fireplaces or wood-burning stoves. Six-bedroom luxury Ridge Top Lodge.
Rates: • $$–$$$. American Plan. Children's rates. Normally a minimum one-week stay, Sunday to Sunday.
Credit Cards: VISA, MasterCard, Discover
Season: Early December to early April
Activities: 40 miles of tilled and tracked cross-country trails through meadows, across ridges, and up valleys. Miles of ungroomed trails and designated snowshoe trails. Retail and rental cross-country shop. Lessons, naturalist-guided ski trips to Yellowstone backcountry. Shuttle service for downhill skiers to Big Sky Resort. Outdoor whirlpool.
Children's Programs: None. Best for children old enough to ski. Toddlers not advised.
Dining: Tremendous log dining room with limited seating open to the public. The food consistently receives rave reviews. Old-fashioned sleigh ride to a cabin in the woods for dinner. The cabin is lit by kerosene lanterns, and food is cooked on a magnificent 100-year-old wood cookstove. Guests enjoy a prime-rib dinner and musical entertainment before their ride back to the ranch. Be sure to ask about the excellent weekly trail buffet lunch.
Entertainment: Several evening programs throughout the winter, including naturalist presentations on grizzly bears and the greater Yellowstone ecosystem. Weekly musical programs also featured.
Summary: World-class cross-country skiing near Yellowstone National Park and downhill skiing at nearby Big Sky Resort. Dependable snow and meticulously groomed trails. Sleigh rides and dining room open to the public on a limited basis. Winter guided fly-fishing trips. Great for conferences. Major airline connections. Check out interactive ski trail map—weather and ski conditions available on the Internet. Video available.

See color photos, pages 250–251.

Triple Creek Ranch
Darby, Montana

Triple Creek Ranch is one of the world's true luxury hideaways. Small, intimate, with personal service second to none, all the trappings that embrace a winter wonderland come alive here. The spirit at Triple Creek is just as magical as the surroundings. Together with an incredible staff, general managers Wayne and Judy Kilpatrick serve up the best of the best. Guests enjoy relaxing in true luxury with crackling fires and gourmet cuisine, coupled with all the outdoor winter activities, including cross-country skiing, snowmobiling, snowshoeing, horseback riding, and sledding, not to mention the heartwarming joys of the Christmas and New Year holidays. Winter, summer, or fall, Triple Creek is truly a slice of heaven and a piece of paradise.

Address: 5551 West Fork Road K, Darby, Montana 59829
Telephone: (406) 821-4600; fax: (406) 821-4666
E-Mail: triplecreekinfo@graphcom.com
Internet: triplecreekranch.com
Airport: Missoula, 74 miles. Private planes to Hamilton with 4,200-foot runway. Helicopter pad at ranch. Airport pickup available.
Location: 12 miles south of Darby, 74 miles south of Missoula
Memberships: Relais & Chateaux
Awards: Relais & Chateaux, *Hideaway Report* Top 10 U.S. Resort Hideaways 1997 and The Hospitality Award 1997
Medical: Marcus Daly Memorial Hospital, Hamilton. Emergency medical helicopter service available.
Conference: 36, executive telecommuting facilities.
Guest Capacity: 28 singles, 21 couples
Accommodations: 18 cozy-to-luxurious cedar log cabins. All have fireplaces and refrigerators stocked with an array of complimentary beverages and a full supply of liquor. Each cabin has satellite TV/VCR. Luxury cabins have handsome, handcrafted, king-size log beds; double steam showers; and private decks with hot tubs overlooking the forest. Daily housekeeping and laundry service.
Rates: • $$$$–$$$$$$. American Plan. No minimum stay. Single rates. All fine wine and liquor complimentary.
Credit Cards: VISA, MasterCard, American Express, Discover
Season: Year-round, all holidays
Activities: While snowmobiling is a specialty, there's also a variety of cross-country skiing and downhill opportunities for both beginning and advanced skiers. Cross-country trails at the ranch are set with a snowmobile, or you may ski into the Bitterroot National Forest with all kinds of backcountry experiences. Downhill skiing at Lost Trail Powder Mountain (28 miles away) with shuttle service provided. Be sure to ask about incredible all-day snowmobiling with gourmet luncheons and snacks. Snowshoeing and horseback riding too! Heated outdoor Jacuzzi.
Children's Programs: Children under age 16 allowed only when entire ranch is reserved by a family or group.
Dining: Gourmet meals with menus featuring Montana beef, seafood flown in from the coast, and wild game. Special diets never a problem. Full room service available. Extensive wine list and full bar. Open to the public on very limited basis.
Entertainment: Informal evening program. Occasional live music. Main lodge with library and full complimentary bar.
Summary: Adults only, year-round luxury in Montana's wilderness. Personal service second to none! Relaxed or active winter paradise—you decide. Superb cuisine, fine wine, and amenities. Excellent for small corporate groups and family reunions. Executive telecommuting available in cabins. Triple Creek is tops!

See color photos, pages 258–259.

Brooks Lake Lodge
Dubois, Wyoming

THE DUDE RANCHERS' ASSOCIATION

Wyoming Dude Rancher's Association

History, romance, magnificence: Brooks Lake captures the spirit and tradition of one of North America's great winter sporting lodges. It's a winter Shangri-la high in the Wyoming Rockies. The lodge is located about 63 miles northeast of Jackson, famous for Les Grand Tetons named by early French explorers. If you drive from the small towns of Dubois or Jackson, Brooks Lake staff will meet you at the trailhead just off Togwotee Pass Highway; their warm smiles are just the beginning. From this point, guests are shuttled by snowmobile five miles to the lodge. Some prefer to cross-country ski or dogsled in. Whatever you decide to do, you're in for the time of your life. Whether you're sitting by one of the blazing fires in the midst of a snowstorm or exploring the magical mountain splendor on a crisp blue-sky day, you'll never forget the Brooks Lake Lodge.

Address: 458 Brooks Lake Road, Drawer K, Dubois, Wyoming 82513
Telephone: (307) 455-2121; fax: (307) 455-2121 (call first)
Internet: http://www.guestranches.com (and click on Brooks Lake Lodge)
Airport: Jackson, 60 miles
Location: 60 miles northeast of Jackson off Highway 287/26, 23 miles west of Dubois off Highway 287/26
Memberships: The Dude Ranchers' Association, Wyoming Dude Rancher's Association, Association of Historic Hotels of the Rocky Mountain West
Medical: Jackson, 60 miles
Conference: 30 (overnight); 125 (day only)
Guest Capacity: 30
Accommodations: Six comfortable lodge rooms with a distinctive motif and exquisite hand-crafted lodgepole furnishings. Six cabins nestle in the spruces behind the lodge, with wood-burning stoves, electric heat, and private baths with bathrobes. Several have wonderful old clawfoot bathtubs. The massive log lodge is furnished with wicker, antiques, and handcrafted works by Wyoming artists. No telephones or TVs in rooms. There is a separate spa cabin.
Rates: • $$$. American Plan. Snowmobiles, dogsledding, and liquor extra. No minimum stay.
Credit Cards: VISA, MasterCard, American Express
Season: Late December to mid-April. Open for lodging Wednesday through Sunday.
Activities: The lodge is situated at 9,200 feet in the midst of the awesome Pinnacle formation of the Absaroka Mountains, the Brooks Mountain to the west, and the Continental Divide to the north. You may cross-country ski, snowmobile (all guided trips), snowshoe, or with prior arrangement, take a thrilling dogsled ride. Guests usually use the lodge as a base camp for myriad outdoor adventures. Overnight trips into Yellowstone National Park by snowmobile are available, too. Ask about Sublette Meadow, Bear Cub Pass, Austin Peak, and bighorn sheep viewing.
Children's Programs: None, but kids are welcome. Younger children should be accompanied by a nanny if parents wish to be active outdoors.
Dining: Hearty regional Western cuisine and health-conscious meals. Delicious homemade soups and freshly baked breads. Lunches open to the public arriving by skis, dogsled, or snowmobile. Liquor and wine served.
Entertainment: The Diamond G Saloon is a gathering place before and after dinner. At 6 p.m., hors d'oeuvres are served. A game of pool, darts, or a natural history video. Evening poetry readings (guests recite their favorite poems, too) and occasional local entertainment.
Summary: The Brooks Lake Lodge winter experience is magical. And talk about snow...Old West beauty, warmth, and mountain splendor. Superb accommodations, great food, and terrific hospitality. You'll cherish your time here for the rest of your life! Lodging open Wednesday through Sunday. Lunches open to the public. Five-mile trip in winter to lodge by skis, snowmobiles, or dogsled (with prior arrangement).

See color photos, pages 282–283.

Brush Creek Ranch
Saratoga, Wyoming

THE DUDE RANCHERS' ASSOCIATION

Wyoming Dude Rancher's Association

Brush Creek Ranch is one of Wyoming's old-time cattle ranches. Just outside the town of Saratoga and overlooking the Platte Valley, the ranch offers the charm and intimacy that you might expect to find on a ranch in the winter. Today, Kinta and Gibb Blumenthal offer a winter experience with very relaxed, easygoing, and independent programs for families, couples, and singles. Brush Creek offers cross-country skiing, horse-drawn sleigh rides, dogsledding, snowshoeing, and great sledding opportunities for children. With several different packages to choose from you may also enjoy off-ranch snowmobile tours through Wyoming's Snowy Range Mountains, just 15 minutes away.

Address: Star Route, Box 10, Saratoga, Wyoming 82331
Telephone: (800) 726-2499, (307) 327-5241; fax: (307) 327-5384
E-Mail: kblumen@csn.net
Internet: http://www.duderanch.org/brush creek
Airport: Denver, 195 miles; Laramie, 65 miles. Airport pickup is extra.
Location: 100 miles west of Laramie. Call for details.
Memberships: Colorado Cross-Country Ski Association, The Dude Ranchers' Association, Wyoming Dude Rancher's Association
Medical: Clinic in Saratoga, 16 miles
Guest Capacity: 24
Accommodations: Guests stay in either the main lodge, built in the early 1900s with a New England white-sided and green-trimmed charm, or in two historic log-cabin duplexes with private baths. The main lodge has a wonderful personality with small, cozy library and fireplace.
Rates: • $$. Full American Plan. Children's rates. Two-night minimum stay.
Credit Cards: VISA, MasterCard
Season: December through March
Activities: You're on your own to do as much or as little as you wish. The ranch will help you coordinate and organize both on- and off-ranch activities. Cross-country skiers enjoy over five miles of snowmobile-prepared trails and miles of untracked skiing opportunities through the cattle in the meadows, by the creek, or on thousands of acres of wonderful backcountry. Equipment available through local outfitter, or bring your own. Be sure to ask about the incredible snowmobiling in the Medicine Bow National Forest, just up the road from the ranch.
Children's Programs: Children are their parents' responsibility. Luckily, it's a kids' winter wonderland. Ice skating (BYOS).
Dining: Western-style food with a gourmet flair. Take-along lunches for day outings. BYOB.
Entertainment: Very low-key and informal. Most relax by the fire, enjoying conversation and sharing stories. Stargazing.
Summary: A 6,000-acre winter wonderland on one of Wyoming's historic cattle ranches. Great for those who savor peace, quiet, and an unstructured program. Wonderful family atmosphere and warm, sincere hospitality. Nearby: charming Western town of Saratoga and Wyoming's Snowy Range Mountains.

See color photos, page 281.

The Hills Health and Guest Ranch
108 Mile Ranch, British Columbia, Canada

SUPER, NATURAL BRITISH COLUMBIA®

Pat and Juanita Corbett had a vision of creating one of the most extensive cross-country ski complexes in North America, coupled with an award-winning spa program. Today, their facility, perched on a hill, is nearly in the center of a maze of trails that wind in all directions. The Hills is part of a community-wide 130-mile trail system. The complex has hosted such major Canadian events as the Cariboo Marathon (western Canada's largest, with more than 1,000 skiers), the Canadian Junior Championship, the B.C. Cup Race, the Kahlua Treasure Hunt on skis, the Timex, and the Skiathlon. At the Hills, you can ski hut-to-hut and among other lodge facilities. Pat and Juanita have opened membership at the Hills to the community. With a membership, families can use the indoor pool, two whirlpools, dressing rooms, and saunas. They keep busy at the Hills; they like what they do, and it shows. Their staff is extremely friendly and helpful. Juanita's Kentucky warmth and charm are contagious.

Address: Box 26, 108 Mile Ranch, British Columbia, Canada V0K 2Z0
Telephone: (250) 791-5225; fax: (250) 791-6384
E-Mail: thehills@bcinternet.net
Internet: http://www.grt-net.com/thehills
Airport: Williams Lake
Train: 100-Mile House
Location: Eight miles north of 100-Mile House off Highway 97, 50 miles south of Williams Lake, 290 miles north of Vancouver
Membership: Canada West Ski Areas Association, British Columbia Guest Ranchers' Association, International Spa & Fitness Association
Medical: 100-Mile House Hospital, eight miles
Conference: 150; 4,300-square-foot meeting space
Guest Capacity: 150
Accommodations: 20 chalets (sunrise or sunset views) line the ridge, with a road up the middle. Each has a full kitchen, small living/dining area, color television, upstairs and downstairs bedrooms, porch, and daily maid service. Two lodges with 26 rooms.
Rates: • $$–$$$. European/American packages available. Children's and group rates available.
Credit Cards: VISA, MasterCard, American Express
Season: December through March (open Christmas)
Activities: Full cross-country ski program, 130 miles of machine-groomed and double-tracked trails, 20 miles of skating trails, ski shop with rentals/sales and ski school, sleigh rides, full spa facilities. Winter spa facilities include exercise room, aerobics studio, power walking, weights, massage, facials, pedicures, nutritionist, and personal training.
Children's Programs: Children are the responsibility of their parents. Swimming class for all ages. Baby-sitting available.
Dining: Fully licensed dining room. Chef prepares wonderful meals in the Trails End Dining Room. Full spa meals.
Entertainment: The weekend dinner music is one of the most delightful features of the Corbetts' operation. Several very talented professional musicians are part of the musical family. Sleigh rides, Indian tepees, and musical entertainment.
Summary: Full cross-country ski program with world-class grooming equipment featuring double-tracked and skating trails, downhill skiing, snowboard park, dogsledding, snowmobiling, ice-skating, along with an international, award-winning adventure spa program. Wellness and fitness workshops. Full ski shop with instruction. Professional entertainment. German and French spoken.

Appendix

RANCHES LISTED ALPHABETICALLY

ADDITIONAL RANCHES

United States

Other properties you might want to consider are listed here by state:

Sprucedale Ranch
Alpine, Arizona, Winter: P.O. Box 880 K, Eagar, Arizona 85925; Summer: HC 61, Box 10, Alpine, Arizona 85920, (520) 333-4984

Circle Bar B Guest Ranch
Goleta, California, 1800 Refugio Canyon Road, Dept. K, Goleta, California 93117, (805) 968-1113

Muir Trail Ranch
Lakeshore, California, P.O. Box 269 K, Ahwahnee, California 93602, (209) 966-3195 (winter)

Avalanche Ranch
Redstone, Colorado, 12863 Highway 133, Drawer K, Redstone, Colorado 81623, (970) 963-2846

Cherokee Park Ranch
Livermore, Colorado, P.O. Box 97K, Livermore, Colorado 80536, (970) 493-6522, (800) 628-0949

Focus Ranch
Slater, Colorado, P.O. Box 51 K, Slater, Colorado 81653, (970) 583-2410

Forbes Trinchera Ranch
Fort Garland, Colorado, P.O. Box 149 K, Fort Garland, Colorado 81133, (719) 379-3264

Sky Corral Ranch
Bellvue, Colorado, 8233 Old Flowers Road, Dept. K, Bellvue, Colorado 80512, (970) 484-1362

Sylvan Dale Ranch
Loveland, Colorado, 2939 N. County Road 31D, Dept. K, Loveland, Colorado 80538, (970) 667-3915

Indian Creek Guest Ranch
Northfork, Idaho, HC 64, Box 105A Drawer K, Northfork, Idaho 83466, (208) 394-2126

Wapiti Meadow Ranch
Cascade, Idaho, H.C. 72 K, Cascade, Idaho 83611, (208) 633-3217

Spur Cross Ranch
Golconda, Nevada, P.O. Box 38K, Golconda, Nevada 89414; Reservations only (800) 651-4567

Vermejo Park Ranch
Raton, New Mexico, P.O. Drawer E, Dept. K, Raton, New Mexico 87740, (505) 445-3097

Roseland Ranch
Stanfordville, New York, Hunns Lake Road, Dept. K, Stanfordville, New York 12581, (914) 868-1350

Logging Camp Ranch
Bowman, North Dakota, HC1 Box 27 K, Bowman, North Dakota 58623, (701) 279-5501

Bald Eagle Ranch
Bandera, Texas, P.O. Box 1177 K, Bandera, Texas 78003, (210) 460-3012

Prude Ranch
Fort Davis, Texas, Box 1431 K, Fort Davis, Texas 79734, (800) 458-6232

Pack Creek Ranch
Moab, Utah, Box 1270 K, Moab, Utah 84532, (435) 259-5505; fax: (435) 259-8879 (bed-and-breakfast)

Rockin' R Ranch
Antimony, Utah, Box 120012 K, Antimony, Utah 84712, (435) 624-3250

Darwin Ranch
Jackson, Wyoming, P.O. Box 511 K, Jackson, Wyoming 83001, (307) 733-5588; call for fax number

David Ranch
Daniel, Wyoming, Box 5, Dept. K, Daniel, Wyoming 83115, (307) 859-8228; fax: (307) 367-2864

Deer Forks Ranch
Douglas, Wyoming, 1200 Poison Lake Road, Drawer K, Douglas, Wyoming 82633, (307) 358-2033; call for fax number

Rafter Y Ranch
Banner, Wyoming, 325 Wagon Box Road, Drawer K, Banner, Wyoming 82832, (307) 683-2258; call for fax number

Terry Bison Ranch
Cheyenne, Wyoming, 51 I-25 Service Road East, Dept. K, Cheyenne, Wyoming 82007, (307) 634-5347, (307) 634-4171; call for fax number

Turpin Meadow Ranch
Moran, Wyoming, P.O. Box 379 K, Moran, Wyoming 83013, (307) 543-2496, (800) 743-2496; fax: (307) 543-2850

Canada

Big Bar Guest Ranch
Clinton, British Columbia, Canada, P.O. Box 27 K, Clinton, British Columbia, Canada V0K 1K0, (250) 459-2333

Black Cat Guest Ranch
Hinton, Alberta, Canada, Box 6267 K, Hinton, Alberta, Canada T7V 1X6, (403) 865-3084

Rafter Six Ranch Resort
Seebe, Alberta, Canada, P.O. Box K, Seebe, Alberta, Canada T0L 1X0, (403) 673-3622

TL Bar Ranch
Trochu Alberta, Canada, Box 217 K, Trochu, Alberta, Canada T0M 2C0, (403) 442-2207

Elkin Creek Guest Ranch
North Vancouver, British Columbia, Canada, 4462 Marion Road, Dept. K, North Vancouver, British Columbia, Canada V7K 2V2, (604) 984-4666

Flying U Ranch
70 Mile House, British Columbia, Canada, Box 69 K, N. Greenlake, 70 Mile House, British Columbia, Canada V0K 2K0, (604) 456-7717

Sundance Guest Ranch
Ashcroft, British Columbia, Canada, Box 489 K, Ashcroft, British Columbia, Canada V0K 1A0, (604) 453-2422/2554

Fly-fishing

Elktrout Lodge
Kremmling, Colorado, P.O. Box 614 K, Kremmling, Colorado 80459, (970) 724-3343

Eagle Nest Lodge
Hardin, Montana, P.O. Box 509 K, Hardin, Montana 59034, (406) 362-4270

Spotted Bear Ranch
Kalispell, Montana, 2863 Foothill Road, Drawer K, Kalispell, Montana 59901, (800) 223-4333

SPECIAL RANCH HIGHLIGHTS

Accessible Only by Boat, Horseback, Helicopter, Plane, or Train
Crystal Creek Lodge, Alaska
Kachemak Bay Wilderness Lodge, Alaska
Grand Canyon Bar Ten Ranch, Arizona
Tall Timber, Colorado
Molokai Ranch, Hawaii
Klick's K Bar L Ranch, Montana

Adults Only (Check with ranch on age limits and opportunities for families who book entire property)
Double JJ Resort Ranch, Michigan
Happy Hollow Ranch & Zeemering Farms Ltd., Michigan
Triple Creek Ranch, Montana
Garrett Creek Ranch, Texas
Flying A Guest Ranch, Wyoming
Flying S Ranch, Wyoming

Adults Only (Special Weeks/Months)
Crystal Creek Lodge, Alaska
Kachemak Bay Wilderness Lodge, Alaska
Grapevine Canyon Ranch, Arizona
The Horseshoe Ranch on Bloody Basin Road, Arizona
Lazy K Bar Guest Ranch, Arizona
Price Canyon Ranch, Arizona
Rancho de la Osa, Arizona
Scott Valley Resort and Guest Ranch, Arkansas
Coffee Creek Ranch, California
Highland Ranch, California
Howard Creek Ranch, California
C Lazy U Ranch, Colorado
Colorado Trails Ranch, Colorado
Drowsy Water Ranch, Colorado
Lake Mancos Ranch, Colorado
Lost Valley Ranch, Colorado
McNamara Ranch, Colorado
Powderhorn Guest Ranch, Colorado
Rawah Ranch, Colorado
San Juan Guest Ranch, Colorado
Seven Lakes Lodge, Colorado
Vista Verde Ranch, Colorado
Waunita Hot Springs Ranch, Colorado
Wilderness Trails Ranch, Colorado
Hidden Creek Ranch, Idaho
Moose Creek Ranch, Idaho
Teton Ridge Ranch, Idaho
Double JJ Resort Ranch, Michigan
Happy Hollow Ranch & Zeemering Farms Ltd., Michigan
Bear Creek Lodge, Montana
Big Hole River Outfitters, Montana
Boulder River Ranch, Montana
Crazy Mountain Ranch, Montana
Diamond J Ranch, Montana
Hargrave Cattle and Guest Ranch, Montana
Hawley Mountain Guest Ranch, Montana
JJJ Wilderness Ranch, Montana
Laughing Water Ranch, Montana
Lone Mountain Ranch, Montana
Mountain Sky Guest Ranch, Montana
RJR Ranch, Montana
The Lodge at Chama, New Mexico
Pinegrove Dude Ranch, New York
Ponderosa Cattle Company and Guest Ranch, Oregon
Cibolo Creek Ranch, Texas
Garrett Creek Ranch, Texas
Woodside Ranch, Wisconsin
Bitterroot Ranch, Wyoming
Canyon Ranch, Wyoming
Crescent H Ranch, Wyoming
Flying S Ranch, Wyoming
Gros Ventre River Ranch, Wyoming
The Hideout at Flitner Ranch, Wyoming
High Island Ranch and Cattle Company, Wyoming
Hunter Peak Ranch, Wyoming
Kedesh Ranch, Wyoming
Lazy L & B Ranch, Wyoming
Lozier's Box R Ranch, Wyoming
Paradise Guest Ranch, Wyoming
Red Rock Ranch, Wyoming
R Lazy S, Wyoming
Savery Creek Thoroughbred Ranch, Wyoming
Seven D Ranch, Wyoming
T-Cross Ranch, Wyoming
Triangle C Ranch, Wyoming
UXU Ranch, Wyoming
Echo Valley Guest Ranch, British Columbia, Canada

Advanced Riding Programs
Circle Z Ranch, Arizona
Elkhorn Ranch, Arizona
Grapevine Canyon Ranch, Arizona

The Horseshoe Ranch on Bloody Basin Road, Arizona
Lazy K Bar Guest Ranch, Arizona
Merv Griffin's Wickenburg Inn and Dude Ranch, Arizona
Rancho de la Osa, Arizona
Rancho de los Caballeros, Arizona
Tanque Verde Ranch, Arizona
White Stallion Ranch, Arizona
Scott Valley Resort and Guest Ranch, Arkansas
Alisal Guest Ranch, California
Howard Creek Ranch, California
Hunewill Circle H Ranch, California
C Lazy U Ranch, Colorado
Colorado Trails Ranch, Colorado
The Home Ranch, Colorado
Laramie River Ranch, Colorado
Latigo Ranch, Colorado
Lost Valley Ranch, Colorado
McNamara Ranch, Colorado
Rawah Ranch, Colorado
San Juan Guest Ranch, Colorado
Seven Lakes Lodge, Colorado
Skyline Guest Ranch, Colorado
Wilderness Trails Ranch, Colorado
Bar H Bar Ranch, Idaho
Hidden Creek Ranch, Idaho
Double JJ Resort Ranch, Michigan
Happy Hollow Ranch & Zeemering Farms Ltd., Michigan
Bonanza Creek Country, Montana
Circle Bar Guest Ranch, Montana
Covered Wagon Ranch, Montana
Elkhorn Ranch, Montana
Hargrave Cattle and Guest Ranch, Montana
Horse Prairie Ranch, Montana
JJJ Wilderness Ranch, Montana
Mountain Sky Guest Ranch, Montana
RJR Ranch, Montana
Cottonwood Ranch, Nevada
Aspen Ridge Resort, Oregon
Ponderosa Cattle Company and Guest Ranch, Oregon
Cibolo Creek Ranch, Texas
Flying L Guest Ranch, Texas
Bitterroot Ranch, Wyoming
Breteche Creek Ranch, Wyoming
Brush Creek Ranch, Wyoming
Cheyenne River Ranch, Wyoming
CM Ranch, Wyoming
Eatons' Ranch, Wyoming
Flying A Guest Ranch, Wyoming
Flying S Ranch, Wyoming
H F Bar Ranch, Wyoming
High Island Ranch and Cattle Company, Wyoming
Lazy L & B Ranch, Wyoming
Lost Creek Ranch, Wyoming
Lozier's Box R Ranch, Wyoming
Paradise Guest Ranch, Wyoming
Savery Creek Thoroughbred Ranch, Wyoming
TA Guest Ranch, Wyoming
T-Cross Ranch, Wyoming
Triangle C Ranch, Wyoming
Vee Bar Guest Ranch, Wyoming
Homeplace Guest Ranch, Alberta, Canada

Airstrip (on or near ranch)
Crystal Creek Lodge, Alaska
Kachemak Bay Wilderness Lodge, Alaska
Circle Z Ranch, Arizona
Flying E Ranch, Arizona
Grand Canyon Bar Ten Ranch, Arizona
Kay El Bar, Arizona
Lazy K Bar Guest Ranch, Arizona
Merv Griffin's Wickenburg Inn and Dude Ranch, Arizona
Rancho de los Caballeros, Arizona
Lost Spur Guest Ranch, Arkansas
Alisal Guest Ranch, California
Coffee Creek Ranch, California
Hunewill Circle H Ranch, California
Coulter Lake Guest Ranch, Colorado
Deer Valley Guest Ranch, Colorado
Drowsy Water Ranch, Colorado
4UR Ranch, Colorado
The Home Ranch, Colorado
King Mountain Ranch Resort, Colorado
La Garita Creek Ranch, Colorado
Latigo Ranch, Colorado
T-Lazy-7 Ranch, Colorado
Wind River Ranch, Colorado
Molokai Ranch, Hawaii
Diamond D Ranch, Idaho
Teton Ridge Ranch, Idaho
Twin Peaks Ranch, Idaho
Double JJ Resort Ranch, Michigan
Happy Hollow Ranch & Zeemering Farms Ltd., Michigan
Crazy Mountain Ranch, Montana
Diamond J Ranch, Montana
Laughing Water Ranch, Montana
Lazy K Bar Ranch, Montana
Nine Quarter Circle Ranch, Montana

RJR Ranch, Montana
63 Ranch, Montana
White Tail Ranch, Montana
Cottonwood Ranch, Nevada
Pinegrove Dude Ranch, New York
Rocking Horse Ranch Resort, New York
Clear Creek Ranch, North Carolina
Greenhorn Creek Ranch, North Carolina
Aspen Ridge Resort, Oregon
Flying M Ranch, Oregon
Ponderosa Cattle Company and Guest Ranch, Oregon
Cibolo Creek Ranch, Texas
Hidden Valley Guest Ranch, Washington
Woodside Ranch, Wisconsin
Brush Creek Ranch, Wyoming
CM Ranch, Wyoming
Crescent H Ranch, Wyoming
Flying S Ranch, Wyoming
H F Bar Ranch, Wyoming
Lazy L & B Ranch, Wyoming
Lozier's Box R Ranch, Wyoming
TA Guest Ranch, Wyoming
T-Cross Ranch, Wyoming
Triangle X Ranch, Wyoming
Echo Valley Guest Ranch, British Columbia, Canada
The Hills Health and Guest Ranch, British Columbia, Canada
Springhouse Trails Ranch, British Columbia, Canada
Three Bars Ranch, British Columbia, Canada
Top of the World Guest Ranch, British Columbia, Canada

Balloon Ranches
La Garita Creek Ranch, Colorado
Vista Verde Ranch, Colorado

Bring Your Own Horse
Flying E Ranch, Arizona
Price Canyon Ranch, Arizona
Rancho de los Caballeros, Arizona
Scott Valley Resort and Guest Ranch, Arkansas
Alisal Guest Ranch, California
Coffee Creek Ranch, California
Highland Ranch, California
Hunewill Ranch, California
McNamara Ranch, Colorado
Bar H Bar Ranch, Idaho
Teton Ridge Ranch, Idaho
Double JJ Resort Ranch, Michigan
Happy Hollow Ranch & Zeemering Farms Ltd., Michigan
Bear Creek Lodge, Montana
Bonanza Creek Country, Montana
Lake Upsata Guest Ranch, Montana
RJR Ranch, Montana
Triple Creek Ranch, Montana
Cottonwood Ranch, Nevada
Ridin-Hy Ranch, New York
Aspen Ridge Resort, Oregon
Flying M Ranch, Oregon
Obstinate J Ranch, Oregon
Ponderosa Cattle Company and Guest Ranch, Oregon
Blue Bell Lodge & Resort, South Dakota
Triple R Ranch, South Dakota
Hidden Valley Guest Ranch, Washington
Woodside Ranch, Wisconsin
Breteche Creek Ranch, Wyoming
Flying S Ranch, Wyoming
Kedesh Ranch, Wyoming
Lozier's Box R Ranch, Wyoming
Savery Creek Thoroughbred Ranch, Wyoming
TA Guest Ranch, Wyoming
T-Cross Ranch, Wyoming
The Hills Health and Guest Ranch, British Columbia, Canada
Homeplace Guest Ranch, Alberta, Canada
Springhouse Trails Ranch, British Columbia, Canada
Three Bars Ranch, British Columbia, Canada

Buffalo Ranch (Have buffalo)
Circle Bar Guest Ranch, Montana
The Lodge at Chama, New Mexico
Blue Bell Lodge & Resort, South Dakota

Cattle Roundups, Cattle Drives
Grand Canyon Bar Ten Ranch, Arizona
Grapevine Canyon Ranch, Arizona
The Horseshoe Ranch on Bloody Basin Road, Arizona
Merv Griffin's Wickenburg Inn and Dude Ranch, Arizona
Price Canyon Ranch, Arizona
Tanque Verde Ranch, Arizona
Alisal Guest Ranch, California
Hunewill Circle H Ranch, California
Coulter Lake Ranch, Colorado
La Garita Creek Ranch, Colorado
Lost Valley Ranch, Colorado
San Juan Guest Ranch, Colorado

Tarryall River Ranch, Colorado
Vista Verde Guest and Ski Touring Ranch, Colorado
Molokai Ranch, Hawaii
Bar H Bar Ranch, Idaho
Twin Peaks Ranch, Idaho
Circle Bar Guest Ranch, Montana
Crazy Mountain Ranch, Montana
G Bar M Ranch, Montana
Hargrave Cattle and Guest Ranch, Montana
Horse Prairie Ranch, Montana
Klick's K Bar L Ranch, Montana
Lazy K Bar Ranch, Montana
Nine Quarter Circle U Rankin Ranch, Montana
Sweetgrass Ranch, Montana
Cottonwood Ranch, Nevada
Pinegrove Dude Ranch, New York
Aspen Ridge Resort, Oregon
Obstinate J Ranch, Oregon
Ponderosa Cattle Company and Guest Ranch, Oregon
Triple R Ranch, South Dakota
Grand Canyon Bar Ten Ranch, Utah
Bitterroot Ranch, Wyoming
Breteche Creek Ranch, Wyoming
Brush Creek Ranch, Wyoming
Cheyenne River Ranch, Wyoming
The Hideout at Flitner Ranch, Wyoming
High Island Ranch and Cattle Company, Wyoming
Lozier's Box R Ranch, Wyoming
Vee Bar Guest Ranch, Wyoming
Three Bars Ranch, British Columbia, Canada
Top of the World Guest Ranch, British Columbia, Canada

Cattle Work
Grand Canyon Bar Ten Ranch, Arizona
Grapevine Canyon Ranch, Arizona
The Horseshoe Ranch on Bloody Basin Road, Arizona
Lazy K Bar Guest Ranch, Arizona
Merv Griffin's Wickenburg Inn and Dude Ranch, Arizona
Price Canyon Ranch, Arizona
White Stallion Ranch, Arizona
Hunewill Circle H Ranch, California
Rankin Ranch, California
The Home Ranch, Colorado
Latigo Ranch, Colorado
Lost Valley Ranch, Colorado
Wilderness Trails Ranch, Colorado
Bar H Bar Ranch, Idaho
Turkey Creek Ranch, Missouri
B Bar Guest Ranch, Montana
Bonanza Creek Country, Montana
C_B Cattle and Guest Ranch, Montana
Circle Bar Guest Ranch, Montana
G Bar M Ranch, Montana
Hargrave Cattle and Guest Ranch, Montana
Horse Prairie Ranch, Montana
Lazy K Bar Ranch, Montana
63 Ranch, Montana
Sweet Grass Ranch, Montana
Cottonwood Ranch, Nevada
Aspen Ridge Resort, Oregon
Obstinate J Ranch, Oregon
Ponderosa Cattle Company and Guest Ranch, Oregon
Bitterroot Ranch, Wyoming
Breteche Creek Ranch, Wyoming
Brush Creek Ranch, Wyoming
Cheyenne River Ranch, Wyoming
The Hideout at Flitner Ranch, Wyoming
High Island Ranch and Cattle Company, Wyoming
Lozier's Box R Ranch, Wyoming
Red Rock Ranch, Wyoming
Savery Creek Thoroughbred Ranch, Wyoming
Seven D Ranch, Wyoming
TA Guest Ranch, Wyoming
T-Cross Ranch, Wyoming
Vee Bar Guest Ranch, Wyoming
Homeplace Guest Ranch, Alberta, Canada
Echo Valley Guest Ranch, British Columbia, Canada
Three Bars Ranch, British Columbia, Canada
Top of the World Guest Ranch, British Columbia, Canada

Childrens' Programs
Lazy K Bar Guest Ranch, Arizona
Merv Griffin's Wickenburg Inn and Dude Ranch, Arizona
Rancho de los Caballeros, Arizona
Tanque Verde Ranch, Arizona
Alisal Guest Ranch, California
Coffee Creek Ranch, California
Rankin Ranch, California
Aspen Canyon Ranch, Colorado
Aspen Lodge Ranch Resort, Colorado
Bar Lazy J, Colorado
C Lazy U Ranch, Colorado
Colorado Trails Ranch, Colorado

Deer Valley Ranch, Colorado
Drowsy Water Ranch, Colorado
Elk Mountain Ranch, Colorado
Flathead Lake Lodge, Colorado
4UR Ranch, Colorado
The Historic Pines Ranch, Colorado
The Home Ranch, Colorado
King Mountain Ranch Resort, Colorado
La Garita Creek Ranch, Colorado
Lake Mancos Ranch, Colorado
Lane Guest Ranch, Colorado
Laramie River Ranch, Colorado
Latigo Ranch, Colorado
Lazy H Guest Ranch, Colorado
Lost Valley Ranch, Colorado
Peaceful Valley Ranch, Colorado
Rainbow Trout Ranch, Colorado
San Juan Guest Ranch, Colorado
Tarryall River Ranch, Colorado
Tumbling River Ranch, Colorado
Vista Verde Ranch, Colorado
Wilderness Trails Ranch, Colorado
Wind River Ranch, Colorado
Wit's End Guest and Resort Ranch, Colorado
Molokai Ranch, Hawaii
Hidden Creek Ranch, Idaho
Moose Creek Ranch, Idaho
Double JJ Resort Ranch, Michigan
El Rancho Stevens, Michigan
Beartooth Ranch and JLX, Montana
Elkhorn Ranch, Montana
Hargrave Cattle and Guest Ranch, Montana
JJJ Wilderness Ranch, Montana
Lone Mountain Ranch, Montana
Mountain Sky Guest Ranch, Montana
Nine Quarter Circle Ranch, Montana
RJR Ranch, Montana
White Tail Ranch, Montana
Pinegrove Dude Ranch, New York
Ridin-Hy Ranch Resort, New York
Roaring Brook Ranch and Tennis Resort, New York
Rocking Horse Ranch Resort, New York
Clear Creek Ranch, North Carolina
Earthshine Mountain Lodge, North Carolina
Rock Springs Guest Ranch, Oregon
Flying L Guest Ranch, Texas
Reid Ranch, Utah
Woodside Ranch, Wisconsin
Double Diamond X Ranch, Wyoming
H F Bar Ranch, Wyoming
Heart Six Ranch and Buffalo Valley Cabins, Wyoming
Laughing Water Ranch, Wyoming
Lazy L & B Ranch, Wyoming
Lost Creek Ranch, Wyoming
Paradise Guest Ranch, Wyoming
Seven D Ranch, Wyoming
Triangle C Ranch, Wyoming
Triangle X Ranch, Wyoming
UXU Ranch, Wyoming
Top of the World Guest Ranch, British Columbia, Canada

Christian Ranches
Deer Valley Ranch, Colorado
Lazy Hills Guest Ranch, Texas
Waunita Hot Springs Ranch, Colorado

Cigar-Friendly
Kachemak Bay Wilderness Lodge, Alaska
Rancho de la Osa, Arizona
Rancho de los Caballeros, Arizona
Coffee Creek Ranch, California
Lane Guest Ranch, Colorado
Lost Valley Ranch, Colorado
T-Lazy-7 Ranch, Colorado
Diamond D Ranch, Idaho
Teton Ridge Ranch, Idaho
Double JJ Resort Ranch, Michigan
El Rancho Stevens, Michigan
Turkey Creek Ranch, Missouri
The 320 Guest Ranch, Montana
Circle Bar Guest Ranch, Montana
Diamond J Ranch, Montana
Klick's K Bar L Ranch, Montana
White Tail Ranch, Montana
Cataloochee Ranch, North Carolina
Aspen Ridge Resort, Oregon
Ponderosa Cattle Company and Guest Ranch, Oregon
Rock Springs Guest Ranch, Oregon
Cibolo Creek Ranch, Texas
Dixie Dude Ranch, Texas
Woodside Ranch, Wisconsin
Absaroka Ranch, Wyoming
Bill Cody Ranch, Wyoming
Breteche Creek Ranch, Wyoming
Brooks Lake Lodge, Wyoming
Canyon Ranch, Wyoming
Double Diamond X Ranch, Wyoming
Eaton's Ranch, Wyoming
H F Bar Ranch, Wyoming
The Hideout at Flitner Ranch, Wyoming
High Island Ranch and Cattle Company, Wyoming

Lozier's Box R Ranch, Wyoming
Paradise Guest Ranch, Wyoming
R Lazy S Ranch, Wyoming
TA Guest Ranch, Wyoming
T-Cross Ranch, Wyoming
UXU Ranch, Wyoming

Conference Opportunities (*Large conference facilities)
Crystal Creek Lodge, Alaska
Kachemak Bay Wilderness Lodge, Alaska
Grapevine Canyon Ranch, Arizona
Kay El Bar, Arizona
Lazy K Bar Guest Ranch, Arizona
Merv Griffin's Wickenburg Inn and Dude Ranch, Arizona
Rancho de la Osa, Arizona
Rancho de los Caballeros, Arizona*
Tanque Verde Ranch, Arizona*
White Stallion Ranch, Arizona
Lost Spur Guest Ranch, Arkansas
Scott Valley Resort and Guest Ranch, Arkansas
Alisal Guest Ranch, California*
Coffee Creek Ranch, California
Greenhorn Creek Ranch, California
Rankin Ranch, California
Aspen Canyon Ranch, Colorado
Aspen Lodge Ranch Resort, Colorado
C Lazy U Ranch, Colorado
Colorado Trails Ranch, Colorado
Coulter Lake Ranch, Colorado
Deer Valley Ranch, Colorado
Diamond J on the Fryingpan Lodge & Guest Ranch, Colorado
4UR Ranch, Colorado
The Historic Pines Ranch, Colorado
The Home Ranch, Colorado
King Mountain Ranch Resort, Colorado
La Garita Creek Ranch, Colorado
Lake Mancos Ranch, Colorado
Laramie River Ranch, Colorado
Latigo Ranch, Colorado
Lazy H Guest Ranch, Colorado
Lost Valley Ranch, Colorado
North Fork Ranch, Colorado
Old Glendevey Ranch, Colorado
Peaceful Valley Ranch, Colorado
Rawah Ranch, Colorado
Skyline Guest Ranch, Colorado
Tall Timber, Colorado
Tarryall River Ranch, Colorado
Vista Verde Ranch, Colorado
Wind River Ranch, Colorado
Wit's End Guest and Resort Ranch, Colorado
Molokai Ranch, Hawaii
Diamond D Ranch, Idaho
Hidden Creek Ranch, Idaho
Moose Creek Ranch, Idaho
Teton Ridge Ranch, Idaho
Twin Peaks Ranch, Idaho
Double JJ Resort Ranch, Michigan
El Rancho Stevens, Michigan
Happy Hollow Ranch & Zeemering Farms Ltd., Michigan
Turkey Creek Ranch, Missouri
B Bar Guest Ranch, Montana
Bear Creek Lodge, Montana
Boulder River Ranch, Montana
Circle Bar Guest Ranch, Montana
Crazy Mountain Ranch, Montana*
Diamond J Ranch, Montana
Elkhorn Ranch, Montana
Flathead Lake Lodge, Montana
Hargrave Cattle and Guest Ranch, Montana
Hawley Mountain Guest Ranch, Montana
Horse Prairie Ranch, Montana
JJJ Wilderness Ranch, Montana
Klick's K Bar L Ranch, Montana
Lake Upsata Guest Ranch, Montana
Laughing Water Ranch, Montana
Lone Mountain Ranch, Montana
Mountain Sky Guest Ranch, Montana
Nine Quarter Circle Ranch, Montana
Parade Rest Ranch, Montana
Pine Butte Guest Ranch, Montana
Seven Lazy P Ranch, Montana
The 320 Ranch, Montana
Triple Creek Ranch, Montana
White Tail Ranch, Montana
The Lodge at Chama, New Mexico
Pinegrove Dude Ranch, New York*
Roaring Brook Ranch and Tennis Resort, New York*
Rocking Horse Ranch, New York*
Cataloochee Ranch, North Carolina
Clear Creek Ranch, North Carolina
Earthshine Mountain Lodge, North Carolina
Aspen Ridge Resort, Oregon
Baker's Bar M Ranch, Oregon
Flying M Ranch, Oregon
Ponderosa Cattle Company and Guest Ranch, Oregon
Rock Springs Guest Ranch, Oregon
Blue Bell Lodge & Resort, South Dakota
Triple R Ranch, South Dakota

Cibolo Creek Ranch, Texas
Dixie Dude Ranch, Texas
Flying L Guest Ranch, Texas
Garrett Creek Ranch, Texas (exclusive conference ranch year-round)*
Lazy Hills Guest Ranch, Texas
Reid Ranch, Utah
Hidden Valley Guest Ranch, Washington
Woodside Ranch, Wisconsin
Bill Cody Ranch, Wyoming
Brooks Lake Lodge, Wyoming
Canyon Ranch, Wyoming
CM Ranch, Wyoming
Crescent H Ranch, Wyoming
Double Diamond X Ranch, Wyoming
Eatons' Ranch, Wyoming
Gros Ventre River Ranch, Wyoming
Heart Six Ranch and Buffalo Valley Cabins, Wyoming
H F Bar Ranch, Wyoming
The Hideout at Flitner Ranch, Wyoming
Hunter Peak Ranch, Wyoming
Kedesh Ranch, Wyoming
Lost Creek Ranch, Wyoming
Paradise Ranch, Wyoming
Red Rock Ranch, Wyoming
Savery Creek Thoroughbred Ranch, Wyoming
Seven D Ranch, Wyoming
TA Guest Ranch, Wyoming
Triangle X Ranch, Wyoming
Triangle C Ranch, Wyoming
UXU Ranch, Wyoming
Vee Bar Guest Ranch, Wyoming
Brewster's Kananaskis Guest Ranch, Alberta, Canada
Echo Valley Guest Ranch, British Columbia, Canada
The Hills Health and Guest Ranch, British Columbia, Canada
Three Bars Ranch, British Columbia, Canada

Corporate Groups, Meetings, Retreats Only
The Wild Horse Creek Ranch, Idaho (winter only)
Garrett Creek Ranch, Texas
Reid Ranch, Utah

Cross-Country Skiing
Aspen Lodge Ranch Resort, Colorado
C Lazy U Ranch, Colorado
The Home Ranch, Colorado
Latigo Ranch, Colorado
Skyline Guest Ranch, Colorado
T-Lazy-7 Ranch, Colorado
Vista Verde Ranch, Colorado
Wit's End Guest and Resort Ranch, Colorado
Teton Ridge Ranch, Idaho
Double JJ Resort Ranch, Michigan
B Bar Ranch, Montana
Lone Mountain Ranch, Montana
Triple Creek Ranch, Montana
Aspen Ridge Resort, Oregon
Woodside Ranch, Wisconsin
Brooks Lake Lodge, Wyoming
Brush Creek Ranch, Wyoming
Triangle C Ranch, Wyoming
Triangle X Ranch, Wyoming
The Hills Health and Guest Ranch, British Columbia, Canada

English Cross-Country Jumping
Savery Creek Thoroughbred Ranch, Wyoming

English Riding
Rancho de los Caballeros, Arizona
Tanque Verde Ranch, Arizona
White Stallion Ranch, Arizona
Alisal Guest Ranch, California
Coffee Creek Ranch, California
Highland Ranch, California
Howard Creek Ranch, California
C Lazy U Ranch, Colorado
Latigo Ranch, Colorado
McNamara Ranch, Colorado
El Rancho Stevens, Michigan
Happy Hollow Ranch & Zeemering Farms Ltd., Michigan
Triple Creek, Montana
Hidden Valley Guest Ranch, Washington
Bitterroot Ranch, Wyoming
Savery Creek Thoroughbred Ranch, Wyoming
Homeplace Guest Ranch, Alberta, Canada
Springhouse Trails Ranch, British Columbia, Canada

Fly-Fishing (Guided programs available; *extensive)
Crystal Creek Lodge, Alaska*
Kachemak Bay Wilderness Lodge, Alaska
Scott Valley Resort and Guest Ranch, Arkansas
Alisal Guest Ranch, California
Bar Lazy J, Colorado

Colorado Trails Ranch, Colorado*
Diamond J on the Fryingpan Lodge & Guest Ranch, Colorado*
4UR Ranch, Colorado
The Home Ranch, Colorado
Laramie River Ranch, Colorado
Latigo Ranch, Colorado
Lost Valley Ranch, Colorado
Powderhorn Guest Ranch, Colorado
Seven Lakes Lodge, Colorado*
Tall Timber, Colorado
Vista Verde Ranch, Colorado
Wilderness Trails Ranch, Colorado
Diamond D Ranch, Idaho
Hidden Creek Ranch, Idaho
Teton Ridge Ranch, Idaho
Twin Peaks Ranch, Idaho
Bear Creek Lodge, Montana
Big Hole River Outfitters, Montana*
Boulder River Ranch, Montana
C_B Cattle and Guest Ranch, Montana
Diamond J Ranch, Montana*
Flathead Lake Lodge, Montana
Horse Prairie Ranch, Montana
Klick's K Bar L Ranch, Montana
Lone Mountain Ranch, Montana*
Mountain Sky Guest Ranch, Montana
Nine Quarter Circle Ranch, Montana
Parade Rest Ranch, Montana*
RJR Ranch, Montana
The 320 Ranch, Montana
Triple Creek Ranch, Montana*
White Tail Ranch, Montana
The Lodge at Chama, New Mexico
Aspen Ridge Resort, Oregon
Obstinate J Ranch, Oregon
Absaroka Ranch, Wyoming
Allen's Diamond 4 Ranch, Wyoming
Bitterroot Ranch, Wyoming
Brush Creek Ranch, Wyoming*
Canyon Ranch, Wyoming
Crescent H Ranch, Wyoming*
Flying A Guest Ranch, Wyoming
H F Bar Ranch, Wyoming
High Island Ranch and Cattle Company, Wyoming
Moose Head Ranch, Wyoming
R Lazy S Ranch, Wyoming
Seven D Ranch, Wyoming
T-Cross Ranch, Wyoming
Triangle X Ranch, Wyoming
UXU Ranch, Wyoming

Foreign Language

Circle Z Ranch, Arizona—Spanish
Grand Canyon Bar Ten Ranch, Arizona—Spanish, French, German, Portuguese
Grapevine Canyon Ranch, Arizona—Czechoslovakian
The Horseshoe Ranch on Bloody Basin Road, Arizona—Spanish, French, German
Price Canyon Ranch, Arizona—Spanish
Rancho de la Osa, Arizona—Spanish
Tanque Verde Ranch, Arizona—Spanish, French, German, Italian, Japanese
White Stallion Ranch, Arizona—Spanish, German, Norwegian, Swedish
Alisal Guest Ranch, California—Spanish, French, German, Italian
Coffee Creek Ranch, California—Spanish, Dutch, German
Highland Ranch, California—French, Italian
Howard Creek Ranch, California—Italian, Dutch, German
Rankin Ranch, California—Spanish
C Lazy U Ranch, Colorado—Spanish, French, German
The Home Ranch, Colorado—Spanish, French, German
Laramie River Ranch, Colorado—French
Latigo Ranch, Colorado—Spanish
Peaceful Valley Ranch, Colorado—German
Rainbow Trout Ranch, Colorado—Portuguese, Swahili
Seven Lakes Lodge, Colorado—Spanish
Hidden Creek Ranch, Idaho—German
Idaho Rocky Mountain Ranch, Idaho—Spanish
El Rancho Stevens, Michigan—Multilingual
Happy Hollow Ranch & Zeemering Farms Ltd., Michigan—French, German, Dutch
Diamond J Ranch, Montana—Spanish
Hargrave Cattle and Guest Ranch, Montana—German
Horse Prairie Ranch, Montana—Spanish, German, Portuguese
The Lodge at Chama, New Mexico—Spanish
Pinegrove Dude Ranch, New York—Spanish, Portuguese
Rocking Horse Ranch, New York—Spanish
Baker's Bar M Ranch, Oregon—Spanish
Ponderosa Cattle Company and Guest Ranch, Oregon—French, German
Blue Bell Lodge & Resort, South Dakota—Multilingual
Cibolo Creek Ranch, Texas—Spanish

Dixie Dude Ranch, Texas—Spanish
Lazy Hills Guest Ranch, Texas—Spanish
Reid Ranch, Utah—Spanish
Bitterroot Ranch, Wyoming—French, German
Brush Creek Ranch, Wyoming—German
Double Diamond X Ranch, Wyoming—Spanish, German
Flying S Ranch, Wyoming—French
The Hideout at Flitner Ranch, Wyoming—Spanish, French, German, Dutch, Japanese
Lost Creek Ranch, Wyoming—Interpreters available
Savery Creek Thoroughbred Ranch, Wyoming—Spanish, French
Vee Bar Guest Ranch, Wyoming—Interpreter available
Homeplace Guest Ranch, Alberta, Canada—German
Echo Valley Guest Ranch, British Columbia, Canada—French, German, Japanese, Swedish, Thai
The Hills Health and Guest Ranch, British Columbia, Canada—German, French, Italian
Springhouse Trails Ranch, British Columbia, Canada—German

Group/Motivational Retreats
Alisal Guest Ranch, California
Earthshine Mountain Lodge, North Carolina
Garrett Creek Ranch, Texas

Handicapped/Wheelchair Accessible
Merv Griffin's Wickenburg Inn and Dude Ranch, Arizona
Rancho de la Osa, Arizona
Rancho de los Caballeros, Arizona
Tanque Verde Ranch, Arizona
Alisal Guest Ranch, California
Coffee Creek Ranch, California
Greenhorn Creek Ranch, California
Aspen Lodge Ranch Resort, Colorado
C Lazy U Ranch, Colorado
The Historic Pines Ranch, Colorado
The Home Ranch, Colorado
Lane Guest Ranch, Colorado
Laramie River Ranch, Colorado
Latigo Ranch, Colorado
Lost Valley Ranch, Colorado
Peaceful Valley Ranch, Colorado
T-Lazy-7 Ranch, Colorado
Wind River Ranch, Colorado
Wit's End Guest and Resort Ranch, Colorado
Hidden Creek Ranch, Idaho
The Wild Horse Creek Ranch, Idaho
Double JJ Resort Ranch, Michigan
El Rancho Stevens, Michigan
Turkey Creek Ranch, Missouri
B Bar Guest Ranch, Montana
Crazy Mountain Ranch, Montana
Diamond J Ranch, Montana
Lone Mountain Ranch, Montana
The 320 Guest Ranch, Montana
Pinegrove Dude Ranch, New York
Roaring Brook Ranch and Tennis Resort, New York
Rocking Horse Ranch, New York
Cataloochee Ranch, North Carolina
Clear Creek Ranch, North Carolina
Earthshine Mountain Lodge, North Carolina
Ponderosa Cattle Company and Guest Ranch, Oregon
Blue Bell Lodge & Resort, South Dakota
Triple R Ranch, South Dakota
Flying L Guest Ranch, Texas
Hidden Valley Guest Ranch, Washington
Woodside Ranch, Wisconsin
Bill Cody Ranch, Wyoming
Brooks Lake Lodge, Wyoming
Double Diamond X Ranch, Wyoming
Heart Six Ranch and Buffalo Valley Cabins, Wyoming
TA Guest Ranch, Wyoming
Triangle X Ranch, Wyoming
Vee Bar Guest Ranch, Wyoming
Brewster's Kananaskis Guest Ranch, Alberta, Canada
The Hills Health and Guest Ranch, British Columbia, Canada
Three Bars Ranch, British Columbia, Canada

Historic–National Register of Historic Sites
Kay El Bar, Arizona
63 Ranch, Montana

Horse Drives
Klick's K Bar L Ranch, Montana
Lazy K Bar Ranch, Montana
Cottonwood Ranch, Nevada
Rock Springs Guest Ranch, Oregon
High Island Ranch and Cattle Company, Wyoming
Lozier's Box R Ranch, Wyoming

Hot Springs

Coulter Lake Ranch, Colorado
Deer Valley Ranch, Colorado
4UR Ranch, Colorado
San Juan Guest Ranch, Colorado
Waunita Hot Springs Ranch, Colorado
Idaho Rocky Mountain Ranch, Idaho
Klick's K Bar L Ranch, Montana
Baker's Bar M Ranch, Oregon
Brush Creek Ranch, Wyoming

Large Outdoor Business/Group Barbecues

Merv Griffin's Wickenburg Inn and Dude Ranch, Arizona
Rancho de los Caballeros, Arizona
Tanque Verde Ranch, Arizona
Scott Valley Resort and Guest Ranch, Arkansas
Alisal Guest Ranch, California
Aspen Lodge Ranch Resort, Colorado
Peaceful Valley Ranch, Colorado
T-Lazy-7 Ranch, Colorado
Wit's End Guest and Resort Ranch, Colorado
Molokai Ranch, Hawaii
Double JJ Resort Ranch, Michigan
El Rancho Stevens, Michigan
Crazy Mountain Ranch, Montana
Flathead Lake Lodge, Montana
The 320 Guest Ranch, Montana
Roaring Brook Ranch and Tennis Resort, New York
Rocking Horse Ranch, New York
Cataloochee Ranch, North Carolina
Clear Creek Ranch, North Carolina
Flying M Ranch, Oregon
Rock Springs Guest Ranch, Oregon
Blue Bell Lodge & Resort, South Dakota
Flying L Guest Ranch, Texas
Lazy Hills Guest Ranch, Texas
Reid Ranch, Utah
Crescent H Ranch, Wyoming
Lost Creek Ranch, Wyoming
TA Guest Ranch, Wyoming
Triangle C Ranch, Wyoming
Vee Bar Guest Ranch, Wyoming
Brewster's Kananaskis Guest Ranch, Alberta, Canada
Homeplace Guest Ranch, Alberta, Canada
Top of the World Guest Ranch, British Columbia, Canada

Large Tours

Merv Griffin's Wickenburg Inn and Dude Ranch, Arizona
Scott Valley Resort and Guest Ranch, Arkansas
Aspen Lodge Ranch Resort, Colorado
Peaceful Valley Ranch, Colorado
Wit's End Guest and Resort Ranch, Colorado
Blue Bell Lodge & Resort, South Dakota
Double JJ Resort Ranch, Michigan
Pinegrove Dude Ranch, New York
Roaring Brook Ranch and Tennis Resort, New York
Flying L Guest Ranch, Texas
Reid Ranch, Utah
Woodside Ranch, Wisconsin
TA Guest Ranch, Wyoming
Vee Bar Guest Ranch, Wyoming

Mountain Bike–Friendly

Flying E Ranch, Arizona
Lazy K Bar Guest Ranch, Arizona
Rancho de la Osa, Arizona
Rancho de los Caballeros, Arizona
Tanque Verde Ranch, Arizona
White Stallion Ranch, Arizona
Scott Valley Resort and Guest Ranch, Arkansas
Alisal Guest Ranch, California
Coffee Creek Ranch, California
Greenhorn Creek Ranch, California
Hunewill Circle H Ranch, California
Rankin Ranch, California
Aspen Lodge Ranch Resort, Colorado
Aspen Canyon Ranch, Colorado
Bar Lazy J Ranch, Colorado
Deer Valley Ranch, Colorado
Diamond J on the Fryingpan Lodge & Guest Ranch, Colorado
Drowsy Water Ranch, Colorado
Elk Mountain Ranch, Colorado
4UR Ranch, Colorado
King Mountain Ranch Resort, Colorado
La Garita Creek Ranch, Colorado
Lake Mancos Ranch, Colorado
Latigo Ranch, Colorado
Lazy H Guest Ranch, Colorado
Peaceful Valley Ranch, Colorado
Rainbow Trout Ranch, Colorado
San Juan Guest Ranch, Colorado
Seven Lakes Lodge, Colorado
Skyline Guest Ranch, Colorado
T-Lazy-7 Ranch, Colorado

Vista Verde Ranch, Colorado
Wind River Ranch, Colorado
Wit's End Guest and Resort Ranch, Colorado
Diamond D Ranch, Idaho
Hidden Creek Ranch, Idaho
Idaho Rocky Mountain Ranch, Idaho
Moose Creek Ranch, Idaho
Teton Ridge Ranch, Idaho
Double JJ Resort Ranch, Michigan
Turkey Creek Ranch, Missouri
Bear Creek Lodge, Montana
Beartooth Ranch and JLX, Montana
Bonanza Creek Country, Montana
Boulder River Ranch, Montana
C_B Cattle and Guest Ranch, Montana
Circle Bar Guest Ranch, Montana
Covered Wagon Ranch, Montana
Crazy Mountain Ranch, Montana
Diamond J Ranch, Montana
Flathead Lake Lodge, Montana
Laughing Water Ranch, Montana
Lone Mountain Ranch, Montana
Parade Rest Ranch, Montana
The 320 Guest Ranch, Montana
White Tail Ranch, Montana
Cottonwood Ranch, Nevada
The Lodge at Chama, New Mexico
Roaring Brook Ranch and Tennis Resort, New York
Earthshine Mountain Lodge, North Carolina
Aspen Ridge Resort, Oregon
Rock Springs Guest Ranch, Oregon
Blue Bell Lodge & Resort, South Dakota
Cibolo Creek Ranch, Texas
Flying L Guest Ranch, Texas
Reid Ranch, Utah
Hidden Valley Guest Ranch, Washington
Allen's Diamond 4 Ranch, Wyoming
Bill Cody Ranch, Wyoming
Bitterroot Ranch, Wyoming
Brooks Lake Lodge, Wyoming
Canyon Ranch, Wyoming
Crescent H Ranch, Wyoming
Flying A Guest Ranch, Wyoming
Gros Ventre River Ranch, Wyoming
Heart Six Ranch and Buffalo Valley Cabins, Wyoming
The Hideout at Flitner Ranch, Wyoming
Hunter Peak Ranch, Wyoming
Kedesh Ranch, Wyoming
Lazy L & B Ranch, Wyoming
Moose Head Ranch, Wyoming
Paradise Guest Ranch, Wyoming
Red Rock Ranch, Wyoming
Seven D Ranch, Wyoming
TA Guest Ranch, Wyoming
Triangle C Ranch, Wyoming
UXU Ranch, Wyoming
Vee Bar Guest Ranch, Wyoming
Echo Valley Guest Ranch, British Columbia, Canada
The Hills Health and Guest Ranch, British Columbia, Canada
Three Bars Ranch, British Columbia, Canada
Top of the World Guest Ranch, British Columbia, Canada

Mountain Flying Instruction
Flying S Ranch, Wyoming

Naturalist Programs & Talks
Kachemak Bay Wilderness Lodge, Alaska
Merv Griffin's Wickenburg Inn and Dude Ranch, Arizona
Rancho de la Osa, Arizona
Rancho de los Caballeros, Arizona
Tanque Verde Ranch, Arizona
White Stallion Ranch, Arizona
Alisal Guest Ranch, California
The Home Ranch, Colorado
Laramie River Ranch, Colorado
Latigo Ranch, Colorado
Rawah Ranch, Colorado
Seven Lakes Lodge, Colorado
Vista Verde Ranch, Colorado
Molokai Ranch, Hawaii
Hidden Creek Ranch, Idaho
Double JJ Resort Ranch, Michigan
B Bar Guest Ranch, Montana
Big Hole River Outfitters, Montana
Horse Prairie Ranch, Montana
Lone Mountain Ranch, Montana
Nine Quarter Circle Ranch, Montana
Pine Butte Guest Ranch, Montana
RJR Ranch, Montana
Seven Lazy P Ranch, Montana
Triple Creek Ranch, Montana
Cottonwood Ranch, Nevada
Earthsine Mountain Lodge, North Carolina
Cibolo Creek Ranch, Texas
Allen's Diamond 4 Ranch, Wyoming
Breteche Creek Ranch, Wyoming
Brooks Lake Lodge, Wyoming
Crescent H Ranch, Wyoming
Gros Ventre River Ranch, Wyoming
Paradise Guest Ranch, Wyoming

Seven D Ranch, Wyoming
Echo Valley Guest Ranch, British Columbia, Canada

Ocean Activities
Molokai Ranch, Hawaii

Old West Town
Double JJ Resort Ranch, Michigan
Crazy Mountain Ranch, Montana

Pets Allowed
Price Canyon Ranch, Arizona
Scott Valley Resort and Guest Ranch, Arkansas
Howard Creek Ranch, California
Lane Guest Ranch, Colorado
T-Lazy-7 Ranch, Colorado
Teton Ridge Ranch, Idaho
The Wild Horse Creek Ranch, Idaho
Covered Wagon Ranch, Montana
Diamond J Ranch, Montana (bird dogs only)
Lake Upsata Guest Ranch, Montana
Laughing Water Ranch, Montana
The 320 Guest Ranch, Montana
White Tail Ranch, Montana
Flying M Ranch, Oregon
Obstinate J Ranch, Oregon
Woodside Ranch, Wisconsin
Canyon Ranch, Wyoming
Hunter Peak Ranch, Wyoming
Spear-O-Wigwam Ranch, Wyoming
The Hills Health and Guest Ranch, British Columbia, Canada
Springhouse Trails Ranch, British Columbia, Canada

Platform Tennis
RJR Ranch, Montana

Professional Rodeo Arena
Molokai Ranch, Hawaii

Ranch Bed-and-Breakfast Inn (Yearly and seasonal)
Howard Creek Ranch, California
Aspen Canyon Ranch, Colorado (winter only)
Coulter Lake Guest Ranch, Colorado (winter only)
Lazy H Guest Ranch, Colorado
McNamara Ranch, Colorado
Peaceful Valley Ranch, Colorado
San Juan Guest Ranch, Colorado
Skyline Guest Ranch, Colorado (winter only)
Bar H Bar Ranch, Idaho
Moose Creek Ranch, Idaho
Happy Hollow Ranch & Zeemering Farms Ltd., Michigan
Bear Creek Lodge, Montana
Laughing Water Ranch, Montana (winter only)
RJR Ranch, Montana
Earthshine Mountain Lodge, North Carolina
Lazy Hills Guest Ranch, Texas
Hidden Valley Guest Ranch, Washington
Woodside Ranch, Wisconsin
Bill Cody Ranch, Wyoming
Cheyenne River Ranch, Wyoming
Hunter Peak Ranch, Wyoming
Savery Creek Thoroughbred Ranch, Wyoming
Vee Bar Guest Ranch, Wyoming
The Hills Health and Guest Ranch, British Columbia, Canada

Ranch Resorts
Merv Griffin's Wickenburg Inn and Dude Ranch, Arizona
Rancho de los Caballeros, Arizona
Tanque Verde Ranch, Arizona
Alisal Guest Ranch, California
Aspen Lodge Ranch Resort, Colorado
C Lazy U Ranch, Colorado
Colorado Trails Ranch, Colorado
Deer Valley Ranch, Colorado
The Home Ranch, Colorado
King Mountain Ranch Resort, Colorado
Lane Guest Ranch, Colorado
Lost Valley Ranch, Colorado
Peaceful Valley Ranch, Colorado
Tall Timber, Colorado
Wit's End Guest and Resort Ranch, Colorado
Double JJ Resort Ranch, Michigan
El Rancho Stevens, Michigan
Turkey Creek Ranch, Missouri
Diamond J Ranch, Montana
Flathead Lake Lodge, Montana
Lone Mountain Ranch, Montana
Mountain Sky Guest Ranch, Montana
The 320 Guest Ranch, Montana
The Lodge at Chama, New Mexico
Pinegrove Dude Ranch, New York
Ridin-Hy Ranch Resort, New York
Roaring Brook Ranch and Tennis Resort, New York
Rocking Horse Ranch, New York

Aspen Ridge Resort, Oregon
Rock Springs Guest Ranch, Oregon
Blue Bell Lodge & Resort, South Dakota
Flying L Guest Ranch, Texas
Lazy Hills Guest Ranch, Texas
Reid Ranch, Utah
Woodside Ranch, Wisconsin
The Hideout at Flitner Ranch, Wyoming
Lost Creek Ranch, Wyoming
Echo Valley Guest Ranch, British Columbia, Canada
The Hills Health and Guest Ranch, British Columbia, Canada
Three Bars Ranch, British Columbia, Canada

Ride on Your Own Without Wrangler (At ranches' discretion; generally for experienced riders only)
Flying E Ranch, Arizona (BYOH)
Bar H Bar Ranch, Idaho
Happy Hollow Ranch & Zeemering Farms Ltd., Michigan
Bear Creek Lodge, Montana
Sweet Grass Ranch, Montana
Cottonwood Ranch, Nevada
Aspen Ridge Resort, Oregon
Baker's Bar M Ranch, Oregon
Flying M Ranch, Oregon
Cheyenne River Ranch, Wyoming
Eatons' Ranch, Wyoming
H F Bar Ranch, Wyoming
The Hideout at Flitner Ranch, Wyoming
High Island Ranch and Cattle Company, Wyoming
Lozier's Box R Ranch, Wyoming
Savery Creek Thoroughbred Ranch, Wyoming
TA Guest Ranch, Wyoming
Vee Bar Guest Ranch, Wyoming
Springhouse Trails Ranch, British Columbia, Canada

RVs
Price Canyon Ranch, Arizona
Lost Spur Guest Ranch, Arkansas
Double JJ Resort Ranch, Michigan
Flying M Ranch, Oregon
Blue Bell Lodge & Resort, South Dakota
Lazy Hills Guest Ranch, Texas
The Hills Health and Guest Ranch, British Columbia, Canada
Springhouse Trails Ranch, British Columbia, Canada

Snowmobiling
Aspen Canyon Ranch, Colorado
Coulter Lake Guest Ranch, Colorado
Skyline Guest Ranch, Colorado
T-Lazy-7 Ranch, Colorado
Wit's End Guest and Resort Ranch, Colorado
Hidden Creek Ranch, Idaho
Moose Creek Ranch, Idaho
The Wild Horse Creek Ranch, Idaho
Double JJ Resort Ranch, Michigan
Crazy Mountain Ranch, Montana
Triple Creek Ranch, Montana
White Tail Ranch, Montana
Aspen Ridge Resort, Oregon
Brooks Lake Lodge, Wyoming
Brush Creek Ranch, Wyoming
Gros Ventre River Ranch, Wyoming
Heart Six Ranch and Buffalo Valley Cabins, Wyoming
The Hideout at Flitner Ranch, Wyoming
Rimrock Ranch, Wyoming
Triangle C Ranch, Wyoming
Triangle X Ranch, Wyoming
Vee Bar Guest Ranch, Wyoming
The Hills Health and Guest Ranch, British Columbia, Canada

Snow Polo
T-Lazy-7 Ranch, Colorado

Spa/Body/Mind
Hidden Creek Ranch, Idaho
Lost Creek Ranch, Wyoming
Echo Valley Guest Ranch, British Columbia, Canada
The Hills Health and Guest Ranch, British Columbia, Canada

Wilderness Pack Trips (*Specializes)
Circle Z Ranch, Arizona
Grand Canyon Bar Ten Ranch, Arizona
Coffee Creek Ranch, California
Laramie River Ranch, Colorado
Old Glendevey Ranch, Colorado
Skyline Guest Ranch, Colorado
T-Lazy-7 Ranch, Colorado
Wit's End Guest and Resort Ranch, Colorado
Diamond D Ranch, Idaho
Hidden Creek Ranch, Idaho
Teton Ridge Ranch, Idaho
Twin Peaks Ranch, Idaho
Circle Bar Guest Ranch, Montana

JJJ Wilderness Ranch, Montana
Klick's K Bar L Ranch, Montana
Laughing Water Ranch, Montana
Nine Quarter Circle Ranch, Montana
Seven Lazy P Ranch, Montana*
White Tail Ranch, Montana
Cottonwood Ranch, Nevada
Absaroka Ranch, Wyoming
Allen's Diamond 4 Ranch, Wyoming*
Bitterroot Ranch, Wyoming
Castle Rock Ranch, Wyoming
CM Ranch, Wyoming
Double Diamond X Ranch, Wyoming
Flying S Ranch, Wyoming
Heart Six Ranch and Buffalo Valley Cabins, Wyoming
H F Bar Ranch, Wyoming
The Hideout at Flitner Ranch, Wyoming
Hunter Peak Ranch, Wyoming
Lazy L & B Ranch, Wyoming
Lozier's Box R Ranch, Wyoming
Paradise Guest Ranch, Wyoming
Rimrock Ranch, Wyoming*
Seven D Ranch, Wyoming
Spear-O-Wigwam Ranch, Wyoming
T-Cross Ranch, Wyoming
Trail Creek Ranch, Wyoming
Triangle C Ranch, Wyoming
Triangle X Ranch, Wyoming*
UXU Ranch, Wyoming
Homeplace Guest Ranch, Alberta, Canada
Brewsters Kananaskis Guest Ranch, Alberta, Canada
Echo Valley Guest Ranch, British Columbia, Canada

Winter Activities
Coffee Creek Ranch, California
Aspen Canyon Ranch, Colorado
C Lazy U Ranch, Colorado
Coulter Lake Guest Ranch, Colorado
Diamond J on the Fryingpan Lodge & Guest Ranch, Colorado
The Home Ranch, Colorado
Old Glendevey Ranch, Colorado
Peaceful Valley Ranch, Colorado
San Juan Guest Ranch, Colorado
Skyline Guest Ranch, Colorado
T-Lazy-7 Ranch, Colorado
Wit's End Guest and Resort Ranch, Colorado
Hidden Creek Ranch, Idaho
Idaho Rocky Mountain Ranch, Idaho
Moose Creek Ranch, Idaho
Double JJ Resort Ranch, Michigan
Happy Hollow Ranch & Zeemering Farms Ltd., Michigan
B Bar Guest Ranch, Montana
Covered Wagon Ranch, Montana
Crazy Mountain Ranch, Montana
Triple Creek Ranch, Montana
The Lodge at Chama, New Mexico
Pinegrove Dude Ranch, New York
Ridin-Hy Ranch Resort, New York
Rocking Horse Ranch Resort, New York
Cataloochee Ranch, North Carolina
Earthshine Mountain Lodge, North Carolina
Aspen Ridge Resort, Oregon
Hidden Valley Guest Ranch, Washington
Woodside Ranch, Wisconsin
Brooks Lake Lodge, Wyoming
Brush Creek Ranch, Wyoming
Canyon Ranch, Wyoming
Gros Ventre River Ranch, Wyoming
Heart Six Ranch and Buffalo Valley Cabins, Wyoming
The Hideout at Flitner Ranch, Wyoming
Rimrock Ranch, Wyoming
Trail Creek Ranch, Wyoming
Triangle X Ranch, Wyoming
Triangle C Ranch, Wyoming
Vee Bar Guest Ranch, Wyoming
The Hills Health and Guest Ranch, British Columbia, Canada

Women Only (Mostly)
McNamara Ranch, Colorado

Workshops
Kachemak Bay Wilderness Lodge, Alaska—Naturalist, Photography
Grapevine Canyon Ranch, Arizona—Horse Clinics, Cutting Clinics, History Week
Lazy K Bar Guest Ranch, Arizona—Women's Week, Kids' Camp
Merv Griffin's Wickenburg Inn and Dude Ranch, Arizona—Horse Clinics, Art, Nature
Rancho de la Osa, Arizona—Photography, Painting, Historical
Tanque Verde Ranch, Arizona—Naturalist
White Stallion Ranch, Arizona—Elderhostel, Photography
Hunewill Circle H Ranch, California—Watercolor
Bar Lazy J, Colorado—Fishing Clinic
C Lazy U Ranch, Colorado—Horsemanship
Colorado Trails Ranch, Colorado—Fly-Fishing

Diamond J on the Fryingpan Lodge & Guest Ranch, Colorado—Clinics
4UR Ranch, Colorado—Fishing
The Home Ranch, Colorado—Natural Horsemanship
La Garita Creek Ranch, Colorado—Photography
Laramie River Ranch, Colorado—Naturalist
Latigo Ranch, Colorado—Photography
Rankin Ranch, Colorado—Drawing and Watercolor, Stamp and Sticker, Western Week
San Juan Guest Ranch, Colorado—Photography
Vista Verde Ranch, Colorado—Fitness, Photography
Wind River Ranch, Colorado—Spiritual, Christian
Diamond D Ranch, Idaho—Crafts
Hidden Creek Ranch, Idaho—Riding, Native American, Spiritual, Mind, Body
Moose Creek Ranch, Idaho—Wild Mustang Program
Double JJ Resort Ranch, Michigan—Corporate Team-Building
Bear Creek Lodge, Montana—Cooking
Boulder River Ranch, Montana—Fishing, Art, Working Cow Horses
Circle Bar Guest Ranch, Montana—Art, History, Photography
Flathead Lake Lodge, Montana—Art
Horse Prairie Ranch, Montana—Lewis and Clark Expedition
Lake Upsata Guest Ranch, Montana—Nutrition
Laughing Water Ranch, Montana—Western Dance
Lone Mountain Ranch, Montana—Fly-Fishing, Photography, Quilting, Nature, Cross-Country Skiing
Mountain Sky Guest Ranch, Montana—Horse, Fly-Fishing
Nine Quarter Circle Ranch, Montana—Quilting
Parade Rest Ranch, Montana—Fly-Fishing Schools
Pine Butte Guest Ranch, Montana—Nature
63 Ranch, Montana—Photography
White Tail Ranch, Montana—Photography
Cottonwood Ranch, Nevada—Holistic Ranch Management
Roaring Brook Ranch and Tennis Resort, New York—Conferences
Obstinate J Ranch, Oregon—Horsemanship/Competition
Rock Springs Guest Ranch, Oregon—Photography
Cibolo Creek Ranch, Texas—Cooking, Photography
Lazy Hills Guest Ranch, Texas—Rug-Hooking
Reid Ranch, Utah—Reading, Computers
Allen's Diamond 4 Ranch, Wyoming—Learn to Pack Vacation
Bitterroot Ranch, Wyoming—Riding, Horse-Training
Breteche Creek Ranch, Wyoming—Horsemanship, Ornithology, Writing
Crescent H Ranch, Wyoming—Fly-Fishing School (June and September)
Eatons' Ranch, Wyoming—Artist in Residency
The Hideout at Flitner Ranch, Wyoming—Horse, Photography, Geoscience
High Island Ranch and Cattle Company, Wyoming—Basket-Weaving
Hunter Peak Ranch, Wyoming—History, Nature
Lozier's Box R Ranch, Wyoming—Horsemanship
Seven D Ranch, Wyoming—Photography, Art
TA Guest Ranch, Wyoming—Historic Preservation
Triangle C Ranch, Wyoming—Photography, Art
UXU Ranch, Wyoming—Painting, Photography, Cooking
Homeplace Guest Ranch, Alberta, Canada—Nature on Horseback, Historic Bar U Ranch Ride
Echo Valley Guest Ranch, British Columbia, Canada—Birding, Indian Culture, Spa
The Hills Health and Guest Ranch, British Columbia, Canada—Wellness
Three Bars Ranch, British Columbia, Canada—Horsemanship

GUEST RANCH ASSOCIATIONS

Arizona Dude Ranch Association
P.O. Box 603 K
Cortaro, AZ 85652
(520) 297-0252
Circle Z Ranch
Elkhorn Ranch
Flying E Ranch
Grapevine Canyon Ranch
The Horseshoe Ranch on Bloody Basin Road
Ironhorse Ranch
Kay El Bar
Lazy K Bar Guest Ranch
Merv Griffin's Wickenburg Inn and Dude Ranch
Price Canyon Ranch
Rancho de la Osa
Rancho de los Caballeros
Sprucedale Guest Ranch
Tanque Verde Ranch
White Stallion Ranch

Colorado Dude and Guest Ranch Association
P.O. Box 2120 K
Granby, CO 80446
(970) 887-3128
(970) 724-3653
(Directory-ordering line)
Aspen Canyon Ranch
Aspen Lodge Ranch Resort
Bar Lazy J Guest Ranch
Buffalo Horn Ranch
C Lazy U Ranch
Cherokee Park Ranch
Colorado Trails Ranch
Coulter Lake Guest Ranch
Deer Valley Ranch
Drowsy Water Ranch
Echo Canyon Guest Ranch
Elk Mountain Ranch
Focus Ranch
Harmel's Ranch Resort
The Historic Pines Ranch
King Mountain Ranch Resort
Lake Mancos Ranch
Laramie River Ranch
Latigo Ranch
Lazy H Guest Ranch
Lost Valley Ranch
North Fork Ranch
Old Glendevey Ranch
Peaceful Valley Lodge
Powderhorn Guest Ranch
Rainbow Trout Ranch
Rawah Ranch
San Juan Guest Ranch
7 W Guest Ranch
Sky Corral Ranch
Skyline Guest Ranch
Sylvan Dale Guest Ranch
Tarryall River Ranch
Tumbling River Ranch
Vista Verde Ranch
Waunita Hot Springs Ranch
Whistling Acres Guest Ranch
Wilderness Trails Ranch
Wind River Ranch

The Dude Ranchers' Association
P.O. Box 471 K
LaPorte, CO 80535
(970) 223-8440
Arizona
Circle Z Ranch
Elkhorn Ranch
Flying E Ranch
Grapevine Canyon Ranch
The Horseshoe Ranch on Bloody Basin Road
Ironhorse Ranch
Kay El Bar
Lazy K Bar Guest Ranch
Rancho de la Osa
White Stallion Ranch
Arkansas
Scott Valley Resort and Guest Ranch
California
Coffee Creek Ranch
Hunewill Circle H Ranch
Colorado
Bar Lazy J Guest Ranch
C Lazy U Ranch
Cherokee Park Ranch
Colorado Trails Ranch
Coulter Lake Guest Ranch
Drowsy Water Ranch
Echo Canyon Guest Ranch
Elk Mountain Ranch
The Home Ranch
Lake Mancos Ranch
Laramie River Ranch
Latigo Ranch
Lazy H Guest Ranch
Lost Valley Ranch
North Fork Ranch
Old Glendevey Ranch
Powderhorn Guest Ranch
Rainbow Trout Ranch
Rawah Ranch
San Juan Guest Ranch
7 W Guest Ranch
Sky Corral Guest Ranch
Skyline Guest Ranch
Sylvan Dale Guest Ranch
Tarryall River Ranch
Tumbling River Ranch
Vista Verde Ranch
Waunita Hot Springs Ranch
Whistling Acres Guest Ranch
Wilderness Trails Ranch
Idaho
Hidden Creek Ranch
Moose Creek Ranch
Twin Peaks Ranch
Wapiti Meadow Ranch
Montana
Beartooth Ranch and JLX
Bonanza Creek Country Boulder River Ranch
C_B Cattle and Guest Ranch
Circle Bar Guest Ranch
Diamond J Ranch
Elkhorn Ranch
Flathead Lake Lodge
G Bar M Ranch
Hargrave Cattle and Guest Ranch
Hawley Mountain Guest Ranch
Horse Prairie Ranch
JJJ Wilderness Ranch
Klick's K Bar L Ranch
Laughing Water Ranch
Lazy K Bar Ranch

Mountain Sky Guest Ranch
Nine Quarter Circle Ranch
Pine Butte Guest Ranch
Seven Lazy P Ranch
63 Ranch
Sweet Grass Ranch

Nevada

Spur Cross Ranch

New Mexico

Hartley Guest Ranch
Baker's Bar M Ranch
Rock Springs Guest Ranch

South Dakota

Triple R Ranch

Texas

Bald Eagle Ranch

Wyoming

Absaroka Ranch
Brooks Lake Lodge
Brush Creek Ranch
Crossed Sabres Ranch
David Ranch
Double Diamond X Ranch
Eatons' Ranch
Flying A Guest Ranch
Gros Ventre River Ranch
Heart Six Ranch and Buffalo Valley Cabins
The Hideout at Flitner Ranch
High Island Ranch and Cattle Company
Kedesh Ranch
Lazy L & B Ranch
Lozier's Box R Ranch
Moose Head Ranch
Paradise Guest Ranch
R Lazy S Ranch
Red Rock Ranch
Rimrock Ranch
Schively Ranch
Seven D Ranch
Spear-O-Wigwam Ranch
T-Cross Ranch
Trail Creek Ranch
Triangle C Ranch
Triangle X Ranch
Two Bars Seven Ranch

Canada

Homeplace Ranch
Three Bars Cattle & Guest Ranch
Wild Rose Ranch & Resort

Idaho Guest & Dude Ranch Association

HC 72 K
Cascade, ID 83611
(208) 633-3217

Diamond D Ranch
Granite Creek Guest Ranch
Hidden Creek Ranch
Idaho Rocky Mountain Ranch
Indian Creek Guest Ranch
Moose Creek Ranch
Shepp Ranch
Twin Peaks Ranch
Wapiti Meadow Ranch
Western Pleasure Guest Ranch

Montana Dude Ranch Association

300 Thompson River Road
Marion, Montana 59925
(406) 858-2284

B Bar Ranch
Bonanza Creek Country
C_B Cattle and Guest Ranch
Circle Bar Guest Ranch
Covered Wagon Ranch
Crazy Mountain Ranch
Elkhorn Ranch
Flathead Lake Lodge
Hargrave Cattle and Guest Ranch
Hawley Mountain Guest Ranch
Horse Prairie Ranch
JJJ Wilderness Ranch
Laughing Water Ranch
Lone Mountain Ranch
Lonesome Spur Guest Ranch
Mountain Sky Guest Ranch
Nine Quarter Circle Ranch
Pine Butte Guest Ranch
Rich Ranch
RJR Ranch
Schively Ranch
Seven Lazy P Ranch
Spotted Bear Ranch
White Tail Ranch

Texas Guest Ranch Association

900 Congress Avenue, Suite 201, Drawer K
Austin, TX 78701
(512) 474-2996

Abundare River Ranch
B Bar B Ranch Inn
Bald Eagle Ranch, Inc.
Bar H Dude Ranch
Bill Bates Cowboy Ranch
Cibolo Creek Ranch
Dixie Dude Ranch
Dos Vaqueros
Flying L Guest Ranch
Garrett Creek Ranch
Lazy Hills Guest Ranch
Loma De Blanca
Mayan Dude Ranch
Nueces Canyon Inn and Bed & Breakfast
Reagan Wells Ranch, Inc.
Running R Guest Ranch Inc.
Selah Inn at the Ranch
Silver Spur Dude Ranch
Southfork Ranch & Conference Center
Texas Lil's Dude Ranch
Twin Elm Guest Ranch
X Bar Ranch

Wyoming Dude Rancher's Association

P.O. Box 618
Dubois, WY 82513
(307) 455-2584

Absaroka Ranch
Allen's Diamond Four Ranch
Bitterroot Ranch
Blackwater Creek Ranch
Box R Ranch
Brooks Lake Lodge
Brush Creek Guest Ranch
Crossed Sabres Ranch
Darwin Ranch
David Ranch
Eatons' Ranch
Flying A Ranch
Gros Ventre River Ranch
Heart Six Ranch
High Island Ranch
Kedesh Dude Ranch

Lazy L & B Ranch
Moose Head Ranch
Paradise Guest Ranch
R Lazy S Ranch
Rafter Y Ranch
Red Rock Ranch
Savery Creek Ranch
Schively Ranch
Spear-O-Wigwam Ranch
T-Cross Ranch
Triangle X Ranch
Vee Bar Guest Ranch

British Columbia Guest Ranchers' Association
P.O. Box 3301 K
Kamloopf, British Columbia
V2C6B9, Canada
(250) 374-6836
Big Bar Guest Ranch
Chilcotin Holidays Guest Ranch
Chilko Lake Ranch
Echo Valley Guest Ranch
Elkin Creek Guest Ranch
Moondance Guest Ranch
Stiefelknecht Ranch
Sundance Guest Ranch
The Hills Guest Ranch
Top of the World Ranch Ltd.
Wild Rose Ranch

BUREAUS OF TOURISM

Alabama
(334) 242-4169
(800) 252-2262
(Nationwide, Alaska, and Hawaii)

Alaska
(907) 465-2012
(907) 465-2287 Fax

Arizona
(800) 842-8257
(602) 542-4068 Fax

Arkansas
(501) 682-7777
(800) 828-8974
(501) 682-1364 Fax

California
(916) 322-2881
(800) 862-2543
(916) 322-3402 Fax

Colorado
(303) 832-6171
(800) 265-6723
(303) 832-6174 Fax

Connecticut
(860) 258-4355
(800) 282-6863
(860) 270-8077 Fax

Delaware
(302) 739-4271
(800) 441-8846
(302) 739-5749 Fax

District of Columbia
Washington, D.C.
(202) 789-7000
(202) 789-7037 Fax

Florida
(904) 488-5607
(904) 487-0132 Fax

Georgia
(404) 656-3590
(800) 847-4842
(404) 651-9063 Fax

Hawaii
(808) 586-2550
(808) 586-2549 Fax

Idaho
(208) 334-2470
(800) 635-7820
(208) 334-2631 Fax

Illinois
(312) 814-4732
(800) 226-6632
(312) 814-6581 Fax

Indiana
(317) 232-8860
(800) 289-6646
(317) 233-6887 Fax

Iowa
(515) 242-4705
(800) 345-4692
(515) 242-4749 Fax

Kansas
(913) 296-7091
(800) 252-6727
(913) 296-6988 Fax

Kentucky
(502) 564-4930
(800) 225-8747
(502) 564-5695 Fax

Louisiana
(504) 342-8100
(800) 334-8626
(504) 342-8390 Fax

Maine
(800) 533-9595
(207) 287-5701 Fax

Maryland
(800) 543-1036
(410) 333-6643 Fax

Massachusetts
(617) 727-3201
(800) 447-6277
(617) 727-6525 Fax

Michigan
(517) 373-0670
(888) 784-7328
(517) 373-0059 Fax

Minnesota
(612) 296-2755
(800) 657-3700
(612) 296-7095 Fax

Mississippi
(601) 359-3297
(800) 927-6378
(800) 873-4780 Fax

Missouri
(800) 877-1234

Montana
(800) 847-4868
(406) 471-3026 Fax

Nebraska
(402) 471-3791
(800) 228-4307
(402) 471-3026 Fax

Nevada
(702) 687-4322
(800) 638-2328
(702) 687-6779 Fax

New Hampshire
(603) 271-2343
(603) 271-2629 Fax

New Jersey
(609) 292-2470
(800) 537-7397

New Mexico
(505) 827-7400
(800) 733-6396
(505) 827-7402 Fax

New York
(800) 225-5697
(212) 827-6237 Fax

North Carolina
(919) 733-4171
(800) 847-4862
(919) 733-8582 Fax

North Dakota
(701) 328-2525
(800) 435-5663
(701) 328-4878 Fax

Ohio
(614) 466-8844
(800) 282-5393
(614) 466-6744 Fax

Oklahoma
(405) 521-3981
(800) 652-6552
(405) 521-3992 Fax

Oregon
(503) 986-0000
(800) 547-7842
(503) 986-0001 Fax

Pennsylvania
(717) 787-5453
(800) 847-4872
(717) 234-4560 Fax

Rhode Island
(401) 789-4422
(800) 556-2484
(401) 277-2102 Fax

South Carolina
(803) 734-0122
(800) 346-3634
(803) 734-1409 Fax

South Dakota
(605) 773-3301
(800) 732-5682
(605) 773-3256 Fax

Tennessee
(615) 741-2159
(800) 836-6200
(615) 741-7225 Fax

Texas
(512) 462-9191
(800) 888-8839
(512) 936-0089 Fax

Utah
(801) 538-1467
(800) 200-1160
(801) 538-1399 Fax

Vermont
(802) 828-3237
(800) 837-6668
(802) 828-3233 Fax

Virginia
(804) 786-2051
(800) 847-4882
(804) 786-1919 Fax

Washington
(360) 586-2088
(800) 544-1800

West Virginia
(304) 558-2766
(800) 225-5982
(304) 588-0108 Fax

Wisconsin
(608) 266-2345
(800) 432-8747
(608) 266-3403 Fax

Wyoming
(307) 777-7777
(800) 225-5996
(307) 777-6904 Fax

Alberta, Canada
(403) 427-4321
(800) 661-8888
(403) 427-0867 Fax

British Columbia, Canada
(604) 663-6000
(800) 663-6000

WESTERN MUSEUMS

Amon Carter Museum
3501 Camp Bowie Blvd.
Fort Worth, TX 76107
(817) 738-1933

Autry Museum of Western Heritage
4700 Western Heritage Way
Los Angeles, CA 90027
(213) 667-2000
(213) 660-5721 Fax

Buffalo Bill Historical Center
P.O. Box 1000
Cody, WY 82414
(307) 587-4771

Buffalo Bill Museum
P.O. Box 1000
Cody, WY 82414
(307) 587-4771

C.M. Russell Museum
400 13th Street North
Great Falls, MT 59401
(406) 727-8787
(406) 727-2402 Fax

Cody Firearms Museum
720 Sheridan Avenue
Cody, WY 82414
(307) 587-4771
(307) 587-5714 Fax

Cowboy Artists of America Museum
1550 Bandera Highway, Box 1716
Kerrville, TX 78028
(830) 896-2553
(830) 896-2556 Fax

Desert Caballeros Western Museum
21 North Frontier Street
Wickenburg, AZ 85390
(520) 684-2272
(520) 684-5794

Eiteljorg Museum of American Indians and Western Art
500 West Washington Street
Indianapolis, IN 46204
(317) 636-9378
(317) 264-1724 Fax

Frederic Remington Art Museum
303 Washington Street
Ogdensburg, NY 13669
(315) 393-2425
(315) 393-4464 Fax

Gilcrease Museum
1400 North Gilcrease Museum Road
Tulsa, OK 74127
(918) 596-2700

Joslyn Art Museum
2200 Dodge Street
Omaha, NE 68102
(402) 342-3300
(402) 342-2376 Fax

Lea County Cowboy Hall of Fame and Western Heritage Center
Campus of New Mexico Junior College
5317 Lovington Highway
Hobbs, NM 88240
(505) 392-5518
(505) 392-5871 Fax

Montana Historical Society
225 North Roberts Street
Helena, MT 59620
(406) 444-2694
(406) 444-2696 Fax

Museum of Fine Arts
107 West Palace Street
Santa Fe, NM 87501
(505) 827-4455
(505) 827-4473 Fax

Museum of Indian Arts and Culture
710 Camino Lejo
Santa Fe, NM 87501
(505) 827-6344
(505) 827-6497 Fax

Museum of International Folk Art
706 Camino Lejo
Santa Fe, NM 87501
(505) 827-8350
(505) 827-6349 Fax

National Cowboy Hall of Fame
1700 N.E. 63rd Street
Oklahoma City, OK 73111
(405) 478-2250
(405) 478-4714 Fax

National Museum of Wildlife Art
Across from National Elk Refuge
Highway 89
P.O. Box 2984
Jackson, WY 83001
(307) 733-5771

Palace of the Governors
On the Plaza,
105 Palace Avenue
Santa Fe, NM 87501
(505) 827-6483
(505) 827-6427 Fax

Phoenix Art Museum
1625 North Central Avenue
Phoenix, AZ 85004-1625
(602) 257-1880
(602) 253-8662 Fax

Plains Indian Museum
P.O. Box 1000
Cody, WY 82414
(307) 587-4771

Pro Rodeo Hall of Fame and Museum of the American Cowboy
101 Pro Rodeo Drive
Colorado Springs, CO
80919-2396
(719) 528-4761
(719) 548-4876 Fax

The R.W. Norton Art Gallery
4747 Creswell Avenue
Shreveport, LA 71106
(318) 865-4201
(318) 869-0435

The Rockwell Museum
111 Cedar Street
Corning, NY 14830
(607) 937-5386
(607) 974-4536 Fax

Sid Richardson Collection of Western Art
309 Main Street
Fort Worth, TX 76102
(817) 332-6554
(817) 332-8671 Fax

Stark Museum
712 Green Avenue
P.O. Box 1897
Orange, TX 77630
(409) 883-6661
(409) 883-3530 Fax

Whitney Gallery of Western Art
P.O. Box 1000
Cody, WY 82414
(307) 587-4771

Woolaroc Museum
Route 3, Box 2100
P.O. Box 1647
Bartlesville, OK 74003
(918) 336-0307
(918) 336-0084 Fax

WAGON TRAINS

In addition to a ranch vacation, you may want to consider a wagon-train adventure. The wagon-train operators listed below offer trips that take you back to the time when pioneers crossed the Plains. In most instances, you'll travel by covered wagon, experiencing the bumps and splendor of days gone by. You'll dine on delicious, fresh, chuck-wagon food and enjoy some modern conveniences, including showers and restrooms. (This varies considerably, so check with the outfitter.) Sleep under the stars, listen to the distant howls of coyotes, smell pungent sage, and, most of all, relive history. Each of these outfitters will happily send you information and references.

Flint Hills Overland Wagon Train Trips
Ervin E. Grant
Box 1076 K
El Dorado, KS 67042
(316) 321-6300

Fort Seward Wagon Trains, Inc.
Phylis Klein Knecht
Box 244 K
Jamestown, ND 58402
(701) 252-6844

Honeymoon Trail Co.
Mel Heaton
Honeymoon Trail Co.
HC65 Box 9 K
Moccasin, AZ 86022
(520) 643-7292

National Trail Ride and Wagon Train Association
Art Howell
P.O. Box 8625 K
Gadsden, AL 35902
(205) 442-0230

Oregon Trail Wagon Train
Gordon and Patty Howard
Route 2, Box 502 K
Bayard, NE 69334
(800) 228-4307, (308) 586-1850

Rocking P Ranch
Bruce and Corrine Prins
RR #3, Box 192 K
Sisseton, SD 57262
(605) 698-4559

Teton Country Wagon Train
Wilson Thomas
P.O. Box 10307 K
Jackson, WY 83002-0307
(888) 734-6101

Wagons West
Peterson-Madson-Outfitters
P.O. Box 1156 K
Afton, WY 83110
(800) 447-4711, (307) 886-9693

Western Dakota Ranch Vacations
HCR1, Box 9 K
Wall, SD 57709
(605) 279-2198
(10-person minimum)

RANCH CAMPS

One of the most exciting experiences for any young person is to spend the summer, or at least part of the summer, at a ranch camp. Since *Ranch Vacations'* first edition was published, I've often been asked about ranch camps by parents seeking summer camps for their children. Today, ranch camps provide a healthy, happy, summer environment that will, without a doubt, broaden each child's experiences. These camps provide opportunities for youngsters to be in the outdoors, exposing boys and girls to refreshing challenges, both educationally and developmentally. Since it would be impossible to list all the ranch camps throughout North America, and remembering the old adage "less is more," I've chosen to list just a few camps below. Each has a fine reputation and has been in the ranch-camp industry for many years. As with all the other ranch properties in this guide, I recommend that you contact the camp and talk with them directly. Ask for references. Each of the camps listed below will be delighted to provide you with all the information you need to help you select the best ranch camp for your children.

Brush Ranch Camp
P.O. Box 5759 K
Santa Fe, NM 87502
(505) 757-8821, (800) 722-2843

Cheley Colorado Camps
P.O. Box 6525 K
Denver, CO 80206-0525
(303) 377-3616 (winter)
(970) 586-4244 (summer)
(800) 226-7386 (summer/winter)

Elk Creek Ranch
31A Academy Street K
South Berwick, ME 03908
(302) 587-3902 (summer)
(207) 384-5361 (winter)

Jameson Ranch Camp
P.O. Box 459 K
Glennville, CA 93226
(805) 536-8888

Sanborn Western Camps
P.O. Box 167 K
Florissant, CO 80816
(719) 748-3341

Teton Valley Ranch Camp
Jackson Hole
P.O. Box 3968 K
Jackson, WY 83001
(307) 733-2958
(307) 733-2978 (winter only)

TOP 20 PRCA RODEOS

Professional Rodeo Cowboys Association, 101 Prorodeo Drive, Colorado Springs, Colorado 80919, PRCA Media Dept.; (719) 593-8840
Women's Professional Rodeo Association, Route 5, Box 698, Blanchard, Oklahoma 73010; (405) 485-2277

Date	City	Event
Mid-January	Denver, CO	National Western Stock Show and Rodeo
Late January	Fort Worth, TX	Southwestern Exposition and Stock Show Rodeo
Early February	El Paso, TX	Southwestern International Rodeo
Early February	San Antonio, TX	San Antonio Livestock Exposition Rodeo
Mid-February	Houston, TX	Houston Livestock Show and Rodeo
Late February	Tucson, AZ	La Fiesta de los Vaqueros
Mid-March	Pocatello, ID	Dodge National Circuit Finals Rodeo
Mid-May	Cloverdale, B.C., Canada	Cloverdale Rodeo
Early June	Reno, NV	Reno Rodeo
Early July	Calgary, Alberta, Canada	Calgary Stampede
Early July	Greeley, CO	Greeley Independence Stampede
Late July	Cheyenne, WY	Cheyenne Frontier Days
Mid-July	Salinas, CA	California Rodeo
Early August	Dodge City, KS	Dodge City Days Rodeo
Mid-August	Colorado Springs, CO	Pikes Peak or Bust Rodeo
Mid-September	Albuquerque, NM	New Mexico State Fair Rodeo
	Pendleton, OR	Pendleton Round-up Rodeo
Late September	San Francisco, CA	Grand National (Cow Palace) Rodeo
Late September–Early October	Oklahoma City, OK	State Fair Championship Rodeo
Early December	Las Vegas, NV	National Finals Rodeo

ANNUAL WESTERN EVENTS
IN THE UNITED STATES AND ALBERTA AND BRITISH COLUMBIA, CANADA

The following is a selection of annual Western events. These events and dates are subject to change. Contact the appropriate Tourism Office listed to verify dates.

Date	City	Event
ALABAMA		
Late January	Town Creek	National Field Trials
Early March	Gadsden	Alabama Wagon Train
	Opp	Opp Jaycee Rattlesnake Rodeo
Late March	Montgomery	Southeastern Livestock Exposition Rodeo and Livestock Week
Mid- to Late April	Bridgeport	Indian Day
	Clayton	Little Britches Rodeo
Late April	Alexander City	Lone Eagle's Legacy
	Decatur	Annual Racking Horse Spring Celebration
Late June	Clayton	Stetson Hoedown Rodeo
Late July	Selma	Selma Jaycee's Annual Rodeo
Early August	Gadsden	Boys Club Annual Rodeo
Mid- to Late August	Gadsden	Cherokees of Northeast
	Alabama	Indian Powwow Festival
Mid-September	Huntsville	Ole Time Fiddling and Bluegrass Convention
Late September	Winfield	Mule Days
	Decatur	Racking Horse World Celebration
Late September to Early October	Mobile	Greater Gulf State Fair PRCA Rodeo
Early to Mid-October	Montgomery	South Alabama State Fair
	Birmingham	Alabama State Fair
	Athens	Annual Tennessee Valley Old Time Fiddlers Convention
Early November	Montgomery	Southern Championship Charity Horse Show
Late November	Atmore	Annual Poarch Band of Creek Indians' Thanksgiving Day Pow-wow
ALASKA		
Early February	Anchorage	Anchorage Fur Rendezvous
Early April	Juneau	Annual Alaska Folk Festival
Late May	Delta Junction	Buffalo Wallow Statewide Square Dance Festival
Mid-August	Palmer	Alaska State Fair
	Kodiak	Alaska State Fair and Rodeo
	Fairbanks	Tanana Valley State Fair
	Haines	Southeast Alaska State Fair and Rodeo
Early July	Skagway	Soapy Smith's Wake

Date	City	Event
ARIZONA		
Early January	Phoenix	Arizona National Livestock Show
	Phoenix	Wrangler Bull Rider's Main Event
	Scottsdale	Wild Horse & Burro Auction
Mid-January	Bullhead City	Turquoise Circuit Finals Rodeo
Late January	Mesa	High Noon's Wild West Collector's Show & Auction
		Cave Creek/Carefree County Ho Down Week
Late January to Early February	Scottsdale	Jaycees' Parada del Sol Rodeo Week
Early February	Ajo	Fiddlers Old-Time Contest
	Camp Verde	Saddlebag All Women Pony Express
	Safford	Oldtime Fiddlers' Contest
	Scottsdale	Parada del Sol Rodeo Dance
	Scottsdale	PRCA Rodeo
	Sierra Vista	Cowboy Poetry & Music Gathering
	Wickenburg	Gold Rush Days
	Yuma	Hospice of Yuma Roping Roundup & Barbecue
	Yuma	Yuma Jaycees Silver Spur Rodeo
	Yuma	Silver Spur Rodeo, Parade and Fiesta
Early to Mid-February	Yuma	Cowboy Skills
	Scottsdale	All Arabian Horse Show and Sale
	Wickenburg	Gold Rush Days and Rodeo
Mid-February	Buckeye	Helz-A-Poppin' Senior Pro Rodeo
	Casa Grande	O'odham Tash
	Pioneer	Pioneer Celebration Days
	Scottsdale	All Arabian Horse Show
Late February	Goodyear	Goodyear Rodeo Days
	Tucson	La Fiesta de los Vaqueros Rodeo (PRCA)
	Tucson	Tucson Rodeo Parade
March	Tucson	SAILA Open & Junior Livestock Show
Early March	Apache Junction	Lost Dutchman Days
	Florence	Founders Day & College Rodeo
	Phoenix	Jaycees' Rodeo of Rodeos Parade
	Phoenix	"Drug Free" Charity Rodeo
Mid-March	Phoenix	Jaycees Rodeo of Rodeos
	Scottsdale	Festival of the West
Late March	Globe/Miami	Copper Dust Stampede Rodeo
	Scottsdale	Ben Johnson's Pro & Celebrity Ropin' for Kids
Mid-April	Cave Creek	Fiesta Days
	Kearny	Pioneer Days
	Scottsdale	Cowboys for Kids Celebrity Rodeo & Auction
May	Eagar/Springerville	Marlen Rogers Family Fun Days
	Page	Lake Powell Rodeo
	Payson	PRCA Pro Rodeo
	Safford	AJRA Rodeo

Date	City	Event
May	Sonoita	Bull-O-Ramaz
Mid-May	Phoenix	PRCA Rodeo
Early May	Sedona	Cinco de Mayo
Early May to Mid-June	Flagstaff	Trappings of the American West
	Tucson	Arizona Boys Chorus Mother's Day Concert
Late May	Prescott	George Phippen Memorial Day Western Art Show & Sale
Late May	St. Johns	High Country Stampede Rodeo
	Tombstone	Wyatt Earp Days
June to August	Flagstaff	Hopi and Navajo Craftsman Exhibitions
June	Payson	Junior Rodeo
Early to Mid-June	Flagstaff	Trappings of the American West
Mid-June	Flagstaff	Pine Country Pro Rodeo
Mid-June to Early July	Flagstaff	Festival of Native American Arts
Late June	Prescott	PRCA Rodeo
July	Prescott	Frontier Days & World's Oldest Rodeo
	Tuba City	Youth Fair
Early July	Prescott	Prescott Rodeo Photo Workshop
	Window Rock	Fourth of July Celebration PRCA Rodeo & Powwow
	Taylor	Fourth of July Celebration
	Eagar/Springerville	Round Valley Western July Fourth Celebration
Mid-July	St. Johns	Pioneer Days
	Snowflake	Pioneer Days Celebration
August	Chinle	Central Navajo Fair
	Fredonia	Northern Arizona Fair
	Payson	Rodeo Parade and Dance
	Safford	Gila Valley Pro Rodeo
	Whiteriver	White Mountain Apache Tribal Fair & Rodeo
	Winslow	West's Best Rodeo
Mid-August	Prescott	Arizona Poets Gathering
	Payson	World's Oldest Continuous PRCA Rodeo
	Tucson	Desert Thunder Rodeo (PRCA)
Late August	Taylor	Sweet Corn Festival
	Payson	PRCA Rodeo
Late August to Early September	Sonoita	Labor Day Rodeo
	Springerville/Eagar	5K Cowboy & Indian Art Show
	Springerville/Eager	Valle Redondo Days
September	Dilcon	Southwestern Navajo Nation Fair
	Douglas	Chochise Country Fair
	Ft. Huachuca	Huachuca Mountain Open Rodeo
	Payson	State Championship Old Time Fiddlers Contest
	Safford/Thatcher	Gila Valley Cowboy Poet Round-up
	Scottsdale	Arizona State Firefighters Benefit Rodeo
Early September	Window Rock	Navajo Nation Fair

Date	City	Event
Mid-September	Holbrook	Navajo County Fair
Late September	Holbrook	All Indian Rodeo Cowboy Association Rodeo & Pow Wow
October	Benson	Butterfield Overland Stage Days
	Kingman	Andy Devine Days & PRCA Rodeo
	Marana	Founder's Day Parade & Rodeo
	Phoenix	Original Coors Rodeo Showdown
	Phoenix	Arizona State Fair
	Scottsdale	Allied Signal Cliff Garrett Memorial Rodeo & Dance
	Tuba City	Western Navajo Fair
	Tucson	John Walker Memorial Rodeo
	Vail	Rincon Valley Festival—Old Spanish Trail
Early October	Phoenix	PRCA Rodeo
	Willcox	Rex Allen Days—PRCA Rodeo
Mid-October	Tombstone	Helldorado Days
Mid-October to Late November	Phoenix	Cowboy Artists of America Show
November	San Carlos	Veteran's Memorial Fair, Pageant & Rodeo
Early November	Sells	Sells All-Indian Rodeo
Late December to Early January	Phoenix	Arizona National Livestock Show
ARKANSAS		
Year-round	Toltec Mounds	Native American Events
Mid-April	Cabot	Old West Daze
Late May	Fort Smith	Old Fort Days Barrel Racing Futurity
	Crossett	Arkansas High School Rodeo Regionals
Late May to Early June	Shirley	Homecoming and Rodeo
Early June	Booneville	National Trails Day Equestrian Ride
	Huntsville	Hawgfest Pig Race, Rodeo, Music
	Newport	Riverboat Days and State Catfish Cooking Contest (Rodeo)
Mid-June	Mountain View	Western Music Weekend
	Calico Rock	IRA Championship Rodeo
	Dardanelle	PRCA Rodeo
	Siloam Springs	Rodeo and Parade
Early July	Springdale	Rodeo of the Ozarks
Mid-July	Clarksville	Round-up Club Rodeo
Late July	Fort Smith	Commissary Charity Hunter-Jumper Show
Early August	Mena	Polk County Rodeo
	Crossett	Rodeo Roundup Day
	Clinton	Bull Riding Spectacular
Late August to Early September	Clinton	Arkansas Championship Chuck Wagon Races
September	Clarksville	Round-up Club Junior Rodeo
Mid-September	Fort Smith	Arkansas/Oklahoma State Fair
	Harrison	Northwest Arkansas District Fair and PRCA Rodeo

Date	City	Event
Mid-September	Mountain View	Arkansas Old Time Fiddlers Association State Championship Competition
	DeQueen	Sevier County Fair and Rodeo
	Jonesboro	Northeast Arkansas District Fair Rodeo
	Marshall	Searcy County Fair and Rodeo
Late September	Pine Bluff	Southeast Arkansas Livestock Show and Rodeo
Late September to Early October	Texarkana	Four States Fair and Rodeo
Early October	Little Rock	Arkansas State Fair and Livestock Show
CALIFORNIA		
Early January	Rancho Murietta	PRCA Rodeo
Late January	Red Bluff	Red Bluff Bull Sale/Ranch Rodeo
Mid-February	Kernville	Whiskey Flat Days
	Indio	Riverside County Fair and National Date Festival
Late February	Palm Springs	Mounted Police Rodeo and Parade
Mid-March	Red Bluff	Red Bluff Winter Roundup
Late March	Alturas	Livestock Market Spring Ranch Horse and Range Bull Sale
Late March to Early April	San Francisco	Junior Grand National Livestock Exposition and Rodeo
	San Jose	World's Toughest Rodeo
April	Chowchilla	Western Stampede
	King City	King City Riding Club Junior Rodeo
Early April	Oakdale	PRCA Rodeo
Mid-April	Bakersfield	Kern County Horse Show Classic on the Green
	Red Bluff	PRCA Rodeo
Late April	Auburn	Wild West Stampede (PRCA)
	Clovis	Clovis Rodeo (PRCA)
	Springville	Frontier Days
	Springville	Springville Sierra Rodeo
May	Marysville	Marysville Stampede
Early May	Borrego Springs	Cinco de Mayo Celebration
	Calexico	Cinco de Mayo Celebration
	Cottonwood	Cottonwood Rodeo Week
	Delano	Cinco de Mayo Celebration
	San Jose	Cinco de Mayo Celebration
	Santa Maria	Cinco de Mayo Celebration
	Sonoma	Cinco de Mayo Celebration
	Valley Springs	Snyder's Pow Wow
Mid-May	Angels Camp	Calaveras County Fair, Frog Jumping Jubilee and Rodeo
	King City	Salinas Valley Fair
	Redding	Redding Rodeo Week (PRCA)
	Sonora	Mother Lode Roundup Parade and Rodeo

Date	City	Event
Late May	Bishop	Mule Days Celebration
	Yucca Valley	Grubstake Days and PRCA Rodeo
Late May to Early June	Santa Maria	Elks Rodeo and Parade
June	Quincy	California State High School Rodeo Championships
Mid-June	Livermore	Livermore Rodeo (PRCA)
	Sonora	PRCA Rodeo
Late June	Folsom	Folsom Championship PRCA Rodeo
July	Santa Barbara	Horse and Flower Show (PRCA)
	Fortuna	Fortuna Rodeo, "Oldest, Longest, Most Westerly"
Mid-July	Merced	Merced County Fair
	Plymouth	Amador County Fair
Late July	Susanville	Doyle Days Rodeo
	Salinas	The California Rodeo
	Bridgeport	Art Festival and Rodeo
Early August	Paso Robles	California Mid-State Fair
	Santa Barbara	Old Spanish Days
	Grass Valley	Nevada County Fair
	Quincy	Plumas County Fair
Mid-August	Susanville	Lassen County Fair
	Truckee	Truckee Rodeo (PRCA)
	Inglewood	PRCA Rodeo
	San Juan Capistrano	PRCA Rodeo
Mid-August to Early September	Sacramento	California State Fair
Late August	Norco	PRCA Rodeo
	Ventura	PRCA Rodeo
Early September	Lancaster	Antelope Valley Fair, Alfalfa Festival and Rodeo
	Barstow	Calico Days Stampede Rodeo
Late September	Bishop	Tri-County Fair and Wild West Weekend
	Poway	PRCA Rodeo
	Bakersfield	Kern County Fair and PRCA Rodeo
Early October	Santa Rosa	PRCA Rodeo
Mid-October	City of Industry	Industry Hills Charity Pro Rodeo
Late October	San Francisco	Grand National Rodeo, Horse and Stock Exposition
Early November	Death Valley	Death Valley Encampment
Mid-November	Brawley	Cattle Call & PRCA Rodeo
COLORADO		
Mid-January	Steamboat Springs	Cowboy Downhill
	Denver	National Western Stock Show and Rodeo (PRCA)
June to August	Durango	Durango Pro Rodeo Series
	Steamboat Springs	Cowboys' Roundup Rodeo
Mid-June	Grand Junction	Colorado Stampede
	Colorado Springs	Pikes Peak Little Britches Rodeo

Date	City	Event
Late June to Late August	Snowmass	Snowmass Stables Rodeo
Late June	Evergreen	Rodeo Weekend
	Greeley	PRCA Rodeo
July	Canon City	Royal Gorge Rodeo
Early July	Greeley	Biggest Fourth of July Rodeo
	Greeley	Independent Stampede Greeley Rodeo
	Durango	Cowgirl Classic
Mid-July	Estes Park	Rooftop Rodeo
	Gunnison	Cattlemen's Days, Rodeo and Celebration
Late July	Monte Vista	Ski-Hi Stampede Rodeo
Early August	Colorado Springs	Pikes Peak or Bust Rodeo
	Loveland	Larimer County Fair and Rodeo
Mid-August	Rifle	Senior Pro Rodeo
Late August	Pueblo	Colorado State Fair, Livestock Show and Rodeo
Early September	Durango	Ghost Dancer All-Indian Rodeo
Early October	Durango	Family Ranch Rodeo

DISTRICT OF COLUMBIA

Late October	U.S. Air Arena	Washington International Horse Show

FLORIDA

January to October (Last weekend each month)	Davie	5-Star Pro Rodeo Series (PRCA)
Early to Mid-February	Kissimmee	Edition Silver Spurs Rodeo
	Tampa	Florida State Fair PRCA Rodeo
	Hollywood	Seminole Tribal Fair and Rodeo
Early February	Homestead	Frontier Days Rodeo
Mid-March	Arcadia	PRCA Rodeo
July	Kissimmee	Silver Spurs Rodeo
Early July	Arcadia	PRCA Rodeo
Early September	Ocala	PRCA Rodeo
	Okeechobee	PRCA Rodeo
Late September	Tallahassee	Native American Heritage Festival
Mid-October	Orlando	Pioneer Days
	Davies	Sunshine State Pro Rodeo Championship
Early November	Okeechobee	PRCA Rodeo

GEORGIA

Early July	Chatsworth	Appalachian Wagon Train
Early October	Chatsworth	Georgia State and Red Carpet Championship Mule-Draft Horse Frolic
Early November	Chatsworth	North Georgia International Horse Trials

IDAHO

Mid-March	Pocatello	Dodge National Circuit Finals Rodeo
Late April	Lewiston	Lewiston Rodeo: Dogwood Festival
Mid-June	Weiser	National Old Time Fiddlers' Contest

Date	City	Event
Late June to Early July	Rupert	July 4th Celebration—IMPRA Rodeo
Early July	Grangeville	Grangeville Rodeo
Early July	Hailey	4th of July Hailey Days of the Old West
	Salmon	Salmon River Days Rodeo
Mid-July	Nampa	Snake River Stampede
Late July	Caldwell	Canyon County Fair
	Glenns Ferry	Elmore County Fair, ICA Rodeo
	Montpelier	Oregon Trail Rendezvous Pageant
	Preston	That Famous Preston Night Rodeo, PRCA Rodeo
Late July to Early August	Grace	Caribou County Fair & Rodeo, PRCA Rodeo
	Rupert	Minidoka County Fair & Rodeo
August	Caldwell	U.S. Team Roping Championships (USTRC) Northwest Finals
Early August	CascadeValley	County Fair & Rodeo
	Downey	South Bannock County Fair
	Fort Hall	Shoshone-Bannock Indian Festival
	Homedale	Owyhee County Fair
Early August	Idaho Falls	War Bonnet Round Up, PRCA Rodeo
	Jerome	Jerome County Fair & Rodeo
Early August	Lewiston	PRCA Rodeo
	New Plymouth	Payette County Fair & Rodeo
	Rexburg	Madison County Fair
	Rupert	Minidoka County Fair & Rodeo
Mid-August	Burley	Cassia County Fair & PRCA Rodeo
	Caldwell	Caldwell Night Rodeo
	Emmett	Gem County Fair & Rodeo
	Gooding	Gooding County Fair & Rodeo
	Montpelier	Bear Lake County Fair
	Pocatello	North Bannock County Fair
	Preston	Franklin County Fair
	Terreton	Mud Lake Fair & IMPRA Rodeo
Mid to Late August	Boise	Western Idaho Fair & Rodeo
Late August	Coeur d'Alene	North Idaho Fair & Rodeo
	Sandpoint	Bonner County Fair
	Spalding	Nez Perce Cultural Days
	Filer/Twin Falls	County Fair & PRCA Rodeo
Late August to Early September	Blackfoot	Eastern Idaho State Fair
Early September	Ketchum	Ketchum Wagon Days Celebration
	Lewiston	Lewiston Roundup
Mid-September	Lewiston	Nez Perce County Fair
	Orofino	Clearwater County Fair & Lumberjack Days

ILLINOIS

Date	City	Event
Early January	Peoria	World's Toughest Rodeo
Late January	Moline	World's Toughest Rodeo
	Rockford	World's Toughest Rodeo
Mid-March	Rosemont (Chicago)	World's Toughest Rodeo

Date	City	Event
Late March	Springfield	World's Toughest Rodeo
Early September	Palestine	PRCA Rodeo
INDIANA		
Mid-February	Evansville	World's Toughest Rodeo
Late October	Fort Wayne	World's Toughest Rodeo
IOWA		
Early February	Cedar Rapids	World's Toughest Rodeo
Late May to Early June	Cherokee	Cherokee Rodeo
Late June	Edgewood	Edgewood Rodeo Days
Early August	Sidney	Iowa Championship Rodeo
September	Audubon	Operation T-Bone
Early September	Fort Madison	Tri-State Rodeo Festival
Mid-September	Cherokee	Cherokee Rodeo
KANSAS		
Early May	Hays	Spring Rodeo, FHSU
Early June	Fort Scott	Good Ol' Days Celebration
	Garden City	Beef Empire Days
Mid-July	Pretty Prairie	PRCA Rodeo
Late July	Wichita	Mid-America Inter-Tribal Indian Powwow
Late July	Manhattan	PRCA Rodeo
Early August	Dodge City	Dodge City Days (PRCA Rodeo)
	Phillipsburg	Kansas Biggest Rodeo
Mid-August	Abilene	Central Kansas Free Fair and Wild Bill Hickok Rodeo
Mid-September	Hutchinson	PRCA Rodeo
Late September	Medicine Lodge	Indian Summer Days
Early October	Medicine Lodge	Indian Peace Treaty Pageant (Every three years; next in 2000)
KENTUCKY		
Early and Mid-February	Bowling Green	Kyana Quarter Horse Show
Early February	Bowling Green	Championship Rodeo
Mid-April	Lexington	Ha'Penny Horse Trials
	Lexington	Spring Horse Affair
	Henderson	Tri-Fest
Late April	Lexington	Rolex Kentucky CCI 3-Day Event
Early May	Louisville	The Kentucky Derby
	Lexington	Kentucky Spring Horse Show II
Mid-May	Lexington	Kentucky Spring Horse Show
	Lexington	High-Hope Steeplechase
Early June	Lexington	The Egyptian Event
Early July	Lexington	Lexington Junior League Horse Show
Mid-July	Grayson County	Kentucky State Fiddlin' Festival
Late July	Lexington	Wild Horse & Burro Adoption & Exposition

Date	City	Event
Mid-August	Lexington	Hunter/Jumper Show
	Louisville	Kentucky State Fair, Horse Show and Rodeo
	Harrodsburg	Pioneer Days Festival
	Lexington	Lexington Grand Prix
Late August to Early September	Lexington	Yamaha All-Arabian Combined Classic I & II
Early November	Louisville	PRCA Rodeo
LOUISIANA		
Mid-January	Lake Charles	Calcasieu Parish Junior Livestock Show
Early February	Lake Charles	Southwest District Livestock Show and Rodeo
Late February	Covington	Dixie Trail Riders
Late March	Lake Charles	Silver Spur Riders Club
Late April	Lake Charles	Silver Spur Riders Club
Mid-May	Lake Charles	Tennessee Walking and Racking Horse Show
Late May	Lake Charles	Silver Spur Riders Club
Mid-June	Lake Charles	Silver Spur Riders Club
Early July	Lake Charles	Silver Spur Riders Club
Early August	Lake Charles	Silver Spur Riders Club
Mid-September	Lake Charles	Silver Spur Riders Club
October	Angola	Angola Prison Rodeo
Mid-October	Raceland	LaFourche Parish Agriculture Fair and Livestock Show
	Lake Charles	Silver Spur Riders Club
Mid-November	Lake Charles	Silver Spur Riders Club
Mid-December	Lake Charles	Silver Spur Riders Club
MAINE		
January	Kingfield	White World
MARYLAND		
Early May	Crownsville	Dave Martin Championship Rodeo and Anne Arundle County Fair
Early July	McHenry	American Indian Inter-Tribal Cultural Organization Powwow
Early August	Cordova	St. Joseph Jousting Tournament and Horse Show
Early September	Easton	Tuckahoe Championship Rodeo
Mid-September	Fort Meade	Southwest Fest
MICHIGAN		
Mid-January	Detroit	World's Toughest Rodeo
Mid-July	Iron River	Upper Peninsula Championship Rodeo
MINNESOTA		
Early February	St. Paul	World's Toughest Rodeo
Early April	Mankato	World's Toughest Rodeo
Early May	Crookston	Great Northern Horse Extravaganza

Date	City	Event
Mid-June	Granite Falls	Western Fest Rodeo
Late June	Buffalo	Buffalo Rodeo
	Park Rapids	PRCA Rodeo
Mid-July	Detroit Lake	Little Britches Rodeo
Mid-September	Shakopee	PRCA Rodeo
MISSISSIPPI		
Early February	Jackson	Jackson Dixie National Livestock Show and Rodeo and Western Festival
Early May	Tunica	PRCA Rodeo
Late May	Natchez	Adams County Sheriff's Rodeo
Late July to Early August	Philadelphia	Neshoba County Fair
Mid-September	Natchez	Shriner's Pro Rodeo
MISSOURI		
Late June to Early July	Kansas City	Kansas City Rodeo
Early September	Independence	Santa-Cali-Gon Days
Early August	Sikeston	Jaycee Bootheel Rodeo
Mid-August	St. Joseph	Trails West!
Early November	Kansas City	American Royal Livestock, Horse Show and Rodeo
MONTANA		
Mid-January	Great Falls	PRCA Rodeo
Early February	Billings	Northern Rodeo Association Finals
Early February	Helena	Race to the Sky Sled Dog Race
Mid-February	Anaconda/Butte	Big Sky Winternational Sports Festival
Mid-March	Great Falls	C.M. Russell Auction of Original Western Art
Late March	Whitefish	North American Ski Laser Championships
Mid-May	St. Ignatius	Buffalo Feast and Pow Wow
	Miles City	Miles City Bucking Horse Sale
Late May	Virginia City	Spring Horseback Poker Run
	Hardin	Custer's Last Stand Re-enactment
Early June	Forsyth	Forsyth Horse Show and Rodeo
June to August	Laramie	Laramie River Rodeo
Early June to Late August	Billings	Billings Night Rodeo (nightly)
Mid-June	Bozeman	College National Finals Rodeo
Late June	Great Falls	Lewis & Clark Festival
	Hamilton	Bitterroot Festival of the American West
Early July	Red Lodge	Home of Champions Rodeo
	Butte	Butte Vigilante Rodeo Roundup
	Landers	Old Timers' Rodeo
	Livingston	PRCA Rodeo
	Harlowton	July 4th Celebration and Rodeo
	Ennis	Fourth of July Rodeo
	Red Lodge	Home of Champions Rodeo
	Wolf Point	PRCA Rodeo

Date	City	Event
Mid-July	Bannack	Bannack Days
	Browning	North American Indian Days
	Deer Lodge	Western Heritage Days
	Libby	Libby Logger Days
	Polson	Kerr Country Rodeo
Late July	Lewistown	Central Montana Horse Show Fair and Rodeo
	Helena	Last Chance Stampede and Fair
	Red Lodge	Red Lodge Mountain Man Rendezvous
Late July to Early August	Great Falls	Montana State Fair and Rodeo
Early August	Missoula	Western Montana Fair & Rodeo
	Glendive	Dawson County Fair and Rodeo
	Red Lodge	Festival of Nations
	Riverton	Fremont County Fair and Rodeo
	Buffalo	Johnson County Fair and Rodeo
	Pine Bluffs	Trail Days
Mid-August	Lewiston	Montana Cowboy Poetry Gathering
	Billings	Montana Fair
	Kalispell	PRCA Rodeo
	Plentywood	Sheridan County Fair and Rodeo
Late August	Dillon	Beaverhead County Fair & Jaycee Rodeo
	Plains	Sanders County Fair and Rodeo
	Roundup	Roundup Cattle Drive
	White Sulphur Springs	Labor Day Rodeo and Parade
Early September	Reedpoint	Running of the Sheep—Sheep Drive
	Dillon	PRCA Rodeo
Late September	Libby	Nordicfest
October	Billings	Northern International Livestock Exposition and Rodeo
Early October to November	West Yellowstone	Cross-Country Fall Camp
Mid-October	Billings	PRCA Rodeo
NEBRASKA		
Mid-February	Lincoln	World's Toughest Rodeo
Mid-June	North Platte	Celebration and Buffalo Bill Rodeo
Late July	Burwell	Nebraska's Big Rodeo
Early July	Crawford	Crawford Rodeo
	Chadron	Fur Trade Days and Buckskin Rendezvous
Late July	Winnebago	Indian Pow Wow
Mid-August	Ogallala	Ogallala Roundup Rodeo
Late August	Sidney	Cheyenne County Fair
	Gordon	Sheridan County Fair and Rodeo
September	Bayard	Chimney Rock Pioneer Days
Mid-September	Ogallala	Indian Summer Rendezvous
Late September	Omaha	River City Roundup and World Championship Rodeo
Early October	Valentine	Cowboy Poetry Gathering

Date	City	Event
NEVADA		
Every other weekend except during August	Mesquite	Peppermill Year-Round Roping Competition
Late January	Elko	Cowboy Poetry Gathering
	Reno	Biggest Little Cutting Horse in the World Competition
March	Dayton	Dayton Cowboy Poetry & Western Art Show
Early March	Carson City	Cowboy Jubilee & Poetry
	Reno	Reno Ranch Rodeo
Late March	Laughlin	USPA Invitational Rodeo
	Minden	Cowboy Culture Weekend
	Reno	Beefmaster and Romagnola Cattle Show/Sale
Early April	Logandale	Clark County Fair
Late April	Reno	Western National Angus Futurity
Early May	Reno	HN Spanish Rodeo
	Las Vegas	PRCA Rodeo
Mid-May	Reno	Nevada Junior Livestock State Show
	Las Vegas	Helldorado Days and Rodeo
	Wells	Buckaroo Rodeo
Late May	Mesquite	Mesquite Days
	Reno	Showcase of the West Horse Show
June	Pahrump Valley	Over the Hill Stampede Rodeo
Early June	Carson City	Kit Carson Rendezvous & Wagon Train
	Las Vegas	PRCA Rodeo
Mid-June	Reno	BLM Horse Event
	Reno	Wild Horse and Burro Show
Late June	Reno	Reno Rodeo (PRCA)
July	Ely	Lund Rodeo
	Virginia City	Way It Was Rodeo
Early July	Fallon	Silver State International Rodeo
	Fallon	International Invitational High School Rodeo
	McDermitt	Twin States Ranch Hand Rodeo
	Reno	Region III Arabian Horse Show
Mid-July	Fallon	All Indian Stampede and Pioneer Days
	Reno	Convention Rodeo and Barbecue
	Reno	Dressage in the Sierra
	Elko	Silver State Stampede Rodeo (PRCA)
Late July	Elko	Native American Festival
August	Elko	Western Folklife Round-up
	Lovelock	World Fast Draw Championship
Early August	Reno	Limousin Cattle Show
	Reno	Appahann Appaloosa Horse Show
Mid-August	Reno	Nevada and Zone II Paint Horse Show
	Ely	White Pine Country Days Fair and Pony Express Days and Horse Races
Late August	Reno	Nevada State Fair
	Yerington	Spirit of Wovoka Days Pow Wow

Date	City	Event
Late August to Early September	Elko	Elko County Fair and Horse Races
	Winnemucca	Buckaroo Heritage Western Art Roundup
September	Lund	Duckwater Classic Roping
	Virginia City	Virginia City Camel Races
Early September	Fallon	Nevada Cutting Horse Spectacular
(Labor Day)	Winnemucca	Nevada's Oldest Rodeo & Western Art Round-up Show and Sale and Tri-County Fair
Early September	Reno	Silver Sire Breeders Horse Show/Sale
	Reno	NSHA Horse Show
Mid-September	Pahrump Valley	Harvest Festival, Parade & Rodeo
	Reno	National Reining Cowhorse Association Snaffle Bit Futurity Competition
	Winnemucca	Pari-Mutuel Thoroughbred, Quarter Horse and Mule Racing Events
Late September	Ely	Whitepine High School Rodeo
	Reno	Bullnanza
	Elko	Spring Creek Ranch Hand Rodeo
Late October	Beatty	Great Beatty Burro Races
	Carson City	Nevada Day Celebration
	Nixon	Pyramid Lake Nevada Day Open Rodeo
	Reno	Western States Celebration
	Reno	ACTRA Team Roping
Early November	Minden	Rhymer's Rodeer Cowboy Poetry
	Reno	National Senior Pro Rodeo Finals
Early December	Las Vegas	National PRCA Finals Rodeo
	Las Vegas	NFR Bucking Horse and Bull Sale
Mid-December	Reno	Hereford Cattle Show and Sale
	Reno	American Shorthorn Cattle Show and Sale
Late December	Reno	Buck 'n' Ball New Years Eve Rodeo
NEW JERSEY		
Late May to Late September	Woodstown	Cowtown Rodeo, PRCA (Weekly)
Late May to Mid-October	Netcong	Wild West City—Replica of Dodge City
NEW MEXICO		
Early January	Red River	Red River Winterfest
Late February	Chama	High Country Winter Carnival
	Angel Fire	Angel Fire Winter Carnival Festival Weekend
Late March	Shakespeare	New Mexico Renegade Ride
Mid-April	Truth or Consequences	Ralph Edwards Fiesta and Rodeo
Mid-May	Deming	Fiddlers' Contest
Late May	Silver City	Endurance Horse Ride
	Cloudcroft	Mayfair Hayrides and Rodeo

Date	City	Event
Early June	Clovis	Pioneer Days Celebration and PRCA Rodeo
	Fort Sumner	Old Fort Days
	Mescalero	Apache Indian Maidens' Puberty Rites and Rodeo
	Las Vegas	Rails and Trails Days
	Farmington	Sheriff Posse Rodeo
Mid-June	Cloudcroft	Western Roundup
	Dulce	All-Indian Rodeo
	Taos	San Antonio Corn Dance
	Gallup	Lions Club Western Jubilee Week and Rodeo
Late June	Taos	Rodeo de Taos
	Tucumcari	PisRodeo de Taos Jubilee Week and Rodeo
Late June to Early July	Clayton	Rabbit Ear Roundup Rodeo
Early July	Cimarron	Cimarron Rodeo
	Eunice	Eunice Fourth of July Celebration and Junior Rodeo
	Santa Fe	Rodeo de Santa Fe
	Taos	Taos Pueblo Powwow
Mid-July	Carlsbad	Western Days and AJRA Rodeo
	Dulce	Little Beaver Roundup Rodeo
	Galisteo	Galisteo Rodeo
	Ruidoso	Billy The Kid–Pat Garrett Historical Days
Late July	Las Vegas	Fort Union's Santa Fe Trail Days
	Taos	Fiesta de Santiago y Santa Ana
August	Lovington	Lea County Fair and PRCA Rodeo
	Gallup	Inter-Tribal Indian Ceremonial and Rodeo
Early August	Los Alamos	Los Alamos County Fair and Rodeo
Mid-August	Capitan	Lincoln County Fair
	Santa Fe	Indian Market
	Albuquerque	Bernalillo County 4-H Fair and Rodeo
September	Albuquerque	New Mexico State Fair and Rodeo
	Santa Fe	Fiesta de Santa Fe
Early September	Socorro	Socorro County Fair and Rodeo
	Ruidoso Downs	All American Futurity
	Clayton	Hayden Rodeo
Late September	Lovington	Days of Old West Ranch Rodeo
	Las Cruces	Southern New Mexico State Fair and Rodeo
	Roswell	Eastern New Mexico State Fair and Rodeo
Late September	Deming	Southwestern New Mexico State Fair
	Taos	The Old Taos Trade Fair
	Taos	San Geronimo Day Trade Fair
Early October	Ruidoso	Cowboy Symposium
Mid-October	Carlsbad	Alfalfa Fest (Mule Races, Largest Parade, and Hayride)
Late October	Truth or Consequences	Old-Time Fiddlers Contest
Mid-November	Hobbs	Llano Estacado Party and Cowboy Hall of Fame and Western Heritage Center Introduction Banquet
Late November	Albuquerque	Indian National Finals Rodeo

Date	City	Event
Late December	Taos	The Matachines Dances at Taos Pueblo
NEW YORK		
Late May	Saratoga Springs	Dressage at Saratoga
Early June	Apalachin	Otsiningo Pow Wow and Indian Craft Fair
	Elmont	The Belmont Stakes
	Kinderhook	Columbia County Carriage Days
Late June	Lake Placid	Lake Placid Horse Show
Early July	Sandy Creek	Oswego County Fair & Horse Show
	Lake Placid	I Love New York Horse Show
Mid-July	Brookfield	Madison County Fair
	Lowville	Lewis County Fair
	Pulaski	Cowboy Round Up
Late July	Cazenovia	Horse Driving Competition
	Queens	Thunderbird American Indian Mid-Summer Pow Wow
Early August	Attica	Attica Rodeo
	Gerry	Rodeo
Late August	Bridgehampton	Hampton Classic Horse Show
	Howes Cave	Iroquois Indian Festival
	Rhinebeck	Dutchess County Fair
	Syracuse	The Great New York State Fair
Early September	Ballston Spa	All American Professional Rodeo
Late October	Manhattan	National Horse Show
NORTH CAROLINA		
Mid-January	Raleigh	Midwinter Quarter Horse Show
Early February	Raleigh	Southern National Draft Horse Psull
Late March	Raleigh	North Carolina Quarter Horse Association Spring Show Championship Rodeo
	Pinehurst	Kiwanis Charity Horse Show
	Raleigh	Great Smokies Pro Rodeo
	Oak Ridge	Oak Ridge Easter Horse Show & Fiddlers Convention
	Fayetteville	Shrine Club Rodeo
Early April	Blowing Rock	Opening Day Trout Fishing Derby
	Southern Pines	Moore County Pleasure Horse Drive Show
	Pembroke	Spring Racking Horse Show
	Pinehurst	Harness Horse Racing Matinee
	Raleigh	Appaloosa Horse Show
Mid-April	Raleigh	Easter Bunny Quarter Horse Circuit
Mid-April	Tryon	Tryon Thermal Belt Chamber of Commerce Horse Show
Late April	Asheville	Carolina Mountains Arabian Show
Early May	Statesville	Tarheel Classic Horse Show
	Asheville	Southern Horse Fair (PRCA)
Mid-May	Burnsville	Jaycees Championship Rodeo
	Monroe	Mid-Atlantic Championship Rodeo
	Raleigh	NC All Arabian Horse Show
	Southern Pines	Sandhills Combined Driving Event

Date	City	Event
Late May	Union Grove	Old Time Fiddlers' and Bluegrass Festival
	Raleigh	Southern States Morgan Horse Show
	Tryon	Tryon Horse Show
Early June	Raleigh	Capitol Dressage Classic
	Wilmington	Sudan Horse Patrol Coastal Plains Horse Show
Mid-June	Love Valley	Junior Showdown
	Raleigh	Appaloosa Horse Show
Late June	Love Valley	Frontier Week Rodeo
	Andrews	Wagon Train
	Raleigh	NC Hunter Jumper Association Show
	Pembroke	Racking Horse Show
Early July	Hayesville	Clay County Rodeo
	Sparta	Lions Club Horse Show
Mid-July	Love Valley	Junior Showdown
	Raleigh	NC State 4-H Horse Show
	Waynesville	Waynesville Lions Club Horse Show
Late July	Waynesville	Trail Riders Horse Show
	Raleigh	NC All Amateur Arabian Horse Show
	Raleigh	Raleigh Summer Hunter Jumper Show
	Asheville	Carolina Mountains Summer All Arabian Horse Show
	Blowing Rock	Blowing Rock Charity Horse Show
	Tryon	Tryon Thermal Belt Chamber of Commerce Horse Show
Early August	Robbins	Farmer's Day & Wagon Train
	Waynesville	Fraternal Order of Police Horse Show
Early September	Mocksville	Lake Myers Rodeo
Mid-September	Monroe	Mid-Atlantic Championship Rodeo
	Raleigh	NC State Championship Charity Horse Show
Late September	Asheville	Carolina Mountains Fall All Arabian Horse Show
Early November	Pinehurst	Fall Horse Carriage Drive
Late November	Raleigh	Eastern Quarter Horse of NC Show & Futurity

NORTH DAKOTA

Early March	Valley City	North Dakota Winter Show and Rodeo
Mid-April	Grand Forks	Native American Days
Mid-May	Beach	Beaver Creek Ranch Round-up & Branding
Late May	Medora	Dakota Cowboy Poetry Gathering
Early June	Bottineau	Old Time Fiddlers Contest
Mid-June	Fessenden	Parimutuel Horse Racing
Mid-June	Williston	Fort Union Trading Post Rendezvous
Late June	Jamestown	Fort Seward Wagon Train
Early July	Dickinson	Rough Rider Days
	Mandan	Rodeo Days
Late July	Taylor	Taylor Horsefest
	Devil's Lake	Fort Totten Days

Date	City	Event
Early August	Sentinel Butte	Champions Ride Rodeo, Home on the Range for Boys
Mid-August	West Fargo	Pioneer Days
September	Bismarck	United Tribes International Pow-Wow
Early September	Dickinson	NDRA Rodeo
Late September	Jamestown	Buffalo Days
Late October	Bismarck	Badlands Circuit Finals Rodeo
OHIO		
Mid-January	Dayton	World's Toughest Rodeo
Early March	Cleveland	World's Toughest Rodeo
Mid-March	Toledo	World's Toughest Rodeo
October	Columbus	All-American Quarter Horse Congress
OKLAHOMA		
January to December	Sallisaw	Parimutuel Mixed Breed Horse Racing
Mid-January	Tulsa	Longhorn World Championship Rodeo
Late January	Oklahoma City	International Finals Rodeo
February to May	Oklahoma City	Parimutuel Thoroughbred Horse Racing
Early February	Oklahoma City	Wild Horse Adoption
Early March	Guthrie	Timed Event Championship of the World
	Tulsa	Super Bull Tour
Mid-March	Oklahoma City	Western Heritage Awards
Mid-April	Guthrie	'89er Days and PRCA Rodeo
	Oklahoma City	Centennial Horse Show
Late April	Checotah	Duvall Jackpot Steer Wrestling
May to July	Oklahoma City	Parimutuel Quarter Horse Racing
Early May	Oklahoma City	Non Pro Cutting Horse Show
	Guymon	Pioneer Days and PRCA Rodeo
Mid-May	Guthrie	Ben Johnson Pro Celebrity Rodeo
Late May	Boley	Boley Rodeo and BBQ Festival
	Guthrie	OCA Range Round-up
	Henryetta	Bullchallenge
	Hugo	PRCA Rodeo
	Idabel	Oklahoma Championship Chuckwagon Races
	Oklahoma City	Chuckwagon Festival
June to August	Pawnee	Pawnee Bill Wild West Show
Early June	Boise City	Santa Fe Trail Daze
	Yukon	Chisholm Trail Festival
Mid-June	Claremore	Will Rogers Stampede Rodeo
	Oklahoma City	National Appaloosa Horse Show
	Pawhuska	Cattlemen's Convention
	Pawhuska	Ben Johnson Memorial Steer Roping
Mid-June	Shawnee	State 4-H Horse Show
July to August	Tulsa	Parimutuel Mixed Breed Horse Racing
Early July	Shawnee	International Finals Youth Rodeo

Date	City	Event
Mid-July	Oklahoma City	National Reining Horse Derby
	Pawhuska	International Roundup Club Cavalcade
	Tulsa	Palomino Horse Breeders of America World Championship Horse Show
Late July	Woodward	Elk's Rodeo (PRCA)
August	Bixby	Wild West Extravaganza
Early August	Clearview	Clearview Memorial Rodeo
	Lawton	Rangers PRCA Rodeo
	Okmulgee	Invitational Rodeo
	Tulsa	Morgan Horse Extravaganza
Mid-August	Freedom	Freedom Rodeo
	Pawnee	Pawnee Bill Memorial Rodeo
	Ponca City	101 Wild West Days PRCA Rodeo
	Tulsa	Intertribal Pow Wow of Champions
Late August	McAlester	Oklahoma State Prison Rodeo
	Vinita	Will Rogers Memorial Rodeo
September	McAlester	Pittsburgh County Intertribal Pow Wow and Oklahoma State Prison Rodeo
September to November	Oklahoma City	Parimutuel Thoroughbred Horse Racing
Early September	Altus	Great Plains Stampede Rodeo
	Chelsea	Clem McSpadden's Bushyhead Labor Day Pasture Roping
	Elk City	Rodeo of Champions
	Enid	Cherokee Strip Stampede PRCA Rodeo
	Guthrie	Pro Bull Riders' Tour Challenge
	Henryetta	Living Legends Rodeo
Early October	Oklahoma City	Grand National and World Championship Morgan Horse Show
Mid-October	Oklahoma City	Festival of the Horse
	Guthrie	Dodge Prairie Circuit Finals Rodeo
	Oklahoma City	National Children's Cowboy Festival
Late October	Oklahoma City	U.S. Team Roping Championships
Early November	Shawnee	Southwest Dressage Championships
Mid-November	Oklahoma City	World Championship Quarter Horse Show
Late November	Guthrie	National Finals Steer Roping Championship & Women's National Finals Rodeo
Early December	Oklahoma City	National Reining Horse Futurity
	Oklahoma City	World Championship Barrel Racing Futurity

OREGON

Mid-January	Portland	Pro Rodeo Classic
Late January	Portland	AG Show
Late April	Salem	AG Fest
	Salem	Oregon State Fair & Stallion Show
Mid-May	Tygh Valley	Tygh Valley Rodeo
	Rogue Valley	Rogue Valley Roundup
	Salem	Salem Rodeo
Late May	Jordan	Big Loop Rodeo
June	La Grande	Eastern Oregon Livestock Show

Date	City	Event
Early June	Sisters	June Rodeo
	Union	PRCA Rodeo
Mid-June	Roseburg	PRCA Rodeo
Late June	Tillamook	Dairy Festival and Rodeo
Late June	Eugene	PRCA Rodeo
July	La Grande	Catherine Creek Junior Rodeo and Elgin Stampede
Early July	St. Paul	St. Paul Rodeo
	Molalla	Molalla Buckeroo
Mid-July	Prineville	Crooked River Roundup
	Philomath	Frolic and Rodeo Festival
	The Dalles	PRCA Rodeo
Late July	Joseph	Chief Joseph Days Rodeo
August	La Grande	Oregon Trail Days Blue Mountain Rodeo
Early August	Madras	Jefferson County Fair and Rodeo
	Hermiston	PRCA Rodeo
	Hillsboro	PRCA Rodeo
Mid-August	Canby	PRCA Rodeo
Late August	Grant County	Grant County Fair and Rodeo
	Philomath	Pee Wee Rodeo
	Salem	Oregon State Fair and Rodeo
September	Burns	Harnay Fair and Rodeo
Early September	Lakeview	Lake County Fair and Roundup
Mid-September	Pendleton	Pendleton Roundup
October	Portland	Pacific International Livestock Show and Rodeo
Mid-October	Klamath Falls	Klamath Basin Horse Show
Late October	Madras	Cutting Horse Show
	Central Point	PRCA Rodeo
	Prineville	Central Oregon Cutting Horse Show

PENNSYLVANIA

Date	City	Event
Late May	Devon	Devon Horse Show and County Fair
Early June	New Castle	Pennsylvania Appaloosa Association Horse Show
Mid-June	Meridian	Butler Rodeo
	New Castle	Arabian Horse Show
	New Castle	Tri-State Reining Association Horse Show
Late June	Shartlesville	Professional Rodeo
	Kellettville	Trail Ride
	Ridgeway	Independence Day Festival
Mid-July	Benton	Frontier Days and Rodeo
Late July	Mercer	Jefferson Township Fair
	Driftwood	Tom Mix Roundup
	Kellettville	Allegheny Mountain Championship Rodeo
	New Castle	Quarter Horse Association Horse Show
	New Castle	Lawrence County Charity Horse Show
Mid-August	No. Washington	North Washington Rodeo (PRCA)
	New Castle	Quarter Horse Association Horse Show
Late August	Shartlesville	Professional Rodeo
Early September	Coatesville	Buffalo Bill Days & Western Horse Show

Date	City	Event
Mid-October	Harrisburg	Pennsylvania National Horse Show
Late October	Harrisburg	Pennsylvania 4-H Horse Show
	Uniontown	Old-Time Fiddlers State Championship
SOUTH CAROLINA		
Mid-March	Aiken	Steeplechase and Harness Races
	Santee	Elloree Trials
Early August	Blacksburg	Ed Brown Rodeo
Early November	Camden	Colonial Cup International Steeplechase
SOUTH DAKOTA		
Late January	Rapid City	Black Hills Stock Show and Rodeo
Early May	Brookings	Jackrabbit Stampede Rodeo
Mid-June	Sturgis	High School Rodeo
Early June	Lake City	Fort Sisseton Historical Festival
July	Wall	Wall Roundup Days
Early July	Belle Fourche	Black Hills Roundup
	Mobridge	PRCA Rodeo
Mid-July	Sturgis	Sturgis Livestock Rodeo
	Mitchell	Corn Palace Stampede Rodeo
Early August	Deadwood	Days of '76"
	Watertown	Pro Bowl Rodeo
	Rapid City	PRCA Rodeo
TENNESSEE		
Late April	Paris	World's Biggest Fish Fry Rodeo
Mid-May	Nashville	Iroquois Steeplechase
Early June	Wartrace	Strolling Jim Memorial Horse Show Heyday
Early July	Smithville	Old Time Fiddlers' Jamboree and Crafts Festival
Late July	Clarksville	Walking Horse Show
Early August	Murfreesboro	International Grand Championship Walking Horse Show
Late August	Gray	Appalachian Fair
	Shelbyville	Tennessee Walking Horse National Celebration
Late September	Memphis	Midsouth Fair and Exposition, Rodeo
TEXAS		
Mid-January to Early February	Fort Worth	Southwestern Exposition Livestock Show and Rodeo
Early February	El Paso	Southwestern Livestock Show and Rodeo
	San Antonio	Livestock Show and Rodeo
	Los Fresnos	PRCA Rodeo
Mid-February to Early March	Houston	Houston Livestock Show and Rodeo
Late February	Yoakum	Rodeo

Date	City	Event
Late February to Early March	Brownsville	Charro Days
	Alpine	Cowboy Poetry Gathering
Mid-March	San Angelo	Stock Show and Rodeo
	Shamrock	St. Patrick's Day Celebration
	Austin	PRCA Rodeo
Mid-March	Mercedes	Rio Grande Valley Livestock Show & Rodeo
Late March	Austin	Livestock Show & PRCA Rodeo
	Palestine	Dogwood Trials Festival and Rodeo
	Lubbock	PRCA Rodeo
	Nacogdoches	PRCA Rodeo
April to September	Mesquite	Mesquite Rodeo (Every Friday and Saturday)
Early April	Richmond	Spring Roundup
Mid-April	San Antonio	Fiesta San Antonio
Mid-April	Corpus Christi	PRCA Rodeo
	Poteet	Strawberry Festival
Late April	Edna	PRCA Rodeo
	Lufkin	PRCA Rodeo
	Corpus Christi	Buccaneer Days Rodeo
Mid-May	Jasper	PRCA Rodeo
	Abilene	Western Heritage Classic
Early June	Fort Worth	Chisholm Trail Roundup
	Gladewater	PRCA Rodeo
	Yoakum	Tom-Tom Festival Parade & Rodeo
Mid-June	Abilene	Texas High School Rodeo Finals
Mid-June to Late August	El Paso	Viva! El Paso"
Late June	Stamford	Texas Cowboy Reunion
	Pecos	West of Pecos Rodeo (PRCA Approved)
	Big Spring	Cowboy Reunion and Rodeo
Early July	Pecos	PRCA Rodeo
Mid-July	Jacksonville	PRCA Rodeo
	Pampa	PRCA Rodeo
Early August	Dalhart	XIT Rodeo and Reunion
Mid-August	Sonora	PRCA Rodeo
Late August	Fredericksburg	Gillespie County Fair & Carnival
Early September	Boys Ranch	Cal Farley's Boys Ranch Rode
	Abilene	West Texas Fair & Rodeo
	Grand Prairie	National Championship Indian Pow Wow
Mid-September	Abilene	PRCA Rodeo
	Brenham	Washington County Fair
Late September	Lubbock	Panhandle South Plains Fair
Late September to Mid-October	Dallas	State Fair of Texas, Rodeo and Livestock Show
October	Lubbock	Texas Tech Intercollegiate Rodeo
Early October	Waco	Heart O' Texas Fair and Rodeo
Mid-October	Angleton	PRCA Rodeo
December	Lubbock	Candlelight Christmas at the Ranch

Date	City	Event
Late December	Odessa	Sand Hills Hereford and Quarter Horse Show and Rodeo
UTAH		
Early March	Tremonton	Cowboy Poetry "Do"
Early May	Tremonton	PRCA Rodeo
Late May	Parowan	Iron County Cowboy Days & Poetry Gatherin'
June	Roosevelt	Rough Rider Days
Early June	Helper	Butch Cassidy Days Celebration
	Moab	Butch Cassidy Days Celebration
Mid-June	Pleasant Grove	PRCA Rodeo
Late June	Lehi	PRCA Rodeo
	Oakley	PRCA Rodeo
Late June to Late July	Vernal	"Cassidy" Outdoor Musical
Early July	Ft. Duchesne	Ute Indian Pow Wow
	Price	Black Diamond Stampede PRCA Rodeo
Early July	Oakley	Oakley Rodeo
	Vernal	Dinosaur Roundup Rodeo
	Belton	PRCA Rodeo
	West Jordan	PRCA Rodeo
Mid-July	Salt Lake City	"Days of '47" Celebration and Rodeo
	Nephi	Ute Stampede
	Vernal	PRCA Rodeo
Late July	Statewide	Centennial Pioneer Day Celebrations
	Ogden	PRCA Rodeo
	Spanish Fork	PRCA Rodeo
Late July to Early August	Logan	Centennial Festival of the American West
August	Statewide	County Fairs
Early August	Morgan	Morgan County Rodeo and Fair
	Farmington	Davis County Fair and Livestock Show
	Richfield	Sevier County Fair Garden City Annual
	Bear Lake	Raspberry Days
	Castle Dale	Emery County Fair
	Logan	Cache County Fair and Rodeo
	Price	Carbon County Fair and International Days
	Spanish Fork	Utah County Fair
	Heber City	Wasatch County Fair and Rodeo
Mid-August	Minersville	Beaver County Fair
	Tooele	Tooele County Fair
	Monticello	San Juan County Fair and Junior Livestock Show
	Hurricane	Washington County Fair
	Duchesne	Duchesne County Fair and Rodeo
	Park City	Park City Ride 'n' Tie
	Park City	North American Supreme Championship Sheep Dog Trials
	Orderville	Kane County Fair
	Coalville	Summit County Fair

Date	City	Event
Mid-August	Ogden	Weber County Fair
	Junction	Piute County Fair
	Loa	Wayne County Fair
	Randolph	Rich County Roundup Days
Late August	Tremonton	Box Elder County Fair and Rodeo
	Manti	Sanpete County Fair
Early September	Cedar City	Iron County Fair
	Moab	La Sal Mountain Horse and Rider Endurance Race
	Parowan	Iron County Fair
Early September	Park City	Lewis Field Rodeo Challenge
	Hooper	Tomato Days and Rodeo
Early September	Cedar City	Southwest Livestock Show
	Salt Lake City	Utah State Fair
	Brigham	Peach Days
Mid-September	St. George	Dixie Roundup
Late October to Early November	Antelope Island	Buffalo Roundup State Park
November	Ft. Duchesne	Ute Thanksgiving Pow Wow
Early November	St. George	Southern Utah Endurance Ride
Mid-November	Moab	Western Poetry Writers Party and Reading Celebration
	Ogden	PRCA Rodeo
Late November to January 1	Salt Lake City	250,000 Christmas Lights Turned on at Historic Temple Square
Late November	Moab	Mountain Man Rendezvous
	Santa Clara	Thanksgiving Day Rodeo
Mid-December	Salt Lake City	Crossroads of the West Gun Show

VERMONT

Date	City	Event
Early May	South Woodstock	All Breed Horse Fair & Trade Show
Late May	Manchester	Bennington County Horse Show
	Barton	Memorial Day Weekend
Late June	Brookline	New Brook Horse Show
Early July	Tunbridge	Vermont Morgan Horse AssociationHeritage
Days		
Early to Mid-July	Killington	Killington Mountain Horse Show
Mid-July	Killington	Vermont Summer Classic–Equestrian Summer Showcase
Late July	Waitsfield	Valley Class–Equestrian Summer Showcase
	South Woodstock	Vermont 100 Mile Endurance Run & Ride
Late July to Early August	Waitsfield	Sugarbush Horse Show
Late July to Early September	North Hero	Hermann's Royal Lipizzan Stallions
Early August	Waitsfield	Mad River Festival–Equestrian Summer Showcase
	Bellows Falls	Vermont State Championship Old Time Fiddlers' Contest

Date	City	Event
Mid-August	Stowe	Midsummer Festival–Green Mountain Equestrian Finale
	Weybridge	Vermont Day Open House
Late August	Stowe	Midsummer Festival–Green Mountain Equestrian Finale
	Tunbridge	Lippitt Country Show
Late September	Bridgeport	Krawczyk Horse Farm Open Barn and Sale
WASHINGTON		
Early January	Yakima	PRCA Rodeo
Early June	Roy	Roy Pioneer Rodeo
	Bickleton	Alder Creek Picnic and Rodeo
Mid-June	Bremerton	Little Britches Rodeo
	Colville	Fort Colville Days and Rodeo (PRCA)
Late June	Darrington	Darrington Timber Bowl Rodeo
Late June	Oakville	Oakville Rodeo
Early July	Sedro Woolley	Logger Rodeo
	Oakville	Oakville Rodeo
	Toppenish	Toppenish Pow Wow and Rodeo
Mid-July	Cheney	Rodeo Days
Late July	Deer Park	Deer Park WRA Rodeo
Early August	Longview	PRCA Rodeo
Mid-August	Omak	Stampede and Suicide Race (PRCA)
	Moses Lake	PRCA Rodeo
Late August	Bremerton	Kitsap County Fair
	Kennewick	PRCA Rodeo
September	Puyallup	Western Washington Fair and Rodeo
Early September	Walla Walla	Southeastern Washington Fair & Frontier Days
	Ellensburg	Kittitas County Fair & Ellensburg Rodeo
Mid-September	Othello	Othello PRCA Rodeo
Late September	Yakima	Central Washington State Fair
	Puyallup	PRCA Rodeo
WISCONSIN		
Late February	Cable	American Birkebeiner
May to September	Statewide	Indian Powwows
Mid-June	Milwaukee	Wonago World Championship Rodeo
Late June	Richland Center	High School Rodeo State Finals
Early July	Manawa	PCRA All-American Rodeo of Rodeos
	Spooner	PRCA Rodeo
Mid-July	Spooner	Heart of the North Rodeo
Late July	Hayward	Lumberjack World Championships
Late August	Lac Du Flambeau	PRCA Rodeo
Early September	Kellner (Wood City)	Little Britches Rodeo
	Praire du Chien	Villa Louis Carriage Classic
	Superior	Great Northern Classic Rodeo
Late November	Madison	World's Toughest Rodeo

Date	City	Event
WYOMING		
Late January	Torrington	Shrine Cutter Races
	Riverton	Wild West Winter Carnival
	Jackson	All American Cutter Races
Late January to Mid-February	Lander	Wyoming State Winter Fair
Early February	Western Wyoming	International Rocky Mountain Stage Stop Sled Dog Race
Mid-February	Gillette	Camplex Winter Western Trade Show and Rodeo
	Saratoga	Don E. Erickson Memorial Cutter Races
	Casper	Cowboy State Games
	Casper	Winter Sports Festival
Late February	Rock Springs	Desert Dust Winter Stampede PRCA Rodeo
Late February	Jackson	Cowboy Ski Challenge
Mid-March	Jackson	Celebrity Ski Extravaganza
Mid-March	Cheyenne	Cowboy Poetry Reading
Late March	Rawlins	Cowboy Poetry Gathering
Mid-April	Cody	Cowboy Songs & Range Ballads
Late April	Casper	Bull Riders Only
Early May	Newcastle	Living History Days
Mid-May	Cheyenne	Regional College Rodeo
	Rock Springs	Cowboy Poetry Music Festival
Mid-May	Rock Springs	All Girl Rodeo
	Jackson	Elk Antler Auction
Late May	Worland	Best Bull Riders Only
	Jackson	Old West Days
Early June	Crowheart	Big Wind Pow Wow
	Cody	Summer Nite Rodeos Begin
Mid-June	Casper	Cowboy State Games
	Greybull	Days of '49
	Hulett	Hulett Rodeo
	Lander	Popo Agie Rendezvous
	Cody	Frontier Festival
	Cheyenne	Happy Jack Mountain Music Festival
	Sheridan	Bozeman Trail Days
	Gillette	Cowboy Days
	Encampment	Woodchopper's Jamboree
	Chugwater	Chugwater Chili Cook-Off
Late June	Lovell	Mustang Days
	Casper	Platte Bridge Encampment
	Fort Washakie	Shoshone Pow Wow and Indian Days
	Green River	Flaming Gorge Days
	Cheyenne	Super Day
	Douglas	Jackalope Days
	Medicine Bow	Medicine Bow Days, Rodeo, Parade & Craft Fair
	Cody	Plains Indian Pow Wow
	Casper	World Open Atlatl & Primitive Skills Contest
	Riverton	Trail Ride

Date	City	Event
Early July	Riverton	1838 Mountain Man Rendezvous
	Cody	Cody Stampede Days
	Laramie	Jubilee Days
	Lander	Pioneer Days
	Guernsey	Old Timers Rodeo
	South Pass	Old Fashioned Fourth of July
	Laramie	Professional Women's Rodeo
	Ten Sleep	Ten Sleep Rodeo
Mid-July	Casper	PRCA Rodeo
	Lander	Arapaho Sundance
	Lusk	Legend of Rawhide
	Green River	Overland Stage Stampede Rodeo
	Douglas	Ft. Fetterman Days
	Casper	Central Wyoming Fair & Rodeo
	Sheridan	Sheridan-WYO Rodeo
	Riverton	Rendezvous WRA Rodeo
Late July	Cheyenne	Cheyenne Frontier Days
	Rock Springs	Red Desert Round up Rodeo
Early August	Pine Bluffs	Pine Bluffs Trail Days
Mid-August	Douglas	Senior Pro Rodeo
Mid-August	Dubois	Whiskey Mountain Buckskinner Rendezvous
Late August	Cody	Buffalo Bill Festival
	Rock Springs	Great Wyoming Polka & Heritage Festival
Late August	Evanston	Bear River Mountain Man Rendezvous
	Cody	Senior Pro Rodeo
	Lusk	Senior Pro Rodeo
	Douglas	PRCA Rodeo
Early September	Fort Bridger	Mountain Man Rendezvous
	Evanston	Cowboy Days
	Laramie	Territory Days
	Evanston	Cowboy Days
	Sheridan	Don King Days
Mid-September	Kaycee	Deke Latham Memorial PRCA Rodeo
Late September	Cody	Buffalo Bill Celebrity Shootout
Mid-October	Riverton	Cowboy Poetry Festival
Late October	Casper	PRCA Rodeo Finals
Mid-November	Rock Springs	WY Rodeo Association Finals
Late November	Cheyenne	Cheyenne Christmas Parade
	Gillette	NRCA Finals Rodeo & Trade Show
Early December	Fort Casper	Candlelight Tour & Christmas with the Frontier Soldiers
Late December	Casper	Cowboy Shootout
	Jackson	Torchlight Parade

ALBERTA

Mid-March	Medicine Hat	PRCA Rodeo
Late March	Edmonton	Northlands Super Rodeo (PRCA)
	Calgary	PRCA Rodeo
Late April	Lethbridge	Whoop-Up Quarter Horse Circuit
	Red Deer	Silver Buckle Rodeo
	Grande Prairie	Whispering Pines Rodeo

Date	City	Event
Late May	Red Deer	Westerner Spring Quarter Horse Show
Late May to Early June	Calgary	The National Horse Show, Spruce Meadows
Early June	Grande Prairie	PRCA Rodeo
	Marwayne	PRCA Rodeo
Mid-June	Innistail	PRCA Rodeo
Late June	Ponoka	PRCA Rodeo
	Sundre	PRCA Rodeo
	Wainwright	PRCA Rodeo
Late June to Early July	Ponoka	Ponoka Stampede
	Airdrie	PRCA Rodeo
Early July	Calgary	The Invitational Horse Show, Spruce Meadows
		PRCA Rodeo
	Calgary	Calgary Exhibition and Stampede
Mid-July	Red Deer	Westerner Days
Mid- to Late July	Edmonton	Edmonton's Klondike Days
Late July to Early August	Medicine Hat	Exhibition and Stampede
Early August	Lethbridge	Whoop-Up Days
	High Level	PRCA Rodeo
	Medicine Hat	PRCA Rodeo
	Strathmore	PRCA Rodeo
Mid-August	High Level	PRCA Rodeo
Early September	Calgary	The Masters Horse Show, Spruce Meadows
Early November	Edmonton	Canadian Finals Rodeo (PRCA)
Late December	Hobbema	PRCA Rodeo

BRITISH COLUMBIA

Mid-April	Kamloops	Kamloops Professional Indoor Rodeo
Late April	Williams Lake	Williams Lake Indoor Rodeo
May	Clinton	Clinton Rodeo
	100 Mile House	Little Britches Rodeo
	Metchosin	Luxton Rodeo
	Lillooet Lake	Lillooet Lake Rodeo
May	Keremeos	Elks Rodeo
	Kelowna	Black Mountain Rodeo
	Ashcroft	Ashcroft Rodeo
Mid-May	Houston	Pleasant Valley Rodeo
	Keremeos	Keremeos Elks Rodeo
	Falkland	PRCA Rodeo
Late May	Cloverdale	Cloverdale Rodeo
June	Doe River	Doe River Rodeo
	Prince George	Prince George Rodeo
	Riske Creek	Riske Creek Rodeo
Early June	Hudson's Hope	Hudson's Hope Rodeo
	Kispiox	Kispiox Valley Rodeo
	Burns Lake	Eagle Creek Stampede
	Stewart	Stewart Rodeo

Date	City	Event
Mid-June	Ashcroft	Ashcroft & Dist. Stampede
	Smithers	Bulkley Valley Rodeo
Late June	Roe Lake	Interlakes Rodeo
	Salmon Arm	Shuswap Rodeo
	Williams Lake	Williams Lake Stampede Rodeo
July	Anaheim Lake	Anaheim Lake Stampede
	Clinton	Clinton Old Timers' Rodeo
Early July	Bella Coola	Bella Coola Rodeo/Dance
	Bridge Lake	Bridge Lake Stampede
Mid-July	Merritt	Merritt Mountain Rodeo
	Quesnel	Billy Barker Days Festival and Rodeo
	Summerland	Summerland Trail Riders Rodeo
Late July	Coombs	Coombs Rodeo
August	Dawson Creek	Dawson Creek Rodeo
	Port St. John	North Peace Rodeo and Fair
Early August	Abbotsford	Agri Fair
	Fort St. James	Baxter Memorial Rodeo
	Chilliwack	Chilliwack Rodeo
Mid-August	Courtenay	Comox Valley Roping Club
	Riske Creek	Riske Creek Rodeo
Late August	Princeton	Princeton Rodeo
	Riske Creek	Jack Palmentier Frontier Days
	Williams Lake	Cariboo Fall Fair
	Vancouver	PRCA Rodeo
Late August to Early September	Barriere	North Thompson Fall Fair
Early September	Armstrong	PRCA Rodeo
September	Merritt	Merritt Rodeo
Mid-September	Port Alberni	Port Alberni Fall Fair

We Want To Hear From You

Guidebooks are like children, constantly growing and changing. One of the joys of writing this guide has been receiving many letters from our readers. Your thoughts and ideas are important to us.

Leading travel guides are great largely because of the suggestions their authors receive from readers. So tell us about your favorite ranch, your not-so-favorite ranch, and new ranches you've discovered. We're also curious about what additional information you would like to see in future editions. We hope that you'll continue to share your comments with us. Please write us at:

Gene Kilgore's Ranch Vacations
Worldwide Ranch Headquarters
P.O. Box 1919
Tahoe City, California 96145
E-Mail: ESKilgore@aol.com

Thank you.